Encyclopedia of the Chicago Literary Renaissance

JAN PINKERTON
and
RANDOLPH H. HUDSON

Facts On File, Inc.

Encyclopedia of the Chicago Literary Renaissance

Facts On File, Inc.
132 West 31st Street
New York NY 10001

Library of Congress Cataloging-in-Publication Data
Pinkerton, Jan, 1934–
Encyclopedia of the Chicago Literary Renaissance / Jan Pinkerton and Randolph H. Hudson
p. cm.
Includes bibliographical references (p.   ) and index.
ISBN 0-8160-4898-3
1. American literature—Illinois—Chicago—Encyclopedias. 2. Authors, American—Homes and haunts—
Illinois—Chicago—Encyclopedias. 3. Chicago (Ill.)—Intellectual life—20th century—Encyclopedias.
4. Authors, American—20th century—Biography—Encyclopedias. 5. American literature—
20th century—Encyclopedias. 6. Chicago (Ill.)—In literature—Encyclopedias. I. Title.
PS285.C47P56 2004
810.9'977311—dc22
2003063114

Text design by Joan M. Toro
Cover design by Cathy Rincon

Printed in the United States of America

VB FOF 10 9 8 7 6 5 4 3 2 1

This book is printed on acid-free paper.

CONTENTS

INTRODUCTION

Chicago is the "Literary Capital of the United States," announced H. L. Mencken in the London *Nation*. The year was 1920; the previous decade in the Windy City had offered a startling outburst of poetry and fiction, ranging from celebrations of vital, if grimy, city landscapes to exposés of small-town dysfunction—exposés soon to be labeled "the revolt from the village." The decade also saw an entrepreneurial spirit, giving the English-speaking world two internationally influential avant-garde periodicals. Originality and freshness in American literature, Mencken concluded, comes now from "under the shadow of the stockyards."

Carl Sandburg's poem "Chicago" appeared in the March 1914 issue of *Poetry* magazine, alarming readers with its unconventional opening line— "Hog-Butcher for the World"—as well as its working-class subject matter and its "unpoetic" free verse. Two months later, Theodore Dreiser published the second of his epic volumes on the prototypical Chicago tycoon, a man ruthlessly exploiting his way to fortune and power. In the next year, 1915, Edgar Lee Masters, a partner in Clarence Darrow's Chicago law firm, published his free-verse *Spoon River Anthology*, a collection of bitter graveyard monologues exposing the often sordid lives of small-town dwellers. In 1919, Sherwood Anderson, another rural refugee, produced his *Winesburg, Ohio*, a collection of stories describing yet another set of repressed, damaged lives. The two new literary journals, *Poetry* and *Little Review*, presented local authors to the world, as well as soon-to-be-hailed figures of international modernism.

The Chicago Renaissance was a creative outburst of fiction and poetry in a midwestern, or "western," city in the early decades of the 20th century. The western locale was crucial because Chicago was far from Boston or New York—far from the 19th-century world of letters, far from an American establishment that still looked to England for precedent and validation. In fiction, Chicago writers rejected what they considered timid East Coast realism; in poetry, they rejected conventional versifying and its pervasive, lingering Victorianism. They embraced instead the radical theories of literary naturalism and the radical poetic techniques of free verse and imagism. They found also a new subject matter—tales of the farmlands they left behind, no longer seen as pastoral or picturesque; tales of the city to which they fled, now seen as squalid and amoral. The term *Renaissance* was soon applied to their work, although the creative outburst was a birth, not a rebirth; Chicago was a new city, built on swampland, without a past.

The major writers of the Chicago Renaissance came from the rural Midwest—Dreiser from Indiana, Anderson from Ohio, Sandburg, Masters, and Vachel Lindsay from downstate Illinois. Willa Cather, a figure not always identified with Chicago—who nevertheless placed three of her novels in the city—came from Nebraska; Edna Ferber arrived in Chicago from Wisconsin. These writers escaped their small-town roots, seeking urban freedom, although they spent the next portion of their lives dwelling on those roots, dissecting them, exorcising them. Poets Masters and Lindsay rarely went further than their village pasts, rarely turning to the city for subject matter; Sandburg actively celebrated his new urban landscape. Fiction writers Dreiser, Anderson, Cather, and Ferber portrayed both village and city, and they were joined by two other novelists who focused on the city in one specific work—Frank Norris, whose *The Pit* depicted the economic forces behind the worldwide distribution of grain, and Upton Sinclair, whose *The Jungle* exposed the criminally negligent and exploitative meatpacking industry.

The greatest years of the Chicago Renaissance lay between 1912, when *Poetry* magazine was founded, and 1919, when *Winesburg, Ohio* appeared—although Dreiser's *Sister Carrie* had appeared earlier and many of the great Anderson stories were to appear later. Some critics cite the starting point as 1890, since by that time a body of fiction, including the work of native-born Henry Blake Fuller and Wisconsin-born Hamlin Garland, as well as pioneering journalism, had been appearing in the aftermath of the devastating Great Fire of 1871. Other critics choose 1900 as the starting point, claiming that literary expression up to that time had maintained its gentility, its conventional ethos; *Sister Carrie* appeared precisely at the century mark. Yet by 1930, historians agree, the Great Depression brought the original flourishing to an end. Dreiser and Anderson continued to produce important work—and a new group of writers, Richard Wright, Nelson Algren, Saul Bellow, were on the horizon—but the original creative breakthrough, as epitomized by Sandburg's "Chicago," had long subsided.

Behind the Chicago Renaissance is the history of a suddenly burgeoning metropolis, driven by access to the Great Lakes and potential access to the Mississippi River. The new settlement grew from 50 adventurers in 1830 to a million and a half residents in 1890; during that time, a "vast ruck of life," as Dreiser wrote, sprang up on "the dark marshes of a lake shore." Chicago is said to have been the fastest-growing city in the world between 1860 and 1900; along with the rural dwellers swarming in from the countryside, immigrants—close to 70 percent of the population in 1890—were pouring in from overseas. The new arrivals dug canals and tunnels, laid railroad tracks, toiled in factories, slaughtered animals in the stockyards; they helped the owners of those enterprises to build vast fortunes. The literarily oriented small-towners, turning to journalism, law, and advertising for financial support, began to reflect in their writing the rawness and dynamism they saw around them, as well as the narrowness and oppression of the rural existence from which they had come.

In the political and economic arena, Chicago had become the most radical city in America, capital of the nation's anarchism and scene of rancorous and deadly labor strife. The first bomb ever thrown in a labor dispute detonated in Haymarket Square in 1886; four anarchists were subsequently hanged. The radical trade union, the Industrial Workers of the World, or "Wobblies," was born in Chicago in 1905; its leader, William "Big Bill" Haywood, convicted of sedition in 1917 by Chicago judge Kenesaw Mountain Landis—soon to become baseball commissioner—jumped bail while awaiting retrial and escaped to the Soviet Union.

The school for writers was the newspapers; higher education was generally irrelevant. Dreiser, Sandburg, Ring Lardner, and Ben Hecht—who later became Hollywood's highest-paid screenwriter—began as Chicago journalists. The second tier of Chicago Renaissance writers, many of them achieving national popularity through syndicated daily columns, remained journalists most of their lives—Eugene Field, popular versifier and commentator on the ways of the elite; Finley Peter Dunne, sardonic observer of politicians through his persona, Irish bartender Mr. Dooley; George Ade, recorder of human foibles in the "Stories of the Streets and of the Town" column, illustrated by line drawings from cartoonist John T. McCutcheon.

For one brief moment during the first decades of the 20th century, Chicago was a motion picture capital, introducing to the world Gloria Swanson, Ben Turpin, Wallace Beery, and Francis X. Bushman—cinema's first matinee idol—before the industry moved westward to the sunny weather of California; Charlie Chaplin made an early film in Chicago. Carl Laemmle and Adolph Zukor, Chicago nickelodeon owners, began seeking an increased volume of product for their showcases; they started to make and distribute films on their own, eventually founding Universal Pictures and

Paramount Pictures. Chicagoan Edgar Rice Burroughs began to write his popular Tarzan stories in 1912, later to make a film star of Chicago Olympic swimmer Johnny Weissmuller. When Prohibition and its accompanying criminal underworld came to the city in the 1920s, Chicago pulp-fiction writer W. R. Burnett created the gangster novel, starting with *Little Caesar;* Ben Hecht soon wrote the screenplay for *Scarface,* invoking the life of mobster Al Capone, and the early seeds of film noir were sown. The phrase *public enemies* was coined in Chicago.

For another brief moment, the city was the nation's jazz capital; Jelly Roll Morton, Joe "King" Oliver, and Louis Armstrong came north from New Orleans in the early 1920s, inspiring local talent such as Benny Goodman, Gene Krupa, and Lionel Hampton. Chicago-born theatrical impresario Florenz Ziegfeld Jr. staged his first presentation at his father's theater in 1893, featuring Eugen Sandow, the European strongman. The Marx brothers, touring the Midwest vaudeville circuit, lived in Chicago for 10 years, between 1910 and 1920. In a more elite theater world, what became known as the "little theater" movement began at the Little Theater in Chicago's Fine Arts Building, founded in 1912, presenting experimental drama, rejecting the popular commercial stage.

From the august new University of Chicago, established in 1892 by funds from industrialist John D. Rockefeller, fresh intellectual voices were soon heard. The first sociology department in the nation found a home in the campus's faux-gothic buildings; philosopher John Dewey formulated his ideals of progressive education in the university's Laboratory School; maverick economist Thorstein Veblen fulminated against the businessman's greed and irresponsibility, establishing the concept of "conspicuous consumption." At the same time, reformer Jane Addams, founding her "settlement house," Hull-House, in 1889, sought to improve the lives of the poor—not by charity, but by bringing educated women into the neighborhood, and by demonstrating that diverse social classes can live together in mutual benefit. Veblen, scorning Addams and her fellow upper-middle-class do-gooders, called Hull-House a propaganda tool.

Writers of the Chicago Renaissance helped make possible a modern national literature. Theodore Dreiser led the way out of repressive moral strictures; in the process, his novels presented a cross section of American lives, ranging from the poverty-stricken to the wealthy and powerful. Sherwood Anderson revolutionized the short story, ridding it of the "poison plot," capturing moments of intensity that helped shape the tales of writers to follow. Carl Sandburg turned once-radical poetic techniques into accepted and everyday practices. Edgar Lee Masters fathered the revolt-from-the-village movement that inspired writers for the next several decades, including Sinclair Lewis, the first American to win the Nobel Prize in literature. *Little Review,* which gave early publication to Anderson—and, like Dreiser, fought censorship battles—folded in 1929, but *Poetry* magazine persists valiantly to the present, its future newly assured in 2002 by the gift of $100 million from the midwestern Lilly pharmaceutical fortune.

Entries in *The Encyclopedia of the Chicago Renaissance* cover all significant Chicago-connected writers of the period from 1880 to 1930, as well as writers of other locales and periods relevant in terms of influence or contacts. Included also are their works, summarized at a length appropriate to their importance, and descriptions of major characters in these works. Other references describe places, buildings, historical events, historical figures, terms, and phrases—matters of primary or ancillary importance to students of the Chicago Renaissance. Cross-references are indicated by small capital letters; in the biographical entry for Masters, for example, a reference to Clarence DARROW indicates an entry on Darrow in the D section. Photographs of significant figures, historic scenes, and buildings of interest are scattered throughout the text. The chronology section provides a time line for the city's history, as well as dates of literary significance through the year 1930.

A

Abbott, Robert S.
(1870–1940) *publisher, founder of the*
Chicago Defender

Born on St. Simon's Island, Georgia, growing up
in Savannah, Abbott graduated from Hampton
Institute in Virginia in 1896. Moving to Chicago, he
received a degree from KENT COLLEGE OF LAW; in
May 1905, he returned to the printing-trade knowledge gained at Hampton, launching the CHICAGO
DEFENDER, destined to become a major African-
American newspaper. Charging two cents a copy,
printing and distributing the paper himself, he hired
his first full-time employee five years later. During
WORLD WAR I, Abbott began to tout job opportunities for Southern blacks in the North, helping to foster the GREAT MIGRATION of African Americans to
Chicago and other northern cities; the *Defender* was
the first black newspaper to claim wide national
readership. Abbott, who died at the age of 71, is said
to have been Chicago's first black millionaire.

Abraham Lincoln: The Prairie Years
Carl Sandburg
(1926)

Originally planned as a one-volume biography for
children, the work grew to become a two-volume
popular biography for adults; it traces Abraham
LINCOLN's life up to his leaving SPRINGFIELD, Illinois, for the presidential inauguration in Washington. The volumes were dedicated to Sandburg's

parents, "Workers on the Illinois Prairie." Giving
the poet his first financial success, the biography
was followed by the four-volume *Abraham Lincoln:
The War Years*, completed in 1939, winning the
Pulitzer Prize for history the next year.

Sandburg's work serves as a milestone in the
20th-century mythologizing of Lincoln—beginning
with the president's log cabin origins, culminating
in his becoming the embodiment of all virtues, including honesty and sympathy for the underdog.
The biography has been called an "Illinois pastoral," in which an idealized figure is presented as
growing out of an idealized natural environment;
Sandburg, identifying with Lincoln, is said to have
been writing his own personal pastoral as well.
Sherwood ANDERSON declared the work "too full of
horse collars," replete with a tiresome "earthy
earthiness." The critic Edmund Wilson, calling the
book "insufferable," quotes descriptions of Lincoln's
mother and his legendary love Ann RUTLEDGE—
both women about whom little is known—and declares that the author is not compiling Lincoln
folklore, but rather actively contributing to it.

"Abraham Lincoln Walks at Midnight"
See THE CONGO AND OTHER POEMS.

Adams, Franklin P.
(1881–1960) *writer, journalist*

Born in Chicago, graduating from the ARMOUR
INSTITUTE, Adams worked as a reporter for the

Chicago Journal in 1903–04. Moving to New York, he became the well-known F. P. A., author of the "Conning Tower" column in the *New York Evening Mail*. In 1910, assuming the New York Giants' point of view, Adams wrote his famous rhyme about the CHICAGO CUBS' infield, lamenting that the three infielders—shortstop Joe Tinker, second baseman Johnny Evers, and first baseman Frank Chance—were destroying the opposition with their double plays. The "saddest of possible words," he concludes—in what becomes the poem's refrain—are "Tinker to Evers to Chance."

Addams, Jane
(1860–1935) *social reformer and activist*

Founder of HULL-HOUSE in Chicago, Addams was a pioneer in the SETTLEMENT HOUSE movement in the United States. Born to a prosperous farmer and businessman whose ancestors, wishing to avoid family mix-ups, had long ago added an extra *d* to the name, Addams grew up in Cedarville, a small town in northwestern Illinois. Childhood spinal tuberculosis left her with back problems that troubled her throughout her life. Attending Rockford Female Seminary, she once vied in an intercollege debate with her contemporary William Jennings BRYAN, a student at downstate Illinois College.

Traveling in Europe in 1888, Addams toured Toynbee Hall, a settlement house in the slums of London; the visit inspired her and a college friend, Ellen Gates Starr, to establish a similar institution in Chicago. The guiding concept at Toynbee Hall, where Oxford University graduates lived alongside the poor, was to provide, instead of charity, a mutual uplift for all involved. In 1889, Addams and Starr, seeking quarters in Chicago, found a once-grand mansion, owned by a family named Hull, in an area of run-down housing, crowded with German, Italian, Irish, and Bohemian immigrants. Gathering other educated, idealistic young women to join them, they began reaching out to the surrounding community. Among the recruits was Florence KELLEY, arriving in 1891 after fleeing an abusive marriage; Kelley, one of the few married women associated with Hull-House, was actively involved in women's and children's labor issues.

She is credited with turning Addams toward a more outspoken role in broadly based political matters.

Although Addams had independent means, she constantly sought further funding; among her talents was an ability to befriend the wealthy and gain financial support from them. One young woman, Mary Rozet Smith, the daughter of a prosperous manufacturer, became not only a major contributor to Hull-House, but also a close companion of Addams; from 1890, when Smith first arrived at Hull-House, until her death in 1934, the women spent many years together.

Addams was meanwhile gaining national prominence, touring and lecturing, writing for publications such as the *Atlantic Monthly* and the new

Jane Addams, by the time of this 1924 photograph, was devoting her efforts to international peace and relief activities. *(Chicago Historical Society)*

American Journal of Sociology, founded at the UNI-
VERSITY OF CHICAGO. Her first best-selling book,
the 1902 DEMOCRACY AND SOCIAL ETHICS, collecting lectures and articles, declared that democracy must have an ethical basis; the volume she
claimed as her favorite, the 1909 THE SPIRIT OF
YOUTH AND THE CITY STREETS, dealt sympathetically with the problems of urban young people. Her
most famous work is the autobiography of 1910,
Twenty Years at Hull-House. In 1912, at the national convention of the newly founded PROGRES-
SIVE PARTY, held in Chicago, Addams seconded
Theodore ROOSEVELT's presidential nomination,
becoming the first woman to play such a role, at a
time when women were unable to vote. Among
the items in the Progressive Party's platform were
an eight-hour day, the abolition of child labor, and
the vote for women. After Roosevelt's defeat, she
continued to campaign for women's suffrage, becoming vice president of the NATIONAL AMERICAN
WOMAN SUFFRAGE ASSOCIATION. In the same
year, *A New Conscience and an Ancient Evil,* a treatise deploring young women's being coerced into
prostitution, became a best-seller.

When WORLD WAR I broke out in Europe in
1914, Addams opposed American involvement;
she traveled in 1915 to The Hague, Netherlands,
to chair the International Congress of Women, a
conference adopting the principles of the Woman's
Peace Party, a group she had earlier helped to establish. She subsequently toured European capitals
to urge an end to hostilities. Her pacifism continued as the United States entered the conflict in
1917, and she came under severe criticism for her
views; for the first time her status as a revered national figure began to wane, and fewer donors were
willing to support her institution on Chicago's
West Side. Racial tensions increased in the neighborhood as well, spurred by the RACE RIOTS of July
1919. By then Addams was spending less time at
Hull-House, devoting herself increasingly to peace
efforts, including the presidency of the WOMEN'S
INTERNATIONAL LEAGUE OF PEACE AND FREEDOM,
established in 1919. During the 1920s, despite
health problems, her activities included meeting
with pacifists internationally, supporting independence movements in Ireland and India, and advocating worldwide relief endeavors. In 1930, she

published her second volume of autobiography,
The Second Twenty Years at Hull-House, a work
showing less optimism than her previous effort. In
1931, she became the first American woman to
win the Nobel Peace Prize; she died four years later
at the age of 74.

The criticism of Addams has been that she was
too middle-class in her outlook, that she was trying
to inculcate the poor with her own bourgeois values. Moreover, as time passed, her model for social
activism became outdated; the problems of the
poor came to be seen as the government's province,
beyond the capacity of individual do-gooders—and
her private fund-raising could never match government resources. Yet as a national figure, as part of
what has been called the PROGRESSIVE MOVEMENT,
Addams set a personal example of high-mindedness
and selfless striving. The public sector took over
the role that she herself had played, and yet
through her efforts, a favorable climate for dedication and service had been established.

The Jane Addams Memorial Park, housing a
sculpture featuring six black granite pillars, designed by Louise Bourgeois, was dedicated in 1996.
The pillars depict human hands in various configu-
rations, reflecting Addams's statement that nothing is "so fraught with significance as the human
hand."

Ade, George
(1866–1944) *journalist, humorist, playwright*

Born in Kentland, Indiana, Ade arrived in Chicago
in 1890 after graduating from Purdue University.
Joining his college friend John T. MCCUTCHEON,
who was establishing himself as a political cartoonist, Ade found a position on the morning edition of
the CHICAGO DAILY NEWS, later named the *Chicago
Record.* In November 1893, he began a regular column, "STORIES OF THE STREETS AND OF THE
TOWN," humorous pieces on topics ranging from
junk shops to boardinghouses; along with another
feature writer, Eugene FIELD, Ade helped to make
the *Record* a widely read and influential paper. Taking further advantage of his popularity, the paper
began publishing "Stories of the Streets and of the
Town" in a series of paperbacks.

In 1895, Ade created the character of Artie Blanchard, a wisecracking office boy; the next year a collection, *Artie: A Story of the Streets and the Town*, published by STONE AND KIMBALL, was praised by William Dean HOWELLS, America's reigning literary critic. Ade was soon creating other popular characters, including Pink Marsh, an African-American bootblack who becomes a Pullman porter; *PINK MARSH: A STORY OF THE STREETS AND THE TOWN* appeared in 1897. Today these pieces are considered dated, in that they make use of DIALECT WRITING—as does the work of another important newspaper columnist, Finley Peter DUNNE—and such usage, ostensibly reproducing the speech of its subjects, has subsequently been viewed as condescending.

A set of humorous tales, *FABLES IN SLANG*, followed, first as a column, then as a book collection; the fables spelled out a moral at the end, such as, "Those who Marry to escape Something usually find Something Else," or, "To insure Peace of Mind, Ignore the Rules and Regulations." The stories were taken up in newspaper syndication, continuing for decades; further books, bearing titles such as *Forty Modern Fables*, eventually added up to 13 volumes in the series. One of the pieces, "The Fable of the Two Mandolin Players and the Willing Performer," was plagiarized by Theodore DREISER for a passage in *SISTER CARRIE*; Ade later said he was proud of the work of his fellow Hoosier.

In 1900, Ade left the *Record*; his next step was to write for the theater. Working with the young composer Alfred G. Wathall, he provided the libretto and lyrics for a musical comedy—or operetta, or light opera, as it was called at the time—THE SULTAN OF SULU. Opening in March 1902 at the STUDEBAKER THEATER in Chicago, the show moved on to a successful run in New York. The next year, Ade provided the libretto and words for another Chicago hit that moved to Broadway, *PEGGY FROM PARIS*, with music by William Lorraine. The Chicago-to-New York theatrical venturing continued—in 1904 with the nonmusical play *The County Chairman*, in 1905 with the musical THE SHO-GUN, music composed by Gustav Luders; Ade and Luders became an established team on Broadway, and other hits followed. In 1917, an Ade play

dating from 1905, *The College Widow*—another Broadway success—was rewritten as a musical for Jerome Kern, the composer who would later set Edna FERBER's *SHOW BOAT* to music.

In 1903, Ade published a selection of "Stories of the Streets and of the Town" columns in *In Babel: Stories of Chicago,* a volume prompting critic H. L. MENCKEN to declare that two or three of the stories are among the best written in America; the collection included the subsequently anthologized "EFFIE WHITTLESY." William Dean Howells, writing about Chicago authors in the same year, singled out Ade as the potential creator of the "great American novel"—echoing Hamlin GARLAND, who as early as 1895 had urged Ade to write an extended work of fiction. Howells later included one of the *In Babel* pieces, "Effie Whittlesy," in his 1920 anthology, *The Great Modern American Stories*. In 1905, Ade moved to an Indiana farm, located 15 miles from his birthplace, where he would live for the next four decades; among continuing projects were screenplays for the ESSANAY FILM MANUFACTURING COMPANY, adapting his fables for short one-reel films. Actress Gloria SWANSON made her movie debut in the 1915 *The Fable of Elvira and Farina and the Meal Ticket.* Thomas Meighan, the actor who had starred in the play *The College Widow,* since transformed into a leading man in silent films, recruited Ade to write scenarios for several movies, including the 1922 *Our Leading Citizen.* Ade died in rural Indiana at the age of 78.

In 1920, H. L. Mencken, naming Chicago as "The Literary Capital of the United States," listed five authors, including Ade, as important figures in American literature; he cited, in order, Sherwood ANDERSON, Theodore Dreiser, Edgar Lee MASTERS, Carl SANDBURG, and Ade. Yet of these writers, Ade is the one who is forgotten today; his works are now seen as slight, as popular expressions of a long-ago era, bound to a particular time and place.

Further Reading

Kelly, Fred C. *George Ade: Warmhearted Satirist.* Indianapolis: Bobbs-Merrill Company, 1947.

Tobin, Terence, ed. *Letters of George Ade.* West Lafayette, Indiana: Purdue University Studies, 1973.

Adler, Dankmar

(1844–1900) *architect and engineer*

Born in Germany, arriving in Detroit in 1854, Adler moved to Chicago at the age of 17, where his father was rabbi of the K.A.M. congregation, the original Jewish congregation in Chicago. In 1862, he enlisted to fight in the CIVIL WAR, serving as an army engineer; he was wounded the following year at Chickamauga, Tennessee. In 1882, he teamed with Louis SULLIVAN to form the firm of ADLER AND SULLIVAN, designing many of Chicago's important buildings. Adler was the expert on technical matters, including foundations, ventilation, and acoustics; the 4,000-seat theater in the AUDITORIUM BUILDING was praised internationally for its acoustics—as was New York's Carnegie Hall, acoustically engineered by Adler in 1891. The brother-in-law of Emil HIRSCH, an influential Reform rabbi, Adler designed the new K.A.M. temple in 1891; it would later become the Pilgrim Baptist church, home of the father of gospel, Thomas A. DORSEY.

Adler and Sullivan

The architecture firm was founded by Dankmar ADLER, a resident in Chicago at the time of the GREAT FIRE, and Louis SULLIVAN, a postfire arrival originally from Boston. Adler's role was as engineer, technical innovator, and businessman; Sullivan's role was as visionary artist. The firm is best known for the AUDITORIUM BUILDING, a 10-story structure of 1889, combining office space with a hotel and a grand theater. Another feat was the 1892 Schiller Building, housing the GARRICK THEATER, noted for its Sullivan-designed interiors; like so many Adler and Sullivan creations, the building and theater have been demolished. Another important structure, subsequently demolished as well—in 1972, amid protests—was the CHICAGO STOCK EXCHANGE BUILDING of 1894; its Trading Room and entrance arch have been reassembled within the domain of the ART INSTITUTE. Frank Lloyd WRIGHT, considering Sullivan his mentor, worked for Adler and Sullivan from 1888 to 1893. The partnership dissolved in 1895, and Sullivan's career went into decline.

Adler Planetarium

This planetarium, the first in America, opening in 1930, was funded by Max Adler, a SEARS, ROEBUCK AND COMPANY executive, brother-in-law of Julius ROSENWALD. It was built to meet an oft-expressed concern, that city lights make natural skies invisible. Using an instrument developed by a German optical engineering firm, the planetarium projected a representation of the skies onto a domed ceiling. The first director of the institution was NORTHWESTERN UNIVERSITY professor Phillip Fox, who later headed the MUSEUM OF SCIENCE AND INDUSTRY.

"Adventure" *See* WINESBURG, OHIO.

Alarm

This anarchist weekly paper, published between 1884 and 1889, was sponsored by the INTERNATIONAL WORKING PEOPLE'S ASSOCIATION, an anarchist-influenced labor organization founded in 1883. Its first editor was Albert PARSONS; a frequent contributor was Lucy PARSONS, whose well-known piece, "TO TRAMPS," appeared in the first issue. Lucy Parsons's article, encouraging the poor to take up violence against the rich, was subsequently distributed as a leaflet; a copy was introduced during the HAYMARKET AFFAIR trial as evidence for the prosecution, illustrating the dangers of ANARCHISM.

Alden, Roberta

A character in Theodore DREISER's novel AN AMERICAN TRAGEDY, Roberta, a young woman who is unselfish and kind, differs from the other girls with whom protagonist Clyde GRIFFITHS becomes involved. Clyde appreciates Roberta's generous qualities, and yet he forgets them when the rich and beautiful Sondra FINCHLEY becomes seemingly obtainable. Roberta is a poor working girl, the daughter of an impoverished farmer; fearful of losing Clyde, she lets him seduce her—unlike Sondra, unlike his previous infatuation, Hortense BRIGGS. When Roberta becomes pregnant and increasingly insists that he marry her, Clyde plots her murder; her actual death by drowning is ambiguously accidental, although her lover is convicted and sentenced to die.

Aldington, Richard
(1892–1962) *English poet, novelist, biographer*

A member of the imagist movement (see IMAGISM), along with American expatriate poets Ezra POUND and Hilda DOOLITTLE—or H.D., as she became labeled—Aldington was championed by Pound, who sent his work to Harriet MONROE, editor of the new POETRY magazine. Monroe published three of Aldington's poems in the second issue of November 1912, helping to place the magazine at the forefront of MODERNISM. His work also appeared in Pound's 1914 anthology, *Des Imagistes,* and in Amy LOWELL's three volumes of 1915–17, *Some Imagist Poetry.* Aldington and H. D. married in 1913; they separated after his service in WORLD WAR I. His antiwar novel, *Death of a Hero,* appeared in 1929. Aldington's later years were devoted to literary history and biography.

Algren, Nelson
(1909–1981) *writer*

Algren, Richard WRIGHT, Saul BELLOW, and Gwendolyn BROOKS are the major writers of the post–Chicago Renaissance generation. Algren, born in Detroit, coming to Chicago at the age of three, graduated from the University of Illinois journalism school in 1931. Two years later, he became a member of the Chicago John Reed Club, part of a national network of organizations for working-class artists and writers. Wright, also a member, served as model for the character Dill Doak in Algren's first novel, *Somebody in Boots,*

published in 1935. Although achieving international cachet through his affair with the French writer and feminist Simone de Beauvoir, Algren kept his fiction situated at the lower end of the social scale. *Never Come Morning,* set in a poor Polish-American neighborhood, appeared in 1942; *The Man with the Golden Arm,* its protagonist a drug addict, in 1949. His 1951 poetic harangue, *Chicago: City on the Make,* invokes Carl SANDBURG's "Chicago" and Sandburg's laughing worker—the "heavy-shouldered laugher"—but adds that the city's laughter "has grown metallic," that the city is no longer in spiritual health.

Altgeld, John Peter
(1847–1902) *governor of Illinois*

Serving only one term, Altgeld is famed for pardoning three HAYMARKET AFFAIR anarchists, thereby destroying his political career. Born in Germany, brought as a child to Ohio, Altgeld served briefly in the CIVIL WAR; he later became county attorney in Savannah, Missouri. Moving to Chicago in 1875, prospering in real estate, he returned to political activity in the 1880s; his 1884 book, OUR PENAL MACHINERY AND ITS VICTIMS, argued for a greater understanding of the causes of crime, detailing the criminal-justice system's favoring of the rich over the poor. In 1892, elected governor of Illinois, Altgeld was urged by Clarence DARROW and others to pardon the remaining Haymarket prisoners, convicted six years previously on what was considered perjured testimony. Altgeld signed their pardons in 1893, knowing that his career would be damaged; the public outcry was clamorous—calling him an anarchist, a socialist, a "foreigner"—and he was defeated in the next election. Joining Darrow's law firm, he was seen as a man broken by his act of conscience. He died at the age of 54, shortly after giving a speech opposing the South African Boer War. His body, lying in state in the Chicago Public Library, was viewed by thousands.

The poet Vachel LINDSAY, whose family home in SPRINGFIELD stood next to the governor's mansion, wrote that he had often gazed as a teenager out of his bedroom window at the man he considered a hero, then a martyr; Lindsay eulogized

Altgeld in his poem, "THE EAGLE THAT IS FORGOT-TEN." Theodore DREISER, in his novel THE TITAN, bases his Swedish-born Governor Swanson on Altgeld; as Altgeld had done, Swanson vetoes a bill in the Illinois state legislature, passed through bribery, that would have extended a corrupt magnate's streetcar franchises in Chicago. In *The Titan,* the governor is depicted as a thoughtful idealist, a man who understands that his political career will not last. Howard Fast's 1946 novel, *The American,* is a fictionalized biography of Altgeld.

America

This literary magazine was founded by Chicagoans Hobart C. Chatfield-Taylor and Slason Thompson and published between 1888 and 1891. The periodical was politically conservative, espousing anti-immigration and anti-Roman Catholic positions; its literary stance was similarly conservative, arguing against the influence of "foreign" realists such as Émile ZOLA. The magazine presented work by Hamlin GARLAND, James Whitcomb RILEY, and others; its most famous publication was Eugene FIELD's poem "LITTLE BOY BLUE."

American Federation of Labor

A labor organization founded in Columbus, Ohio, in 1886, the year of the HAYMARKET AFFAIR, the AFL grew out of the older Federation of Organized Trades and Labor Unions. Composed of loosely affiliated craft unions, led by Samuel L. GOMPERS, the organization emphasized negotiation and collective bargaining, avoiding larger political and ideological issues. The growing criticism was that it excluded unskilled workers, an exclusion based on the ground that such workers could be readily replaced in a strike, thereby undermining the union's negotiating position. As the industrial era progressed, as unskilled workers became increasingly hired for routine assembly-line work, the AFL's stance was seen as reactionary; unskilled workers were deemed in particular need of protection. The AFL came under attack by more revolutionary unionism, notably represented by the INDUSTRIAL

WORKERS OF THE WORLD, or "Wobblies," an organization founded in Chicago in 1905. In a 1912 textile workers' strike in Lawrence, Massachusetts, the AFL took a position directly opposed to that of the IWW. In the 1930s, dissidents from the AFL founded the industry-based Congress of Industrial Organizations, or CIO, an organization achieving particular success in the automobile and steel industries; the two unions merged in 1955.

Yet African Americans had long been decrying the near-total exclusion of black workers from trade unionism. A. Philip RANDOLPH, founder of the BROTHERHOOD OF SLEEPING CAR PORTERS, once called the American Federation of Labor "the American Separation of Labor." His union eventually joined the AFL in 1935.

American Railway Union

A labor organization founded in 1893, headed by Eugene V. DEBS, the American Railway Union became an early labor union to organize by industry, rather than by craft or skill, as had been the practice of the AMERICAN FEDERATION OF LABOR. The rationale for the industrywide organization was to create labor solidarity by including all workers, eliminating the hierarchy of the skilled over the unskilled—although African-American service workers, employed as porters by the PULLMAN PALACE CAR COMPANY, were never considered for membership; a distinction was maintained between service workers and "productive" workers.

In 1894, the ARU called the PULLMAN STRIKE, directed against the Pullman company. Federal troops, sent by President Grover CLEVELAND, broke the strike, and Debs, convicted under ANTITRUST legislation, was imprisoned for six months. The ARU, never receiving support from the AFL, soon dissolved.

The American Songbag
Carl Sandburg
(1927)

Presenting African-American spirituals, cowboy songs, hobo songs, and other examples of regional diversity—many never having been in print before—Carl SANDBURG's collection of American folk songs contains nearly three hundred songs, including words, melody, and accompaniments. The collection contributed to the popularity of such pieces as "She'll Be Comin' Round the Mountain," "Frankie and Johnnie," "Blow the Man Down." A song from the Bahamas, "The Wreck of the Sloop John B," published with a musical arrangement by Alfred G. Wathall—the composer of George ADE's *THE SULTAN OF SULU* 25 years previously—achieved popularity through the folk groups the Weavers and the Kingston Trio; the Beach Boys contributed their version in 1966.

An American Tragedy
Theodore Dreiser
(1925)

DREISER's most commercially successful novel, *An American Tragedy* is based on a real-life 1906 murder case in upstate Herkimer County, New York; the man involved was executed two years later. Dreiser updated the time to an era closer to his own, although he kept the geographical locale, having spent a month scouting the Andirondack region during the summer of 1923. In the novel he turns the town of Cortland into Lycurgus, and Big Moose Lake becomes Big Bittern; he visited Sing Sing prison as well. In his earlier novel, *THE FINANCIER*, Dreiser had already described lengthy court scenes, drawn from real life; in this case he had the advantage a more sensational trial, detailing sex and murder rather than financial proceedings.

The first book of the novel, relating the early career of Clyde GRIFFITHS, is the author's creation, having nothing to do with the real-life murderer. Dreiser is providing his own version of his protagonist's early experience, once again recasting the poverty of his own youth. H. L. MENCKEN later suggested that this portion of the novel be skipped by the impatient reader, although the segment can be considered valuable for establishing Clyde's weaknesses and limitations. Originally published as a two-volume set, the work reaches well over 800 pages.

Synopsis

BOOK I

At the dusk of a summer day in Kansas City, a street preacher, his wife, and four children, ages seven through 15, set up a portable organ and campstool in an alley near a downtown thoroughfare. The family sing a hymn together, although the 12-year-old boy, Clyde Griffiths, sings only halfheartedly. He is thinking about his family's lifestyle, their poverty, their being unlike other people; their home is a mission housed in a shabby wooden building. Clyde thinks also about an uncle, Samuel Griffiths, whom he has never met, who lives a far different life, as a rich businessman in upstate New York.

Clyde, as he grows older, wishes to escape his existence, but it is his older sister Hester, or Esta, who makes the first move; she disappears one night, eloping with a young man. The matter is hushed up within the family, but Clyde, now 16 years old, is increasingly determined to find his own freedom as well. Through persistence, he obtains a position as a bellhop at a leading hotel, and his life changes as a result. Not only does he have money, but he learns about the larger world, readily abandoning the teachings of his sheltered background; his fellow bellhops introduce him to restaurants, liquor, and brothels.

Meeting a girl named Hortense BRIGGS, Clyde tries to impress her, taking her out, buying her gifts. But when Esta, pregnant, is abandoned by her lover, Mrs. Griffiths rents her a room nearby, and Clyde reluctantly gives his mother the money he would rather spend on Hortense. Although partially realizing that Hortense is trying to manipulate him, he is unable to resist her—until an automobile accident terminates the relationship. A joy ride in an illegally borrowed car ends in a fatal mishap, and Clyde and Hortense escape the police by going their separate ways.

BOOK II, CHAPTERS I–X

Samuel Griffiths, owner of the Griffiths Collar and Shirt Company of Lycurgus, New York, has prospered as his younger brother, Clyde's father, has not. Samuel's family includes his son Gilbert, who works in the family business; they spend their summers at a nearby fashionable lake resort. On a business trip to Chicago, Samuel is accosted by his nephew, Clyde, now a bellhop at an upscale men's club; Clyde introduces himself, and Samuel takes a liking to him, inviting him to come to Lycurgus to see about a job. Back at home, Samuel tells Gilbert that Clyde looks like him, if a bit taller; Gilbert, the family heir, is not pleased by the potential rivalry.

Clyde, it turns out, had fled Kansas City in a boxcar, going first to St. Louis, then Chicago; his next destination is Lycurgus, where he can upgrade his position in the world. Gilbert Griffiths receives him coolly at the factory, giving him a lowly position in a basement room; Clyde is disappointed, although he knows he has no choice. Finding lodging in a rooming house, he realizes the other boarders are impressed that he is related to one of the town's leading families—and yet he himself has had no contact with the family, except to be given a laborer's job. He becomes friendly with a fellow boarder, who introduces him to a girl with whom he is about to pursue a relationship—until a letter of invitation arrives from the Griffiths. Clyde is invited to a Sunday supper, and he loses interest at once in his recent acquaintances.

On that Sunday evening he meets not only the rest of the family, but also a friend of one of the sisters, Sondra FINCHLEY; he is enraptured by her beauty, her fashion, her obvious wealth. Yet when Mrs. Griffiths introduces him as a nephew who must make his own way in the world, Sondra acts dismissively toward this young man who is her social inferior. Samuel Griffiths understands that poverty will ensure that his nephew continues to be neglected by the family.

BOOK II, CHAPTERS XI–XXI

Samuel decides that Clyde should at least be given a better position at the factory; he instructs Gilbert to find him a supervisory position. As a result Clyde becomes the head of a room where all 25 workers are women; Gilbert reminds Clyde to behave as a gentleman, to be strictly businesslike. Clyde is delighted by his new job and salary, resolving to stay away from the women who work for him.

One of the women is Roberta ALDEN, who has moved to Lycurgus from a poverty-stricken farm, hoping to find work and help support her family; she lives in a boardinghouse run by a strict religious couple. It is summertime, and the employees take advantage of the nearby lakes for boating or swimming—although the Griffithses and the Finchleys, Clyde knows, go to more exclusive areas for golf, tennis, riding, and dancing; he feels both loneliness and resentment. On a Sunday afternoon outing he chances upon Roberta and a friend and persuades them to go canoeing with him, breaking the rule about not associating with women at work. He and Roberta are soon agreeing on evening meeting places, and they agree, too, that they are in love. Roberta must find new lodgings, as she faces constraints in her present situation; she finds a new room, located on the ground floor, which has a connection to the outside. Yet she refuses to let Clyde into her room; he becomes angry, and at work the next day he ignores her, paying attention to other women. Heartbroken, she writes him a note, asking him to come to her that night, and they become lovers.

BOOK II, CHAPTERS XXII–XXXI

Clyde feels he is now a man of the world, and since he can have Roberta, he can surely have others as well. The Griffiths family has been ignoring him, and yet he continues to imagine himself staying at a resort with the elite of Lycurgus. One evening, as he walks along the street where the wealthy live, he catches sight of Sondra Finchley in her chauffeured car; she mistakes him for Gilbert and calls out to him, offering him a ride. When she recognizes her error, she instructs her chauffeur to drive him to where he lives, an address that embarrasses him; he tries to take advantage of the opportunity to ingratiate himself with her. She finds him more pleasing than Gilbert, wondering why the Griffithses do not seem interested in him.

Sondra decides to champion Clyde within her set, and she persuades a friend to invite him to a dinner and dance at her home; Clyde is surprised and thrilled. Yet he feels overwhelmed at the party, as the men begin talking of universities, but he soon realizes that they are too interested in themselves to pay attention to his academic deficiencies. As for Sondra, he realizes she is more refined than Hortense Briggs, although hardly less self-centered; he exults when she puts her arm in his as they go in to dinner. For her part, she is pleased that Clyde has handled himself well and proved acceptable to the others.

Clyde is now part of the social life of the town. Roberta, unaware of his new success, becomes disturbed as he breaks engagements with her, as he seems increasingly indifferent; his excuse is that the Samuel Griffithses have finally taken him up. She goes home for Christmas, confiding to her mother that she has been seeing Clyde, although not admitting the nature of the relationship; her brother-in-law points out a society item in the newspaper, naming Clyde as a guest at a party that was not a Griffiths family event. Roberta is devastated, wondering which girl he was with, wondering if he will eventually desert her. Yet when she returns to Lycurgus, his excuses are so tender and convincing that she is temporarily assuaged.

BOOK II, CHAPTERS XXXII–XL

Late one evening, Sondra invites Clyde into the kitchen of her home. Seeing him impressed by its opulence, she understands all the more that he is entranced by her and what she represents. She knows her parents would never approve of him, and yet she enters into the glow of his love for her, feeling even a reciprocal glow.

Roberta tells Clyde that she is pregnant. Seeking a drugstore remedy, he goes to Schenectady, where he would not be recognized; he is turned down by one pharmacist, but another sells him an expensive potion—which fails to work. Seeking a doctor, Clyde asks a clerk in a men's clothing store for the name of a physician who might oblige, and he is given a name. Clyde refuses to go with Roberta to the doctor, saying he cannot risk his reputation in the family firm, although he is far more concerned about his reputation with his new friends. The doctor is sympathetic but turns Roberta down in her request. She continues to implore Clyde to marry her, but the idea is repugnant to him, especially now that he has prospects for allying himself with Sondra and improving his status in life. His re-

solve is strengthened by a chance meeting with Roberta's father. On an automobile outing with his friends, Clyde asks for directions at a rundown farmhouse and sees Roberta's family name on the mailbox; speaking with the ill-dressed farmer, he is all the more appalled that Roberta wants him to marry into that family—when all the wealth of Sondra and her friends is spread before him.

BOOK II, CHAPTERS XLI–XLVII

Summer has arrived, and the Finchleys have gone to their lakeside home; Sondra expects weekend visits from Clyde. Yet Roberta is growing desperate, and Clyde suggests she return to her home, implying that a wedding trip will follow. While Sondra is sending him frivolous love letters, Roberta is sending letters that are despairing and anguished. Then Clyde notices a newspaper article about a lake boating accident involving a man and a woman; he reads that an upturned rowboat was found, along with two hats in the rushes along the shore, after which a woman's body was found—but so far no man's body. Although he is horrified by the thought, Clyde realizes that a similar occurrence could rid him of his troubles; he knows that Roberta cannot swim. He dwells on the idea during the weekend at the Finchleys' summer home, when Sondra suggests that the two of them run away and get married—although she changes her mind, remarking that she will not be of age until the fall, that her parents could dissolve such a marriage; she and Clyde should thus wait a few months.

Roberta writes that she is returning to Lycurgus, insisting that she and Clyde marry at once. Clyde worries about her causing trouble with the Griffithses; he promises he will come and get her, after which they will be married. He has already made up his mind what to do; he has spotted a suitably lonely lake area and will take Roberta there.

Clyde tells Roberta he has met a minister at one of the lake resorts. They will register at a nearby hotel as Mr. and Mrs. Carl Graham or Clifford Golden; he plans to bring along a camera and tripod, suggesting they go out in a boat to take pictures. She will leave her bag at the lodge; he will take his bag for the purpose of carrying the camera.

He will also purchase an extra hat, to leave one behind, as described in the newspaper story.

Traveling separately at first, Clyde and Roberta arrive at their destination. Renting a boat, Clyde rows them to an isolated spot, stopping briefly onshore to leave off his bag; they go out on the lake again for another picture. He knows now that the time has come, that he must leap to one side of the boat and rock it vigorously. Yet he pauses, feeling a paralysis of will, and Roberta, thinking he is about to fall, reaches out to him, seeking to take his hand. He responds by lashing out—not to hurt her, but to free himself from her touch—and the camera in his hand strikes her, knocking her backward; he reaches to assist her, and the boat capsizes. He has not willfully caused the mishap.

They are both in the water, and his action now is to save himself. She calls out to him, but he does nothing. It was an accident, he tells himself, and his only culpability is in not rescuing her afterward; he did not cause her death in the first place. Moreover, if he tries to rescue her, he might himself be drowned. He swims to the shore. Taking the tripod from his bag and hiding it under a log, he begins the long walk through the woods.

BOOK III, CHAPTERS I–VIII

The county coroner first hears the news about the woman's body, and the politically ambitious district attorney, Orville W. Mason, takes over the case. The suspicion of murder is strong, since marks on the woman's face suggest that she was struck. Moreover, the body of the man has not been found—he registered under different names at different places—and his bag is gone from the lodge, although the woman's bag is still there. Mason, speaking to Roberta's parents, learns that their daughter had mentioned Clyde Griffiths, nephew of the wealthy Samuel Griffiths; a mailman says Roberta had given him letters addressed to Clyde Griffiths. Mason finds the letters at Clyde's boardinghouse, as well as letters from Sondra Finchley; he now knows the motive for murder.

Clyde, stumbling through the woods, meets three men; they greet him in a friendly fashion, but he worries that they will remember him. The next day, taking a boat and a train, he arrives at the resort where Sondra and the others are staying, although once he is there, he has trouble acting naturally. When he hears the report of a drowning, he finds it almost impossible to hide his shock; he had not expected Roberta's body to be found so soon. He worries about the wet suit of clothing that is still in his bag; he weights it with a stone and throws it into the lake. The next morning, when a newspaper story suggests that the drowning was murder, he feels even more frightened; he reads that a young man, similar to the descriptions given of Carl Graham and Clifford Golden, was seen later in the woods.

Sondra and her friends take a camping trip to a nearby lake, and Clyde tries to appear happy and carefree. He hears shots in the woods—they are from a sheriff's posse, signaling to one another—and he slips away from the camp. He knows he should run, and yet he does not want to leave Sondra. A sheriff's deputy accosts him, announcing his arrest; Clyde denies all charges. His one plea is that the deputy not take him back to the camp where Sondra is, where she can see him as he is now, a captive of the law.

BOOK III, CHAPTERS IX–XVI

Orville Mason arrives at the camp and, seeing the beautiful and rich Sondra, understands why Clyde chose her over Roberta. Meeting with the deputy outside of the camp, he begins questioning his prisoner; Clyde denies knowing Roberta at all. Yet when Mason says they must go to the camp to collect his belongings, Clyde admits knowing her, although denying he killed her; he says that going to the lake was her idea and that he was trying to persuade her to let go of him. The deputies gather his belongings without bringing him to the camp.

The gray suit, said by witnesses to have been worn by Clyde when he rented the boat, is not found. He says he had no such suit, insisting that the one he is wearing now is what he wore on the boat; he had it cleaned and pressed at a local tailor shop. The subject of straw hats—relevant in an era when men customarily wore hats—comes up as well. Clyde wore a hat away from the lake, and yet he left one on the lake where he had "drowned"; he claims he had been in the area previously and had found the one he had left before.

A search of the lake area turns up a camera tripod; Mason suggests that this implement was used to strike Roberta, knocking her from the boat. Clyde denies he had a camera or tripod with him, and yet a search of the lake bottom brings up a camera. An assistant district attorney, hoping to help the case along, decides to prove that the camera delivered the blow; visiting the morgue, he secures a few hairs from the dead woman's head, then threads the hairs inside the lid of the camera. Mason and the coroner, although wondering why they had not noticed the hairs before, know now that they have conclusive evidence of murder.

As the newspapers make much of the case, Samuel Griffiths consults his lawyers, concerned that a nephew bearing the family name has been accused of murder. Meanwhile, Sondra Finchley's father realizes—once Sondra confesses her closeness to Clyde—that he must take action as well; her name must not come out in the trial. Griffiths sends lawyers to interview Clyde in his cell; they decide, since he has already lied so much, that his case is hopeless. Yet a member of the local Democratic Party, dismayed at seeing the Republican Mason gain favor with the electorate, recommends he call in the Democrat-connected law firm of Belknap and Jephson; Alvin Belknap is particularly sympathetic to Clyde, but both agree that the case is difficult. The suggestion of an insanity plea is made, then rejected; the men begin to put together a story, considering the facts as well as the lies Clyde had previously told. The overall story will be that Clyde took Roberta to the lake, planning to persuade her to release him, even offering to pay her expenses. Then he began to feel sorry for her, offering to marry her; the accident occurred when she jumped up in gratitude, causing the boat to capsize.

BOOK III, CHAPTERS XVII–XXVI

Belknap and Jephson wish to bring some of Clyde's family to the trial, to show support and to attest to his good character. Yet no members of the Samuel Griffiths family care to step forward, and they do not wish the western branch of the family, Clyde's socially embarrassing parents, to appear. Clyde's parents have moved their mission to Denver, where they are raising Esta's child, passing him off as an orphan whom they adopted in Kansas City; Clyde discourages his mother from attending the trial.

Belknap and Jephson coach Clyde for his upcoming courtroom appearance, not only on how to respond to questions, but on how to keep looking pleasant and confident, never seeming frightened or cowed. As the trial begins, it becomes clear that the name of Sondra Finchley will never be mentioned; she will be referred to as Miss X, an example of the privileges granted to the economically powerful. The witnesses, starting with Roberta's father, are questioned, and damaging evidence is presented, including the retrieved camera, displaying two strands of Roberta's hair; the dead girl's unhappy letters are read to the jury as well.

When Clyde takes the stand, he tries his best to answer as he has been instructed. Yet Mason speaks convincingly as he piles up evidence of the young man's murderous intent; he catches the defendant in various details, such as when he picked up maps and hotel brochures. When the proceedings conclude, the jury returns the expected verdict of guilty.

BOOK III, CHAPTERS XVII–XXIV

Samuel Griffiths, having paid for Belknap and Jephson's defense of his nephew, has no interest in paying for an appeal. Clyde's mother arrives from Denver, feeling troubled and dubious as her son maintains his innocence. When the sentence of death is pronounced, he is removed to a death-row penitentiary, where he finds himself among a new group of prisoners, all condemned to die. His mother tries to raise appeal money from churches in the area, but members are suspicious of her unordained street-preaching status, and they are convinced as well of her son's guilt. She raises a small sum of money, and Belknap and Jephson agree to file an appeal. Meeting a fellow independent evangelist, Duncan McMillan, she asks him to talk to Clyde; McMillan urges Clyde to repent, although the prisoner continues to maintain his innocence.

A message finally arrives from Sondra. It is typed and unsigned, saying that she feels sorrow, that she wishes him freedom and happiness; Clyde falls into a deep depression. He finally begins telling McMillan the truth about Roberta; he admits he intended to harm her, admitting, too, that he could have saved her. McMillan is disturbed by the confession.

Clyde's appeal is turned down. The only hope lies with the newly elected governor, who might be persuaded to commute the sentence from death to life imprisonment. The governor agrees to meet with McMillan and Clyde's mother; he surmises that McMillan is a truthful man, and he asks him if he knows of any fact that might weaken the trial testimony. McMillan pales and grows silent, knowing of no such fact, knowing that Clyde gave deliberately false testimony. He finally replies that he is a spiritual, not a legal, adviser. The governor, convinced of the defendant's guilt, refuses any commutation of the sentence, and Clyde is executed shortly thereafter. McMillan wonders if he will ever again have peace of mind.

A final brief section of the book, entitled "SOUVENIR," describes the dusk of a summer day in San Francisco—during which a street preacher and his wife, along with several others, including a young boy, cross a busy thoroughfare, set up a portable organ, and sing a hymn together. Dreiser is recapitulating the opening of his novel. Mr. and Mrs. Griffiths are in a new city, but they are pursuing the same activities as 10 years earlier—and this time they have with them a young boy, Esta's son. Dreiser continues the parallels; the passersby in San Francisco make comments similar to those made in Kansas City, and Mr. Griffiths's comments on the listeners' attentiveness are similar to those made 10 years earlier. Yet Mrs. Griffiths lets the boy buy an ice cream cone, realizing perhaps that she must not restrain him too much, that she should be "more liberal" with him.

Critical Reception

Most reviews of *An American Tragedy* were favorable. The English writer H. G. Wells called it "one of the very greatest novels of this century"; an American reviewer labeled it "the best novel yet written by the greatest of American novelists." The academic critic Stuart P. Sherman, who had previously deplored Dreiser's immorality, noted

that the author had finally become a "good moralist," portraying the shame and anguish of Roberta Alden—and then allowing her, unlike his earlier heroines, to be punished for her sexual sins.

The English novelist Arnold Bennett addressed stylistic issues, declaring that the author "evidently despises style, elegance, clarity, even grammar"—although Bennett acknowledged, too, the power of Dreiser's prose, his "unrelenting grip" on the reader. H. L. Mencken noted stylistic problems also, calling the work "a vast, sloppy, chaotic thing"; yet he added that in human terms it is "full of solemn dignity."

Two years later, in Boston, the censorship issue was raised in regard to this and other novels. Sinclair LEWIS's *Elmer Gantry* and Upton SINCLAIR's *Oil!* were banned from bookstores, and *An American Tragedy* was said to be under consideration for a similar prohibition. The publisher, hoping for favorable national publicity, made a point of selling the novel and inviting arrest; he was convicted and fined, and the lengthy appeal process kept the work out of Boston bookstores for several years.

A dramatization of the novel by Patrick Kearney became a New York stage success in 1926; a later theatrical version, *The Case of Clyde Griffiths*, emphasizing social-class conflict, proved too political for audience appeal. A Hollywood movie version was proposed in 1930 for Russian director Sergei Eisenstein, renowned for his 1925 *Potemkin*; yet a communist filmmaker was eventually deemed unacceptable, and the 1931 *An American Tragedy* was directed by Josef von Sternberg. The much-lauded, and retitled, *A Place in the Sun* appeared in 1951, starring Montgomery Clift, Elizabeth Taylor, and Shelley Winters.

Ames, Bob

A character in Theodore DREISER's novel SISTER CARRIE, Ames who is a cousin of Carrie's neighbor in New York, is given little space in the story. Yet he is the one who keeps Carrie aspiring, who keeps pointing her toward higher and more worthy goals. Coming from Indianapolis, employed by an electrical company—and thus a man of the future—Ames surprises Carrie by remarking that people spend too much money on luxury items; he adds that he himself would not care to be rich, or at least not so rich as to spend money foolishly. These are all new ideas to Carrie. Later, he encourages her to be a dramatic actress, as opposed to a comic actress; he claims she is capable of serious expression, of qualities that would be of value to others. At the end of the novel, the possibility remains that Carrie will continue to see him.

"Among the Corn Rows"   See MAIN-TRAVELLED ROADS.

anarchism

This antigovernment political doctrine advocates a stateless and cooperative society. Anarchism holds that the state fosters injustice and inequality and must therefore be abolished; taking its place would be voluntary agreements or associations. The movement reached its height in the last years of the 19th century, coexisting with the more structured SOCIALISM.

Chicago, the nation's most radical city, was the capital of American anarchism. Its fervor was fed by German Americans and German immigrants, then the city's, as well as the nation's, largest ethnic group. Using the recently invented dynamite as a weapon of protest, anarchists had already carried out assassinations in Europe; one of the doctrines was "principled murder," or assassination for the greater good. Johann MOST, a German anarchist agitator touring the nation in the early 1880s, distributed his pamphlet, *The Science of Revolutionary Warfare,* giving instructions for the manufacture of bombs. Advocating "propaganda by deed," or acts of terrorism, Most helped found the anarchist-influenced labor organization, the INTERNATIONAL WORKING PEOPLE'S ASSOCIATION. Its weekly periodical, ALARM, was edited by Albert PARSONS, who was hanged after the HAYMARKET AFFAIR.

When President William MCKINLEY was shot and killed by an anarchist in Buffalo in 1881, the movement's chief American spokesperson, Emma GOLDMAN, was held temporarily in Chicago; she was released when no evidence could be found against her. After the Haymarket Affair of 1886, in which anarchists were accused of throwing a bomb that killed seven policemen, sentiments against anarchism continued to run high; the movement was seen as dangerous in a way that other radical thought, such as socialism, had not yet been perceived. Anarchist Alexander Berkman, an associate of Goldman's, made an attempt on the life of steel executive Henry Clay Frick in Pennsylvania in 1892; released from prison, he made a yet less successful attempt on the John D. ROCKEFELLER family in 1914.

After WORLD WAR I and the Russian revolution, communism replaced anarchism as the predominant "foreign" radicalism. A latter-day case involving anarchists took place in Dedham, Massachusetts, where two Italian-born anarchists, Nicola Sacco and Bartolomeo Vanzetti, were arrested in 1920 and charged with murdering two men in a payroll holdup; Sacco and Vanzetti were convicted and executed in 1927. Observers viewed these executions as a repeat of the unjust Haymarket executions of several decades earlier.

Anarchism was often associated with forward-looking movements in the arts; it was seen as antibourgeois and anticensorship. Its rival, socialism, was often viewed by artists as too doctrinaire, too "scientific"; Margaret ANDERSON, enthralled by the anarchist oratory of Goldman, said she "could never listen to the socialists." Goldman herself was accused of turning anarchism from a political statement to the mere advocacy of self-expression.

Novelist Frank NORRIS, writing from a California perspective—and finding no glamour in radical activity—had already taken a conservative position on anarchism in his 1901 novel, *The Octopus.* He describes the stranglehold that the railroads had gained over farmers, and yet a character who preaches anarchist violence is disdained; his anarchist, a saloon-keeper, who goaded one man to attempted murder and another to inadvertent murder, is viewed as a pernicious influence, a man who is "poisoning the farmers' bodies with alcohol and their minds with discontent."

In Carl SANDBURG's poem "Dynamiter," collected in the 1916 CHICAGO POEMS, the poet makes a point of sympathetically humanizing his revolutionary figure. He reports sitting with an anarchist in a German saloon, listening to him talk of his wife, his family, and the cause of the working class. The poet remembers this man, "an enemy of the nation," as simply a lover of life and laughter.

Andersen, Arthur
(1885–1947) *founder of accounting firm*

Born in Plano, Illinois, the son of Norwegian immigrants, Andersen received an accountancy degree from the University of Illinois in 1908; he became a professor of accounting at NORTHWESTERN UNIVERSITY four years later. In 1913, he cofounded Andersen, DeLany and Company, which became Arthur Andersen and Company in 1918; among his clients were utility firms controlled by Samuel INSULL. Known for wearing a yellow rose in his lapel, he died at the age of 61. The Andersen company subsequently became an elite leader in the accounting profession; in 2002, after a series of corporate scandals, including a conviction for obstruction of justice, the firm ended its 89-year role as an auditor of public companies.

Anderson, Gilbert M.
(1880–1971) *silent film actor, cofounder of the Essanay Film Manufacturing Company*

As "Broncho Billy," Anderson was the movies' first cowboy star, leading the way for William S. Hart, Tom Mix, and others to follow. Born Gilbert Maxwell Aronson in Little Rock, Arkansas, he initially performed in VAUDEVILLE under the stage name of Max Anderson. In the groundbreaking film of 1903, *The Great Train Robbery*, produced by the Thomas Edison Company in New Jersey, Anderson played the posse leader, tracking down a gang of robbers. Coming to Chicago to join the Selig Polyscope Company, he worked as both actor and director; William SELIG sent him to California to seek out authentic western scenery. In 1907, he

and George K. Spoor formed their ESSANAY FILM MANUFACTURING COMPANY, named after their S-and-A initials; it was under Essanay auspices that Anderson starred in the first Broncho Billy western in 1909. Nearly 300 popular Broncho Billy films followed, filmed by Essanay in Colorado and California; Anderson retired the character in 1915. Moving to California, he directed films for a new comic, Stan Laurel, but never regained his earlier eminence.

Anderson, Margaret
(1886–1973) *founder and editor of* Little Review

Born in Indianapolis, Anderson attended Western College for Women in Oxford, Ohio, and moved to Chicago in 1908 at the age of 22; she immediately impressed bohemian circles with her "unearthly red-gold beauty." After working on a religious journal, she joined the staff of the DIAL, the prominent literary magazine of the day. In 1914, she founded the LITTLE REVIEW, naming it after the LITTLE THEATER MOVEMENT. Having gathered minimal funding and offering no payment to contributors, she rented an office on the ninth floor of the FINE ARTS BUILDING, the venue of Maurice BROWNE's LITTLE THEATRE and the LITTLE ROOM.

Meeting Emma GOLDMAN, admiring her oratory, Anderson declared herself an advocate of ANARCHISM. Drawn by the cultural appeal of the doctrine, as purveyed by Goldman, she saw anarchism less as a political issue than as a matter of defiance and freedom of expression; her enthusiasm for Goldman cost her financial support. Always short of funds, Anderson spent one summer, along with her sister, her sister's children, and others, on a Lake Michigan beach north of the city, living in makeshift tents. In 1916, Jane HEAP, a painter, joined her as lover and coeditor of the magazine. In the same year, the two women left for California, pursuing financial backing; from there they published the famous September blank issue, consisting of 64 mostly empty pages. They returned to Chicago in the fall, then moved to New York by the end of the year. In 1917, Anderson took up the offer of expatriate American poet Ezra POUND to become "foreign editor"; Pound secured her financial support as well, from New York lawyer and art patron John Quinn. Receiving a new work from Pound, James JOYCE's *Ulysses*, she began serial publication of the novel in 1918; the *Little Review* provided the first appearance of this work by the then-unknown author. Under laws established by Anthony COMSTOCK, the United States Post Office seized and burned the magazine on four different occasions, on the grounds that it purveyed obscenity through the mails; Anderson and Heap faced criminal charges. The resulting sentence was reduced from jail time to a fine, but Anderson, whose relationship with Heap was ending, became increasingly determined to leave the country.

In 1923, she accompanied French singer Georgette Leblanc, who became her companion, to Paris. By this time Anderson and Heap were studying the teachings of the Russian mystic George GURDJIEFF, a cult figure in artistic and intellectual circles. Heap had taken over most of the editing of the *Little Review*, turning its focus to international movements such as surrealism and cubism; yet the magazine was waning, and its last issue appeared in 1929. The following year Anderson published the first volume of her autobiography, *My Thirty Years' War*. During the German occupation of France, Leblanc died, and Anderson, returning to America, met on shipboard Dorothy Caruso, widow of the tenor Enrico Caruso; Caruso became her companion until Caruso's death in 1955. The second volume of Anderson's autobiography, *The Fiery Fountains*, telling of her relationships with Heap and Leblanc, appeared in 1951. Returning to France, Anderson lived as a recluse, publishing in 1961 *The Unknowable Gurdjieff*, an advocacy of the mystic's views, and in 1969 *The Strange Necessity*, her final autobiographical volume.

The ascendency of Anderson within the Chicago Renaissance was short-lived. Appearing briefly on the scene, drawing to her a range of modernist and experimental artists, she soon moved on to other locales and interests. In a city associated with REALISM, even NATURALISM, she sought out imagination and creativity, leaving behind a spirited, feminine leavening to the city's early 20th-century expression.

Anderson, Sherwood
(1876–1941) *writer*

Author of the epochal WINESBURG, OHIO, Anderson is an important figure in the history of the American short story, as well as one of the major writers of the Chicago Renaissance. Born in Camden, Ohio, growing up in Clyde, Ohio, he drew material for fiction from his hometown for the rest of his life. After the death of his mother in 1895, he moved to Chicago, finding work in a warehouse; he returned to Ohio at the outbreak of the SPANISH-AMERICAN WAR, enlisting in an Ohio infantry regiment and serving four months of noncombat duty in Cuba. Back in Chicago in 1900, Anderson worked as an advertising copywriter, marrying in 1904; two years later, he returned to his native state, establishing himself in business, eventually heading a mail-order paint-manufacturing business in Elyria, Ohio. A turning point in his life came in November 1912, when, three days after walking out of his company office, he was found wandering and dazed in Cleveland. After hospitalization, he returned to Chicago, leaving his business and eventually his family.

At the age of 36, Anderson found literary companionship in Chicago, becoming part of an informal group known as the FIFTY-SEVENTH STREET GROUP, or the Jackson Park colony; Carl SANDBURG, Margaret ANDERSON, Ben HECHT, and Floyd DELL were among the members. A new impetus to creativity came two years later, in the spring of 1915, when a Chicago lawyer, Edgar Lee MASTERS, published a volume of poetry, SPOON RIVER ANTHOLOGY; a collection of gravestone monologues, *Spoon River* offered a new picture of small-town America, revealing it as a place of dysfunction and repression. Using similar subject matter, Anderson began writing the stories collected four years later in *Winesburg, Ohio*.

In 1916, he published WINDY MCPHERSON'S SON, a novel he had brought with him in manuscript from Ohio; its first portion is set in a

Winesburg-like small town. In the same year he married Tennessee MITCHELL, a music teacher and sculptor who had been the mistress of Masters. In 1917, he published MARCHING MEN, another Ohio manuscript, a novel that would continue to puzzle critics; they called it proletarian at first, then fascist. Meanwhile, the stories that would go into *Winesburg* were appearing in small magazines, including LITTLE REVIEW; the collected volume was published in 1919. The follow-up to *Winesburg,* appearing in 1920, was the novel POOR WHITE, considered the best of Anderson's full-length fiction.

In 1921, a benefactor took the author and his wife to Europe, where he met Gertrude STEIN and James JOYCE; Anderson would later give the young Ernest HEMINGWAY, whom he had met in Chicago, a letter of introduction to Stein in Paris. In the same year he published THE TRIUMPH OF THE EGG, a collection of tales and poems that received critical praise; another collection, HORSES AND MEN, appeared two years later. Leaving his second wife in 1922, going to Reno, Nevada, for a divorce—Clarence DARROW was his Chicago lawyer—he married again in 1924; his novel of 1923, MANY MARRIAGES, depicts the dissolution of a long-term marriage. For the next several years, Anderson spent time in New Orleans, producing in 1925 his best-selling novel DARK LAUGHTER, a work depicting African Americans in a manner that would be considered stereotyped today; Hemingway, the writer he had once helped, parodied *Dark Laughter* in his TORRENTS OF SPRING the following year.

Anderson continued to produce short stories, novels, poems, and essays throughout the 1920s; SHERWOOD ANDERSON'S NOTEBOOK gathered essays and stories in a 1926 collection. Yet by the end of the decade, his work was receiving less acclaim and reaching a smaller audience; in 1927, he bought two weekly newspapers in rural Virginia, settling into writing journalistic pieces, collected in the volume *Hello Towns.* In 1929, he separated from his third wife, the same year that his second wife, Tennessee, was found dead in her Chicago apartment, possibly from an overdose of sleeping pills; he married for a fourth time in 1933. His final important collection of stories, DEATH IN THE WOODS, appeared in 1933; the title piece, first pub-

Sherwood Anderson, in this portrait from about 1922, had recently published a well-received story collection, *The Triumph of the Egg.* (*Chicago Historical Society*)

lished in 1926, has become a classic in American short fiction. During the GREAT DEPRESSION of the 1930s, spurred by the interests of his new wife, he became involved in social causes, lending his support to labor agitation in Virginia and Kentucky. Early in 1941, while on a goodwill tour to South

America, he fell ill on shipboard; taken to hospital in Colón, Panama, he died of peritonitis at the age of 64.

Anderson's greatest achievement is as an innovator of the English-language short story, an area in which American writers have predominated. Avoiding conventional plots and the plot-driven tale—the ultimate example, as Anderson noted, being the work of O. Henry, or William Sydney PORTER—Anderson created stories that capture instances of heightened awareness and perception, leading the short-story genre away from the tenets of REALISM. In the post-*Winesburg* tales, he began exploring the process of narration and narrative techniques, focusing on the reporting of events and on the evolving perceptions of the reporter. Anderson's fiction influenced a range of 20th-century writers, including the sometimes-sneering Hemingway, as they strove to reach beyond realism, beyond specific events, to moments of understanding and revelation.

Further Reading

Townsend, Kim. *Sherwood Anderson*. Boston: Houghton Mifflin Company, 1987.

White, Ray Lewis, ed. *The Achievement of Sherwood Anderson*. Chapel Hill: University of North Carolina Press, 1966.

Williams, Kenny J. *A Storyteller and a City: Sherwood Anderson's Chicago*. DeKalb: Northern Illinois University Press, 1988.

Andersonville

A Confederate prison camp for captured Union soldiers during the CIVIL WAR, officially named Camp Sumter, the prison was established near Andersonville, Georgia, early in 1864. The facility held 45,000 soldiers, nearly 13,000 of whom died of starvation or disease; its commander was the one Confederate officer executed for treason after the war. In "The Book of the Grotesque," the introductory tale in Sherwood ANDERSON's *WINESBURG, OHIO*, a man who had once been a prisoner at Andersonville weeps when he thinks of his brother who died there. MacKinlay KANTOR's Pulitzer Prize–winning novel of 1955, *Andersonville*, portrays a fictionalized version of the camp.

Anglin, Margaret
(1876–1958) *actress, producer*

Born into a politician's family in Ottawa, Canada, Anglin made her debut on the New York stage in 1894. Her roles ranged from Shakespeare's Cleopatra to Euripides' Medea to the heroine in *The Count of Monte Cristo*, playing opposite popular actor James O'Neill, father of playwright Eugene O'NEILL. Taking on the duties of manager, she undertook the staging of William Vaughn MOODY's 1906 play, *THE GREAT DIVIDE*, first in Chicago, then in New York; the role of Ruth Jordan in the play has been called one of her most memorable achievements. Anglin remained active on the stage in the 1940s, playing in Lillian Hellman's wartime drama, *Watch on the Rhine*.

"Another Wife"   See DEATH IN THE WOODS.

Anti-Imperialist League

An organization formed to fight American territorial expansion, the league was founded in 1898 after the SPANISH-AMERICAN WAR. It opposed all U.S. expansion after the defeat of Spain, including acquisition of the Philippines; in the years following the war, American troops were continuing to fight Philippine rebels—who had previously fought against Spain—for control of the nation. The word *imperialism*, deriving from the Latin word for empire, refers to the rule by one nation or society over another; in modern times the term has referred to colonial expansion by European powers, beginning with the age of navigation in the 15th century.

Rallies led by the Anti-Imperialist League took place in Chicago in 1899, supported by Henry B. FULLER, William Vaughn MOODY, and other literary figures; an important national spokesman was the writer Mark Twain. Industrialist Andrew Carnegie backed the aims of the league, offering to buy the Philippines for $20 million, afterward giving the nation its freedom; Democratic candidate William Jennings BRYAN placed the issue of imperialism in the party's platform in the 1900 presidential election. Two poems by Moody, "ODE IN A TIME OF HESITATION" and "ON A SOLDIER FALLEN IN THE PHILIPPINES," were widely read after their publication in the *Atlantic Monthly* in 1900 and 1901; the league collected "Ode" and other poems in a volume entitled *Liberty Poems Inspired by the Crisis of 1898–1900*. Failing to win the support of organized labor or to receive other broadly based endorsement, the league eventually dissolved.

Anti-Saloon League

The first group bearing this name, the Ohio Anti-Saloon League, was founded in 1893 in Oberlin, Ohio; two years later, a National Anti-Saloon League was organized in Washington, D.C. Committed to sponsoring temperance legislation, as well as to enforcing existing laws, the league chose to work within the current political framework, supporting "dry" candidates from either party; it differed in this matter from the PROHIBITION PARTY, founded as a separate party nearly 25 years earlier. Baptist John D. ROCKEFELLER was a major contributor to the Anti-Saloon League; poet Vachel LINDSAY toured the league's lecture circuit in central Illinois in the first decade of the 20th century. Because of its nonpartisanship, the league became a stronger political force than the Prohibition Party, as the nation headed toward PROHIBITION after WORLD WAR I.

Lindsay's popular poem of 1914, "The Drunkard's Funeral," collected in *THE CHINESE NIGHTINGALE AND OTHER POEMS*, features a repeated mourners' chorus, "The saloon must go, / The saloon must go."

antitrust

The corporate TRUST—a combining of enterprises, concentrating of economic power, eliminating competition, and fixing prices—burgeoned after the CIVIL WAR. The Sherman Anti-Trust Act, passed in 1890, banned combination acting "in restraint of trade," becoming the first national antitrust measure; Senator John Sherman of Ohio considered the PULLMAN PALACE CAR COMPANY one of the nation's greatest malefactors. Yet during the law's first decade, actions were brought most frequently against unions, not businesses; Eugene V. DEBS's arrest during the PULLMAN STRIKE came when his union boycott was ruled in violation of the Sherman act. The redirecting of antitrust activity against business was spurred by Theodore ROOSEVELT, taking up the cause of "trust-busting" after becoming president in 1901. The first major antibusiness action, occurring in 1904, broke up a combination of railroads; the most famous case was against John D. ROCKEFELLER's Standard Oil Company, brought by the federal government in 1908, resulting in the Supreme Court's breakup of the company in 1911. The Clayton Antitrust Act of 1914, amending and supplementing the Sherman act, excluded labor unions from the restraint-of-trade ban.

"An Apology for Crudity"   *See SHERWOOD ANDERSON'S NOTEBOOK.*

The Appeal to Reason

This socialist weekly newspaper, founded in Kansas City in 1896, moving a year later to Girard, Kansas, became an important political voice in the early years of the new century. Floyd DELL first read the paper as a teenager in Quincy, Illinois, joining the Socialist Party at the age of 16. In 1904, the periodical sent Upton SINCLAIR to Chicago to investigate conditions in the stockyards; it published the resulting novel, *THE JUNGLE*, in serial installments before its publication in book form. Toward the end of the work, Sinclair depicts his protagonist, Jurgis RUDKUS, as awakening to the promise of SOCIALISM; Jurgis learns about *The Appeal to Reason*, about how a former Colorado real-estate speculator started to publish the four-page weekly to benefit the "American working-mule." In 1917, the magazine broke ranks with other socialist groups, supporting American entry into WORLD WAR I.

Appleton, Tom "Tony"

A character in Sherwood ANDERSON's story "The Sad Horn Blowers," collected in HORSES AND MEN, Tom, a housepainter and paperhanger, is one of many versions of Anderson's father. Like that other housepainter, Windy MCPHERSON of WINDY MCPHERSON'S SON, Tom is an embarrassment to his children—as well as an incompetent horn player in village celebrations; in this particular story the townspeople put up with his playing in the local band because they like him. His career downfall comes when he spills two pots of hot coffee over himself, sustaining burns that keep him from working. Later, Tom's son, Will APPLETON, comes across another "sad horn blower," an old man who is trying to assert himself by blowing his cornet, while realizing, too, that he is no longer relevant in life.

Appleton, Will

The principal character in Sherwood ANDERSON's story "The Sad Horn Blowers," collected in HORSES AND MEN, Will leaves his hometown of Bidwell, Ohio—the fictional town featured in the novel POOR WHITE, as well as in other Anderson stories—after his mother dies and his father can no longer work. He finds factory work in Erie, Pennsylvania. Receiving a letter from his older sister, learning that she is marrying, he realizes that his home will be gone, that he will now be on his own in the world. The title of the story refers to two amateur horn blowers, or cornet players, who have impinged on Will's life—his father, who plays poorly, and an old man at his boardinghouse, who is too old to play. The old man urges Will to assert himself, to blow the horn loudly.

Arbeiter Zeitung

Because of the constraints imposed by owners of mainstream newspapers, the foreign-language press in Chicago became by default the radical press. Arbeiter Zeitung, a German-language daily newspaper, "the worker's newspaper," turned from SOCIALISM in the early 1880s to an active espousal of ANARCHISM, becoming a focus of the HAYMARKET AFFAIR trial. Its editor, German-born August SPIES, stood as one of the accused anarchists; the paper's offices were searched, and calls to violent action were found, further incriminating the defendants.

Archie, Dr. Howard

A character in Willa CATHER's novel THE SONG OF THE LARK, based on a real-life doctor in Cather's home town of Red Cloud, Nebraska, Dr. Archie first treats the young Thea KRONBORG for pneumonia, then establishes a friendship with her. He soon realizes that Thea is different from the rest of her family, as well as from the town of Moonstone, Colorado. Unhappily married, he accepts his role as mentor and helper to Thea, aiding her as she rises to fame in the artistic world—a world he himself never understands, although he intuitively understands that she possesses personal greatness. Archie first helps Thea to become established in Chicago; later, he travels to New York to lend her money for study in Germany. His wife dies, and his status in the world improves from a silver mine investment, and yet his role continues to be the supporter and admirer of this remarkable woman—a role seemingly bringing him all the contentment he needs.

The Arena

This short-lived Boston magazine was an early publisher of Hamlin GARLAND. Founded in 1889 by Benjamin O. Flower, father-in-law of Hutchins HAPGOOD, the magazine ran articles supporting the theories of Henry GEORGE and other radical and POPULIST causes. After publishing some of Garland's short stories on midwestern farm life—considered too harsh for established outlets—the periodical sponsored the first publication of Garland's MAIN-TRAVELLED ROADS, issuing a paperbound edition in 1891.

Armour, Philip D.
(1832–1901) *meatpacker*

Born on a farm in New York State, traveling briefly to the gold fields of California, Armour settled in the meatpacking business in Milwaukee; his first fortune came from speculating on pork futures at the end of the CIVIL WAR. Arriving in Chicago in 1875, the same year as his rival-to-be, Gustavus F. SWIFT, he became known for his detailed organization and efficient operation. While Swift's name is associated with refrigeration technology, Armour's is linked to a particular decree—that no part of an animal should be wasted, that previously discarded animal parts, from horns to hooves to internal organs, should be turned into buttons, soap, candles, glue, oleomargarine, and digestive aids. Upton SINCLAIR's novel THE JUNGLE provides a version of the dictum: "Use everything about the hog except the squeal." In 1893, at the urging of a clergyman, Frank W. GUNSAULUS, Armour founded the ARMOUR INSTITUTE, a technical school, later the Illinois Institute of Technology. After the SPANISH-AMERICAN WAR of 1898, his company was accused of having sold tainted canned meat to the United States Army. Armour died in Chicago at the age of 68.

Known also as a grain speculator, Armour was a figure in the failed attempt of Joseph Leiter to corner the wheat market in 1897–98—an event that became the basis for Frank NORRIS's 1903 novel THE PIT. Robert HERRICK's novel of two years later, THE MEMOIRS OF AN AMERICAN CITIZEN, presents a fictional meatpacker who is accused of selling tainted meat during the war; the same charge, bolstered by graphic details about diseased cattle, appeared in 1906 in *The Jungle*.

Armour Institute

A technical school, later the Illinois Institute of Technology, the Armour Institute was founded in 1893 by Philip D. ARMOUR. It was established for young men to receive technical training, offering courses in mechanical and electrical engineering. In arrangement with the ART INSTITUTE, it established the Chicago School of Architecture; in 1903, the school began offering the nation's first course in fire protection engineering. The long-term president was Frank W. GUNSAULUS, the clergyman whose sermon on philanthropy had inspired the school's founding. In 1940, the Armour Institute merged with the LEWIS INSTITUTE to form the Illinois Institute of Technology; the original 1893 building, still standing on the IIT campus, was restored in 1992.

Armstrong, Hannah   *See* SPOON RIVER ANTHOLOGY.

Armstrong, Louis
(1898–1971) *trumpeter, jazz innovator, singer*

Born in New Orleans, performing in clubs in the city's Storyville district, Armstrong first came to Chicago in 1922. He joined cornetist Joe "King" OLIVER, who had earlier established his Creole Jazz Band in various BRONZEVILLE venues. In the next two years, Armstrong is credited with extending the vocabulary of JAZZ, establishing himself also as an improvisor and a soloist. He made his first acoustical recording for the Paramount Record Company in Chicago 1923; moving to New York, he returned to Chicago to make a series of records that have been recognized as milestones in the history of jazz. During his early years in the city, he saw performances by Bill "Bojangles" Robinson, the African-American singer and dancer presenting a model for his own all-around-entertainer act; at the VENDOME theater in Chicago, Armstrong perfected his Reverend Satchelmouth routine, gaining the nickname of "Satchmo." Music historians have recognized also the role of his wife, Chicago pianist Lillian "Lil" HARDIN, in his musical development.

Arnett, Justice   *See* SPOON RIVER ANTHOLOGY.

Art Deco

This style of art is also called art moderne. Flourishing in the 1920s and 1930s, the style received its name from a Paris exhibition of 1925, the

Exposition Internationale des Arts Décoratifs et Industriels Modernes, or *arts décoratifs*. Art Deco—the abbreviated label was not used until the 1960s—incorporated industrial and machine forms into interior design, furnishings, decorative arts, and architecture; it emphasized a streamlined look, making use of glass, chrome, aluminum, and industrial metals. In architecture the style promoted sleek lines and glossy surfaces, often in multicolored hues. The 1930 CHICAGO BOARD OF TRADE building, designed by Holabird and Root, represents the Art Deco style, exemplified also in its streamlined statue of Ceres, Roman goddess of grain, extending from the top of the building.

Art Institute of Chicago

This renowned museum and school was founded as the Chicago Academy of Fine Arts in 1879 and renamed in 1882. The Art Institute of Chicago moved to its current home, the former Memorial Art Palace of the WORLD'S COLUMBIAN EXPOSITION, after the fair closed in 1893. The downtown structure, although removed from the South Side fair grounds, was designed in the same ÉCOLE DES BEAUX-ARTS style as the rest of the exposition palaces; Frank Lloyd WRIGHT, sharing the views of his mentor, Louis SULLIVAN, called it "a stupid building." The school of the Art Institute, featuring such popular teachers as Lorado TAFT, a Beaux-

The Art Institute, shown here in 1918, included a museum and an art school; Walt Disney attended the school in 1917. *(Chicago Historical Society)*

Arts-trained sculptor, became the largest art school in the world. Artist-turned-poet Vachel LINDSAY studied at the Art Institute in 1901–03, artist Georgia O'Keeffe in 1905–06, and movie animator Walt Disney in 1917. The museum itself has long been noted for its extensive collections, including 19th-century French paintings donated by civic-minded businessmen and social leaders; one of the best-known works is Georges Seurat's "Sunday Afternoon on the Grande Jatte."

In Willa CATHER's *THE SONG OF THE LARK*, Thea KRONBORG finds a haven in the Art Institute, going once a week, always looking at "her picture," Jules BRETON's "The Song of the Lark," In Theodore DREISER's *THE "GENIUS,"* Eugene WITLA comes from a small town in Illinois to attend the school; at that time, in 1889, the Art Institute had not yet moved to its postfair location.

art nouveau

A style of art flourishing in the late 1890s and early 1900s—embodying a florid, linear, asymmetrical, often dreamlike quality—art nouveau was seen as a reaction against 19th-century industrialism and mass production; critics considered it erotic and degenerate as well. The movement found a Chicago outlet in the CHAP-BOOK, published by the firm of STONE AND KIMBALL between 1894 and 1898; one of the illustrators of the *Chap-Book* was Aubrey Beardsley, an English artist noted for his linear style. Louis SULLIVAN, despite his severe "form follows function" edict, made use of art nouveau detail in his architecture, exemplified in the wrought-iron ornamentation of the Carson, Pirie, Scott and Company store. Later, the style known as ART DECO brought back an industrial mode, reembracing the machine, finding sleekness in the streamlined and aerodynamic.

Arts and Crafts movement

Combining artistic activity with social reform, the Arts and Crafts movement, led by Englishman William MORRIS, began in the latter decades of the 19th century; it soon spread its influence to the United States. The emphasis was on workmanship and skill, on the use of natural materials, fabrics, and dyes; the enemy was factories and industrialization, said to have made craft obsolete. In the social arena, workers were seen as no longer valued for their skills; they were relegated to factory production and readily exploited, considered replaceable and interchangeable in the assembly line. The solution was a form of SOCIALISM that respected the sanctity of labor, that flourished through cooperation and profit sharing. The creation of quality goods was what mattered, not the creation of wealth.

Morris's Kelmscott Press produced hand-bound books that influenced the Chicago publishers STONE AND KIMBALL and WAY AND WILLIAMS. The early work of architect Frank Lloyd WRIGHT, emphasizing artistic integrity, making use of indigenous materials, followed the principles of the Arts and Crafts movement. An inevitable reaction came as critics questioned the abandoning of the machine, as artists found a role for the machine in their productions.

The young Carl SANDBURG felt the influence of Morris and his American disciple Elbert HUBBARD; Sandburg wrote briefly for the periodical *To-Morrow*, associated with Morris disciple Oscar Lovell TRIGGS. At the same time, Thorstein VEBLEN, Triggs's colleague at the UNIVERSITY OF CHICAGO, was defending machines and industrialization, labeling anti-industrial efforts as archaic and decadently romantic.

"At the Branch Road"   *See MAIN-TRAVELLED ROADS.*

Auditorium Building

This masonry structure, considered ADLER AND SULLIVAN's triumphant work, was built in 1889 at MICHIGAN AVENUE and Congress Parkway. The 10-story building, topped by a 17-story tower, included a theater, a hotel, a restaurant, a ballroom, and an office building; the commercial spaces were to subsidize the theater. At the time of construction, the Auditorium was the largest private building in the

In June 1888, the Republican National Convention met at the partially completed Auditorium Building, nominating Benjamin Harrison for president. *(Chicago Historical Society)*

country; the theater, seating more than 4,000, became the nation's largest concert hall. Louis SULLIVAN, designing one of the last great wall-bearing buildings, used iron beams to support the high ceilings of the theater; the acoustics, considered among the best in the world, were engineered by Dankmar ADLER. Frank Lloyd WRIGHT called the theater "the greatest room for music and opera in the world—bar none." The Auditorium Building was one of the earliest structures to be wired completely for electrical lighting.

The opening night audience included President Benjamin HARRISON; musical celebrations included a cantata composed to the words of Harriet MONROE, as well as the renowned opera diva Adelina PATTI's rendition of "Home, Sweet Home." The Auditorium served as the first home the CHICAGO SYMPHONY ORCHESTRA, although orchestra founder Theodore THOMAS, considering the theater too large, urged construction of a new ORCHESTRA HALL. The touring Damrosch Opera Company presented works of Richard WAGNER at the theater in the 1890s, pleasing Chicago's large German population; the CHICAGO OPERA COMPANY was established in the Auditorium in 1910. The theater closed during World War II, when the building served as a serviceman's center; a refurbished hall was opened in 1967.

In Hamlin GARLAND's 1895 novel, *ROSE OF DUTCHER'S COOLLY*, the girl from rural Wisconsin hears the Chicago Symphony Orchestra for the first time at the Auditorium, feeling thrilled by the music of Wagner. In the opening chapter of Frank NORRIS's 1903 novel THE PIT, Laura DEARBORN hears Charles Gounod's opera *Faust* in the theater, and in Willa CATHER's 1915 *THE SONG OF THE*

Louis Sullivan designed an elaborately ornamented interior for the Auditorium theater, as shown in these boxes. *(Chicago Historical Society)*

LARK, Thea KRONBORG hears her first symphony concert at the Auditorium, also including Wagner, whose music becomes part of her life.

Austin, Mary
(1868–1934) *fiction writer, essayist*

Known for her southwestern settings, yet producing a midwestern REVOLT FROM THE VILLAGE novel that foreshadowed both Willa CATHER's *THE SONG OF THE LARK* and Sinclair LEWIS's *Main Street,* Austin was born and raised in rural Carlinville, Illinois. When she was 20, she and her family moved to homestead land in the California desert; except for a decade in New York City, she lived the rest of her life in California and New Mexico. Her best-known work, the 1903 *The Land of Little Rain,* is a compilation of nature descriptions and folklore; an active environmentalist, Austin pressed also for Native American rights and the preservation of Native American and Spanish-American culture. Among her California associates were Charlotte Perkins GILMAN, with whom she shared public disapproval in having abandoned a husband and child, and MUCKRAKING writer Lincoln STEFFENS, with whom she entered into a relationship and whom she fictionalized in several works.

Her novel *A WOMAN OF GENIUS,* appearing in 1912, is autobiographical in its depiction of a repressive small midwestern town, shown as particularly constricting the lives of women. Written in New York, where Austin became acquainted with Sinclair Lewis, the novel presents many of the problems that Lewis described eight years later in *Main Street.* Yet since her heroine is an aspiring actress, the work foreshadows even more closely Willa Cather's *The Song of the Lark;* Austin's actress, freeing herself of her small town, goes on to Chicago, then to New York, setting the path that Cather's singer will follow three years later.

"An Awakening"   *See* WINESBURG, OHIO.

B

Back of the Yards *See* PACKINGTOWN.

Baker, Ray Stannard
(1870–1946) *journalist, writer*

Baker, born in Lansing, Michigan, graduated from
Michigan State College. He served later as a reporter
for the CHICAGO RECORD from 1892 until 1897. As a
protégé of George ADE, he took over the popular
"STORIES OF THE STREETS AND OF THE TOWN"
columns in Ade's absence. In 1902, writing for MC-
CLURE'S MAGAZINE, he covered a coal miners' strike
in Pennsylvania, helping to push that periodical along
the path toward MUCKRAKING; in 1906, he and Lincoln STEFFENS, Ida M. TARBELL, and others turned
the new *The American Magazine* into a further muckraking outlet. In 1907, Baker pursued yet another direction, assuming the pen name of David Grayson
and publishing *Adventures in Contentment,* the first of
what would be nine volumes of tranquil country
sketches. In 1919, after WORLD WAR I, he served as
director of the American press bureau at the Paris
peace conference; he subsequently wrote an eight-
volume life of President Woodrow WILSON, receiving
the Pulitzer Prize for biography in 1940.

Balaban, Barney
(1887–1971) *founder of the Balaban and
Katz theater chain*

Born in the MAXWELL STREET area of Chicago, the
son of Russian-Jewish immigrants, Balaban first
teamed with his brother in 1908 to buy a theater
on the near South Side. In 1915, he and Sam Katz
began their partnership that would lead to the
building of the ever-expanding BALABAN AND
KATZ chain of opulent movie palaces. In 1935, a
decade after his firm had merged with Adolph
ZUKOR's production company, Paramount Pictures,
Balaban became Paramount president. The stage
and film actor Bob Balaban is his nephew.

Balaban and Katz

A Chicago-based movie-theater chain, known for
the elegance of its showcases, as well as for early
forms of air-conditioning—and ushers who wore
red uniforms and white gloves—Balaban and Katz
began in 1908. In that year, Barney BALABAN and
his brother started purchasing venues to showcase
the increasingly popular motion pictures; they
were joined in 1915 by Sam Katz. Two years later,
the team built their first new theater. The chain's
flagship became the opulent CHICAGO THEATER,
built in 1921 on State Street in the LOOP; another
luxury venue was the 1925 UPTOWN THEATER, located on the North Side. The chain ultimately
numbered 125 theaters. In 1925, Balaban and
Katz merged with the Famous Players-Lasky Corporation, a company founded by ex-Chicagoan
Adolph ZUKOR, producing films under the name of
Paramount Pictures; Barney Balaban became president of Paramount in 1935. Legal troubles arose
in the late 1940s, when the company faced AN-

TITRUST actions; movie theaters were ordered by the U.S. Supreme Court to sever ties with the studios that produced the movies. Eventually, the Balaban and Katz chain was bought by Canadian-based Cineplex Odeon; a large portion of the original showcases have been demolished.

Balmer, Edwin
(1883–1959) *writer, editor*

Best remembered as the coauthor, along with Philip Wylie, of the science fiction classic *When Worlds Collide,* Balmer wrote a series of crime and detective novels during his years as a Chicago journalist. Born in the city, becoming a reporter for the CHICAGO TRIBUNE in 1903, he served as editor of the Chicago-based periodical *Red Book* from 1927 until 1949. With his brother-in-law William MacHarg, he wrote a set of detective stories featuring Luther Trant, claimed to be America's first fictional scientific criminologist; Trant, making use of X rays and microscopes, developed also a new crime-solving device, the lie-detector. Balmer's 1925 thriller, *That Royle Girl,* became the basis for the legendary lost movie, the 1925 THAT ROYLE GIRL, shot partly in Chicago, starring W. C. Field and directed by D. W. GRIFFITH. Balmer and Wylie's *When Worlds Collide* became an apocalyptic movie in 1951.

Barker, Amanda   *See SPOON RIVER ANTHOLOGY.*

Barriers Burned Away
E. P. Roe
(1872)

ROE's novel is set against the background of the GREAT FIRE. A Presbyterian minister in New York, Roe came to Chicago immediately after the disaster, gaining material for a detailed description of the event and its aftermath; the novel first appeared serially in the magazine *New York Evangelist.* In the story, a Christian man, loving a wealthy woman who is a nonbeliever, saves her during the fire, leading her along with others to the lake shore. There, at the lakefront, social inequalities are leveled, and the barriers of class and status are burned away; the woman accepts her rescuer's faith, and a new spirit of brotherhood prevails. A silent movie from the novel appeared in 1925.

Bates, Susan

A character in Henry B. FULLER's novel WITH THE PROCESSION, based in part on the real-life Bertha Honoré PALMER, Mrs. Granger Bates is depicted as the leader of Chicago society. Although opulent in her lifestyle—and determined to remain the leader of the social "procession"—she is presented sympathetically; she takes her charitable work seriously, and she remembers the days when her manner of living was more modest. A special room in her mansion is furnished in the style of the room she once occupied in her carpenter father's house. Among her charities is a summer camp in Wisconsin for city children; she insists that members of society do more than give money, that they participate personally in their altruistic enterprise. She manages to increase the social conscience of Cecilia Ingles, the young, beautiful wife of an older man—who serves also as the enigmatic society icon of Fuller's previous novel, THE CLIFF-DWELLERS. Mrs. Bates appears briefly in *The Cliff-Dwellers* as well; in both works she is a patron of the Charity Ball, as was the real-life Mrs. Palmer.

Baum, L. Frank
(1856–1919) *writer*

Lyman Frank Baum remains famed for THE WONDERFUL WIZARD OF OZ, published in Chicago in 1900, inspired in part by the WORLD'S COLUMBIAN EXPOSITION. Born in Chittenango, New York, participating as a young man in acting and playwriting, Baum moved in 1888 to Aberdeen in the Dakota Territory, where he bought and edited a weekly newspaper; he moved to Chicago in 1891 to join the staff of the *Chicago Evening Post.*

Mother Goose in Prose, published in 1897 by the firm of WAY AND WILLIAMS, was his first book for children; Maxfield Parrish, producing book drawings for the first time, was its soon-to-be-famous illustrator. For his next volume, *Father Goose: His Book,* Baum collaborated with illustrator Arthur W. W. DENSLOW; when their small Chicago publisher, George M. Hill Company, was unwilling to pay for color plates, Baum and Denslow paid for the plates themselves. The book proved a success, although the publisher again required payment for the illustrations of their next volume, originally titled "The Emerald City"; the work appeared in 1900 as *The Wonderful Wizard of Oz.* Baum and Denslow later dissolved their partnership, Denslow going on to publish *Denslow's Scarecrow and the Tin-Man* in 1904. Baum, using a new illustrator, John R. Neill, published *The Marvelous Land of Oz* the same year; Neill became the illustrator of 32 Oz books, writing and illustrating three of his own.

A stage musical, THE WIZARD OF OZ, opened in Chicago in 1902; it subsequently achieved a long New York run, becoming a staple of touring companies. Turning to the new motion pictures, Baum began to work with William N. SELIG of the Selig Polyscope Company, scripting a series of short movies on Oz themes; in 1910, Selig released four Oz-inspired one-reelers. Moving to California the same year, Baum established Oz Film Manufacturing Company; the firm proved unsuccessful, although at the same time he was publishing a series of girls' stories, using the pen name of Edith Van Dyne. Baum died in Hollywood at the age of 63; his last book, *Glinda of Oz,* was issued posthumously. After his death his publisher hired the writer Ruth Plumly Thompson to continue the Oz series, keeping Neill as illustrator; the last official Oz book appeared in 1963.

Beery, Wallace
(1885–1949) *film actor*

Comedian and character actor, Beery played his first movie roles for the ESSANAY FILM MANUFACTURING COMPANY. Born in Kansas City, Missouri, he began his career at Essanay in 1914 and achieved popularity with a series of one-reel comedies, performing as "Sweedie," a Swedish maid, in women's clothes. The 1915 *Sweedie Goes to College,* placing Sweedie as a servant in a girls' college dormitory, featured also the Chicago-born Gloria SWANSON. Beery and Swanson were married from 1916 to 1918. Moving with the film industry to Los Angeles, Beery won an Academy Award for the *The Champ* in 1931; other roles of the 1930s included an alcoholic waterfront character in *Tugboat Annie* and Long John Silver in *Treasure Island.*

Beiderbecke, Leon Bismarck "Bix"
(1903–1931) *jazz cornetist, composer*

Born in Davenport, Iowa, Beiderbecke, at the age of 15, heard Louis ARMSTRONG play on a Mississippi River showboat. Sent to school in the Chicago suburb of Lake Forest, spending his time in the city's JAZZ clubs, he first played professionally with the Wolverine Orchestra, a Chicago band named after Jelly Roll MORTON's "Wolverine Blues"; he toured with other midwestern groups before moving to New York. His active musical career, shortened by bootleg alcohol during the years of PROHIBITION, lasted six years; he died of pneumonia at the age of 28. "In a Mist" remains his best-known composition; "Davenport Blues" reflects his origins. Dorothy Baker's 1938 novel, *Young Man with a Horn,* is loosely based on his life; the 1950 movie starred Kirk Douglas.

Bellamy, Edward
(1850–1898) *utopian writer*

Bellamy is the author of the most significant work in American utopianism, the widely read *Looking Backward, 2000–1887,* published in 1888. Born in Massachusetts, the son of a Baptist minister, he achieved instant fame with his novel set in the future. Bellamy clubs sprang up across the nation, including one organized by novelist and critic William Dean HOWELLS. Espousing SOCIALISM, *Looking Backward* rejects the Marxist idea of a class struggle, suggesting that the achievement of a socialist state—the placing of corporations under government ownership—comes from common sense, from voluntary benevolence; society's principal virtue is cooperation, not competition, and the tenets of SOCIAL DARWINISM are overlooked. Other beneficent utopias followed this work, including William MORRIS's 1891 *News from Nowhere* and Howells's 1894 *A Traveler from Altruria*. In contrast is Jack LONDON's work of 1907, *The Iron Heel*—also looking back, although in this case over many centuries—in which a socialist society is established only after hundreds of years of bloody rule by the capitalist Oligarchy, or Iron Heel.

Edward Bellamy was a cousin of Francis Bellamy, advocate of CHRISTIAN SOCIALISM and author of the U.S. Pledge of Allegiance.

Bell and Howell

A pioneering motion-picture equipment company founded in 1907 by ESSANAY FILM MANUFACTURING COMPANY employees Donald J. Bell and Albert S. Howell, the firm became an early producer of movie cameras and projection equipment. Placing the first movie camera on the market in 1910, Bell and Howell played a crucial role in the standardizing of cinematography; the company became the standard supplier of equipment to Hollywood. The modern firm, headquartered in suburban Lincolnwood—having left the movie industry in the 1970s—is a developer of electronic communication and processing.

Bellow, Saul
(1915–   ) *Post–Chicago Renaissance novelist*

Born near Montreal, coming to Chicago at the age of nine, Bellow graduated from NORTHWESTERN UNIVERSITY in 1937. His first novel, *Dangling Man*, appeared in 1944; his breakthrough work was *The Adventures of Augie March*, published in 1953. *Augie*, the exuberant tale of a boy's seeking to find his way in the world, begins, "I am an American, Chicago-born." Bellow's later novels include the 1964 *Herzog*, the 1970 *Mr. Sammler's Planet*, the 1975 *Humboldt's Gift*; the last work received a Pulitzer Prize. Serving for many years as professor at the UNIVERSITY OF CHICAGO, Bellow won the Nobel Prize in literature in 1976.

Bentley, Jesse; Louise   *See* WINESBURG, OHIO: "Godliness."

Berczynskas, Marija

A character in Upton SINCLAIR's novel THE JUNGLE, the cousin of Ona RUDKUS, Marija comes with her family and Jurgis RUDKUS from the forests of Lithuania. A strong and determined woman, she finds work in a packinghouse but is laid off because of her outspokenness. Ultimately she finds a place in a house of prostitution. When Jurgis discovers her situation, he urges her to leave; yet she has nowhere to go, and, like the other women in the brothel, she is hooked on drugs.

Bertram Cope's Year
Henry Blake Fuller
(1919)

A novel by Henry Blake FULLER, this privately printed work was ignored in Fuller's lifetime, probably in part because of its gay theme, which, although never fully specified, was recognizable. Today, to contemporary readers, the theme seems positively advertised.

The Chicago suburb of Churchton—its name suggesting, as Fuller intended, prominent religious edifices—is modeled on EVANSTON; the unnamed university is the Methodist-founded NORTHWESTERN UNIVERSITY. Fuller notes that in 1840 Churchton consisted of a single tavern, undoubtedly finding irony in the fact that the new university's charter, enacted 11 years later, banned alcohol within a four-mile radius of the campus.

In a novel that has little to do with business endeavors—unlike his earlier THE CLIFF-DWELLERS and WITH THE PROCESSION—Fuller yet introduces his standard criticism of the business mentality; the young businessman is shown as condescending to the university instructor Bertram COPE, assuming that his own occupation presents the norm against which men are to be measured. Fuller also continues his recurring theme of the businessman father and his artistic son; Basil RANDOLPH, a gentleman stockbroker by inheritance, cares little for business, and Arthur LEMOYNE, musician and actor, rejects the family business outright, persuading his father to give up on preparing him for an inherited occupation.

Bertram Cope's Year is in many ways a backward-looking novel, reminiscent of the genteel fiction of Henry James—even as it appeared the same year as Sherwood ANDERSON's ground-breaking WINESBURG, OHIO. Yet the work can be said to look to the future as well, pursuing its clear, if obliquely labeled, gay theme. In 1998, the novel received its first reprinting since the original publication.

Synopsis

CHAPTERS 1–5: "COPE AT A COLLEGE TEA," "COPE MAKES A SUNDAY AFTERNOON CALL," "COPE IS 'ENTERTAINED,'" "COPE IS CONSIDERED," "COPE IS CONSIDERED FURTHER"

Bertram Cope, a newly arrived university instructor in the suburb of Churchton, attends a reception where he meets Mrs. Medora PHILLIPS, a wealthy fortyish widow, and Basil Randolph, a fiftyish bachelor. Both Mrs. Phillips and Randolph are on the lookout for protégés—Mrs. Phillips to add to her socially glamorous entourage, Randolph to offer personal friendship and wisdom. Bertram joins Mrs. Phillips at her home for tea, and yet as she talks, he mentally composes a letter to his friend Arthur, whom he has left behind in Wisconsin. Several young women are in attendance, including Amy, a violinist, Carolyn, a poet, and Hortense, a painter; Cope speaks flippantly of being on Parnassus—the mount sacred to Apollo and the Muses, goddesses of the arts—and Hortense responds with a frown, implying that he is being insincere. In an era when all music is performed live, Amy entertains the guests by playing the violin, and Carolyn reads poetry; Cope is prevailed upon to sing, accompanying himself on the piano. Later, as he leaves, Mrs. Phillips remarks that he seems not to care for the young women, that he fails to find them clever or interesting. In his mind he continues writing the letter to Arthur, saying that he misses his friend and wishes his friend would come to Churchton.

Randolph finds out Cope's address and walks by the young man's modest boardinghouse; he no-

tices lighted windows and wonders which window is his. Later, he visits Mrs. Phillips, and they agree that Cope is charming, if somewhat self-centered. Randolph discreetly learns as much as he can about the young man, not wishing to seem too interested.

Joseph FOSTER, an invalid relative of Mrs. Phillips, confined to a wheelchair, lives on the upper floor of her house; Randolph regularly visits and reads to him. When Randolph goes up to the third floor, Foster says he is glad to have a man in the house, since it is usually full of women. Foster mentions that he has heard Mrs. Phillips's new protégé singing, although he has not met the young man; he finds that he sings with a "cool correctness." Both men speak wistfully of how young students condescend to older men, acting carelessly and thoughtlessly toward them.

CHAPTERS 6–9: "COPE DINES—AND TELLS ABOUT IT," "COPE UNDER SCRUTINY," "COPE UNDERTAKES AN EXCURSION," "COPE ON THE EDGE OF THINGS"

Cope begins his actual letter to Arthur, saying that he misses him. When he speaks of being "gay," he is using the then-standard sense of the word, meaning not only merry or lively, but also, as here, partaking in social pleasures. Cope tells Arthur of a dinner at Mrs. Phillips's mansion, where he met Randolph once more, as well as a man in a wheelchair. He mentions Hortense, the artist, a niece of Mrs. Phillips, who is "a bit tonguey"; wit in a woman, he remarks, makes him uncomfortable. He adds that Randolph expressed hopes of hearing him sing, but he made it clear that he needed his regular accompanist—and Cope pleads once more for Arthur to come to Churchton, where they can live together.

Cope continues his letter later, saying that Randolph has since called on him, providing a pleasant distraction from his students. Cope has in turn called on Randolph, finding that the older man lives in a handsomely decorated apartment; Randolph has invited him to dinner and the theater in the city. Cope reports that they spoke of Shakespeare and Bacon, Randolph explaining how proving Bacon's authorship could become like a parlor game; one selects the letters of a text by an arbitrary formula, then makes those letters provide a hidden message, buried in the text. Cope concludes his letter by insisting that Arthur be in Churchton by January.

Mrs. Phillips asks Randolph about his dinner and theater engagement with Cope; Randolph speaks lightly, although Mrs. Phillips detects feeling in his words. She announces a Sunday excursion to the INDIANA DUNES, the scenic lakefront area where she owns a house; she adds that her car will be full and Randolph should come by train, bringing Cope with him.

On Sunday morning Randolph and Cope leave the Indiana train station and begin the walk to the house. Arriving at the lake shore, they contemplate a swim; Cope sheds his clothes and wades in. He asks Randolph about the other guests and learns that the three girls will be among them; he remarks that he has no knack with girls, nor is he eager to acquire such an ability.

CHAPTERS 10–12: "COPE AT HIS HOUSE PARTY," "COPE ENLIVENS THE COUNTRY," "COPE AMIDST CROSS PURPOSES"

Mrs. Phillips leads the guests in a nature appreciation walk, although she is appreciating Cope's appearance as well. Among the group is a young businessman who assumes that a business life is the highest pursuit for men, that other pursuits, such as Cope's academic endeavors, are inferior. Seeking to escape the man, Cope ends up walking with Amy Leffingwell, the violinist, also an instructor at the university. Back at the house he sings to a gramophone record, winning admiration from Amy and others. Yet he has a class to teach the next morning, and he and Randolph return to Churchton.

Cope receives a letter from Arthur Lemoyne, in which Arthur mentions taking a trip to Green Bay with a young man who has just bought a roadster; Cope reads the passage "darkly." However, he is comforted when Arthur says he is thinking of moving to Churchton, although he will have to find employment; perhaps, Arthur suggests, someone among the faculty or trustees could find him a place in the library or registrar's office. Later, Cope learns that Randolph's brother-in-law is a university trustee. Meanwhile, Cope and Randolph mention to each other their need to obtain larger living quarters; Randolph's unspoken motive is to have more room for overnight guests, such as Cope; Cope's unspoken motive is to have Arthur come and live with him.

CHAPTERS 13–15: "COPE DINES AGAIN— AND STAYS AFTER," "COPE MAKES AN EVASION," "COPE ENTERTAINS SEVERAL LADIES"

Mrs. Phillips invites Cope, who avoids alcohol, to a dinner at which she serves wine. Having had a busy day and eaten little lunch, Cope takes a few sips of burgundy and comes close to fainting; he is led to a sofa in the library to lie down.

Randolph, visiting Joe Foster, tells him of his intent to move to larger quarters. He is planning also to take Cope on a weekend trip to the downstate Indian Rock area; he knows of a fine hotel on the river. Cope calls off the trip at the last minute, saying that he has unexpected work to do and that family members are coming to town. Feeling let down and hurt, Randolph goes to Mrs. Phillips's home and talks again to Foster, although he refrains from speaking of his disappointment.

Cope has been absent from the classroom, and his landlady and others are worried about his health. Mrs. Phillips and Amy Leffingwell call on him, although they find that he seems well enough. He tells them he is moving, and he brings out photographs from Wisconsin, where he had previously lived. Mrs. Phillips notices a young man in the pictures, and Cope identifies him as the friend who will be coming to live with him in January. Mrs. Phillips remarks later to Amy that she is glad he likes *somebody*.

Cope resumes his letter to Arthur. He writes that seeing new scenery with "Mr. R." would have been good for him, but he acknowledges that Arthur has "first claim." So he gave up Indian Rock for Arthur—although Arthur, he adds, did not give up Green Bay for him. Yet he is missing his friend more than ever.

CHAPTERS 16–18: "COPE GOES A-SAILING," "COPE AMONG CROSS-CURRENTS," "COPE AT THE CALL OF DUTY"

Cope happens to meet Amy on campus one Sunday afternoon—less than accidentally on her part—and walking along the lakefront, they decide to rent a sailboat. After a few minutes out on the lake, the boat capsizes, and they are forced to swim to shore, a hundred yards away. She untangles him from the sail, and he supports her at first in swimming, although by the end she is supporting him. Yet she tells Mrs. Phillips that he was brave and strong, implying that he saved her life. She and Cope are now viewed by many as a couple.

Randolph invites Cope for dinner in his new apartment, and he learns for the first time that his move into new rooms is to accommodate a friend arriving from Wisconsin. He wonders if his own acquisition of larger quarters was for nothing, and Cope, in turn, wonders if Randolph's connection with the university board of trustees might help find employment for Arthur.

Social convention dictates that Cope pay a call at Mrs. Phillips's house to inquire after Amy, although he has taken his time in doing so. When he calls, Foster has been brought downstairs, and the invalid understands what is happening; he observes the insistent Amy, as well as the withdrawing Cope, who seems to be trying to remove himself from the company. Foster notes also the young businessman, George Pearson, who covertly disparages Cope while showing an interest in Amy. Hortense is watching as well, and when she finds Cope seated at a library table, she demands that he speak to her, that he stop ignoring her. She has a great personal interest in him, and yet she is implying, too, that he is disengaged from a household that has treated him hospitably.

Amy has written a song for him to sing, and he obliges, although refusing to sing more; Mrs. Phillips suggests he provide some other entertainment, such as a recitation, or the telling of a story. Bowing to pressure, he notices a decorative collection of dried leaves, and he begins to put together a rustic folktale. His story tells of a group of wood nymphs, "a nice enough lot of girls" but who have one great disadvantage in that they have no thumbs—a tale today's readers would find patently Freudian. Amy later accompanies Cope to the door, taking his hand affectionately. He walks home flustered, feeling that her hand was one of possession.

CHAPTERS 19–21: "COPE FINDS HIMSELF COMMITTED," "COPE HAS A DISTRESSFUL CHRISTMAS," "COPE, SAFEGUARDED, CALLS AGAIN"

Amy continues contriving to meet Cope on campus, as well as sending him notes. Despite her delicate-seeming exterior, she is, the author comments—slipping into his occasional first-person plural "we" or "us"—basically stubborn and tenacious. So the

atmosphere has changed at Mrs. Phillips's household, and expectation is in the air—although Mrs. Phillips herself is not pleased, as she wants Cope to continue being part of her domain, not to be diverted elsewhere.

Foster tells Randolph of Amy's obvious expectations, and Randolph is upset, wondering also about the arrival of Cope's friend from Wisconsin; Foster has understood all along the older man's reason for moving into his larger apartment. Cope, meanwhile, is trying to remember what he had said to Amy to make her assume they were engaged; perhaps he had used the word *wait,* and she took it to mean more than he had intended. Whatever it was, she had then put her face up to his, expecting to be kissed, and he, feeling pity at her expression when he hesitated, had lightly brushed her lips. Now he is feeling dismay and repugnance at what seems to be unfolding before him. Modern readers, thrust into an earlier era, must realize that he is following a gentlemanly code of honor, still governing polite society at the time.

Cope writes to Arthur about what has happened, and his friend replies that he must "nip it." During the Christmas holiday, Cope visits his family downstate, and Arthur joins him, determined to help Cope extricate himself from his entrapment. Returning together to Churchton, they establish their new living arrangements. When they call on Mrs. Phillips, Arthur is introduced, and Mrs. Phillips notes how proprietary the young man is toward Cope; she remarks on the matter to Foster, who passes the remark on to Randolph—who makes his own "astringent" comment. The young businessman, George Pearson, is in attendance as well, boasting about a business success he has achieved. Cope and Arthur together sing the ballad "Larboard Watch," Arthur providing the piano accompaniment. Cope is now singing as Churchton listeners have never heard him sing—with animation and feeling. Foster, once disappointed by the quality of Cope's vocalizing, notices in surprise, and he notices Mrs. Phillips's enthusiasm as well.

CHAPTER 22–23: "COPE SHALL BE RESCUED," "COPE REGAINS HIS FREEDOM"

Foster, describing the evening, tells Randolph that Cope kept away from Amy the whole time, aided by his newly arrived friend. He mentions that the businessman, Pearson, is interested in Amy. As a result Randolph hosts a dinner party for Pearson, Mrs. Phillips, and others, at which Pearson is led to understand, with Mrs. Phillips's help, that Amy does not really care much for Cope. The goal is that Pearson will pursue Amy himself.

Amy telephones Cope, suggesting that they talk, but she finds him unresponsive and ends the conversation. Arthur comes back from the university dramatic club, pleased that he has landed a part in a play. He helps Cope draft a letter to Amy, ending the engagement, but before Cope sends it, Amy writes her own letter, asking for the same result; soon she is seen wearing a ring from Pearson. As the two men return to their lodgings one evening, Arthur throws his arm around Cope's shoulder, and "Urania" looks down kindly upon them.

The author, at this point, is declaring himself—to those who are knowledgeable. Closing the chapter with the name of Urania, the muse of astronomy, Fuller is making his subject matter clear to those who have attained a specialized knowledge—that "Uranian," or "Uranism," is a term used to denote male homosexuality. In the 1860s, the German lawyer Karl Heinrich Ulrichs, noting the distinction made in Plato's *Symposium* between two aspects of Aphrodite, the Greek goddess of love, had pointed out that it is the Uranian, or heavenly, Aphrodite who oversees love between men; Ulrich thereby coined a new term. Fuller's reference would be understood by many, but not universally understood.

CHAPTERS 24–26: "COPE IN DANGER ANEW," "COPE IN DOUBLE DANGER," "COPE AS A GO-BETWEEN"

Mrs. Phillips is sympathetic to Cope, suggesting that he has been unfairly treated by Amy, although she is kind to Amy as well, who will soon be safely removed from the scene. She takes Cope to the opera, happy to have him sitting decoratively in her box. When Cope subsequently calls at the house, Hortense brings out a secret portrait of him that she has been painting, claiming she needs him to pose so she can finish it; she has set up a studio near the town square.

Cope comes to her studio, and Randolph drops by as well. The older man still feels proud of

his dinner party, by which he has helped free Cope from his engagement. He reminds the younger man that he has not yet met Arthur, and Cope promises that the two of them will call on him, although he knows Arthur has no interest in meeting a man he sees as a rival.

Carolyn, the poet, has published some impassioned verses, and the object of her passion is recognizable as Cope. Arthur, seeing the poems, feels annoyed; he considers Hortense and Carolyn—and Mrs. Phillips, too—all to be further rivals for Cope. He argues with his friend over these displays of female affection, but the two men reconcile as Cope, tearful, puts his arm around Arthur's shoulder.

Cope persuades Arthur to accept Randolph's dinner invitation, reminding him that the older man's university connections might help him find a job. Yet when Randolph and Arthur meet, they dislike and distrust each other immediately. Arthur understands that Randolph has been trying to replace him as Cope's friend, and Randolph sees for the first time that Cope is totally absorbed by Arthur. When Cope asks Randolph to use his influence to get Arthur a job, the older man makes no promises.

Later, when Randolph tells Foster that he does not care for Lemoyne, Foster replies that he himself does not care for Cope. He tells Randolph not to help Lemoyne, reminding him that the two young men accepted his invitation only because they wanted something from him. Foster tells Randolph that Cope cares nothing for him, that Cope's thoughts are only for Lemoyne; Randolph is forced to admit that Cope is cold and selfish. Foster then goes further, saying that Randolph is being a fool to do anything for either of them. Nevertheless, Randolph uses his influence to obtain Lemoyne a job in the university administration offices.

CHAPTERS 27–30: "COPE ESCAPES A SNARE," "COPE ABSENT FROM A WEDDING," "COPE AGAIN IN THE COUNTRY," "COPE AS A HERO"

Cope arrives at Hortense's studio for one further sitting, making clear that it is his last. Hortense upbraids him again for his indifference; he responds by saying he is willing to be friends with everyone, but offers nothing more to anyone. She predicts that his friendship with Lemoyne will not last, that he will eventually need something different, something better.

Mrs. Phillips tells Randolph that he has won; he has triumphed with Cope because he obtained a job for Cope's friend. Meanwhile, Amy and Pearson marry, and Mrs. Phillips decides to send Hortense away for a time, since her niece has shown publicly her feelings for Cope. Mrs. Phillips invites Cope for another excursion to the Dunes; Arthur is busy rehearsing for his musical comedy, *The Antics of Annabella,* in which he plays a comic female role, a practice not unusual at the time. Since Amy and Hortense are gone, Mrs. Phillips sees Carolyn as the only young woman to make a claim on Cope; yet Carolyn, she decides, is less aggressive, not threatening to her domain.

While the group is staying at the Dunes, an intruder breaks into the house at night. Cope calls out, and Mrs. Phillips's chauffeur grapples with the intruder and chases him away—and yet Carolyn and Mrs. Phillips both see Cope as their savior. He protests otherwise, but they continue to proclaim his heroism.

CHAPTERS 31–33: "COPE GETS NEW LIGHT ON HIS CHUM," "COPE TAKES HIS DEGREE," "COPE IN A FINAL VIEW"

Cope comes home from the Dunes to find Arthur's costumes strewn about, and he feels discomfort in seeing wigs, lingerie, and ladies' shoes. Arthur insists that everything must be done right.

At the actual performance Arthur does everything all too well. His "mincing ways" are too feminine for the roughly humorous college men playing the other women's roles, including the "hearty young lads" in the chorus. Randolph describes the performance later to Foster, who expresses satisfaction that Randolph has never cared for Lemoyne; he wishes again that he had never cared for Cope, either.

However, Randolph does not yet know what happened after the performance. It turns out that Lemoyne, when presented with a bouquet of roses, continued in his feminine character, smiling and pirouetting; then, offstage, while still in female clothing, he accosted another performer, a man dressed in male clothing. The outraged man pushed him off, shoving him against the scenery, shouting at him to keep away. As a result Lemoyne is out of

the drama club, out of the university, out of Churchton. He is back in Winnebago, Wisconsin.

Cope is preparing to receive his graduate degree. He has seen little of Mrs. Phillips or Randolph recently, and Foster, speaking to Randolph, says that Cope is showing the standard ingratitude of the young. Randolph and Mrs. Phillips attend the graduation ceremonies together, having become "reconciled competitors." They congratulate Cope, and when he introduces them to his parents, his impersonal manner makes the parents think they are merely casual acquaintances.

A perfunctory letter from Cope arrives at the Phillips house, addressed to Carolyn, adding brief regards to Mrs. Phillips; Cope says he has obtained a position at a university in the East. He mentions a brief visit to Winnebago but gives no indication that Lemoyne will join him in his new location. Foster asks Randolph if he is going to "cultivate" a new young man next year, and Randolph says he is not; Foster, approving, remarks again that the young do not appreciate the old.

Mrs. Phillips tells Randolph that Cope will eventually marry Carolyn; having "prospects," he will need respectability in order to advance in his career. Randolph disagrees, saying that Lemoyne will eventually join him. The two of them agree, however, that young people merely tolerate and use them, that Cope was hardly worth the trouble they made over him.

Critical Reception

The novel was barely noticed when it appeared. Several years later, the writer Carl Van Vechten remarked that if Theodore DREISER had written it, it would have been suppressed—a tribute to Fuller's greater subtlety, his tendencies toward indirection and understatement. In a retrospective on the author published in 1970, the critic Edmund Wilson called the novel his best work, claiming that it "is not really a book about homosexuality"—a notion challenged by recent readers.

At issue also has been the interpretation of Cope himself, determining how negatively he should be viewed. Foster, Randolph, and Hortense consider him cold and selfish, and yet, as Fuller demonstrates throughout the novel, these characters are making uncommon demands on him. Defenders of Cope assert that he cannot be blamed for his attractiveness, nor for the fact that men and women desire him. Moreover, he remains untouched by self-importance; he never claims the heroism attributed to him in the lake accident, and he feels embarrassed when Mrs. Phillips acts as if he were the one who chased away the Dunes intruder, reminding her that it was the chauffeur who acted heroically. He also meets consistent standards of politeness and propriety; even after Hortense speaks to him angrily in the studio, he responds with an "instinctive heed" to niceties.

A relevant question is whether Joseph Foster's words of condemnation are valid, or whether Foster should be seen as an embittered man, lashing out at youth from the perspective of age and impotence. A further question is whether Cope's seeming lack of perception is a willed lack of perception—that is, whether he purposely shuts himself off from others or simply remains clueless. Even if his imperceptiveness is willed, the issue is whether it can be seen as a necessary self-defense; Cope is facing a world rife with possessive and lustful men and women.

Biddlebaum, Wing   *See under* WINESBURG, OHIO: "Hands."

The Birth of a Race

Intending to counteract the racist movie *The Birth of a Nation*, Chicagoan Emmett J. Scott formed a production company to make a movie depicting African-American life sympathetically; its target was the pro-Ku Klux Klan propaganda of D. W. GRIFFITH's 1915 film. The movie premiered in November 1918 at the Blackstone Theater. The Illinois state legislature, responding also to the Griffith film, passed a bill banning racially inflammatory material on either stage or screen.

Black Hawk
(1767–1838) *Sauk Indian warrior*

Born near what is now Rock Island, Illinois, Black Hawk fought on the side of the British during the

War of 1812. By the late 1820s, the Sauk and Fox nation, living in northern Illinois and southern Wisconsin, was driven across the Mississippi River into Iowa by the advance of white settlers; they concluded a treaty with the U.S. government in 1830. In April 1832, hoping to reclaim Illinois territory, Black Hawk led 200 warriors and their fami-

The 50-foot statue of Sauk warrior Black Hawk, created by Lorado Taft, stands on a promontory over the Rock River in northwest Illinois. *(Chicago Historical Society)*

lies once more across the river, opposed by Illinois militia and federal troops. Defeated in August at Bad Axe River, Wisconsin, he eventually returned to Iowa, dying there at the age of 71.

Juliette KINZIE, in her 1856 narrative, WAU-BUN: THE "EARLY DAY" IN THE NORTH-WEST, describes the Black Hawk conflict from the vantage point of her home at Fort Winnebago, Wisconsin; Kinzie, wife of an Indian agent, laments the lot of Native Americans, "gradually dispossessed of the broad and beautiful domains of their forefathers." Abraham LINCOLN was a member of the Illinois militia and participated in the Black Hawk war.

A monumental statue of the warrior by Lorado TAFT, erected in 1911, stands on a bluff overlooking the Rock River in Oregon, Illinois.

"Blacklisted"   See CHICAGO POEMS.

Black Sox scandal

Eight members the CHICAGO WHITE SOX baseball team—soon to be popularly named the Black Sox—were bribed by gamblers to lose the 1919 World Series to the Cincinnati Reds; team owner Charles A. COMISKEY was later criticized for the low salaries he paid to his players. The most noted player was Joseph Jefferson "Shoeless Joe" Jackson, an illiterate athlete, called at the time the greatest natural ballplayer in the game's history. As a result of the scandal—and in an effort to improve the image of the game—Chicago federal judge Kenesaw Mountain LANDIS was persuaded to become the first baseball commissioner.

Blackstone Hotel

The Blackstone Hotel on South MICHIGAN AVENUE achieved national fame in 1920, serving as the site of the original "smoke-filled room." Built in 1909 by Benjamin H. Marshall, an architect known for luxury design, the hotel stands 23 stories, featuring ÉCOLE DES BEAUX-ARTS ornamentation, a grand ballroom, and marble staircases. Opera diva Mary GARDEN lived in a suite at the hotel during her years in Chicago. In the early morning of June 11, 1920, leaders at the Republican Party National Convention, after long deliberation, nominated a compromise candidate for the presidency, Warren G. HARDING of Ohio; the deal makers reportedly emerged from the hotel suite amid billows of cigar smoke, and a newsman wired to the Associated Press that Harding was chosen "by a group of men in a smoke-filled room."

In Edna FERBER's 1917 novel, FANNY HERSELF, the heroine is taken to lunch at the Blackstone, dining in its "splendid room," hearing the sounds of its fountain, observing the lily blossoms floating on the water. In Willa CATHER's 1925 novel, THE PROFESSOR'S HOUSE, Godfrey ST. PETER and his wife, enjoying a lake view, stay in a suite at the Blackstone.

Blood, A. D.   See SPOON RIVER ANTHOLOGY.

The Blood of the Prophets
Edgar Lee Masters
(1905)

Like much of Edgar Lee MASTERS's early work, the collection of verse was privately printed and published under a pseudonym, in this case "Dexter Wallace"; as a practicing lawyer, Masters believed that being identified as a poet would harm his legal career. Reviewed by Emma GOLDMAN in her journal *Mother Earth*, the book included antiwar poems written in response to the SPANISH-AMERICAN WAR.

Blue, Angela

A character in Theodore DREISER's autobiographical novel THE "GENIUS," Angela is a 25-year-old attractive and conventionally minded schoolteacher in Wisconsin when she first meets Eugene WITLA, a man five years her junior. After a long engagement—during which time Eugene becomes involved with other women as well—they marry, and she joins him in New York. Soon it becomes clear that she lacks the sophistication to fit into his artistic circles, although she is a devoted wife and provides support when he suffers an emotional collapse. Yet her jealousy and anger surface when she learns of his other relationships, and she becomes increasingly shrill and nagging. Eugene feels sympathy for her, although he regrets the marriage. Angela decides to bear a child to bind him to her, but by then he is overwhelmed in his last great infatuation, with the 18-year-old Suzanne DALE. That relationship fails, as Suzanne's mother keeps Eugene and her daughter separated; he has meanwhile separated from Angela, who dies in childbirth, leaving him with a daughter.

Angela is based on Dreiser's wife, with whom he lived in an increasingly hostile relationship; his marriage ended as he pursued an 18-year-old girl. Angela's maiden name of Blue is a version of Dreiser's wife's maiden name of White. The character shares qualities also with Aileen BUTLER in the Frank COWPERWOOD trilogy; in THE TITAN, Aileen, like Angela, fails to fit properly into a social milieu and expresses strong jealousy—suggesting that Aileen, even if officially modeled on the wife of Charles T. YERKES, is based, like Angela, on Dreiser's wife as well.

Bodenheim, Max
(1892–1954) *poet, playwright, novelist*

Born Maxwell Bodenheimer in Hermanville, Mississippi, Bodenheim moved with his family to Chicago in 1900. His verse, influenced by IMAGISM, first appeared in POETRY in August 1914, later in LITTLE REVIEW and Alfred KREYMBORG's periodicals *Glebe* and OTHERS. Bodenheim collaborated with Ben HECHT in the short-lived CHICAGO LITERARY TIMES, a periodical presenting literary humor and satire. A novel, *Replenishing Jessica*, achieved best-selling status in 1925, aided by obscenity charges brought by John S. Sumner and the NEW YORK SOCIETY FOR THE SUPPRESSION OF VICE. Bodenheim's friendship with Hecht ended when the latter published in 1926 the novel *Count Bruga*, featuring a readily recognizable eccentric poet. Bodenheim spent his last decades in New York City, pursuing a chosen lifestyle of near

destitution. In the 1930s, he was barred from the Federal Writers' Project, accused of lying about his one-time ties with the Communist Party; by then he was sinking terminally into alcoholism and homelessness. At the age of 61, Bodenheim, along with his wife, was murdered in a derelict hotel by a former mental patient.

The Bomb
Frank Harris
(1909)

Providing a fictional account of the HAYMARKET AFFAIR, this novel by Frank HARRIS identifies the bomb thrower, naming the real-life Rudolph Schnaubelt, a German immigrant. Schnaubelt, known to have fled Chicago after the bombing—and long rumored to have been the guilty party—becomes the novel's first-person narrator. He tells of receiving the bomb from Louis Lingg, another real-life anarchist, then describes the novel's central action; he throws the bomb over his shoulder, purposely stumbling to the ground to escape harm. In the ensuing confusion, he makes his way to a railroad depot and boards a train to New York; he eventually goes on to Liverpool and the Continent. Harris expands also on the character of Louis Lingg, the youngest of the anarchists, who committed suicide in his jail cell with explosives that had been smuggled to him; he died at the age of 23. In the novel Lingg becomes a thoughtful, idealistic spokesman for ANARCHISM.

Bond, Carrie Jacobs
(1862–1946) *songwriter*

The first important woman writer of popular songs, Bond was also the first woman composer to achieve wealth from her work. Born in Janesville, Wisconsin, moving to Chicago in 1894 after her husband's death, she established a shop that sold sheet music, including her own self-published work; one of the locations was in the FINE ARTS BUILDING. Specializing in popular sentimental songs—as did her contemporary Paul DRESSER— she wrote more than 400 songs, including "I Love

You Truly" and "A Perfect Day." Her autobiography, *Roads of Melody,* appeared in 1927; she died in California at the age of 84.

"The Book of the Grotesque"   *See* WINESBURG, OHIO.

Booth, John Wilkes
(1838–1865) *actor, assassin of President Abraham Lincoln*

Born in Maryland, the son of Junius Brutus Booth Sr., patriarch of a prominent acting family, John Wilkes Booth was the younger brother of Edwin Booth, one of America's first great Shakespearean actors. In 1862, three years before the murder of President LINCOLN, the younger brother, never considered as accomplished an actor as the elder, played in Shakespeare's *Richard III* and *The Merchant of Venice* at the MCVICKER'S THEATRE in Chicago. Expressing Confederate sympathies during the CIVIL WAR, Booth turned his attention afterward to the Union president, carrying out the assassination in a Washington theater on Good Friday, April 14, 1865. Less than two weeks later, he was shot during a pursuit in rural Virginia. When Lincoln's funeral train came to Chicago on May 1, actors playing at the McVicker's issued a statement expressing outrage at their fellow thespian, agreeing that Chicago theaters should be closed until after the funeral services. The McVicker's was destroyed six years later in the GREAT FIRE.

Booth, William
(1829–1912) *English founder of the Salvation Army*

Opening an evangelical mission among the poor in London's East End in 1865, Booth worked to bring social relief as well as a Christian message. As the missions spread beyond London, he adopted an organization along military lines, complete with ranks and uniforms. The first SALVATION ARMY came to America in 1879, establishing headquarters in Philadelphia. Vachel

LINDSAY's poem "GENERAL WILLIAM BOOTH ENTERS INTO HEAVEN," drawing upon memories of Salvationists in his native SPRINGFIELD, brought the poet his first fame, becoming one of the staples on his lecture circuit.

Boyington, William W.
(1818–1898) *architect*

A major figure in pre-GREAT FIRE architecture, Boyington came to Chicago in 1853. He designed hotels and commercial buildings, including CROSBY'S OPERA HOUSE—all structures that were destroyed in the fire. He is best known today for the WATER TOWER AND PUMPING STATION, stone buildings that survived the fire; they currently maintain their historic status amid the high-rises of MICHIGAN AVENUE. Frank NORRIS in *THE PIT* apotheosizes the nine-story Boyington-designed CHICAGO BOARD OF TRADE BUILDING, a postfire structure of 1885, likening it to a "monstrous sphinx"; the building was demolished in 1929. Another notable Boyington structure is the Joliet state prison, south of Chicago, built in 1858; the limestone fortress, although no longer serving as a correctional facility, has been permanently recorded in two Blues Brothers' movies.

Bradley, Jessie

A character in Henry B. FULLER's novel THE CLIFF-DWELLERS, a woman of little personal wealth, Jessie spends much of her life among the rich; her expensive tastes become a problem for her husband, George OGDEN. Her extravagance brings Ogden to financial disaster, leading him to "borrow" money illegally from the bank that employs him. Eventually she dies, freeing him to marry a more suitable woman.

Bradwell, Myra
(1831–1894) *lawyer, publisher*

Founder of the *Chicago Legal News,* Bradwell was an early champion of a woman's right to practice law, as well as of women's suffrage. Born in Vermont, coming to Chicago in 1854, she founded the periodical in 1868, turning it into a platform for feminist causes, including advocacy on behalf of Mary Todd LINCOLN. A lawyer's wife, Bradwell challenged in 1870 the Illinois statute that barred women from practicing law; the Illinois Supreme Court denied her suit, citing "the natural and proper timidity and delicacy which belongs to the female sex." In 1873 the United States Supreme Court upheld the Illinois decision, ruling that the Constitution did not guarantee a citizen's right to practice a profession. In 1875 when the widow of the assassinated president was committed to a mental institution by her son, Robert Todd LINCOLN, Bradwell and the *Chicago Legal News* were instrumental in securing her release.

Brainard, Abbie

A character in Henry B. FULLER's novel *THE CLIFF-DWELLERS*, Abbie, the older daughter of ruthless businessman Erastus M. BRAINARD, has managed to escape the family greed and rapacity; she is the woman whom George OGDEN, as he later understands, should have married. Ogden had fastidiously looked elsewhere, seeing that her family was tainted by divorce and other seemingly inappropriate behavior. When Abbie and Ogden finally marry—after both are financially ruined—she is content to live an unpretentious existence.

Brainard, Erastus M.

A character in Henry B. FULLER's novel *THE CLIFF-DWELLERS*, Brainard, an unscrupulous financier, comes from what is called Egypt—a reference, not favorable, to southern Illinois and its city of Cairo. Like many successful businessmen in fiction, he comes from an obscure rural background; the author suggests he once preached at Methodist camp meetings. His extensive business holdings range from real estate to electric companies to western mines. Brainard dies by the hand of his younger son Marcus BRAINARD, the artist of the family, whom he had rejected for his non-businessman's qualities. Critics have suggested that he was modeled in part on Fuller's own grandfather and father. Although not so fully developed a character, Erastus Brainard foreshadows other fictional tycoons, including Van HARRINGTON in Robert HERRICK's *MEMOIRS OF AN AMERICAN CITIZEN* and Frank COWPERWOOD in Theodore DREISER's trilogy.

Brainard, Marcus

A character in Henry B. FULLER's novel *THE CLIFF-DWELLERS*, Marcus is a businessman's son whose interests are artistic, leading him to reject the business world; he is rejected in turn by his father. Estranged from his family, Marcus secretly meets with his sister Abbie BRAINARD; she sees sadly that he is inebriated and, grasping his hand, notes the thinness of the fingers—fingers that once delicately held a drawing pencil. Not long afterward, Marcus stabs his father and hangs himself.

Brandeis, Fanny

A character in Edna FERBER's novel *FANNY HERSELF*, Fanny is the author's most autobiographical figure. The daughter of a Hungarian immigrant merchant, Fanny grows up in Winnebago, Wisconsin, part of the town's small Jewish community. After her father's death, her mother, Molly BRANDEIS, takes over the family store, and Fanny sees before her a strong, effective businesswoman, whom she will emulate throughout her life. Moving to Chicago, she takes a buyer's position for Haynes-Cooper, a mail-order firm. Always successful, never encountering setbacks, Fanny is unapologetic for her drive and ambition; as a woman, as a Jew—although on one occasion she denies her Jewishness—she knows she is compensating for centuries of discrimination and repression. Yet she feels sympathy for less-fortunate working women, particularly the immigrant women in the garment trades. Her escape from the contradictions between an affluent lifestyle and her working-woman sympathies comes in the novel's facile ending; Fanny marries a Jewish man from her hometown who has become a New York newspaper columnist and gives up business for art, a talent she had displayed from her youth.

Readers have noted that Ferber shows a greater emotional investment in Fanny when the character is acting as the take-charge business-woman, organizing, restructuring, and innovating, than when she is expressing concern for the down-trodden or love for her husband-to-be. In one early episode, meeting the buyer she will soon surpass, a man who needs the income to support his family, Fanny lets settle over her face "the mask of hardness that was so often to transform it."

Brandeis, Molly

A character in Edna FERBER's novel FANNY HER-SELF, Molly is a reconfiguring of Emma MCCHES-NEY, the traveling saleswoman, the character Ferber had created earlier in a series of popular short stories. Emma, the first notable business-woman to appear in American fiction, is depicted as a divorced single mother, fiercely energetic, cleverly outwitting her rivals; Molly Brandeis is her Jewish version, a widowed single mother, the hard-working owner of a novelty store in Winnebago, Wisconsin. Both women are based on Ferber's mother. The protagonist, Fanny, at one point invokes Molly's spirit, which she sees as going back generations, all the way to the biblical matriarch, Sarah—"repressed women, suffering women, troubled, patient, nomadic women." Molly is formidable, driving away a snobbish customer, but she is kindly as well, befriending other customers, chatting, and giving advice. After Molly dies, Fanny carries on the family tradition of shrewdness and hard work, tempered by sympathy for others.

Brandeis, Theodore

A character in Edna FERBER's novel FANNY HER-SELF, Theodore is an aspiring concert violinist. The brother of Fanny BRANDEIS, he is the family member for whom Fanny and her mother, Molly

BRANDEIS, sacrifice their comfort; they scrimp on expenditures in order to send him to Germany for musical study. After their mother dies, Fanny continues to support him, although she is suspicious of the German woman he marries; he soon has a child as well. Theodore comes back to America for a concert tour after a 10-year absence, bringing his daughter, but leaving behind his wife, who has taken up with another man; Fanny takes her brother in, happy to be reconciled with her remaining family. He tells her of the anti-Semitism he has faced in Europe. Yet after WORLD WAR I breaks out, he suddenly returns to Germany with his daughter, claiming that he still loves his wife, that if necessary he will stay and fight for Germany. Like his old violin teacher in Winnebago, Wisconsin, he is ruining his life, Fanny understands, for a woman. Appearing in 1917, the novel anticipates future expressions of German anti-Semitism.

Brander, Senator George Sylvester

Brander is a character in Theodore DREISER's novel JENNIE GERHARDT. The novel's heroine, Jennie GERHARDT, works in a Columbus, Ohio, hotel, where she meets the middle-aged senator, who lives in the hotel when he is not in Washington. Taken by her innocence, Brander helps her and her impoverished family; when her brother, Bass, is caught stealing coal from a railroad yard, Brander intervenes to free him and pays the fine. Jennie's gratitude causes him to lose his strictly paternal stance, and the two briefly become lovers. Called to Washington, Brander promises to marry Jennie, but he is stricken with typhoid and dies. Jennie subsequently gives birth to a daughter, VESTA.

Breton, Jules
(1827–1906) *French painter*

Known for his scenes depicting rural life, Breton is invoked by Willa CATHER in her 1915 novel, *THE SONG OF THE LARK*; the novel's title comes from his painting of the same name. Showing a peasant girl listening alone in a field at sunrise, the 1884 work was exhibited in the Art Palace of the WORLD'S COLUMBIAN EXPOSITION in 1893; it later became part of the ART INSTITUTE's collection. In the Cather novel the music student Thea KRON-BORG visits the work regularly, seeking inspiration in its tribute to music.

The Briary-Bush
Floyd Dell
(1921)

A continuation of the autobiographical novel MOON-CALF, this work follows the hero, Felix Fay, from the fictional small city of Port Royal—the real-life Davenport, Iowa—to Chicago, where he arrives at the age of 21. The novel centers on Felix's troubled marriage to a woman resembling author Floyd DELL's first wife, Margery CURREY, including their living in studios converted from shops left over from the WORLD'S COLUMBIAN EXPOSITION. A brief interlude toward the end of the volume gives a version of Dell's affair with actress Elaine HYMAN, who broke with Dell to follow Theodore DREISER to New York. The book's title comes from a song that the fictionalized character, Elva Macklin, sings to Felix about the briary-bush "that pricks my heart so sore"; the singer in the song vows that if he ever gets out of the prickly shrub, he will never get in again—and yet Elva tells Felix that he will get in again, that people indeed go back to the briary-bush.

Briggs, Hortense

A character in Theodore DREISER's novel AN AMERICAN TRAGEDY, Hortense, appearing only in Book I, presents a foreshadowing of Sondra FINCH-LEY, the woman whom Clyde GRIFFITHS pursues in Books II and III. Realizing the power she has over Clyde, the self-centered Hortense consciously exploits him for what she can gain; Clyde understands what she is doing but cannot resist. The pattern is repeated with Sondra, although with the difference that Sondra represents wealth and status as well.

Bronzeville

The Bronzeville area was one of the first established African-American neighborhoods in Chicago. In the 1850s, the African-American community numbered about 50; by the time of the CIVIL WAR, fugitive slaves and free blacks brought the figure to nearly a thousand. By 1890, the black population in Chicago approached 15,000, settled in scattered areas, mostly on the South Side; no clearly defined African-American neighborhood yet existed.

After WORLD WAR I, Chicago became a destination for African Americans arriving from the South, and the city's black population grew from 45,000 in 1910 to 235,000 in 1930. The area became more strictly demarcated, and the term *Black Belt* was applied by UNIVERSITY OF CHICAGO sociologists as they launched their studies in demographic patterns; the term *Bronzeville* is attributed to an editor of the CHICAGO BEE. The original boundaries, from Twelfth Street south to Thirty-first Street, later extended farther south; the main north-south thoroughfare was State Street, and the east-west commercial center became Forty-seventh Street. The area's JAZZ clubs drew both blacks and whites during PROHIBITION; a popular venue was the LINCOLN GARDENS, a dance hall at Thirty-first and Cottage Grove. "Jelly Roll" MORTON arrived in the early years of the century, Joe "King" OLIVER in 1918. At the same time, Oscar DEPRIEST, the first post-RECONSTRUCTION black congressman, began to build his political organization at Unity Hall, former home of a Jewish social organization, subsequently considered the birthplace of African-American politics in the North. Another well-known structure in Bronzeville is the Eighth Regiment Armory, headquarters of the nation's first all-black army regiment; the Victory Monument, a statue erected in 1926, honors the "Fighting Eighth." LIBERTY LIFE INSURANCE COMPANY, the first African-American–owned insurance business in the North, merged with other companies in 1929 to form Supreme Life Insurance Company; the Supreme Life Building has been called the Gateway to Bronzeville.

Chicago's black residents established their own shops, restaurants, churches, clubs, and theaters, having little contact with whites. Many of the city's whites, immigrants from overseas, had little knowledge or understanding of African Americans—a situation often translating into intolerance and hostility, as expressed in the violent RACE RIOTS of 1919. The area declined as the LOOP became less segregated and as middle-class blacks moved farther south, many to the suburbs.

Fenton JOHNSON's poem "Aunt Jane Allen" evokes Bronzeville's State Street in the early decades of the 20th century. "State Street is lonely today," the piece begins, because the old woman who used to hobble along it "has driven her chariot to Heaven."

Brooke, Rupert
(1887–1915) *English poet*

One of the famed WORLD WAR I poets, Brooke died in the same month that several of his war sonnets appeared in POETRY magazine. First celebrated as a poet at Cambridge University, he came briefly to Chicago in 1914, visiting his friend Maurice BROWNE and meeting with Harriet MONROE and Margaret ANDERSON; Anderson wrote later of his "girl's beauty," noting that everyone turned to look at him as he walked down MICHIGAN AVENUE. His work appeared in *Poetry* in April 1915, just after he died of blood poisoning on the Greek island of Skiros.

Brooks, Gwendolyn
(1917–2000) *poet*

The major poet of the post–Chicago Renaissance generation, Brooks succeeded Carl SANDBURG as Illinois Poet Laureate in 1968. Born in Topeka, Kansas, moving as a girl to Chicago, Brooks began contributing regularly to the CHICAGO DEFENDER in 1934. Her first collection, *A Street in Bronzeville*, appeared in 1945, followed in 1949 by the long poem *Annie Allen*, which won the Pulitzer Prize for poetry; Brooks is the first African American to win the award. In the late 1960s, her writing became increasingly political, and she turned to smaller, African-American

publishing houses as an outlet for her work. Her most-quoted poem is the brief "We Real Cool," presenting the words of young high school dropouts, concluding, "we die soon."

Brotherhood of Sleeping Car Porters

An African-American labor union, the Brotherhood of Sleeping Car Porters began in New York City. In the 1920s, the PULLMAN PALACE CAR COMPANY was the largest private employer of black Americans in the United States; the porters, or service workers, had historically been

The largest local union of the Brotherhood of Sleeping Car Porters was in Chicago, home of the Pullman Palace Car Company; this poster dates from 1928. *(Chicago Historical Society)*

African American. Despite labor progress elsewhere, the Pullman company had long suppressed unionizing efforts among the porters; the AMERICAN RAILWAY UNION and the AMERICAN FEDERATION OF LABOR had been of little help to black workers. A. Philip RANDOLPH, a New York social activist, having the advantage of not being a Pullman employee—and thus not being subject to dismissal—launched the Brotherhood of Sleeping Car Porters in New York City in August 1925. The first national convention was held in Chicago in 1929; as the home of the Pullman company, Chicago became the home also of the largest and strongest local union in the brotherhood. Despite critics who saw the AFL as a stronghold of racial prejudice, the new union eventually affiliated with the older craft union in 1935. In 1937, 12 years after its founding, the brotherhood won concessions in hours and wages from the Pullman company; by the 1940s it was considered the nation's most important black political institution. The A. Philip Randolph Pullman Porter Museum, located in the historic town of PULLMAN, was founded in 1995.

"The Brothers"   *See* DEATH IN THE WOODS.

Browne, Francis Fisher
(1843–1913) *founder and editor of the* Dial, *bookstore owner*

Born in Vermont, Browne moved to Chicago in 1867 after serving in the CIVIL WAR. Becoming an editor for the A. C. McClurg and Company publishing firm, he founded the periodical DIAL in 1880, aimed originally at advertising McClurg publications. Soon the *Dial* became the leading national literary journal of its day; Browne took over ownership in 1892. His bookstore in the FINE ARTS BUILDING, operating from 1907 to 1912, featured an interior designed by Frank Lloyd WRIGHT; Margaret ANDERSON worked as a clerk in the store during her early days in Chicago. Browne also contributed to the ever-burgeoning list of Abraham LINCOLN volumes, publishing *The Every-day Life of Abraham Lincoln* in 1886.

Browne, Maurice
(1881–1955) *founder of the Little Theatre, pioneer in the little theater movement*

Born in England, Browne met a Chicago woman, Ellen VAN VOLKENBURG, in Florence, Italy, and came to Chicago to marry her in 1912. He established a theater company for his wife, an amateur actress, in the FINE ARTS BUILDING, relying on wealthy patrons to support the company's productions. When the LITTLE THEATRE closed in February 1917, Browne and Van Volkenburg left Chicago, eventually divorcing. Browne returned to London, where he produced R. C. Sherriff's WORLD WAR I drama, *Journey's End;* when the play became a success, he sent it on a world tour, including an engagement in Chicago. After quarreling with London associates, Browne became artist-in-residence at the University of California in 1949. He eventually returned to England, living on a pension from ex-wife Van Volkenburg; he died at the age of 74.

In Theodore DREISER's novel THE TITAN, Browne appears as the theater director Lane Cross—"a rake at heart," Dreiser suggests, whose true qualities are hidden by his smooth exterior.

Bryan, William Jennings
(1860–1925) *politician and orator*

Born in Salem, Illinois, moving in 1887 to Lincoln, Nebraska, Bryan became recognized as leader of the FREE SILVER movement, advocating unlimited coinage of silver to relieve the burdens of the farmers; the GOLD STANDARD was seen as the tool of rich Easterners, oppressing the agricultural Midwest. At the age of 36, Bryan delivered his famous "cross of gold" speech, condemning the gold standard—"You shall not crucify mankind on a cross of gold"—at the Democratic National Convention in Chicago in 1896. He was defeated that year by Republican William MCKINLEY; further unsuccessful bids for the presidency came in 1900 and 1908. Appointed secretary of state by President Woodrow WILSON in 1913, he resigned his post two years later, favoring American neutrality during WORLD WAR I.

The famed last act of Bryan's life was the 1925 Scopes, or "monkey," trial, testing the teaching of evolution in the Tennessee public schools. John T. Scopes, a biology teacher charged with including evolution in his curriculum, was defended by Clarence DARROW; Bryan aided the prosecution. During the trial, Darrow, who had long felt enmity toward Bryan—starting with Bryan's leading the Democrats to defeat in 1896 and 1900—subjected his opponent to severe cross-examining on matters of fundamentalist biblical interpretation. Scopes, although convicted, was later acquitted on appeal. Bryan died just five days after the trial, said by some to have been "hounded to his grave" by the agnostic Darrow.

William Jennings Bryan ran as Democratic presidential candidate for the third and last time in 1908, the date of this poster. *(Chicago Historical Society)*

Edgar Lee MASTERS, who had attended the Democratic convention in 1896, wrote later of the crowds cheering Bryan, of the hopes raised in the heartland for Bryan's victory. Harriet MONROE, who also attended the convention, recalled in her autobiography that a particular morning session was filled with ineffectual speakers—but then in the afternoon the audience felt electrified by the powerfully built young man, whose voice "could be heard to the last row of the highest gallery." She admits she had never heard of Bryan, but the gathering listened spellbound while the cross-of-gold oration "rolled out toward the resounding roof."

A teenage Vachel LINDSAY, living in SPRINGFIELD, heard Bryan speak on the campaign trail that year; he regarded the orator, along with John Peter ALTGELD, as one of the heroes of his youth. Several of Lindsay's poems pay tribute to Bryan, including "When Bryan Speaks," collected in THE CHINESE NIGHTINGALE AND OTHER POEMS, and "Bryan, Bryan, Bryan, Bryan," collected in *The Golden Whales of California and Other Rhymes in the American Language*. Theodore DREISER took a negative view of Bryan the politician in THE TITAN of 1914; citing the foolishness of preaching "a new doctrine of deliverance," he suggests that Bryan, offering his panacea for the human condition, stood on the wrong side of history.

Bryant, William Cullen
(1794–1878) *poet, newspaper editor*

An admired poet of the early 19th century, the Massachusetts-born Bryant was also one of the founders of the antislavery Republican Party. His best-remembered poem, "Thanatopsis," a meditation on death, appeared in the *North American Review* in 1817, establishing him as an important figure in American romanticism. "Earth," presenting voices from the graveyard, prefigures Edgar Lee MASTERS's SPOON RIVER ANTHOLOGY; "The Prairies," written after a journey west in 1832, provides an early description of the phenomenon that Carl SANDBURG would celebrate in the first decades of the following century. Serving for 50 years as editor of the *New York Evening Post*, Bryant introduced Abraham

LINCOLN at Lincoln's first New York address in 1860, leading the way to his receiving the Republican presidential nomination.

The Bulwark
Theodore Dreiser
(1946)

Inspired by a young woman who told tales of her austere Quaker father, Theodore DREISER began this posthumously published novel in 1915, working on the volume sporadically over the next three decades. Sympathetically portraying the plain-living Society of Friends, the author is said to have been attracted by the sect's similarities to his mother's Mennonite community. The story concerns an upright Quaker patriarch—"a bulwark of the older and better order of things"—who grudgingly allows affluence into his life, who then watches as his children fall from righteousness into luxurious living, immorality, hedonism, and suicide. The youngest daughter returns to her father as he nears death, receiving a Quaker-style spiritual revelation not unlike the Hindu-style revelation received by Berenice FLEMING in Dreiser's other posthumous novel, THE STOIC. The work received mixed reviews when it appeared, leading critics to discuss retrospectively the career of the recently deceased writer.

Burnett, Frances Hodgson
(1849–1924) *English-American author of children's fiction*

Although two of her famous works, the 1886 *Little Lord Fauntleroy* and the 1911 *The Secret Garden*, have been reproduced endlessly on stage and screen, Burnett wrote also a lesser-known tale centering on the WORLD'S COLUMBIAN EXPOSITION— *Two Little Pilgrims' Progress: A Story of the City Beautiful*, published in 1895. Comparing the WHITE CITY of the world's fair to the Celestial City of John Bunyan's 17th-century *A Pilgrim's Progress*, the story follows a set of twins as they make their rounds of the sights. Burnett describes that new phenomenon, night-time electric illumination, appearing like "myriads of diamonds, all alight."

Burnett, W. R.
(1899–1982) *crime novelist*

Capitalizing on the new underworld brought about by PROHIBITION, Burnett helped create a new genre of gangster fiction. Born in Springfield, Ohio, coming to Chicago in 1927, he worked as a hotel desk clerk, gaining opportunity for close-up observation of criminal activity. His first novel, *Little Caesar*, published in 1929, traces the rise and fall of a hoodlum; it became a film of the same name two years later, bringing stardom to actor Edward G. Robinson. Burnett, writing nearly three dozen novels, pursued a Hollywood scriptwriting career as well, turning many of his works into films, including *High Sierra* and *The Asphalt Jungle*. The 1931 movie *Little Caesar* remains a separate entity from the 1932 *Scarface*; Burnett worked on the latter screenplay but was replaced by another Chicagoan, Ben HECHT.

Burnham, Daniel H.
(1846–1912) *architect, city planner*

The New York-born Burnham, who came with his family to Chicago in 1855, has been called the city's master builder. Working briefly for William LeBaron JENNEY, he joined with John Wellborn ROOT in 1873 to establish the firm of BURNHAM AND ROOT. After Root's death in 1891, Burnham became the principal overseer of planning and construction for the WORLD'S COLUMBIAN EXPOSITION of 1893; the firm became D. H. Burnham and Company. Later Burnham buildings in Chicago include the 1895 Reliance Building, noted for its large windows, admitting an unprecedented natural light, made possible by the new steel-frame construction. Among structures outside of Chicago are the 1902 triangular Flatiron Building in New York City, the 1903 Merchant's Exchange Building in San Francisco—a structure that withstood the city's 1906 earthquake—and the 1907 Union Station in Washington, D.C. Department stores besides MARSHALL FIELD AND COMPANY include Selfridge's in London, Gimbels in New York, Wanamaker's in Philadelphia, and Filene's in Boston.

In 1909, fulfilling a commission from the Commercial Club of Chicago, Burnham created the *Plan of Chicago*, the first comprehensive development plan drawn up for a major American city. "Make no little plans" was his famous injunction. The far-reaching proposal was to keep the LAKE MICHIGAN shoreline open, breaking the precedent of most waterfront cities, which had allowed lakefronts and waterways to be taken over by manufacturing and industrial concerns. Burnham's vision called also for central planning and centralization, culminating in a domed municipal complex, a system of boulevards and parks, and a series of islands along the lakefront created from landfill, linked to the city by bridges; most of these recommendations were never carried through. Burnham has been criticized as elitist, in that his plan presented no means for alleviating slums and crowded housing; he declared that some day public housing would have to be built, although he never pursued the issue. Montgomery WARD was an important figure in lakefront preservation as well. Burnham died while traveling abroad, in Heidelberg, Germany, at the age of 65.

The architect Tom Bingham in Henry B. FULLER's novel WITH THE PROCESSION is modeled in part on Burnham.

Burnham and Root

Formed in 1873, the architectural firm brought together two young men still in their 20s, Daniel H. BURNHAM and John Wellborn ROOT. Root came to be seen as the creative visionary, Burnham as the innovative administrator. The firm is credited with the first SKYSCRAPER built in Chicago, the 10-story Montauk Building, completed in 1882, making use of Root's "floating foundation," providing stability in the city's marshy soil; it was clad also in terra-cotta, or fired clay, for the purpose of fire-proofing. The building was demolished in 1902. Another of the firm's structures housed the ART INSTITUTE in 1887, before that establishment moved into new quarters in 1893; the building was razed in 1929. Another historic structure no longer standing is the Rand-McNally Building, the world's first all-steel-frame

structure; built in 1890 for the RAND MCNALLY COMPANY, it incorporated new steel technology, including the use of rivets for fastening. The 21-story Masonic Temple, the world's tallest structure when built in 1892, complete with roof garden, was demolished in 1939. Among the company's still-standing buildings are THE ROOKERY of 1888 and the MONADNOCK BUILDING of 1891. After Root's sudden death in 1891, the firm became D. H. Burnham and Company.

Hamlin GARLAND's 1895 novel, ROSE OF DUTCHER'S COOLLY, depicts the newly arrived Wisconsin farm girl as ascending to the heights of the Masonic Temple. In Theodore DREISER's THE "GENIUS," the protagonist, arriving in the city in the late 1880s, takes drawing classes at the old, now demolished, Burnham and Root Art Institute.

Burroughs, Edgar Rice
(1875–1950) *author of science fiction and adventure tales*

Burroughs came to fame through his character Tarzan, the English child raised by apes in the African rain forest. Born in Chicago, writing for a business magazine, Burroughs published his first piece of "pulp" fiction—a term referring to the cheap paper used in popular magazines and books—in the magazine *The All-Story*; the work, originally titled "Under the Moons of Mars," appeared in book form in 1912 as *A Princess of Mars*. His next effort, *Tarzan of the Apes*, appearing also in *The All-Story*, received book publication in 1914. Although declaring later that he wrote *Tarzan* with the help of Henry M. Stanley's 1890 *In Darkest Africa*—the book that inspired Vachel LINDSAY's poem "The Congo"—Burroughs had also, as a teenager, visited the Dahomey Village, an African-inspired exhibit at the WORLD'S COLUMBIAN EXPOSITION in 1893. For more than a quarter of a century, he produced a new Tarzan work almost yearly; the first of many films, *Tarzan of the Apes*, appeared in 1918. Chicagoan Johnny WEISSMULLER made his first Tarzan movie in 1932. Moving to Southern California in 1919, Burroughs formed his own corporation, Edgar Rice Burroughs, Inc.; the Los Angeles suburb of Tarzana bears the name of his creation. He died in California at the age of 74.

Bushman, Francis X.
(1883–1966) *cinema's first matinee idol*

Born in Baltimore, Bushman joined the ESSANAY FILM MANUFACTURING COMPANY in 1911 after establishing himself as a stage actor. He soon became the company's handsome leading man, starring in dozens of films, including *The Eye That Never Sleeps*—a reference to the Allan PINKERTON detective agency—the George ADE-scripted *The Fable of the Bush League Lover Who Failed to Qualify,* and the George Barr MCCUTCHEON-inspired *Graustark.* In 1916, Bushman starred in a popular *Romeo and Juliet,* along with actress Beverly Bayne, who had become his frequent leading lady. Yet his deep secret, kept from his public, was that he had a wife and five children; exposure of that fact, along with a divorce to marry Bayne, ruined his career. He made a partial a comeback in the 1925 *Ben-Hur;* his later career was in radio soap opera.

Butler, Aileen

A character in Theodore DREISER's Frank COWPERWOOD trilogy Aileen who first appeared in THE FINANCIER, is the daughter of Edward Malia BUTLER, a man of lowly origins who becomes a powerful figure in Philadelphia politics. Despite her father's wealth, she is conscious of her lack of ultimate respectability; Dreiser reminds the reader frequently that the family is Irish and Catholic. Yet her youth and beauty captivate the young financier Cowperwood, who is already married to a woman five years older than he; Cowperwood and Aileen begin a clandestine affair. When her enraged father learns about the relationship, he actively contributes to Cowperwood's downfall; as the financier's misappropriation of public funds is revealed, Butler makes sure that Cowperwood is convicted and given the maximum sentence. Aileen admires the man she considers brilliant but mistreated, including

by her own father, and remains devoted to Cowperwood throughout his imprisonment; she follows him to Chicago and marries him after his wife seeks a divorce.

In THE TITAN, published two years later, the author's depiction of Aileen shifts. At issue now is her desire to be accepted into society, a matter not even to be contemplated in Philadelphia; she begins to feel her social inadequacies. She has only her beauty to rely on, lacking both cleverness and sophistication; as a character remarks, "She is not exactly coarse, but not clever enough." Eventually Cowperwood's financial dealings cause scrutiny of her past, and the scandal of her previous life surfaces as well, dooming all hopes of her entering into society. Cowperwood begins to pursue affairs outside of marriage, and Aileen becomes no longer the confident and secure woman she had been in *The Financier*; she launches into a fierce physical attack on Rita SOHLBERG, one of her husband's mistresses. Later, she drifts into her own unsatisfactory affairs; her suicide attempt occurs when Cowperwood, hoping to marry Berenice FLEMING, asks for a divorce.

In THE STOIC, as her husband moves to England and seeks control of the London subway system, Aileen sees her status partially restored; Cowperwood wishes to maintain the appearance of respectability. Yet he has moved Berenice to England as well, and he secretly employs a charming but impoverished social figure, Bruce Tollifer, to distract Aileen, to feign interest in her, keeping her occupied while he himself spends time with Berenice. Aileen ultimately finds out about the scheme and feels humiliated, breaking off with Tollifer. When Cowperwood falls fatally ill, she agrees to carry out his charitable wishes, but after his death the estate is caught up in litigation so that nothing is left for charity, as well as little for her. Living alone in a New York apartment, she dies of pneumonia several years later.

As the character of Cowperwood is based on the real-life transportation magnate Charles T. YERKES, so Aileen Butler Cowperwood is a reflection of Yerkes's wife—and yet she resembles the character of Angela BLUE, the protagonist's wife in the autobiographical THE "GENIUS." Biographical evidence suggests that Aileen, in her lack of sophistication, in her jealous outburst, is modeled on Dreiser's wife as well.

Butler, Edward Malia

A character in Theodore DREISER's novel THE FINANCIER, Butler of Irish immigrant stock, has risen to become one of the controlling figures in Philadelphia politics. Starting out by hauling away garbage free of charge, using it to feed his animals, he begins collecting money for the task; his next step is to become the city's authorized garbage collector, turning the practice into a citywide monopoly. Other lucrative contracts follow, obtained by bribery; soon he is paving streets, building bridges, constructing sewers, and ultimately becoming a municipal power broker. Butler's wife is portrayed as a transplanted peasant woman, devoted to her religion; it is the next generation that is seen as adapting to the times, including two prominent sons and a younger daughter who marries appropriately. Yet the older daughter, Aileen BUTLER, brings disgrace to the family through her liaison with Frank COWPERWOOD. Butler's revenge on Cowperwood ensures that the financier is imprisoned for financial misdeeds—misdeeds that Butler, a corrupt politician, would otherwise not have taken seriously. He dies six months after Cowperwood goes to prison, a death attributed to his daughter's continuing defiance.

Butler, Jim

This character in Hamlin GARLAND's story "Under the Lion's Paw," collected in MAIN-TRAVELLED ROADS, started out in the grocery business in Rock River, Iowa; he soon learned that profits lie in land speculation. Butler is the owner of the farm that Timothy HASKINS rents and improves and who then doubles the price once the improvements have made the land doubly valuable. Butler represents the evils that Henry GEORGE, along with his disciple Garland, saw as destroying the economy of the West.

Buttered Side Down
Edna Ferber
(1912)

In Edna FERBER's first collection of stories, the settings are either small-town Wisconsin, where Ferber lived as a girl, or in Chicago, where she lived in her 20s. The tales alternate between praising small-town life and indicating instead a preference for the big city. Most of the city-dwelling characters have come originally from rural Wisconsin or Iowa; they tend to be working girls engaged as clerks in retail establishments, selling shoes, gloves, and lingerie. Several stories feature Jewish heroines, counteracting the otherwise semiautobiographical Irish heroine of Ferber's previously published novel, DAWN O'HARA—as well as the idealized portrait of her mother in the contemporaneous Emma MCCHESNEY tales. "The Homely Heroine," set in her hometown of Appleton, Wisconsin, is Ferber's first published story, appearing in Everybody's Magazine in 1910; the heroine, Pearlie Schultz, is seen again in "The Leading Lady." Another tale, "One of the Old Girls," presents a woman who has achieved the high position of buyer for a Chicago department store—the same occupation held by other Ferber heroines—and turns down a marriage proposal; she defends her single life, claiming that marriage would confine her and threaten her hard-won financial independence.

Butterworth, Clara

A character in Sherwood ANDERSON's novel POOR WHITE, Clara is the daughter of Thomas BUTTERWORTH, the Ohio village's richest man. She has little sympathy for her father's investing in factories, for his pushing the town into a new industrial age. Many of her ideas come from a fellow woman student at the state university, the "mannish" Kate CHANCELLER, who criticizes the social and economic system of the day. Feeling obliged to marry, Clara looks to Hugh MCVEY, the inventor who has caused the town to build its factories. She continues to react negatively to industrialization—until an unhinged craftsman, feeling himself bypassed by machines, attacks her husband. At that point her instincts as wife and mother take over, and she automatically becomes a defender of the new era that her husband represents.

Butterworth, Thomas

A character in Sherwood ANDERSON's novel POOR WHITE, Thomas is a farmer who owns a thousand acres of land and is already the richest man in Bidwell, Ohio. Yet he seizes new opportunities as they arrive, promoting inventions, building factories— even as his fellow townspeople lose their life savings in one of his projects. Tom considers himself a man of the future, a man who is ultimately benefiting the community by bringing in industry and prosperity. Seeing himself also as the town's leading citizen, he wants to make sure his daughter marries well.

"Buttons"   See CHICAGO POEMS.

C

Campbellites

Members of the religious group, known also as Disciples of Christ, or Church of Christ, included the families of Vachel LINDSAY and George ADE. Beginning in the late 18th century as an offshoot of Presbyterianism, led in the next century by the charismatic Alexander Campbell, the Disciples of Christ called themselves simply Christians, rejecting denominational labels, following a "primitive" Christianity; they practiced adult baptism and shunned church hierarchy or authority. Hiram College in Hiram, Ohio, where Lindsay enrolled, was founded in 1850 as a Campbellite institution; President James A. GARFIELD, a Disciples of Christ lay preacher, taught at Hiram College in the late 1850s. Lindsay concludes his 1920 collection, *The Golden Whales of California and Other Rhymes in the American Language,* with a three-part work entitled "Alexander Campbell"; he recreates the voice of the prophet, exhorting renegades, prodigals, and blasphemers to return to the river and repent.

Camp Douglas

A prison for Confederate soldiers during the CIVIL WAR, located on the South Side of Chicago, the camp was originally a federal military training ground, established on land once owned by Stephen A. DOUGLAS, Illinois Democratic senator. Between 1862 and 1865, the facility held 26,000 Confederate prisoners, often ill and starving. As many as 6,000 men are said to have died at Camp Douglas; their bodies were buried in what is now LINCOLN PARK, then reburied in Oak Woods cemetery on the South Side. On Memorial Day, May 30, 1895, a monument was dedicated at Oak Woods, in a ceremony attended by President Grover CLEVELAND and veterans of both Confederate and Union armies. The Southern equivalent to Camp Douglas was ANDERSONVILLE in Georgia, in which 13,000 Union soldiers are said to have died of disease and malnutrition.

capitalism

In this economic system, the means of production and supply are privately owned. In its modern form, capitalism dates from the Industrial Revolution, originating in Great Britain in the 18th century; at that time, manufacturing began to replace ownership of land as the prime generator of wealth. The new industries, producing goods in unprecedented quantities, relied also on unprecedented quantities of human labor; social critics deplored the disparity between the earnings of the small group of owners and the earnings of the mass of laborers. Karl Marx, espousing SOCIALISM, called for the public ownership of industry; to achieve that goal, he and many of his followers saw the necessity of class struggle, of revolution, to overthrow the existing system. Adherents of ANARCHISM spoke also of revolution, although their solutions were not as systematic as those of socialists and—

in a term once considered interchangeable—communists. Anticapitalism in America ranged from labor agitation, including that of the radical INDUSTRIAL WORKERS OF THE WORLD union, to the mild-mannered socialist utopianism of Edward BELLAMY and William Dean HOWELLS.

Capone, Alphonse "Al"
(1899–1947) *Chicago-based gangster*

The establishment of PROHIBITION in 1920 allowed criminals to build a powerful underworld empire; rivalry between gangs caused the violence for which Chicago became known. Capone, born in Italy, growing up in New York, arrived in Chicago along with Prohibition; he kept headquarters in the Lexington Hotel on South MICHIGAN AVENUE and controlled, it is said, an extensive and brutal crime syndicate. The nickname "Scarface" came from a knife wound on his jaw, the result of a fight in New York. The notorious ST. VALENTINE'S DAY MASSACRE, allegedly masterminded by Capone, took place in 1929. His eventual conviction, for income tax evasion, sent him to prison in 1931; paroled in 1939, he died of syphilis in Florida at the age of 48. The Lexington Hotel was demolished in 1995.

Capone and his associates became models for a new set of characters in fiction and film. W. R. BURNETT's *Little Caesar*, published in 1929, began the focusing on Capone-like protagonists; the film of the same name, starring Edward G. Robinson, appeared two years later. The 1932 movie *Scarface*, portraying the life and death of a similar gangster, written by ex-Chicagoan Ben HECHT and starring ex-Chicagoan Paul MUNI, was completed earlier than *Little Caesar* but released later, having encountered censorship problems because of its violence. Another well-known gangster movie, *The Public Enemy*, starring James Cagney, appeared in 1931.

In 1941, exiled German playwright Bertolt Brecht wrote a parable of Adolf Hitler's rise to power, *The Resistible Rise of Arturo Ui*, choosing a Chicago hoodlum as his Hitler stand-in. In the 1960s, the popular *The Untouchables* television series revived the Chicago gangster image, bringing a

defamation lawsuit from the Capone estate. Director Brian De Palma remade *Scarface* in 1983, followed by *The Untouchables* as a movie, starring Kevin Costner, Sean Connery, and Robert De Niro—as Capone—in 1987.

Carpenter, Belle   *See under* WINESBURG, OHIO: "An Awakening" and "Respectability."

carpetbagger

This term was applied to Northerners going south after the CIVIL WAR, presumably for predatory motives. The label suggests that they brought their possessions in carpetbags, or cheap suitcases, intending to take advantage of the defeated Confederacy. Observers have claimed that the term, implying chicanery, gave Southerners an excuse to reject the efforts of RADICAL REPUBLICANS to enforce Constitutional guarantees for African Americans.

In Sherwood ANDERSON's novel *POOR WHITE*, a man comes to an Ohio town who had been "a carpet-bag Governor of a southern state." Following the generally accepted image, he is portrayed as admitting to cheating Southerners and making a considerable amount of money. Anderson returns to the figure in a 1923 magazine article titled "King Coal," collected in *SHERWOOD ANDERSON'S NOTEBOOK*; an old man once came to his Ohio town from the postwar South, bringing with him "unlawful moneys" and "a good deal of rascality."

Carson, Edith

A character in Sherwood ANDERSON's novel *MARCHING MEN*, Edith is a Chicago milliner, or hatmaker. When she meets protagonist Beaut MCGREGOR, she reminds him of a woman he once cared for in his hometown of Coal Creek, Pennsylvania. Edith is older than McGregor, and like the undertaker's daughter in Coal Creek, she is seemingly frail. She maintains a long-term platonic relationship with McGregor, although the restraint is on his side, not hers. When he announces he will marry Margaret ORMSBY, Edith asserts herself for the first time, challenging the wealthy and beautiful Margaret; the latter recognizes her claim and backs down. Yet Edith disappears from the novel as soon as she wins her victory; her married life with McGregor is never mentioned.

Cassatt, Mary
(1844–1926) *American Impressionist painter*

Recognized as an important 19th-century figure, Cassatt is known to historians also as the creator of the long-lost mural for the WORLD'S COLUMBIAN EXPOSITION of 1893. Born in Pittsburgh, after spending time as a girl abroad with her family, Cassatt sailed for Paris in 1865 at the age of 21, planning to live on her own and become an artist—an unprecedented undertaking for a woman of the era. The principal art academy of France, the ÉCOLE DES BEAUX-ARTS, was not open to women, and Cassatt was forced to turn to private instruction. Holding her first exhibition at the Paris Salon in 1872, she was later invited by French painter and sculptor Edgar Degas to exhibit with the Impressionists. Her subject matter always remained the same, centering on women and children. Degas himself painted her in "Mary Cassatt at the Louvre," portraying Cassatt and her older sister, Lydia, looking at a group of paintings in the Louvre's grand gallery.

In 1892, Bertha PALMER, traveling to Paris as representative of the Board of Lady Managers for the world's fair, asked Cassatt to undertake another unprecedented project for a woman, painting a large mural. It was to be called "Modern Women," placed under the glass roof of the Women's Building, a facility demonstrating women's achievements over the years. The other end of the hall was reserved for "Primitive Women," painted by a more conventional artist, Mary Fairchild MacMonnies. Palmer's instructions were that "Primitive Women" should depict female servitude, while "Modern Women" should depict female progress, notably in education and the arts. Palmer, already a collector of impressionist art—works that would eventually find their way to the ART INSTITUTE—realized that Cassatt, although

never having undertaken such a project, would be an appropriate nontraditional artist for a nontraditional subject.

Using bright colors, Cassatt depicted young women in three separate scenes, one showing women "plucking the fruits of knowledge or science." Yet when the mural was placed high on the wall, the figures appeared small and unclear, and the colors were said to clash with other displays in the building; the public generally disapproved. At the close of the fair, the Cassatt and McMonnies murals went into storage, no specific plans being made for their preservation; the storage company is assumed to have disposed of them. Cassatt's reputation is high today, and feminists applaud her determination to succeed in a male-dominated art world—although some object to her mother-and-child subject matter, seeming to exalt traditional women's roles.

Cather, Willa
(1873–1947) *novelist*

Although she never lived in Chicago, Cather is often included among the figures of the Chicago Renaissance because of her use of the city as a setting for three novels, as well as her recurring REVOLT FROM THE VILLAGE themes. Born in Winchester, Virginia, Cather moved with her family at the age of nine to Red Cloud, Nebraska, and graduated from the University of Nebraska in 1895. In March of that year, she visited Chicago for the first time, seeing five productions of the touring Metropolitan Opera Company of New York; this experience began her lifelong love of opera. Her three Chicago novels, published 10 years apart, are the 1915 THE SONG OF THE LARK, the 1925 THE PROFESSOR'S HOUSE, and the 1935 *Lucy Gayheart.*

Cather found her first job outside of Nebraska at the *Home Monthly,* a women's magazine published in Pittsburgh; she next worked at the *Pittsburgh Daily Leader.* In 1901, she accepted a high school teaching post, hoping to have more time for writing. A Pittsburgh friend, Isabelle McClung, invited her to live in the McClung family house; Isabelle's father, a prominent judge, had presided over the trial of Alexander Berkman, lover of Emma GOLDMAN, the anarchist charged in the attempted murder of industrialist Henry C. Frick. Cather lived with the McClungs for five years; Isabelle is said to have remained the most important person in her life. In 1905, Cather published the story collection *The Troll Garden,* including the much-anthologized piece, "Paul's Case." The next year, accepting an offer from MCCLURE'S MAGAZINE, she moved to New York, joining companion Edith Lewis, a fellow Nebraskan.

In 1912, the novelist made her first trip to the Southwest, traveling to Arizona and New Mexico; the Southwest became an important setting for her fiction, including portions of two Chicago novels, *The Song of the Lark* and *The Professor's House.* Yet in keeping with her revolt-from-the-village credentials, she returned periodically to a rural Midwest locale; *O Pioneers!* and *My Ántonia,* published in 1913 and 1918, depict a stark farm life on the Nebraska prairie, and the long first segment of *The Song of the Lark,* substituting Colorado for Nebraska, is set in a small town on the plains. Twenty years later, *Lucy Gayheart* depicts a heroine once more escaping a town near the Nebraska-Kansas border and moving on to Chicago.

In 1913, Cather interviewed the Swedish-American opera singer Olive FREMSTAD for *McClure's,* and the Minnesota-raised Fremstad became the inspiration for *The Song of the Lark,* as well as a personal friend. In 1922, the author ventured a WORLD WAR I novel, *One of Ours,* which became a best-seller, giving her financial security for the first time; the work won a Pulitzer Prize. In 1927, Cather published the acclaimed *Death Comes to the Archbishop,* set in New Mexico, followed in 1931 by *Shadows on the Rock,* set in Quebec; the author's last major work was the 1940 *Sapphira and the Slave Girl,* presenting a pre–CIVIL WAR South, portraying for the first time her earliest childhood setting. Cather died in New York City at the age of 73.

Although her ties to the Chicago Renaissance are less strong than those of other writers of the era, Cather understood, like them, that the city was the place to find freedom from inhibiting influences, to foster artistic expression. Yet her seemingly conservative views—despite her repudiation of small-town values—have come under attack from politically oriented critics. She depicts midwestern farmers as struggling against the elements, against nature itself, never suggesting—in the manner, say, of Hamlin GARLAND—that economic factors contribute to their problems; she ignores the social and political issues that came to the forefront during the GREAT DEPRESSION. In *Sapphira and the Slave Girl,* she has been accused of downplaying the issue of slavery, of romanticizing the antebellum South. Yet in recent years critics have reevaluated her once more, viewing her anew as a lesbian writer, finding fresh viewpoints from which to analyze her themes and her choice of subject matter. Cather remains today a major American fiction writer of the first half of the 20th century, standing unsurpassed in storytelling, in creating visionary, often tragic panoramas of life.

Further Reading

Acocella, Joan. *Willa Cather and the Politics of Criticism.* Lincoln: University of Nebraska Press, 2000.

Gerber, Philip. *Willa Cather: Revised Edition.* New York: Twayne Publishers, 1995.

Stout, Janis P. *Willa Cather: The Writer and Her World.* Charlottesville: University Press of Virginia, 2000.

Catherwood, Mary Hartwell
(1847–1902) *novelist*

Known originally as the author of historical romances, Catherwood is best remembered today for *THE SPIRIT OF AN ILLINOIS TOWN,* published in 1897. Born in Ohio, moving to Milford, Illinois, she earned recognition through her novels of the French in North America, including the 1889 *The Romance of Dollard,* drawing on the work of historian Francis Parkman. Depicting 17th-century NEW FRANCE as representing a time of graciousness and nobility, Catherwood's work helped spur a wave of historical romances, as well as romances of fictitious geography, such as George Barr MC-CUTCHEON's 1901 GRAUSTARK. Her *Lazarre,* published also in 1901, drew on another romantic fiction—that the dauphin, heir of the French throne, son of the beheaded Louis XVI, had been brought to America to live among the Indians; Mark Twain had already drawn on that tradition in creating his confidence men, the Duke and the Dauphin, in *The Adventures of Huckleberry Finn*.

In a well-publicized debate with Hamlin GARLAND at the CONGRESS OF AUTHORS coinciding with the 1893 WORLD'S COLUMBIAN EXPOSITION, Catherwood defended "romance" against Garland's REALISM; she spoke for the romantic ideals of honor and nobility of spirit. The conservative DIAL supported her views, as did the newspaper columnist Eugene FIELD. Garland spoke also against sentimentality—a quality that has since been ascribed to Catherwood's *The Spirit of an Illinois Town*, published four years later.

Chanceller, Kate

A character in Sherwood ANDERSON's novel POOR WHITE, Kate is a student at the state university along with Clara BUTTERWORTH. She is a woman who swears like a man, who is "in her nature a man." Befriending Clara, she speaks of things that Clara has not thought about, such as women's roles and society's expectations of women; Kate is a socialist as well, talking about economic issues such as free trade and protectionism. She is also planning to find work—an activity not necessarily appropriate for a woman who has the economic means to attend a university. Although Kate holds back in displays of affection, Clara is vaguely aware that their friendship is more than simply friendship.

Channing, Christina

A character in Theodore DREISER's novel THE "GENIUS," Christina, an aspiring opera singer, presents a new type of woman to the young Eugene WITLA. Teaching him about music and the musical world, she engages him in a brief physical relationship, then goes off to pursue her career; she has understood that combining a career and marriage is not possible for a woman, and she has found Eugene useful only for the passing moment. As an American singer, she follows, too, the necessary

course of the day, going off to Europe to gain recognition and then returning, validated, to a career in her native country; Thea KRONBERG, the singer-protagonist of Willa CATHER's THE SONG OF THE LARK—a novel published the same year as *The "Genius"*—follows the same transatlantic path. Later, Christina, returning from Europe, sees and admires Eugene's gallery exhibit; she remembers her lover fondly, although acknowledging that the past is gone, feeling no regrets. Eugene at the same time notes her name in the newspapers, hailing her as a new and rising talent in opera; he himself is by then suffering a nervous breakdown.

The Chap-Book

A literary magazine first appearing in May 1894 and resembling the English periodical, *The Yellow Book*, *The Chap-Book* reflected turn-of-the-century aestheticism, a conscious revolt against the presumed high-minded seriousness of the Victorian era. The title is a self-deprecating term, referring to inexpensive books sold by itinerant peddlers. Published twice monthly by the firm of STONE AND KIMBALL, the periodical featured Chicago writers, as well as international figures such as French poets Paul Verlaine and Stéphane Mallarmé and English writers Thomas Hardy and H. G. Wells; it serialized American novelist Henry James's *What Maisie Knew*. Illustrations by Aubrey Beardsley, a major English artist of the ART NOUVEAU movement, appeared in many issues; one of its advertising posters was by French artist Henri de Toulouse-Lautrec. The magazine continued for four years, until July 1898.

Chaplin, Charlie
(1889–1977) *major motion picture star*

Born in London to a theatrical family, Chaplin first came to America with a touring company in 1910. Making his initial film in 1914, he signed that year with the ESSANAY FILM MANUFACTURING COMPANY in Chicago; his one Chicago-made movie, *His First Job*, filmed in 1915, included comedian Ben TURPIN and a teenage Gloria SWANSON. The

Little Tramp, his signature character, was introduced later the same year in *The Tramp*, made for the California branch of the Essanay studios; Chaplin continued making Little Tramp silent movies through 1936. In 1943, he married the daughter of playwright Eugene O'NEILL. Criticized for his left-wing politics, Chaplin spent the last 25 years of his life in Switzerland.

The comedian was a favorite actor of poet and movie fan Carl SANDBURG. Writing about a Chaplin movie in the 1915 *INTERNATIONAL SOCIALIST REVIEW,* Sandburg points out that the actor, portraying a purposefully incompetent worker, turns work into sabotage, into passive protest. Later, when Sandburg became movie reviewer for the *CHICAGO DAILY NEWS,* he wrote admiringly of "the world's greatest Charlie"; his poem "Without the Cane and the Derby," collected in *Slabs of the Sunburnt West,* expands on a profile he wrote for the *Daily News* in 1921. The real Chaplin, Sandburg declares, when seen without his comic props, is a quiet and serious man.

Cheerful by Request
Edna Ferber
(1918)

The stories in this collection by Edna FERBER are set mainly in Chicago or small-town Wisconsin. The tales follow in the tradition of O. Henry, or William Sydney PORTER, relying on plot twists, tidy coincidences, and surprises; the endings, conforming to popular sentimental standards, are either happy or bittersweet. One of the pieces, "The Gay Old Dog," found a place in the volume *Best American Short Stories of 1917;* it became a silent movie in 1919. Another story, "The Eldest," about a woman who has sacrificed for her family, was turned into a play by the author and performed by the PROVINCETOWN PLAYERS in 1920. "The Woman Who Tried to Be Good" features one-time brothel owner Blanche Devine, who, although retired from her profession, still receives scorn from the community, even after a selfless act of kindness; she appears also in the novel *FANNY HERSELF.* Two stories provide further echoes of *Fanny,* portraying businesswomen

specifically identified as Jewish. "The Girl Who Went Right" depicts a young woman who, like Fanny, denying her Jewishness to her employer, goes on to prove her understanding of business. In "Sophy-as-She-Might-Have-Been," a Jewish woman buyer from a Chicago retail store expresses a strong interest in business: "I don't know anything but business. It's the only thing I care about." Ferber stands among the earliest authors depicting women succeeding in business, if within circumscribed areas.

"Chicago"   *See* CHICAGO POEMS.

Chicago
Maurine Watkins
(1926)

Reflecting the new world of gangsters brought about by PROHIBITION—and soon popularly portrayed in fiction, theater, and film—this play by Maurine WATKINS draws on two real-life murder cases of 1924. Watkins, a reporter for the *CHICAGO TRIBUNE,* covered the trials of two women accused of murdering their lovers; both defendants, benefiting from extensive media coverage—including that provided by Watkins—were acquitted by all-male juries. The play debuted in New York in 1926; it is credited with inspiring Ben HECHT and Charles MACARTHUR to write their own murder-and-newsroom drama, *THE FRONT PAGE,* in 1928.

A silent film was made in 1927; a version titled *Roxie Hart,* starring Ginger Rogers, appeared in 1942. In the latter film, Hecht served as uncredited screenwriter. The John Kander and Fred Ebb stage musical, *Chicago,* premiered in New York in 1975; the movie *Chicago* won the Best Picture Academy Award in 2003.

Chicago Bee

An African-American newspaper founded to rival the *CHICAGO DEFENDER,* the *Chicago Bee* was established as a weekly in 1926 by Anthony Overton, a food-products and toiletries manufacturer.

On its staff was Chandler OWEN, cofounder with A. Philip RANDOLPH of the New York socialist publication *Messenger*. The paper has been credited with popularizing the term BRONZEVILLE. Ceasing publication in 1940, it left behind its headquarters, built in 1931, which have been restored and opened as the Chicago Bee Branch of the Chicago Public Library.

Chicago Board of Trade

The world's first commodities trading organization, the Chicago Board of Trade was established in 1848 by a group of farmers and businessmen. Serving as an exchange for commodities—articles for trade or commerce—the CBOT became the marketplace for the wheat and corn grown by farmers of the surrounding region; it soon dealt in livestock and other commodities as well. The expansion of the telegraph led to the futures market; speculators began buying and selling claims on agricultural products that they did not physically possess. The trading floor, or pit—"the marketplace of the world"—became the scene of fortunes made or lost in a matter of minutes. Carl SANDBURG, visiting the city from downstate Illinois in 1896, at the age of 18, later wrote about watching "the grain gamblers throwing fingers and yelling prices." Lucy PARSONS and others referred to the institution as the "Board of Thieves." Yet it is claimed that futures trading gave benefits to farmers, shifting the risk of future price changes from the growers to the speculators.

The 1930 Chicago Board of Trade Building, featuring a rooftop representation of Ceres, Roman goddess of grain, replaced the previous building on the same spot, the structure romanticized by Frank Norris in *The Pit*. *(Chicago Historical Society)*

Chicago Board of Trade Building

One of two successive buildings standing on the same site on South La Salle Street, the first Board of Trade Building, built in 1885 by William W. BOYINGTON, one of Chicago's early architects, was a nine-story structure housing a high-ceilinged trading hall, or "pit." The hall featured 80-foot windows, stained-glass skylights, and a spectators' gallery. The building was often criticized for its eclectic mix of styles, including a rooftop copper weather vane in the form of a ship; Henry B.

FULLER's novel of 1893, THE CLIFF-DWELLERS, presents a naïve man from the countryside, who praises the structure, causing the authorial voice to brand him as a "simple soul." The building provided the setting for Frank NORRIS's 1903 novel, THE PIT; Norris saw it as a symbol of larger forces, describing it as "crouching on its foundations, like a monstrous sphinx with blind eyes."

A second building, designed by the firm of Holabird and Root, was completed in 1930. Exemplifying ART DECO style, the structure is topped by a 32-foot aluminum statue of Ceres, the Roman goddess of grain and agriculture.

Chicago Cubs

A National League baseball team, the outgrowth of an earlier organization, the Cubs received their name in 1902. In that same year the legendary double-play infield trio—shortstop Joe Tinker, second baseman Johnny Evers, and first baseman Frank Chance—was formed, immortalized by Franklin P. ADAMS in the verse lamenting "Tinker to Evers to Chance." The Cubs merged with the Chicago Whales of the Federal League in 1915, and the team moved into the Whales's Weeghman Park, built the previous year. William WRIGLEY Jr., becoming sole owner of the Cubs in 1921, renamed the park WRIGLEY FIELD in 1926. The Wrigley family owned the Cubs until 1996, when the team was sold to the owners of the CHICAGO TRIBUNE.

Chicago Daily News

A major Chicago newspaper, founded in 1875 by Melville E. STONE, the *Daily News* became the city's most influential paper by the end of the 19th century. The afternoon tabloid was seen as the workingman's friend, having sided with the strikers in the GREAT STRIKE of 1877; for its first 30 years, it cost a penny a copy. The related morning paper was the *Chicago Morning News,* later renamed the *Chicago News-Record,* then the *Chicago Record;* the papers became the forum for many important Chicago writers. Victor F. LAWSON, who bought the *Daily News* from Stone, heading it until 1926, hired Finley Peter DUNNE, Eugene FIELD, George ADE, and political cartoonist John T. MC-CUTCHEON; editor Henry Justin Smith hired Ben HECHT, Carl SANDBURG, and James T. FARRELL. Later, the paper passed into the hands of the Marshall FIELD family; after a hundred years of existence, it was folded in 1978 into the *Chicago Sun-Times.*

Chicago Day Book

A tabloid newspaper started by publishing magnate E. W. Scripps in 1911, the *Day Book* tested the idea that a publication could survive without advertising. Targeting the workingman, the paper was small in size, fitting without folding into a pocket; Ben HECHT described it as having "a most unprofessional look and equally strange content." Carl SANDBURG worked on the paper from 1913 to 1917; its editor was Don MacGregor, later involved in the Colorado "coal wars" and killed in Mexico, as memorialized by Sandburg in his "Memoir of a Proud Boy," collected in CORNHUSKERS. The *Day Book* ceased publication in 1917.

Chicago Defender

An African-American newspaper founded by Robert S. ABBOTT in 1905, the *Chicago Defender* became the most important black publication in the United States, as well as the most widely read newspaper among African Americans in the South; it was carried along southern routes by Pullman porters. Promoting Chicago as the promised land, the paper has been credited in part for the GREAT MIGRATION, the movement of blacks into Chicago after WORLD WAR I. Outspoken about lynchings and segregation laws, the *Defender* was also the first black newspaper to carry a comic-strip page. William Foster, an early Chicago African-American filmmaker, wrote for the *Defender;* Langston HUGHES wrote a column for more than 20 years. Reaching a circulation high of 160,000 in the 1930s, the paper lost readership in recent decades as other African-American media outlets grew.

Chicago Literary Times

This periodical was published by Ben HECHT and Max BODENHEIM and underwritten by the publishing firm of COVICI-MCGEE. Appearing between March 1923 and June 1924, the biweekly eight-page tabloid included parodies, criticism, and humor. Among the figures lampooned were Sherwood ANDERSON and Carl SANDBURG; Hecht's list of the world's worst books included J. M. Barrie's *Peter Pan* and Karl Marx's *Das Capital,* as well as

William Dean HOWELLS's *The Rise of Silas Lapham.* Illustrators included Hecht's friend, the subsequently celebrated German expatriate artist Georg Grosz.

Chicago Opera Company

Originally performing at New York's Manhattan Opera House, the Chicago Opera Company came to Chicago and the AUDITORIUM BUILDING theater in 1910; it was sponsored by Harold McCormick, son of reaper inventor Cyrus MC-CORMICK, and his wife, Edith, daughter of John D. ROCKEFELLER. In November of its initial season, renowned soprano Mary GARDEN, performing her Dance of the Seven Veils in Richard Strauss's opera *Salome*, scandalized audiences, causing Mrs. Rockefeller to request that the last of four scheduled presentations be canceled. Soprano Rosa RAISA, long associated with the company, first appeared in Chicago in 1913.

In 1921, the organization commissioned an opera from Russian composer Serge PROKOFIEV; *The Love of Three Oranges* received its world premiere, conducted by the composer, in December of that year. In 1922, the company was reorganized as the Chicago Civic Opera under the leadership of Samuel INSULL. Insull oversaw the building of the CIVIC OPERA HOUSE in 1929; it opened a few days after the stock-market crash. The company dissolved in 1932.

In Willa CATHER's 1925 novel *THE PROFESSOR'S HOUSE*, Godfrey ST. PETER and his wife enjoy French composer Ambroise Thomas's opera *Mignon*, performed by the company at the Auditorium.

Chicago Poems
Carl Sandburg
(1916)

In this first volume by Carl SANDBURG, the opening section consists of 55 poems separately titled "Chicago Poems"; it contains some of the most famous American verse. The second section, titled "Handfuls," begins with the oft-quoted "Fog."

Many of these poems were first published in PO-ETRY magazine. The work followed untraditional practices at the time, combining an "unpoetic" FREE VERSE—poetry without meter or rhyme—with a content that was also deemed "unpoetic," evoking urban grime and squalor. Writing for the dust jacket, Edgar Lee MASTERS declared that the poetry "prophesies of Industrial America, Business America." Although Sandburg's images of the city were unconventional for poetry, they had been anticipated in the fiction of Theodore DREISER and Frank NORRIS. Norris's *THE PIT*, published in 1903, refers to Chicago as crude and brutal, while yet "sane and healthy and vigorous."

Synopses of Selected Poems

"CHICAGO"
This poem is the key work of the Chicago Renaissance. Leading off the March 1914 issue of POETRY, the piece startled readers with its very first line, "Hog Butcher for the World"—raising at once the issue of poetic content. The stanza continues in a personification of the city, endowing it with human qualities, naming its various industrial roles; the second stanza indicates that the city itself is being addressed. The poet repeats the common accusations—you are "wicked," "crooked," "brutal"—and agrees with the charges; his subsequent refrain, using the first-person "I have seen" and citing examples, provides his own personal verification. Yet the poet turns then to the accusers, addressing them, answering their charges. The city is now seen as a sturdy worker, singing, cursing, brawling, laughing amid dust and smoke. Instead of the downtrodden worker depicted elsewhere—including in some of Sandburg's other poems—the worker here, as well as the city he represents, embodies a strong and manly ideal.

"LOST"
A sole boat in the lake at night, sounding its whistle, is personified, depicted as plaintively seeking harbor; it is likened to a lost child, crying, seeking the maternal breast. The poem follows what European and American writers, discovering the Japanese HAIKU in the early years of the 20th century, perceived as one of the mandates of the

haiku—to record a keenly observed moment. Like the preceding "Chicago," the poem appeared in the March 1914 *Poetry*.

"HALSTED STREET CAR"

Halsted Street is the thoroughfare on which Jane ADDAMS's HULL-HOUSE stands; these riders of public transportation are largely immigrant workers. The "cartoonists" are the political cartoonists of the newspapers; the poet is challenging them to capture the riders' tired despair, letting the public realize the plight of a large portion of the city's population. Yet it is at seven o'clock in the morning that Sandburg depicts the riders, when they have yet to face the day's work; their appearance on the evening trip is to be imagined.

Theodore DREISER's heroine in *SISTER CARRIE*, when she first comes to Chicago, lives with her sister in the Halsted Street area.

"FISH CRIER"

MAXWELL STREET was the center of a large outdoor market of largely Jewish merchants, many of them of recent Eastern European origin. That the peddler is "terribly" glad suggests an ambiguity, as does his "north wind" voice. One thing he is glad of, according to the poet, is "that God made fish"; readers have detected a criticism in those words, in that the fish crier himself is not a maker or builder—as opposed to other Chicago workers who labor to build skyscrapers and railroads.

"Pavlowa" is a reference to the popular Russian ballerina Anna Pavlova, who made her American debut in 1910. In Edna FERBER's 1917 novel, *FANNY HERSELF*, the heroine makes sketches of people she sees, one of them an old bearded fish vender: "It took a thousand years of suffering and persecution and faith to stamp that look on his face," an admirer remarks.

"HAPPINESS"

Professors and executives, who are representatives of the intellectual and financial elite, do not understand what the immigrant workers—those who have toiled in harsh conditions all week long—understand when they celebrate their day off, when they spend their day of freedom with their families.

Although Sandburg might have resented the designation, this poem can be called an example of PRIMITIVISM, using a less "civilized" group for the purpose of criticizing those who are presumably overcivilized. The poet can be accused of condescension, of bestowing a blessing—which is his, the privileged poet's, to bestow. The DES PLAINES RIVER, the original portage connection with the CHICAGO RIVER, runs to the west of the city.

"BLACKLISTED"

In the 1950s, a blacklist named those not to be hired because of alleged communist sympathies; in Sandburg's day, a blacklist named those not to be hired because of union sympathies. During the labor troubles of the earlier era, union members or union sympathizers were systematically blacklisted by many companies. Yet as the poem suggests, in the days before Social Security numbers, a man could readily change his name—and this man will do so because he needs a job. In Clarence DARROW's novel of 1905, *AN EYE FOR AN EYE*, a railroad worker changes his name after participating in the PULLMAN STRIKE, managing to get a job in the switchyards.

"CHILD OF THE ROMANS"

The railroad worker, laboring 10 hours a day, keeps the roadbed smooth so that travelers can enjoy the luxury of the dining car. While he stops for a moment to eat his bread and bologna, the travelers speed by, enjoying steak, strawberries, and éclairs. The worker, referred to as "the dago shovelman," is a child of the once-grand Romans; Sandburg, on various occasions, makes use of what are now considered ethnic or racial slur words—in an era when such slur words could still be used to imply an ironic sympathy. Uppermost in the poet's mind is the Marxist doctrine declaring that the true creator of wealth—and thus the true deserver of wealth, as opposed to the railroad passengers—is the laboring man.

"THE RIGHT TO GRIEF"

A favorite theme of sentimental literature has been the death of a child; Sandburg was aware of the highly popular "Little Boy Blue" of Eugene FIELD. The poet here acknowledges the grief felt for the millionaire's dead child, although he calls it a "perfumed sorrow"; the millionaire cannot write a check to buy off Death, but he can use his checkbook to solve many of life's other troubles. So the poet prefers to extend his empathy to the laboring man's dead child, the daughter of the "stockyards hunky"; the term is an uncomplimentary reference to a Hungarian or Bohemian, used in the same semi-ironic way as "dago" in the preceding "Child of the Romans." The poet is mourning the family's poverty as well; the family can be glad now for no more doctor bills. When the priest says, "God have mercy on us all," the implications are for the larger group—for all the impoverished workingmen who must now go back to their degrading, exploitative toil.

"A FENCE"
After the luxurious mansion has been built, it must be protected by a fence. Workers are now putting up the iron bars that will keep people out—including the needy, the hungry, and the very men who built it, as well as their families. Only Death and Rain can pass through those bars—and, ominously, Tomorrow. That last word is a warning that the revolution will come, that the property of the rich will be taken away from them. The doctrines of SOCIALISM looked upon private property with suspicion, especially opulent private property; not only is the homeowner protecting his inordinate wealth, but he is excluding others from his unjustly gotten gains.

"MAMIE"
The title character feels confined in her small Indiana town, seeing it as ordinary and unromantic—and she sees, too, the trains that run regularly to Chicago. Yet having arrived in the big city, she has found herself confined, like so many other girls from small towns in the Midwest, to a six-dollar-a-week shopgirl's job. She wonders if there is another bigger, more romantic place to which the trains run.

"LIMITED"
The poet is making a play on the word *limited*. A limited train makes a limited number of stops before reaching its destination; it provides a high-

speed and elite form of travel. Carrying a thousand passengers, this particular train includes dining, sleeping, and smoking cars. Yet one day the coaches will be scrap metal, and the passengers will be dust. Meanwhile, a man in the smoking car, when asked where he is going, replies, "Omaha." In naming his immediate destination, he is showing his limited point of view.

Sandburg read this poem to the celebrants at a dinner for the visiting William Butler YEATS in 1914, an event sponsored by *Poetry* magazine. The ironic final line was undoubtedly effective in a public presentation—although on this particular occasion Vachel LINDSAY startled the audience subsequently with his recitation of the yet-unpublished "THE CONGO."

"IN A BACK ALLEY"
Newsboys amuse themselves by pitching pennies in an alley—pennies that bear the image of Abraham LINCOLN. Thus society carelessly remembers this great man, the man who loved humankind, who asked for "malice toward none." The president loved the newboys—in 1916, the phrase *lover of boys* lacked the pedophilic resonance it has today—as he loved all humanity. Sandburg, eventually the renowned biographer of Lincoln, spells out more of Lincoln's virtues in "Knucks," published in his next volume, CORNHUSKERS.

"DYNAMITER"
The anarchist is sitting and talking peaceably in a German saloon, and the poet, refraining from mentioning his violent deeds, feels no need to defend him. Sandburg's stance is to present this man, whom the public sees as an enemy, as he appears in the saloon, a family man, a lover of life and laughter. Yet the reference in the final line to "red blood," echoing the seemingly innocent "red-blooded" heartiness of the man's storytelling, can be read as an acknowledgment of the man's violence.

The poet identified the real-life subject as Anton Johansson, a man once suspected in a labor-dispute bombing at the *Los Angeles Times* in 1910. Hapgood HUTCHINS had already written about Johansson in his 1907 *The Story of an Anarchist*.

"UNDER A HAT RIM"

The poet, although immersed in an urban setting, draws upon the city's lakeside imagery. Walking along a city street, he catches a glimpse of a face under a hat—and sees a shipwrecked soul, clutching to fragments of a sinking vessel; this urban dweller is desperate, drowning. Yet the fragment of the ship that he clings to is a stateroom door, indicating that he is not a workingman—as evidenced, too, by the rimmed hat—but rather a man of substance. This poem, although longer than a traditional haiku, ends with the brief, haikulike image of the broken door.

"READY TO KILL"

When the poet looks at the statue of the famous general on horseback, he decides that statues should be built instead to the farmer, the miner, the factory worker—to the laboring man, who does the work of the world. Only if those other memorials are built, the poet says, will he look with ease on the general who seems ready to kill, to shed blood. Yet Sandburg notes that this blood runs over "the sweet new grass of the prairie"; he is foreshadowing the poems of his subsequent volume, *Cornhuskers*, where the prairie is seen as a symbol of regeneration and renewal.

"TO A CONTEMPORARY BUNKSHOOTER"

Originally titled "Billy Sunday," naming the contemporary evangelist William "Billy" SUNDAY, the poem appeared in both THE MASSES and the INTERNATIONAL SOCIALIST REVIEW in September 1915. When the publisher of *Chicago Poems* accepted the piece for the 1916 volume, he requested, fearing a libel suit, that the name be dropped. Other changes softened the poem's presumed antireligious impact; "This Jesus guy" becomes simply "This Jesus," and "the hell" is omitted from "What the hell do you know about Jesus?"

"SKYSCRAPER"

The piece renders poetically what Henry B. FULLER had already presented in his novel of 1893, THE CLIFF-DWELLERS—an urban skyscraper as a microcosm, as containing a full range of human activity. Multitudes of people pour in and out of the structure every day, giving it a living soul, and although the building consists, too, of elevator cables, tubes, wires, pipes, girders, and pilings, the souls of the workers who constructed the building are there as well—even the soul of the hod carrier now out of work, or of the bricklayer in prison for shooting a man while drunk. As for the man who fell from a girder and broke his neck, his soul has gone into the very stones of the building.

The cares and sorrows of each current worker, whether stenographer or executive, make a contribution to the whole; the skyscraper is not only a monument to the men who constructed it, but also the sum of its current inhabitants, whether of high or low status. Unlike in "The Right to Grief," where the poet downplays the grief of the millionaire, here the man whose name is written on the door—and thus of higher status than the laborer—is given sympathy when he thinks of his dead child. At the end of the day, when the floors empty, the soul of the building is still evident—as the structure looms now in "smoke and stars" over the sleeping city. Even when separated from human activity, it has its own mystical soul.

"FOG"

Standing first in the "Handfuls" section, this poem is an imitation of the Japanese haiku; it is a short verse recording a brief, striking perception. The poet can also be said to be practicing personification, endowing an inanimate object, fog, with an animal's sensibility. Because of its brevity—and because of its freshness at a particular time and place in literary history—the poem is one of the most recited pieces in the American canon.

"MURMURINGS IN A FIELD HOSPITAL"

This poem appears in the section "War Poems." America had not yet entered WORLD WAR I, and Sandburg, a writer for socialist periodicals, which generally denounced the war as a capitalist plot, produced a series of antiwar poems. Yet after U.S. entry into the conflict, he supported American military efforts, although continuing to write, often under a pseudonym, for socialist papers as well.

The poem records the statements of a wounded soldier, who now wants only simple things, like the playthings of childhood. What he does not want are "iron cold" things, that is, weapons. The soldier is seeking an escape from present reality and a return to the simple prewar past; those idealized images are agrarian images, as in "the new crock of butter." The poet, when conveying past perfection, is choosing a pastoral setting, far from any urban scene.

"BUTTONS"
The progress of World War I—as yet a faraway war, one in which Americans are not yet involved—is shown by colored buttons placed on a wall map in a newsroom. A laughing young man climbs a ladder and casually moves the buttons. Yet those casual moves, the poet knows, even moving just one inch at a time, represent thousands of men lying wounded and dead. This is war as seen from a distance, by those who never come near it, who can still respond without horror.

"SALVAGE"
The poet is addressing William MORRIS, English poet and social reformer, who died in 1896; Morris has been spared, Sandburg says, from seeing the devastation of the current war. As founder of the Society for the Preservation of Ancient Buildings, Morris not only loved the old buildings now being destroyed, but he also sought a return to the ideals of the medieval workman; advocating socialism, he emphasized the importance and value of labor. Sandburg speaks of cathedral stones carved by workmen who are joyful in their craft, "singing while they hammered." These lines echo the conclusion of "Chicago," where the city itself becomes a boisterous, laughing workman.

"WARS"
The last of the "War Poems" section, this work at first seems a standard exercise in pessimism—that is, lamenting that wars will never cease, that wars simply change in technology; what changes is that horses give way to motors, and swords give way to guns. The poet then imagines future warfare, featuring technology as yet undreamed of—"silent wheels" and "silent hurlers"—in which even more men die. In the old wars thousands of men fol-

lowed kings; in the new, or current, wars, millions of men follow kings. Yet the final line breaks the rhetorical pattern; instead of kings "quarreling," as they have done in both old and new wars, kings in future wars are "kicked under the dust"—and millions of men follow "great causes" instead. In other words, a revolution will come; leaders will fall, and the millions of men will struggle toward their dream.

This work assumes a common view of the time, that social change will come only through strife, through warfare and revolution. The poem predates the Russian revolution of 1917.

"WHO AM I?"
The sweeping first-person "I," derivative from Walt WHITMAN, becomes not a poetic persona, but rather a personification of Truth—although the reader is not aware of that identity until the last line. Up to that point the "I" is all-expansive, reaching from the stars to the "foam of primal things," talking to God, knowing both horror and beauty—and then, as an ironic anticlimax, knowing man's rebellion against a "Keep Off" sign. Man, the poet is saying, revolts against the exclusionary tactics of the privileged. The final line reminds the reader that Truth can never be captured or confined, that it will always escape to proclaim itself.

The poem can be read in conjunction with "A Fence," in which the poet documents the building of a keep-off device around a mansion for the privileged. As Truth cannot be confined, neither can privilege be made impregnable.

"SOILED DOVE"
The poem appears in a group labeled "Shadows," pieces dealing with prostitution. In this piece the woman, a showgirl from a Florenz ZIEGFELD chorus, was not "a harlot" until she married a corporation lawyer; she had never taken money from anyone before. Yet she loved the man she married, although he loved other women as well. So the money she now takes from him goes toward keeping up her looks, while he keeps other women—and while he tries, too, to undermine the government's interstate commerce commission. The woman is the "soiled dove" of the title,

and yet that title is ironic; her soiling is only because of the man she married. Like anyone connected to a corporation, he is the one who is unclean.

"GONE"

This is the last poem in the "Shadows" group. The people of the town do not know where Chick Lorimer, a local girl, has gone; they all loved her, a "wild girl" who had dreams and who packed her trunk and left. Presumably she was seeking her fortune in the city; yet the context makes clear that she ended up in a life of prostitution.

"I AM THE PEOPLE, THE MOB"

This poem and "Government" appear in the last section of *Chicago Poems*, labeled "Other Days." Although the poet again seems to be adopting Whitman's first-person inclusiveness, the "I" is not self-referential, but rather a personification of the mob, of the people speaking collectively. Yet in the fourth stanza Sandburg turns to the image of the prairie, not the city—because the prairie, the seed ground, dies and then renews itself. The prairie demonstrates another quality as well, in that it forgets the storms passing over it. The conclusion is that this "I" persona—the people, as well as the seed ground that produces the people—must remember the storms, must remember the wrongs committed against it. Then the people will gain their rightful power.

"GOVERNMENT"

This poem is less positive than the immediately preceding "I Am the People, the Mob." The institution of government is indicted here, and since the poet names policemen and militiamen, he is referring to both local and national governments. They are corrupt and callous because they are made up of men. The previous poem expressed hope of corrective action, once the people remember; yet here, since new governments are formed from old governments, they are all the same. No hope of progress is possible because the new governments are still human and will always be so. This poem represents an anarchist more than a socialist view, forgoing socialist optimism that a better society can be built.

Critical Reception

The "Chicago Poems" stirred a strong reaction when they first appeared in *Poetry*. The periodical DIAL urged readers "to rally around the old standards," to oppose these new forms of verse. The pieces were deemed technically unsound, full of "ragged lines," and the content was declared improper: "This author would be more at home in the brickyard than on the slopes of Parnassus."

When *Chicago Poems* was published in book form two years later, it met similar criticism. The *Boston Transcript* decried its "ill-regulated speech that has neither verse or prose rhythms"; the *Dial*, while praising some of the "highly sensitized impressionist poems," criticized others, claiming them to be written by a "mobocrat." Amy LOWELL found Sandburg both a gifted poet and a writer who indulged in excessive violence and propaganda.

The Chicago Race Riots, July 1919
Carl Sandburg
(1920)

This collection of articles by Carl SANDBURG originally appeared in the CHICAGO DAILY NEWS. The articles were later published in pamphlet form. The RACE RIOTS of 1919 claimed 38 lives in various parts of the city, beginning with the death of a young black swimmer at a Chicago beach. In his introduction to the collection, Sandburg puts the blame on a lack of police protection of black citizens, as well as on poverty that creates fear and hate among white workers. The police are "ignorant of Lincoln, the Civil War, the Emancipation Proclamation," he writes, and hoodlums arise from a "gaunt involuntary poverty." His poem "Hoodlums," written that July and collected in SMOKE AND STEEL, recreates the violent thoughts of a white rioter.

Chicago River

Originally flowing into Lake Michigan, declared the smallest river upon which any great city was ever built, the sluggish Chicago River traversed only a brief distance; a continental divide, sending waters westward, lay only a few miles away. In 1848, the ILLINOIS AND MICHIGAN CANAL crossed that divide, connecting the river and the Great Lakes to tributaries of the Mississippi River and ultimately the Gulf of Mexico. In 1900, in an unprecedented large-scale public-works feat, the flow of the river was reversed, marking the first time a river flowed away from its mouth. The river was engineered to go backward into the Sanitary and Ship Canal, then into the Illinois River, then on into the Mississippi River; locks placed at the mouth of the Chicago River restricted the flow of water out of LAKE MICHIGAN. The purpose of the project was to end pollution of the lake and the city's water supply, ending as well the frequent outbreaks of typhoid fever and cholera.

Unlike the lakefront, the riverfront was never protected from industry; commercial traffic filled the river, and manufacturing and commercial structures, including meatpacking plants and grain elevators, covered the riverbanks. In the 1914 novel THE TITAN, Theodore DREISER describes the river as "filthy," noting "its black, oily water." In THE "GENIUS" of the following year, he speaks of "black, mucky water churned by puffing tugs"; the banks are "lined by great red grain elevators and black coal chutes and yellow lumber yards." In recent times the river craft have been largely pleasure boats, and the banks of the river have been reclaimed for public use.

Chicago School of Architecture

This group of architects is credited with developing the modern skyscraper. After the GREAT FIRE of 1871, business leaders asked for new structures worthy of a great metropolis; the buildings would be required to soar upward, as LAKE MICHIGAN and the two branches of the CHICAGO RIVER imposed boundaries on desirable land. William Le Baron JENNEY, a former CIVIL WAR engineer, was the first to arrive, pioneering the use of the steel frame; the firms of BURNHAM AND ROOT, ADLER AND SULLIVAN, and Holabird and Roche

followed. Heavy masonry buildings were constructed initially, looming as high as their load-bearing walls would allow; the AUDITORIUM BUILDING and the MONADNOCK BUILDING are admired examples. Then came the steel-supported SKYSCRAPER, allowing walls to be thinner and windows larger, bringing in new light, establishing new concepts of beauty and proportion. Henry Blake FULLER's 1893 novel THE CLIFF-DWELLERS and Carl SANDBURG's poems "Skyscraper," collected in the 1916 CHICAGO POEMS, and "Prayers of Steel," collected in the 1918 CORNHUSKERS, are among celebrations of the new structures, equating their height with ambition and mastery.

Chicago School of Fiction

This title was bestowed by William Dean HOWELLS, writing in the prestigious Boston-based *North American Review* in May 1903. Howells, a leading literary critic of the era, headed his piece, "Certain of the Chicago School of Fiction." Declaring that natural democratic sentiments exist in the Midwest, he claimed that Chicago writing exemplifies these sentiments; the city's authors represent "what America has been doing and saying" since the Declaration of Independence. Among the writers Howells names are Henry Blake FULLER, Robert HERRICK, Hamlin GARLAND, and George ADE; he makes no mention of Theodore DREISER, whose *SISTER CARRIE*, appearing in 1900, had been suppressed by its publisher.

Chicago Stock Exchange Building

Designed by Louis SULLIVAN of ADLER AND SULLIVAN and considered one of his masterpieces, the 13-story building was completed in 1894 and was razed in 1972. In its destruction, it tragically took the life of an architecture buff, Richard Nickel, who was buried in the ruins while trying to retrieve some of the building's fragments. The Trading Room stands reconstructed within the ART INSTITUTE; the terra-cotta entrance arch has been reassembled nearby.

Chicago Symphony Orchestra

German-born Theodore THOMAS, who toured American cities with his orchestra throughout the 1870s and 1880s, was asked by Chicago businessmen in 1891 to establish a permanent orchestra in the city. The Chicago Orchestra, as it was first called, gave its initial concert in October of that year in the AUDITORIUM BUILDING. Considering the theater too large for audience rapport, Thomas urged the construction of a smaller venue; ORCHESTRA HALL was built in 1904. After Thomas's death early in 1905, the orchestra was led for the next 37 years by Frederick Stock.

Chicago Theater

This 3,600-seat movie palace, opened by BALABAN AND KATZ in 1921, was second in size only to the theater of the AUDITORIUM BUILDING. It originally showed both movies and stage shows, according to the practice at the time. The five-story lobby and grand staircase were designed in French Baroque style; the exterior was fashioned as a replica of the Arc de Triomphe in Paris. Carl SANDBURG, reviewing movies for the CHICAGO DAILY NEWS, called the theater Babylonian. Closed in 1985, the structure was saved the next year from demolition; it was subsequently refurbished for live entertainment. The restored 1921 Wurlitzer pipe organ became the first musical instrument in Chicago to be given landmark status.

Chicago Tribune

Founded in 1847, the city's oldest and largest newspaper became an establishment voice by the last years of the 19th century; the *Tribune* remains today the best-known Chicago paper. Originally supporting nativist, anti-immigrant views, the newspaper was taken over eight years later by Joseph MEDILL, who began promoting a downstate lawyer, Abraham LINCOLN, in state and national politics. In 1893, when Governor John P. ALTGELD pardoned the three remaining anarchists convicted in the HAYMARKET AFFAIR, the *Tribune* was among Altgeld's strong critics. In 1903, it hired cartoonist John T.

MCCUTCHEON, a mainstay of the paper for years; Ring LARDNER began writing his sports column in 1913. Medill's grandson, Robert R. MCCORMICK, took over the paper in 1911. In 1922, in a competition seeking designs for a new Tribune Tower, plans submitted by modern architects Eliel Saarinen and Walter Gropius were overlooked, resulting in the construction of a backward-looking Gothic building, modeled in part on France's Rouen Cathedral.

Chicago White Sox

Brought to Chicago from St. Paul, Minnesota, in 1900, the team was named the White Stockings—adopting the name of an earlier Chicago team—by owner Charles A. COMISKEY; in 1902, the name was shortened to White Sox. Comiskey Park was

The Chicago Theater, shown here in 1927, was the flagship of the Balaban and Katz movie-theater chain. *(Chicago Historical Society)*

built on the South Side in 1910, a stadium that remained in operation until 1990. In 1919, the BLACK SOX SCANDAL tarnished baseball's reputation; it was partially restored two years later when Chicago Judge Kenesaw Mountain LANDIS took over as new baseball commissioner.

Chicago window

The new steel-frame construction in SKYSCRAPERS made large windows possible, even on the highest floors, thereby allowing unprecedented natural light. What became known as the Chicago window, an innovation of the 1890s, consisted of a stationary window flanked on either side by smaller glass panes; the smaller panes could be opened to allow for ventilation. The window was pioneered by the firm of Holabird and Roche in the 1894 Marquette Building, which still stands.

"Child of the Romans"   *See* CHICAGO POEMS.

Children of the Market Place
Edgar Lee Masters
(1922)

This novel by Edgar Lee Masters deals favorably with the life of Stephen A. DOUGLAS, the Illinois senator who became an opponent of Abraham LINCOLN, and is the only fiction by Masters that is not autobiographical. Masters's earlier views of Lincoln, as expressed in *SPOON RIVER ANTHOLOGY* and *MITCH MILLER,* had been positive; in this work, Masters turns against the president, seeing him as an upholder of "the market place" and commercialism. Douglas, on the contrary, is seen as the spokesman of an idealized rural agrarianism.

The Chinese Nightingale and Other Poems
Vachel Lindsay
(1917)

This volume is Vachel LINDSAY's last widely read and quoted book of verse; the title poem ap-

peared in the February 1915 issue of POETRY. Two pieces, placed under the heading "To Jane Addams at the Hague," were first published in a Chicago newspaper after the sinking of the British ocean liner LUSITANIA in May 1915; ADDAMS was attending the International Congress of Women at The Hague, Netherlands, which called for a repudiation of war. Another poem in the collection, "The Broncho That Would Not Be Broken," is quoted in MacKinlay KANTOR's novel DIVERSEY.

Christian socialism

This term is applied to doctrines combining SOCIALISM and Christian ideals. Focusing on social betterment, Christian socialists claimed Christ as the first socialist; for some, inspiration came also from the writings of Leo TOLSTOY. The Society of Christian Socialists, receiving support from various Protestant groups, was established in 1889; one of the founders was Francis Bellamy, author of the Pledge of Allegiance and cousin of utopian writer Edward BELLAMY. Another set of reformist advocacies—also within the fold of liberal Protestantism, yet avoiding political terminology—became known as the social gospel movement.

Opposition to Christian Socialism came from conservative Christians such as Russell H. Conwell, author of the 1888 *Acres of Diamonds*; Conwell, a Baptist minister and indefatigable public lecturer, found a justification of capitalism within Christian doctrine. Evangelists Dwight L. MOODY and William "Billy" SUNDAY, preaching individual salvation, provided a further counteremphasis to broadly based social action.

In Robert HERRICK's 1905 novel, *THE MEMOIRS OF AN AMERICAN CITIZEN,* the narrator's wife becomes interested in a clergyman preaching Christian socialism; when the cleric attacks the narrator directly in a Sunday morning service, the couple leave the church. In 1909, Vachel LINDSAY declared, "I believe in Christ the Socialist"—an ideology not seen as incompatible with his lecturing that year for the ANTI-SALOON LEAGUE.

"The Circuit Judge"   *See* SPOON RIVER ANTHOLOGY.

The Circuit Rider
Edward Eggleston
(1874)

Focusing on an evangelistic practice that Edward EGGLESTON himself once undertook, the novel looks back to earlier times, to 19th-century Ohio; the characters remember not the CIVIL WAR, but the Revolutionary War. Circuit riders were Methodist preachers assigned to travel a frontier area, or circuit, holding open meetings and services. Eggleston makes clear that these times were crude, that men of the frontier were coarse and violent. He presents his dedicated Methodist preachers—whom he acknowledges to be unrefined—while reminding the reader of the necessary role they played: "Without them, there must have been barbarism." Joseph KIRKLAND's *ZURY: THE MEANEST MAN IN SPRING COUNTY*, set after the WAR OF 1812 in rural Illinois, evokes a similar harsh era.

Civic Opera House

An opera house and office building, the last great cultural edifice built before the GREAT DEPRESSION, the Civic Opera House was erected by Samuel INSULL, owner of electric, gas, and transportation companies. The structure, located on the bank of the CHICAGO RIVER, combined two large theaters with a 42-story office building; it opened on November 4, 1929, shortly after the Stock Market crash. The market collapse and its fallout soon led to Insull's financial ruin. Insull, the product of a lower-middle-class English upbringing, had decreed one major innovation in his opera house—banning viewers' boxes, the traditional seating for the wealthy, from the sides of the auditorium, confining them to the rear. The soprano Rosa RAISA sang Giuseppe Verdi's *Aida* on opening night; acoustics and sightlines were declared excellent. The new structure replaced the AUDITORIUM BUILDING as a prime venue for grand opera and other major musical events.

Civil War

The great conflict of American history, fought from 1861 to 1865, the war resonated through the nation's literature for over a century. The main issue was slavery; the South seceded from the Union to maintain this institution, and the North, led by President Abraham LINCOLN, fought to preserve the Union, ending slavery as well. The total casualties in the war were greater than in any other American conflict; midwestern towns and villages, as described in the work of Chicago Renaissance writers, suffered great losses among their young men, as well as the loss of men to work the farms. Hamlin GARLAND's collection of tales of depressed farming conditions, *MAIN-TRAVELLED ROADS*, includes the story of a farm gone to near-ruin when the father—in reality, Garland's own father—goes off to war. In Sherwood ANDERSON's first novel, *WINDY MCPHERSON'S SON*, the former Union sergeant, Windy MCPHERSON—another character modeled on an author's father—never finds his place back in the normal world, becoming a boastful drunk, recounting again and again his tales of battle. In the prologue to Anderson's *WINESBURG, OHIO*, an old soldier, who had been a prisoner in the Georgia prison camp at ANDERSONVILLE, weeps when he thinks of his brother who died there of starvation; the Winesburg story "Godliness" recounts the hardships of a farm family after four of its sons are killed in war. In Edgar Lee MASTERS's graveyard in *SPOON RIVER ANTHOLOGY*, one young man, Knowlt Hoheimer, who died at Missionary Ridge in Tennessee, is memorialized by a marble statue on a pedestal bearing patriotic words—a monument far grander that of the man who died in the less-than-glorious SPANISH-AMERICAN WAR. Accounts of the war often center on that favorite mythic figure, the martyred President Lincoln, assassinated by John Wilkes BOOTH, a Southern partisan, just days after the conflict ended.

Cleveland, Grover
(1837–1908) *22nd and 24th president of the United States*

Serving two nonconsecutive terms, elected in 1884 and again in 1892, Democrat Cleveland presided over an era of labor strife, including the HAYMAR-KET AFFAIR, as well as midwestern agricultural discontent. In the PULLMAN STRIKE of 1894, Cleveland called out federal troops to intervene—over the protest of Governor John Peter ALTGELD—on the grounds that railroad strikers were halting the movement of the United States mail; he was drawing on the precedent set by President Rutherford B. HAYES during the GREAT STRIKE of 1877. Rural unrest, demonstrated by the million votes received by the POPULIST PARTY in 1892, continued throughout Cleveland's second term, leading to the Democratic Party's nomination of the farm-supported William Jennings BRYAN in 1896. The resulting battle, pitting East versus West, ended in the East's triumph and the presidency of Republican William MCKINLEY.

The Cliff-Dwellers
Henry Blake Fuller
(1893)

The work has been called the first American novel about modern city life; the title likely came from a volume published earlier in the year on the American Southwest, Gustaf Nordenskiold's *The Cliff Dwellers of the Mesa Verde.* FULLER applies the term *cliff-dwellers* to those people inhabiting the new skyscrapers of Chicago, buildings soaring upward in the wake of the GREAT FIRE. His specific focus is on an office building called the CLIFTON BUILDING, modeled on the 1891 MONADNOCK BUILDING; the name of the protagonist, George OGDEN, reflects Chicago's first mayor and railroad builder, William Butler Ogden. Fuller's villainous financier, Erastus M. BRAINARD, becomes one of many unscrupulous businessmen portrayed in the new novel of American urban REALISM.

Synopsis

INTRODUCTION; CHAPTERS I–III
An extraordinary phenomenon has arisen in the city of Chicago: the Clifton Building. It soars to the height of 18 stories, using 10 elevators to facilitate the daily cliff-climbing of its inhabitants. These inhabitants include bankers, lawyers, brokers,

realtors, insurance agents, clerks, cashiers, stenographers, errandboys, janitors, and scrub-women; they number 4,000 souls. Life in the Clifton is so complete within itself that few outside excursions are necessary in telling of the lives of the Cliff-Dwellers.

George Ogden, a man in his early 20s, has recently arrived from New England and obtained a job at the Underground National Bank, headquartered at the Clifton. He meets a young woman visiting the Clifton, Jessie BRADLEY, as well as another young woman, Mayme Brainard, the daughter of his employer, Erastus M. Brainard, owner of the bank. Mayme, he learns, is enamored of Russell Vibert, a noted soloist at the Episcopalian church, St. Asaph's. Another occupant of the Clifton is Eugene McDowell, a real estate entrepreneur who is engaged to marry Ogden's sister.

Erastus Brainard has business interests far beyond those of the bank, including streetcars and electric companies; he has been accused of manipulating city councils and state legislatures as well. Yet he cannot stand up to his daughter Mayme, and one day Ogden hears her declaring to her father that she will marry Vibert; Ogden knows that Vibert, although admired at St. Asaph's for his tenor voice, is a lowly clerk in an insurance office—and that he is an unpleasant man as well. Yet the 18-year-old Mayme is as determined in love as her father has been in business.

CHAPTERS IV–V
Ogden visits the 12th-floor office of McDowell, his future brother-in-law; McDowell has persuaded Ogden's parents to transfer their assets from New England to Chicago, investing in Chicago real estate. Ogden, meanwhile, visiting Brainard's house, has met Brainard's older daughter, Abbie BRAINARD; Abbie treated him pleasantly, while the older son, Burton, proved to be rude and imperious.

Having lunch at the café in the Clifton, Ogden finds himself served by Cornelia MCNABB, a young woman who had once waited tables in his boardinghouse. Cornelia is a small-town Wisconsin girl trying to get on in the big city; among her self-improvement efforts is a course in shorthand and typewriting. She mentions to Ogden a woman whose name she often sees in the newspaper, Mrs. Arthur J. Ingles, or Cecilia INGLES; she envies such a woman, whose dinner parties are written up in the papers and whose elegant gowns are described in detail. Ogden says he has never met Mrs. Ingles. Cornelia makes clear that her ambitions for upward mobility are endless.

CHAPTERS VI–VII

A fellow lodger in Ogden's rooming house, an insurance adjuster named Brower, works for the same company, Ogden learns, as Russell Vibert—the man whom Mayme Brainard has now married. Brower raises the question: Is it better for a man of modest circumstances to marry a rich girl or a poor girl? The alternatives are debated, and it is suggested that the natures of the two people involved make the difference. Ogden meets Jessie Bradley again at a social function; Arthur J. Ingles is there as well—whom Ogden learns is the man who owns the Clifton—along with his architect, Atwater. The latter, it turns out, once gave employment to Marcus BRAINARD, the younger son of the tycoon; Marcus had a talent for drawing, Atwater remarks, but none for business—for which his father rejected him, giving everything instead to his older son, Burton. Marcus has since taken to drink. Ogden, hearing of this family turmoil, decides he will refrain from calling on Abbie Brainard.

CHAPTERS VIII–IX

Eugene McDowell is worrying about the 10-acre subdivision in which he has invested, where the land is low-lying—or, as rivals say, a swamp—and potential buyers can see it only after the weather is dry. Meanwhile, his father-in-law, George Ogden's father, has died suddenly, leaving no will; the old man's attention had been taken up in the transfer of his property to Chicago. The younger Ogden, unacquainted with local laws, is happy to leave probate matters to McDowell. Yet associates begin to notice that McDowell seems to be prospering, despite having limited resources.

One day Ogden sees Cornelia McNabb working at the Underground bank; she has been employed by Burton Brainard, now vice president of the firm. She tells Ogden she has seen the name of Arthur J. Ingles on a door in the building, and she

asks more about Mrs. Ingles. Ogden says again he has never seen her; perhaps, he suggests humorously, the newspapers have made her up.

In an office of the Underground bank Abbie Brainard has come to plead with her father for the sake of Mayme, whose husband, Russell Vibert, has physically abused her; Vibert has also lost his job with the insurance firm. Yet Erastus Brainard, still angry at the daughter who defied him, will do nothing for either. He mentions that another offspring of his, Marcus, has disappointed him as well, dabbling in drawing and music; Abbie asks accusingly why her father never gave Marcus an education, that is, the kind of education that would have helped him.

CHAPTERS X–XV

Ogden pays a visit to McDowell, querying about property settlements; McDowell speaks of taxes and special assessments, and Ogden, although disturbed, assumes that his brother-in-law is acting for the best. One evening he pays a visit to the Brainard house, hoping to talk to Abbie alone, but other guests are there as well. When he returns home to his boardinghouse, his fellow roomer, Brower, tells him he saw Burton Brainard that night, sitting in a theater box with Cornelia McNabb. Meanwhile, Vibert has abandoned his wife, and Brainard sets attorneys on him in a divorce suit; Mayme must go into exile among relatives downstate. The publicity surrounding the case makes Ogden shrink once more from the thought of linking himself to Abbie Brainard and her dysfunctional family.

One day at the office, Erastus Brainard offers George a promotion and a raise, even a vacation. George assumes the old man has mellowed because of the forthcoming marriage of his son Burton and Cornelia McNabb; Erastus has no objections to such a marriage because a daughter-in-law—as opposed to a son-in-law—can be molded and shaped. George takes his vacation at a lake in Wisconsin, where Jessie Bradley and her family are expected to visit. He now realizes, because of his promotion, that he has the means to marry. He contemplates Abbie Brainard, but then thinks of her divorced sister and her banished brother, as well as of her other brother, Burton, whose impending marriage to Cornelia McNabb proves a certain family coarseness. Then Jessie Bradley appears.

CHAPTERS XVI–XIX

George Ogden and Jessie Bradley marry, although Brainard, to George's surprise, allows him no time off for a wedding trip. The couple rent a house, and Jessie is soon hosting receptions and luncheons, hiring florists and caterers. One day, when George comes home from work, he is told he has just missed Cecilia Ingles; in mock wonder, he asks if there really is such a person. He is noticing, however, that Jessie is buying expensive furnishings for their home; she is insisting also that new front doors be installed, consulting with Atwater, the fashionable architect. Worried about finances, Ogden realizes that McDowell's settling of his father's estate is favoring McDowell, not himself.

When Jessie makes plan for a musical evening at their house, she asks George to put a notice in the newspaper, listing the guests, and George, scanning the list, protests that various friends of theirs have been excluded; she replies that Cecilia Ingles does not care for those friends. Although noticing that his wife seems increasingly pale and tired, George feels an increasing estrangement.

CHAPTERS XX–XXI

Mrs. Erastus Brainerd dies, and Marcus, the errant son, never appears at the funeral. Abbie secretly arranges to meet him one evening in a park; when he appears, she sees his unsteady walk and bloodshot eyes. He announces menacingly that he will kill his father, then disappears into the night.

George's old friend Brower discusses George's marriage with another acquaintance. When he and George once debated the merits of rich girls and poor girls, Brower says, they left out one kind of girl—namely, the girl in moderate circumstances who spends all her time visiting wealthy relatives and friends. That's the kind George married, and as a result, he is a disappointed man.

Yet Jessie is not only frail by now—the unspoken assumption is tuberculosis—but she soon gives birth to a daughter; not long after, the daughter dies. Ogden continues trying to get funds from his father's estate, even a loan on some worthless property. When his efforts come to nothing, he spends a sleepless night and resolves to get his own temporary "loan" from the Underground National Bank.

CHAPTERS XXII–XXIV

Ogden is caught in embezzlement, and Brainard fires him. As an anguished Abbie stands by, Brainard tells Ogden that he, Brainard, promoted Ogden because Abbie asked him to; Abbie had always been her father's only real comfort in life. But then, Brainard continues, he watched as Ogden passed her over for another—for a woman who ruined him with her extravagance. When someone reminds the group that the wife is dying, Ogden, upset, rushes toward the elevator, requesting the floor for McDowell's office. Ogden picks up a chair in the office and smashes it over McDowell's head.

That evening Marcus Brainard comes to his father's house. After grappling with his brother, Burton, he plunges a paper-cutter into his father's throat. He escapes through a window. Brainard, after lingering for a few days, dies, and Marcus is found hanged in the stable.

No formal steps are taken against Ogden. When Jessie dies, Ogden moves into a new neighborhood and establishes himself in a real-estate business, putting his bitter experience with McDowell to use. Burton Brainard, proving helpless in business without his father, loses his money, and soon the whole family, including Abbie, is impoverished. One evening Ogden visits his friend Brower, who persuades him to see Abbie Brainard; within a month they marry. Not long afterward, at a public function, they see a grand party entering a theater box; Abbie asks George who they are, and he identifies them as Mr. and Mrs. Atwater, the architect and his wife, and then as Mr. Ingles, who owns the Clifton—but, he says, he has never seen the other woman. Yet he knows who she is. That magnificent young woman, radiating splendor, is Cecilia Ingles. She is the woman for whom the Clifton was built.

Critical Reception

The novel was praised by William Dean HOWELLS and others for its urban realism, although it never reached a wide audience. Historically, the work can be considered the beginning of Chicago literature, although readers at the time noted the negative image the author presented of the city.

Cosmopolitan magazine, finding that the novel depicted seriously the city's social conditions, deemed Fuller an able chronicler, "though scarcely a sympathetic one." The DIAL praised the work's realism, declaring the novel to have value both as a story and as a social document.

The Cliff-Dwellers can be understood today as a melancholy, somewhat misogynist work. At the end Ogden has not fallen from great heights, as the Marshall family will fall in Fuller's next work, WITH THE PROCESSION, and yet he is a man whose ambitions have never been fulfilled. He is brought to what Fuller calls a "middlingness" by the forces of greed and acquisitiveness around him—and by his choice of a woman, one who was too weak to resist those forces.

Fuller's novel gives an early description to a unique urban phenomenon—the emptying of great buildings at the end of a day. Frank NORRIS's novel of a decade later, THE PIT, uses images similar to Fuller's; the crowd, Norris writes, "poured out incessantly," becoming "a mass, slow-moving, black." Edna FERBER's 1917 novel, FANNY HERSELF, describes a similar scene, noting first a trickle, then a stream, then a flood, and finally a torrent, inundating the streets and sidewalks, "filling every nook and crevice, a moving mass."

Cliff-Dwellers' Club

This club for writers and artists was established in 1907 by Hamlin GARLAND; its name came from the novel by Henry Blake FULLER. The group was reserved for men only and differed in this respect from the LITTLE ROOM. In 1909, the club moved to quarters at the top of ORCHESTRA HALL. POETRY magazine's oft-described dinner for William Butler YEATS was held at the club in 1914; Louis SULLIVAN completed his *Autobiography of an Idea* there shortly before his death in 1924. To counterbalance the all-male atmosphere of the Cliff-Dwellers, sculptor Nellie Walker established a women-only Cordon Club in the FINE ARTS BUILDING in 1915. In 1995, nearly 90 years after its founding, the Cliff-Dwellers' Club was exiled to a nearby building, the result of an Orchestra Hall renovation.

The Clifton

This fictional building served as the principal setting of Henry B. FULLER's novel THE CLIFF-DWELLERS. Based on the recently completed MONADNOCK BUILDING, this SKYSCRAPER is presented as a microcosm, a self-contained world. Fuller placed as much action there as possible, sometimes to the novel's detriment; his exposition in the first few chapters, achieved as various people drop by offices in the building, creates a somewhat confusing clutter of characters. Carl SANDBURG explored the skyscraper-as-microcosm concept later in "Skyscraper," part of his CHICAGO POEMS.

Cobb, Henry Ives
(1859–1931) *architect*

Designer of the NEWBERRY LIBRARY and the suburban campus of Lake Forest College, Cobb is best known as architect of the Gothic-style limestone buildings of the UNIVERSITY OF CHICAGO. Born in Brookline, Massachusetts, he came to Chicago in 1881 after attending the Massachusetts Institute of Technology. An early commission was the vast, turreted home of Potter PALMER on the North Side, built in 1882; Cobb also designed the massive Federal Building, housing courtrooms and the U.S. post office, filling a city block, completed in 1905. Both structures have since been demolished. For the University of Chicago campus, Cobb planned seven quadrangles, its buildings resembling those of Oxford University in England; the campus—called the Gray City, in contrast to the White City of the nearby WORLD'S COLUMBIAN EXPOSITION—provided an American prototype for what became known as college Gothic. Also for the university, Cobb designed the Yerkes Observatory in Williams Bay, Wisconsin, a gift to the institution by transportation magnate Charles T. YERKES.

In Theodore DREISER's novel SISTER CARRIE, the popular upscale bar of Fitzgerald and Moy's is located opposite the "imposing" Federal Building.

Cochran, Lester

A character in Sherwood ANDERSON's story "Unlighted Lamps," collected in THE TRIUMPH OF THE EGG, Cochran, the town doctor, knows he is soon to die of heart disease. He knows, too, that he has never been able to express his feelings—to his wife, who left him and their child years before, or to his daughter, who is now grown up. When his wife told him she was pregnant, he remained silent, believing no words could express what he felt; a former actress, she decided she could no longer live with him in the small town of Huntersburg, Illinois. Despite rumors that she ran off with another man, the truth is that Cochran took her to Chicago so that she could find work in a theatrical company; he gave her money, still unable to express his feelings at the loss of her. He has been generous to his patients in Huntersburg; his daughter learns of his attending a laborer's son without charge, giving the family money for medicine. On the night of his death he had resolved to talk to his daughter, to tell her about her mother, about his feelings, but returning from delivering the child of a farmer's wife, he dies on the stairs coming up to her.

Cochran, Mary

This character is featured in two Sherwood ANDERSON stories collected in THE TRIUMPH OF THE EGG. "Unlighted Lamps" depicts Mary in her home town of Huntersburg, Illinois; "The Door of the Trap" brings her to a small college in Union Valley, Illinois. Both stories came originally from an uncompleted novel.

All her life Mary has felt estranged from the townspeople of Huntersburg; they know that her mother left her and her father when she was a child, and they continue to gossip about her mother. The story is that she ran off with a young man, and Mary has overheard a woman suggesting that she—who has now grown up, having reached the age of 18—will be just like her mother: "Like mother, like daughter"; Mary in fact slaps a young man when he follows her. Yet her main problem is that her father, suffering from a heart condition,

might die at any time; she regrets their lack of emotional closeness, blaming herself for the seeming distance between them. Her father dies before further words can be spoken.

At college in Union Valley, Mary becomes drawn into the world of Hugh WALKER, a mathematics professor. Hugh invites her to his home, and soon she is part of the household, taking his two young sons on excursions and eating dinner with the family; his wife seems not to mind. In this particular story, Mary's role is secondary to Hugh's role; her function is to be part of his world, to live within his perspective. Hugh suddenly kisses her and tells her never to come back; he understands that she is free, that she is not yet trapped by ties—that she is not, like him, one of the imprisoned.

Colter, Cyrus
(1910–2002) *writer*

Along with Richard WRIGHT, Willard MOTLEY, and Gwendolyn BROOKS, Colter represents the first generation of post–Chicago Renaissance African-American writers. Born in Nobleville, Indiana, Colter graduated from the Chicago–KENT COLLEGE OF LAW in 1940 and pursued a professional and government career for three decades, serving as head of the Illinois Commerce Commission from 1950 until 1973. Literary recognition came in 1970 with the publication of the short-story collection *The Beach Umbrella*, followed by the novels *The River of Eros* and *The Hippodrome*; Colter taught at NORTHWESTERN UNIVERSITY from 1973 until 1978. "The Beach Umbrella," his most-anthologized story, tells of a family man who finds a day of pleasure on a LAKE MICHIGAN beach, escaping briefly through the status provided by a bright red-and-white beach umbrella; reality inevitably intrudes at the end of the day when he tries to sell the umbrella and realizes he must meet the demands of his family by taking an exhausting job in the steel mills.

Columbian Exposition   *See* WORLD'S COLUMBIAN EXPOSITION.

Comiskey, Charles A.
(1859–1931) *baseball player and team owner*

The son of a Chicago alderman, Comiskey became a player for the St. Louis Browns in 1882 and is said to have established basic principles of major-league first-base playing. In 1900, he brought a baseball team to Chicago from St. Paul, Minnesota, naming it the Chicago White Stockings, later CHICAGO WHITE SOX; his South Side stadium, Comiskey Park, was built in 1910. Nine years later, Comiskey's reputation was tarnished in the BLACK SOX SCANDAL, in which his players threw the World Series for $10,000 from gamblers; Comiskey was felt to have severely underpaid his players. Ring LARDNER's collection of tales, YOU KNOW ME AL, featuring a sometime White Sox player, depicts the team owner's reputed stinginess. Comiskey Park was replaced by a new, neighboring stadium in 1991.

Comstock, Anthony
(1844–1915) *censorship crusader*

Born in Connecticut, serving with the Union Army in the CIVIL WAR, Comstock was responsible for the passage in 1873 of strict legislation against sending obscene matter through the United States mail. In the same year, he founded the NEW YORK SOCIETY FOR THE SUPPRESSION OF VICE, a private organization chartered by the state to implement antiobscenity laws; his work was carried on after his death by John S. Sumner, responsible for the banning of Theodore DREISER's THE "GENIUS" and the suppression of LITTLE REVIEW's publication of James JOYCE's *Ulysses*. The term *Comstockery* has come to mean prudish and zealous censorship.

"The Congo"   *See THE CONGO AND OTHER POEMS.*

The Congo and Other Poems
Vachel Lindsay
(1914)

In the second published book of poetry by Vachel Lindsay, the title piece is one of the two poems—

the other being "GENERAL WILLIAM BOOTH ENTERS INTO HEAVEN"—that made the author famous as a poet, lecture-circuit reciter, and early spoken-recording artist. A last-minute addition to the volume was "Abraham Lincoln Walks at Midnight," one of several antiwar poems written after WORLD WAR I began in August 1914. Two poems, "Yet Gentle Will the Griffin Be" and "The Strength of the Lonely," are among those chosen by American composer Jake Heggie for his Lindsay-based song cycles, *Songs to the Moon* and *The Moon Is a Mirror*.

Synopses of Selected Poems

"THE CONGO"

The poet has said that the piece began with a sermon in the First Christian Church of SPRINGFIELD, Illinois, telling of the drowning of a missionary in the Congo River; Lindsay was familiar also with Joseph Conrad's novel, *Heart of Darkness*, the tale of a journey up the Congo River, and H. M. Stanley's *In Darkest Africa*, a journalist's account of his finding the missionary David Livingstone. The poem's refrain, referring to the Congo River as "a golden track," is traceable to Lindsay's boyhood copy of the Stanley book, featuring on its cover a black map of Africa traversed by the golden line of a river; it is the same book that Edgar Rice BURROUGHS read before writing his tales of Tarzan.

Each section of the poem starts with Lindsay's envisioning of an African-American scene, followed by a presumed parallel Congo scene. In the first section, the American scene depicts a saloon, and the African equivalent presents a gathering of "tattooed cannibals"; the poet also imagines Leopold, the exploitative king of Belgium, burning in hell for his brutal colonial policies. The second section moves from an American gambling hall to an African witch-doctor's "cake-walk" performance—Lindsay's African prototype for the 19th-century African-American step. The third section of the poem moves from a black American revival meeting to the conversion of the entire Congo nation to Christianity.

Written in 1913, the poem had not yet been published when Lindsay recited it at POETRY magazine's banquet honoring William Butler YEATS early in 1914. In its naïve flamboyance, the piece is a classic modern example of PRIMITIVISM.

"FACTORY WINDOWS ARE ALWAYS BROKEN"

People throw bricks at factory windows, and yet no one throws stones at chapel windows, which proves that something is wrong with factories. The poet points to no specifics, and yet he is writing at a time of labor agitation; it is also an era of anti-industrial, anti-mass-production sentiments, as expressed by William MORRIS and others, decrying the replacement of craftsmanship by factory labor.

"Yahoo" refers to the debased humans of Jonathan Swift's 18th-century satire *Gulliver's Travels;* the linking of "rotten" and "Denmark" points to Shakespeare's *Hamlet*'s claim that "something is rotten in the state of Denmark." The poem, illustrating Lindsay's often-purposeful simplicity, has been occasionally anthologized.

"EUCLID"

Euclid, the Greek father of mathematics, once drew a circle on the sand; he then added boundaries and enclosures to the circle, illustrating to the other wise men the principles of geometry. A child stands by, watching silently, seeing instead "round pictures of the moon." Lindsay is contrasting the old men's analytical reasoning with the child's wondering over nature. Written in 1912, the poem precedes by a decade the famous Edna St. Vincent Millay sonnet "Euclid alone has looked on Beauty bare"—a poem praising, in contrast, the beauty of mathematics.

"YET GENTLE WILL THE GRIFFIN BE"

Subtitled "What Grandpa Told the Children," the poem describes the moon as a griffin's egg; the griffin is a mythical beast, often seen as a protective symbol, which combines the head and wings of an eagle with the body of a lion. As the egg hatches, the creature stretches across the sky, and little boys shout with delight—although little girls hide and cry. But the griffin is gentle; it laps up the Milky Way like a cat.

"THE STRENGTH OF THE LONELY"

Subtitled "What the Mendicant Said," the poem compares the moon to a mendicant, or monk. The monk's cell is the sky, and his strength is that of men who make vows, defying the perils of life. Like snow or dew, they leave no sorrow behind, only the blue of the heavens.

"ABRAHAM LINCOLN WALKS AT MIDNIGHT"

The figure of the dead president, Abraham LINCOLN, walks the land in mourning, pacing up and down near the courthouse, lingering until the coming of dawn. He wears his old-fashioned suit and hat, making him a quaint figure in the city of Springfield, where he was buried half a century before. He cannot sleep because another war, World War I, has broken out—yet another war in which men must die. Peasants are fighting for their warlords, and dreadnaughts, or battleships, are taking over the seas. The poet draws on the image of the unquiet spirit that cannot rest until wrongs are righted. Here the spirit of the martyred president cannot rest until "the Workers' Earth"—a socialist vision shared by many writers of the day—brings peace to the land; then he may sleep upon his hill again.

Critical Reception

Because it seemed fresh and original, because it appeared to carry on the tradition of the by-then revered Walt WHITMAN, the poem "The Congo," as well as the volume in which it appeared, received favorable commentary. Later, civil-rights sensibilities turned the piece into an embarrassment, although the African-American poet Langston HUGHES, to whom Lindsay had once lent support, defended the poet. In 1991, the critic Elizabeth Hardwick called the poem "the supreme folly" of Lindsay's career, as well as a "most extraordinary embarrassment in our cultural history."

"Abraham Lincoln Walks at Midnight" is one of the few Lindsay pieces that has survived, buoyed by the Lincoln myth, as well as by its antiwar sentiments.

Congress of Authors

This symposium, part of the WORLD'S COLUMBIAN EXPOSITION, met in July 1893 at the new lakefront building, the Memorial Art Palace, now the ART INSTITUTE. The Congress was opened by the Southern writer George Washington Cable. Among papers read were those of novelist Mary Hartwell CATHERWOOD, espousing romantic fiction, and the response of Hamlin GARLAND, making a defense of literary REALISM. Eugene FIELD, writing about the event in his "Sharps and Flats" column—headed "The Battle of the Realists and Romanticists"—declared his dislike of Garland's "dungfork"; he preferred Catherwood's picturesque, dashing heroes to Garland's heroes, who, he wrote, "sweat and do not wear socks."

conspicuous consumption

This phrase was coined by Thorstein VEBLEN, a UNIVERSITY OF CHICAGO economist, in his 1899 volume, THE THEORY OF THE LEISURE CLASS. Veblen put the label on what he considered one of the negative consequences of CAPITALISM, the inordinate accumulation of wealth; such accumulation, he declared, is then followed by an inordinate display of that wealth. This display, made in a competitive spirit, automatically fosters further display, and the never-ending cycle continues. Veblen gave emphasis to the role of the capitalist's wife, caught up in her practice of competitive ostentation. Feminist Charlotte Perkins GILMAN later criticized women's fashion on similar grounds, noting that it was men's wealth—wealth provided by men, not women—that subsidized female fashion.

Cook, George Cram
(1873–1924) *writer, theater innovator*

Born in Davenport, Iowa, Cook attended the University of Iowa, Harvard University, and the University of Heidelberg, then taught at the University of Iowa before joining an Iowa regiment during the SPANISH-AMERICAN WAR in 1898. Teaching briefly afterward at Stanford University, he returned to Davenport in 1903 to pursue a life of tilling the soil, following the model of the Russian novelist Leo TOLSTOY. In 1911, he came to Chicago to join fellow Davenportian Floyd DELL on the staff of the

FRIDAY LITERARY REVIEW; he later married Susan GLASPELL, another Davenport native. When the couple moved to New York, Cook continued to send a weekly "New York Letter" to the *Literary Review*. Cook and Glaspell were instrumental in founding the PROVINCETOWN PLAYERS, first in Massachusetts, then in New York City, as well as in achieving recognition for the playwright Eugene O'NEILL. They left the Provincetown Players in 1922, going to Greece to live a presumably simple life, although it was said that Cook moved principally to escape the recently enacted PROHIBITION law; he died two years later. Cook appears in Dell's autobiographical novel MOON-CALF as Tom Alden.

Cooke, Jay
(1821–1905) *financier*

The failure of Cooke's banking firm, Jay Cooke and Company, set off the PANIC OF 1873; the collapse provided partial background for Theodore DREISER's THE FINANCIER. Born in Ohio, founding his firm in Philadelphia in 1861, Cooke was called "the pillar of the nation," having financed the CIVIL WAR by putting together the sale of federal bonds. His company closed its doors in September 1873, after attempting unsuccessfully to expand its recently acquired Northern Pacific Railroad. Thousands of banks and businesses collapsed in the aftermath, bringing about the nation's most severe economic depression up to that time.

Coolidge, Calvin
(1872–1933) *30th president of the United States*

Born in Vermont, Coolidge served as governor of Massachusetts before his election to the vice presidency in 1920. He became president upon the death of Warren G. HARDING in 1923 and served a subsequent term as well. Declaring that "the business of America is business," Republican Coolidge was admired by some for a taciturn honesty; others say he encouraged the stock market speculation that led to the crash of 1929 and the GREAT DEPRESSION.

Cope, Bertram

The principal character in Henry B. FULLER's novel *BERTRAM COPE'S YEAR*, Cope is a young man from downstate Illinois, a graduate of an institution modeled on NORTHWESTERN UNIVERSITY; he returns to his alma mater to teach and pursue a graduate degree. A handsome young man, he attracts both men and woman, although his real affection, as people gradually learn, is for the young Arthur LEMOYNE, whom he had known in Wisconsin; Arthur soon joins him in suburban Churchton. Modern readers see a veiled candor in Fuller's dissection of a homosexual relationship; they find the characterizations convincing, noting only the absence of a forthright label. In contrast to the flamboyant Arthur, Cope is presented as a conservative figure—abstaining from alcohol, becoming embarrassed by Arthur's antics—who might perhaps eventually marry. He conforms to social conventions, even becoming temporarily trapped in an "engagement," the result of following a gentlemanly code of honor. Critics have called him unsympathetic, in that the novel's other characters find him cold and unresponsive; yet he can be said to be protecting himself against their determined, insistent pursuit.

Copperheads

This term, invoking poisonous snakes, was applied to Northerners sympathetic to the South during the CIVIL WAR especially to Democrats opposing the policies of Abraham LINCOLN. In the 1864 presidential election, as the war continued, many Democrats called for negotiations with the Confederacy; Northerners felt that the Copperheads were prolonging the war, encouraging the South not to abandon its struggle. Massachusetts clergyman Edward Everett Hale had already published in the *Atlantic Monthly,* late in 1863, the anonymous story "The Man Without a Country," inspired by a Copperhead leader's remark that he did not wish to live in a country with Lincoln as president; Hale's story is about an army lieutenant, charged with treason, who says he never wants to hear of the United States again, and his sentence—to his ultimate regret—is to live the rest of his life on shipboard, isolated from news of his native land. Another literary response to Copperhead politics came from Ohio journalist David Ross Locke, who published, beginning in 1864, fictional letters from a character named Petroleum Vesuvius Nasby, a Copperhead preacher who reveals himself as ignorant and corrupt.

Cornhuskers
Carl Sandburg
(1918)

In this second book of poetry, Carl SANDBURG, having established himself as an urban poet with *CHICAGO POEMS*, returns to his rural roots. Although urban settings still appear—some of the poems were left over from earlier years—Sandburg is now chanting of the plains and the PRAIRIE; Abraham LINCOLN becomes a subject, as the poet is gradually transforming himself into a celebrator of Americana and American folk heroes.

Discussions of late-autumn cornhusking, done by hand, appear frequently in the literature of the rural Midwest. The protagonist in Joseph KIRKLAND's 1887 novel, *ZURY: THE MEANEST MAN IN SPRING COUNTY,* remarks that husking corn is an unpleasantly cold job, requiring one to take hold of "one bitter-cold ear after another." Sherwood ANDERSON's story of 1917, "An Untold Lie," collected in *WINESBURG, OHIO,* notes the chapped and painful hands of a man husking corn in late October. Hamlin GARLAND, recalling the farm toil of his youth, speaks of husking corn "in a savage November wind, with your boots laden with icy slush and your fingers chapped and bleeding." A solution—for the prosperous Ohio farmer of an earlier era—is depicted in Edward EGGLESTON's 1878 novel, *THE CIRCUIT-RIDER,* in which a farmer holds a corn-shucking party; teams of neighbors compete to shuck, or husk, the most corn, and whiskey flows. In Sandburg's poem "Prairie," the cornhuskers wear leather on their hands.

Synopses of Selected Poems

"PRAIRIE"

The opening poem of the volume contrasts sharply with "Chicago," the opening poem of the previous volume; it is also one of the longest of the poet's works. Sandburg turns to the landscape from which many Chicago writers, including himself, originally emerged; he focuses on what he considers an enduring, timeless land that will last longer than any man-made city.

The poem begins with the first-person "I," and at this point the "I" is the poet himself; he was born on the prairie, and the prairie gave him his song. The geological history of the land is reviewed, then the routine of farming upon its soil. The city is mentioned only briefly; within its walls the pistons and wheels of the train sound noisily, but out on the prairie the train glides by like a phantom, the soil soothing its sounds.

In the next section, the "I" becomes the prairie itself, which will endure when cities and men are dust. The prairie addresses the pioneers who came to it, as well as the Indians who came before them. This land, too, has lasted through wars, and at this point the prairie becomes a morally neutral entity; it speaks of Appomattox, a site from the CIVIL WAR, of Valley Forge from the Revolutionary War, of Marne and Verdun from WORLD WAR I, and it claims that all these names are beautiful. Indeed, says the land, "I take peace or war." The prairie then asks rhetorically if one has ever seen its sunset over a cornfield, or heard its threshing crews yelling or cornhuskers singing—all of which takes place on the land.

The next section returns to the geological development of the prairie, starting with the rivers that cut their paths across it. Then cities sprang up; smoke from wigwams became smoke from smokestacks, and the call of the wild duck became the whistle of the steamboat. Yet these changes have occurred within a thousand years, and such a stretch of time—as I, the prairie, knows—is short. What are steel mills and steel workers after a thousand years?

The Pioneer Limited train is crossing Wisconsin in a snowstorm; the fireman waves to the teacher and to the schoolboy on a bobsled. The farmer, meanwhile, is fattening his hogs, and then—because this is the cycle of life and death that occurs on the land—he is slaughtering them. On a summer morning the farmer and his daughter ride in a wagon carrying radishes and eggs to

sell; beside the road the corn that was once knee-high is now head-high. The prairie is claiming all these people and activities as its own, including the cornhuskers; even the phantoms of yellow roosters, of old hunting dogs, of old workhorses are part of what belongs to the prairie—as are the mockingbirds that sing and the farm families that sing, even as an ice storm pounds on the windows. The prairie girl sings as spring returns to the land.

In the last two sections, the "I" is once more the poet; he is the son of the prairie, the mother whom he has always loved. He might speak of new cities or new people, but he is also the brother of the cornhuskers who say simply, at day's end, that tomorrow is a day—that is, that the ever-renewing present, as the prairie has always known, is all that matters.

"ILLINOIS FARMER"
The farmer, whose life was spent growing corn on the land, will now sleep underneath that land. The wind that blew through the cornsilk in the autumn, the wind that brought snow to the corncrib in the winter—this force will now blow over the spot where he lies. The poet asks for respect for this man; his life might have been considered narrow, but he worked the land and nurtured the produce of the land.

"LOCALITIES"
The poet starts by naming places in the West, including Cripple Creek, Colorado, the home of miners and gamblers; these are places he has never been. He then mentions seeing three White Horse taverns, one in the East, two in the Midwest—and that name reminds him of a tavern called White Pigeon, where he once stopped in a village that was just a crossroads.

The poet focuses next on two Illinois locations—one on a riverbank, where boys run barefoot in the leaves, the other in his own home county, where boys with Swedish names find hazel nuts in the autumn. These are the places that are meaningful to him. As for those boys with Swedish names, some now work locally, some have joined the navy, and some have left home; their mothers no longer await their return.

This is a poem of nostalgia, focusing on the poet's boyhood home. Sandburg is aware of the popularity of nostalgic verse at the time, particularly the work of James Whitcomb RILEY, the Indiana poet famous for his rural images of barefoot boys and swimming holes. Yet in rejecting traditional rhyme and meter, he is distancing himself as well from popular childhood evocations.

"FIRE-LOGS"

Nancy Hanks is Abraham Lincoln's mother. The poet echoes annunciation scenes—that is, scenes that tell a woman of the child she will bear, the child that is destined for greatness. The poet asks the woman to dream first of a beautiful child, then of a tall man, who will be the great president himself. Sandburg was aware of the long-standing tradition that Hanks herself was of illegitimate birth.

"MEMOIR OF A PROUD BOY"

Coal miners had struck against the John D. ROCKEFELLER-controlled Colorado Fuel and Iron Company in Ludlow, Colorado, in 1913. National guardsmen later attacked their encampment, setting fire to the tents, resulting in 22 deaths, including those of women and children. The man whom Sandburg is celebrating in the poem—a journalist he had known from his days on the CHICAGO DAY BOOK—led an uprising by the miners, undertaking a political role that was new to him. "Mother Jones" is the well-known labor agitator, Mary Harris "Mother" JONES, at that time a woman in her mid-70s; she was jailed in Trinidad, Colorado, for three months. The journalist, whose "Scotch name" was Dan MacGregor, fled to Chihuahua, a state in northern Mexico, taking part in that country's revolution; he was killed by Carranzistas, followers of one-time revolutionary Venustiano Carranza, opposed by the more adamant revolutionary Pancho Villa. Floyd P. Gibbons, a war correspondent in Mexico for the CHICAGO TRIBUNE, wrote the account to which Sandburg is referring. The poet names two purveyors of entertainment who would have wrung drama from the story—D. W. GRIFFITH, the silent-film director, and Victor Herbert, the composer of operettas. The lost poems and stories are pieces that McGregor had been writing along with his journalism.

"SOUTHERN PACIFIC"

Collis P. Huntington was one of the railroad builders whose networks, including the Southern Pacific company, controlled transportation in the West. Blithery is the fictional railroad worker, the man who laid the ties and tracks for the Southern Pacific. In death each man dreams of railroads at the level he interacted with them in life—as owner, as laborer—and yet both sleep in a coffin of the same size. In this juxtaposing of the rich and the poor, Sandburg returns to the subject matter of CHICAGO POEMS.

"WASHERWOMAN"

The concluding phrase, "the Last Great Washday," suggests the poet's humorous response to the woman's religion, as does her singing of humankind's final days while rubbing underwear. That she is a member of the SALVATION ARMY draws only gentle mocking in this poem—a mild application of the tenet of Marxist SOCIALISM that religion is the opiate of the people, that religion causes one to accept his or her current woes, since the joys of heaven are forthcoming. Moreover, the "wrongs" the woman contemplates are those she herself has committed—whatever their nature, whatever their degree of seriousness—not those committed against her as a member of the working class. The poem was published after Vachel LINDSAY's evocation of the Salvation Army in "GENERAL WILLIAM BOOTH ENTERS INTO HEAVEN," including references to the hymn in which one washes away one's sins.

"PORTRAIT OF A MOTORCAR"

The car is a long, luxury model, and Danny the driver is the chauffeur. The first two lines of the poem give the vehicle animal qualities—of a racing dog, of an eagle—and yet Danny sees the car in sexual terms; he dreams of it when he dreams of women. The car is a machine interacting with a member of the working class, but in this case it is not exploiting him; it is energizing and vitalizing him.

"PRAYERS OF STEEL"

The supplicant in these prayers is steel personified—an inanimate object given human voice. The steel prays first to be hammered into a crowbar, razing old buildings, destroying old walls and foundations. Then it prays to be a spike, driven into girders, holding the SKYSCRAPER together. Its final prayer is to be fastened by red-hot rivets to the central girders so that it will be the "great nail" holding the building in the sky. The poet, who earlier in the volume celebrated the permanent qualities of the prairie, is here celebrating the dynamism of the city.

"LAWYER"

In this piece of near-prose, Sandburg is mocking a defense lawyer—in an era when lawyers were portrayed as defending the white-collar guilty, not the working man or the disadvantaged; the disadvantaged could not afford such defenders. As the courtroom waits in suspense, the lawyer prepares to ask for a new trial if the verdict is guilty, proclaiming that the verdict is absurd. Maurine WATKINS's play of 1926, CHICAGO, presents a famously smooth and successful defense lawyer.

"THREE BALLS"

A sign consisting of three balls indicates a pawn shop, a place where people get loans on their possessions; the pawnbroker sells the items if they are not retrieved within a period of time. A month earlier the poet passed the window of the shop, seeing three battered items that had been pawned and never recovered; they are seemingly family keepsakes, two of them representing the family religion. Now the poet passes the window again, and the items are still for sale. Not only did the original owners not retrieve them, for whatever reason, but one else has wanted them, either.

"KNUCKS"

SPRINGFIELD, Illinois, is Abraham Lincoln's city, where the great man was laid to rest, where he is still remembered. The poet, looking in a store window, sees a set of knucks, or iron knuckles used for fighting; the proprietor says he sells "a carload a month." Thinking of Lincoln's Second Inaugural Address, offering "malice toward none," the poet realizes that everyone in town is "for Abe and the 'malice to none' stuff"—but he knows that such words are simply accepted parlance;

they have nothing to do with reality. If people really held no malice, they would have no need of iron knuckles.

Like "Fire-Logs," the poem shows Sandburg's turning to his new Lincoln subject matter. Edgar Lee MASTERS, a fellow poet from Lincoln territory, quotes a longer passage from the well-known address—"With malice toward none, with charity for all"—in his "Anne Rutledge" monologue in SPOON RIVER ANTHOLOGY, published three years earlier.

"SHENANDOAH"

The Shenandoah Valley in Virginia is the site of several Civil War campaigns. Using this name as the title of a poem, as well as of a group of poems, Sandburg indicates that his subject is war—although not only the Civil War, but the contemporaneous World War I as well.

"Shenandoah" speaks of the gray rider wearing the gray uniform of the Confederacy, and the blue rider wearing the blue uniform of the Union. The sun once shone on both, "wondering"—that is, puzzling over the conflict below. Now the riders are piled together in the dust of the valley, and no one remembers their colors. Yet the climbing blue flowers are "wondering," and a midnight purple violet claims the sun, finding a place among the old dreams of the blue and gray riders.

"GRASS"

The poet evokes famous conflicts of the past. The battle of Austerlitz was Napoleon's great victory, Waterloo his final defeat; Gettysburg was a battle of the Civil War, Ypres and Verdun of World War I. And the grass—like the prairie in the first poem of the volume—is the force that persists, that covers the past and maintains an eternal presence. When tourist trains take visitors to the battlefield sites, the visitors are not sure where they are; they need to be reminded—because the grass has done its job so well. As opposed to a common 19th-century view of the natural world, in which nature is seen as sympathetic to man, the natural world here is neutral; moreover, its neutrality gives a message to man—that his battles, his passions, do not much matter.

"Grass" is one of Sandburg's most frequently anthologized pieces.

"FLANDERS"

Flanders is an area of Europe, extending along the North Sea, shared by Belgium, France, and Holland; it was a scene of continuous fighting in World War I. The poet is aware, as are his readers, of the oft-quoted poem, "In Flanders Fields," evoking the voices of fallen soldiers, by the Canadian John McCrae, published in 1915. At one time, Sandburg says, Flanders was known only to those who lived there, who dwelt peacefully on farmland and dairyland. Later, during the war, people were still not sure exactly where it was; if an American was asked, he would reply in a slang phrase—a phrase incongruous with the scene of the farmgirl sitting quietly by the window, washing wooden bowls. The carnage of war, too, is incongruous with such a scene.

"OLD TIMERS"

Here the "I" is the universal soldier—or rather, the man conscripted for reluctant duty; this man, the generic military conscript, has been called up from ancient times to the present. His role was not always the hero's role; for the Persian king Xerxes, fighting the Greeks, he cleaned pans on the soup wagon. For the Greek Miltiades, he carried a spear, and for the Roman Caesar, he drove horses. For Sweden's Charles XII and for France's Napoleon Bonaparte, he served at a more lowly level; he was a horseshoer in their armies—although for Bonaparte he trimmed the feet of the general's horse. Then Abraham Lincoln sent him to war, and he drove a wagon and team; at Spotsylvania Court House, in rural Virginia, his arm was shot off. So his service has been varied, and yet—as the final line of the poem repeats the opening line—he has always been the reluctant conscript; he has always been the man forced to fight the world's battles.

"HOUSE"

Immediately following "Old Timers" is a poem expressing the opposite view—the eagerness of men to go to war. Old Joe, a veteran of the Civil War, lives upstairs from two Swedish families, and on cold winter nights he tells the Swedish sons about the battles he fought, about the fierce Union victories where men on both sides were slaughtered in the rain and the darkness. The boys go downstairs, their heads filled with images of guns and battle, and one boy wishes there were a war now so that he could be a soldier. The poet makes no comment, relying on the reader's sense of irony to supply the appropriate response.

Critical Reception

The Nation, reviewing the volume, commented on "half-cooked free verse," but criticism was generally muted; the book won a half-share of the annual prize given by the Poetry Society of America. The involvement of the United States in World War I affected the reception of the work; the last piece in the volume, "The Four Brothers," a blatantly anti-German, pro-American poem, had already led off the November 1917 issue of POETRY, coming at a time when war fervor was high. Sandburg had become unabashedly pro-American by this time, and the patriotism of the final poem deterred critics who had once worried about his working-class subject matter.

The influence of Walt WHITMAN becomes increasingly clear in these poems. Many of the pieces are longer than those of the earlier volume; the lines are longer, and the accumulation of detail is greater. In terms of subject matter, "The Prairie" can be compared to a work by the 19th-century American poet William Cullen BRYANT, whose "The Prairies" appeared in 1832; that piece, treating this new landscape—a landscape previously undescribed in English-language poetry—is more traditional and orderly than the sprawling, organizationally challenged work of Sandburg.

Corthell, Sheldon

A character in Frank NORRIS's novel THE PIT, Corthell is a maker of stained glass and a musician; as an artist, he stands aloof from the business activity of the city. Laura DEARBORN, before she marries Curtis JADWIN, feels the attraction of Corthell; at one point a friend predicts they will marry, as they have their love of art and beauty in common. The son of a businessman, enjoying a private income, Corthell is far from impoverished;

yet it is the manly businessman, Jadwin, who triumphs in winning Laura, even though he lacks artistic sensibilities. Later, when Jadwin is distracted by market speculations, Corthell renews his suit, and Laura feels temptation—and, according to some readers, succumbs—but once again the pursuer of masculine activity wins out.

Corthell shares a similarity with two earlier Henry B. FULLER characters, Marcus BRAINARD in the 1893 THE CLIFF-DWELLERS and Truesdale MARSHALL in the 1895 WITH THE PROCESSION; these sons of businessmen also reject business for art. Yet unlike them, Corthell is not estranged from his family; his function is to represent one of Laura's choices between two types of men and two ways of life.

Coughlin, John "Bathhouse"
(1860–1938) *alderman of the first ward*

Nicknamed for once being a masseur at a bathhouse—an institution serving a socially acceptable function in a plumbing-scarce era—Coughlin, along with Michael "Hinky Dink" KENNA, presided over the LEVEE, the city's notable vice district. The EVERLEIGH SISTERS are said to have paid him large sums of money for protection. Elected in 1892, he served as alderman for 46 years; he was known also for writing and publicly reciting bad poetry. Coughlin and Kenna are named in Upton SINCLAIR's THE JUNGLE as "proprietors of the most notorious dives in Chicago." In Theodore DREISER's THE TITAN, they appear under the names Patrick "Emerald Pat" Kerrigan and Michael "Smiling Mike" Tiernan. Edna FERBER mentions Coughlin in several works; when she refers in FANNY HERSELF to "Bath-House John's groggery" as lying "almost in the shadow of the City Hall," she is suggesting municipal corruption.

Court, Landry

A character in Frank NORRIS's novel THE PIT, Court is a member of a brokerage firm, a lesser figure than the grand speculator Curtis JADWIN. Court nevertheless demonstrates the power of "the Pit," the hold exercised by business activity, turning men into callous competitors. Normally an ordinary man, Court becomes on the trading floor a figure of action and shrewdness, demonstrating a "male hardness." He cannot compete with the yet-stronger Jadwin for the affection of Laura DEARBORN, but he wins the hand of Laura's sister.

Covici-McGee Company

This publishing company grew out of the Washington Street Bookstore, founded by Romanian immigrant Pascal Covici and former Catholic priest William McGee. The store was a popular gathering place for writers, including Edgar Lee MASTERS, Sherwood ANDERSON, and Ben HECHT. In 1922, Covici turned from bookselling to book publishing, producing as his first title Hecht's collection of columns, *1001 AFTERNOONS IN CHICAGO*; his firm also underwrote Hecht's short-lived weekly periodical, the CHICAGO LITERARY TIMES. In 1928, Covici moved to New York, joining with Donald Friede to form Covici-Friede, a company that lasted until 1938.

Cowley, Elmer   *See under* WINESBURG, OHIO: "Queer."

Cowperwood, Aileen   *See* BUTLER, AILEEN.

Cowperwood, Frank

The principal character in Theodore DREISER's trilogy, THE FINANCIER, THE TITAN, and THE STOIC, Cowperwood is based on the real-life Chicago transportation magnate Charles T. YERKES. Cowperwood is portrayed throughout the series as charming, brilliant, and unbothered by scruples—although he is also generous and free of pettiness. His motto, as declared in the first two novels, is simply, "I satisfy myself." Or, as he puts it in *The Stoic*: "I try to follow the line of self-interest."

In *The Financier*, set in Philadelphia, his empire is built in part on the illegal use of municipal funds; when it topples, he is sent to prison. Yet the problem lies not in the illegality—at that particular time and place, illegality could be overlooked—but rather in an avenging father whose daughter he has made his mistress; the financier, pursuing both sexual and economic goals, has overreached himself. In *The Titan*, set in Chicago, the empire is built largely on bribery, on paying off politicians to obtain city franchises; Cowperwood is ultimately forced by opponents to relinquish control. Again, the problem is overreaching, in that his manipulations have turned other businessmen against him, in that he has been too blatant in his chicanery. Yet another factor obtrudes in this particular case—the climate has changed and illegality is now less easily overlooked. Finally, in *The Stoic*, Cowperwood, shut out of Chicago, turns to London, taking part in the development of the London subway system. Here his dealings, involving shrewdness more than illegality, occupy a lesser portion of the book. When he dies, his holdings are reduced and scattered after five years of legal wrangling.

Although using a real-life model, Dreiser shows the influence also, at least in the two earlier novels, of the concept of the "superman," as expressed by the German philosopher Friedrich NIETZSCHE—and as expounded by Dreiser's friend H. L. MENCKEN, author of a treatise on Nietzsche. In *The Financier* and *The Titan*, Cowperwood proceeds without heed to moral principles, acting as the superior man who transcends such constraints—and in neither novel is he presented as deserving the fall that comes to him; he is the superior man brought down by less-than-visionary inferior men. In *The Titan*, he thinks scornfully of the "plodding" Chicago businessmen who belong to a "humdrum conventional world," a world resenting his spirit, his daring; after the HAYMARKET AFFAIR, he feels no allegiance to the rights of the masses, but rather to the destiny of men like himself, who are sent into the world "to better perfect its mechanism."

Dreiser clearly admires Cowperwood, and although readers of his era might have been scandalized by the character's sexual liaisons, readers today often admire his powerful stance. In *The Financier*, he is given a further sympathetic note

when shown to be deeply moved by his glimpse of President Abraham LINCOLN; the nation's leader has just delivered a solemn speech on a necessary war, and Cowperwood finds his visage sad and meditative: "For days the face of Lincoln haunted him." Nor is Cowperwood presented as vindictive, as stooping to revenge; in *The Titan*, after Governor Swanson—a brief portrait of Governor John Peter ALTGELD—vetoes the bill extending the street-railway franchises, Cowperwood, respecting Swanson's idealism, lends the governor the money he knows he needs.

Cowperwood's love life, like that of Yerkes and Dreiser as well, is busy and varied. The young Aileen BUTLER becomes his mistress during his marriage to his first wife, Lillian COWPERWOOD. After moving to Chicago and marrying Aileen, Cowperwood takes up with a series of women, including Rita SOHLBERG and Stephanie PLATOW; he finally realizes that the ordinary rules of love are not for him, that he is "wholly liberated," sensually and emotionally. It is not until he meets his last great love, Berenice FLEMING, 35 years his junior, that he feels self-doubt for the first time, worrying that she might become interested in a younger man. Yet Berenice turns out to be faithful, always recognizing his superiority, remaining true to his memory after death.

Cowperwood can be compared to his fictional businessmen predecessors, found in the work of Henry B. FULLER, Frank NORRIS, and Robert HERRICK—although Dreiser's character, reflecting later times, is the only sexual predator among the group. The next incarnation of the businessman will appear in Sinclair LEWIS's *BABBITT*; there the Nietzchean man is gone, and in his place stands an unimaginative conformist.

Cowperwood, Lillian

A character in Theodore DREISER's novel *THE FINANCIER*, Lillian Semple is a married woman when the 19-year-old Frank COWPERWOOD meets her; she is five years older, and he appreciates her tall, stately beauty. After her husband dies, he overcomes her reluctance and persuades her to marry him; they have two children.

Cowperwood then becomes disillusioned as Lillian grows older and seemingly more placid and passive—and as he becomes infatuated, too, with the younger and livelier Aileen BUTLER. Lillian first refuses to grant him a divorce, but after he leaves Philadelphia for Chicago—as related in the early chapters of the subsequent novel, THE TITAN—she agrees to the divorce. By then she is "a tall, severe, and rather plain woman." Well provided for financially, she goes to church on Sundays and tries to believe that all is for the best.

Coxey's Army

This group of marchers, protesting unemployment, was organized in 1894 by Ohio businessman Jacob S. Coxey. Suffering from the effects of the PANIC OF 1893, the men left Massillon, Ohio, to march to Washington, D.C.; their purpose was to demand jobs from the federal government. Joined by others along the way, the group, numbering close to 500, was dispersed after reaching the capital; Coxey was jailed for trespassing. Ray Stannard BAKER, among the journalists responding to the march and its aftermath, wrote a sympathetic account of the events in the CHICAGO RECORD. Other "armies" of the unemployed attempted similar treks; Edna FERBER, living as a girl in Ottumwa, Iowa, recalls seeing a contingent of Coxey's army, "a pitiful tatterdemalion crew, floating down the muddy Des Moines River on flat boats and rafts, hungry, penniless, desperate."

Cressler, Charles

A character in Frank NORRIS's novel THE PIT, Cressler was once a wheat farmer who benefited from rising food prices during the CIVIL WAR. After giving up farming and moving to Chicago, he bought a seat on the CHICAGO BOARD OF TRADE; he subsequently lost much of his fortune in an attempt to corner, or monopolize, the wheat market. He vowed never to speculate again. During the course of the novel, he continues to speak against speculation; when his friend

Curtis JADWIN scores a triumph in wheat, he says he would rather Jadwin had lost, as the Pit would then no longer exert its hold over him. Yet he himself is once more lured into the Pit; as a broker remarks, "Once a speculator, always a speculator." Cressler shoots himself when he is wiped out financially.

crime of the century

This term has been applied to the Chicago Loeb-Leopold murder case of 1924, in which two young men, Richard A. Loeb and Nathan F. Leopold, were convicted of murdering 14-year-old Bobby Franks in a "thrill" murder, attempting to commit what they called a perfect crime; their defense was provided by Clarence DARROW. A long-standing foe of capital punishment, Darrow made use of the insanity plea to save his clients from the death penalty. Loeb died in a prison assault in 1936; Leopold, paroled in 1958, died in Puerto Rico in 1971. Alfred Hitchcock's 1948 film, *Rope*, provides a version of the crime; the 1956 novel by Meyer LEVIN, *Compulsion*, gives another fictionalized enactment, followed by the 1959 movie of the same name, featuring Orson Welles as the Darrow figure.

Crosby's Opera House

In 19th-century cities the designation of opera house usually applied to any venue specializing in musical entertainment; *grand opera* was the term for the work of serious European composers. Crosby's Opera House, designed by William W. BOYINGTON, the city's most important pre–GREAT FIRE architect, opened on April 20, 1865—after a postponement caused by the assassination of President Abraham LINCOLN. The 3,000-seat auditorium was the site of the nomination of Ulysses S. GRANT for the presidency in May 1868; the building also housed a music academy founded by the father of Florenz ZIEGFELD Jr. On October 9, 1871, conductor Theodore THOMAS arrived with his touring orchestra, scheduled to perform at the theater; he learned that the structure had just burned to the ground in the still-blazing fire.

Crumbling Idols
Hamlin Garland
(1894)

Appearing under the imprint of STONE AND KIMBALL, this collection of essays by Hamlin GARLAND argues for a literature that is free from the cultural idols that have crumbled—the East, the past, and Europe. The new American literature will be Western, created by writers responding to their terrain, ignoring literary precedents, avoiding forms dictated by the past; Chicago will be in the forefront of this new expression. The result will be an American VERITISM, Garland's regional version of the REALISM of William Dean HOWELLS.

Currey, Margery
(1877–1959) *member of the Fifty-seventh Street Group*

Born in EVANSTON, Illinois, Currey graduated from Vassar College in 1901 and taught in several high schools in the Midwest, including Davenport, Iowa. There she met Floyd DELL, 10 years her senior; they married in Evanston in 1909. Four years later, the couple moved to separate studios in the Fifty-seventh Street area, near JACKSON PARK on the South Side; late in 1913, Dell moved to New York City. After newspaper work in Chicago, Currey eventually moved to the East Coast as well. Sherwood ANDERSON, in his posthumous memoirs, speaks of Currey's kindness when he first tried to make his way into her FIFTY-SEVENTH STREET GROUP; he fails to mention their affair, which took place after her separation from Dell.

D

Dale, Suzanne

A character in Theodore DREISER's autobiographical novel THE "GENIUS," Suzanne is the last of Eugene WITLA's major loves; she is based on a real-life prototype, the woman who broke up Dreiser's own marriage. Witla, nearing 40, married, successful, becomes infatuated by the 18-year-old Suzanne and loses his career in pursuit of her. Suzanne claims to return his love, suggesting that they live together; she is portrayed as free-thinking, telling him he should leave her if he ever tires of her—far from how Eugene's wife is portrayed. Yet she is disillusioned when Eugene gives in to her mother's stipulations that he wait and seek a divorce; she would prefer a dramatic flouting of convention. Eugene agrees to a year's separation, and the relationship is never renewed. As in the case of the other 18-year-old with whom Eugene becomes infatuated, their love is never consummated.

Dark Laughter
Sherwood Anderson
(1925)

Written after ANDERSON's stay in New Orleans, the novel follows a newspaperman as he leaves his wife and job in Chicago and heads southward. Taking factory employment in an Indiana town along the Ohio River, he becomes a gardener to his employer's wife, then the wife's lover. His southerly journey also brings him into contact with African Americans, and the "dark laughter" of the title refers to an imputed African-American spontaneity and exuberance for life—as opposed to white sterility and overcivilization. Influenced by the language of James JOYCE's *Ulysses*, as well as by the fiction of African American Jean TOOMER, Anderson attempts to reproduce, through passages of stream-of-consciousness narrative, his version of naturalness and spontaneity; the result is a stereotyping that makes the work an example of PRIMITIVISM. Ernest HEMINGWAY, the younger writer whom Anderson had once helped, published a parody of the novel, THE TORRENTS OF SPRING, the following year. Yet readers of the 1920s, who made *Dark Laughter* Anderson's only best-seller, cared little about the rhetorical excesses that Hemingway lampooned—and more about the novel's antipuritanism, its presumed "natural" actions. Critic H. L. MENCKEN called the work "one of the most profound novels or our time."

Darrow, Clarence
(1857–1938) *renowned labor and criminal lawyer*

Born in Kinsman, Ohio, Darrow moved to Chicago in 1887, after starting out as a small-town lawyer. In the aftermath of the previous year's HAYMARKET AFFAIR, Darrow sought out aspiring politician John Peter ALTGELD, whose OUR PENAL MACHINERY AND ITS VICTIMS had reached him in Ohio; when Altgeld was elected governor in 1892,

Darrow and others pressed him to pardon the remaining Haymarket anarchists. The governor granted the pardon, although in doing so he irrevocably damaged his own career.

Serving as counsel for the Chicago and Northwestern Railway, Darrow resigned the position in 1894 in the wake of the PULLMAN STRIKE. Taking on the defense of Eugene V. DEBS, president of the new AMERICAN RAILWAY UNION, he lost the case, and Debs went to prison; Darrow committed himself from that point on to maintaining a pro-underdog legal stance. In 1896, when William Jennings BRYAN became the Democratic candidate for president, Darrow ran for Congress; he lost in the general Democratic Party defeat that year and blamed Bryan for the defeat, believing that the presidential candidate, while strong on oratory, was weak in long-term vision. He also disliked what he considered Bryan's religiosity.

Called increasingly to high-profile cases nationwide—including a successful defense of labor leader William HAYWOOD in a 1907 Idaho murder trial—Darrow continued his ongoing campaign against the death penalty; his anti-death-penalty novel, AN EYE FOR AN EYE, appeared in 1905. He became increasingly known also as an orator; at the same time that Vachel LINDSAY was lecturing for the ANTI-SALOON LEAGUE in downstate Illinois, Darrow was proving himself a popular anti-PROHIBITION orator throughout the Midwest. At the same time, a partner in his law practice, Edgar Lee MASTERS, was publishing poetry under a pseudonym.

In 1915, Darrow was called to defend architect Frank Lloyd WRIGHT from accusations that he had violated the Mann Act, a law—sponsored by Chicagoan James Robert Mann—that had been passed by Congress in 1910 to suppress "white slave" traffic, or trade in prostitutes. Wright, whose mistress had been murdered the previous year at his Wisconsin home, was accused of transporting an unmarried woman across state lines from Illinois to Wisconsin; Darrow provided evidence of a personal vendetta by the accuser, and the charges were dropped.

Darrow's most famous Chicago trial arose from the so-called CRIME OF THE CENTURY, the 1924 murder case involving two young men who confessed to killing a teenager, attempting to commit the "perfect crime." Through an insanity plea, Darrow saved the defendants from the death penalty. The next year, he was pitted against the man toward whom he had long felt enmity, William Jennings Bryan. In the Scopes, or "monkey," trial, held in Dayton, Tennessee, a high school biology teacher, John T. Scopes, was charged with violating state law by teaching evolution, a doctrine deemed contradictory to biblical accounts of creation; Darrow took the defense against a prosecution aided by Bryan. Scopes was convicted, although later released on a technicality; Darrow, cross-examining Bryan on the latter's literalist interpretation of the Bible, was considered the true victor. Bryan died five days later.

Darrow spent the later years of his life as a popular lecturer. When he died at the age of 80, his eulogy at a UNIVERSITY OF CHICAGO memorial service rendered verbatim the funeral oration he himself had delivered for John Peter Altgeld in 1902, more than 35 years earlier. His ashes were scattered in the JACKSON PARK lagoon.

The play *Inherit the Wind,* a fictionalized version of the Scopes trial by Jerome Lawrence and Robert E. Lee, appeared in New York in 1955, starring Paul MUNI as the Darrow-based character; a 1960 movie of the same name starred Spencer Tracy. In 1956, Meyer LEVIN's novel *Compulsion* provided a fictionalization of the 1924 murder case, followed by a 1959 movie presenting Orson Welles in the Darrow role.

A Daughter of the Middle Border
Hamlin Garland
(1921)

A continuation of his 1917 autobiographical novel *A SON OF THE MIDDLE BORDER,* this volume begins as GARLAND describes his first winter in Chicago; he speaks also of the disappointing reception of his coming-to-the-city novel, *ROSE OF DUTCHER'S COOLLY.* He admits that his writing subsequently changed; his fiction became less grim as his locales moved farther west, as he began to write about miners, mountaineers, and "the epic side of western life"—works that proved more popular than his harsh early fiction. A recurring figure is that of his father, a CIVIL WAR veteran, a man whose years as a soldier remained the most treasured experience of his life. The volume ends with his father's death, "another soldier of the Union mustered out." Garland received the Pulitzer Prize for biography in 1922.

Dawn O'Hara: The Girl Who Laughed
Edna Ferber
(1911)

In this first novel, Edna FERBER draws upon her experience working for a Milwaukee newspaper, as well as her subsequent nervous collapse and return to her hometown of Appleton, Wisconsin. Her heroine, Dawn, follows a similar pattern, but in reverse; she recuperates first, then finds a newspaper career. Unlike Ferber, who never married, Dawn is forced to recover from marriage to a man who has been confined to a mental institution; she ventures to Milwaukee, finding her position as a reporter. The work is basically a sentimental popular novel; the heroine, although loving another man, refuses to divorce her husband out of loyalty and pity, until an automobile accident finally takes his life. Religious scruples are never a factor in her decision; Dawn, although speaking frequently of her Irish ancestors, makes no reference to the practice of Roman Catholicism. Ferber can be said to be avoiding the Jewish identity she will acknowledge later in the more fully autobiographical *FANNY HERSELF.* Set in a city with a large German population—Ferber later claimed Milwaukee to be "as German as Germany"—*Dawn O'Hara* presents sympathetic German-speaking characters and records multiple German phrases; such views and practices disappeared from popular fiction three years later with the advent of WORLD WAR I.

Dearborn, Laura

This principal character in Frank NORRIS's *THE PIT*, Laura is portrayed as possessing willfulness and a taste for drama, undoubtedly reflecting Norris's effort to take her beyond the conventional heroine's role. Nevertheless, she remains entirely within social and literary conventions; she is "womanly," which means, as she herself says, "to love one's home and to take care of it, and to love and believe in one's husband." Yet when her husband is caught up in the frenzy of the Pit, she becomes selfish and self-centered; she feels sorry for herself, lamenting that she is being left alone. Later, her sister sums up how she should have acted; she should have taken more interest in her husband's work, entering more fully into his life. Laura herself had once, not long after her marriage, concluded that a woman's love is "less a victory than a capitulation"; she repeats the idea as she accompanies her defeated husband westward: "I have won a victory by surrendering." Norris intends no irony in these passages.

Some modern readers assert that Laura commits adultery with the artist Sheldon CORTHELL; such an act would undoubtedly have suited Norris, rendering his heroine all the more poignant in her final victory-by-surrendering. Yet he avoided being explicit, and the audience of his day is likely to have discerned no infidelity, seeing Laura as drawn into a compromising situation, but never actually compromised.

"Death"   *See* WINESBURG, OHIO.

"Death in the Woods"   *See* DEATH IN THE WOODS.

Death in the Woods
Sherwood Anderson
(1933)

This volume constitutes the final short-story collection in the basic Sherwood ANDERSON canon. Many of the pieces were first published in periodicals in the 1920s, including the oft-anthologized title story. In that tale the briefly mentioned experience with dogs in the Illinois woods—as opposed to the central experience of the tale—draws on a personal episode recounted in *SHERWOOD ANDERSON'S MEMOIRS*; the locale is Palos Park, a town outside Chicago, serving also as the setting for "Brothers," collected in THE TRIUMPH OF THE EGG. In the story "The Return," the town of Caxton recalls the Caxton, Iowa, of WINDY MCPHERSON'S SON, although in this case it is in Ohio, a stand-in for Anderson's hometown of Clyde, Ohio. "A Meeting South" is a version of Anderson's encounter with the younger writer William FAULKNER in New Orleans, including an account of Faulkner's spurious war injuries; the retired madam is based on a real-life figure as well.

Synopses of Selected Stories

"DEATH IN THE WOODS"

The unnamed first-person narrator, having witnessed a memorable scene in the woods as a boy, tries to understand that scene as he grows older; he tells and retells the story, interpolating into it his own subsequent experiences. The narration begins in a relatively straightforward manner, and the reader realizes only later that the story is a reconstruction, that the narrator actually saw only the final death scene. His subsequent understanding as a man completes the tale of what he saw as a boy.

An old woman, named only by her last name of Grimes, periodically comes into town, followed by several dogs; she trades eggs for salt pork and other staples, then walks the two or three miles home. Her husband, Jake GRIMES, is generally disliked and is reputed to be a horse thief; their 21-year-old son has already spent time in jail. She herself was once a bound, or indentured, servant to a German farmer, who had imposed himself on her; the narrator notes that bound children, who were orphans, were often cruelly treated. The woman's life has now become a harsh struggle to feed the animals, as well as her husband and son; her only resource is a few chickens that provide eggs. Overworked, she begins to look old and stooped, even before reaching the age of 40.

One cold winter day, the woman goes off to town with her eggs, and the dogs, as usual, follow. The butcher feels sorry for her, giving her some liver and meat. Snow is falling as she heads back out of town; hoping to get home before dark, she takes a shortcut through the woods. In a clearing,

she sits down to rest at the foot of a tree. As the weather clears and a moon illuminates the scene, the woman sleeps. The four dogs begin to run in circles around the tree, stopping now and then to investigate the sleeping figure; they are waiting for her to die. When the woman is finally dead, the dogs tear the bag off her back, dragging her body, facedown, into the open. The dress is torn from her shoulders, and in death she looks like a young girl.

A hunter finds the body and reports back to town; the narrator, hearing the story, goes with his brother and the townsmen into the woods. The two boys have never seen a woman's unclothed body before. The blacksmith spreads his overcoat over the body, gathering it up and taking it back to town. That night, the brother tells the story to the boys' parents, but the narrator is not satisfied with the telling. Later, when he is older, he has the experience of working for a German farmer, and sees how the hired girl fears her employer; the narrator also experiences a night in a forest in Illinois, when a pack of dogs circle about him. Thus, he keeps coming back to that one scene from his childhood, viewed in the cold, moonlit forest. He must keep telling about it; he must keep trying to understand it.

The story appeared in the September 1926 *American Mercury*.

"THE RETURN"

John HOLDEN, a 40-year-old man who has been living in New York City, is returning for the first time to his midwestern hometown of Caxton; he left the town as a young man 18 years earlier, after his mother had died. Driving west in his expensive car, he thinks of the people he will see once more, including Lillian, the girl he left behind. He recalls the night when he walked out with her, just before he went away; she seemed surprised that he left her at the front porch at three o'clock in the morning. Perhaps, he feels, he has always disappointed people—including his wife, whom he married four years after leaving Caxton and who has recently died. He has a 12-year-old son, currently away at a summer camp.

Holden picks up a hitchhiker, a likable 16-year-old boy who is working his way to the West

Coast; leaving the boy off when he stops for the night, he thinks later that he should have invited him to his hotel. Looking for him the next morning, he realizes the boy is gone; he wonders if he was purposely avoiding him. He thinks of his own son, who is often unaware of others, who is casually selfish.

Arriving in Caxton in the early evening, Holden registers at the hotel, then goes for a walk on Main Street. He meets Tom Ballard, whom he had once known, who is now a doctor. These are PROHIBITION years, and Holden offers Tom a drink from a bottle in his room; he realizes the doctor drinks too much. Tom speaks of other townspeople, including Lillian, who has since married and divorced; she seems a little strange these days, Tom says, and has lost much of her looks. The two men go out for a drive, although Tom first suggests another drink; he goes into a drugstore and obtains a medicinal alcoholic potion. He picks up friends whom Holden does not know, suggesting that they go to a roadhouse, a combination dance hall and dining room, where drinks can be bought. A woman named Maud squeezes into the backseat of the car next to Holden, and they share the medicinal alcohol; her fingers occasionally touch his fingers. Inside the roadhouse Tom warns Holden to stay away from Maud, as she and her husband have been arguing about her paying attention to other men.

On the way back, most of the group have drunk too much; Maud presses herself against Holden and puts her hand in his. Once back in the hotel, he decides he must leave, even though it is the middle of the night. He wakes up the clerk and asks that his car be brought around. Heading east again, he lets the motor go at full throttle, bringing the car up to racing speed.

The story was first published in the May 1925 *Century*.

"IN A STRANGE TOWN"

The first-person narrator, a college professor, has taken the train, on a whim, to a nameless small town. He sends the porter on ahead to the hotel with his bags. He notes a tearful widow on the station platform, sending off a coffin on a train; he thinks of death as something "majestic." He takes

a room at the hotel and spends the night; he is married, and yet his wife—who considers him a bit strange—is patient with him. As he sits in his hotel room, he is thinking about a woman student who used to come to his office; he would talk to her, or sometimes they would sit for moments in silence. Then he heard that she was struck and killed by an automobile. He ponders staying in this town another day, or perhaps he will go on to another town.

The story was first published in the January 1930 *Scribner's Magazine*.

"THESE MOUNTAINEERS"

Traveling in the Blue Ridge Mountains, the narrator comes across a small cluster of houses in a mountain hollow. The local store, where he had hoped to purchase edibles, is closed, and an old man invites him to his house, offering him food. The house is small and unclean, and the meal of beans is unclean; the old man is described as evil-looking. The narrator sees a girl living in the house, not over 12 or 13; the man refers to her as a "hell cat," saying she has to have a man—a young man, who lives in the house as well—and he indicates that she is pregnant. The girl looks at the narrator with hatred in her eyes.

Some time later, the narrator returns to the hollow, determined to give the girl money. She is more obviously pregnant now, and he sees the father of her child. The narrator offers the girl a $20 bill, suggesting that she buy some clothes. Refusing the money, she looks at him with a hatred that is even more intense. The narrator leaves, contemplating the hardness of one who is so young.

The story appeared in the January 1930 *Vanity Fair*.

"ANOTHER WIFE"

The first-person narrator, a 47-year-old doctor, has been a widower for two years; he is spending his summer holiday in a mountain town. A woman who lives nearby, 10 years younger, has been visiting him. He is not sure how she views him, and he knows little about her or her past. They go for a walk, and she tells him about studying art in New York and Paris; she speaks of an English novelist she had known in Paris, who had not returned her love. The narrator and the woman embrace, and he decides he wants to marry her. An understanding is reached—and yet he feels caught; he feels both afraid and glad. He thinks to himself that he has a new wife; he has another wife.

The story appeared in the December 1926 *Scribner's Magazine*.

"A MEETING SOUTH"

The unnamed narrator, a midwesterner living in New Orleans, encounters a southern poet, David, who suffers from a painful limp, the result of a wartime plane crash. David carries a bottle of whiskey—as always at that time, illegal—in his hip pocket; the drink is necessary for him to sleep. The narrator introduces David to Aunt Sally, originally, like himself, a midwesterner. Aunt Sally had come to New Orleans years before, opening a successful gambling, drinking, and prostitution establishment; at age 50, having made a good living, she retired. Now, at 65, she seems a motherly figure; she gets along well with David, offering him some of her own whiskey. David, scion of a soon-to-be-bankrupt southern plantation family, claims he can sleep only out of doors; he lies down on the bricks of Aunt Sally's patio and falls asleep. The narrator leaves, and as he walks along the dark street, he thinks of both David and Aunt Sally as aristocrats; he is pleased that the Midwest can produce aristocrats. He hopes that Aunt Sally is actually from his own home state, Ohio, although he knows he should avoid inquiring too closely into her past.

The story first appeared in the April 1925 *DIAL*; it was reprinted in the 1926 *SHERWOOD ANDERSON'S NOTEBOOK*, as well as in the 1933 *DEATH IN THE WOODS*.

Critical Reception

The title story, "Death in the Woods," has since achieved the status of a classic American short story, taking its place alongside *WINESBURG, OHIO*. The other tales in the volume have been generally forgotten. In "The Return," critics have noted what might be called the primal Anderson scene: In a small midwestern town, a young man, whose

mother has just died, takes a long, last evening walk with a young woman; he is leaving the next day for the big city, for a new life. The third-person narration in this tale—differing from the first-person narration in many Anderson stories of the 1920s—echoes *Winesburg* as well.

"In a Strange Town" is recognizable also as an Anderson work—although perhaps for more negative qualities; it can be said to support Ernest HEMINGWAY's impulse, however criticized, to satirize the writer. The style is Anderson at his most mannered, and the story itself can be said to resemble parody, as if the author were doing the satirist's work on his own. In "The Mountaineers," Anderson seems out of his element, psychologically as well as geographically. One of his strengths is in presenting states of mind, and here the principal figure, the mountain girl, is alien to him; she is a character he cannot fathom. Nor is the narrator, in this case—as opposed to many other instances in Anderson's later work—a figure to be explored psychologically. "A Meeting South" is of continuing interest to the student of American literature, in its presentation of an early fictionalized version of William Faulkner.

Debs, Eugene V.
(1855–1926) *labor leader, Socialist candidate for president*

Born in Terre Haute, Indiana, Debs worked for the railroads as a teenager and helped organize a local railroad firemen's union Terre Haute in 1875; in the next decade he served as a member of the Indiana legislature. In 1893, becoming president of the new AMERICAN RAILWAY UNION, he headed an organization rejecting the concept of a union organized by crafts, as represented by the AMERICAN FEDERATION OF LABOR; the ARU was open to all workers, whether skilled or unskilled—although "workers" meant manufacturing workers, not service workers, who were mostly African American. During the 1894 PULLMAN STRIKE, Debs was arrested for defying a federal injunction against continuing the strike; he was sent to prison for six months in Woodstock, Illinois, outside of Chicago.

In 1898, Debs took the lead in establishing what became the SOCIALIST PARTY OF AMERICA, becoming the party's presidential candidate in 1900 and again in 1904. The following year, he helped found the INDUSTRIAL WORKERS OF THE WORLD in Chicago, although he later withdrew because of the union's radical stance. Running as a Socialist candidate again in 1908 and 1912, he received nearly a million votes in the latter election; he declined to run in 1916. In June 1918, arrested under the WORLD WAR I Espionage Act for criticizing the military draft, Debs insisted that the law was unconstitutional; he allowed no other defense than the constitutionality issue, and as a result, he spent two and a half years in prison. In 1920, running for president a fifth time—from his cell in the Atlanta Penitentiary—he garnered another near-million votes. Debs received a pardon from President Warren HARDING late in 1921; his health damaged in prison, he died five years later in Elmhurst, a Chicago suburb, at the age of 70.

Deere, John
(1804–1886) *inventor of the steel plow*

Born in Rutland, Vermont, a blacksmith by trade—as had been the father of reaper inventor Cyrus MCCORMICK—Deere began to manufacture a steel plow in Grand Detour, Illinois, in 1837. The thick prairie soil was resistant to wooden or cast-iron plows, and Deere provided an implement enhanced by strong steel cutting edges. In 1848, he moved to Moline, Illinois, on the Mississippi River, thereby gaining ready access to transportation; his factory was soon producing plows and other farm implements. Along with the McCormick reaper, the Deere plow helped open up the midwestern PRAIRIE to agriculture.

De Koven, Reginald
(1859–1920) *composer*

Creator of popular operettas, De Koven is best known today for the wedding favorite "Oh Promise Me." Born in Middletown, Connecticut, a

clergyman's son, he settled in Chicago in 1882; he served as music critic for the *Chicago Evening Post* between 1889 and 1912. His greatest success, the operetta *Robin Hood,* opened in Chicago in 1890; the song "Oh Promise Me," which had been written earlier, was interpolated into the production to please one of the singers. Other light musicals included *Rob Roy* and *Maid Marian;* De Koven's two serious operas were *The Canterbury Pilgrims,* premiering in New York in 1917, and *Rip Van Winkle,* opening in Chicago in 1920.

Dell, Floyd
(1887–1969) *writer, editor*

Born in Barry, Illinois, Dell moved with his family to Quincy, Illinois, and then to Davenport, Iowa, and came to Chicago in 1908; he found a reporter's job on the *Chicago Evening Post.* In 1911, at the age of 24, he became editor of the *Post's* literary supplement, the FRIDAY LITERARY REVIEW; his friend from Iowa, George Cram COOK, soon joined him as an assistant. In 1909, he married Margery CURREY, 10 years his senior; they separated in 1913, as he pursued the actress Elaine HYMAN, who subsequently formed a liaison with Theodore DREISER. Later that year, Dell left Chicago for New York, bringing with him the manuscript of Sherwood ANDERSON's first novel, WINDY MCPHERSON'S SON; he was instrumental in getting the novel published. In the same year, his own first book appeared, *Women as World Builders,* a collection of essays about Charlotte Perkins GILMAN, Jane ADDAMS, Emma GOLDMAN, and others, aiming to espouse the cause of feminism—although contemporary readers find the views condescending and paternalistic; writing about Gilman, Dell expresses ambiguity over "independent work" for women with children.

His move to New York led him increasingly to political issues; he took over the editorship of the socialist periodical THE MASSES. In 1916, he became involved also with the PROVINCETOWN PLAYERS, a theatrical group carrying on the Chicago-initiated LITTLE THEATER MOVEMENT; founders included fellow former Iowans and Chicagoans George Cram Cook and his third wife, Susan GLASPELL. Former Chicago actress and former lover Elaine Hyman, now known as Kyra Markham, became associated with the group, as well as the poet and sometime actress Edna St. Vincent Millay, who began a relationship with Dell. In 1918, Dell, Max Eastman, and three others associated with *The Masses* were tried under the WORLD WAR I Espionage Act, accused of antiwar activities; the trial—and a subsequent trial as well—ended in a hung jury. In 1919, Dell married again. The following year he published his best-selling autobiographical novel, MOON-CALF, recounting his boyhood in small-town Illinois and Iowa; in 1921, THE BRIARY-BUSH continued the story, bringing his protagonist to Chicago. A novel published in 1927, *An Unmarried Father*, became the basis for a successful Broadway play, *Little Accident;* two movie versions of the play followed. In the same year, Dell also published a biography of a man he had long admired, Upton SINCLAIR, praising Sinclair's exposures of injustice and hypocrisy in social and economic life. In 1933, the autobiography *Homecoming* appeared, covering much of the material already presented as fiction in *Moon-Calf* and *The Briary-Bush*—sometimes with less candor, sometimes more. Two years later, Dell moved to Washington, D.C., taking a position with the Writers Project of the newly established Works Project Administration; he remained in the post for 12 years. He died in Bethesda, Maryland, at the age of 82.

In Dreiser's THE TITAN, Dell appears as the drama critic Gardner Knowles, "smug and handsome," seducer of the actress Stephanie PLATOW.

Further Reading

Clayton, Douglas. *Floyd Dell: The Life and Times of an American Rebel*. Chicago: Ivan R. Dee, 1994.

Democracy and Social Ethics
Jane Addams
(1902)

Collecting a series of lectures, many published as articles in *Atlantic Monthly, American Journal of Sociology*, and other periodicals, Jane ADDAMS declares in this volume that democracy must be grounded in a "social ethic." Refuting the tenets of SOCIAL DARWINISM, she speaks of the social causes of poverty, affirming the basic equality of all Americans; she declares that the good must be extended to all classes of society—and that all classes must contribute to that good. This early popular volume expresses an optimism that Addams would not always maintain.

Denslow, Arthur W. W.
(1856–1915) *artist, illustrator*

Denslow's fame lies in his collaboration with L. Frank BAUM on THE WONDERFUL WIZARD OF OZ, published in Chicago in 1900. Born in Philadelphia, Denslow published his first illustration 1872 in *Hearth and Home*, the magazine edited by Edward EGGLESTON; he was later one of the illustrators for Mark Twain's 1880 volume, *A Tramp Abroad*. In 1893, he came to Chicago for the WORLD'S COLUMBIAN EXPOSITION, working for the *Chicago Herald;* he sketched scenes from the fair for the newspaper. Later, he established a studio on the ninth floor of the FINE ARTS BUILDING, achieving recognition for his RAND MCNALLY COMPANY advertising posters, as well as for covers and decorations for MONTGOMERY WARD AND COMPANY catalogues. Elbert HUBBARD sought his services in Aurora, New York, for the Roycroft Press, and he illustrated two 1899 Roycroft publications, *The Rime of the Ancient Mariner* and *The Rubáiyát of Omar Khayyám*.

Denslow first collaborated with Baum on the 1899 *Father Goose: His Book*, a verse collection. Denslow and Baum supplied the money to the publisher for color plates, and the book, featuring bright illustrations unprecedented in children's literature, became a success; the team also made up-front payments for their next book, tentatively called "The Emerald City." Appearing in 1900 as *The Wonderful Wizard of Oz*, the volume became one of the best-selling children's books of all time; its use of color revolutionized publishing practices in children's literature. The two men collaborated on a total of three books; Denslow never again achieved the success he gained with the *Oz* volume.

"Departure"   *See* WINESBURG, OHIO.

DePriest, Oscar
(1871–1951) *politician*

Born in Florence, Alabama, coming to Chicago in 1889, DePriest was elected Second Ward alderman in 1915. He was the first African-American alderman in Chicago. Two years later, he was indicted for accepting bribes to allow houses of prostitution and gambling to operate, including those from the owner of the PEKIN THEATER; defended by Clarence DARROW, he was acquitted. In 1928, DePriest was elected as a Republican to the U.S. House of Rep-

Oscar DePriest was the first post-Reconstruction African American to serve in Congress; he was elected in 1928. (*Chicago Historical Society*)

resentatives, the first African-American member of Congress since RECONSTRUCTION; after serving two terms, he was defeated in 1934 by a Democratic candidate, who became the first black Democrat to serve in Congress. During the GREAT DEPRESSION, African-American voters were shifting from the Republican to the Democratic party.

Des Imagistes
(1914)

This poetry anthology was originally collected as the fifth issue of the periodical *Glebe*, published earlier in 1914 by Alfred KREYMBORG. Its contents consisted of poems sent from London by Ezra POUND—most of which had appeared previously in POETRY magazine, causing Harriet MONROE to threaten legal action. Among the poets represented are Pound, Richard ALDINGTON, H.D., James JOYCE, and William Carlos WILLIAMS; because only one poem by Amy LOWELL appeared in the anthology, Lowell published her own collections of imagist poetry; her three volumes of *Some Imagist Poets* excluded verse by Pound.

Des Plaines River

Flowing into the Illinois River, which in turn flows into the Mississippi River, the Des Plaines River is part of the Mississippi system; it lies a short few miles from the CHICAGO RIVER, which is part of the separate Great Lakes system. Indians had long used portage, or the carrying of canoes, to traverse the low divide between the two water systems; French explorers Louis JOLIET and Jacques MARQUETTE followed the same practice in their 1673 journey up the Mississippi to LAKE MICHIGAN.

In 1869, as the railroads began spreading out from the new city of Chicago, William Le Baron JENNEY and Frederick Law OLMSTED completed the first "railroad suburb," the village of Riverside, located along the Des Plaines River on the Burlington-Northern railway line. Leaving the riverbank free and open, Olmstead laid out streets following the river's curve. Writer Ring LARDNER lived in Riverside between 1914 and 1917. Carl

SANDBURG's poem "Happiness," collected in CHICAGO POEMS, presents an immigrant family enjoying a Sunday afternoon by the Des Plaines River.

Dewey, John
(1859–1952) *educator, philosopher*

Born in Burlington, Vermont, Dewey received a Ph.D. from Johns Hopkins University and came to the philosophy department of the UNIVERSITY OF CHICAGO in 1894. Two years later, he established the institution's University Elementary School, or Laboratory School, to demonstrate new progressive ideas in education; the data gathered went into his 1889 *School and Society*. In the realm of education, the term *progressive*—a catchword in many fields at the time—meant to downplay authority, to adopt a child-centered point of view, to refuse to impose ideas and interests on children; among Dewey's precepts were "learning by doing," educating the "whole" child, making schools a "preparation for life." Later critics accused Dewey of introducing permissiveness into education, of denying the importance of discipline and rigor. In 1904, he moved to Columbia University in New York, turning from educational innovation to broader philosophical and social issues. He died in New York City at the age of 93.

Dial

A literary magazine originating in Chicago in 1880, sponsored by the publishing firm of A. C. McClurg and Company, the monthly *Dial* was edited by Francis Fisher BROWNE. Its name came from the Boston periodical of the 1840s, associated with New England writers Margaret Fuller and Ralph Waldo Emerson. Browne bought the magazine from McClurg in 1892; when he died in 1913, it was carried on by his son. During the early years, its editorial policy was conservative, reacting negatively to the new POETRY magazine, calling it "a futile little periodical." In regard to the FREE VERSE of Carl SANDBURG and others, it declared that "even doggerel has its rhythm."

The *Dial* moved to New York in 1918. Under new editorial policies, the periodical became a major outlet for contemporary poetry—in effect, supplanting the once-dominant *Poetry*. In the 1920s, it published the work of Ezra POUND, William Butler YEATS, William Carlos WILLIAMS, and Wallace STEVENS, including Stevens's famed "The Emperor of Ice Cream." Its major achievement came in November 1922 when it presented the first American appearance of T. S. ELIOT's "The Waste Land," the poem that would become a touchstone of MODERNISM. In 1926, poet Marianne MOORE became editor; in 1929—like that other Chicago-born magazine, LITTLE REVIEW, which had also moved away from its birthplace—the *Dial* ceased publication.

dialect writing

Dialect writing is prose or poetry that alters spelling to follow a speaker's pronunciation. Once popular, dialect writing is used rarely today, not only because readers find it inaccessible, but also because it is considered condescending, if not mocking; the pronunciation it renders is nonstandard—due to the speaker's national origin, region, or social class—and thus the nonstandard spelling is seen as inviting ridicule. Dialect is often associated with southern writers and African-American speech, and yet all regions of the country have been subject to the practice; historians point to the Yankee dialect used by New England poet James Russell Lowell in *The Biglow Papers* of 1848.

An early midwestern novel of 1871, Edward EGGLESTON's THE HOOSIER SCHOOLMASTER, employs Indiana dialect, rendering it in a mild and readable form. Yet nearly inaccessible to modern readers is the speech recorded in Joseph KIRKLAND's regional novel of 1887, ZURY: THE MEANEST MAN IN SPRING COUNTY; the central-Illinois dialect is "phonetically exact," according to Hamlin GARLAND, and yet the author sacrificed readability to accuracy. Garland himself, publishing MAIN-TRAVELLED ROADS four years later, used western speech patterns, although generally less obtrusively. A popular writer of mild Indiana dialect was

James Whitcomb RILEY, whose nostalgic and sentimental poems were once widely read. The African-American dialect poetry of Paul Laurence DUNBAR has been praised for its humor and its folklore origins, although it has been criticized for its stereotyping as well.

In late 19th-century Chicago, immigrant speech offered yet another field for dialect writing. The best-known practitioner, Finley Peter DUNNE, employed immigrant Irish speech in his columns for the *Chicago Evening Post.* Besides the goal of humor, Dunne claimed that by speaking through a persona, he could comment more pungently on local and national politics; he could make controversial points he might otherwise withhold.

Another justification for dialect writing has been found in its presumed democratic qualities; in conveying the speech of the common man, it gives voice to those otherwise excluded from literature. Yet again the issue of condescension arises; George ADE, another newspaperman employing dialect—writing humorous columns presenting a wide range of characters, including the African American Pink Marsh—presents his characters with obvious affection, and yet the modern reader sees an unconscious sense of superiority along with the affection.

An example of dialect writing can be found in the various spellings of the word *Indiana*, as it occurs throughout the literature of the region. In *The Hoosier Schoolmaster,* the spelling is Injeanny; in "Under the Lion's Paw," from *Main-Travelled Roads,* it is Ingyannie; to Dunne's Irish spokesman, Mr. Dooley, it becomes Injyanny. Readers today find such spellings both incomprehensible and intimidating. Ring LARDNER, presenting his letters written by a fictional semiliterate baseball player in *YOU KNOW ME AL,* always spelled the place names, such as Milwaukee and Los Angeles, correctly—even though his ballplayer, demonstrating multiple lapses in spelling otherwise, would not have been able to do so. In 1927, when Carl SANDBURG published his *AMERICAN SONGBAG,* a collection of songs and ballads from all regions of the nation, he spoke frankly in his preface of "the butcheries of words" required for an accurate rendering of the songs.

Dingman, Agnes

This character in Hamlin GARLAND's story "At the Branch Road," collected in *MAIN-TRAVELLED ROADS,* is the daughter of an Iowa farmer. Agnes marries a neighboring farmer after her fiancé, Will HANNAN, caught up in a series of misunderstandings, leaves the area. When Will returns seven years later, he finds Agnes, now the mother of a child, ill and weak; she is abused by her husband, as well as living an impoverished existence. Will decides she is "a dying woman" unless she can rest under his care. Taking her child, she flees with him.

Diversey
MacKinlay Kantor
(1928)

In this first novel by MacKinlay KANTOR, a young newspaperman from Iowa comes to Chicago, looking for a job; he befriends a bootlegger and gangster at his rooming house. Gradually, he becomes entangled with the criminal class that supplies liquor to the city—a new subject for novels set during PROHIBITION. The work also depicts the local government corruption brought about by the new underworld, as well as the milieu of working-class boardinghouses, buses, and el trains. As with much fiction of the period, the social drinking of illegal liquor is described; in *Diversey,* the characters drink at parties and at a speakeasy, or illegal drinking establishment. Diversey is the name of an east-west thoroughfare on the North Side.

Donnelley, R. R.
(1836–1899) *publisher, printer*

Founder of the Lakeside Press and the R. R. Donnelley Company, Richard Robert Donnelley became a national figure in publishing and printing. Born in Ontario, Canada, coming to Chicago in 1864, he founded Lakeside Publishing and Printing Company in 1870, followed by R. R. Donnelley and Sons in 1882; the Donnelley company printed the city's first telephone directory in 1886, then went on to print catalogues for MONTGOMERY WARD AND COMPANY and SEARS, ROEBUCK AND COMPANY. In 1903, after Donnelley's death, the Lakeside Press began issuing its annual holiday series, the Lakeside Classics, volumes that have become collector's items; the first volume was Benjamin Franklin's *Autobiography*, considered appropriate because of Franklin's background as a printer. The Lakeside Press Building of 1897, designed by Howard Van Doren SHAW, still stands in Printer's Row, south of the LOOP; the million-square-foot plant on the Near South Side, built by Shaw in 1912, is said to have been the largest structure in the country devoted to printing. The company has served as printer for popular national magazines, including *Life, Look, Time, Ebony, Popular Mechanics, Readers Digest, TV Guide, People,* and *Sports Illustrated* and continues as a major printer today.

Doolittle, Hilda
(1886–1961) *poet*

Born in Pennsylvania, briefly engaged to Ezra POUND, Doolittle, dropped out of Bryn Mawr College and moved to London in 1911, where she joined Pound and his literary circle. Under the name "H.D. Imagiste," Pound sent her poems to POETRY, where her work, an exemplum of IMAGISM, first appeared in January 1913; Pound promoted also the English poet Richard ALDINGTON, whom Doolittle married in 1913. Her work appeared in Pound's 1914 anthology, DES IMAGISTES, and in Amy LOWELL's 1915 anthology, *Some Imagist Poets*. After separating from Aldington, and after bearing a daughter in 1919, she became the companion of Winifred Ellerman, a wealthy woman writing under the name Bryher. In the 1930s, Doolittle was analyzed by Sigmund Freud; in the 1940s, she took up spiritualism. Her *End to Torment*, a memoir of Pound, written during his post–World War II incarceration, was published posthumously in 1979.

Dorsey, Thomas A.
(1899–1993) *composer, choir director*

Dorsey is known as the father of African-American gospel music, first developed in Chicago. Born in Georgia, the son of a Baptist minister, he arrived in Chicago in 1918, becoming a pianist in nightclubs and speakeasies, using the name Georgia Tom; he led a backup band for Gertrude "Ma" RAINEY. He turned later to sacred music, organizing a gospel choir at the Pilgrim Baptist Church on South Indiana Avenue, the largest and most influential black church of the time, formerly the ADLER AND SULLIVAN-designed K.A.M. TEMPLE. His best known piece, "Precious Lord, Take My Hand," was written in 1932 after the death of his wife in childbirth. Dorsey died in Chicago at the age of 93.

Douglas, Stephen A.
(1813–1861) *politician, orator*

Known as "the Little Giant," Douglas is remembered today as an opponent of Abraham LINCOLN in the pre–CIVIL WAR debate over slavery. Born in Vermont, Douglas moved to rural Illinois in 1833 and became a Democratic congressman, then a U.S. senator from Illinois. Advocating western expansion, envisioning a national rail system, he called for the federal government to grant lands to states for the building of railroads; his influence led to development of the ILLINOIS CENTRAL RAILROAD, linking Chicago and Cairo, Illinois, later extending farther southward. Coining the term *popular sovereignty*, Douglas became identified with the doctrine of states' rights; he was instrumental in passage of the Kansas-Nebraska Act of 1854, providing that new territories decide independently whether or not to allow slavery within their borders. In 1858, the downstate lawyer Lincoln, running as a Republican against Douglas for the Senate, challenged his opponent to a series of debates, presenting a strong antislavery position; Douglas retained his seat in the election, but the debates gave Lincoln his first national prominence. At the outbreak of the Civil War, Douglas denounced Southern secession and supported Lincoln's course of action; he died of typhoid fever not long afterward. CAMP DOUGLAS, the Union prison camp for Confederate soldiers during the war, was built on land he had owned in Chicago. As the Lincoln legend grew, Douglas's reputation suffered.

Edgar Lee MASTERS's novel of 1922, CHIL-DREN OF THE MARKET PLACE, provides a defense of Douglas, demonstrating the poet's increasing animus against Lincoln; the book sold poorly.

Douglass, Frederick
(1818–1895) *African-American abolitionist*

Douglas came to Chicago late in life, in 1893, when he denounced the WORLD'S COLUMBIAN EXPOSITION for excluding the achievements of black Americans. Born into slavery near Easton, Maryland, Douglass escaped as a young man to New Bedford, Massachusetts. He published his autobiography, *Narrative of the Life of Frederick Douglass*, in 1845; depicting the life of a runaway slave, the *Narrative* became a major document in the antislavery movement. Establishing a base in Rochester, New York, Douglass published the abolitionist *North Star* for 17 years; a further autobiography, *My Bondage and My Freedom*, appeared in 1855. During the CIVIL WAR, he organized black regiments to fight in the Union cause. In 1893, arriving in Chicago, Douglass served as commissioner of the Republic of Haiti pavilion; Haiti's island of Hispaniola had provided the first landing for Christopher Columbus, whom the fair was unambiguously celebrating. Douglass allied in Chicago with Ida B. WELLS, both figures denouncing the fair as excluding the achievements of black Americans; they protested as well the U.S. government's failure to provide protection from lynching and discrimination. Referring to "the Negro problem," Douglass declared: "There is no Negro problem"; the problem, he argued, is that Americans do not live up to the ideals of their Constitution. He introduced also the young poet Paul Laurence DUNBAR, reading a poem, "Colored Americans," written for the occasion. Douglass died less than two years later at the age of 77.

Dreiser, Theodore
(1871–1945) *novelist*

Labeled both a naturalist and a realist, Dreiser was the principal writer challenging the pervasive "gen-teel tradition" of American literature; he described working-class life, presenting a series of characters who ignore religious and social conventions. Born in Terre Haute, Indiana, the son of a German immigrant father and an American-born Mennonite mother, Dreiser came to Chicago in 1887 at the age of 15; through a benefactor's generosity, he spent a year at Indiana University in 1889–90. Becoming a reporter for the *Chicago Globe,* he moved next to a newspaper in St. Louis; after sojourns in Toledo, Cleveland, and Pittsburgh, he arrived in New York City late in 1894, during a time of economic depression. Joining the ranks of the down-and-out, he experienced the poverty and helplessness that would go into his depiction of George HURSTWOOD in SISTER CARRIE.

Through the connections of his older brother, Paul DRESSER, an actor and songwriter who had "Americanized" his name, Dreiser became editor of a music-publishing magazine; in 1897, leaving the periodical, he turned to freelance writing. His novel SISTER CARRIE, drawing on the life of his sister Emma, appeared in 1900—although the work was suppressed by its publisher; reader Frank NORRIS had accepted the manuscript, but publisher Frank Doubleday, returning from Europe, had deemed the novel immoral and inappropriate, and it received a minimal printing. Dreiser suffered a nervous breakdown—as does the artist-protagonist in the autobiographical novel THE "GENIUS"—and found himself unable to continue his next manuscript; like his fictional alter ego, he worked for a period of time in a railroad carpentry shop. Returning to the world of letters, he served as editor successively of *Smith's* magazine, *Broadway Magazine,* and a women's periodical, *The Delineator.* In 1907, a new publishing firm reissued *Sister Carrie;* the reviews, generally favorable, acknowledged Dreiser as an important writer.

His next novel, JENNIE GERHARDT, appearing in 1911, dealt with another young woman, based on another sister. At the same time, he was writing *The "Genius,"* the autobiographical work that would cause publishing problems because of its account of multiple sexual liaisons. By then Dreiser had separated from his wife and was pursuing an 18-year-old woman—as does the protagonist *The "Genius"*—whose family persuaded her to go abroad; she remained as an impossible ideal for the nearly 40-year-old author.

In 1912, Dreiser published THE FINANCIER, the first of three novels fictionalizing the life of Charles T. YERKES, the Chicago streetcar magnate. Yerkes's early years had been spent in Philadelphia, culminating in a prison term for irregularities involving public funds; Dreiser, using the name Frank COWPERWOOD, detailed his protagonist's financial life, drawn from Philadelphia newspaper records, and extrapolated on the character's personal life as well. The same year he returned to Chicago to research the next phase of Yerkes's career, interviewing those who had known the businessman, making use of records at the NEWBERRY LIBRARY. Dreiser also entered into a friendship with Edgar Lee MASTERS, known then as a partner in Clarence DARROW's law firm; the two men visited the downstate locales that would later appear in SPOON RIVER ANTHOLOGY. While in Chicago, Dreiser met also the actress Elaine HYMAN, beginning a relationship that would continue in New York. In 1914, THE TITAN, the second volume of the Cowperwood trilogy, appeared; the final volume, THE STOIC, would not be published until after Dreiser's death, three decades later.

The autobiographical novel The "Genius" appeared in 1915. Although featuring a visual instead of a literary artist, the tale paralleled Dreiser's career up to that point; its depictions of a bitter marriage and a series of liaisons with other women reflected the author's life as well. Because of the novel's sexual frankness, its sale was halted by the NEW YORK SOCIETY FOR THE SUPPRESSION OF VICE, the organization that would later destroy copies of the LITTLE REVIEW that serialized James JOYCE's Ulysses.

In 1919, Dreiser was called on by a distant cousin, a young married woman named Helen Richardson, who was an aspiring actress, hoping for a career in Hollywood; Dreiser, receiving a screenwriting offer, set out with her for California. Helen soon received small movie roles, including a part in Rudolph Valentino's The Four Horsemen of the Apocalypse; Dreiser began working on the novel that would become AN AMERICAN TRAGEDY, based on a real-life murder case in upstate New York. Three years later, he and Helen traveled to New York, researching sites in the Adirondacks for his novel; from that point on, the couple moved back and forth between the two coasts.

The publication of An American Tragedy in 1925 gave Dreiser, at the age of 54, his first major commercial success. Most reviews were enthusiastic, citing the author as the greatest American novelist of the era—although the double-volume set was banned in Boston in 1927; the publisher, hoping for favorable national publicity, purposely provoked a court case, but the novel was kept unavailable in that city for several years.

During the 1930s, Dreiser identified himself with communism, although he also managed to be quoted making various anti-Semitic statements. In the last years of his life he was unable to complete his two long-undertaken novels, THE BULWARK, first begun in 1915, and The Stoic, the final Cowperwood volume. The two novels, undergoing varying degrees of editing, were published posthumously in 1946 and 1947. After his wife's death in 1942, Dreiser married Helen Richardson; he died of a heart attack in California at the age of 74.

The standard criticism of Dreiser has been to speak of his lumbering, often infelicitous prose; he has been accused of overloading his novels with details, creating stretches of tedium and monotony. Sherwood ANDERSON, while declaring him a great writer, conceded that "no more awkward writer ever lived." In defending Dreiser's style, critics have emphasized his reportorial qualities, noting the power that his prose achieves cumulatively, so that the "human document," as H. L. MENCKEN once called it, becomes forceful and overwhelming. These effects have made Dreiser more successful as a novelist than as a writer of short fiction.

He is also important in American literature for challenging moral strictures and censorship. Anderson, dedicating a volume to Dreiser, wrote that because of him, "those who follow will never have to face the road through the wilderness of Puritan denial"; that road, Anderson added, is one "that Dreiser faced alone." Anderson's first fiction began appearing at the time that The "Genius" was being held up in courts.

Edgar Lee Masters included "Theodore the Poet" in his Spoon River Anthology, paying tribute to his admired friend. The poem is an anomaly in

Masters's collection, in that it is not a graveyard monologue; the poet imagines Dreiser as a boy studying a crawfish hiding in its burrow—a boy who grows up to study men and women hiding in the burrows of the great cities.

Further Reading

Gerber, Philip. *Theodore Dreiser Revisited.* New York: Twayne Publishers, 1992.

Lingeman, Richard. *Theodore Dreiser: At the Gates of the City 1871–1907.* vol. 1. New York: G. P. Putnam's Sons, 1986.

———. *Theodore Dreiser: An American Journey 1908–1945.* vol. 2. New York: G. P. Putnam's Sons, 1990.

Dresser, Paul

(né Dreiser; 1858–1906) *actor, songwriter*

Born in Terre Haute, Indiana, 13 years older than his brother, Theodore DREISER, Dresser—changing his name to sound more "American"—joined a touring minstrel show at the age of 16. He performed in Chicago and elsewhere as a blackface singer, composing comic songs for the troupe and later moved to New York, achieving success as an actor, singer, and songwriter. One of his popular compositions, "ON THE BANKS OF THE WABASH," written in 1897, was later designated the Indiana state song; some of the lyrics are said to have been written by his brother. Other well-known works include "Just Tell Them That You Saw Me," "My Mother Told Me So," and "My Gal Sal"; the last immortalized the name of a brothel proprietor in Evansville, Indiana, with whom Dresser had once lived, who had briefly supported his mother and siblings. "My Gal Sal," written in 1905, was made a hit by Louise Dresser, née Louise Kerlin, a woman Dresser had claimed as his sister and whose theatrical career he launched; Louise Dresser is one of several likely inspirations for the later depiction of Carrie MEEBER in his brother's SISTER CARRIE.

Dresser was a top songwriter in America in the late 1890s. Before the coming of the phonograph, sheet music was the means of spreading and popularizing music, and Dresser founded and owned a song-publishing firm. Yet as the popularity of his sentimental ballads waned—especially as ragtime, a forerunner of JAZZ, came to the fore—Dresser, having pursued an indulgent lifestyle, died penniless at the age of 47.

His life was portrayed, with little accuracy, in the 1942 movie *My Gal Sal*, starring Victor Mature as Dresser and a singing-dubbed Rita Hayworth.

"Drink"   *See* WINESBURG, OHIO.

Drouet, Charles

A character in Theodore DREISER's SISTER CARRIE, Drouet is Carrie MEEBER's first lover, the man who rescues her from poverty. Although charming, he is presented as shallow and careless; Carrie realizes also that he has no intention of marrying her. He leaves, if reluctantly, when he learns that Carrie has been seeing his friend George HURSTWOOD. Later, after Carrie has become a successful New York actress, Drouet calls on her, assuming that their relationship can be renewed; when she makes clear her lack of interest in him, he is last seen in his usual pursuit of pleasure. Unlike Carrie and Hurstwood, he does not change significantly; his role in life undergoes no major alteration.

Dround, Henry I.

This character appears in Robert HERRICK's novel *THE MEMOIRS OF AN AMERICAN CITIZEN.* Like David MARSHALL in Henry B. FULLER's *WITH THE PROCESSION*, Henry Dround is a once-successful businessman whose sense of honor has prevented him from keeping up with a rapacious new era. His meatpacking company faces ruin—except that his wife, Jane DROUND, without his knowledge, spurs employee Van HARRINGTON on to bold, unscrupulous action, thereby saving the company.

Dround, Jane

A character in Robert HERRICK's novel *THE MEMOIRS OF AN AMERICAN CITIZEN,* Jane is the feminine counterpart of the main character, Van HAR-RINGTON, whom the reader is supposed to judge as morally reprehensible. Jane is to be judged as reprehensible as well, although modern readers have a hard time doing so; she is a strong woman, and it is she, set against Harrington's weak and childlike wife, who encourages the businessman-narrator, who hardens his will as he resolves to build his expanding empire. Moreover, she is the outsider—although, because of her wealth and position, she is not necessarily perceived as such—because she is the daughter of a legendary half-breed trader, who made a fortune dealing with the Indians and the government.

A common 19th-century practice in fiction was to portray wholesome heroines as blond, while the alluring, if ultimately unsuitable, women were brunet; Herrick, placing Jane in the exotic category, is drawing on this tradition. He likely felt, too, that his readers would find her dangerous qualities more credible if they were embodied in such a woman. Yet modern readers note the problems she faces; as a woman she is tightly bound to society, and all she can do is live through a man. She has reveled in Harrington's success, in his power: "I have lived a man's life," she says in satisfaction. Herrick is not suggesting a modern-day gender confusion, but rather the idea that a strong woman can exert her strength only vicariously. The author depicts the two characters as soulmates, making the veiled suggestion that they should have been lovers.

Dudley, Herman

The first-person narrator and principal character in Sherwood ANDERSON's story "The Man Who Became a Woman," collected in HORSES AND MEN, the young Herman has left his respectable family background and become a "swipe," or groom, on the horse-racing circuit. The sexual ambiguity suggested in the story's title is implied in various ways—from the love that Herman acknowledges for the older Tom MEANS, from Herman's never having been with a woman, from his visit to a saloon where his mirrored reflection seems to be that of a girl, from the drunken stable-hands' taking the

young man for a girl one night in the stable loft. In the last climactic scene, running from the men in the darkness, Herman comes upon an old slaughterhouse grounds; he falls into the skeleton of a horse, its ribs enfolding and terrifying him. The fright of the experience frees him from his confusion; he says good-bye to the gelding he has been grooming and leaves the life of horseracing. He eventually marries.

Dunbar, Paul Laurence
(1872–1906) *African-American poet and novelist*

In 1893, at the age of 21, Dunbar was invited to Chicago for the WORLD'S COLUMBIAN EXPOSITION and shared a platform with the aging spokesman Frederick DOUGLASS; his recitation of his poem "Colored Americans" came after Douglass's speech on "The Race Problem in America." Born in Dayton, Ohio, Dunbar achieved early notice with two privately printed volumes, the 1982 *Oak and Ivy* and the 1895 *Majors and Minors;* the latter volume, praised by critic William Dean HOWELLS, brought Dunbar to national attention. Howells wrote the introduction to the poet's next collection, *Lyrics of Lowly Life,* published in 1896, a well-received volume employing DIALECT WRITING and folk materials. Other works include an 1898 collection of short stories, *Folks from Dixie,* and a novel, *The Sport of the Gods,* published in 1902. He died of tuberculosis in Dayton at the age of 33. His *Complete Poems* appeared in 1913.

One of Dunbar's most anthologized poems is "We Wear the Mask," a nondialect work; the poet speaks of the duplicity that African Americans must practice, the public hiding of true feelings, behind "the mask that grins and lies." Yet his original fame came from dialect poems, works for which he has been criticized; he himself expressed reluctance in employing dialect, although he understood it to be the source of his popularity. In Langston HUGHES's 1930 novel NOT WITHOUT LAUGHTER, a character keeps Dunbar's *Complete Poems* on her shelf, yet criticizes the poet for the image he creates of African Americans, condemning his focusing on lower-class life and speech.

Dunne, Finley Peter
(1867–1936) *journalist, humorist*

A native Chicagoan, Dunne began his newspaper career in 1884 at the age of 16. Covering baseball news for the CHICAGO DAILY NEWS, he is credited with expanding baseball coverage from a listing of statistics to a narrative reporting of events; he is credited also with coining the term *southpaw* for a left-handed pitcher. In 1892, working for the *Chicago Evening Post,* he wrote his first story in Irish dialect, following the then popular practice of DIALECT WRITING. In October of the next year, he created the character Martin J. Dooley, or Mr. Dooley, a tavern owner in the Irish community of Bridgeport. Mr. Dooley initially restricted his commentary to local topics and personages, such as Charles T. YERKES or George M. PULLMAN; he later went on to national figures, including William Jennings BRYAN, Theodore ROOSEVELT, and President William MCKINLEY. The first collection of columns, *Mr. Dooley in Peace and War,* was published in 1898; *Mr. Dooley in the Hearts of His Countrymen* appeared the following year. In 1900, Dunne moved to New York, continuing to write columns for national syndication; the hundreds of Mr. Dooley tales eventually filled 10 separate volumes.

Dunne claimed that dialect usage allowed him to say things that might otherwise get him in trouble, such as "to call an alderman a thief." When President Grover CLEVELAND sent troops to Chicago during the PULLMAN STRIKE, Mr. Dooley pointed out George M. Pullman's seeming privileges: "This here Pullman makes th' sleepin' cars an' th' Constitootion looks afther Pullman." During the Philippines conflict after the SPANISH-AMERICAN WAR, Mr. Dooley remarks that a man who sends a country to war—he is referring to President McKinley—ought to do some of the fighting himself; a listener wonders if Mr. Dooley is antiexpansionist, at which point the tavern owner threatens to "smash in ye'er head." Mr. Dooley expresses candid opinions, but he is officially too unsophisticated to take responsibility for them.

In Edna FERBER's 1917 novel *FANNY HERSELF,* the Irish priest in Winnebago, Wisconsin, is depicted as reading Mr. Dooley; in the last portion of her 1926 SHOW BOAT, set in a Chicago of earlier times, Ferber mentions "Pete Dunne," George ADE, and others, spotted at a local restaurant. Like Ade, Dunne is a once-famous writer whose name is barely known today.

Du Sable, Jean Baptiste Point
(1745–1818) *first non-Indian resident of the site that is now Chicago*

Of part-African heritage, believed to have been born in Haiti to a French father and Haitian mother, Du Sable arrived in the Midwest from Quebec; his wife was a member of the POTAWATOMI nation. Records are scarce, but he is known to have run a trading post in what is now Michigan City, Indiana, in the late 1770s; he lived in Detroit in the early 1880s. In about 1784, he established a fur-trading post at the mouth of the CHICAGO RIVER, expanding his holdings to include a mill, a smokehouse, and a dairy. In 1800, he sold his property and left the area; the next buyer was John KINZIE, later a survivor of the FORT DEARBORN massacre. Parish records in St. Charles, Missouri, indicate that Du Sable died there at the age of 72.

The Du Sable League was formed in Chicago in 1928 to commemorate the city's first settler; a representation of Du Sable's house was shown at the 1933 world's fair in Chicago.

Dutcher, John

A character in Hamlin GARLAND's novel *ROSE OF DUTCHER'S COOLLY,* "pappa John" is the prototypical sturdy midwestern farmer, a taciturn man, yet a devoted father to his only child, Rose DUTCHER. His wife died when Rose was young, and he continues to worry about his daughter's welfare; her religious instruction, about which he cares little, is not at issue, but rather her moral instruction—her protection from the natural, or "pagan," forces experienced by those who live amid nature. Later, John Dutcher agrees to support her educational ambitions, little realizing that she will no longer be content to remain at home; he weeps when he understands she will leave him permanently.

In economic terms, Dutcher is prosperous, making him better off than the farmers whose harsh lives Garland described in the earlier stories of MAIN-TRAVELLED ROADS. In an obvious self-reference, Garland has his character Warren MASON remark about "the new school of fiction" that makes farmers into "heroic sufferers"; Mason, a city man, rejects such depictions, as seemingly does Garland himself in this work.

Dutcher, Rose

The principal character in Hamlin GARLAND's novel ROSE OF DUTCHER'S COOLLY, Rose, having lost her mother as a child, grows up with her father and aunt on an isolated Wisconsin farm. Her independence and superiority of character are evident at an early age, as well as her physical beauty. Her first significant experience comes when she sees a traveling circus and falls in love at a distance with a handsome acrobat; she contemplates this new ideal, which inspires her to greater ambitions. When Doctor Thatcher, from the state capital of Madison, visits her school and is impressed by her scholarship, she tells of her wish to be a writer; Thatcher makes it possible for her to go to a preparatory school and then to the University of Wisconsin. Her next step is Chicago, where she goes, not to work, but to experience the larger world; her father continues to support her. She aspires to be a writer, although her poems are considered derivative by Warren MASON, the man she eventually marries. Her time in the city is taken up by social activity, and she meets professional and intellectual figures who are overwhelmed by her "promise." Yet she makes no effort to become economically self-sufficient, and the reader is forced to see her triumph in the big city, the culmination of her aspirations since childhood, as simply the making of an advantageous marriage.

Critics have noted references in the novel to Rose's sexuality, to her "pagan" sensibilities in her natural childhood setting; while on the farm, Rose is portrayed as responding to sexual impulses, although never in specific terms, never with a loss of "virtue." Once she comes to Chicago, she acts as properly as any late-Victorian maiden; the institution of marriage is questioned by her associates—as are traditional gender roles, as is matrimonial fidelity—and yet she is portrayed as maintaining the proper, sentimentally appropriate virtues for a young woman of culture.

dynamite

Invented by Swedish chemist Alfred B. Nobel in 1866, the new explosive was hailed by revolutionary groups as a democratic weapon because it could be wielded by the common man. Johann MOST, arriving in America in 1882, distributed his *Science of Revolutionary Warfare,* giving instructions for making dynamite bombs. "A pound of dynamite is worth a bushel of bullets," declared Haymarket anarchist August SPIES. Lucy PARSONS's article of 1884, "TO TRAMPS," speaks of the tools of warfare that "Science has placed in the hands of the poor man"; Parsons concludes her exhortation: *"Learn the Use of Explosives!"*

"Dynamiter"   See CHICAGO POEMS.

E

"The Eagle That Is Forgotten"
(1911)

This poem by Vachel LINDSAY is a tribute to Governor John P. ALTGELD, one of Lindsay's boyhood heroes. Defeated politically for pardoning the remaining anarchists of the HAYMARKET AFFAIR, Altgeld was viewed by many as hero and martyr; he died in 1902 at the age of 54.

The poet addresses the governor as the "eagle," referring not only to a national emblem, but to a classical symbol of strength as well. Yet in the passage of time, the poet laments, this eagle is no longer remembered. As for his foes, they rejoiced secretly when they buried him, even though they put on a show of mourning. As for the others—the poor, the scorned—they mourned him truly, but now they have forgotten him as well. Yet "a hundred white eagles," the poet declares, have arisen as sons of this eagle; these are men who carry on his valor, his zeal. It is better "to live in mankind"—that is, to live one's ideals in actual human life—than "to live in a name." Altgeld's name is forgotten, but his wisdom and valor live on.

This poem, finding newspaper publication, is what led Harriet MONROE to write to Lindsay, soliciting work for her new magazine POETRY. In a later poem about his other boyhood hero, William Jennings BRYAN—"Bryan, Bryan, Bryan, Bryan," collected in the 1920 *The Golden Whales of California and Other Rhymes in the American Language*—Lindsay will again use the eagle image for Altgeld, linking Bryan with "Altgeld the Eagle."

Eastland disaster

On July 24, 1915, the ship *Eastland* was chartered to bring Western Electric employees and their families to a company picnic in Michigan City, Indiana. While the ship remained in its Chicago docking, passengers crowded to one side to watch a passing boat, and the *Eastland* capsized, drowning more than 800 people, becoming the worst maritime disaster in Chicago history. In September, Carl SANDBURG wrote an article in the INTERNATIONAL SOCIALIST REVIEW, blaming greedy businessmen, as well as the secretary of commerce, for allowing the use of the boat, an "unstable ancient hoodoo tub." A temporary morgue for victims, set up at the Second Regiment armory on West Washington Street, was later transformed into Harpo Studios by television personality Oprah Winfrey.

École des Beaux-Arts

This renowned art school in Paris, dating to 1648 but established under its present name in 1796, stood in the 19th century as the upholder of the French academic tradition. In architecture, the tradition meant the imitation of classical and Renaissance forms, including domes, arches, columns, and colonnades; this doctrine triumphed in the buildings of the WORLD'S COLUMBIAN EXPOSITION of 1893. Louis SULLIVAN, who had studied briefly at the École and rejected its teachings, designed for the fair his anomalous, multicolored Transportation Building; it was positioned away from the others. The ART INSTITUTE, built at the same time, maintains the neoclassical style, as do the original Chicago Public Library, the FIELD MUSEUM OF NATURAL HISTORY, the SHEDD AQUARIUM, and the MUSEUM OF SCIENCE AND INDUSTRY.

Edwards, Tom

This character appears in Sherwood ANDERSON's story "An Ohio Pagan," collected in HORSES AND MEN. Tom is an orphan who has rejected schooling, preferring an outdoors way of life, first as a caretaker and driver of horses, then as a member of a threshing crew. Yet he feels yearnings in his soul, and being impressed by the powerful Christian faith of his employer, he sees the young god Jesus walking in the fields. Soon the subject of his visions shifts, however, and he sees the forms of women in nature—in trees, clouds, and water. He realizes he must pursue schooling, as he will then be fit for a woman; he has become a pagan, not a Christian, and he sees women, not Jesus, in the world about him.

"Effie Whittlesy"
George Ade
(1886)

First published as one of the "STORIES OF THE STREETS AND OF THE TOWN" columns in the *CHICAGO RECORD*, this short story by George ADE was collected in the 1903 volume *In Babel: Stories of Chicago*. William Dean HOWELLS later included the story his 1920 anthology, *The Great Modern American Stories*. After a Chicago woman hires a maid, the woman's husband realizes that the maid is from his rural hometown; he begins treating her as an equal, not as a servant—and the wife insists that she be let go. The husband complies, giving the woman train fare back home. Howells, in his introduction, noting that the small town is being swallowed up by the city, declares the short tale to be important to American fiction, to be "of a value far beyond most American novels."

"The Egg"   *See* THE TRIUMPH OF THE EGG.

Eggleston, Edward
(1837–1902) *novelist, early midwestern writer*

Born in Vevay, Indiana, Eggleston spent a brief period as a circuit-riding minister for the Methodist church. In the late 1960s, living in EVANSTON, Illinois, he edited several religious-based periodicals. Moving to New York in 1870, editing the monthly magazine *Hearth and Home*, he gained sudden fame by serializing in its pages his novel THE HOOSIER SCHOOLMASTER—written, he claimed, to fill space in the magazine; it appeared in book form in 1871 and achieved great popular success. Depicting crude, often mean-spirited backwoods folks in a southern Indiana locale, the novel goes beyond the practices of LOCAL COLOR, to what the author called "provincial realism"; it incorporates DIALECT WRITING as well. In 1874, Eggleston published THE CIRCUIT RIDER, set in early 19th-century Ohio, and three years later THE GRAYSONS: A STORY OF ABRAHAM LINCOLN. Although pioneering in rural REALISM, the author followed plot formulas that today are considered sentimental.

In the preface to *The Hoosier Schoolmaster*, Eggleston notes that the rural people depicted in literature so far have been New Englanders; it is Easterners' customs and manners that have filled American volumes. Foreshadowing Hamlin GARLAND by 20 years, he advocates not only realism, but regionalism as well, proclaiming that western states—meaning, in 1870, midwestern states—provide equally worthwhile material. Fifty years after Eggleston's declaration, Sherwood ANDERSON makes the same case in the 1921 story "Milk Bottles," collected in HORSES AND MEN.

Eighteenth Amendment   *See* PROHIBITION.

Eliot, T. S.
(1888–1965) *major poet of modernism*

Born in St. Louis, educated at Harvard University, Eliot moved to England in 1914; in his early years abroad, fellow expatriate poet Ezra POUND provided support and encouragement. At Pound's urging, Harriet MONROE published Eliot's breakthrough poem, "The Love Song of J. Alfred Prufrock," in POETRY in 1915—although her conservative tastes led to the delay of nearly a year; after Monroe arbitrarily cut a line from another piece, Eliot stopped submitting work to the magazine. With the publication of "The Waste Land" in 1922—in the former Chicago magazine, the DIAL—the poet entered the century's literary pantheon as a major voice of MODERNISM; the work was followed by a large output of poetry, essays, and drama. Eliot received the Nobel Prize in literature in 1948. His collection of light verse, *Old Possum's Book of Practical Cats*, published in 1939, became the basis of the long-running theater musical *Cats*.

Emerald City

The fictional city in L. Frank BAUM's THE WONDERFUL WIZARD OF OZ, Emerald City is a sham metropolis, a façade—not the grand and powerful capital that the travelers from afar had expected; the city is green because the people wear green spectacles. An inspiration for Emerald City is said to have been the "White City," the buildings of the WORLD'S COLUMBIAN EXPOSITION; Baum and his illustrator, Arthur W. W. DENSLOW, were aware that the gleaming buildings, made from painted plasterboard, were fragile and temporary. Politically minded readers have identified Emerald City as an allegorical version of Washington, D.C., and the travelers represent COXEY'S ARMY, coming into a capital that is seemingly powerless to aid them.

Emma McChesney & Company
Edna Ferber
(1915)

This collection of short fiction gathers the final stories featuring Edna FERBER's vibrant business-woman, Emma MCCHESNEY. The volume suffers in comparison with the two earlier collections, in that the long-divorced Emma succumbs to matrimony and conjugal happiness. She goes so far as to follow temporarily the wifely expectation of giving up work and staying at home; becoming a grandmother, she temporarily plays a grandmotherly role as well. Reacting against both of these restraints, Emma returns to her natural persona, that of an energetic woman of business, although the briskness and edge of her earlier characterization is gone.

Erik Dorn
Ben Hecht
(1921)

This autobiographically based novel by Ben HECHT tells of a newspaper reporter who travels from Chicago to Berlin and leaves his wife for another woman. Reviewers considered it racy for its time, although its mannered narrative style caused it to be labeled as unintelligible and opaque as well. Readers noted also that the romanticized hero, portrayed as being desired by three different women, seems only to half-understand his narcissism; several years later, critic Stuart Sherman, referring to *Erik Dorn* and a later work, *Humpty Dumpty*, accused Hecht of "an atrophy of the normal emotional faculties." In the novel, the poet Old Carl is Carl SANDBURG—as the poet Lief Lindstrum will be in Hecht's later novel, *Gargoyles*—and Warren Lockwood, a fellow writer, is modeled on Sherwood ANDERSON. In his 1954 autobiography, *A Child of the Century*, Hecht writes that his seven-year friendship with Anderson ended when the older writer read *Erik Dorn*, then enigmatically terminated their friendship. In 1927, the novel was reprinted in a Modern Library edition.

Essanay Film Manufacturing Company

For a brief period, at the end of the first decade of the 20th century, Chicago was a motion-picture capital, producing perhaps one-fifth of the world's movies. The reigning studio was Essanay, founded in 1907; its name, spelling out the initials *S* and *A*, came from the names of cofounder George K. Spoor and William G. ANDERSON. The studio established some of the early traditions of cinema, presenting a new set of celebrities to the public as well. Anderson, calling himself Broncho Billy, became the screen's first cowboy; Francis X. BUSHMAN, handsome and muscular, became the first matinee idol. Comedian Ben TURPIN, featured in the studio's initial movie, went on to fame for pratfalls and crossed eyes; comedian Wallace BEERY, soon to marry Essanay bit player Gloria SWANSON, starred in the company's early popular comedy series, *Sweedie, the Swedish Maid,* wearing woman's clothing and a blond wig. The greatest silent comedian of all, Charlie CHAPLIN, made one film for the Chicago studio, the 1915 *His New Job,* before making California his preferred location.

Ring LARDNER and George ADE wrote screenplays for Essanay; Louella PARSONS, born in Freeport, Illinois, worked for the studio before becoming a Hollywood gossip columnist. Katherine Anne PORTER, trying for an acting career before achieving fame as a writer, spent six months in Chicago in 1914, working as an extra in Essanay productions. Two Essanay employees, Donald J. Bell and Albert S. Howell, established BELL AND HOWELL, the firm that supplied the nation's motion-picture equipment.

In 1908, Essanay built studios on Argyle Street on the North Side; its rival was the earlier-established firm, also located on the North Side, the Selig Polyscope Company. Founder William N. SELIG drew on Chicago writer L. Frank BAUM for *Oz* stories, as well as pioneered in newsreel distribution. Yet the moment for midwestern filmmaking soon passed; both firms were out of business by the end of the century's second decade. In the case of Essanay, the loss of Chaplin, as well as legal problems—and the fact that sunny weather was sending the entire film industry to the West Coast—led to its closing in 1917.

"Euclid"   *See* THE CONGO AND OTHER POEMS.

Evanston

This suburb north of Chicago is the home of NORTHWESTERN UNIVERSITY, founded in 1855. The city provides the milieu for two novels with academic settings. In Henry B. FULLER's 1919 BERTRAM COPE'S YEAR and Willa CATHER's 1925 THE PROFESSOR'S HOUSE, the suburb is called, respectively, Churchton and Hamilton. Evanston was also the home of Frances E. WILLARD, president of the WOMEN'S CHRISTIAN TEMPERANCE UNION.

Everleigh sisters, Ada
(1876–1960) and
Minna
(1878–1948) *owners of a legendary upscale brothel*

Born in Kentucky under the name of Lester, Minna and Ada Everleigh toured with a theatrical company until they arrived in Chicago in 1899. They bought and redecorated a 50-room mansion on South Dearborn Street, in what was known as the LEVEE district, opening it as the Everleigh Club in February 1900. The establishment became increasingly exclusive, catering to the wealthy, requiring recommendation for admittance; then-lawyer Edgar Lee MASTERS was among the clients. The Everleigh sisters claimed the highest standards among their employees, allowing no alcohol or drug addiction—in contrast to the practice described by Upton SINCLAIR in THE JUNGLE, in which a character is kept addicted to drugs to make her a willing brothel worker. Potential scandal came to the Everleigh Club in 1905, when the sole heir to a department store fortune, Marshall Field II, was shot, allegedly on the club's premises; the matter was hushed up, leaving rumors to continue flourishing, as in Masters's poem "Rosie Roberts" in SPOON RIVER ANTHOLOGY, and in Sherwood ANDERSON's novel MARCHING MEN. The club was closed in an antivice campaign by Mayor Carter Harrison Jr. in 1911. The sisters retired to New York City, and the building was razed in 1933.

An Eye for an Eye
Clarence Darrow
(1905)

Written to serve DARROW's lifelong campaign against the death penalty, the novel is set on the night before a workingman is to be hanged for murder. The work records the prisoner's story as he tells it through the night to a visitor; the prisoner is presented as a decent man, provoked to violence by poverty. Darrow illustrates another favorite theme as well, that the judicial system favors the rich over the poor.

F

Fabian Society

Founded in 1883, this English socialist organization took its name from a Roman general who practiced diversion and avoidance, not confrontation. The Fabian Society repudiated the concept of class struggle and revolution; it set as its goal a gradually developing SOCIALISM. Among the founders were the married couple Beatrice and Sidney Webb; the Webbs visited HULL-HOUSE in 1898. Other members included playwright George Bernard Shaw and poet Rupert BROOKE. Alice HAMILTON, observing the Webbs at Hull-House, wrote later that their theoretical radicalism seemed contradicted by what she herself saw in practice— that is, their apparent snobbery; Hamilton made note of their "total lack of democratic feeling."

"Fables in Slang"

Starting as newspaper columns, later appearing in magazines and other formats, George ADE's fables were brief humorous tales, followed by humorous "morals," or lessons. Ade was following the example of ancient Greek writer Aesop and 17th-century French poet Jean de La Fontaine—as well as the selections of fables presented in McGuffey's Readers, the standard children's textbook of the day. Ade's first fable, published in 1897 in the CHICAGO RECORD, was titled "The Fable of Sister Mae, Who Did as Well as Could Be Expected"; its moral concluded that "Industry and Perseverance

Bring a Sure Reward." The first book collection, *Fables in Slang,* was published in 1899 by STONE AND KIMBALL; further volumes, including *More Fables* and *Forty Modern Fables,* appeared between 1900 and 1920. ESSANAY FILM MANUFACTURING COMPANY turned nearly 60 Ade fables into short films between 1915 and the studio's closing in 1917. In the 1930s, the author revised his earlier fables for newspaper syndication, continuing the popularity of tales that had been written three decades previously; the fables were drawn in a syndicated comic strip as well. In 1932, a collection of sports material, *The Omnibus of Sport,* edited by Grantland Rice, included Ade's "The Fable in Slang of the Caddy Who Hurt His Head While Thinking."

"Factory Windows Are Always Broken"
See THE CONGO AND OTHER POEMS.

Fanny Herself
Edna Ferber
(1917)

An immensely popular novelist and playwright for more than half a century, Edna FERBER wrote this semiautobiographical novel early in her career, at the age of 31. Running serially in *The American Magazine* before book publication, the work deals at length with her Jewish identity, a theme she had often avoided. At a time when writers were still dealing in stereotypes and expressing casual anti-Semitism—and would continue to do so for another four or five decades—Ferber tells of the temple in her Wisconsin town, its rabbi, its congregation, as well as anti-Semitic incidents experienced by the town's small Jewish community. Although Winnebago, Wisconsin, is the real-life Appleton, Wisconsin, the anti-Semitic tribulations of the character Clarence HEYL come from Ferber's girlhood in the town of Ottumwa, Iowa; she relates these experiences in her 1938 autobiography, *A Peculiar Treasure*.

The volume introduces to the American novel a successful businesswoman, Fanny BRANDEIS. Fanny consciously strives to make money in a male-oriented corporate world; her mother, Molly BRANDEIS, having taken over the family store, had provided the precedent. Like Ferber's character in an earlier series of short stories, Emma MCCHESNEY, Molly is based on Ferber's mother; in the novel, when Emma, the traveling saleswoman, visits the Brandeis store, Ferber is having two versions of her mother meet each other. A further identifiable figure is Rabbi Kirsch of the prosperous Chicago synagogue, based on Emil HIRSCH, a well-known reform rabbi. The Chicago mail-order firm of Haynes-Cooper combines MONTGOMERY WARD AND COMPANY and SEARS, ROEBUCK AND COMPANY.

Synopsis

CHAPTERS 1–4

When Ferdinand Brandeis dies, his general store, located in Winnebago, Wisconsin, is heavily in debt; Brandeis had been a dreamer, not a businessman. His widow, Molly, 38 years old, takes over running the business, although the women at the small Congregation Emanu-el find it inappropriate for her to work. Yet soon she is off to Chicago on her first buying trip, taking with her 13-year-old Fanny. Among her purchases is a dusty, leftover set of 200 religious figures; Molly, knowing that Winnebago is two-thirds Catholic, brings the figures back to her store, washes them, displays them in the window, and sells them within a week. Her $400 profit lets Molly know that she can succeed.

Fanny realizes she is different from other children in Winnebago; she stays out of school on Jewish holidays, and she goes to temple on Friday night and Saturday morning. On the Day of Atonement, she attends services, where her 15-year-old brother, Theodore BRANDEIS, plays the violin, stirring the congregation with the "poignant wail" of his instrument. Fanny fasts for 24 hours; Molly disapproves of a young person's fasting but praises Fanny, not because of her seeming piety, but because she did what she set out to do.

Carrying back from the library a copy of Émile ZOLA's novel *The Ladies' Paradise*, Fanny comes across a group of schoolboys tormenting the thin, sickly Clarence Heyl, jeering at him, knocking him into the mud. They ridicule the name Clarence—and then they call him "the Name"; the Name, although Ferber does not specify it, is the anti-Semitic "sheeny." Fanny, enraged, sets upon the bullies and breaks up the altercation. Later, she talks to her mother about the Zola novel, which tells of the coming of the modern department store in Paris, putting small stores out of business; her mother has talked about her own similar situation, in which midwestern mail-order businesses are hurting small-town merchants. Although Fanny refers to *The Ladies' Paradise* as a work of "social protest," it has also been seen as a celebration of the department store and the rise of consumer culture—and she is "thrilled and fascinated" by it.

CHAPTERS 5–7

A famous violinist, Levine Schabelitz, comes to Winnebago to give a concert, and Theodore's teacher arranges for his pupil to play for him. Schabelitz says that Theodore must go to Dresden to study. Molly decides she and Fanny must scrimp in expenditures and finance his study abroad. Fanny has meanwhile sketched a humorous caricature of Schabelitz, which the violinist sees and appreciates.

Theodore leaves, and Molly and Fanny begin their self-denying existence; Molly devotes her life all the more resolutely to the store. In high school, Fanny writes a thesis, "A Piece of Paper," based on research at a local paper mill, in which she finds hundreds of girls working in rag-rooms filled with dust, breathing lung-damaging air. She gains access to the mill by taking a job there, insisting she must actually work on the spot to get her reportage right. In her thesis, she dramatizes the human cost of making a single piece of paper, and her teacher, impressed, shows her work to the editor of the local newspaper; the editor labels it as socialistic and anarchistic. After graduation, Fanny begins working in the store, and she realizes she is good at selling, at judging people's tastes, at understanding their wants. The store is profitable now, and most of the money goes to Theodore. Fanny meets her mother's old friend Emma McChesney, the traveling saleswoman.

Theodore has been gone six years. He writes to announce his marriage to a performer in a Vienna music hall; he needs money, which Molly cables to him. Yet Molly becomes less spirited in her business, and Fanny takes over the buying; she supervises the window displays and makes changes in the store's format. That year the store has its most successful Christmas season; the two women work hard, staying open until 10 or 11 at night. After Christmas is over, Molly becomes ill. Fanny, alarmed, calls a doctor, who tells her that her mother has pneumonia. To Fanny's grief, Molly is soon dead.

CHAPTER 8

The town of Winnebago pays respect to Molly Brandeis. A new resolve is forming in Fanny's mind; she will not keep up the store, but instead make something of herself in the larger world. Nor will she allow handicaps such as race or religion to stand in the way; she will become a successful woman, achieving money and status. Yet the "thousands of years of persecution behind her" give her a sense of sympathy with the downtrodden, and she will use that understanding to help overcome her obstacles.

She sells Brandeis' Bazaar, planning to leave Winnebago. She learns that the Chicago mail-order firm of Haynes-Cooper needs someone to run the infants' wear department. She knows that the small-town merchant feels threatened by the mail-order houses, and yet she knows, too, that opportunities exist there. Before she leaves, she

visits Father Fitzpatrick of the local Catholic church, a longtime friend of her mother's; she tells him of her plans to join Haynes-Cooper in Chicago. He remarks on her talent for drawing and laments that it was not developed further, since the money went for Theodore's study, not hers. Fanny asks, "Who ever heard of a woman cartoonist!" They speak of her Jewishness, which she labels a handicap, although Father Fitzpatrick calls it an asset, saying that being persecuted, being hounded from place to place, leaves a mark on people, differentiating them, making them more emotional and sensitive. She visits Rabbi Thalmann as well, seeing photographs of his confirmation classes; she is in none of the pictures, as she had never taken formal steps toward avowing her creed. At the last Friday night service she attends, a stranger comes down the aisle, whom Fanny realizes is Clarence Heyl, back from the West, where he has distinguished himself as a naturalist. The welcoming he receives from the congregation keeps him from following after Fanny, as she disappears into the hotel where she is staying her final night in Winnebago.

CHAPTER 9

Fanny is interviewed by Michael Fenger, general manager of Haynes-Cooper, a man who lives by system and efficiency. Fenger knows her history and believes she can bring growth to the infants' wear department, which is not performing as successfully as it should. The department needs a woman, he says, even though he never employs a woman if he can help it. He then asks for an opinion of an etching on the wall, and Fanny replies honestly that she does not like it, that it is too flowery, using too many lines. Fenger agrees, and then asks if she is a Jew. After a moment, Fanny replies that she is not; Fenger smiles for the first time, commenting that he cannot blame her for getting rid of "excrescences," since being a woman in business is handicap enough. He tells her that suggestions will be welcome, and she offers one right away. She has already toured the enormous 15-story building, and she has seen stock boys and stock girls walking miles every day as they fill bins and carry orders. She suggests they do what the paper boy in Winnebago used to do: wear roller skates. Fenger acts at once to implement the suggestion, telling Fanny she has earned six months' salary in the last five minutes.

She meets the current buyer in the department, and she already feels sorry for him, knowing she will surpass him. At her next meeting with Fenger, she outlines the changes that need to be made, noting that the infants' wear department does not understand women, particularly women who work in mills and factories, who live on farms, who live in isolated villages. Her working at Brandeis' Bazaar has taught her that these women like lacey, ribboned clothing for their babies, and these garments must be attractive, even as the prices are kept low; she suggests a "mother's guide" as well, to answer questions and give advice. The situation changes when Fenger invites Fanny to have dinner with him; she refuses, knowing he is married—and knowing, too, that any such activity could spoil her long-laid-out career plans. He makes amends by inviting her to dine with him and his wife at his home. Fanny understands that by having lied to him earlier, demonstrating her lack of integrity, she had made herself vulnerable.

CHAPTERS 10–12

Fanny has dinner with Mr. and Mrs. Fenger, the latter a semi-invalid; she feels a sympathy for her supervisor. Among the guests is a young mechanical engineer whom Fanny thinks of as Fascinating Facts; the young man takes her home in his roadster, or open car. Receiving a letter from Theodore, she learns that his wife is pregnant; he needs money. Fenger promises Fanny a raise in salary, a reward for the success she has achieved in her department. She receives an unexpected telephone call from Clarence Heyl, who is stopping in Chicago on his way to New York; she has no interest in seeing him, but he forces himself into her office, declaring that he has become strong because of her, because of her fighting spirit. He invites her to come with him on a Sunday trip to the INDIANA DUNES.

Arriving at Fanny's apartment, Clarence sees the sketches she has made, including one of an old fish vendor. He says she has no business working in

a mail-order house when she can draw like that. During their excursion at the dunes, she agrees that sometimes she feels she should walk away from Haynes-Cooper; he tells her that next time the feeling comes she should take a train for Denver, and he gives instructions on how to reach his well-stocked retreat in the Rocky Mountains. He tells her again, too, that any newspaper in the country would use her sketches. When they part for the evening, Clarence makes clear, although he is headed at the moment for New York, that he will see her again.

Father Fitzpatrick comes to visit Fanny at Haynes-Cooper, taking her to lunch at the BLACKSTONE HOTEL. Sitting by a window in the luxurious restaurant, the priest asks her to name the most interesting thing she views from her seat; she indicates a man shivering outside in the cold, wishing she had not just ordered lobster thermidor. Father Fitzpatrick grasps her hand, saying delightedly that she is still the same person, that Haynes-Cooper has not spoiled her.

CHAPTER 13

A year has passed since Molly Brandeis's death. Instead of joining the congregation of the famed Dr. Kirsch—who speaks on politics, not religion, at least not as she has understood religion—Fanny finds her way to an orthodox Russian Jewish synagogue on the West Side; it is a bare, dim house of worship, where the rabbi intones the traditional prayer for the dead.

For the first time, Fanny is off to New York on a buying trip. She strikes a deal with a clothing manufacturer, but the firm hesitates when she insists on a narrow time frame; she suggest that the company speed up its workroom. Then, out on the street again, she looks up at the manufacturing lofts and sees women at their sewing machines, working relentlessly, mechanically; they are not like the women of leisure back in Winnebago, sitting on their porches and stitching peacefully. She is accosted by a man in tattered clothing asking for money, and she gives him a five-dollar bill. A fellow buyer mentions a column she has seen in a New York newspaper, full of human-interest material; Fanny knows it is Clarence Heyl's column. She tells herself she will not get in touch with Clarence while she is in New York, but she telephones him just before she is leaving for Chicago. Meeting her at Grand Central Station, he speaks again of her drawings, learning, to his disappointment, that she has done no sketching in recent months. Realizing, too, that she traverses the city alone, he instructs her in self-defense, teaching her how to accomplish an effective uppercut.

Back in Chicago, touring the Haynes-Cooper facilities, Fanny comes upon a girl sorting bundles as they come down a chute; the work is hectic, requiring fast thinking and acting. Fanny learns that the girl, Sarah Sapinsky, makes seven dollars a week, that her family requires most of her wages, that she is discontented and on the brink of trouble. Fanny's next general memo, proposing improvements in operations and in merchandising, declares also that seven dollars a week is not a living wage; that particular suggestion is ignored.

CHAPTERS 14–15

Having moved from the South Side to the North Side, living now in expensive quarters, Fanny is a successful, prosperous businesswoman. Yet as she works relentlessly, her soul seems to have shriveled. The young man dubbed Fascinating Facts asks her to marry him, and she replies that a woman like her is unlikely to marry. Michael Fenger continues to admire her, a man in turn she admires as an astute businessman.

Fanny takes her first trip to Europe for the firm, and Clarence Heyl sees her off on the ocean voyage. He declares again that she should not be working in commerce, that she is becoming hardened and shrewd. He compares her with social activist Jane ADDAMS and MUCKRAKING writer Ida TARBELL, saying that either of those women could have been successful in business, but they chose to pursue more worthy causes; Addams, he adds, is "the most radiantly beautiful woman I have ever seen." Fanny, reduced to tears, responds that she now has what she once strove for, that she is happy, that he should leave her alone.

Returning to New York, she learns that Theodore is coming to America on a concert tour. She learns also that Clarence, whose popular col-

umn is now nationally syndicated, has returned to the Colorado mountains for the summer. A women's suffrage parade, meanwhile, is taking place, and Fanny sees a group carrying a banner, "Garment Workers. Infants' Wear Section"; these are the women who make the clothes she buys for Haynes-Cooper. She notes the girl carrying the banner, a Russian Jew, representing the misery of Siberian prison camps, the horror of pogroms, or organized massacres of Jews; she sheds tears once more. When Fenger, who is in New York, takes her and a colleague to tea, she has him stop while she rushes into a stationery store; she sees Fenger as representing Big Business, and for the moment she is loathing Big Business. Back in her hotel, using the stationery, she sketches the girl in the parade, catching the details of her shabby clothes, yet finding the triumph in her face. Going to Heyl's New York paper, imperiously making her way into the editorial office, she shows the picture to the editor and says she wishes he would use it. Impressed, the editor promises that his paper next morning, showing the sketch, will outshine all the others in their coverage of the parade. He offers her a job, but she refuses. Going home amid Jewish riders on the subway, she says to herself that these are her people.

CHAPTERS 16–19

WORLD WAR I has started, and Theodore arrives on the last ship from Germany. With him is his baby daughter and a nursemaid, but not his wife; Fanny learns that she has taken up with another man. Yet when Fanny suggests that he will never see her again, he responds that he wants her.

Theodore is scheduled to begin a concert tour, playing first with the CHICAGO SYMPHONY ORCHESTRA. His manager arrives from Germany on a Holland boat, telling Fanny that Theodore's wife is now alone and starving; he also says that Schabelitz, the violinist Theodore once met in Winnebago, has sent a warning to him not to let a woman destroy his career. Fenger, meanwhile, announces that Nathan Haynes, founder of Haynes-Cooper—having listened to sociologists and philanthropists—has instituted a profit-sharing plan; as a result, the firm will no longer be properly run, Fenger believes, and he is selling his shares.

Fanny is pleased that wages at Haynes-Cooper will rise; she tells Fenger about a girl named Sarah Sapinsky, whose wage was too low to support her family, who left the firm for a life of prostitution. Fenger proposes that he and Fanny form a new company together.

A letter arrives for Theodore, postmarked Vienna; Fanny hides it. After the Chicago performance, he leaves for Cleveland, insisting on taking his daughter with him. Fanny takes the train on Sunday to the Fengers' summer home on the North Shore, where Fenger renews his business proposal; after speaking of Haynes's "socialistic slop," he says that the two of them can be a national power in five years' time. Fanny is hesitant, saying she has lost interest in the mechanics of business. Fenger admits for the first time that his wife is not there; he grasps Fanny's shoulder, swinging her toward him, declaring his love for her. Fanny, protesting, remembers the uppercut that Clarence once taught her, and she follows his instructions. Fenger slumps to the floor, and she rushes from the house to the train station.

Arriving home, she finds a telegram from Theodore. He has found the letter she hid, and he and his daughter are on their way back overseas; he will return to America with his wife, or he will stay and fight for Germany. Fanny, feeling the shock, knows she must join Clarence Heyl at his retreat in the Rocky Mountains; she takes a train to Denver, then another train, then a steam automobile. She learns that Clarence has left for the East, but she finds his cabin and settles into its comfort. She refreshes herself in new surroundings, rethinking her life, forgetting Haynes-Cooper and Fenger. Venturing out one day, she is caught in a snowstorm—and is rescued by a returning Clarence Heyl. Clarence carries her to a warm cabin and is soon speaking of their future life together; Fanny wonders if his editor will still give her the drawing job he once offered.

Critical Reception

The work achieved only moderate sales. The *DIAL* offered praise, calling *Fanny Herself* "the most serious, extended and dignified" of Ferber's volumes, although the reviewer noted the seemingly contrived ending; the novel tells, the reviewer added—in what today reads strangely—of "the ascent of a forceful and persistent race." A silent movie, *No Woman Knows*, appeared in 1921. Although widely read in her day, Ferber has long been dismissed as a popular writer, and her work has been generally forgotten since her death; the University of Illinois Press reprinted the novel in 2001.

Fantazius Mallare
Ben Hecht
(1922)

This novel by Ben HECHT is a fantasy-world story of an artist driven to madness. An imitation of the morbid "decadent" movement of late 19th-century European writers, it was published in a limited edition by the Chicago firm of COVICI-MCGEE. Hecht, Covici-McGee, and the illustrator were charged with obscenity by the U.S. postal authorities and subsequently fined. Because of the work's negative publicity, Hecht was fired from the *DAILY NEWS*, terminating his popular daily column, "1001 Afternoons in Chicago." A further publication, also in a limited edition, appeared in 1924, *The Kingdom of Evil: A Continuation of the Journal of Fantazius Mallare.*

Farrell, James T.
(1904–1979) *novelist*

A member of the post–Chicago Renaissance generation, Farrell published his first novel, *Young Lonigan*, in 1932. Featuring an Irish-American boy growing up on Chicago's South Side, it was followed by *The Young Manhood of Studs Lonigan* in 1934 and *Judgment Day* in 1935, completing the trilogy. The middle volume, taking its protagonist from high school in 1917 through the next dozen years, briefly re-creates—using the white participants' point of view—the RACE RIOTS of 1919. Farrell unflinchingly depicts the racism and mob mentality of the protagonist and his friends.

Faulkner, William
(1897–1962) *major southern author*

Best known for his novels set in the fictional Yok-napatawpha County, Mississippi, including *The Sound and the Fury* (1929) and *Absalom! Absalom!* (1936), Faulkner was aided in his early career by the older writer Sherwood ANDERSON. Meeting Faulkner in New Orleans late in 1924, Anderson was instrumental in the publication of Faulkner's first novel, *Soldier's Pay;* the older writer also suggested that the younger man—who at that time had not yet written about his native region—go home and "write about that little patch up there in Mississippi." Anderson fictionalized his encounter with Faulkner in "A Meeting South," published in the DIAL in 1925, collected the next year in SHERWOOD ANDERSON'S NOTEBOOK, and published again in the 1933 DEATH IN THE WOODS.

The two authors later became estranged; Faulkner wrote a parody of Anderson's style in the 1926 *Sherwood Anderson and Other Famous Creoles,* a collaboration with Faulkner's artist friend William Spratling. Faulkner's volume appeared several months after the publication of another parody of Anderson, the novel THE TORRENTS OF SPRING, written by a writer whom Anderson had also once helped, Ernest HEMINGWAY. In 1929, Faulkner dedicated his novel *Sartoris* to Anderson, "through whose kindness I was first published"; several decades later, after Anderson's death, he wrote of the older author's ready generosity to aspiring writers. Faulkner won the Nobel Prize in literature in 1949.

"A Fence"   *See* CHICAGO POEMS.

Fenger, Michael

A character in Edna FERBER's novel FANNY HERSELF, the general manager of the mail-order firm Haynes-Cooper, Fenger represents system, organization, and "efficiency, efficiency, efficiency." He therefore appreciates Fanny BRANDEIS, who is not only efficient, but clever and resourceful; he

would rather hire a man, he makes clear, but he realizes she is the right person to employ as a buyer for the infants' wear department. It is to Fenger that she denies her Jewishness during her initial interview. Yet later, when she hears him speaking on the telephone in faultless, modulated English, she understands that his language usage is an acquired faculty; he is playing the same game that she is playing, the implication being that he is Jewish as well. Fanny realizes also that the etchings on the wall—which she had earlier criticized—are of his making, an effort to overcome the barreness of his youth. The reader learns later that as a boy he had been a machine attendant in a Racine woolen mill; working his way into an office job, he married the owner's daughter.

Eventually, Fenger becomes the villain of the novel, in that he is unsympathetic to the plans of Nathan Haynes, the company's founder, to share the profits; Fenger also, although a married man, makes a romantic overture to Fanny, to which she responds with a knock-out blow. Yet his villainy, coming toward the end of the novel, seems a contrivance; its purpose is to drive Fanny out of her business activity, which suddenly seems heartless to her—although such activity has been relished throughout the narrative—and into the morally neutral field of art, as well as into the socially acceptable institution of matrimony.

Ferber, Edna
(1885–1968) *novelist, short-story writer, playwright*

Ferber was a popular American writer for more than half a century, recreating locales that ranged widely across the nation. Her first fiction is set in Wisconsin and Chicago, and perhaps her best fiction, the novel FANNY HERSELF, dwells in those early settings. Born in Kalamazoo, Michigan, the daughter of an immigrant Hungarian father and an American-born mother, Ferber moved with her family to Chicago, then to Ottumwa, Iowa, then to Appleton, Wisconsin. At the age of 17, she began to write for a newspaper in Appleton; a year and a half later, she became a reporter for the *Milwaukee*

Journal, a position she held for five years. Suffering an apparent nervous breakdown, she returned to her parents' home in Appleton; after her father's death she moved to Chicago in 1909. She began publishing stories the following year; her first novel, DAWN O'HARA: THE GIRL WHO LAUGHED, appeared in 1911, and her first collection of stories, BUTTERED SIDE DOWN, was set mainly in Wisconsin and Chicago, in 1912. In the next several years she wrote a series of 30 tales about a traveling saleswoman, Emma MCCHESNEY; the character is based on her mother, who had run the family dry-goods store in Wisconsin. The stories appeared over a five-year period in popular magazines and were collected into three volumes: *Roast Beef Medium, Personality Plus,* and EMMA MCCHESNEY & CO. President Theodore ROOSEVELT was an admirer of Emma McChesney. Ferber collaborated with George V. Hobart to create a play, *Our Mrs. McChesney,* which opened in New York in 1915, starring Ethel Barrymore.

Fanny Herself, published in 1917, her most autobiographical novel, tells of a young Jewish woman's upbringing in a Wisconsin town, followed by her moving to Chicago to work in a mail-order firm. Another collection of stories, CHEERFUL BY REQUEST, set mostly in Wisconsin or Chicago, appeared in 1918, and GIGOLO, including more midwestern tales, was published in 1922. Her 1924 novel, *So Big,* set in Chicago and suburbs, originally serialized as "Selina" in the *Women's Home Companion,* won a Pulitzer Prize the following year; Ferber was first Jewish writer to win the award.

Moving to New York, working with playwright George S. Kaufman, she turned a 1922 short story set in Chicago, "Old Man Minick"— collected in *Gigolo*—into a play, *Minick,* first performed in 1924. Her familiarity with the Barrymore acting family led to further plays cowritten with Kaufman, the 1927 *The Royal Family* and the 1932 *Dinner at Eight;* these works, despite her disclaimer, are based on the Barrymore family legend. The hero of *Dinner at Eight* is modeled on actor John Barrymore, who, essentially playing himself, starred in the screen version the following year. Ferber's 1926 novel, SHOW BOAT, set partially in Chicago, became the basis for the classic Jerome Kern–Oscar Hammerstein II musical, produced the next year by Florenz ZIEGFELD Jr. *Show Boat* opened in New York on December 27, 1927, followed on December 28 by the opening of *The Royal Family.*

A forerunner of the later popular novelist James Michener, Ferber perfected the technique of acclimating herself to a locale and then writing about it; her settings, besides Wisconsin and Chicago, include the Mississippi River, Oklahoma, Connecticut, Michigan, Texas, and Alaska. *Cimarron,* the most widely read book of 1930, is set in Oklahoma, although she claimed to have spent little time there; the description of the newspaper office, she noted, came from her days at the *Appleton Daily Crescent.* Ferber wrote two volumes of autobiography, the 1938 *A Peculiar Treasure* and the 1963 *A Kind of Life;* she died at the age of 81.

Because she was popular with a mass audience, because she was seen as facile and sentimental, Ferber has been placed outside the critical canon. Her pioneering trait was her creating women who flourish in careers, who compete successfully with men—although, readers have noted, these women are always single women; even the formidable Fanny BRANDEIS, when she marries, relinquishes business for art. Ferber herself downplayed her role as a Jewish woman writer; although returning to Jewish themes in her autobiography *A Peculiar Treasure,* she relegated these themes in fiction principally to scattered short stories and the novel *Fanny Herself.*

Ferris, George Washington
(1859–1896) *inventor of the Ferris wheel*

A native of downstate Galesburg, home of Carl SANDBURG, Ferris set out to surpass the engineering achievement of the Paris Eiffel Tower, the product of an earlier world's fair. Constructed on the MIDWAY PLAISANCE, the entertainment area of the WORLD'S COLUMBIAN EXPOSITION, the Ferris wheel, illuminated at night by 3,000 electric light bulbs, stood 26 stories high; it offered a ride that lasted 10 minutes. Subsequently appearing at several other fair sites, the wheel was eventually sold for scrap metal. Ferris died bankrupt at the age of 37.

Field, Eugene
(1850–1895) *poet, journalist*

Remembered today for children's poetry, Field was the first of the popular daily newspaper columnists. Born in St. Louis, Field attended Williams College in Massachusetts and Knox College in Galesburg, Illinois, and held newspaper jobs in St. Louis, Kansas City, and Denver; in 1883, he was recruited to work for the respected morning edition of the CHICAGO DAILY NEWS, later known as the CHICAGO RECORD. He is credited with creating the first daily newspaper column in America, "Sharps and Flats," an influential series ranging between humor and seriousness, between verse and personal commentary; like most newspaper writing at the time, it was unsigned. Referring to the UNION STOCK YARDS, as well as disparaging the cultural pretensions of the newly rich, Field named Chicago "Porkopolis." Theodore DREISER, looking back on his own career, recalled that as a young man he read Field's "Sharps and Flats" and decided that he, too, wanted to write. The journalism of Field and his colleagues became the model—as opposed to a more traditional and genteel literary culture of the East—for aspiring midwestern writers.

At the CONGRESS OF AUTHORS of the WORLD'S COLUMBIAN EXPOSITION in 1893, Field took sides during a notable debate on REALISM in fiction, held between Hamlin GARLAND and Mary Hartwell CATHERWOOD; he made clear his preference for the historical romances of Catherwood. In 1894, when Eugene V. DEBS was imprisoned for his part in the PULLMAN STRIKE, Field gave support to the labor leader, at a time when newspapers were generally decrying labor agitation; defending Debs, he cited the man's idealism and integrity.

Field's best-known children's poem is "LITTLE BOY BLUE," a sentimental piece about the death of a child. "Wynken, Blynken, and Nod"—in which the characters sail off in a wooden shoe—first appeared, like so much of his work, in his "Sharps and Flats" column. The poem "The Duel" tells of a conflict between a gingham dog and a calico cat,

concluding, "They ate each other up!" It has been assumed that Field's fellow native of St. Louis, T. S. ELIOT, presenting a calico cat in his *Old Possum's Book of Practical Cats*, was familiar with the piece. Field died suddenly of a heart attack at the age of 45, causing national mourning; it is said that hardly a town exists in America that does not have a Eugene Field School.

Field, Marshall
(1834–1906) *retailer*

Chicago's major retailer, "The Merchant Prince," was born in Conway, Massachusetts, came to the city in 1856, and worked first as a clerk in a wholesale dry-goods firm. In 1867, he and Levi Z. LEITER bought out the retail dry-goods business of Potter PALMER, opening their store in Palmer's newly established State Street business district in 1868. When the GREAT FIRE leveled the area three years later, Field rebuilt and eventually bought out his partner. The current LOOP store, designed by Daniel BURNHAM, was built in 1892; further additions were made in the next several decades. "Give the lady what she wants," became Field's famous motto. His fortune was the largest in Chicago in his day.

In 1905, his only son, Marshall Field Jr., died from a gunshot wound at the age of 37; rumors abounded that he was shot in the EVERLEIGH SISTERS, brothel, although the official verdict was accidental death, brought about while cleaning a gun at home. Edgar Lee MASTERS deals with the subject in "Rosie Roberts," a poem in SPOON RIVER ANTHOLOGY, and Sherwood ANDERSON includes a version of the same incident in his novel MARCHING MEN.

Field donated the land on which the UNIVERSITY OF CHICAGO was built; the FIELD MUSEUM OF NATURAL HISTORY, established in 1921, was another of his legacies.

Field Museum of Natural History

This museum of nature, archaeology, and anthropology was originally housed in the Palace of Fine

Arts in JACKSON PARK. Containing artifacts left over from the WORLD'S COLUMBIAN EXPOSITION, the museum opened in its present building, near downtown, in 1921; it is one of the largest public museums in the country. Along with the SHEDD AQUARIUM and the ADLER PLANETARIUM, it forms a museum campus of classical architecture at the south end of lakefront Grant Park.

Fifty-seventh Street group

This informal group of artists, also referred to as the JACKSON PARK colony, gathered in a cluster of one-story buildings at Fifty-seventh Street and Stony Island Avenue, across from Jackson Park on the city's South Side. The buildings, remnants from the WORLD'S COLUMBIAN EXPOSITION, had served during the fair as shops and studios. In the first decades of the new century, painters, sculptors, and writers—including Sherwood ANDERSON, Carl SANDBURG, Maxwell BODENHEIM, Ben HECHT, and Thorstein VEBLEN—lived or gathered in the area, located near the UNIVERSITY OF CHICAGO. In Margery CURREY's storefront studio, Margaret ANDERSON first received encouragement and support for launching her LITTLE REVIEW; Currey and her estranged husband, Floyd DELL, kept separate adjoining studios. In Sherwood Anderson's novel DARK LAUGHTER, although the area is designated as Forty-seventh Street, the protagonist speaks of the "small low buildings," filled with "people who wrote, made pictures, read books, talked of books and pictures." By the middle of the second decade, the locale for writers and artists began shifting to Chicago's North Side, where the magazine POETRY was located, where Anderson and others lived. The Fifty-seventh Street buildings have since been razed.

The Financier
Theodore Dreiser
(1912)

DREISER's third published novel, *The Financier* is the first in the trilogy of novels featuring Frank COWPERWOOD, a fictionalized version of Chicago

streetcar magnate Charles T. YERKES. Originally envisioned as a single volume, the manuscript grew to the point that the initial portion of Yerkes's life, when the businessman lived in Philadelphia, became the subject of the entire first volume. Dreiser's principal source was Philadelphia newspaper files, although he drew also on a recently published biography of Jay COOKE, another self-made Philadelphia financier, whose fall in 1873 Cowperwood uses to financial advantage. The sequel THE TITAN, covering Cowperwood's Chicago career, appeared in 1914, and the third volume of the trilogy, THE STOIC, tracing his subsequent career in New York and London, appeared after Dreiser's death, published in 1947.

Synopsis

CHAPTERS I–V

Frank Cowperwood, born in 1837, the son of a Philadelphia bank clerk, ponders from an early age such questions as how people live and how life is organized. He receives an answer by watching the tank in a fish market, in which a lobster slowly devours a helpless squid. He feels a touch of sorrow for the squid, but then gazes at the lobster and understands the lesson—that things live on each other, that men live on each other as well.

Watching and listening to his father, the boy learns about banking and brokering. When an uncle, a successful planter in Cuba, asks about his interests, he responds simply, "Money!" Entering into his first business venture at the age of 13, Frank buys seven cases of soap at auction, then sells them at a profit to the neighborhood grocer. Leaving school at the age of 17, he takes a job as bookkeeper for a grain-brokerage company; soon he is soliciting customers, making deals, and steering the firm in new and profitable directions. He goes next to a firm of bankers and brokers.

CHAPTERS VI–XI

Cowperwood meets Semple, a shoe-store owner, who talks about the new transportation facility, streetcars; Cowperwood realizes the potential of this form of public transport, soon to replace omnibuses. Semple's wife, Lillian, interests him as well; she has beauty, an important quality to him. A year later, Semple dies of pneumonia, and Cowperwood pays court to the widow, even though she is older than he; they marry when he is 21 and she 26.

Cowperwood's finances are flourishing. Benefiting from his own efforts and from money left by his uncle, the young man has bought streetcar shares that are increasing in value. Starting his own brokerage business, he learns about ongoing practices in state and municipal financing—that government officials are taking public funds and loaning them interest-free to banks, reaping the profits of speculation for themselves.

The CIVIL WAR begins. A Philadelphian, Jay Cooke, prospers by marketing loans to the federal government; when the state of Pennsylvania needs to raise funds for paying and equipping its quota of troops, Cowperwood hopes to become part of the lending process. He makes overtures to Edward Malia BUTLER, a politically connected contractor. Paying a call on Butler, he meets 15-year-old Aileen BUTLER, a vivacious convent schoolgirl.

CHAPTERS XII–XVIII

Cowperwood and his wife have two children, although Lillian's looks are no longer as striking as they once were. His negotiations with the state are not as profitable as he had hoped, but his alliance with Butler is proving beneficial; he builds an imposing new house for his family and an equally fine house for his parents. Aileen Butler is becoming a charming, spirited young woman.

Cowperwood meets George W. STENER, newly elected city treasurer and member of the Republican Party, the dominant party in Philadelphia. Stener owes his job to the three men who control the city—Butler; Mark Simpson, a U.S. senator; Henry A. Mollenhauer, a businessman. Holding the office of treasurer allows Stener to continue the practice of speculating—and helping others to speculate—with public funds; Cowperwood is designated as the financier to receive these funds. He and Stener profit alike from their illegal activities. Cowperwood ponders the possibility of gaining control of a citywide street-railway system.

The new Cowperwood homes host a housewarming reception and dance; Aileen Butler attends with her family. When she and Cowperwood dance, they reach a tentative understanding.

CHAPTERS XIX–XXIV

Aileen and Cowperwood declare their love for each other. Despite her religious training, she has no compunctions about involving herself with this married man, whom she idealizes; Cowperwood feels no moral restraints at all. He rents a house where they can meet discreetly.

Cowperwood also discreetly makes deals for Stener and others, investing the borrowed city money in profitable streetcar stocks. Public funds totaling $500,000 have been deposited with him. It is now the summer of 1871. Then the unexpected blow occurs—the Chicago GREAT FIRE, occurring in October of that year. The city's commercial section burns to the ground, and a national financial panic sets in. Insurance companies close their doors; the losses of manufacturers, wholesalers, and merchants spread across the nation, to eastern investors and mortgage-holders as well. Deposits are withdrawn, and loans are called in. Cowperwood feels particularly vulnerable because of the thousands of dollars of city funds he has invested.

He pays a visit to Butler, hoping to persuade the contractor and his friends to hold back on calling in loans, in order to support the market; he knows his personal finances will survive if his loans are not called, and he knows they will not be called if the market does not slump drastically. Cowperwood admits to Butler the extent of his drawing from the public treasury, and Butler realizes the potential problems in the upcoming elections for the Republican Party—the party that gives him his contracts for street paving, bridges, viaducts, and sewers.

CHAPTERS XXV–XXX

Butler talks to Mollenhauer, telling him about the $500,000. Mollenhauer turns out to be less interested in saving the Republican Party—he himself is not dependent on it for contracts—than in his personally getting hold of Cowperwood's street-railway stock. Senator Simpson turns out to be secretly interested also in acquiring the streetcar stock.

The next morning, the market is in severe decline, and Cowperwood realizes he needs more money from Stener to sustain his loans. He reminds Stener that the two of them are in this precarious situation together. Yet Mollenhauer has already contacted Stener, and the city treasurer, beholden to this powerful figure, refuses to make any more funds available.

Butler receives an anonymous letter, saying that his daughter, Aileen, is engaged in a liaison with Cowperwood; it gives the address of the rented house. Butler is devastated; feeling vengeful against Cowperwood, he calls in the loan he has made to him, vowing to send him to jail, to break him. Butler confronts Aileen as well, showing her the letter. She denies everything, but he knows she is lying, since her reaction is haughty, not one of genuine protest.

Cowperwood solicits relatives and friends, trying to raise money to cover the loan from Butler. He again asks Stener for money, reminding him of their complicity, but the treasurer is still afraid to cross Mollenhauer. Then Cowperwood finds Stener's clerk and manages to get from him a check for $60,000, secured by bank loan certificates; these are certificates he had acquired earlier but had not yet deposited to the credit of the city—and he had no intention to deposit them since they had already been used for other purposes. The clerk later tries to get the check back, but Cowperwood refuses. Aileen, meanwhile, tells Cowperwood that her father knows about their relationship. Lillian Cowperwood knows, too, as she has received an anonymous letter as well; she resolves to say nothing about it.

CHAPTERS XXXI–XXXVIII

The Cowperwood firm goes into receivership. The ultimate legal problem—the problem that involves possible criminal charges—is not the $500,000 borrowed from the treasury, but rather the $60,000 of unrestored certificates. Butler turns out to be the hard-liner on the matter, to the surprise of Mollenhauer and Simpson; they know nothing about Butler's personal issues.

The Citizens' Municipal Reform Association conducts an investigation, reporting an abuse of public trust. Butler and his associates, protecting the Republican Party, throw blame not on the politician Stener, but on the financier Cowperwood—although it is understood that if Cowperwood is convicted, Stener must be convicted as well. Both men end up being formally charged. Cowperwood and Aileen realize that her father's wish for revenge has been instrumental in pressing the charges.

Butler tries to send his daughter off to Europe, but she refuses to go. Hiring a private detective to shadow her, he learns that she and Cowperwood are meeting in a house of assignation; he arranges to confront them. His subsequent embarrassment of his daughter infuriates her, making her all the more resistant when he demands that she give up Cowperwood and leave the city.

CHAPTERS XXXIX–XLVIII

The trial begins. The judge is a man who will do what his party dictates, and the official line is that Cowperwood is the principal villain, having led Stener astray. Yet the election is over, and the party has not suffered much; the judge wonders why Cowperwood is still the main target. He has heard that Butler has some private grudge against the defendant, but he has no idea of its nature. It is understood that Cowperwood is to be punished, as well as Stener, so that the party appears to be righteously cleansing itself.

The jury is impaneled for Cowperwood's trial, and the district attorney enumerates four separate charges, detailing larceny and embezzlement. The first witness is Stener, who is led to spell out the schemes in which he and Cowperwood participated—that reveal both men's less-than-scrupulous conduct. A succession of witnesses follows, and finally the defendant himself is put on the stand. The sticking point is the $60,000 check; Cowperwood claims not to have known that the loan certificates had not been deposited, but the jury, rightly, does not believe him. Closing speeches are delivered by Cowperwood's lawyer—whose name is Steger, not to be confused with Stener—and the district attorney; the jury leaves to deliberate. Cowperwood hears that Butler has been observing in the courtroom; he knows that the judge, Butler's "emissary," will pronounce the maximum sentence if the jury convicts. The jury returns a guilty verdict; Cowperwood's lawyer asks for a postponement of sentencing, pending a motion to the State Supreme Court for a new trial. The court denies the motion, and the date for sentencing is scheduled; Cowperwood knows he must prepare for prison.

CHAPTERS XLIX–LVI

Lillian Cowperwood is 40 years old by now, and her husband is 35. She has never fully understood his crimes, but she understands her own status at the moment; her husband is going off to prison, and his affections have gone elsewhere as well. He says his good-byes to her and the two children—just as he has already had his final tryst with Aileen. In court, Edward Butler is there to hear the sentencing; Aileen, unknown to him, is there as well. The judge sentences Cowperwood to four years and three months in the state penitentiary; he sentences Stener to four years and nine months.

Cowperwood, eager to act to his advantage, learns quickly the ways of the penitentiary. Under the Quaker-influenced "Pennsylvania System," the prisoners are given solitary confinement; their mandate is to reflect and repent as they live in silence and carry out their labor in individual cells. Cowperwood's labor is the caning of chairs. Yet the guards, he learns, are open to bribery and privilege-granting, and he still has funds; he has engaged a man, Wingate, to front a brokerage firm for him. As a result, Cowperwood is granted more visits than normally allowed, including visits from Aileen, and he is given use of a garden. Sometimes at night he takes a chair outside and looks up at the sky, gazing at the constellations, wondering about the grandeur of the universe—although he himself still believes that he is the mortal destined for grandeur. Dreiser is continuing at this point to draw closely on the life of Charles T. Yerkes, noting that Cowperwood later donated a great telescope to a university, as did Yerkes himself to the UNIVERSITY OF CHICAGO in 1892. One day when his wife visits, Cowperwood decides it is time to ask for a divorce. She has expected such a request, and yet she is resentful, accusing him of thinking only of

his own gratification; she vows not to grant his wish. He knows she will ultimately bend to his will.

CHAPTERS LVII–LIX

Six months after Cowperwood is incarcerated, Edward Butler dies. Aileen's disgrace, as he viewed it, then her turning on him—especially her accusing him of being responsible for her lover's imprisonment—are suggested as the cause of his collapse. Yet Butler is no longer around to oppose a pardon for Cowperwood and Stener, and the two men, having served terms of 13 months, are pardoned in March 1873.

Cowperwood reasserts himself in Wingate's firm, taking over as broker, although officially he is still a broker's agent. Then in September 1873, the financial world is shaken; the banking firm of Jay Cooke, the man who had successfully bankrolled the federal government during the Civil War, fails; it had overextended itself in financing the expansion of the Northern Pacific Railroad. As a result of the failure of both the bank and the railroad enterprise, the PANIC OF 1873 ensues, causing widespread economic ruin.

Cowperwood sees his opportunity. Unlike after the Chicago fire, when he had many holdings, he now has little to lose; he will go "short," that is, sell borrowed stock, anticipating a lower price at repayment. Then, as the market continues to fall, he will buy to satisfy those previous sales. At the end of several days, Cowperwood is once again a millionaire. Three months later, he is on a train speeding west. Two years after that, his firm is operating in Chicago; Lillian Cowperwood has been granted a divorce in Philadelphia, and Aileen Butler, after many trips back and forth, comes permanently to live in Chicago.

Critical Reception

Reviews were favorable, as Dreiser was now recognized as a major writer, making a serious critique of what would be called the GILDED AGE, the era of the rise of capitalism—although he sent no message of reform; the massive financial documentation, as well as the detailing of lengthy trial proceedings, were the work of a reporter, a chronicler of his era, not a polemicist. Most critics have understood also that Dreiser identified with Cowperwood, admiring his strength and energy. *The Financier* has been called one of the great novels of business, although readers often prefer the nonbusiness passages, including the stories of Aileen Butler and Edward Malia Butler.

Finchley, Sondra

A character in Theodore DREISER's novel AN AMERICAN TRAGEDY, Sondra, beautiful and selfish, belongs to the set of rich young people whom protagonist Clyde GRIFFITHS aspires to join. She understands her power over him and is fascinated by that power—as much as by Clyde himself. Hinting that they might elope and marry, she adds that she is not yet of age, that her parents could put an end to her marriage; as a result, they must wait. She is a refined version of Hortense BRIGGS, the girl who had previously infatuated Clyde—while still, like Sondra, withholding her favors—during his earlier life in Kansas City. Hoping ultimately to attain her, Clyde plots murder against Roberta ALDEN, the working-class woman who is pregnant and insisting that he marry her. After Clyde is charged with murder, he hears nothing from Sondra; her name, because of her family's influence, has been omitted from trial testimony. Finally, an unsigned, typed note, expressing "sorrow and sympathy," is delivered to him on death row—a gesture interpreted as feeble and inadequate.

Fine Arts Building

This landmark building on South MICHIGAN AVENUE, built in 1885 as the Studebaker Building, provided a showroom, as well as assembling facility, for the Studebaker Carriage Company; the structure was renovated in 1898 as the Fine Arts Building. Taking advantage of its location across the street from the ART INSTITUTE, offering studios for artists and writers, the building became associated with the era's literary and artistic figures. It was

home to the LITTLE THEATRE and the LITTLE ROOM, as well as the Studebaker Theater and the Chicago Musical College, operated by the father of Florenz ZIEGFELD Jr. Artist's studios were held by Joseph C. LEYENDECKER, soon to become a major commercial artist, and Arthur W. W. DENSLOW, illustrator of THE WONDERFUL WIZARD OF OZ. Francis Fisher BROWNE, founder and editor of the DIAL, operated a bookstore in the building, its interior designed by a young Frank Lloyd WRIGHT. Margaret ANDERSON worked in Browne's store when first coming to Chicago; she later housed her LITTLE REVIEW office in the building. In 1950, the Studebaker Theater was converted to a television studio; in 1981, it reopened as a multiple-screen cinema, showing art films until it closed 20 years later.

In Theodore DREISER's THE TITAN, the structure appears as the New Arts Building; an amateur drama group, called by Dreiser the Garrick Players, is quartered there, and Frank COWPERWOOD surprises his mistress in a tryst on the premises. Willa CATHER's 1935 novel, *Lucy Gayheart*, presents the Arts Building, located on Michigan Avenue, as the setting for the heroine's music studies.

"Fire-Logs"   *See* CORNHUSKERS.

"Fish Crier"   *See* CHICAGO POEMS.

"Flanders"   *See* CORNHUSKERS.

Fleming, Berenice

A character in Theodore DREISER's novels THE TITAN and THE STOIC, Berenice is the daughter of the madam of an upscale house of prostitution in Louisville, Kentucky. She first interests Frank COWPERWOOD as a young girl, appearing to have all the superior qualities that he, a superior man, requires, and she herself is aware of her value. Yet she understands that her mother's past makes her an outcast in society; what she fails to understand until later is that Cowperwood—who is 35 years her senior—is supporting her and her mother in style, hoping eventually to make her his own. When he is ousted from his franchises in Chicago, she comes to him and declares that she will be his; together they will form a union of "beauty and strength and intelligence and courage."

Although sympathizing with his wife, Aileen BUTLER Cowperwood, and resolving to be generous to her, Berenice remains true to Cowperwood throughout the rest of his life, despite his fears of her finding interest in younger men. After his death she spends four years in India, seeking and gaining enlightenment; when she returns to New York, she vows to establish a hospital for the poor, as Cowperwood had once proposed. Dreiser's motive in establishing her as a selfless, giving person is perhaps aimed at leading the reader to approve of Cowperwood as well—although critics have complained of the implausibility of her sudden transformation into a selfless, spiritually aware do-gooder.

The character of Berenice is based on the real-life Emilie Grigsby, a woman many years younger than Charles T. YERKES, the model for Cowperwood. Her background in Louisville was similar to Berenice's, and she followed Yerkes to London and later embraced Hindu mysticism; one of the reasons for the delay in the writing and publication of *The Stoic* was fear of a libel suit from Grigsby.

"Fog"   *See* CHICAGO POEMS.

Fort Dearborn

This army post near the mouth of the CHICAGO RIVER, named after Henry Dearborn, President Thomas Jefferson's secretary of war, was built in 1803; its purpose was to protect the northwestern United States territories. Housing soldiers, civilians, and families, the fort was first commanded by Captain John Whistler, grandfather of painter James McNeil Whistler.

What became known as the Fort Dearborn massacre occurred during the WAR OF 1812, between America and Great Britain, when Indians allied with the British attacked a group of 94 soldiers, women, and children who were evacuating the fort; the group had set out along the lake, planning to go east into Indiana, but were attacked a few miles outside the fort. Fifty-two of the party were killed, the rest taken prisoner; the scalped remains of the dead, still lying in the sand, were discovered by returning troops four years later. The Potawatomi, along with the Chippewa and the Ottawa, controlled the area for the next several years. In 1816, Fort Dearborn was rebuilt, and trading posts and settlements soon followed; the army troops were withdrawn in 1836, and the second fort was razed two decades later.

The most widely promulgated version of the massacre first appeared in a pamphlet of 1844, in which Juliette KINZIE transcribed the recollections of her father-in-law, John KINZIE, who had escaped from the city after the massacre; the material was later included in her narrative *WAU-BUN: THE "EARLY DAY" IN THE NORTH-WEST.* Historians have found inaccuracies in the account, although it remains the principal document on which subsequent accounts have been based. At the actual site of the massacre, near what is now 1800 South Calumet Avenue, George M. PULLMAN commissioned a monument, a statuary group of life-sized figures, in 1893; the monument has since been placed in storage. A reproduction of the fort was included at the 1933 Century of Progress world's fair in Chicago.

Fort Sheridan

This army post 30 miles north of the city was established in 1887, spurred by the HAYMARKET AFFAIR and labor unrest of the previous year. The fort was built on land donated by the Commercial Club of Chicago; its purpose was to maintain order during times of social disruption. The first regiment arrived on November 8, three days before the scheduled Haymarket executions. Named in 1888 for the just-deceased CIVIL WAR hero General Philip Sheridan, who had established martial law in Chicago in the aftermath of the GREAT FIRE, the post served also as a staging ground for troops dis-

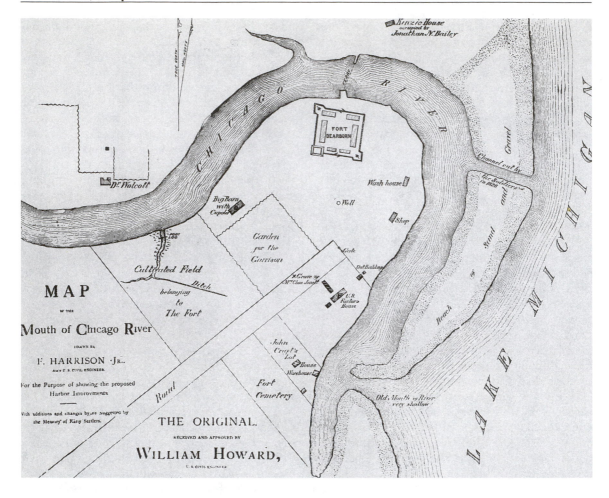

This 1830 map shows the mouth of Chicago River and the rebuilt Fort Dearborn and its accouterments. In 1834, soldiers from the fort cut farther through the river's sandbar, creating a navigable harbor; two years later, the garrison was withdrawn. *(Chicago Historical Society)*

patched during the SPANISH-AMERICAN WAR. It closed in 1993.

Foster, Joseph

A character in Henry B. FULLER's novel BERTRAM COPE'S YEAR, Foster, the half brother of Mrs. Medora PHILLIPS's deceased husband, is a partially blind, wheelchair-bound invalid; he serves as a commentator on the action, the observer who understands character and motive. Issues of homosexuality are never explicitly discussed, and yet Foster is aware of the orientation of Basil RANDOLPH, Arthur LEMOYNE, and Bertram COPE. He realizes Randolph's feelings for the younger Cope and is critical of the young man, knowing that Randolph will be hurt by him. Brooding alone in his top-floor quarters, Foster becomes the proverbial blind-man-who-sees. He laments, too, that the young are careless about the old—perhaps speaking for the 62-year-old author himself. Likely seen as sharing Fuller's sexual orientation as well, Foster is given a brief interlude of joy when a 14-year-old male houseguest befriends him, wheeling him cheerfully about the house.

Foster, Tom   *See under* WINESBURG, OHIO: "Drink."

Franklin, Miles
(1879–1954) *Australian writer*

Best known for the book and movie *My Brilliant Career,* Franklin lived in Chicago between 1906 and 1915. Serving as a journalist and labor activist, she regretted, apparently, that she was thereby deflected from her literary pursuits. Born Stella Maria Sarah Miles Franklin in rural New South Wales, dropping the first three names to avoid gender identification, she published in 1901 the work for which she is now remembered. Featuring the 16-year-old daughter of a poor farmer—like Franklin herself at the time she began writing—the novel served as a protest against a society she considered repressive of women. In 1906, Franklin left Australia for the United States; arriving in Chicago, bearing a letter of introduction to Jane ADDAMS, she met fellow Australian Alice HENRY, who had come to the city earlier in the year. Henry, employed by the Chicago branch of the Woman's Trade Union League, later the NATIONAL WOMEN'S TRADE UNION LEAGUE, brought Franklin into the organization; the women became active in labor agitation and the women's suffrage movement. Late in 1910, during a garment workers' strike against Hart, Schaffner, and Marx, a men's clothing manufacturer, Franklin worked to gain a sympathetic press for the strikers, mainly immigrant women; the labor action, led by Sidney HILLMAN, resulted later in the formation of the Amalgamated Clothing Workers Union. In 1911, Henry and Franklin launched *Life and Labor,* a monthly magazine sponsored by the NWTUL; in the same year Franklin was elected national secretary, later secretary-treasurer, of the organization.

Franklin continued writing fiction, although a short-story collection, *Some Everyday Folk and Dawn,* published in Edinburgh in 1909, received little notice. In 1915, *The Net of Circumstances,* set in Chicago, appeared in London under a pseudonym; in this novel a woman labor investigator, struggling to live in commonplace circumstances, becomes acquainted with a wealthy reformer, a man enjoying luxuries that she could never hope for. The character is said to be based on William Bross Lloyd, the son of Henry Demarest LLOYD, a married man with whom Franklin had a long-standing, presumably platonic, friendship; Lloyd later became a founder of the Communist Labor Party in Chicago. Franklin's other novel with a Chicago setting, the posthumously published *On Dearborn Street,* features a woman who runs a stenography service in the LOOP. This work also introduces a rich young man; his offer of marriage is rejected by the heroine, who harbors suspicions of both men and marriage.

In 1915, Franklin, whose restlessness and ambition had brought her to America, left for England, stirred by the challenges of WORLD WAR I. In 1927, she returned to Australia; she is said never to have spoken of her Chicago years, implying that she regretted them. In her pseudonymous *Cockatoos,* published in the year of her death, she says that her protagonist "had fallen among reformers"—and for an artist, that is "more fatal than for a merchant to fall among bandits." Lacking financial resources to sustain a literary lifestyle, arriving unknown in a city where her only contacts were feminists and reformers, Franklin seemed to regret having allowed herself to be drawn into their social and political activism.

Most Americans first heard of Franklin through *My Brilliant Career,* the 1979 movie directed by Gillian Armstrong; the film brought international recognition to the Australian actors Judy Davis and Sam Neill. As for Franklin's years in Chicago—taking "suffrage trains" to SPRINGFIELD, participating in NWTUL conventions, attempting to ameliorate the lot of strikers, attending the PROGRESSIVE PARTY convention in Chicago in 1912—they remain generally unrecognized.

Further Reading

Coleman, Verna. *Miles Franklin in America: Her Unknown (Brilliant) Career.* London: Angus and Robertson, 1981.

Fraser, Daisy   *See SPOON RIVER ANTHOLOGY.*

Freemasonry

This label is applied to secret fraternal organizations, as well as to their teachings and practices. Believed to have originated with stonemasons and cathedral-builders of the Middle Ages, Freemasonry has long maintained secret orders, or societies, practicing secret ceremonies and rituals. In the 19th century, fraternal orders in America, including those connected with Freemasonry, provided the model for a variety of protest groups. The KNOW-NOTHING MOVEMENT, a collection of secret societies arising in the 1840s, opposed immigration and "foreign" influence. The farm-based GRANGERS, or the National Grange of the Patrons of Husbandry, and the city-based KNIGHTS OF LABOR, or the Noble and Holy Order of the Knights of Labor, began as fraternal organizations; they dropped their commands of secrecy as they developed into voices for rural populism and urban labor agitation. An Anti-Masonic Party, reacting against the concept of secret societies—spurred by the presumed murder of a man who had divulged Masonic practices—operated briefly in the 1820s and 1830s; the party attracted temperance and antislavery followers as well.

free silver

This term was the rallying cry of the movement advocating the free coinage of silver. As agricultural prices declined in the 1870s, the call for unlimited silver coinage arose in western states. Rejecting the GOLD STANDARD, favored by eastern bankers as providing monetary stability, farmers sought an inflationary economy, hoping to ease their burden of debt. Free silver became a cause embraced by the POPULIST PARTY and by Democrat William Jennings BRYAN in his 1896 presidential campaign. William MCKINLEY's victories over Bryan in 1896 and 1900, as well as gains in national prosperity, made free silver a less prominent political issue.

free thought

This term describes the rejection of supernatural or metaphysical concepts. The late-19th-century orator Robert INGERSOLL, "the great agnostic," achieved fame by denying Christian belief, urging historical criticism of the Bible; he helped popularize what became known as humanism and scientific rationalism. Floyd DELL, in his autobiographical novel of 1920, MOON-CALF, writes about a free-thought organization he attended as a young man in the fictionalized Davenport, Iowa.

free verse

Indicating poetry without rhyme or metrical structure, *free verse* is a translation of *vers libre*, applied to the work of 19th-century French poets. Matthew Arnold and Walt WHITMAN were similarly creating poetry in English using the cadence, or speechlike line. The difference between free verse and the blank verse of earlier canonical poets is that Shakespeare and Wordsworth, as examples, while omitting rhyme, nevertheless retained a patterned metrical unit, or "foot." Free verse omits not only rhyme, but metrical structure as well.

The confusion of these two attributes, rhyme and meter, has been a commonly recurring phenomenon. The newspaperman-narrator in Sherwood ANDERSON's "A Man's Story" provides an example; admitting that he tries his hand at verse every now and then, he claims to write both "the rhymed kind and the newfangled vers libre sort"—implying that what is newfangled about free verse is its lack of rhyme. From the 16th century on, much of the great poetry in the English language has lacked rhyme.

Carl SANDBURG used free verse in his famed 1914 "Chicago" poems, receiving both praise and condemnation; the conservative DIAL questioned whether he was writing poetry at all. The work of Ezra POUND and other leaders of IMAGISM and MODERNISM soon established free verse as the poetic mode of the 20th century. Margaret ANDERSON, supporting the unconventional in art as well as her own version of artistic ANARCHISM, declared that free verse is appropriate for expressing a revolutionary consciousness.

Fremstad, Olive
(1871–1951) *Swedish-American soprano*

The model in part for Thea KRONBORG in Willa CATHER's *THE SONG OF THE LARK*, Fremstad was born in Stockholm, Sweden, and came to the United States as a child, growing up in rural Minnesota. Moving to New York, she supported herself as an accompanist for other students—as did the fictional Thea Kronborg in Chicago—and went on for further musical study in Berlin in 1893. Returning to the United States, Fremstad became one of the first major Wagnerian singers at the Metropolitan Opera in New York; she sang at the Metropolitan from 1903 to 1914. Cather interviewed her for MCCLURE'S magazine in 1913 and became a personal friend. When *The Song of the Lark* appeared, Fremstad praised the work for its accurate depiction of an artist's life.

French, Alice   *See* OCTAVE THANET.

Friday Literary Review

Founded in 1909 by the Irishman Francis HACKETT, the weekly supplement of the *Chicago Evening Post* was designated as a vehicle for avant-garde criticism. The *Friday Literary Review* published reviews and essays by Floyd DELL, Margaret ANDERSON, Ben HECHT, and others. Subjects included European playwrights August Strindberg and Arthur Schnitzler, French philosopher Henri Bergson, American poets Ezra POUND and Vachel LINDSAY. In 1911,

Hackett went to New York to write for *The New Republic,* and Dell took over as editor. In 1913, the parent newspaper terminated the separate supplement, reducing the literary section to a double page within the paper itself; Dell left for New York, becoming an editor of THE MASSES.

Friedman, Isaac Kahn
(1870–1930) *novelist, sociologist*

Born in Chicago, graduating from the University of Michigan, Friedman engaged in SETTLEMENT HOUSE work, as well as served on the Faculty of the new SOCIOLOGY department at the UNIVERSITY OF CHICAGO. His collection of stories, *The Lucky Number. A Book of Stories of Chicago Slums,* appeared in 1896. His 1901 novel, *By Bread Alone,* featuring an anarchist character modeled on Emma GOLDMAN, presented a fictionalized version of the Pennsylvania HOMESTEAD STRIKE of 1892, including the involvement of strike-breaking agents sent by Allan PINKERTON.

The Front Page
Ben Hecht, Charles Macarthur
(1928)

This play by Ben HECHT and Charles MACARTHUR, set in the newsroom of the Chicago Criminal Courts Building, covers an evening before the scheduled execution of a murderer. The prisoner escapes, and a star reporter, who had been planning to leave Chicago and take an advertising position in New York, is lured back to his post by the thrill of gaining a scoop; his hard-boiled editor, resorting to ruses, is determined to keep him on the job. The play seems dated to modern readers—in its romanticizing of journalism, in its admiring of newsmen who will stop at nothing to get a story. Among the characters is also the proverbial prostitute-with-a-heart-of-gold, who has befriended the prisoner; she leaps recklessly from a window to avoid saying where he is hiding. The character of the editor is based on Walter Howey, city editor of the CHICAGO TRIBUNE, later of William Randolph Hearst's *Chicago Examiner.*

Playing the editor's role on the New York stage was Osgood Perkins, father of movie actor Anthony Perkins. The play was an immediate success, garnering glowing reviews; the *New York Times* called it "one of the tautest and most unerring melodramas of the day." The published edition—by Hecht's old Chicago friend Pascal COVICI, now teamed in New York with Donald Friede—sold well, an unprecedented accomplishment for an American play. Four movies were subsequently made, beginning with a 1931 version starring Adolphe Menjou as the editor; the most celebrated version of the play is *His Girl Friday,* appearing in 1940, in which the reporter becomes a woman, played by Rosalind Russell, and the editor her ex-husband, played by Cary Grant. Billy Wilder's 1974 movie, restoring the original title, starred Walter Matthau, Jack Lemmon, and Carol Burnett; the renamed *Switching Channels* of 1988, changing the gender of the reporter once again, starred Kathleen Turner and Burt Reynolds. In 2003, playwright John Guare returned the play to the stage in a new version, adapting the film *His Girl Friday* for London's National Theatre.

Frost, Robert
(1874–1963) *poet*

Born in San Francisco, raised in Salem Depot, New Hampshire, Frost spent the first period of his life teaching school, working on a newspaper, and taking up poultry farming. In 1912, at the age of 38, selling his farm, he moved with his family to England; he published his first volume of poetry, *A Boy's Will,* the following year. Meeting Ezra POUND in London, he was championed by the expatriate American poet, who convinced Harriet MONROE to publish his "The Code" in the February 1914 issue of *POETRY;* it became Frost's first American publication. His next collection, *North of Boston,* appeared the same year. Returning to America, Frost gradually gained recognition and awards, winning the Pulitzer Prize for *New Hampshire,* published in 1923.

During the 1920s, comparisons were often made between Frost and Carl SANDBURG, the Illi-

nois poet who by then had established himself as a chronicler of rural scenes, as well as of city scenes. Yet as Sandburg turned increasingly toward "popular" expression, Frost—although himself not a model of elitism or MODERNISM—soon eclipsed Sandburg in critical recognition. He received three more Pulitzer Prizes, including one for his *Collected Poems* of 1930. In 1957, Frost joined with other writers to petition for the dropping of treason charges against Pound, indicted for wartime profascist activities in Italy. In 1961, at the age of 86, Frost took part in the inauguration ceremony of President John F. Kennedy; the poet died in Boston two years later.

Fuller, Henry Blake
(1857–1929) *novelist*

A native Chicagoan, Fuller was the first Chicago-connected writer to gain national recognition. Born into a prominent family, traveling in Europe as a young man, he returned to the city to write two romanticized, semifictional travel books of faraway places. In 1893, he published his first Chicago-based novel, THE CLIFF-DWELLERS, turning to the mode of REALISM promoted by novelist and critic William Dean HOWELLS; the novel focuses on businessmen and their families as they seek wealth and status. Two years later, he published another Chicago novel, WITH THE PROCESSION, a study of the declining fortunes of a once-prominent family. Theodore DREISER later claimed that American realism began with these works; it was Fuller, he wrote, who "pioneered the way to a real expression of American life."

In 1899, the author published a volume of satirical verses, *The New Flag,* attacking President William MCKINLEY and national expansionism after the SPANISH-AMERICAN WAR, lending support to the activities of the ANTI-IMPERIALIST LEAGUE. His collection of stories published in 1901, UNDER THE SKYLIGHTS, included "The Downfall of Abner Joyce," the tale of a minimally disguised Hamlin GARLAND, portrayed as a one-time man of the people who becomes a member of the elite, forgetting his roots. Yet Fuller was never able to recapture the success of his two 1890s novels. In 1919, at the age of 62, he published, through private funding, a remarkable novel, BERTRAM COPE'S YEAR; in this work, the principal male characters are readily identifiable as gay, although never specifically labeled. Some modern readers—although unable to discern the exact spirit in which it was written—assume it was a coded volume intended for the initiated; it received its first reprint in 1998.

Bertram Cope's Year revived an interest in Fuller and his fiction. Readers beginning with that work subsequently sought out his two novels of a quarter-century earlier; they found volumes offering a knotty prose style, as well as considerable erudition, yet rewarding in their depiction of commercial activity and social striving—the world of Chicago business and society that Dreiser would update 20 years later in THE TITAN.

Further Reading

Bowron, Bernard R., Jr. Henry B. Fuller of Chicago: The Ordeal of a Genteel Realist in Ungenteel America. Westport, Conn.: Greenwood Press, 1974.

Scambray, Kenneth. A Varied Harvest: The Life and Works of Henry Blake Fuller. Pittsburgh: University of Pittsburgh Press, 1987.

G

Gale, Zona
(1874–1938) *short-story writer, novelist*

Born in Portage, Wisconsin, Gale graduated from the University of Wisconsin and worked as a reporter on the *Milwaukee Journal*—as would Edna FERBER several years later—before leaving for New York in 1901. As a girl she had lived in OAK PARK, Illinois; architect Frank Lloyd WRIGHT designed her family home in the suburb, and later, after separating from his second wife, he paid brief court to her. Gale's early fiction, set in the mythical Friendship Village, Wisconsin, demonstrates the sentimental conventions of LOCAL COLOR; the greater REALISM of her later work, part of the REVOLT FROM THE VILLAGE movement, has been credited to the influence of Edgar Lee MASTERS's *SPOON RIVER ANTHOLOGY*. Her novel *Miss Lulu Bett*, published in 1920—and compared to Sinclair LEWIS's *Main Street* of the same year—features a protagonist, a woman in her 30s, who is trapped within the conventions of the fictional Warbleton, Wisconsin. In 1921, Gale turned the novel into a successful play, becoming the first woman to win a Pulitzer Prize for drama. She died in Chicago at the age of 64.

Galena and Chicago Union Railroad

This railroad line, the first in Chicago, opened in 1848. Its name deriving partly from Galena, Illinois, a lead-mining center in the northwestern part of the state, the railroad began Chicago's dominance of the nation's transportation. In November of that year, using a small steam engine, the *Pioneer*, the train carried a load of wheat from the DES PLAINES RIVER, running over eight miles of track at 16 miles per hour. As the railroad extended westward and northward, becoming absorbed into the Chicago and North Western Railway, the farmers of the Midwest, who had once brought their grain to Chicago by horse-drawn wagon, were shipping their produce by railway. Within a decade Chicago was the center of the largest railroad network in the world.

The outgrowth of the line is the Union Pacific Railroad, one of the railroads meeting in the historical driving of the "golden spike" in Utah in 1869. The resulting railway was never truly transcontinental, in that the eastern terminus of the Union Pacific was Chicago; yet it connected Chicago to the Pacific Ocean and to Asian trade—in the same year that saw also the opening of the Suez Canal.

In Joseph KIRKLAND's 1887 novel, *ZURY: THE MEANEST MAN IN SPRING COUNTY*, a character excitedly takes on the job of "engine-driver" for the Galena and Chicago railway; he takes charge of the *Pioneer*, pulling a freight train of 20 cars.

Garden, Mary
(1874–1967) *lyric soprano, Chicago-based opera singer*

Born in Aberdeen, Scotland, first coming to the United States at the age of six, Garden and her

Soprano Mary Garden was Chicago's favorite operatic diva. *(Chicago Historical Society)*

Manhattan Opera Company moved to Chicago, becoming the CHICAGO OPERA COMPANY, Garden brought the role of Salomé with her; her performance in November of that year was considered scandalous—and Garden labeled as a "great degenerator of public morals"—and the production was halted after two performances. She remained the reigning diva with the Chicago company from 1910 until 1931, serving as general manager during the 1921–22 season; the highlight of that year was the world premiere of Sergei PROKOFIEV's opera *THE LOVE FOR THREE ORANGES*. Unlike operatic singers who rely on voice alone, Garden—whose vocal abilities were sometimes questioned—was known as a singing actress, praised for her characterizations and for her interpretative gifts. After her retirement from the stage, she conducted master classes, served as a consultant for the movie industry, and traveled the lecture circuit. Her final years were spent in Aberdeen, where she died at the age of 93.

Garfield, James A.
(1831–1881) *20th president of the United States*

In office only between March and September 1881, Garfield was shot by a job-seeker on July 2 and died 80 days later on September 19. Born in rural Ohio, holding CAMPBELLITE and antislavery views, he served in the Union army during the CIVIL WAR; he held a congressional seat before becoming Republican presidential candidate in 1880. Chester A. Arthur succeeded him in office.

Garland, Hamlin
(1860–1940) *fiction writer; essayist*

Born near West Salem, Wisconsin, Garland moved with his family to successive farms in Wisconsin, Minnesota, and Iowa. In 1884, he made his way to Boston, eventually meeting his literary hero, the Ohioan-turned-easterner William Dean HOWELLS. While returning west to see his family in the late 1880s, viewing once more the severe conditions faced by plains farmers, he became a supporter of

family settled in Chicago in 1887. At the age of 22, she went to Paris for musical study; three years later, making her debut at the Opéra-Comique in Gustave Charpentier's opera *Louise,* she became a public celebrity. In 1902, composer Claude Debussy chose her for the lead in the premiere of his opera *Pelléas et Mélisande;* she edged out Georgette Leblanc—later the companion of Margaret ANDERSON—for the role.

Garden's American debut came in 1907, singing in Jules Massenet's *Thaïs* for the Manhattan Opera Company in New York; the soprano later created a sensation in Richard Strauss's *Salomé,* performing her provocative version of the Dance of the Seven Veils. In 1910, when the economic reformer Henry GEORGE; he saw George's *Progress and Poverty*, published in 1879, as explaining the farmers' problems, attributable to the evils of land speculation. Garland's early fiction was set on the "middle border," usually defined as the land between the older western states, such as Indiana and Illinois, and the Rocky Mountains—Wisconsin, Minnesota, Iowa, and the Dakotas.

In 1887, Garland became acquainted with Illinois writer Joseph KIRKLAND, author of ZURY: THE MEANEST MAN IN SPRING COUNTY, after favorably reviewing the novel in a Boston paper; he credited Kirkland with suggesting that he turn to fiction. Kirkland, reminding Garland that he had lived as an actual farmer, performing exhausting physical labor, declared that the younger writer would be uniquely capable of telling the truth about midwestern agriculture. The grim and pessimistic stories of MAIN-TRAVELLED ROADS were the result.

A populist Boston magazine, THE ARENA, first accepted "A Prairie Heroine," a tale depicting the hardships faced by a plains farm woman; later, the magazine's publishing company collected six pieces, turning them into the 1891 *Main-Travelled Roads*. Readers were unprepared for such despairing tales of farm life, reflecting the agricultural depression of the 1880s; the stories refuted literary pastoral ideals, as well as myths of happy agrarian enterprise. The tales became associated, too, with rabble-rousing populism and the POPULIST PARTY—as proven when the following year, the author campaigned for the Populist Party in Iowa during the 1892 presidential election.

In 1893, moving to Chicago, Garland spoke at the CONGRESS OF AUTHORS of the WORLD'S COLUMBIAN EXPOSITION, offering opposition to views expressed by Illinois writer Mary Hartwell CATHERWOOD. Catherwood, author of historical novels about the French in North America, had favored "romance"; Garland objected not only to historical romance, but to false depictions of rural life—which are false, as he quoted himself later, "if they deal only with June sunshine, roses, and strawberries." He coined the term VERITISM, indicating a Western rural REALISM.

Yet Garland soon moderated his populist views, undergoing the change that Henry B.

FULLER describes in the story "The Downfall of Abner Joyce," collected in a 1901 volume, UNDER THE SKYLIGHT; Abner Joyce, a figure modeled on Garland, changes from a populist agrarian—publishing a collection of stories titled *This Weary World*—into a genteel establishment figure. Garland himself had married the sister of the well-known sculptor Lorado TAFT. His CRUMBLING IDOLS, a collection of essays espousing a lukewarm veritism—suggesting little of the harsh rural realism displayed in *Main-Travelled Roads*—appeared in 1894. The following year, he published a commercially unsuccessful novel, ROSE OF DUTCHER'S COOLLY, drawing criticism for its sexual themes.

In 1898, his biography, *Ulysses S. Grant: His Life and Character*, initially serialized in MCCLURE'S MAGAZINE, recounted the life of his boyhood hero. Returning to fiction, Garland began writing popular tales with a far western or Rocky Mountain setting. The autobiographical A SON OF THE MIDDLE BORDER, first serialized in *Collier's Weekly*, appeared in 1917, followed in 1921 by the continuing autobiography, *A Daughter of the Middle Border*. A collection of short fiction, *The Book of the American Indian*, published in 1923, featured illustrations by the late Frederic REMINGTON. Other volumes consisted of reminiscences: *Roadside Meetings, Companions on the Trail, My Friendly Contemporaries,* and *Afternoon Neighbors*. Living the last half of his life as a genial literary eminence, Garland is remembered today for one powerful chronicle of rural hardship, the tales gathered in *Main-Travelled Roads*; that volume, rooted in a specific time and place, remains a valuable historical and sociological document, recording lives the author knew well—his, his family's, his neighbors'—lives that had been devastated by a pitiless natural world and an unjust economic system.

Garrick Theatre

Located in the Randolph Street theater district in the LOOP, housed in ADLER AND SULLIVAN's Schiller Building, the Garrick was noted for its interior metal work and soaring ornamented arches. William Vaughn MOODY's *The Sabine*

Woman, later named THE GREAT DIVIDE, opened there in April 1906, before moving to a successful run in New York. In 1960, the building was demolished, although the theater's façade was salvaged and reconstructed at the Second City Theater on Wells Street. Architecture buff Richard Nickel, who later lost his life in the collapse of the CHICAGO STOCK EXCHANGE BUILDING, made a fruitless effort to save this structure as well.

"General William Booth Enters into Heaven"
Vachel Lindsay
(1913)

This is the poem that made Vachel LINDSAY famous. After years of occasional publication, including self-publication, Lindsay saw the piece appear in the January 1913 issue of POETRY magazine. He had submitted two versions to editor Harriet MONROE, one with musical directions, one without; Monroe chose the more complete version. William BOOTH, founder of the SALVATION ARMY, had died the previous year in London; Lindsay as a boy had watched the Salvation Army band play in front of the courthouse in his hometown of SPRINGFIELD, Illinois.

Instructions at the beginning of the poem indicate that it is to be sung to the tune of "The Blood of the Lamb," a gospel hymn containing the refrain, "Are you washed in the blood of the Lamb?" General Booth is seen leading the way to heaven with his bass drum, followed by the unwashed—lepers, drunks, "drabs," or prostitutes, drug addicts. Although blind when he died, Booth is shown walking commandingly in his faith. Then Jesus comes through the courthouse door, stretching out his hands; the lame are straightened, the eyes of the blind are opened, sinners are made whole. All are set free by the Lamb of God, washed in His blood. In the last stanza, as the instruments turn silent, Booth sees his Master, King Jesus, coming with robe and crown; they stand face-to-face, and then Booth kneels, weeping.

William Dean HOWELLS, editor of the influential *Harper's* magazine, called the piece a "fine brave poem." At Harriet MONROE's dinner for the visiting William Butler YEATS in 1914, the Irish poet praised the poem for its simplicity and "strange beauty." The same year American composer Charles IVES produced a musical setting for the poem.

The "Genius"
Theodore Dreiser
(1915)

Although autobiographical elements exist in other DREISER novels, *The "Genius"* is the most straightforward personal narrative; it tells of a small-town boy who goes to Chicago, moves on to New York, and achieves a modicum of success. Along the way, he endures a troubled marriage, suffers a nervous breakdown, and gains ascendancy in the publishing business. These actions closely parallel Dreiser's career up to that point; in an early version of the novel, the protagonist is a newspaper reporter, not an artist, as Eugene WITLA becomes. Also reflected in the novel is Dreiser's lifelong successive liaisons with women; his pursuit of an 18-year-old girl, as mirrored in the book, is the relationship that broke up his marriage. A further model for the character of Witla is Everett Shinn, a member of the New York "Ashcan School," a group of artists depicting gritty street scenes, bridges, and buildings; like Witla, Shinn produced illustrations for the prestigious magazines of the day, including *Harper's,* and led an active romantic life as well. The direct artistic parallel between Witla and Dreiser is in their allegiance to REALISM; the public is reluctant to accept Witla's realism, as it had been reluctant to accept Dreiser's. The author added the quotation marks in the title to acknowledge an ironic interpretation, although by the end it is suggested that Witla is indeed a certifiable great artist.

Synopsis

BOOK I: YOUTH, CHAPTERS I–VI
In the small town of Alexandria, Illinois, in the late 1880s, young Eugene Witla lives with his parents and older sisters; his honest, thrifty father works as a sewing machine agent. Eugene, not

caring much for school, is far more interested in girls; his courtship of Stella Appleton ends when she wearies of his intensity. Working as a typesetter at the local newspaper, he begins wondering why advertisers fail to use drawings in their ads; he has seen Chicago papers featuring drawings and sketches, even in news stories. He resolves to go to the big city, a hundred miles away.

As in the earlier SISTER CARRIE, Dreiser's protagonist arrives in Chicago by train, entering into an immense, noisy railroad station. Absorbing the overwhelming sights, walking for miles, he finds inexpensive lodging. He undertakes several jobs, then gains employment as a payment collector for a furniture store, providing sufficient money for him to go to art school; he has been sketching railroad yards, factory sites, and riverboats. He enrolls at the ART INSTITUTE, an institution still located, as Dreiser reminds the reader, at its old, less impressive, location. Attending classes in the evening, he takes note of the model who disrobes for his segregated-by-gender drawing class.

BOOK I, CHAPTERS VII–XIX

On a visit to his hometown, Eugene meets the friend of a relative, an attractive schoolteacher from Wisconsin, Angela BLUE. She is five years older than he, although he is not aware of that fact; he makes it clear that he hopes to see her when she visits Chicago. He is progressing in his classes at the Art Institute, becoming friendly with one of the models, Ruby Kenny. When Angela visits Chicago, staying with an aunt on the North Side, Eugene compares Angela to Ruby; he realizes that Angela is superior, that she has a greater depth of feeling, and he proposes marriage to her. Yet as Angela remains in Wisconsin, he continues seeing Ruby, entering into a physical liaison.

A teacher at the Art Institute suggests that Eugene try for newspaper illustration work. Bringing samples of pen-and-ink drawings, he secures a position at an afternoon paper; his city scenes, showing wagons in the street or birds flying over smoke stacks, receive praise. As his confidence grows, he knows he wants Angela as a wife, and yet he would like Ruby to be available as well—ex-

cept that he does not have the money for such an arrangement. He decides to go to New York City, where magazine work is available.

In New York, he sells a drawing of a crowd scene to the weekly magazine *Truth*—a real-life magazine of the era—and succeeds in placing other illustrations as well; yet he understands the difficulty of making an adequate living by such means. After 16 months away from her, he visits Angela in Wisconsin. He admires her family, who are sturdy and honest farmers, and yet their high standards seem alien to him; they do not acknowledge the shifting nature of existence, the subtleties of life. One evening, after the family has retired, Angela lets her passion for him carry her further than she intended, although she ultimately resists; she worries afterward about her near-lapse—while Eugene feels more fully bound to her. Yet she wonders when he will marry her.

BOOK I, CHAPTERS XVIII–XX

On his way East again, Eugene stops in Chicago, but makes no effort to see Ruby. Back in New York, he sells a drawing to *Harper's Magazine*, a major publication; he meets several interesting women as well, including Christina CHANNING, an ambitious singer seeking a place in a European opera company, then hoping to return in triumph to America. Christina lives with her mother, as would be appropriate for a single young woman at the time; yet even after saying that marriage and a career are incompatible for her, she encourages Eugene, inviting him to a summer home in the mountains. There she enters into a physical relationship with him, while making clear that it is temporary, that it is confined to the brief holiday period. Once back in New York, they no longer see each other.

Angela, still living in Wisconsin, continues to worry about Eugene's promise of marriage; she writes anxiously, saying that financial insecurities need not delay their union. Her sister writes Eugene as well, reminding him that Angela would make a wonderful wife. Having heard only casually from Christina, who is now in Europe, Eugene visits Angela again in Wisconsin; there she yields to him physically—making clear, too, that she will kill herself if he fails to marry her. He realizes he must do so, even as he foresees the reaction of his New

York friends, who will find her limited, who will think he has made a mistake. He rents an appropriate studio and plans for the marriage.

BOOK II: STRUGGLE, CHAPTERS I–XXI

Eugene and Angela marry, although he feels he has been compelled against his will. His women friends are surprised, as he had not told them he was engaged. Angela feels chagrin at their surprise, and she feels jealousy as well; their remarks seem condescending and insulting. Meanwhile, one of his paintings receives favorable newspaper notice; encouraged, he approaches a gallery, hoping for a show of his works. The resulting exhibition brings glowing reviews, and a few of the paintings are sold; he and Angela travel to Paris, where he seeks to paint further city scenes. Yet it is there that he begins to grow ill—feeling apprehension, sleeping badly, experiencing nightmares. For the next five or six years, he will be unable to work, suffering from nervous exhaustion.

Packing up their belongings to return to the Midwest, Angela discovers letters that Eugene has kept, from Ruby Kenny and Christina Channing—women she now realizes he was seeing while engaged to her, while claiming his love for her. A recriminatory scene follows; he manages to assuage her, and yet she knows now that she must be watchful. While they stay with his parents in Illinois, Eugene meets a girl, Frieda Roth, 18 years old, and begins an ever-escalating flirtation with her. Angela does not see the stolen kisses, but her suspicions lead to another tempestuous scene; they leave for her parents' home in Wisconsin. Eugene is devastated at losing Frieda.

In the next two years, they wander in and out of Chicago, as well as various southern states, gradually spending the money that Eugene has earned from his paintings. Angela remains in Wisconsin while he returns to New York, trying unsuccessfully to sell some of his pictures from the past. He recalls hearing about a writer who applied to a railroad executive for a job, claiming nervous disability; the executive gave him a laborer's position. Eugene attempts the same tactic, and he gains employment at a railroad carpentry shop. The shop is located outside the city, and he finds lodging with a widow in a

neighboring village. The other workers gradually accept him, in part because he sketches pictures of them.

BOOK II, CHAPTERS XXII–XXX

The widow's daughter, Carlotta WILSON, moves back into her mother's house; Carlotta is a married woman in her early 30s, separated from her professional-gambler husband. Eugene is not immediately drawn to her, but she finds him interesting, inviting him to ride in her chauffeured car; once he understands her intentions, he acts accordingly. He leaves work early to go off with her, finding her love of pleasure irresistible. The idyll is disrupted when her mother discovers the relationship and demands that both of them leave the house.

Angela, deciding that she and Eugene must no longer be separated, arrives to take her place by her husband's side; she finds lodging for them, as Eugene continues to work for the railroad. Yet he continues to see Carlotta as well; she is living now in her New York apartment, and they meet when he takes time off from work. However, the inevitable happens, as Angela discovers one day that he has not been at work, and she finds a note that Carlotta has written him; she has no knowledge as to who the writer is, and she bides her time—until she finally bursts out in rage at the husband who has been deceiving her, initiating another of their turbulent scenes. Yet she is helpless to keep Eugene away from Carlotta, and the lovers continue meeting; they finally drift apart when he begins looking for a job again in the art world and obtains a position as a newspaper artist. Angela is hopeful that she and Eugene can make a new start.

BOOK II, CHAPTERS XXXI–XLIV

Eugene is rising now in the world. He leaves his newspaper job to become art director for an advertising agency; he then becomes advertising manager for a weekly magazine. Angela, meanwhile, is considering having a child, thinking that it might have a sobering effect on her husband. Eugene takes on yet a new position, becoming manager of the editorial, art, and advertising departments of a large publishing firm. He and Angela move into a luxurious apartment on Riverside Drive; he is now a prosperous, powerful figure in artistic and intellectual circles. Yet Angela is less acceptable in such circles, as she is insufficiently clever or sophisticated. Eugene continues to widen his scope, as he begins conferring with a real estate speculator, who is making plans to develop an upscale Long Island seaside resort.

BOOK III: REVOLT, CHAPTERS I–XI

Eugene meets a wealthy widow, Mrs. Emily Dale, becoming part of her social set; six months later, he encounters her 18-year-old daughter, Suzanne DALE—and once again finds himself infatuated. Suzanne becomes another feminine ideal, and he will allow her to change his life. Meanwhile, the proposed seaside resort, complete with hotels, casinos, and clubhouses, has taken his attention as well; he invests all his available capital in the project. At the same time, Angela suffers an attack of "rheumatism," or rheumatic fever, and she is confined for weeks to her bed. Yet the major happening in his life is his overwhelming love for Suzanne; they meet on various innocent occasions—until they reach a tentative understanding, then a full understanding; she claims to return his love. He becomes careless now in his work, which had already been losing his interest to the plans and sketches he was making for the resort.

Suzanne, referring to *Anna Karenina,* the novel by Leo TOLSTOY about adultery, suggests that she and Eugene live together; he is surprised by her free-thinking attitude, knowing the obstacles presented not only by society, but by his wife and her mother as well. One evening, at a concert held in his apartment, Angela sees him embracing Suzanne; she reacts in fury, telling Suzanne that he has had other women before her, that he will never be free to obtain a divorce and marry her. Angela then tells Eugene that she is pregnant; he is shocked, not knowing whether to believe her or not, yet knowing, too, that she is not in good health. Suzanne, meanwhile, says she will tell her mother about her love for Eugene, hoping that Mrs. Dale, who has been heard to profess broad-minded views, will accept an unconventional arrangement between the two of them.

BOOK III, CHAPTERS XII–XIX

Suzanne tells her mother that she might not want to marry, that she might wish to enter into an independent relation with a man. Mrs. Dale is astounded, wondering what books she has been reading; she decides that a trip abroad is the answer. Suzanne says she will take no such trip, and she finally gives her reason; she will stay near the man she loves, and she names him as Eugene Witla. Her mother, in a vehement outburst, brands Eugene as a villain; she declares she will speak to his wife, as well as inform his employer of his villainy. She goes to see Eugene as well, proclaiming that he will never have her daughter. Among the desperate measures she ponders are abducting Suzanne by means of chloroform. She finally devises a more workable scheme; she will pretend to give Suzanne her freedom, yet insist that her daughter sign a waiver of rights to her mother's estate, the signing to take place in the office of legal representatives in Albany. Suzanne, eager to join Eugene, claims to have no interest in an inheritance; she will sign the necessary papers. Her mother's ruse is that the train is not going to Albany, but to Canada.

When Suzanne, riding with her mother and brother, understands the trick being played on her, she refuses to leave the railroad car, a hired car now sidetracked near a private lodge. Mrs. Dale threatens to call a doctor, declaring her insane, and Suzanne finally gives in, realizing that she has no money and no means of transport. Nevertheless, through a servant she manages to get a letter to Eugene, telling him where she is; he sets off on his journey immediately. Arriving at the train station nearest the lodge, he is met by Mrs. Dale, who tries to deflect his purpose; yet he persists and is soon reunited with the beautiful, eager, determined Suzanne.

BOOK III, CHAPTERS XX–XXII

Mrs. Dale convinces Eugene to wait before taking any further steps; for the sake of social appearances, he and Suzanne will remain apart, and he will try to obtain a divorce. Suzanne is disappointed, as she had expected dramatic action; she had expected that the two of them would defy the world, flouting convention, rushing to personal victory. But now Eugene and her mother are talking rationally, planning for the two of them to get married at some future date—and that is not what she wanted. The group leave the lodge, the Dales going to their house in the Berkshires, Eugene going on to New York.

Back at the office, Eugene's employer says that Mrs. Dale, an influential woman, has been to see him, that she is pressuring him to let Eugene go; he mentions other work-related problems that Eugene has been having as well. He offers to let him take a year off, although both men know that his employment at the company has ended. Eugene realizes now that his income, his present prosperous life, is gone. He learns, too, that the seaside resort project is stalled and that he cannot retrieve his investment.

Suzanne begins to ponder her situation. Eugene had always seemed strong and powerful, but now he has not only given in to her mother, but lost his employment as well; Suzanne goes along with her mother's request that she and Eugene remain separated for a year's time. Eugene despairingly realizes that she might never be his.

BOOK III, CHAPTERS XXIII–XXIX, L'ENVOI

His sister Myrtle, having taken up Christian Science, persuades Eugene to see a practitioner; he learns that his troubles are illusions, that carnal beliefs produce evil, and that evil has no reality outside man's thoughts. Yet he feels he cannot give up Suzanne or his hopes of finally attaining her.

Angela goes into a dangerous labor, and doctors perform a cesarean operation; a girl is born. Yet Angela's heart has been weakened by her illness, and she dies not long afterward. Eugene and the baby stay with his sister and her husband. For the next three years, he lives in a gloom that is not broken until he starts painting again.

Suzanne, traveling in Europe, begins to wonder if she ever really loved Eugene. She hears of his wife's death and the birth of his child; she hears, too, that he has risen once more to fame. He has been commissioned to paint grand murals for banks, public buildings, and state capitols. Yet he has decided by now that he can resist the lure of

beauty. One day in New York, he sees, or thinks he sees, Suzanne crossing the street, and yet he refuses to acknowledge her. She thinks he has failed to recognize her, or else he hates her now. It has been five years since they met.

Eugene needs religion no longer, as his soul has regained its health. Moreover, women have reentered his life, and once again violent scenes take place—tears, separations, renunciations. Little Angela is there as well, sharing his studio, along with Myrtle and her husband. One night, reading the English writer Herbert Spencer's words on the immeasurable, unknowable universe, Eugene marvels at the welter of existence, at its richness and color; he looks up at the sky, and "great art dreams" well up in his soul.

Critical Reception

Because *The "Genius"* was Dreiser's fifth novel, the author was a generally known quantity, and reviews divided along expected lines—although more sharply so, because this work presented more overt sexual content. After its publication, Margaret ANDERSON's LITTLE REVIEW called Dreiser "the greatest novelist in the country"; critic John Cowper Powys praised the novel as an American epic revealing a "stupendous life-tide" that flows through "vast panoramic stretches of cosmic scenery." On the opposite side, reviewers spoke of the novel's sordidness and depravity, noting that the narrative reduced humanity to its lowest animal behavior; Eugene was labeled as "pathological." Yet morality was not the only issue; H. L. MENCKEN, long a supporter of Dreiser and his work, questioned the "vague" organization of the novel, finding its contents rambling and shapeless. Floyd DELL called the work "a great and splendid book which contains many dull pages." The background of WORLD WAR I obtruded as well, as some critics made spiteful note of Dreiser's German ancestry.

In 1916, the NEW YORK SOCIETY FOR THE SUPPRESSION OF VICE, the organization founded by Anthony COMSTOCK, threatened prosecution of the publisher, and the volume was withdrawn from bookstores; in 1918, an equivocal court ruling resulted in the publisher's continuing to keep the book from the market. A different firm reissued it in 1923, resulting in respectable sales.

George, Henry
(1839–1897) *economist, founder of the single-tax movement*

Born in Philadelphia, moving to California as a young man, George witnessed frontier land being bought by speculators, who later reaped great profits. He concluded that this increase in land value, a value unearned by the owner, was the cause of the nation's economic and social problems; only a few individuals, rather than the group as a whole, benefited. In his *Progress and Poverty*, published in 1879, George advocated the levying of a single tax, to be placed on the increase in value of land; all other taxes could then be abolished. This single tax would meet the costs of government, he argued, leaving a surplus. George's ideas have been called a mix of radical economics and Jeffersonian idealism—and naïve and inadequate as solutions to complicated problems.

Clarence DARROW, while still a small-town lawyer in Ohio, read and responded favorably to *Progress and Poverty*; Hamlin GARLAND, first reading the book on his parents' midwestern farm, later argued the single-tax message in periodical articles. The work sold millions of copies worldwide. In 1880, George moved to New York City, running unsuccessfully for mayor in 1886 as the candidate of the United Labor Party, aiming his campaign at "landlordism." He died in New York at the age of 58.

Georgians

A group of English poets writing in the second decade of the 20th century, the Georgians, who generally followed conventional poetic practice, were seen as rear-guard practitioners by Ezra POUND and other exponents of MODERNISM. The label refers to the reign of King George V, who came to the throne in 1910; the title *Georgian Poetry* appeared on four separate anthologies published between 1912 and 1922. WORLD WAR I

disrupted—and in some cases, destroyed—the lives and work of many of the poets. Among Georgians published in Harriet MONROE's POETRY magazine were Rupert BROOKE, who died in the conflict, and D. H. LAWRENCE, who would later be celebrated for his fiction.

Gerhardt, Jennie

The principal character in Theodore DREISER's novel *JENNIE GERHARDT*, Jennie, kindhearted and generous, trying to alleviate her family's poverty, becomes involved successively with two wealthy men. Her first liaison, a brief interlude with Ohio's Senator George BRANDER, ends when he dies suddenly of typhoid; 15 years later, their daughter, VESTA, dies of typhoid as well. The second liaison, continuing for years, is with businessman Lester KANE, whose family expects him to marry appropriately; he reluctantly leaves Jennie so that he can retain his inheritance. Jennie is portrayed throughout the novel as loving and self-sacrificing: "Did anything matter except goodness— goodness of heart?" the author asks rhetorically. Modern readers find an excess of sentimentality in the character, who seems to have been one of Dreiser's favorites.

Gigolo
Edna Ferber
(1922)

Originally published in magazines, the stories in this collection by Edna FERBER are set mainly in Chicago; the two tales located in New York feature protagonists originally from the Midwest—from EVANSTON, Illinois, and Kenosha, Wisconsin. The title piece, set in post–WORLD WAR I Europe, specifies midwestern origins as well; its fictional Winnebago, Wisconsin, had already been the locale for Ferber's autobiographical novel, *FANNY HERSELF*. The story "The Sudden Sixties" features a woman who, like the mother in *Fanny*, takes over after the death of her husband and succeeds in the business world. "Not a Day over Twenty-One" repeats a situation from the author's first novel, DAWN O'HARA, in that the heroine's husband, now dead, has remained for years in a mental institution. Another story, "Old Man Minick," tracing the problems of a lonely Chicago widower, was transformed into a play by Ferber and George S. Kaufman, presented as *Minick* on the New York stage in 1924.

Gilded Age

Generally dated between 1870 and 1910, this era takes its title from Mark Twain and Charles Dudley Warner's novel of 1873, *The Gilded Age*. The period was a time of economic expansion and private accumulation of wealth. "Robber barons"—named after feudal lords who once waylaid travelers—helped fuel the CONSPICUOUS CONSUMPTION that Thorstein VEBLEN labeled at the end of the century; the era was a time also of labor agitation and social unrest. Novelists began creating their businessmen-protagonists during this period, starting with William Dean HOWELLS's 1885 *The Rise of Silas Lapham*; Chicago writers, ranging from Henry B. FULLER to Robert HERRICK to Theodore DREISER, made these businessmen a significant part of their fictional territory.

Gilman, Charlotte Perkins
(1860–1935) *feminist, writer*

Gilman is best known today for her story "The Yellow Wallpaper," published in 1892, subsequently a feminist classic. Born in Hartford, Connecticut, the grandniece of abolitionist Harriet Beecher Stowe, Gilman married early, bore a child, and suffered a nervous breakdown—events forming the background for "The Yellow Wallpaper." Also part of the background was the popular "rest cure" of the 1880s, designed for females who are considered too active or too thoughtful; Jane ADDAMS had also once consulted the physician, S. Weir Mitchell of Philadelphia, on his rest-cure therapy. In 1895, Addams hosted Gilman for an extended stay at HULL-HOUSE, although aware that Gilman, by then well known on the lecture circuit, had drawn disapproval for abandoning her husband and daughter. Gilman's *Women and Economics*, published in 1898, asserts that a woman's maternal and household roles hinder her social and economic development; only through economic independence can a woman achieve growth. Other polemics, including *Concerning Children, The Home: Its Work and Influence*, and *Human Work*, argue that new technology, as currently adapted to industry, should be adapted to household drudgery as well; Gilman advocated cooperative, remunerated housekeeping and public child-care. Her magazine, *The Forerunner*, founded in 1909, took up other gender issues, criticizing women's fashion—luxuries paid for by men, indicating an unhealthy social stratification—and alimony for divorced women, another sign, she declared, of women's dependence on men. Her ideas on women's dress are traceable to Thorstein VEBLEN's 1899 volume, THE THEORY OF THE LEISURE CLASS, labeling excesses of fashion as an example of CONSPICUOUS CONSUMPTION. Gilman's fictional utopia, *Herland*, serialized in *The Forerunner* in 1915, depicts a land without men, where women are able, through mutation, to reproduce by virgin birth, bearing only girls; the land is orderly and peaceful. Learning that she had incurable cancer, Gilman committed suicide through an overdose of chloroform at the age of 75.

Sherwood ANDERSON wrote a defense of Gilman's suicide in 1936, published in the periodical *Forum* as "The Right to Die: Dinner in Thessaly."

Glaspell, Susan
(1876–1948) *writer, playwright*

Born in Davenport, Iowa, Glaspell became a reporter for the *Des Moines Daily News* after graduating from Drake University in 1899. Her famous story, "A JURY OF HER PEERS"—originally the play *Trifles*—is based on a murder case she covered for the newspaper. In 1903, she enrolled for graduate work at the UNIVERSITY OF CHICAGO; her short stories set in Chicago include "At the Turn of the Road," focusing on an Iowa girl studying art in the city. Her novel *The Visioning*, published in 1911, features a hero modeled on George Cram COOK, whom she married in 1913. The couple moved to

Provincetown, Massachusetts, and Glaspell, along with Cook, helped found the PROVINCETOWN PLAYERS. *Trifles* was presented by the group in 1916, Glaspell herself playing the leading role; the story "A Jury of Her Peers" was written the following year. Glaspell's play *Alison's House*, inspired by the life of poet Emily Dickinson, won the Pulitzer Prize for drama in 1931. "A Jury of Her Peers" continues as a favorite anthology piece; it appears in the retrospective 1999 collection, *Best American Short Stories of the Century*.

"Godliness"   See WINESBURG, OHIO.

Goldman, Emma
(1869–1940) *anarchist*

Born in what is now Lithuania, Goldman immigrated to Rochester, New York, in 1885, at the age of 16. Responding to the HAYMARKET AFFAIR of 1886 and the executions the following year, she became active in radical circles, advocating ANARCHISM. After an involvement with Johann MOST, the German-born anarchist preaching violence, she met Alexander Berkman, a fellow Lithuanian; she aided him in his plot to assassinate Carnegie Steel manager Henry Clay Frick during the Pennsylvania HOMESTEAD STRIKE in 1892. Berkman managed only to wound Frick, subsequently spending 14 years in prison. In 1901, when President William MCKINLEY was assassinated by an anarchist in Buffalo, Goldman, speaking in Chicago, expressed sympathy for the killer; she was arrested for conspiracy to commit murder, but released a month later for lack of evidence. In 1907, she began publishing the periodical *Mother Earth*, which continued for over a decade; among contributors was the young Ben HECHT. While in Chicago in 1908, she met Ben Reitman, a local physician working among the homeless, known as the "hobo doctor," who became her lover as well as manager of her lecture tours. In 1914, Margaret ANDERSON heard her speak and praised her in the May issue of the *LITTLE REVIEW*; Anderson herself began advocating anarchism, although she favored unrestrained artistic expression more than

political and social upheaval. During WORLD WAR I, Goldman's pacifist activity, including working with draft resisters, put her in prison, along with the recently released Berkman; in 1919, they were deported to Russia. Becoming disillusioned in Russia, Goldman and Berkman left the country, making their way to Berlin, then England, then France. By this time, Goldman was expressing disagreement with American intellectuals still looking favorably on the experiment in SOCIALISM in the Soviet Union.

Theodore DREISER, long an admirer of Goldman, met her in Paris in 1926, suggesting that she write the story of her life, which he called "the richest of any woman's of our century"; she published *Living My Life* five years later. In 1936, a despondent Berkman killed himself; four years later, Goldman suffered a fatal stroke in Canada, and her body was brought to lie near the graves of the Haymarket anarchists in WALDHEIM CEMETERY. Dreiser's 1915 THE "GENIUS" depicts Goldman briefly as a character named Elizabeth Stein.

gold standard

Using gold to indicate the basic monetary unit, a gold standard defines a nation's currency in terms of a fixed weight of gold. An alternative bimetallism, a historically more common system based on two metals, silver and gold. In the United States the Coinage Act of 1873 eliminated coinage of the silver dollar, signaling an end to bimetallism. As a result, the demand for gold rose, increasing its value—and increasing as well the "real" value of mortgages and debts. Midwestern farmers, burdened by debt, suffering from declining agricultural prices, argued for an inflationary monetary policy; such a policy, making money cheaper, would reduce the value of their debt. They advocated a return to bimetallism, increasing the money supply through FREE SILVER, or the unlimited coinage of silver. William Jennings BRYAN's famous "cross of gold" speech of 1896 detailed the harm caused by the nation's reliance on gold; his loss in the presidential election was seen by supporters of William MCKINLEY as a victory for sound money and monetary stability.

Gompers, Samuel
(1850–1924) *labor leader*

Born in London, coming to New York City in 1863, Gompers began his union career as president of a local cigar-makers' union. In 1881, he became a founder of the Federation of Organized Trades and Labor Unions, reorganized in 1886 as the AMERICAN FEDERATION OF LABOR; he served as president of the union until his death four decades later. Convinced that labor causes must be separated from political causes, he focused on specific issues such as wages and hours, rather than on larger issues such as the ownership of the means of production. Dissent from this conservative stance led to the founding of the INDUSTRIAL WORKERS OF THE WORLD in Chicago in 1905. With the coming of WORLD WAR I, Gompers, unlike IWW leaders, supported American military efforts. In Chicago, a park along the north branch of the CHICAGO RIVER was renamed Gompers Park in 1929, four years after his death.

"Gone"   *See* CHICAGO POEMS.

Goodman, Benjamin David "Benny"
(1909–1986) *clarinetist, band leader*

Born in the MAXWELL STREET area of Chicago, Goodman learned to play the clarinet at a synagogue and at HULL-HOUSE. After playing with a Hull-House band, he made his professional debut in 1921; his first solo recording came five years later. Moving to New York, he established in 1934 a "big band," including drummer and fellow Chicagoan Gene KRUPA. The Benny Goodman trio, formed in 1935, consisted of Goodman, Krupa, and African-American pianist Teddy Wilson; performing that year at the Congress Hotel in Chicago, the trio set a milestone in the acceptance of racially integrated ensembles. In 1936, Goodman added Chicagoan Lionel HAMPTON to form a quartet. His epochal big band concert at Carnegie Hall in New York City in 1938, including soloists from the Duke Ellington and Count Basie bands, gave a new respectability to JAZZ.

Goodman, Kenneth Sawyer
(1883–1918) *playwright*

Heir of a lumber fortune, graduate of Princeton University, Goodman collaborated with Ben HECHT to produce one-act plays at the HULL-HOUSE theater. Their cowritten collection, *The Wonder Hat and Other One Act Plays*, appeared in 1925, after Goodman's death from influenza during WORLD WAR I. Hecht writes in his autobiography, *A Child of the Century*, that Goodman dreamed of building a people's theater in the MAXWELL STREET area, bringing free drama to the poor. After Goodman died, his family endowed a theater—although located in the MICHIGAN AVENUE area, far from Maxwell Street; the Goodman Theater, a long-standing Chicago institution, was designed in 1925 by architect Howard Van Doren SHAW and adjoined the ART INSTITUTE. A gleaming new Goodman theater complex, constructed within the restored shells of two earlier theaters, has since been built in the LOOP.

Good Morning, America
Carl Sandburg
(1928)

In this collection of poetry by Carl SANDBURG, the title poem, consisting of 21 sections, is one of the poet's longest works; it is a compendium of Americana ranging from Niagara Falls to statues of war heroes. Critics found the volume, his fifth collection, weaker than earlier volumes, decreeing that the all-inclusive cataloguing, or accumulation of details, revealed vague thinking, not precise observation. By this time, Robert FROST was becoming America's preferred poet of the people, and intellectuals were choosing the MODERNISM of T. S. ELIOT, Ezra POUND, and Wallace STEVENS.

The Gospel of Freedom
Robert Herrick
(1898)

This novel by Robert HERRICK, dealing with financial corruption, stock speculation, and the newly rich, focuses also on what was once called "the new woman." A wealthy young woman tries to achieve personal freedom, as well as influence positively those about her, and she ultimately fails. In the character of the aesthete Simon Erard, Herrick presents an unflattering portrait of Bernard Berenson, his fellow Harvard University student who became a prominent art critic.

"Government"   See CHICAGO POEMS.

Graham, Magrady   See SPOON RIVER ANTHOLOGY.

Grand Army of the Republic

The Union CIVIL WAR veterans' organization, the GAR was founded in 1866; the first post was established in Decatur, Illinois. The organization reached its greatest membership, around three-quarters of a million, in the late 1800s. The GAR was responsible for the adoption of MEMORIAL DAY, originally honoring the Union dead, later honoring the American dead in all wars.

In Frank NORRIS's novel THE PIT, a member of a CHICAGO BOARD OF TRADE brokerage firm is said always to wear a Grand Army button in his lapel; readers of 1903 understood that the button was the mark of a hero. In the rural Iowa of Sherwood ANDERSON's WINDY McPHERSON'S SON, the veteran Windy McPHERSON attends GAR meetings with his fellow former soldiers, telling and retelling stories of war. Hamlin GARLAND, in his 1921 autobiography, DAUGHTER OF THE MIDDLE BORDER, recalls his father as a loyal GAR member, cherishing its "ceremonies and comradeship"; 35 years after the war, the old man tearfully watches a GAR parade in Chicago, a "melancholy procession of time-scarred veterans."

Grangers

This term refers to a network of organizations established for the welfare of farmers. The word *grange* refers to a farm, or a set of farm buildings.

The National Grange of the Patrons of Husbandry, founded in 1867, was originally a secret organization, modeled in the traditions of FREEMASONRY; its purpose was to foster social and educational goals among farmers. The members, or grangers, looked upon their local units, or granges, as providing ways to improve the quality of agricultural life; the motto was "Cooperation, Association, Education." With the decline of agricultural prices in the 1870s, the movement began focusing on political protest—against railroads, banks, and merchants, all of whom were seen as holding farmers in an economic vise. Grangers worked for state laws regulating prices charged by railroads and grain elevators; they set up cooperative elevators, mills, and stores. One of the original goals of MONTGOMERY WARD AND COMPANY was to stock cooperative stores in rural areas. Granger activity, along with that of groups organized under the name of Farmers' Alliances, led to the founding of the POPULIST PARTY.

Grant, Ulysses S.
(1822–1885) *general, 18th president of the United States*

Born in Ohio, educated at West Point, Grant led the Union armies to victory in the CIVIL WAR. Living after the war in Galena, Illinois, he aligned himself with the RADICAL REPUBLICANS during the presidency of Andrew JOHNSON. Reluctantly accepting the Republican nomination to succeed Johnson, he was elected president in 1868 and again in 1872. His administration was marked by corruption and financial scandals, although he himself remained above suspicion; revisionist historians have claimed that much of the criticism against him came from intellectuals such as Henry Adams, disdaining the man who was once a military hero, and from Southern scholars, maintaining loyalty to a lost cause. Hamlin GARLAND's sympathetic biography, appearing in 1898, had early sought to find political prejudice behind the negative views of his boyhood hero.

Grant is credited with enlightened post–Civil War racial policies, including attempts by a Republican-dominated Congress to exert federal power against the Ku Klux Klan in the South—although such efforts in the RECONSTRUCTION era became increasingly ineffectual. Toward the end of his life, suffering from throat cancer, facing financial difficulties, he undertook his memoirs, hoping to provide for his family. The *Personal Memoirs of U.S. Grant*, published in two volumes in 1885–86, is considered a triumph of clear and simple prose; it was a favorite both of Mark Twain and of expatriate writer Gertrude STEIN.

"Grass"   *See* CORNHUSKERS.

Graustark
George Barr McCutcheon
(1901)

A best-seller by Chicago newspaperman George Barr MCCUTCHEON, the novel sends an American abroad—following precedents established by Mark Twain and Henry James—to a fictional East European nation. The hero maintains his innocence and virtue while triumphing over decadent, Old World aristocrats. The novel became the model for stories set in far-off locales, in which democratic values prevail over traditions that are outworn and benighted; an example is the musical comedy appearing the next year, THE SULTAN OF SULU, by fellow Hoosier George ADE. McCutcheon, unlike Ade, had not been abroad when he wrote his work.

The Graysons: The Story of Abraham Lincoln
Edward Eggleston
(1887)

The novel by EGGLESTON is best known for its telling of the murder trial of Tom Grayson, in which the young lawyer Abraham LINCOLN, arguing for the defense, wins his case. Lincoln demonstrates, using an almanac, that no moon had been shining on the night of the murder, thus proving that the presumed eyewitness could not have seen the crime. The story is told again

in Carl SANDBURG's ABRAHAM LINCOLN: THE PRAIRIE YEARS.

Great Depression

Starting with the American stock market collapse of October 29, 1929, the Great Depression lasted for more than a decade; it is considered to have ended during World War II. In that period, businesses and banks failed, and the unemployment rate in the United States rose to 25 percent; the midwestern plains states suffered as well from severe drought and soil erosion, resulting in what became known as the Dust Bowl. In Chicago, the city made few alterations in its plans for another world's fair, A Century of Progress; opening on April 29, 1933, the fair was overseen by Daniel H. Burnham Jr., whose father had directed the 1893 WORLD'S COLUMBIAN EXPOSITION.

The Great Divide
William Vaughn Moody
(1906)

The actress Margaret ANGLIN, appearing with a theater company in Chicago in 1906, read the script of MOODY's play; she decided to mount a Chicago production of the play in April of that year. The original name, *A Sabine Woman*, was changed, since the allusion to a classical story—concerning the rape of a group of women to provide wives for early settlers of Rome—was deemed unfamiliar to general audiences.

The setting is Arizona, where Moody, like Willa CATHER—and Cather's characters Thea KRONBORG and Tom OUTLAND—traveled, finding inspiration in the southwestern landscape and the Native American past. Like Cather in THE SONG OF THE LARK, Moody also exalts strength and power; both writers are popularizing the ideas of the German philosopher Friedrich NIETZSCHE. Moody's heroine, Ruth, an easterner visiting the Southwest, is assaulted by a drunken miner, Stephen Ghent, and yet, despite her protest, she lets him abduct her and eventually marry her; he has led her, she says, "out of a world of little codes and customs into a great new world." In the course of the play social conventions reassert themselves temporarily, and she leaves him, even though she has a child. Yet Ghent eventually regains her, celebrating his new "law," which "is joy, and self-ishness"; his masculine, and Nietzschean, will to power triumphs. This play, the product of a man who had once written verse drama using classical themes, was considered an advance in REALISM for the American stage; it ran in New York for two years. The work was made twice into a silent film, in 1917 and 1924.

Great Fire

In this major Chicago disaster of October 1871, fire destroyed the entire central city, covering a four-mile area and leaving a third of the population homeless. Legendarily beginning when Mrs. O'Leary's cow kicked over a lantern—a legend that has been disproved—the blaze started on the West Side on a dry Sunday evening, October 8, and burned for nearly 30 hours, until rain fell early Tuesday morning. The recently built waterworks, bringing Lake Michigan water to the city, proved inadequate, and the structures of the central business district—including stores, factories, mills, grain elevators, banks, train stations, newspaper of-fices, hotels, theaters, and public buildings—were destroyed. Compared to other great fires of history, the 1666 London fire and the 1812 Moscow fire, the Chicago conflagration covered four times the area of either the London or the Moscow disaster. The Illinois militia and troops of the United States Army, commanded by General Philip Sheridan of CIVIL WAR fame, kept order under martial law for several weeks following. The city was rebuilt in the next 20 years.

One of the most detailed descriptions of the blaze appears in E. P. ROE's novel BARRIERS BURNED AWAY, written by a clergyman who had arrived in Chicago shortly afterward. Harriet MONROE, 10 years old at the time of the fire, recalls in her auto-biography that she ran to the window, finding "the air strangely full of an ashen dust, blinding and odorous." From 80 miles away, George ADE, then at the age of five, later recalled sitting on a fence

in Kentland, Indiana, watching "a blur of illumina-tion in the northern sky."

Theodore DREISER's novel THE FINANCIER presents his protagonist, Frank COWPERWOOD, based on the real-life Charles T. YERKES, as meet-ing his downfall in Philadelphia after the Chicago fire; the ensuing panic caused financial repercus-sions in the East, resulting in the disruption of his fortunes.

A 1938 movie, Darryl F. Zanuck's *In Old Chicago*, starring Tyrone Power, Alice Faye, and Don Ameche, was based on Niven Busch's story "We, the O'Learys," following the O'Leary-cow explanation.

Great Migration

This term refers to the mass exodus of African Americans from the South to Chicago and other northern cities after WORLD WAR I.

The title of Richard WRIGHT's *12 Million Black Voices: A Folk History of the Negro in the United States,* published in 1941, indicates the estimated number of southern blacks who jour-neyed North during and after the war. The choice of Chicago as the destination was spurred by the most widely read black publication in America, the CHICAGO DEFENDER. The area into which the migrants moved was labeled the "black belt," or BRONZEVILLE. A 15-foot statue of a man dressed in simple clothing, carrying a suitcase, stands today in a traffic island on Martin Luther King Drive, representative of the many who made the migration northward.

Great Strike of 1877

This work stoppage became the first national strike in the United States. During a period of economic depression, starting with the PANIC OF 1873, Chicago and other cities witnessed labor unrest and demonstrations by the unemployed. When four railroad companies announced a 10 percent wage cut in June 1877, the workers, although generally unorganized, staged strikes throughout the nation; labor stoppages began in the East and

This engraving, originally published in *Harper's Weekly* on August 18, 1877, shows strikers confronting the militia during the Great Strike of 1877. *(Chicago Historical Society)*

moved westward. In Chicago, strikers fought police and the local militia for three days, culminating in the death of 30 workers. Nationwide, the Great Strike lasted two weeks, after which President Rutherford B. HAYES sent in federal troops to restore the transportation system. The episode was the beginning of a long period of labor agitation in the United States, and Chicago soon became the center of radical ideology. The strike also set a precedent for federal intervention in labor issues; President Grover CLEVELAND pursued a similar course during the PULLMAN STRIKE 17 years later.

In Henry B. FULLER's 1895 novel, WITH THE PROCESSION, a character looks back to the strike of 1877, referring to it as "the railroad riots."

Greek Anthology

This collection of classical verse was first gathered around 80 B.C.E. and supplemented in later collections. The poems of the Greek Anthology are epigrammatic, short and pithy, often satiric. The verse includes first-person graveyard epitaphs, or tombstone inscriptions, in which the deceased sum up their lives. Some speakers refer to each other; some address each other. Edgar Lee MASTERS, reading the Anthology on the recommendation of William Marion REEDY, began writing his own epigrammatic poetry—terse self-portraits, often presenting a paradoxical twist, spoken from a small-town graveyard. Following the

Anthology precedent, Masters created in SPOON RIVER ANTHOLOGY a series of interconnected monologues, often giving two sides of the same story, or two versions of the same event.

Green Mill Gardens

This North Side nightclub opened in 1907 and received its name in 1910—a variation on the name of the Paris nightclub Moulin Rouge, or red mill. The establishment once stood near the studios of the ESSANAY FILM MANUFACTURING COMPANY; it became a movie setting and an actor's gathering place during its first decade. With the coming of PROHIBITION, the Green Mill Gardens came under control of the underworld—a control extending to entertainers as well as to bootleg alcohol; the club gained notoriety in November 1927, when entertainer Joe E. LEWIS, naively moving to a rival establishment, nearly lost his life in a revenge-inspired mob hit. Continuing in the same location in modified form, the Green Mill Lounge was restored in the 1980s, becoming known as a JAZZ venue; the Poetry Slam, part of the national organization, Poetry Slam, Inc., was born there in 1986.

Grierson, Francis
(1848–1927) *writer, celebrator of Abraham Lincoln*

Born in England as Jesse Shepard, growing up in rural Sangamon County, Illinois, Grierson lived much of his life as a European expatriate. His 1909 *Valley of Shadows: Sangamon Sketches,* written in London, speaks in a young person's voice of the environs of SPRINGFIELD in the 1850s; Grierson had heard one of the LINCOLN-Stephen A. DOUGLAS debates in Alton, Illinois, in 1858. The author presents the brooding, often melancholy, spirit of the great man, Lincoln, as the CIVIL WAR approaches; the war is to be seen as God's judgment on slavery. In 1918, Grierson published *Abraham Lincoln: The Practical Mystic,* declaring Lincoln "the greatest practical mystic the world has known for nineteen hundred years."

Griffin, Marion Mahony
(1871–1961) *architect*

Born in Chicago, the second woman to receive an architecture degree from the Massachusetts Institute of Technology—after Sophia G. Hayden, designer of the Women's Pavilion at the WORLD'S COLUMBIAN EXPOSITION—Griffin joined the studio of Frank Lloyd WRIGHT in OAK PARK in 1895. She left in 1909, the same year Wright left his family and studio. In 1912, her husband, architect Walter Burley Griffin, won an international competition to design the new Australian capital of Canberra, and the couple moved to Australia, where they remained for more than 20 years.

Griffith, D. W.
(1880–1948) *film director*

Born in La Grange, Kentucky, son of a Confederate officer in the CIVIL WAR, David Wark Griffith is known as the first major film innovator, as well as maker of the notoriously racist movie *The Birth of a Nation.* In 1909, his short one-reel film, *A Corner in Wheat,* drew upon Frank NORRIS's novel THE PIT—although its depicting the villain's drowning in a cascade of wheat came from Norris's earlier novel *The Octopus.* In 1915, Griffith's Ku Klux Klan–exalting 12 reel, three-hour opus was found offensive by many, and yet the film—presenting the close-up, the cut-away, parallel-action shots, and other subsequently standard cinematic devices—became the basis for future film technique and narrative. In an attempt to counteract the movie's racism, the Chicago-made THE BIRTH OF A RACE was filmed and distributed in 1918.

Griffith's famous lost movie of 1925, THAT ROYLE GIRL, starring W. C. Fields in a dramatic role—listed as one of the American Film Institute's 10 most wanted lost treasures—was filmed partly in Chicago; it was based on a novel by Chicagoan Edwin BALMER.

Griffiths, Clyde

The principal character in Theodore DREISER's novel AN AMERICAN TRAGEDY, Clyde, the son of a street preacher, grows up craving what his parents cannot give him—and what they consider sinful—namely, ease, luxury, beauty, and wealth. He gains his first glimpses of such a world as a bellhop at a hotel in Kansas City; he discovers girls as well, finding himself helpless against their wiles, particularly those of the exploitative Hortense BRIGGS.

Leaving Kansas City after involvement in a fatal automobile accident, Clyde contacts a wealthy uncle in upstate New York, who offers him a factory job. He comes to live in his new town as a poor relation, since the family pays little attention to him; he enters into a liaison with Roberta ALDEN, a working girl in the family factory. Yet his personal attractiveness eventually gains him entrance into town's young social set, and he is taken up by the beautiful and wealthy Sondra FINCHLEY. Sondra, as superficial and self-centered as Hortense Briggs, basks in Clyde's obvious infatuation with her. When Roberta becomes pregnant and insists that Clyde marry her, he can think only of his possible attainment of Sondra, and he plots Roberta's murder by drowning. The circumstances of her actual death are ambiguous, but Clyde is convicted and sentenced to die. He hears no more from Sondra, except for a brief unsigned note.

His downfall has lain in his vulnerability to the allure of love and riches—a vulnerability apparent to the women who have taken advantage of it; they have perhaps even scorned what they see as his submissiveness. He has also carried out his murderous plotting clumsily, leaving a trail of bungling behind him. Dreiser is known to have insisted on the word *tragedy* in the title, and yet the classical connotations of the term—that it is about a great man who has fallen, through a tragic flaw—are not applicable to this man who, although in many ways likable and sympathetic, is persistently ordinary.

Grimes, Jake

This character appears in Sherwood ANDERSON's story "DEATH IN THE WOODS." Grimes's father once owned a sawmill, but he lost everything to drink and women; his son, Jake, attempted a threshing business, but people did not trust him,

believing him to be a thief. Jake's son, in turn, grew up to be his father's drinking partner, as well as his presumed thieving partner. One winter day, when the two men are away from home, their wife and mother meets her death in the woods, dying from cold and from overwork. The townspeople turn against the men, and they leave the area; later the narrator comes upon their abandoned house along a creek, its doors broken. In the story it is the woman, not Jake, who is the central character, and yet her name is never given.

"grotesques"

In the collection WINESBURG, OHIO, Sherwood ANDERSON applies this label to characters who focus on just one truth, excluding others—although his "grotesque" figures are shown to be formed by their society as well, having been warped by small-town repression. The term had been familiar at the time; in March 1915, Margaret ANDERSON's *LITTLE REVIEW* published "Ten Grotesques," poems by Arthur Davison Ficke, and in the same year, a one-act free-verse drama by Cloyd Head, "Grotesques," had been performed at the LITTLE THEATRE. In February 1916, Anderson's "The Book of the Grotesque" appeared in THE MASSES; it would be the opening section of *Winesburg* three years later. In the story "The Egg," collected in THE TRIUMPH OF THE EGG, the narrator refers to deformed chickens as "grotesques," adding that these phenomena can be "born out of eggs as out of people."

Gullible's Travels
Ring Lardner
(1917)

This collection of short stories by Ring LARDNER, originally appeared in the *Saturday Evening Post*. The stories are told by a wisecracking, uneducated Chicago man whose wife has pretensions to advance in society. One tale recounts the couple's vacation trip to Palm Beach, Florida, during which the wife is mistaken for a chambermaid by "Mrs. Potter from Chicago"—a barely disguised reference to Mrs. Potter PALMER, the city's still-prominent social leader. Unlike the earlier *YOU KNOW ME AL*, the first-person stories are presented as spoken, not written, although they continue what has been called "the Lardner idiom," revealing a man who is vain and ignorant. To modern readers the work seems dated, in that the speech patterns and the types of affectation described no longer ring true; the pretense of being interested in grand opera, then mangling the names of operas, composers, and singers, appears less relevant today than in Lardner's era. The title makes reference to Jonathan Swift's 18th-century satire, *Gulliver's Travels.*

Gunsaulus, Rev. Frank W.
(1856–1921) *Congregationalist minister*

His famous sermon, "If I Had a Million Dollars," delivered at the Plymouth Congregational Church when Philip D. ARMOUR was in attendance, resulted in Armour's founding in 1893 of the ARMOUR INSTITUTE; the school provided technical training for young men. Gunsaulus became the first president of the school, a position he held for nearly 30 years. In 1940, the Armour Institute merged with the LEWIS INSTITUTE to become the Illinois Institute of Technology. A hall in the ART INSTITUTE is named after Gunsaulus.

Gurdjieff, George
(1866?–1941) *Greek-Armenian mystic and occultist*

Among Gurdjieff's disciples were Margaret ANDERSON, Jane HEAP, Jean TOOMER, and Olgivanna Wright, third wife of architect Frank Lloyd WRIGHT. Born in Russia, claiming to have gained enlightenment while traveling through Central Asia, Gurdjieff established his Institute for the Harmonious Development of Man in Russia in 1919, then in Fontainebleau, near Paris, in 1922. Among his teachings was the claim that most humans act as if they are asleep; his Fourth Way, as he called it, shows the path to true wakefulness, to an enlightened consciousness. English writer Katherine Mansfield, dying of tuberculosis, came to stay at Fontainebleau before her death in 1923. Anderson and Heap, meeting Gurdjieff in 1924, remained followers the rest of their lives; Toomer, also meeting Gurdjieff in 1924, established a center for his teachings in Chicago in 1926, later initiating a short-lived commune in Portage, Wisconsin.

H

Hackett, Francis
(1883–1962) *editor, biographer, novelist*

Born in Ireland, coming to America in 1902, Hackett worked at MARSHALL FIELD AND COMPANY, then found a position at the *Chicago Evening Post*. In 1909, he established the paper's supplement, the FRIDAY LITERARY REVIEW; two years later, turning the editorship over to Floyd DELL, he left for New York to become literary editor of the *The New Republic*. His biography *Henry the Eighth* was a best-seller in 1929.

haiku

This Japanese poetic form was imitated by Western poets in the early years of the 20th century. The haiku traditionally consists of three lines, containing 17 syllables; it records a striking moment of perception. The IMAGISTS, led by Ezra POUND, made adaptations of the form, praising what they considered its austere pictorial qualities. Pound's most famous haiku adaptation, "In the Station of the Metro," was written in 1912; the poet claimed he had originally composed a poem of 30 lines, then destroyed it—and then composed a poem half that length, then destroyed that version as well—before settling on his final rendition. Carl SANDBURG used versions of the haiku in his "Handfuls" poems, published in the 1916 CHICAGO POEMS; the most famous is the six-line "Fog."

Hainsfeather, Barney   *See* SPOON RIVER ANTHOLOGY.

"Halsted Street Car"   *See* CHICAGO POEMS.

Hamblin, Carl   *See* SPOON RIVER ANTHOLOGY.

Hamilton, Alice
(1869–1970) *physician, Hull-House resident*

Pioneering as a woman physician, living at HULL-HOUSE for nearly four decades, Hamilton was one of the founders in the field of occupational health; she brought to public attention the issues of occupational diseases and industrial poisoning. Born in New York City, she grew up in Fort Wayne, Indiana, and received a medical degree from the University of Michigan; she came to Chicago in 1897 to teach at the Women's Medical School of NORTHWESTERN UNIVERSITY. Among her projects was a study of lead poisoning, documenting its effects, finding that a deleterious use of lead occurred in more than 70 industrial processes; its victims were usually the poor and the foreign-born. In 1919, Hamilton became professor of industrial medicine at Harvard Medical School, receiving a half-time appointment that allowed her to continue living part of the year at Hull-House. Her important textbooks were the 1925 *Industrial Poisons in the United States* and the 1934 *Industrial Toxicology*. Hamilton was with Jane

ADDAMS when the Hull-House founder died in 1935; she herself lived another 35 years, dying at the age of 101.

Hampton, Lionel
(1908–2002) *jazz musician, vibraphonist*

Born in Louisville, Kentucky, Hampton attended a Roman Catholic school for Native American and African-American children in Kenosha, Wisconsin, where he first took up drumming and percussion playing. Attending high school in Chicago, he joined a newsboys' JAZZ band sponsored by the CHICAGO DEFENDER. In 1927, he was persuaded by Louis ARMSTRONG to take up the vibraphone, an electronic version of the xylophone; it soon became his signature instrument. In 1936, clarinetist Benny GOODMAN formed a quartet consisting of Goodman, Hampton, drummer Gene KRUPA, and pianist Teddy Wilson; it became an early integrated jazz combo. Known as a crowd-pleasing showman, Hampton later formed his own band, moving from swing to bebop. He died in New York City at the age of 94.

Hamsun, Knut
(1859–1952) *Norwegian novelist*

In the late 1880s, Hamsun worked in Chicago as a streetcar conductor, then as a farm laborer in North Dakota. Returning to Norway, he wrote in 1890 his best-known novel, *Hunger*, reflecting the school of NATURALISM; he won the Nobel Prize in literature in 1920. During World War II, Hamsun welcomed the German Nazi invasion of Norway, bestowing his Nobel Prize on Nazi functionary Joseph Goebbels. Because of his age, postwar charges of treason were dropped; he died in Norway at the age of 92.

"Hands"   See WINESBURG, OHIO.

Hannan, Will

This character appears in Hamlin GARLAND's story "At the Branch Road," collected in MAIN-TRAVELLED ROADS. As a young man growing up on an Iowa farm, Will lets jealousy and impulsiveness drive him away from his fiancée, Agnes DINGMAN. He subsequently prospers in Texas, acquiring interest in a cattle ranch. When he returns to Iowa and finds Agnes wasted by illness, living a harsh farm life with an abusive husband, he resolves to act on the love he once felt for her; he persuades her and her child to flee with him.

Hansen, Harry
(1884–1977) *journalist*

A Chicagoan for two decades, Hansen produced a memoir in 1923, *Midwest Portraits*, that provided an idiosyncratic view of several Chicago literary figures. Born in Davenport, Iowa, first coming to the city to cover the 1904 Republican national convention, he became a reporter for the CHICAGO DAILY NEWS in 1913; he spent two years in Europe as a correspondent during WORLD WAR I, returning in 1919 to cover the Versailles peace conference. In *Midwest Portraits*, Hanson devotes laudatory sections to Carl SANDBURG and Sherwood ANDERSON, discussing with approval Anderson's recently published and now dismissed novel, MANY MARRIAGES; he reviews also the career of Edgar Lee MASTERS, praising the recently published autobiographical novel SKEETERS KIRBY, calling it Masters's best prose work. In a final section, he lauds Ben HECHT as a "dreamer and poet, scorner and critic," concluding that Hecht is a man of promise. Hansen moved to New York in 1926, becoming literary editor of the *New York World*, producing a widely read syndicated column.

Hapgood, Hutchins
(1869–1944) *writer*

Born in Chicago, living most of his life in the East, Hapgood produced several Chicago-based works; he was also one of the founders of the PROVINCETOWN PLAYERS. In 1905, he researched material in Chicago on the American workingman, spending time at HULL-HOUSE; his *The Spirit of Labor*, published in 1907, featured an anarchist union leader, Anton Johanssen, the figure whom Carl SANDBURG depicted in his CHICAGO POEMS piece, "The Dynamiter." In 1909, Hapgood published *An Anarchist Woman*, centering on his Chicago companion, a former prostitute; in 1912, he provided the introduction to *Prison Memoirs of an Anarchist*, written by Alexander Berkman, one-time companion of Emma GOLDMAN. Hapgood and his wife, Neith Boyce, daughter of the owner of the Boston radical periodical THE ARENA, publicly espoused beliefs in free love and open marriage; Hapgood's play *Enemies*, the story of their marriage, was performed by the author and Boyce for the Provincetown Players in 1916. Theodore DREISER's *A Gallery of Women*, published in 1929, contains an unflattering fictionalized portrait of Hapgood.

"Happiness"   *See* CHICAGO POEMS.

Hard, Tandy   *See under* WINESBURG, OHIO: "Tandy."

Hardin, Lilian "Lil"
(1898–1971) *pianist, jazz composer*

The wife of Louis ARMSTRONG, Hardin has been credited with playing a role in her husband's musical innovation, as well as furthering his career. Born in Memphis, Tennessee, coming to Chicago in 1918, she was hired by Joe "King" OLIVER; playing with his ensemble, she met Armstrong, whom she married in 1924. Between 1925 and 1927, Armstrong, Hardin, and other JAZZ musicians made pioneering acoustical recordings in Chicago; historians suggest that a large portion of the music was written by Hardin, noting that she later sued Armstrong for copyright ownership of some of the material. When her husband moved on to New York, Hardin stayed in Chicago, continuing a career as a nightclub pianist and band leader. She died a month after Armstrong, collapsing while performing at an outdoors tribute to his life and music.

Harding, Warren G.
(1865–1923) *29th president of the United States*

Born in Ohio, elected to the U.S. Senate, Harding received the Republican nomination for president in the early morning of June 11, 1920, in the original smoke-filled room at Chicago's BLACKSTONE HOTEL. Promising a "return to normalcy" after the WORLD WAR I era—and coining a word in the process—Harding won the election in a landslide vote. Late in 1921, he issued a pardon for Eugene V. DEBS, releasing the Socialist Party candidate, who had run against him in prison, from a confinement of more than two and a half years. Harding died suddenly after less than two years in office, succeeded by vice president Calvin COOLIDGE.

Hardy, David   *See under* WINESBURG, OHIO: "Godliness."

Hargus

A character in Frank NORRIS's novel THE PIT, Hargus—no first name is given—is an old trader who lost a fortune two decades earlier in an attempt to corner the market on the CHICAGO BOARD OF TRADE. He had once been "a king all-powerful," Norris writes; he is a foreshadowing of Curtis JADWIN. Although the historical figure of Joseph Leiter provides the immediate background for Jadwin's financial failure, the character Hargus is based on another real-life figure who lost millions of dollars speculating in grain and who in the last years of his life ran a tobacco shop near the Board of Trade building.

Harper, William Rainey
(1856–1906) *founding president of the University of Chicago*

Born in New Concord, Ohio, Harper received a Ph.D. in Old Testament studies from Yale University at the age of 18 and first came to Chicago to teach at the Baptist Union Theological Seminary; he later taught at Yale as professor of Semitic languages and instructor in Hebrew at Yale Divinity School. In 1891, he was persuaded to return to Chicago, becoming president of the new UNIVERSITY OF CHICAGO, funded by Baptist tycoon John D. ROCKEFELLER. Gathering a world-renowned faculty, Harper oversaw the establishment of a prestigious institution, committed to research and scholarship; an early achievement was convincing Chicago businessman Charles T. YERKES to fund the building and equipping of the world's most complete astronomical observatory, established at Williams Bay, Wisconsin. Harper died of cancer at the age of 49.

Harrington, Van

The principal character in Robert HERRICK's novel *THE MEMOIRS OF AN AMERICAN CITIZEN*, Harrington, coming from a small Indiana town, begins his rags-to-riches story with nights of homelessness in Chicago. He gradually rises in the meatpacking business and achieves great wealth, although through methods that are unscrupulous and illegal. As Harrington tells his tale in the first person, Herrick expects the reader to pass judgment on him, to apply his own moral standards, and thus to find Harrington wanting. Yet the character's self-justification often seems convincing, especially since the author allows him twinges of conscience and bouts of loneliness, and readers end up grudgingly admiring him; they have also noted that Harrington, unlike Theodore DREISER's businessman Frank COWPERWOOD, leads an upright family life.

Harris, Frank
(1856–1931) *novelist*

Born in Galway, Ireland, living in both the United States and England, Harris published *THE BOMB*, his first novel, a fictionalized account of the HAYMARKET AFFAIR, in 1908. He had worked in Chicago as a teenager, and in 1907, he returned to the city to revisit locales and read contemporary newspaper accounts of the Haymarket Affair. He drew also upon the experiences of anarchists he had known, giving particular focus in the novel to

the anti-immigrant attitudes that prevailed at the time; he states that nine out of 10 of the men employed at the MCCORMICK REAPER WORKS, where the labor violence started, were foreign born. Harris's best-known work appeared nearly two decades later—the scandalous, long-censored *My Life and Loves,* a self-celebrating autobiography published in three volumes between 1923 and 1927. Floyd DELL, who knew Harris in New York, described him after his death as a "loud, gentle, bombastic old pirate."

Harrison, Benjamin
(1833–1901) *23rd president of the United States*

CIVIL WAR officer and Indianapolis lawyer, grandson of William Henry Harrison, the ninth U.S. president, Republican Benjamin Harrison defeated Democrat Grover Cleveland in 1888. His presidency saw the beginnings of ANTITRUST activity, with passage of the Sherman Anti-Trust act in 1890, although the effects of the law in curtailing trusts would be little felt until the next century. The growing discontents of rural populism and labor agitation led to his defeat after one term, and Cleveland was reelected in 1892. Harrison attended opening night ceremonies at the Chicago AUDITORIUM theater in 1889.

Hartman, Reverend Curtis   *See under WINESBURG, OHIO:* "The Strength of God."

Haskins, Timothy

This character appears in Hamlin GARLAND's story "Under the Lion's Paw," collected in *MAINTRAVELLED ROADS*. Haskins and his family, driven from their Kansas farm by grasshoppers, find an Iowa farm to rent; they hope to be able eventually to buy it. After grueling effort put in by the husband, the wife, and their nine-year-old son, the farm is greatly improved—but then the owner, citing the improvements, doubles his price. Haskins is a victim of unjust land-ownership policies, exemplifying Garland's support of the economic theories of Henry GEORGE;

he represents also the ceaseless, exhausting labor necessary to work a farm on the western plains.

Hately, Constance   *See SPOON RIVER ANTHOLOGY.*

Hatfield, Aaron   *See SPOON RIVER ANTHOLOGY.*

Hayes, Rutherford B.
(1822–1893) *19th president of the United States*

Born in Ohio, Hayes served in the CIVIL WAR and was subsequently elected to Congress. Hayes supported the RADICAL REPUBLICANS in their program for RECONSTRUCTION. Becoming president in a disputed 1876 election, Hayes withdrew the last of the federal troops from southern states, marking the end of Reconstruction. During the GREAT STRIKE of 1877, he send troops to urban areas, bolstering state militias, setting the precedent for Grover CLEVELAND's antistrike actions later in the century.

Haymarket Affair

This epochal event in labor history was until recently referred to as the Haymarket Riot. On May Day, 1886, Samuel GOMPERS, leader of the Federation of Organized Trades and Labor Unions—later the AMERICAN FEDERATION OF LABOR—called for a nationwide strike, demanding an eight-hour work week and increased wages; it

This rendition of the Haymarket Affair bombing appeared in *The Graphic News,* May 16, 1886. *(Chicago Historical Society)*

was the first organized general strike in labor history. In Chicago, a May Day parade took place without incident, but two days later, violence erupted between strikers and nonunion strikebreakers, or "scabs," in front of the MᴄCORMICK REAPER WORKS; two strikers were killed. A rally was called for the following evening, May 4, at Haymarket Square, and as police approached, a bomb was thrown—the first bomb ever employed in a labor dispute—killing seven policemen. The thrower of the bomb was never identified, but in the subsequent trial eight anarchists were condemned, seven facing the death penalty.

August SPIES, German-born publisher of the *ARBEITER ZEITUNG*, a radical German-language newspaper, was one of the men condemned to death; a large cache of explosives was claimed to have been found in the paper's offices after the incident. Another of the condemned men was Albert PARSONS—southern-born, the only native American member of the group—whose widow, Lucy PARSONS, continued long afterward to be active in radical circles. Albert Parsons, during his trial, praised dynamite as "democratic," since it makes everyone equal: "It emancipates the world from the domineering of the few over the many." Spies, Parsons, and two others were hanged on November 11, 1887.

Earlier that year, the federal government had accepted land north of the city, offered by Chicago businessmen, to establish a military base, FORT SHERIDAN; the purpose was to make troops available in case of further strife. In 1889, a monument to the slain policemen, its pedestal designed by architect

The monument to the police in Haymarket Square, unveiled in 1889, has subsequently been relocated several times; since 1976, it has stood in the courtyard of the Chicago Police Academy. *(Chicago Historical Society)*

John Wellborn ROOT, was erected in Haymarket Square. In 1893, Governor John Peter ALTGELD pardoned three remaining anarchists, causing a public outrage that effectively ended his political career.

The event has been said to have initiated a new militance in both labor and politics, as well as increased repressive measures; labor leaders such as Gompers believed the affair set back the labor movement for years. When agitation for an official LABOR DAY was renewed, designating the first day in May, or May Day—as had been adopted elsewhere—Congress, acting in 1894, chose a September date, in what was seen as defiance of the workers' movement.

Robert HERRICK's novel of 1905, *THE MEMOIRS OF AN AMERICAN CITIZEN*, recounts the Haymarket trial in critical terms, presenting its fictional businessman as a member of the jury. Three years later, the Irish-American novelist Frank HARRIS published *THE BOMB,* a novel fictionalizing the happenings of that evening in May, naming the man who, as many people think, actually threw the bomb. Theodore DREISER, writing in 1914 in *THE TITAN,* noted that the Haymarket incident brought to the forefront in America the issues of social class, including the rights of workingmen in the nation's economic development—although its protagonist, Frank COWPERWOOD, dismisses the importance of such matters.

Haywood, William "Big Bill"
(1869–1928) *labor leader*

Haywood is best known as a founder of the INDUSTRIAL WORKERS OF THE WORLD, or "Wobblies," in Chicago in 1905. Born in Salt Lake City, a leader of the Western Federation of Miners, he was accused of inciting violence in a Cripple Creek, Colorado, strike, also of involvement in the dynamite murder of a former governor of Idaho; Chicago lawyer Clarence DARROW traveled to Idaho to defend him successfully. In 1911, Haywood coauthored a pamphlet, *Industrial Unionism,* denouncing gradualism, or step-by-step social progress, arguing that the property rights of CAPITALISM, protected under "capitalist law," should not be respected. He was active in the textile workers' strikes in Lawrence,

Massachusetts, and Paterson, New Jersey, in 1912 and 1913. Clashing with Eugene V. DEBS, he was ousted from the SOCIALIST PARTY OF AMERICA in 1913. During WORLD WAR I, he was convicted of sedition and sentenced to 20 years in prison by Chicago federal judge Kenesaw Mountain LANDIS, who would later become baseball commissioner after the BLACK SOX SCANDAL. Haywood jumped bond while awaiting a new trial, escaping to the Soviet Union. Novelist Theodore DREISER visited him in Moscow in 1927, finding him aged and "beaten"; he died the next year at the age of 59.

H.D.   *See* DOOLITTLE, HILDA.

Heap, Jane
(1883–1964) *coeditor of the Little Review*

Born in Topeka, Kansas, Heap came to Chicago in 1901 to study at the ART INSTITUTE; she achieved recognition as an artist and became a set designer and an actress for the LITTLE THEATRE group. In 1916, she met Margaret ANDERSON, becoming her companion as well as coeditor of *LITTLE REVIEW*; a witty conversationalist, wearing men's clothes, Heap was considered more interesting than the feminine and glamorous Anderson. The two women moved the *Little Review* to New York in 1917, then to Paris in the early 1920s. As Anderson formed a liaison with Belgian opera singer Georgette LEBLANC in 1923, Heap took over editorship of the periodical, continuing it until 1929. She had met, meanwhile, Armenian mystic George GURDJIEFF, who became an important influence in in her life—and in Anderson's, too—and moved to London in the 1930s to teach his beliefs. She died there at the age of 80.

Hecht, Ben
(1894–1964) *journalist, dramatist, screenwriter*

Born in New York City to Russian-Jewish immigrants, later moving with his family to Racine, Wisconsin, Hecht came to Chicago in 1910. He went to work first for the *Chicago Journal,* then the CHICAGO DAILY NEWS; he contributed to LITTLE REVIEW, FRIDAY LITERARY REVIEW, and POETRY. In 1921, he began his daily column, "1001 Afternoons in Chicago," presenting a range of figures, varying in ethnicity and occupation; the column continued the popular newspaper story-sketch that had been introduced the previous century by Eugene FIELD and George ADE. In the same year, he published the novel ERIK DORN, followed in 1922 by FANTAZIUS MALLARE; the latter was seized by U.S. postal authorities for obscenity, and as the result, Hecht lost his job at the *Daily News,* ending his daily column. *1001 AFTERNOONS* appeared in book form in 1922, published by the Chicago firm of COVICI-MCGEE. In 1923, Hecht, along with Maxwell BODENHEIM, began the weekly CHICAGO LITERARY TIMES, underwritten by Covici-McGee; the paper lasted a little over a year. The friendship between Hecht and Bodenheim ended with the publication of Hecht's *Count Bruga* in 1926, an unflattering portrait of a poet modeled on Bodenheim; the novel drew obscenity charges, as had Bodenheim's *Replenishing Jessica* the previous year.

In 1926, at the age of 33, Hecht began scriptwriting for the movies, eventually becoming Hollywood's most highly paid writer. He is credited with initiating the gangster movie, drawing on his knowledge of Al CAPONE and other Chicago underworld figures; his silent film *Underworld,* opening in 1927, won the first Academy Award for a screen story. Making the transition to sound films, Hecht wrote the screenplay for *Scarface,* starring fellow Chicagoan Paul MUNI; the film, made in 1930, was not released until 1932 because of censorship problems regarding violence. Meanwhile, in 1928, the stage play THE FRONT PAGE, cowritten with fellow one-time reporter Charles MACARTHUR, depicting a group of hard-boiled Chicago newspapermen, opened to acclaim in New York; Hecht worked later on the 1940 gender-switching movie version, *His Girl Friday.* His many other screen credits include *Wuthering Heights, Notorious,* and *Spellbound.* A 1954 anecdotal autobiography, A CHILD OF THE CENTURY, became a best-seller, much of it devoted to his Chicago years; three years later, he wrote a memoir of MacArthur in *Charlie: The Improbable Life and Times of Charles MacArthur.* A 1963 personal memoir, *Gaily, Gaily,* returned in part to his early Chicago material. Hecht died of a heart attack in New York City.

Further Reading
MacAdams, William. *Ben Hecht: The Man Behind the Legend.* New York: Charles Scribner's Sons, 1990.

Hemingway, Ernest
(1899–1961) *renowned writer*

Born in the Chicago suburb of OAK PARK, Hemingway spent little time in the city; the setting of his early work was northern Michigan, where his family maintained a summer home. During high school, he is said to have practiced imitating Ring LARDNER, whose baseball stories began appearing in the *Saturday Evening Post* in 1914. After graduation from high school, Hemingway obtained a job on the *Kansas City Star;* in 1918, the last year of WORLD WAR I, he signed up as a Red Cross ambulance driver in Italy, where he was wounded just before his 19th birthday. Returning to Chicago in 1919, he met Sherwood ANDERSON, then enjoying success with WINESBURG, OHIO. Anderson encouraged the younger writer, giving him letters of introduction to American expatriate Gertrude STEIN and Irish expatriate James JOYCE, helping him find a publisher for his story collection, *In Our Time;* Hemingway was considered ungrateful when he published THE TORRENTS OF SPRING, a mock-novel parodying Anderson's DARK LAUGHTER. The work that brought Hemingway international renown was *The Sun Also Rises,* appearing in 1926, confirming him as the voice of what Stein labeled "the lost generation." The novel was followed three years later by *A Farewell to Arms,* and his Spanish Civil War novel, *For Whom the Bell Tolls,* appeared in 1940. Hemingway received the Nobel Prize for literature in 1954; he died a suicide at the age of 61.

Henderson, Alice Corbin
(1881–1949) *poet, associate editor of* Poetry

Acting as initial reader for editor Harriet MONROE, contributing to the editorial section,

Henderson played an important role in the ascendancy of POETRY magazine; she became known for her candor and outspokenness. Among the poets she is credited with discovering are Edgar Lee MASTERS and Carl SANDBURG. In the spring of 1916, suffering from tuberculosis, she moved to Santa Fe, New Mexico, following medical advice; observers agree that her departure deprived the magazine of an important editorial voice. In 1922, Henderson and Monroe engaged in a legal battle over royalties for a revised edition of *The New Poetry,* an anthology presenting work from the periodical; the conflict severed their relationship. *The New Poetry,* originally published in 1917, revised for three subsequent editions, became a basic text of MODERNISM.

Henry, Alice
(1857–1943) *reformer, writer*

Born in Melbourne, Australia, becoming an activist in women's suffrage organizations both in Australia and in England, Henry arrived in the United States in 1906. While speaking that year at a Baltimore convention of the NATIONAL AMERICAN WOMAN SUFFRAGE ASSOCIATION, she met Jane ADDAMS, who invited her to come to Chicago. Staying briefly at HULL-HOUSE, Henry joined the staff of the NATIONAL WOMEN'S TRADE UNION LEAGUE, an organization seeking to improve labor conditions and promote women's suffrage; she served also on the editorial board of the *Union Labor Advocate,* the journal of the Chicago Federation of Labor. When the Chicago chapter of the Women's Trade Union League launched its own journal, *Life and Labor,* in 1911, Henry coedited the periodical, along with fellow Australian Miles FRANKLIN. In 1915, Henry published a treatise on labor history, *Trade Union Women,* followed in 1923 by *Women in the Labor Movement.* In 1926, she left Chicago for California, returning to Australia seven years later; she died there at the age of 85.

Henry, O.   *See* WILLIAM SYDNEY PORTER.

Herndon, William H.
(1818–1891) *law partner and early biographer of Abraham Lincoln*

In his three-volume collection of materials and reminiscences published in 1889, Herndon promulgated many of the stories that became part of the LINCOLN myth, including the romantic tale of Ann RUTLEDGE; the story resulted in Rutledge's remains being moved to the new cemetery in the town of Petersburg, Illinois. Edgar Lee MASTERS—besides adding his own chapter to the Rutledge saga in *SPOON RIVER ANTHOLOGY*—pays tribute in a graveyard monologue to the man he recalled seeing as a boy in downstate Illinois; he presents Herndon as a man who had seen his hero rise from the soil, then hasten on to a tragic destiny.

Herrick, Isabel

This character appears in Hamlin GARLAND's novel *ROSE OF DUTCHER'S COOLLY.* An early example of a professional woman in American fiction, Isabel is an alienist, or medical psychologist, having published a treatise on "nervous diseases." She is foreshadowed in the novel by a woman lawyer from Milwaukee who rescues the young heroine, Rose DUTCHER, from harassment on a train; the lawyer also advises Rose not to marry until she is 30 years old. Isabel herself waits until the age of 33 to marry, having first achieved a professional status. She had long ago lost a young man, the great love of her youth, who had died; she now marries a fellow doctor for companionship and potential motherhood, and being a mother, she claims, will not interfere with her continuing profession. Isabel is presented as an up-to-date, feminist role model for Rose—Rose's own farm-wife mother died years before—although the tale ends without Rose's convincingly finding her own profession.

Herrick, Robert
(1868–1938) *novelist*

Born in Cambridge, Massachusetts, Herrick graduated from Harvard University and came to the UNIVERSITY OF CHICAGO in 1893; he soon began writing novels deploring the crudeness and greed he found about him in his new city. The 1898 THE GOSPEL OF FREEDOM depicts the foolishness and self-indulgence of the newly wealthy; the 1900 THE WEB OF LIFE places the city's corruption against a backdrop of the WORLD'S COLUMBIAN EXPOSITION and the PULLMAN STRIKE; the 1904 *The Common Lot* includes the story of a new hotel, built from inferior material, that burns to the ground, causing loss of life. Herrick's best-known novel is the 1905 MEMOIRS OF AN AMERICAN CITIZEN, telling in ironic first-person narration the rise of a poor Indiana boy to success as a meatpacker, then a United States senator. Herrick's work fits the formulas for REALISM, although his novels were never as popular as those of William Dean HOWELLS—and far less popular than the work of Theodore DREISER, whose Frank COWPERWOOD trilogy also traces the rise of a business tycoon. Retiring from teaching in 1923, Herrick took the post in 1935 of government secretary of the Virgin Islands, where he died three years later.

Hertz, John D.
(1879–1961) *entrepreneur*

Born in Austria, later Czechoslovakia, coming with his family to Chicago at the age of five, Hertz as a young man engaged in amateur boxing under the name of Danny Donnelly. Taking up automobile sales, he founded the Yellow Cab Company in 1915, providing a service that had been considered the province of the wealthy; the color yellow was adopted to identify his cabs, to signify an inexpensive form of transportation that was available to all. In 1923, Hertz took over a car-rental enterprise, renaming it the Yellow Drive-Yourself Corporation; a year later, he sold the company to General Motors. During the PROHIBITION era, rental cars had taken on a negative aura, seen as vehicles for bootlegging, or the transporting of liquor. In 1953, Hertz bought back his company, naming it Hertz Rent-A-Car.

Heyl, Clarence

This character appears in Edna FERBER's novel *FANNY HERSELF*. Protagonist Fanny BRANDEIS,

growing up in a small Wisconsin town, rescues Clarence, her schoolmate, from anti-Semitic bullying. Later, his family sends him to Colorado for his health, and he returns a strong young man, determined to establish a relationship with his one-time defender. Fanny pursues her successful business career, and Clarence becomes a well-known newspaper columnist in New York City; when they reunite, he leads her into expressing her artistic talent, as well as persuades her to marry him. He remains a one-dimensional character, functioning to rescue Fanny from what Ferber feels obliged to disapprove—namely, the pursuit of heartless business practices.

Higbie, Archibald   *See* SPOON RIVER ANTHOLOGY.

"The Hill"   *See* SPOON RIVER ANTHOLOGY.

Hillman, Sidney
(1887–1946) *labor leader*

Serving for 30 years as president of the Amalgamated Clothing Workers of America, one of the largest unions in the country, Hillman came first to prominence in the 1910–11 strike against the Chicago clothing firm of Hart, Schaffner and Marx. Born in Lithuania, coming to the United States as a young man, Hillman settled in Chicago in 1909, employed as a fabric cutter. Supported by residents of HULL-HOUSE and the Chicago chapter of the NATIONAL WOMEN'S TRADE UNION LEAGUE, he led the local garment workers' union, consisting mostly of immigrant women, to a settlement with the clothier in January 1911. Moving to New York City three years later, he became the first president of ACWA, a position he held until his death. In 1935, Hillman and others broke from the AMERICAN FEDERATION OF LABOR to form the Congress of Industrial Organizations, or CIO.

Hindman, Alice   *See under* WINESBURG, OHIO: "Adventure."

Hirsch, Rabbi Emil G.

(1851–1923) *rabbi of Reform Judaism*

Born in Luxembourg, where his father had been chief rabbi, Hirsch came to the United States in 1866. From 1880 until his death, he headed the Sinai Congregation on the South Side, where his influence is said to have led to many of the philanthropic projects of Julius ROSENWALD. In 1892, joining the faculty of the UNIVERSITY OF CHICAGO as professor of rabbinical literature and philosophy, he became the first rabbi to teach at an American university; he edited the periodical *Reform Advocate* from 1891 until his death.

In Edna FERBER's 1917 novel, *FANNY HERSELF,* a prominent Chicago rabbi, modeled on Hirsch, is given the name of Kirsch; the heroine, attending his grand house of worship, finds him speaking about politics in satirical, biting tones. She decides that this is not religion, at least not as she has been taught, but it is certainly "tonic."

Hoheimer, Knowlt   *See SPOON RIVER ANTHOLOGY.*

Holabird, William

(1854–1923) *architect*

Coming from New York to Chicago in 1875, Holabird worked initially for William Le Baron JENNEY; in 1880, he entered into a partnership that included Martin Roche, leading to the founding of Holabird and Roche in 1883. The firm's first major building was the Tacoma, completed in 1889, using large amounts of exterior glass, taking advantage of the wide apertures allowed in the new steel-frame construction; it was demolished in 1929. The still-standing Marquette Building of 1894 features a Holabird and Roche innovation, the CHICAGO WINDOW, again capitalizing on the new light-providing apertures; the Marquette is noted also for its grand rotunda, featuring bronze reliefs memorializing the French Jesuit explorer Jacques MARQUETTE. In 1929, Holabird's son, John A. Holabird, joined with John Wellborn Root Jr., son of pioneering architect John Wellborn ROOT, to form the firm of Holabird and Root, noted for the modern ART DECO version of the BOARD OF TRADE BUILDING, completed in 1930.

Holden, Barry   *See SPOON RIVER ANTHOLOGY.*

Holden, John

In Sherwood ANDERSON's story "The Return," collected in *DEATH IN THE WOODS,* The 40-year-old Holden drives from New York City to the hometown he left 18 years before; he is thinking of all the people he will see, including Lillian, the girl he left behind. Arriving in the evening, he meets an old acquaintance on Main Street, a man who is now a doctor and—even during PROHIBITION—a drunk. The doctor introduces him to people he does not know, taking them to a roadhouse where they can obtain liquor; Holden wonders what he is doing there. Although he feels that in the past he has let people down—the girl at home, the wife who has since died—he is finding no answers, nor connections, in this return to the past. He leaves town abruptly in the middle of the night.

Home Insurance Building

This building is the world's first structure using a partial metal frame. Designed by William Le Baron JENNEY in 1885, the 10-story building relied on load-bearing stone masonry for the first two floors, then on a bolted-iron cage that supported the next several floors. Above the sixth story, Jenney incorporated Bessemer steel beams, fabricated according to a recently developed process; he substituted the steel beams for the more corrosion-prone and fire-vulnerable iron products. The building was razed in 1931.

Homestead Act

This law, passed in 1862, gave public land to private citizens. The Homestead Act has been called one of the most significant pieces of legislation in

American history; it provided landless citizens with 160 acres of property and spurred westward migration. Recipients were required to develop the land and live on it; after five years they owned it. Support for a homestead act was voiced in 1860 by the Republican Party, considering it a way to stop the spread of slavery into new territories; southern states opposed the legislation, but secession from the Union cleared the way for its passage. President Abraham LINCOLN signed the bill on May 20, 1862, making it law beginning the following year. By 1900, homesteaders had claimed 80 million acres of land.

Homestead Strike

Called against the Carnegie Steel Company in Homestead, Pennsylvania, this labor dispute began in June 1892 over a proposed cut in wages. Henry C. Frick, company general manager, hired operatives of Allan PINKERTON's detective agency, and armed conflict between agents and strikers resulted in casualties; Alexander Berkman, an associate of Emma GOLDMAN, made an unsuccessful attempt on Frick's life. Artist Frederic REMINGTON covered the strike for *Frank Leslie's Illustrated Weekly*, depicting the strikers as rioters against law and order.

The Hoosier Schoolmaster
Edward Eggleston
(1871)

This novel is an important early example of midwestern regional fiction; *Hoosier*, a term of unclear origins, refers to Indiana, or a resident of Indiana. Edward EGGLESTON, in his introduction, expresses admiration for James Russell Lowell's use of Yankee, or New England, DIALECT WRITING in *The Biglow Papers*; he declares that he himself is consciously using midwestern dialect, being careful to preserve it accurately. In the novel, a young man comes to teach in a rural school in southern Indiana, replacing two previous teachers, each of whom had been thrashed by his students and driven off; Eggleston's backwoods characters are presented as often crude and mean-spirited, going

beyond the charm and quaintness of standard LOCAL COLOR writing.

Hamlin GARLAND, writing nearly a half-century later in *A SON OF THE MIDDLE BORDER*, tells of reading the serialization of the novel in the magazine *Hearth and Home*. Living with his family on the plains of Iowa, he competed with his sister, he recalls, as to who should read the periodical first. The perennially popular novel was made into a movie in 1935, altering the schoolmaster into a returning CIVIL WAR hero. Eggleston's sequel, *The Hoosier School-Boy*, became a follow-up movie, starring Mickey Rooney, two years later.

Horses and Men
Sherwood Anderson
(1923)

In several stories of this collection, the author's hometown of Clyde, Ohio, becomes Bidwell, Ohio, in several of these stories—as it had been previously in the novel *POOR WHITE* and the story "The Egg," collected in *THE TRIUMPH OF THE EGG*. Further autobiographical elements appear in the racetrack settings; in "The Man Who Became a Woman," the narrator's traveling in a horse-racing circuit mirrors ANDERSON's own activities in 1895, and Tom MEANS, the talkative, story-telling writer-to-be, is the author himself. The background for "An Ohio Pagan" comes from the summer of 1899, when Anderson worked as a thresher after returning from the SPANISH-AMERICAN WAR.

Autobiographical family relationships recur throughout the writer's work; in "The Sad Horn Blowers," Will APPLETON serves as an authorial surrogate, and Tom APPLETON, housepainter, paperhanger, and horn blower, is one of many versions of Anderson's father. The older sister in the story, Kate, keeping the house together after the mother's death, is Anderson's sister Stella. Yet no family obtrudes in "The Triumph of a Modern or, Send for the Lawyer," where the author presents himself as an adult—and as an orphan, beyond the embrace of family. Humorously depicting a faux-artist, he is mocking himself, a sometime painter who, in the early 1920s, mounted shows of his watercolors at bookstores in Chicago and New York.

As with the stories collected in THE TRIUMPH OF THE EGG, the modern reader must remember that an epithet considered racist today was less potent in the 1920s—or at least, more prevalent and accepted in mainstream writing. One assumes, too, that if modern sensibilities had prevailed in 1923, Anderson would likely have altered the potential assault at the end of "The Man Who Became a Woman."

Synopses of Selected Stories

"I'M A FOOL"

The unnamed first-person narrator has held a job as a swipe, or groom, on a horse-racing circuit, but his family persuades him to give up what they consider a disreputable livelihood. He takes a job caring for horses in a delivery business in Sandusky, Ohio. When the races come to Sandusky, however, he takes the day off to see them. Wearing his best clothes, he goes downtown, walking into a hotel and buying 25-cent cigars; he wishes to appear as an important personage, mingling with the sportsmen gathering at the bar. Seeing a well-dressed man putting on airs, he takes offense; he pushes past the man, ordering a whiskey, then another.

Sitting in the grandstand, he finds himself near a young man who is a college man—although not stuck on himself, as so many such men are. Along with the college man are two young women, a girlfriend and a sister, and the sister is remarkably appealing. The college man makes a bet on a horse and loses. Yet in the next race, a horse appears that the narrator knows, and he decides to impress the girl by sharing inside information with her brother, although worrying about the smell of whiskey on his breath; he lights a cigar to disguise the aroma. Then he begins to show off, claiming to be the son of the horse's owner, a wealthy man in Marietta, Ohio; he makes up a first name for himself. He explains how this horse is going to fare in the races—that it will lose the first heat, then do well in the next—and he gives the man money to bet; the man and the two women add their own money as well. The races turn out as predicted, and the new friends are pleased.

The narrator finds, to his delight, that the sister seems to like him. After the races, the four young people go on a picnic, and the narrator has a chance to spend more time with the girl; she gives him a quick kiss before the group must catch their train home. As she gets on the train, she says that they will write to each other.

Now he is furious with himself. She will write to him, he realizes, and the letter will be returned, letting her know that no such person exists in Marietta, Ohio. No explaining will ever set the situation right again. If only, he tells himself, he had not drunk that whiskey in the hotel; if only he had not tried to outdo that man who was putting on airs. Maybe he would not have been such a fool.

"THE TRIUMPH OF A MODERN OR, SEND FOR THE LAWYER"

The *modern* of the title refers to the modern artist, as the first-person narrator likes to style himself. He begins by saying that he was a clerk in a Chicago office until two years ago—although he has always felt the urge to be a painter, or at least to assume the pose of a painter, and he has always been ready to appraise of the paintings of others. Then at the age of 30, he received money from the estate of his aunt, a woman he had never met; he tells how his good fortune came about.

One summer, having a possible inheritance in mind, he travels to the home of his aunt in Wisconsin. He finds that her house is closed up; she suffers from hay fever, he learns, and she spends her summers elsewhere. He goes to a hotel and writes a letter, expressing sorrow at not finding her home. He had hoped, he writes poetically, to find the comfort of his only female relative, wishing to lay his head on her breasts—he uses the plural of the word, avoiding the old-fashioned *bosom*—and then, to his desolation, he finds that she is not there. He pours his eloquence onto seven sheets of paper, finishing with tears in his eyes. When the letter reaches his aunt, a nurse reads the artful pages to her, and the aunt weeps. She feels overwhelmingly drawn to her nephew, and although originally intending to bequeath her money to finding a hay fever cure, she changes her mind. "Send for the lawyer," she tells the nurse.

"THE MAN WHO BECAME A WOMAN"

The first-person narrator, later identified as Herman DUDLEY, is working as a groom at a county fair racetrack in western Pennsylvania. A fellow groom is a would-be writer, Tom MEANS; Herman acknowledges a love for Tom, although he knows not to talk about such feelings. He makes clear also that he is now happily married.

Herman is groom to a gelding, or castrated male horse, named Pick-it-boy; the owner has also added a stallion recently to his stable, O My Man, whose groom is a black man named Burt. All the men working at the track regularly go into town for liquor and women—except the narrator, who has never been with a woman; Tom and Burt laugh at him for his backwardness. Yet Tom has recently left, traveling with his horse to another circuit, and the narrator finds himself troubled; dreaming of women, he feels disturbed as he walks the horses. Sometimes, as he walks Pick-it-boy, the gelding puts his nose up against his face, and he wishes it were a girl.

One Saturday evening the men go off to town, and the narrator promises to keep an eye on the horses. Yet he feels the urge to leave, and he heads down the hill in rain and darkness. Not far from the fairground stand the ruins of an abandoned slaughterhouse, where the bones of animals lie on the ground, where a smell still arises from the old building. The narrator comes upon a saloon in which a dozen miners are drinking; he orders a glass of whisky. Looking at a cracked mirror behind the bar, he sees his face, except that it is a girl's face, the face of a lonesome, scared girl. He orders another whisky.

A big, red-haired man comes into the saloon, carrying a child; the man sets the child down on the bar and orders drinks. The other men begin to laugh at him, calling him "cracked"; the big man, his eyes strange, is muttering under his breath. Another patron begins singing a song about a crack in "the old tin pan," getting up and strutting about as he sings it. The big man strikes out at him, knocking him to the floor with a single blow; he brings his heavy boot down on the man's shoulder, making the bones crunch. Still muttering, he raises his boot again, aiming at the man's face—but the child begins to cry, and the man picks him up and

leaves the room. The narrator, sickened, leaves the saloon as well. He finds his way back to the horses, to the loft of Pick-it-boy's stall, where he will sleep for the night; he removes his wet clothes and tucks himself in among the horse blankets.

He is awakened with a bang; two black men from the tracks, having been drinking, think that his naked body is a woman's, that one of the grooms has brought a woman back to the stables and that such a woman is fair game. Yet the narrator cannot make himself cry out and identify himself; he bolts from the loft, running out the door and into the darkness. He keeps running, still not making a sound, perhaps because he is ashamed of having been turned into a girl. He comes to the old slaughterhouse field, filled with bones; tripping, he falls into a horse's ribbed skeleton. A wave of terror runs through him and burns out "all that silly nonsense about being a girl." The spell is broken. Finding a straw stack in which sheep are sheltered, he crawls in among the animals and goes to sleep.

The next morning, still unclothed, he returns to the stable; the men laugh at him, but Burt, understanding that something has gone wrong, commands them to keep quiet, threatening them with a pitchfork. The narrator gathers up his clothes, gives Pick-it-boy a good-bye kiss, and leaves the horse-racing life forever.

"MILK BOTTLES"

The nameless first-person narrator, who works for a Chicago advertising agency, lives on the top floor of an old house; it is the month of August, and the room is unbearably hot. One night, the narrator walks out onto the street, and a milk bottle comes flying past him, breaking on the pavement; he hears the two actresses on the lower floor complaining about finding a half-filled bottle of spoiled milk on the windowsill. Meanwhile, because of the summer heat, hordes of people are coming outside from their homes, hoping to spend the night on parkland beside the lake. In the darkness, the narrator accidentally knocks over a woman's half-filled milk bottle; he apologizes, but the woman tells him the milk was sour, anyway.

The narrator meets Ed, a colleague at the agency, who insists he come back to his apartment;

Ed wants to show him something he has written. The narrator reads his sheets of paper, covered with poetic effusions, describing the grand, beautiful city of Chicago; he knows that such a city is mythical. He picks up another set of papers and finds himself reading eagerly. But his friend grabs the papers from him and throws them out the window; he had not intended to show that piece to anyone. It was just something, he explains, that he had written after coming home on a crowded, smelly streetcar; he was clearing his head in order to write his literary prose. Yet the narrator knows that those pages were expressing the real life of people, "the kind of thing Mr. Sandburg or Mr. Masters might have done." They had described a half-filled bottle of spoiled milk, standing on a windowsill.

Leaving the apartment, the narrator speculates on what had led to Ed's writing the discarded piece. Earlier in the day, he decides, his boss had asked him to write "snappy" ad copy on the subject of condensed milk. So Ed sat down and thought about milk, focusing on its "sweet fresh" qualities; then he went home to resume writing about the city beautiful. First he made a sandwich from some cold meat in the ice chest, but found that the milk had turned sour. Going out to the alley behind the building, he saw a row of half-filled milk bottles standing on windowsills. Then he wrote angrily, filling a half-dozen sheets of paper. That action made him feel better, and so he went back to writing about his dream city. But that dream city, the narrator knows, is lifeless; what Ed wrote about the milk bottle, on the other hand, was miraculous.

Going himself out into the alley, the narrator looks for those sheets of paper thrown from the window. But they are lost in the litter and rubbish of the alley.

The story, appearing in the March 1921 *Vanity Fair*, was originally titled "Why There Must Be a Midwestern Literature." The title complements the story's reference to H. L. MENCKEN, who had recently called Chicago the literary capital of America; the narrator mentions also the stockyards—as Mencken had done, praising work written "under the shadow of the stockyards." The subtext of the original title is that the genteel liter-

ature of the East must be rejected and replaced; the writers the narrator cites, Carl SANDBURG and Edgar Lee MASTERS, are poets of specifically midwestern locales.

"THE SAD HORN BLOWERS"

Will APPLETON's mother has just died, and the family in Bidwell, Ohio, now consists of Will's father, Tom APPLETON, and three children; Kate, at the age of 20, is the oldest. Tom, a housepainter and paperhanger, is often an embarrassment to his children; he never seems properly dignified, and the townspeople are willing to put up with his cornet-playing in the Bidwell band—which he does poorly—only because they like him. The children worry, too, that he will now marry one of the town's widows. One evening, when Tom takes two coffeepots, along with his cornet, to a neighbor's house, he stumbles on the way, spilling hot coffee over him, burning himself badly.

Tom is unable to work, and so Will heads east on a train to find a factory job in Erie, Pennsylvania. He considers his sojourn temporary, although he worries that his sister might be marrying—and if she marries, his father will remarry, too, and the family will then disappear.

Sitting next to Will on the train is an old man, and at the man's feet is a small leather case. Will assumes that this man also plays the cornet, and he decides, too, that he has no dignity as well. The man begins telling Will about his failures in life; his first wife died, and his second wife, younger than he, has used his money to establish a boardinghouse in a factory district in Erie. Meanwhile, he wants to play his cornet in the evenings, but he cannot, because his playing would disturb the boarders. He has tried to get factory work, but he is too old; he has tried to get a job with a band in Cleveland, but "my lip," he laments, "is no good any more." Returning to the boardinghouse, he invites Will to stay there as well.

Will gets a job at a factory, and several weeks later a letter arrives from Kate, saying that she is getting married. He has carried the letter to his room, and while he is there, the old man comes to see him; the man is determined to assert himself to his wife, and one of his acts will be to blow his cornet. Yet Will has his own problems; he takes a walk along the docks, realizing that he no longer has a home, that he is now out in the world on his own. He returns to the house, and the old man comes again to his room; this time the man carries his cornet, announcing that he is going to play, that he does not care what his wife says. He blows the horn softly, but then stops, saying that his lip is no good. He thrusts the cornet at Will, telling him to blow, to make a loud racket. Will manages several notes, and the man urges him to blow loudly. He pleads with him to make "a deuce of a racket."

"AN OHIO PAGAN"

Tom Edwards, an orphan, lives with a Bidwell, Ohio, farmer who has taken up horseracing. Tom becomes a local hero when he drives a trotting horse to a record-setting win in Columbus. Yet he has received little schooling, and a truant officer singles him out, threatening him and his employer if he does not go to school. Tom sees little use in sitting in a classroom, and he leaves Bidwell in the middle of the night on a freight train. The next summer, he joins a threshing crew, driving a team of farm horses.

His new employer, John Bottsford, has his own three sons working for him as well; they travel around the county, sleeping in the lofts of barns. Bottsford is a religious man, and at night, when he thinks the others are sleeping, he goes down onto the barn floor to pray; Tom listens to his fervent prayers. Since rainy weather has stopped the crew from working, Bottsford asks Jesus for better weather, for warm days.

The warm days come, and as Tom drives the horses, he thinks of the man's prayerful words. In his mind he sees the figure of Jesus, "a young god walking about over the land." Yet other impulses are coming to Tom; as he goes from farm to farm, he sees the women looking at him. The youngest Bottsford son, Paul, seeing them also, says he would like to hold a woman.

One day Bottsford takes his crew to church. The minister speaks of Mary Magdalene, the woman taken in adultery; then he tells of Jesus' temptation by the devil. Tom thinks the temptation must have been Mary's offering of herself to Jesus; he discusses

the matter with Paul, asking if Jesus really refused Mary. Paul reminds him that Jesus was surrounded at all times by 12 disciples.

That evening Tom hears Bottsford praying again. The thresherman's prayers had previously been effective, since no rains had occurred during their three months of work; now a shower is falling, although it is on a Sunday, the day the crew is idle. The thresherman asks Jesus for good weather tomorrow; Tom knows that the rain will not last. He goes out of the barn and sees drops of rain on the grass, lit by the setting sun; the hilltop sparkles as if set in gems. Tom feels that Jesus is there, lying on the grass, looking at him over the edge of the hill.

The threshing season is coming to an end, and Paul will be living in town to attend school; Paul tells Tom he will find a woman in the town. Bottsford has talked to Tom about going to school as well; he says the young man should find out what books have to say. Yet Tom is thinking of Jesus, who goes up into a mountain with his woman, Mary; Tom prays Jesus to bring him a woman.

In the days that follow, the young Jesus seems no longer to walk with him, and Tom begins seeing other visions instead. The trees in the apple orchard become the arms of women, and the apples on the trees become the breasts of women. The clouds in the sky, the bay by Lake Erie, all become forms of women; a stream running toward the bay widens into a woman, and she smiles at him invitingly.

Tom makes a decision. He will leave farm work, and he will go into the city. There he will attend school and learn, making himself fit to have a woman. Even John Bottsford had a woman, he tells himself, and so he will do the same.

This story, originally part of an abandoned novel, first appeared in the collected volume.

"THE MAN'S STORY"

A man named Edgar Wilson has been acquitted of murdering his mistress; another man confessed to the crime. Yet Wilson seems indifferent to the woman's death, as well as to his own near-conviction. The first-person narrator, a Chicago newspaperman, is trying to understand why.

The narrator has picked up various facts about Wilson—that he came originally from the West, although more recently from a small town in Kansas; there he had run away with a druggist's wife. When the couple came to Chicago, they found rooms in an old boardinghouse. The woman took a wardrobe job in a theater, and the man spent his time writing poetry. The narrator has read the man's poetry because he was in the room where the body was found; he saw a copybook of the poetry and took it.

The verse is all about walls, the walls that men erect around themselves—although they want to break them down to reach across to human warmth and beauty. Yet out of madness, they keep building the walls higher and higher. Wilson writes, too, about taking hold of the houses on a street and compressing all the people into one person, and then loving that person. In other words, the narrator realizes, Wilson found what he needed in the woman; she gave herself to him, bringing the world with her, enabling him to express himself.

The narrator explains how he knows the rest of the tale: A hunchbacked girl, living in an adjoining room, kept watching Wilson and the woman through a keyhole. She once saw the woman hanging up washing in the room—and then the man gathering up the wet clothes and throwing them into the muddy yard below. He seemed not to know what he was doing; it was only after the woman had washed the clothes again and hung them up that he realized his actions, and he wept. The woman consoled him, saying that she understood, that he must not be hurt.

One evening the man and woman are walking home from the theater where she works; she is satisfied, as always, simply to be with him. A crazed stagehand appears out of the fog and shoots her with a pistol. Yet Wilson does not hear the shot, nor does he notice that she is hit; the woman, wounded, keeps walking with him. They reach the building and go upstairs, where she lights a fire; Wilson is still unaware that she is dying. She walks toward him, falls, and dies at his feet. He stands for a few minutes, then tries to step over the body; his foot lands on her arm, leaving the mark of his heel.

He goes on outside and stops at a store to buy cigarettes. Finally, as a crowd is coming out of a movie theater, he begins shouting, trying to remember what has happened. He goes back to the boardinghouse, where the woman's body lies; a policeman arrests him.

At the trial, he seems uninterested in the outcome, even when the stagehand confesses. The woman is no longer there, giving him his means of expression, and he is sinking into dumbness. The narrator keeps trying to understand. And if he understands, can he help bring the man to the surface of life again? Or, to ask a more relevant question, which the narrator had already raised at the beginning of the story: Can a man—that is, Anderson's version of the artist—be outwardly callous and unfeeling and yet, in another part of himself, be gentle and sensitive?

The story was first published in the September 1923 DIAL. In the posthumously published *Sherwood Anderson's Memoirs*, the author calls it "one of the finest stories I or any other man ever wrote."

Critical Reception

The collection did not sell well. William FAULKNER, whom Anderson had befriended New Orleans, designated "I'm a Fool" as "the best short story in America"; yet a full appreciation of Anderson's short fiction did not come until a revival of his reputation posthumously.

Critical discussion has since focused on the author's importance in the history of the short story—in combating "the tyranny of the plot," in focusing on techniques of narration. Like the WINESBURG, OHIO pieces, the stories in this collection avoid what Anderson called the "Poison Plot," featuring a further post-*Winesburg* element as well, a focus on the process of narration; the reporting itself is crucial to the story. In "The Man Who Became a Woman," the narrator, while addressing the reader, continues the process of trying to understand himself, to fathom his own psyche amid the happenings he describes; the reader understands, too, that the narrator's older self is speaking, that the older man is recapturing the reactions of the younger man. This technique is used again in "Death in the Woods," collected in the volume of that title, in which the narrator juxtaposes his older and younger selves.

In "The Man's Story," the narrator must use a go-between, the hunchback girl, to bring him knowledge of events he does not see, although he admits to using his imagination as well; this roundabout method of telling the tale further exemplifies the author's avoidance of tidy plot-making. Critics have remarked, too, on the story's being both literally and figuratively about a man's stepping over a woman. Moreover, the answer to the opening question—can a man be both brutal and tender?—is clearly in the affirmative.

In "An Ohio Pagan," the first-person narrator fades away after appearing briefly; from then on, the third-person narration, following the protagonist's point of view, lets the events unfold linearly—perhaps the result of the story's being taken from an abandoned novel. The title of the tale underscores the point that Tom, after his brief exposure to Christianity, has taken up a religion of nature and "natural" love.

Much has been written about gender-identity issues in "The Man Who Became a Woman." That the narrator loves Tom Means, that he is groom to a gelding, that he sees himself as a woman in the all-male bar, that he is later actually mistaken for a woman—these issues of gender confusion are presumably resolved by the end, although the nature of the resolution, the conclusion to be drawn, varies with the critic; a spectrum of psychosexual analyses has been offered. The character Burt, appearing previously in "I'm a Fool," is designated in the earlier tale as a "best friend"; here the narrator speaks of a socially imposed barrier between blacks and whites. In both stories Burt, a black man, is groom to a black stallion—again, in contrast to the narrator's being groom to a gelding.

"Milk Bottles" might be said to argue for REALISM, and yet the references to Sandburg and Masters, as well as the original "Why There Must Be a Midwestern Literature" title, indicate that the issue is regionalism, not realism; the writers singled out are poets who are locally identified. The sour milk in the bottles represents the city and its ugliness—and yet the point is that the ug-

liness is native, regional, and American writers must address the ugliness that surrounds them. Anderson had already made such a declaration in the brief essay "An Apology for Crudity," published in the *Dial* in 1917 and collected in SHERWOOD ANDERSON'S NOTEBOOK; he noted that a major component of the nation's life has become the factory and industrialization, and so "crudity and ugliness" becomes the writer's necessary subject matter.

"House"   See CORNHUSKERS.

House Beautiful

This magazine, initiated in 1897 under the title *The House Beautiful,* was inspired by the ARTS AND CRAFTS MOVEMENT and originally printed by hand. Its first publisher was STONE AND KIMBALL; it was later taken over by the Herbert S. Stone Company. The periodical provided early illustrations of work of the PRAIRIE SCHOOL OF ARCHITECTURE.

Howard, Jefferson   See SPOON RIVER ANTHOLOGY.

Howe, Edgar Watson
(1853–1937) *novelist, regionalist*

Howe's THE STORY OF A COUNTRY TOWN, published in 1883, is an early realistic novel of small-town Midwest life. Breaking with LOCAL COLOR expectations of picturesque characters and settings, it stands as an early REVOLT FROM THE VILLAGE document. Howe, born near Wabash, Indiana, moved with his family at a young age to northwest Missouri, where his father, a Methodist minister, published a newspaper supporting abolition. Settling in 1877 in Atchison, Kansas, where he became publisher and editor of a newspaper, he drew his fiction from his childhood experiences in Missouri. He wrote three later novels and published an autobiography, *Plain People,* in 1929.

Howells, William Dean
(1837–1920) *novelist, critic*

An important writer of fiction, as well as editor of two influential periodicals, Howells became the nation's literary arbiter in the last years of the 19th century. His dictum was REALISM, the presentation of "nothing more and nothing less than the truthful treatment of material"—although his outlook was confined to middle-class concerns, avoiding the harsher perspectives of NATURALISM. Born in Martins Ferry, Ohio, the son of the publisher of an antislavery newspaper, Howells became assistant editor of the *Atlantic Monthly* in Boston in 1866, then editor-in-chief five years later. He produced two important novels during the 1880s, *A Modern Instance* and *The Rise of Silas Lapham,* the latter an early novel featuring a businessman; *A Hazard of New Fortunes* appeared in 1890. Moving to New York, he continued a long-standing association with *Harper's* magazine; in 1894, inspired by Edward BELLAMY's *Looking Backward,* he published the socialist utopian work, *A Traveler from Altruria.*

By the turn of the century, Frank NORRIS and others were advocating naturalism, going beyond a decorous realism. Howells demurred, stating a preference for writers dealing with "the more smiling aspects of life"; these writers, he declared—unlike the Continental novelists whom Norris championed—are "the more American." Reviewing Norris's *McTeague,* he found the novel not to meet the criteria of realism; the work is not true "because it leaves beauty out," because it focuses instead on the brutal and hateful—and thus fails to reflect reality. The next year, Howells ignored Theodore DREISER's *SISTER CARRIE;* he continued overlooking Dreiser in his 1903 article in the *North American Review,* "Certain of the Chicago School of Fiction," bestowing approval on Henry B. FULLER, Robert HERRICK, Hamlin GARLAND, and George ADE.

As the new century progressed, the one-time advocate of truth and realism came to be seen as advocating, instead, the avoidance of truth. In 1930, Sinclair LEWIS, accepting the Nobel Prize in literature, explicitly contrasted the pronouncements of Howells with the practice of his fellow American, Theodore Dreiser; in his speech in Stockholm, Lewis praised Dreiser as the still-unappreciated pioneering writer in America, as the man who had "cleared the trail of Victorian Howellsian timidity and gentility." Just 10 years after his death, Howells's name had become the byword for what was to be avoided and rejected.

In the novel THE PIT, Norris portrays his businessman, Curtis JADWIN, as enjoying his wife's reading aloud to him, including the novels of Howells. Jadwin speaks approvingly of the scheming Bartley Hubbard in *A Modern Instance,* saying he knows plenty of men just like him; he loves the title character of *The Rise of Silas Lapham* "like a brother."

How to Write Short Stories [With Samples]
Ring Lardner
(1924)

This collection, prefaced by a parody of fiction-writing instruction, contains many of LARDNER's most admired stories. Singling out "Champion," reviewer Edmund Wilson declared that the volume should have been titled "The Champion and Other Stories." The story tells of a vicious prizefighter, Midge Kelley, who once threw a match, whose life history has been the abusing of family and friends; one of the piece's ironies is that Kelley receives a glowing write-up in the press—and a final irony is the recognition that if he had not been written up favorably, the newspaper would not have printed the story. The public, Lardner is suggesting, wants to view Kelley as a hero; the concluding words explain, "He's champion." Another critical favorite, "Some Like Them Cold," presents an exchange of courtship letters between a man and a woman, revealing both of them to be fatuous and devious; the story was adapted by Lardner and George S. Kaufman into a successful play, *June Moon,* in 1929. The best known piece is "Alibi Ike," the tale of a baseball player who avoids facing facts, even when the facts reflect on him positively; Ike is one of the more ingratiating of Lardner's characters. A movie of the same name, starring Joe E. Brown and Olivia de Havilland, opened in 1935. In 1949, the movie *Champion* featured Kirk Douglas.

Hubbard, Elbert
(1856–1915) *author and publisher*

Born in Bloomington, Illinois, Hubbard prospered as a soap manufacturer and retired at the age of 35 to devote himself to the principles of William MORRIS and the ARTS AND CRAFTS MOVEMENT. In 1895, he founded an artists' colony, the Roycrofters, in East Aurora, New York; the group—in addition to devoting itself to metalwork, leatherwork, and furniture-making—established the Roycroft Press, noted for the craftsmanship of its books. Among artists contributing to the press was W. W. DENSLOW, already noted for illustrating the Chicago-published THE WONDERFUL WIZARD OF OZ. In 1899, Hubbard published his famed article, "A Message to Garcia," drawing on a reported incident in the SPANISH-AMERICAN WAR. That short piece, telling of a message delivered in the face of great obstacles, concludes with a moral lauding determination and perseverance; it became a favorite of inspirational speakers. Despite the socialist principles of his mentor Morris, Hubbard defended big business, publishing a pamphlet in 1910 that praised the Standard Oil Company and criticized Ida M. TARBELL, author of the MUCKRAKING milestone, HISTORY OF THE STANDARD OIL COMPANY. Along with Chicago publisher Herbert F. Stone, cofounder of STONE AND KIMBALL and fellow espouser of Arts and Crafts principles, Hubbard died in the sinking of the British liner LUSITANIA during WORLD WAR I.

Hughes, Langston
(1902–1967) *African-American writer*

Although associated with the 1920s Harlem Renaissance, Hughes concluded his autobiographical novel of 1930, NOT WITHOUT LAUGHTER, with the arrival of his protagonist in Chicago; he later wrote for more than two decades for the CHICAGO DEFENDER. Born in Joplin, Missouri, living in Lawrence, Kansas, and Lincoln, Illinois, Hughes attended high school in Cleveland; he first visited Chicago in the summer of 1918. In 1925, working as a busboy at a hotel in Washington, D.C., he approached the visiting poet Vachel LINDSAY, leaving poems at his table in the dining room; that evening Lindsay announced to his audience that he had discovered a new poet—not realizing that Hughes had already received recognition, that his first book, *Weary Blues,* had already been accepted by a New York publisher. Although Lindsay was soon to receive scorn for his stereotyping in "The Congo," Hughes wrote favorably of the older poet on his death in 1931.

Influenced by the work of Walt WHITMAN and Carl SANDBURG, Hughes responded to Whitman's "I hear America singing" in words that are often quoted: "I, too, sing America./ I am the darker brother." Another well-known poem, "Harlem"—popularly called "A Dream Deferred"—provided the title for Lorraine Hansberry's Chicago drama, *A Raisin in the Sun;* the play opened at the Blackstone Theater in Chicago in 1958, before going on to success in New York. In November 1942, Hughes began a weekly column for the *Chicago Defender,* soon introducing his best-known character, Jesse B. Semple, or "Simple." The Semple stories, presenting folk wisdom and humor—extending a tradition of Chicago newspaper columns that goes back to Eugene FIELD and George ADE—continued for the next 23 years; the tales are often considered his best fiction. As the author of poetry, fiction, plays, essays, children's books, and newspaper columns, Hughes was the first African American to earn his living as a creative writer.

Hull-House

Having visited the original settlement house of Toynbee Hall in London, Jane addams and Ellen Gates Starr founded Chicago's famed settlement house in 1889. The two women appropriated an old mansion southwest of the LOOP, at Halsted and Polk streets, once owned by a family named Hull. Seeking parallels with Toynbee Hall, which had drawn university men into an impoverished community, Addams and Starr saw Hull-House as a women's equivalent, where educated women would provide a model for poor and working women. Ethnic populations in the area included German, Polish, Russian, Jewish, Italian, and Bohemian.

Addams soon established the first kindergarten in Chicago, as well as the first public playground. Aware of ethnic considerations, she instituted adult instruction in subjects such as Italian art and German history; she also established classes in English poetry and fiction, holding the late-Victorian belief that literature, replacing religion, was a source of moral uplift. Other activities included debating clubs, singing groups, art classes, cooking classes, science clubs, and athletic clubs. Among notable speakers were Clarence DARROW, Frank Lloyd WRIGHT, and John DEWEY.

Soliciting funds from the wealthy, Addams oversaw the expansion of the Hull-House facilities. In 1892, she and labor organizer Mary Kenney established a nearby boardinghouse for working women, eventually housing 50 women; the facility provided an emergency fund to support women while they were out of work or on strike. In 1895, Addams's friend Mary Rozet Smith persuaded her father to finance construction of a new children's school building. Eventually, the Hull-House complex comprised 13 buildings, including schools, art studios, theaters, residences for women, and residences for men.

In 1893, a demographic study of the area, *Hull-House Maps and Papers,* authored by "the Residents of Hull-House," became an important document in the new field of SOCIOLOGY. Modeled on Charles Booth's 1891 *Life and Labour of the People in London,* surveying factors including nationality, occupation, income, and housing, it set the standard for future urban studies by members of the UNIVERSITY OF CHICAGO department of sociology.

Charlotte Perkins GILMAN spent three months at Hull-House in 1895; English socialists Beatrice and Sidney Webb, leaders of the FABIAN SOCIETY, the forerunner of Britain's Labour Party, visited in 1898. Harriet MONROE stayed for three months, staging her plays at the Hull-House theater. Dr. Alice HAMILTON, coming to Chicago to teach at the new Women's Medical School of NORTHWESTERN UNIVERSITY in 1897, lived at the facility for nearly 40 years.

The Hull-House theater, founded 1900, became a forerunner in the LITTLE THEATER MOVEMENT; performances ranged from Monroe's children's operetta, *The Troll's Holiday,* to the American premiere of John Galsworthy's drama *Justice.* Classical Greek plays were acted by Greek immigrants in their native tongue; the young Paul MUNI, coming from a Yiddish theater family, performed on the Hull-House stage. Addams also showed early silent films, charging the same five-cent admission as the local NICKELODEON.

The Chicago chapter of the NATIONAL WOMEN'S TRADE UNION LEAGUE was organized at Hull-House in 1904, employing feminists and labor activists Alice HENRY and Miles FRANKLIN. In the wildcat strike of October 1910 against clothing manufacturer Hart, Schaffner, and Marx—which later expanded into a broadly based strike involving 40,000 garment workers—Hull-House residents and league members supported the workers, mainly women and immigrants, during a bitter winter season; the strike was settled in January 1911, following an agreement between the clothier and local garment workers' union leader Sidney HILLMAN, who went on to become national president of the Amalgamated Clothing Workers of America.

Associated with Hull-House was the story of the "devil-baby," a neighborhood tale claiming that an offspring of Satan was sheltered at the institution; it is said to have arisen when a woman brought a deformed baby to its doors. Addams, understanding that spreading the tale gave women a status in the neighborhood, as well as in their families, wrote about the phenomenon in an October 1916 article in the *Atlantic Monthly;* she included the material in her *The Long Road of Women's Memory,* published the same year.

After WORLD WAR I, Hull-House declined in reputation and prominence; one factor was Addams's unyielding pacifist stand during the war. The RACE RIOTS of 1919 suggested that social palliatives were perhaps ineffectual, that the city's white-ethnic neighborhoods were less than prone to uplift. Moreover, the profession of social work, replacing private efforts, was gaining prominence—as well as the belief that it is the role of the government, not private charities, to solve the problems of the poor. Addams, spending increasingly less time at the institution she had founded, died in 1935.

The original Hull-House—which Edna FER-BER described as "a smoke-blackened red brick pile" amid "smells and dirt and teeming tenements"—still stands as a public museum at 800 South Halsted Street. Most of the rest of the complex was demolished in 1963 to make way for the University of Illinois at Chicago campus. A subsequent Jane Addams Center Hull House, established on the North Side, later gave way after four decades to neighborhood gentrification.

Hunter, Steve

A character in Sherwood ANDERSON's novel POOR WHITE, the son of the jeweler in a small Ohio town, Hunter goes off to a business college in Buffalo, New York. He understands that farming will soon be accomplished by machinery and that this machinery will be built in factories; he wants to build and own these factories. A combination of luck and aggressiveness brings him financial backing to sponsor the inventor Hugh MCVEY. Yet when McVey's first invention fails, Hunter has no hesitation in letting his fellow townspeople lose their invested money; he and partner Tom BUTTERWORTH buy the factory back cheaply, intending to use it in more profitable enterprises. One of the townspeople who lost his life savings, a harness-maker named Joe WAINSWORTH, attacks and wounds Hunter; yet Wainsworth's larger grievance is that industrialization is destroying a long-accepted way of life. The capitalist Hunter, not the inventor McVey, is the figure that the skilled craftsman most resents.

Hurstwood, George W.

This character appears in Theodore DREISER's SISTER CARRIE. As Carrie MEEBER's second lover, Hurstwood replaces Charles DROUET—not only because he is of higher social standing, but because he demonstrates a greater depth and understanding. A married man with grown children, Hurstwood is the manager of a popular "resort," or saloon, a bar catering to a relatively upscale clientele. Infatuated by Carrie, he cannot resist the op-

portunity to abscond with the establishment's money—although fate, as much as willful criminality, provides that opportunity—and by deceptive methods he brings Carrie away with him. Although later restoring the money, he is now on a downward trajectory from which he seems helpless to escape; a contemporary psychologist would note a convincing depiction of clinical depression. Yet Dreiser knows, too, that Hurstwood must fall as Carrie rises; as Carrie becomes a successful actress, Hurstwood ends up a derelict and a suicide.

Hutchins, Robert M.

(1899–1977) *president of the University of Chicago*

At the age of 30, arriving from the Yale Law School, Hutchins became the youngest president of a major university, serving from 1929 to 1945; he continued as chancellor of the UNIVERSITY OF CHICAGO until 1951. His agenda was to support liberal education—as opposed to specialization or vocational instruction; he promoted the Great Books program, or "the Tradition of the West," first instituted at Columbia University. As chairman of the editorial board of the *Encyclopedia Britannica*, brought to Chicago in 1920, Hutchins oversaw the issuing of its series the Great Books of the Western World. The Great Books program, defining an arbitrary canon of literature and philosophy—once a staple of college curricula—has since been criticized as culturally narrow, as ignoring broadly based world traditions.

Hyman, Elaine

(1891–1967) *actress, companion of Theodore Dreiser*

Born in Chicago, attending the ART INSTITUTE, Hyman became an active member of Maurice BROWNE's LITTLE THEATRE company. DREISER is said to have first seen her playing Andromache in the Little Theatre's production of Euripedes' *The Trojan Women*; she had previously been the lover of Floyd DELL. Taking the name of Kyrah Markham, hoping to become a professional actress, Hyman followed Dreiser to New York; she acted briefly with the PROVINCETOWN PLAYERS. Moving to California, she entered into a short-lived marriage with Frank Lloyd Wright Jr., the son of the architect. Returning to New York, she took up a career as an artist and illustrator.

Hyman appears as the character Stephanie PLATOW, member of an amateur theater group, in Dreiser's novel THE TITAN; the critic Gardner Knowles is modeled on Dell, and Dreiser himself appears as Stephanie's lover Forbes Gurney—thus inserting himself into his fictionalized life of Charles T. YERKES. Like Dreiser, Yerkes had multiple mistresses, but none of them present parallels to Hyman. In the novel, Dreiser anticipates the real-life actress's future artistic career by presenting Yerkes as admiring Platow's sketches: "Gifted girl!" he exclaims: "Paints, draws, carves on wood, plays, sings, acts."

The actress is fictionalized also as Elva Macklin in Dell's autobiographical novel, THE BRIARY-BUSH; in Homecoming, a later autobiography, Dell praises Hyman's "extraordinary gift for the expression of beautiful and romantic emotions."

I

"I Am the People, the Mob"   *See* CHICAGO POEMS.

If Christ Came to Chicago!
William T. Stead
(1894)

William T. STEAD, an English journalist who came to Chicago in 1893 for the WORLD'S COLUMBIAN EXPOSITION, published this nonfiction polemic the next year, attacking the city's gambling, prostitution, and corrupt politics. Establishing a contrast with the "White City" of the world's fair, he speaks of the iniquitous "Black City" of the rest of Chicago—although in the last chapter he foresees a future in which Chicago has become the nation's capital. In an idealized future, various goals—including the unifying of all religions, public ownership of department stores, as well as utilities, and an eight-hour working day—have been accomplished.

Illinois and Michigan Canal

This waterway connects the CHICAGO RIVER and the Illinois River. Begun in 1836 and completed in 1848, the canal was financed by eastern capital, using land ceded to the state of Illinois by the federal government; its purpose was to link the Great Lakes and the Gulf of Mexico. The canal replaced the portage path of the Indians, who had long car-
ried canoes across the low continental divide between the Chicago River and the DES PLAINES RIVER, which flowed into the Illinois River, a tributary of the Mississippi; as early as 1674, French explorer Louis JOLIET, making use of the portage, had suggested that a canal be dug to facilitate transportation. The Indian path had traversed only several miles; the canal extended 96 miles, all the way to the Illinois River. Much of the labor was provided by Irish immigrants, settling in the neighborhood called Canalport, subsequently Bridgeport. Creating the longest inland waterway in the world, the canal brought grain and other agricultural products, grown by farmers in the West, into the city, to be shipped eastward by way of Lake Michigan.

Six months after its opening, the GALENA AND CHICAGO UNION RAILROAD, harnessing a locomotive, the *Pioneer*, made a 10-mile run from Chicago to the Des Plaines River, returning with a load of grain. In the same year that it opened, the canal had already begun its decline in importance.

Illinois Central Railroad

This historically important railway was built on public lands granted by the federal government, benefiting from Stephen A. DOUGLAS's efforts in the United States Senate. As a result, the Illinois Central Railroad set the pattern for future federal support of nationwide railroad expansion. Opening in 1856, running between Chicago and Cairo,

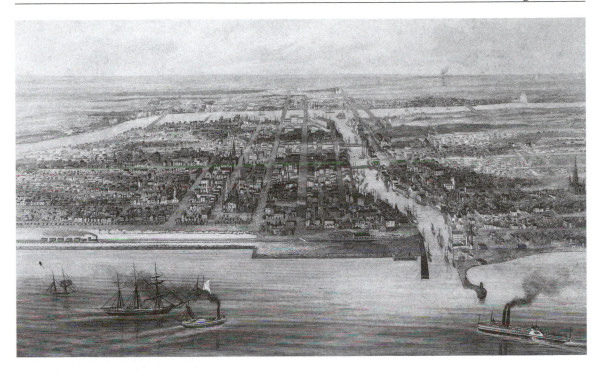

This 1856 cityscape shows the Illinois Central Railroad in the process of polluting the lakefront. Early in the next century, the tracks would be covered and landfill extended into the lake to provide parkland. *(Chicago Historical Society)*

Illinois, the route at the time was the longest in the world; it would soon extend to New Orleans. Joseph KIRKLAND came to Illinois that year as an Illinois Central official; spending time in the neighborhood of Danville, before settling in Chicago, he gathered experience for his novel of early Illinois, ZURY: THE MEANEST MAN IN SPRING COUNTY.

In 1852, the Illinois Central was allowed to run a track along LAKE MICHIGAN on Chicago's South Side, violating the earlier established principle that the lakefront was to remain open and free. Edna FERBER, who had moved to Chicago in 1909, describes in FANNY HERSELF the Illinois Central as puffing "contemptuous cinders into the great blue lake." In 1912, its tracks were depressed as part of a landfill park construction—the railroad "was being disciplined," wrote Harriet MONROE—and the efforts of Daniel H. BURNHAM and Montgomery WARD to maintain a public lakefront were vindicated.

"Illinois Farmer"   *See* CORNHUSKERS.

"I'm a Fool"   *See* HORSES AND MEN.

imagism

A set of specific poetic practices, imagism became a brief literary movement. In 1912, the American poet Ezra POUND named as "Imagistes," a group of poets, including himself, who employed clear, precise, concrete images. Pound declared that by providing glimpses of objects—and presenting these glimpses in spare, economical language—poets could reveal basic truths. Imagist poetry proclaimed an avoidance of abstraction, vagueness, emotional verbiage, and conventional diction—qualities said to encumber the repudiated Victorian poetry; its medium was FREE VERSE. The poetry has been linked with the Japanese HAIKU, a form adapted by Western poets at the beginning of the 20th century. Much of the early imagist verse appeared in POETRY magazine; Pound sent editor Harriet MONROE the work of Richard ALDINGTON and H.D., as well as his own pieces, and his 1914 anthology, *Des Imagistes*, consisted largely of poems already published in the Chicago magazine. Poet Amy LOWELL, accused of trying to take over leadership of the imagist movement, published her own *Some Imagist Poets* in three volumes between 1915 and 1917. Poet Witter Bynner once criticized the minimalism of the movement: "These people wring tiny beauties dry."

"In a Back Alley"   *See* CHICAGO POEMS.

"In a Strange Town"   *See* DEATH IN THE WOODS.

Indiana Dunes

Now a national park, the dunes are located at the southern end of LAKE MICHIGAN. By the end of the 19th century, the area had become a popular place for an outing; Edgar Lee MASTERS began his liaison with Eunice TIETJENS after meeting her at a POETRY magazine excursion. The dunes also became a locale for early motion-picture companies to film western landscapes or the supposed Sahara. In the 1917 novel FANNY HERSELF, Edna FERBER describes the dunes as combining "mountains of sand" with woods and flowers: "blue lake, golden sand-hills, green forest, in one." In Henry B. FULLER's novel BERTRAM COPE'S YEAR, published two years later, his party of suburbanites takes two separate excursions to a summer home in the dunes.

Industrial Workers of the World

A radical labor union founded in Chicago in 1905, the IWW, or "Wobblies," rejected the craft-union structure of the AMERICAN FEDERATION OF LABOR. Organizing by industry instead of by groups of skilled workers, the IWW sought to unite all workers in an industry, skilled and unskilled, in the name of solidarity; the defunct AMERICAN RAILWAY UNION had followed that model. Among the founders of the new organization were William "Big Bill" HAYWOOD, bringing to Chicago his delegates from the Western Federation of Mines union, Eugene V. DEBS, Lucy PARSONS, and Mary Harris "Mother" JONES. The IWW doctrines were militant and uncompromising, employing the rhetoric of class war, or war between the capitalist and working classes. The union's greatest success was the 1912 strike in the textile mills of Lawrence, Massachusetts, an action arousing national sympathy as it publicized the exploitation of women and children. Another historic engagement was the 1913 strike by miners in Ludlow, Colorado; Carl SANDBURG invokes the event in "Memoir of a Proud Boy," collected in CORNHUSKERS. As the United States entered WORLD WAR I, the IWW came increasingly under attack, accused of interfering with the war effort; in Chicago in 1918, a group of one hundred Wobblies were convicted and sent to prison. After the war, membership in the union declined; Haywood, sentenced to 20 years imprisonment, jumped bail and escaped to Russia, where he lived until his death in 1928.

Ingersoll, Robert G.
(1833–1899) *antireligious polemicist*

A lawyer serving as attorney general of Illinois from 1867 to 1869, Ingersoll was forced to give up politics because of his religious stance. Advocating FREE THOUGHT, called "the American Voltaire," he became to many observers a respected orator, questioning Christian beliefs, popularizing critical and historical study of biblical texts. Clarence DARROW, himself an agnostic, was an admirer.

In Willa CATHER's 1915 novel THE SONG OF THE LARK, a railway man reads Ingersoll's speeches in the upper bunk of his caboose, while others play poker below him; his generosity later gives the heroine her chance for a music education. In Sinclair LEWIS's 1920 novel *Main Street*, a small college in Minneapolis finds that it must continue to combat the "heresies of Voltaire, Darwin, and

Robert Ingersoll." Floyd DELL's novel of the same year, MOON-CALF, includes the portrait of a young man, brought up in strict Methodism, who finds illumination in the works of Ingersoll, delighting in "the vision of a free humanity" offered by the freethinker.

Ingles, Cecilia

This character appears in Henry B. FULLER's novels *THE CLIFF-DWELLERS* and *WITH THE PROCESSION*. In the earlier novel, Mrs. Arthur J. Ingles, wife of the owner of the monumental CLIFTON building, is the woman whom no one ever seems to see; it is her great wealth that sets her off from the others. The protagonist George OGDEN finally sees her in a theater box—the symbol of the grand, the unobtainable. In *With the Procession*, Cecilia Ingles no longer serves a larger symbolic function; she is presented as a shallow-minded society wife, whom Susan BATES must educate in the virtues of altruism and charitable works.

Insull, Samuel
(1859–1938) *public utilities, transit system magnate*

Born in London, Insull came to the United States in 1881, serving as inventor Thomas Edison's private secretary. He organized the Edison General Electric Company, managing a growing industrial empire that would include the Chicago Edison Company. Coming to Chicago in 1893, Insull consolidated existing electricity firms, working toward providing electric service for a mass market; he built generators, extended power lines, and established a centralized electric supply. Eventually, he took over streetcar lines and railway companies, converting some of the latter to electricity for the first time. After WORLD WAR I, he took over and reorganized the People's Gas Light & Coke Company; eventually, his companies were operating in 30 states. His cultural project was the CIVIC OPERA HOUSE, which opened two weeks after the stock market crash of 1929. After that event, his empire began to crumble, and in the midst of allegations

of illegal financial manipulation, he fled the country. Extradited from Greece, he faced charges and was acquitted, although from that time on he spent most of his life in Europe. He died of a heart attack in a Paris subway station at the age of 78.

International Harvester   *See* McCORMICK REAPER WORKS.

International Socialist Review

The Chicago-based periodical, published by the firm of Charles H. KERR, first appeared in July 1900. The journal was initially devoted to Marxist theory, although when Kerr took over as editor in 1908, the *Review* became geared toward practical working-class issues. Supporting the INDUSTRIAL WORKERS OF THE WORLD, it placed on its masthead "The Fighting Magazine of the Working Class." Carl SANDBURG wrote extensively for the periodical, often anonymously or under a pseudonym. The periodical folded when it was banned from the mails during WORLD WAR I.

International Working People's Association

This anarchist organization was founded in 1883 in Pittsburgh by Albert PARSONS, August SPIES, Johann MOST, and others. Its platform called for violence and revolutionary action. In 1884, the organization established the periodical ALARM in Chicago, naming Parsons as editor; Parsons's wife, Lucy PARSONS, wrote much of the content. For several years, the Chicago IWPA held counter–Thanksgiving Day marches past the mansions of Prairie Avenue, demonstrating against the excesses of the rich and well fed.

The Iron Heel
Jack London
(1907)

This polemical novel by Jack LONDON is set in the future, in the year 419 B.O.M.—Brotherhood of

Man. Purporting to be the presentation of a manuscript written seven centuries earlier and recovered only recently, *The Iron Heel* covers the years 1912 to 1932, including the time of brutal oppression in Chicago. The socialist B.O.M. era finally comes about after three centuries of cruel tyranny by the Oligarchy, or Iron Heel, the capitalist-dominated ruling class. The first revolt against the Oligarchy takes place in Chicago, a city of bitter labor relations, where "the revolutionary spirit" is strong, and yet the Chicago Commune—a tribute to the Paris Communes, or insurrectionary governments, of 1792 and 1871—is squelched by the mercenary soldiers of the Iron Heel. Sherwood ANDERSON's novel MARCHING MEN shows the influence of London's work; both novels have been seen as forecasts of fascism.

Iroquois Theatre

This theater, which had opened just five weeks previously, became the site of a devastating fire on December 30, 1903. During a matinee for children, featuring the comedian Eddy Foy, the blaze started with an exploding floodlight; the flames spread, and the audience discovered that most of the exits were blocked. Approximately 600 people died; among those who escaped were two young sons of architect Frank Lloyd WRIGHT. The resulting public outcry demanded the enforcement and upgrading of theater safety codes. The Iroquois later reopened as the Colonial Theater, which was demolished in 1925 to make way for the BALABAN AND KATZ–owned ORIENTAL THEATER, now the Ford Center for the Performing Arts.

Ives, Charles
(1864–1954) *composer*

An insurance executive, Ives worked in musical isolation throughout most of his life; his classical music received few performances until the 1940s. He turned often to Americana, such as brass bands and revival meetings, and in 1914 he set to music a condensed version of Vachel LINDSAY's poem "General William Booth Enters into Heaven." Instead of using the SALVATION ARMY's tune, "Are You Washed in the Blood of the Lamb?"—the words that Lindsay used as a refrain—Ives incorporated another well-known hymn tune, "There Is a Fountain Filled with Blood."

"I Want to Know Why"   See THE TRIUMPH OF THE EGG.

J

Jackson Park

This South Side park, conceived by Frederick Law OLMSTED in 1869, was named after Andrew Jackson, seventh president of the United States. Jackson Park was planned as part of a system to include Washington Park and the connecting link of the MIDWAY PLAISANCE; the area remained a marshy site until developed for the WORLD'S COLUMBIAN EXPOSITION of 1893. A building left over from the fair, the Palace of Fine Arts, became the original locale of the FIELD MUSEUM OF NATURAL HISTORY; in 1933, the structure was restored to become the MUSEUM OF SCIENCE AND INDUSTRY. The FIFTY-SEVENTH STREET GROUP, sometimes known as the Jackson Park colony, moved into nearby shops and storefronts, also remaining from the fair.

Jadwin, Curtis

Jadwin is the principal male character in Frank NORRIS's novel THE PIT. A wealthy man who rose from humble rural roots, he is portrayed as personally admirable, as well as admired by others; financiers of the day consult him and seek his friendship. That the beautiful and intelligent Laura DEARBORN chooses him over two attractive younger men further proves his superiority. Although deficient in an appreciation of the arts—aesthetics being incompatible, Norris seems to be saying, with business or commerce—his masculine strength compensates for his lack of artistic sensi-

bilities; he is, as Laura declares, "a great, strong, kind-hearted man." His flaw is that he lets himself be drawn into the excitement and challenge of the Pit, into vast schemes and manipulations on the CHICAGO BOARD OF TRADE. Triumphing on several occasions, winning great fortunes, he comes to believe in his infallibility, brushing aside warnings that grand-scale speculation will destroy him—as it eventually does. Humbled at the end, moving west to start a new life, Jadwin remains one of the more likable of fictional businessmen.

Jadwin, Laura   See DEARBORN, LAURA.

jazz

This African-American musical form began in New Orleans in the last quarter of the 19th century. Jazz came to Chicago—and to its first national prominence—after WORLD WAR I. The new music arrived in Chicago in 1918, brought by Joe "King" OLIVER; its previous venue, the New Orleans red-light district of Storyville, had been closed down by the United States Navy. In 1922, Oliver invited Louis ARMSTRONG to join his group; during his next two years in Chicago, Armstrong created major innovations in jazz performance and improvisation. "Jelly Roll" MORTON, an important popularizer of the music, also followed the route from New Orleans to Chicago. By a twist of history, the coming of jazz to the North coincided with the coming of PROHIBITION; the music's association with speakeasies, or underworld clubs, where illegal liquor flowed, helped give jazz a negative image. The 1920s were called the Jazz Age—a popular dance, the Charleston, derived from the music—and at the same time the decade was the age of illicit liquor. Local white musicians who took up the idiom, including Bix BEIDERBECKE, Benny GOODMAN, and Gene KRUPA, joined what might be called a 1920s version of the counterculture. The first sound movie, appearing in 1927, was *The Jazz Singer,* featuring white singer Al Jolson in minstrel blackface makeup.

Jenney, William Le Baron
(1832–1907) *architect*

Father of the modern SKYSCRAPER, the first architect to use a steel frame to support a building, Jenney changed urban landscape and the history of building design. Born in Massachusetts, educated in Paris, he built roads and bridges as an engineer for the Union army in the CIVIL WAR. In 1867, he came to Chicago, opening architectural offices the following year; in 1869, he and his partner published a well-received text, *Principles and Practice of Architecture.* In the same year, Jenney and landscape architect Frederick Law OLMSTED completed what has been called the first planned suburban community, the village of Riverside, 11 miles outside of Chicago. Jenney's HOME INSURANCE BUILDING, built in 1885, was the first structure to receive partial support from a steel skeleton; it led to his fully steel-framed Second Leiter Building, completed in 1891 to house a department store, later a SEARS, ROEBUCK AND COMPANY store. The Second Leiter Building, still standing, is noted for its simplicity and economy, seen as a foreshadowing of modernist structures to come.

Jennie Gerhardt
Theodore Dreiser
(1911)

Beginning his second novel early in 1901, shortly after *SISTER CARRIE* was published, DREISER felt discouraged by his publisher's suppression of the first novel and collapsed into a nervous breakdown. He discarded much of the manuscript, not returning to it until 1910. As the title character of *Sister Carrie* is modeled on one of Dreiser's sisters, the title character of this work, Jennie GERHARDT, is modeled on another sister, whose pregnancy caused family turmoil. Jennie's brother, Sebastian, or "Bass," is based on Dreiser's brother Marcus Romanus, or "Rome," who became a gambler and an alcoholic. The strict Lutheranism of the father, William Gerhardt, mirrors the strict Roman Catholicism of Dreiser's father; of all of the author's works, this novel most fully portrays his family as it grew up in small-town poverty.

The novel continues to show the influence of NATURALISM; the larger forces in humankind's existence—in Jennie's case, the condition of poverty—determine the life of an individual character. Dreiser exhibits an understanding of business and finance in this work, a knowledge revealed more fully in THE FINANCIER, the volume published the following year. The character of Samuel M. Ross, the real estate speculator, is based on Samuel Eberly Gross, a Chicago construction and real estate mogul active in the closing decades of the 19th century.

The episode of Bass's stealing coal from a railroad car reflects actions not uncommon in the era—although the accepted, legal practice was to gather stray coal from along the tracks; the older children in Dreiser's family were sent out to gather coal during times of poverty. A fictional precedent for stealing coal appears in Clarence DARROW's 1905 novel *AN EYE FOR AN EYE,* in which a character claims to have got through a winter by taking coal from the railroads; Sherwood ANDERSON's novel *POOR WHITE* depicts railroad workers regularly throwing coal off a car onto a widow's property, helping her out in hard times.

Synopsis

CHAPTERS I–VIII
In the fall of 1880, 18-year-old Genevieve, or Jennie, Gerhardt and her mother find work at a hotel in Columbus, Ohio, seeking to support their ailing

father and husband, as well as four younger children. An older brother, Bass, makes four dollars a week working for a freight-car builder; the children scavenge coal in the railroad yards. Jennie, doing laundry for Senator George BRANDER, who stays at the hotel when not in Washington, attracts the senator with her kindness and innocence; realizing her family's financial straits, he sends goods and gifts at Christmas. Jennie's feelings toward the senator, 30 years older than she, are genuine fondness and admiration. Then Bass, caught throwing coal down from a railroad coal-car to his waiting siblings, is arrested, jailed, and fined. Senator Brander hears the tale from a distraught Jennie and pays the fine, securing Bass's release. As Jennie expresses her gratitude, Brander forgets the scruples he had carefully maintained, and a euphemistically described seduction takes place. The senator, leaving for Washington, gives her $100 and promises, in full sincerity, to send for her and marry her. Then the news comes that he has suddenly died.

CHAPTERS IX–XXII

Jennie's strict German Lutheran father, learning of her pregnancy, demands that his daughter leave his house; Bass finds her a room elsewhere. The elder Gerhardt, feeling he can no longer face his neighbors, decides to go to Youngstown to look for work. Bass fixes on Cleveland as the place he will find work, realizing he could give his family, and Jennie, shelter there; he secures a position in a cigar store. Jennie returns home to bear her daughter, whom she names Vesta; she goes on to Cleveland, finding employment as a servant in a wealthy household. Mrs. Gerhardt, the younger children, and Vesta move to Cleveland. On a Christmas visit William Gerhardt acknowledges his granddaughter to the extent of insisting that she be baptized.

Working in the household, Jennie attracts the attention of a frequent visitor, a man in his mid-30s named Lester KANE. He says he can help her, and she finds him appealing, although she knows she cannot reciprocate his interest, nor can she tell him about her child. Then Gerhardt senior, who has been sending money from Youngstown, suffers a disabling accident; he is forced to return to his family. Jennie realizes she must accept Kane's help;

when he suggests they go away to New York for several weeks—telling her family that her employer needs her services on a trip—she agrees.

CHAPTERS XXIII–XXXIV

Jennie enjoys her sojourn with Lester to New York, although she worries about not having told him about her daughter. For his part, Lester worries about where he can more or less permanently hide Jennie from his family, who want him to settle into an appropriate marriage. Jennie tells her own family that she and Lester are marrying; his new presumed status as husband gives her a cover to help her family financially. She finds them a house that includes, for the first time in their experience, the luxury of a bathroom.

During the next three years, Jennie leads a life that seems peculiar to her family. She continues to live at home, periodically taking trips with the man they have been told is her husband. Lester still knows nothing about her daughter. Then Mrs. Gerhardt sickens and dies, and Lester is sent by his family to Chicago to open a branch of their carriage-manufacturing business. This is his opportunity to install Jennie in an apartment, where he himself will live, although officially establishing residence at a hotel. Jennie secretly makes arrangements for a woman in Chicago to take care of Vesta, who is now five years old; Jennie will visit her daughter during the day when Kane is at work.

The couple have established a mutually satisfying relationship; Jennie loves Lester, and he loves her "in his own way." Jennie realizes, too, that since she has kept her daughter's existence a secret for so long, it would be all the more difficult now to tell him the truth about her past. Yet the secret is revealed when Vesta's caretaker bursts upon them one evening, telling Jennie that her daughter is ill; the illness turns out not to be serious, but Lester, shocked, has doubts about his relationship with Jennie. He nevertheless realizes his emotional dependence on her and makes no changes, acknowledging that the daughter must live with them. Matters continue quietly until his sister, visiting unexpectedly, learns of his living arrangement with Jennie; Lester becomes estranged from his disapproving family.

CHAPTERS XXXV–LIII

Kane rents a house in the fashionable suburb of Hyde Park, and Jennie brings her father to live with them. Yet rumors abound, and a newspaper prints an account of a wealthy businessman's marrying a servant girl—presumably a flattering account, although the Kane family knows that the couple is not married. When Lester's father dies, the terms of his will keep Lester from his full inheritance if he remains in his current situation; he has three years to take definitive steps. Traveling abroad with Jennie, he meets Letty Gerald, the woman his family had once wanted him to marry; she is now a wealthy widow. He recognizes their affinity in class and status, but he still understands that his greatest comfort is with Jennie. He has never told her the terms of his father's will.

Lester finds out that his older brother, now controlling the family firm, is buying up carriage companies to form a monopoly; any efforts to compete with him would be fruitless. He enters into a real estate project and loses much of his remaining capital. Letty Gerald, not sure whether Lester is really married or not, moves to Chicago; Lester admits he is not married, and Letty urges him to leave Jennie, to reinstate his rightful place within his family and claim his family fortune. The elder Gerhardt dies, never knowing that Jennie had not been properly married. Lester's brother sends a lawyer to call on Jennie and tell her about Lester's financial situation and his impending disinheritance; she knows that she and Lester must part.

CHAPTERS LIV–LXII

Jennie and Vesta find a house in a small lakeside town north of Chicago. They will be well provided for financially, although Jennie is heartbroken. Lester prospers in the business world and marries Mrs. Gerald. Jennie suffers new sorrows when Vesta, 15 years old, contracts typhoid fever and dies. Lester comes to comfort her, then drifts back into his affluent world, letting his wife persuade him to move to New York to join that city's social elite. Jennie adopts two orphan children from an asylum.

Years pass, and Lester, now nearing 60, returns to Chicago on business while his wife is abroad; falling ill, he asks for Jennie. She stays at his bedside until he dies several days later. Heavily veiled, she attends his funeral service, then watches as his body, surrounded by his wife and family members, is put on a train to Cincinnati for burial. Jennie thinks hopelessly of the future.

Critical Reception

H. L. MENCKEN hailed *Jennie Gerhardt* as a great novel, indisputably American, although "so European in its method"—that is, reflecting the realistic style of authors such as Honoré de Balzac and Émile ZOLA. Floyd DELL, writing in the Chicago *FRIDAY LITERARY REVIEW,* found the work sympathetic and poignant, lauding "the long-sustained simplicity of the narrative." Fewer moral objections were raised than in the case of *Sister Carrie;* Jennie, unlike Carrie, pays for her sins. One critic declared that Jennie's story "makes the reader's heart ache with the helpless pity of it all." *Carrie* had elicited no such response.

Subsequent critics have noted that *Jennie Gerhardt* is more explicit in sexual matter than *Sister Carrie.* Although not forthright by modern standards, the novel depicts its heroine as being sexually attracted to Lester Kane—an element missing in Carrie's feelings for her lovers. Yet Jennie turns out to be impossibly kind and virtuous; Dreiser, as if to counterbalance her frankness of feeling, has removed all other complexities from her character.

Johnny Appleseed and Other Poems

Vachel Lindsay

(1928)

A gathering of poems chosen for children's reading, the volume was illustrated by George Richards, a friend of Vachel LINDSAY's from art school in New York City. In addition to the three-part "In Praise of Johnny Appleseed," the collection presents such previously published titles as "The Congo" and "ABRAHAM LINCOLN WALKS AT MIDNIGHT." Johnny Appleseed, born John Chapman, was the early 19th-century figure who distributed apple seeds and saplings to frontiersmen, preaching the religion of Swedish mystic Emanuel Swedenborg along the way.

Johnson, Andrew
(1808–1875) *17th president of the United States*

Born in North Carolina, serving as senator from Tennessee, Johnson remained loyal to the Union after his state seceded to the Confederacy. In 1862, President Abraham LINCOLN appointed him military governor of Tennessee; in 1864, he became Lincoln's running mate. After the president's assassination, less than two months into the new term, Johnson inherited the task of presiding over postwar RECONSTRUCTION. In 1868, having followed a policy considered too moderate by RADICAL REPUBLICANS, he was impeached, or charged with misconduct, by the House of Representatives; the Senate, requiring a two-thirds vote for conviction, failed to convict him by a one-vote margin. During the previous year, Johnson's secretary of state, William H. Seward, had negotiated the purchase of Alaska from Russia, further carrying out, in the minds of many, the commands of MANIFEST DESTINY.

Johnson, Fenton
(1888–1958) *African-American poet*

Born in Chicago, son of a Pullman porter, Johnson attended both the UNIVERSITY OF CHICAGO and NORTHWESTERN UNIVERSITY and taught briefly at the State University of Louisville. He subsequently moved to New York City to study journalism at Columbia University. Returning to Chicago, he published two short-lived magazines between 1916 and 1920, *The Champion Magazine* and *The Favorite Magazine,* writing most of the material himself under pen names. His early poetry, making use of dialect, shows the influence of Paul Laurence DUNBAR; his free-verse pieces appeared in POETRY and in Alfred KREYMBORG's periodical OTHERS. Contemporary critics—citing a phrase of James Weldon Johnson—find his strongest work his "poems of despair." The availability of Johnson's poetry has generally been limited to anthologies; the small group of anthologized pieces includes "The Banjo Player," "The Scarlet Women," "A Negro Peddler's Song," and the despairing "Tired."

Johnson, Jack
(1878–1946) *African-American boxer*

Born in Galveston, Texas, Johnson became the first black heavyweight champion in 1908. Moving to Chicago in 1911, he was charged the following year with transporting a woman across state lines for immoral purposes—a woman who had once been employed at the EVERLEIGH SISTERS' establishment. The narrator in Sherwood ANDERSON's story "I'm a Fool," collected in *HORSES AND MEN,* says that the African-American groom, Burt, has "soft, kind eyes"—but in a fight "could hit like Jack Johnson."

Joliet, Louis
(1645–1700) *French explorer*

The Quebec-born Joliet (or Jolliet) and the French-born Jesuit Jacques MARQUETTE were the first Europeans to view the future site of the city of Chicago. In 1673, journeying north into the upper Mississippi River system, Joliet and Marquette portaged—carried their canoes, following Indian practice—from the Illinois River to the CHICAGO RIVER, reaching the shores of LAKE MICHIGAN. Joliet had previously journeyed through the Great Lakes from the north, from NEW FRANCE, but French explorers and fur traders had not yet understood the near accessibility of those inland seas to the Mississippi system. Following his 1673 trip, Joliet envisioned a canal across the short portage route, linking the Great Lakes and the Mississippi; the administrators of New France showed little interest. One hundred seventy-five years later, the new city of Chicago oversaw the building of the canal.

Jones, Mary Harris "Mother"
(1837–1930) *labor spokesperson*

Born in Cork, Ireland, Mary Harris came to Toronto, Canada, in the early 1850s; her father worked for the railroads. In 1860, she took a teaching job in Michigan, then went on to Chicago, where she worked as a dressmaker.

Moving to Memphis, she married an ironworker, George Jones, in 1861; he and their four children died in a yellow fever epidemic in Memphis in 1867. Returning to Chicago at the age of 33, she began a dressmaking business, working for rich clients, seeing the contrast between the wealthy and the poor. The GREAT FIRE of 1871 destroyed her possessions.

During the 1890s, as the recession caused by the PANIC OF 1893 deepened, Jones turned to social causes, lending aid in 1894 to COXEY'S ARMY, a group of jobless men marching on Washington to seek relief from unemployment. The same year, the United Mine Workers union called a nationwide coal strike, and Jones became the miners' spokesperson, rallying crowds and leading marches. From that point on, she lived a life of travel, appearing wherever labor agitation arose; by the turn of the century, as a woman in her 60s, she had taken on the persona of "Mother" Jones. In Chicago in 1905, she helped found the INDUSTRIAL WORKERS OF THE WORLD, or "Wobblies." In 1913, she participated in what became known as the Colorado coal wars, conflicts in which mine operators and national guardsmen opposed striking miners in Ludlow, Colorado. Until slowed down by age, Jones continued to travel extensively, appearing in Illinois, Pennsylvania, New Jersey, Ohio, Michigan, Arizona, Texas, Colorado, and West Virginia—wherever a cause was to be supported.

One cause she failed to support was women's suffrage. Jones saw economic issues as more important than women's issues; her overriding concern was the just distribution of wealth. If such a goal were achieved, she believed—revealing a less-than-modern social conservatism—a woman could stay at home and raise her children properly; Emma GOLDMAN expressed a similar view, declaring that the power of capitalism is so great that the vote, any person's vote, is worthless. Jones also resented the middle-class privileges of suffrage supporters, refusing to give credit to reformers, such as Jane ADDAMS, who came from bourgeois backgrounds. She doubted as well the interest of the American woman in radical politics, believing the average woman might vote more conservatively than her husband. Jones never supported the right of women for birth control, for reproductive freedom.

In *The Autobiography of Mother Jones*, written in Chicago, published by the firm of Charles H. KERR in 1925, Jones misstates the year of her birth; other inaccurate statements include the claim that she was born on May 1, the international workers' holiday. She died at the age of 93 in Washington, D.C., and is buried in the nation's only union-owned cemetery, the Union Mine Cemetery in Mount Olive, Illinois.

Carl SANDBURG evokes Mother Jones in "Memoirs of a Proud Boy," collected in CORNHUSKERS.

Joyce, James
(1882–1941) *Irish novelist*

Joyce is one of the principal figures of MODERNISM, exerting a lasting influence on narrative technique and on the use of language in fiction. Born in Dublin, leaving Ireland in 1904, he subsequently lived in Trieste, Paris, and Zurich. Ezra POUND included Joyce's poetry in the *DES IMAGISTES* volume of 1914, the same year that his acclaimed collection of stories, *Dubliners*, appeared. Harriet MONROE published five pieces by Joyce in *POETRY* in 1917. His novel *Ulysses*, first serialized in 1918 in Margaret ANDERSON's *LITTLE REVIEW*, is considered, along with T. S. Eliot's *The Waste Land*, a basic document of modernism. The novel also incurred obscenity charges; copies of the *Little Review* were seized by the United States Post Office, and in 1920 Anderson and her co-editor Jane HEAP were tried and sentenced to a fine. Published in book form in Paris in 1922, *Ulysses* continued to be banned in the United States until 1933. Joyce's final work, *Finnegans Wake*, considered the culmination of High Modernism, appeared in 1939; the author died in Zurich at the age of 58. Among American novels incorporating Joycean stream-of-consciousness techniques—as famously exemplified in *Ulysses* character Molly Bloom's unpunctuated interior monologue—was Sherwood ANDERSON's *DARK LAUGHTER*, published in 1925; paying specific tribute to *Ulysses*, Anderson depicts his protagonist as recalling the scene of Molly Bloom in her bedroom and "her night of animalism."

The Jungle
Upton Sinclair
(1906)

In 1904, the Kansas-based socialist periodical THE APPEAL TO REASON sent Upton SINCLAIR to Chicago to report on the meatpacking industry. The resulting novel, dedicated "To the Workingmen of America," was serialized in the magazine before its publication in book form. The author's purpose was to make a case for SOCIALISM; *The Jungle* exposes the meatpacking industry, including its use of child labor, and deals also with prostitution, discrimination against immigrants, sexual harassment in the workplace, and—after putting its protagonist briefly on the road—the exploitation of rural farm workers. Yet as in most radical thinking of the time, African Americans are kept outside the circle of "workingmen"; their role in the novel is as strike-breakers, and their depiction perpetuates negative stereotypes.

Synopsis

CHAPTERS 1–2
A joyous Lithuanian wedding is taking place on a Sunday, held in the back room of a saloon in PACKINGTOWN. Jurgis RUDKUS, a packing-house worker, is marrying Ona, a young girl who is not quite 16. Among the celebrators are Ona's cousin Marija BERCZYNSKAS, her stepmother, Elzbieta LUKOSZAITE, and Jurgis's father, Antanas. At the end of the feasting and dancing, Elzbieta holds out a hat, into which guests are expected to contribute; the festivities cost more than a worker's income for a full year. Yet the ways of the new country have broken traditional feelings of obligation, and the amount collected is insufficient. Jurgis's response—as always when bills mount—is the stoic "I will work harder." The celebration lasts until two o'clock in the morning, although that same morning at seven o'clock, the guests will have to be at work; just one minute's tardiness means losing an hour's pay.

Jurgis had come to America with a group of 12 adults and children from the forests of Lithuania; he had never seen a city before. The immigrants, arriving in the stockyards area, overcome by its "raw and crude" odors, find a boardinghouse, where as many as 14 people share a single room; each boarder must furnish his own mattress, although the mattresses are often used in shifts. The inside of the house is filthy; outside, holes have been dug and filled with festering garbage.

CHAPTERS 3–4
An acquaintance gives the newcomers a tour of the stockyard operations. Jurgis learns that railroads bring in 25,000 head of cattle, hogs, and sheep daily; the dressed meat then leaves by rail from the other side of the packing-house. He watches the killing of the hogs, as well as the assembly line that scrapes the carcass, splits it, and eviscerates it; several hundred men partake in the dressing of one hog. The guide repeats the oft-quoted statement: "They use everything about the hog except the squeal." A government inspector is checking for tuberculosis in the hogs, feeling glands in the neck—although he carelessly lets dozens of carcasses pass by untouched and unexamined. Jurgis hears about secret rooms where spoiled meats are doctored.

Jurgis is hired at once because of his robust appearance. His job in the "killing beds" is to sweep the entrails of cattle into a trap; he wades in blood amid an overpowering stench. Marija obtains a job labeling cans. Jurgis's father, Antanas, also wants work, but no one will hire a man of his age.

The family members see advertisements about owning their own home, paying only a down payment and a monthly rate. A Lithuanian-speaking salesman shows them a house, featuring four rooms, lying a mile and a half south of the yards; it is brand-new, the salesman insists. Worrying about being swindled, the family members find a lawyer, who assures them there are no tricks in the contract. They turn over their carefully hoarded money brought with them from Lithuania.

CHAPTERS 5–6
A plant foreman offers Antanas a job, as long as he hands over to him one-third of his wages. Although suffering from lung trouble, Antanas agrees; he wants to be useful to his family. His

This photograph of women working in a canning department in the Union Stock Yards dates from 1917—11 years after Upton Sinclair, in *The Jungle,* described his character Marija as finding employment labeling cans in the stockyards. *(Chicago Historical Society)*

work is cleaning refuse meat out of the traps, putting it back with the rest of the meat. The family is learning about what happens to meat that is not fit to eat, including meat from cows that have died in freight cars from distant states; it is put in with the rest, scattered about so it will not be noticed.

Jurgis and Ona are hoping to marry, but they have no money for the type of wedding that Elzbieta insists upon; Ona will have to find a job. Meanwhile, they learn from a neighbor about the house they have bought; it is not new, as had been claimed, and has already been resold four times. The company owning the houses assumes that buyers will not able to keep up their payments; it then repossesses the property. The neighbor fur-

ther horrifies the family by mentioning the interest they have to pay on unpaid principal—an expense the family had not understood; a visit to the agent confirms this further monthly payment. Ona has all the more reason now to work, as well as her half brother Stanislovas, who is 14 years old. Labor laws prohibit children under 16 from working, and so Elzbieta takes Sanislovas to the priest to certify that he is two years older. The boy is assigned to run a machine filling cans with lard; his pay is five cents an hour.

CHAPTERS 7–9
The wedding takes place, leaving Jurgis and Ono $300 in debt. Meanwhile, the children are not well; the family fails to realize that their house has

no sewer, that the sewage of 15 years has been collecting in a cesspool beneath the flooring. Antanas, working in a damp, unheated cellar, is also ill; suffering coughing fits, he dies after severe hemorrhaging. Moreover, winter arrives, and family members must walk a mile and a half through snowdrifts to the packing-houses; streetcars are too expensive. Stanislovas becomes particularly fearful of the cold, having seen the ears of a fellow child worker, after a long walk to work, actually break off from the cold.

Marija's canning factory temporarily shuts down, leaving its employees without income; the packing-houses are also running shorter hours, and Jurgis begins listening to the union representatives. A plant watchman suggests that he take out naturalization papers; he readily becomes a citizen, repeating an oath he does not understand. The man then tells him to register to vote; the local political boss delivers the stockyards regularly to his candidate.

Jurgis learns more about the stockyards—about the diseased beef that killed U.S. soldiers during the SPANISH-AMERICAN WAR; he learns, too, how the packing-houses welcome tuberculosis in cattle, since it makes them fatten more quickly. He also hears—in the example that became famous to readers of the novel—of the men who work near open vats and on occasion fall into a vat. When that accident occurs, there is no need to fish the men out; only their bones will be left, and the rest will go into the market as "pure" lard.

CHAPTERS 10–14

Ona gives birth to a son; going back to work as soon as possible, she loses only a week's wages. Jurgis slips and injures his ankle at work, and soon the ankle swells so that he can neither walk nor work. His income is now gone, and the two younger boys, ages 10 and 11, have to go out into the city to sell newspapers. When Jurgis is able to work again, he finds his old job is gone; he no longer appears able-bodied, and the only position he can obtain is at the lowest level, in the fertilizer plant. This is the place where the waste is brought, and the product permeates the bodies of the workers, making it impossible to remove the stench. The

boys, meanwhile, are learning to smoke cigarette butts, as well as not bothering to come home at night; they know how to direct visitors to "Hinky-dink's" saloon—a reference to the corrupt politician Michael "Hinky Dink" KENNA—as well as to the LEVEE, the area noted for its houses of prostitution. Their mother, Elzbieta, now seeks work, too, finding a position running a sausage machine; well-dressed onlookers come to this spot to watch, staring at her as if she were "some wild beast in a menagerie."

Elzbieta learns about the spoiled meat that goes into sausage; if the meat is moldy and white, it is dosed with borax and glycerine. Rats often run over it, and they are fed poisoned bread. Then both the rats and the bread, as well as rat dung, go into the hoppers along with the spoiled meat. Ona, meanwhile, is pregnant again; she is also developing a cough, but she must continue working.

CHAPTERS 15–19

One night, Ona does not come home; she explains the next morning that she could not get through the snow, that she went home with a friend. When Ona does not come home again, Jurgis finds the friend and learns that Ona has never stayed with her. He forces the truth from his wife, learning that her boss, Connor, threatened to fire her if she did not go with him to a house of prostitution. Furious, seeking revenge, Jurgis rushes out of the house to find Connor; he beats the man savagely. The police arrest him.

In jail, Jurgis—called "the stinker" by fellow prisoners because of his fertilizer smell—meets an inmate named Jack Duane, a thief and safecracker. When Stanislovas comes to visit, Jurgis learns that Marija has cut her hand and is unable to work, that Connor has fired both Ona and Stanislovas from their jobs, that Elzbieta's sausage department has shut down. Elzbieta is now begging from door to door, asking for food.

When Jurgis is released, he finds that his house is occupied by another family; his own family has lost everything. He learns they have gone back to the boardinghouse where they first stayed; it is in that boardinghouse that Ona's new baby dies, then Ona herself.

CHAPTERS 20–22

Jurgis has been blacklisted in the packing-house because of his confrontation with Connor. A well-dressed woman, seeing one of the children eating food from a garbage dump—she is a "settlement worker"—hears the family story and gives Jurgis a letter to take to a superintendent at the steel mills. He obtains a job at the mill, shifting rails; yet the mills are 15 miles away, and he is forced to find lodging nearby. He comes back to the old boarding-house once a week to see his small son, in whom he takes great pride. Yet one Saturday evening when he comes home, he sees a crowd gathered; he learns that his son has fallen off a wooden sidewalk and drowned in the sunken street.

Devastated, Jurgis sets out down the road and keeps walking. He comes to a railroad crossing and hops onto a passing freight car; he will get farther and farther away from Packingtown. Out in the countryside, leaving the train, he sees the natural world; he finds a stream and bathes in it, washing his clothes—dreaming that he might get rid of the fertilizer smell.

He is living now as a tramp, sleeping in barns, negotiating with farmers to chop wood in return for a meal. He learns to eat berries, to find apples in orchards, to catch chickens. Reaching Missouri at the end of July, he learns of the need for labor at harvesting time. He joins a work gang, then spends his money in town on a Saturday night. Yet he realizes that farm labor is seasonal, that once November comes farmers can no longer keep their employees.

CHAPTERS 23–25

In the fall, Jurgis returns to Chicago. Keeping away from the stockyards, he looks for jobs elsewhere; he finds work digging railway tunnels downtown. Yet an accident leaves him with a broken arm, and he can no longer work. When his money is gone, he is forced to go out to the streets to beg for food and lodging against the bitter cold.

One evening, when he is begging in the theater district, he accosts a well-dressed young man wearing a silk hat and an overcoat with a fur collar. The man is inebriated, friendly and sympathetic. When he hears that Jurgis is hungry and has no home, he invites him to his own home for supper.

Pulling out a roll of money, he gives a bill to Juris, who sees that it is a $100 bill, and tells him to call a cab and keep the change. Soon the two men are heading in a cab toward Lake Shore Drive. When they arrive at a mansion, the young man tells a servant to pay the cab driver, and so Jurgis still retains the bill. The servants are upset at his presence, but they do the young man's bidding and bring a meal, complete with bottles of wine. When the young man falls asleep, the servants tell Jurgis to leave, threatening to call the police.

Jurgis's problem now is changing the $100 bill. After a long walk, he finds a saloon and a bartender who takes it—and who then denies he ever had it; no one, he knows, would believe that a man in such clothing would have a $100 bill. Jurgis assaults the bartender, the police are called, and Jurgis is once more in jail.

There he again meets the thief Jack Duane; Duane suggests they team up when they are released. He knows a pawnbroker who will buy goods for a third of their value. They await a victim in a dark street, selecting a man who looks prosperous; he turns out to have money and a gold watch. Soon Jurgis is becoming acquainted with the criminal world, which extends, he learns, to politicians and civil servants and corporation lawyers. He himself becomes politically connected, receiving pay to pick up fraudulent city payroll checks. An election is coming up, and he is given a job in a packing-house, where he had once been black-listed; he is to help deliver Packingtown votes to the right candidate. Distributing notices and posting placards, escorting workers to the polls—where they vote several times, as he himself does—he helps buy a corrupt election.

CHAPTERS 26–29

Union activity is increasing, and members call a strike against the packing-houses. For political reasons, Jurgis stays on the job, although he is attacked as a "scab." Other strike-breakers are recruited, and at this point in the novel, the author reverts to the prejudices of the day, describing the strike-breakers as "a throng of stupid black Negroes and foreigners." Meanwhile, Jurgis runs into Connor and assaults him again—and because Connor is a powerful man politically, Jurgis cannot avoid arrest; he skips bail and heads to the other side of town.

He is reduced once more to begging. Meeting a woman he had known from Packingtown, he learns where Marija is living; she is a prostitute in a brothel. He learns, too, that Stanislovas is dead, killed by rats after falling asleep from the workman's beer he had been drinking. Elzbieta and the other children live nearby, supported by Marija's earnings. Marija tells him she takes morphine; the madam hands out drugs when women first come to her establishment, confirming them in the habit that keeps them on the job.

Still trying to find work, Jurgis happens into a meeting hall, where a large audience is gathering. He is tired and begins to nod off, until a well-dressed woman urges him, to his surprise, to listen; she addresses him gently as "comrade." He begins to take heed of the speaker, who is describing how humanity has been "caught beneath the wheels of the juggernaut of Greed."

The speech is long and dramatic, and Jurgis finds himself enthralled, transformed. Although never having thought much about religion, he has now had a soul-shaking experience. He stays after the program is over, and the speaker, finding out that he is Lithuanian, tells "Comrade Ostrinski," who speaks Lithuanian, to talk to him. Ostrinski, a tailor, takes Jurgis to his home and speaks about socialism. At this point, the author describes Ostrinski sympathetically as a man of a "despised and persecuted race"—although earlier references to Jews had partaken of the usual stereotyping. Ostrinski tells Jurgis that the socialist movement is worldwide, that it ranges from Japan to Argentina to France; it is a new religion of humanity. Jurgis realizes he has been wandering in the wilderness, but now he has come to the mountain top.

CHAPTERS 30–31

Jurgis finds Elzbieta, telling her about the revolution to come, but she is not interested. She is impervious to ideas; life for her has become simply "the hunt for daily bread." He obtains a job as a hotel porter, and his employer turns out to be an organizer for the Socialist Party; the two men are now "Comrade Jurgis" and "Comrade Hinds."

Hinds speaks of the Beef Trust, the Coal Trust, the Steel Trust, the Oil Trust, lamenting that Henry Demarest LLOYD's exposé of the Standard Oil Company was not properly appreciated. Jurgis begins to read about socialism and its history; he becomes acquainted with THE APPEAL TO REASON, the journal telling tales of capitalist exploitation— the very journal that had sent the author to Chicago to investigate the meatpacking industry.

Jurgis goes to Marija, telling her that he has a job and she can leave her work. She refuses; she can do nothing else, she claims, and she is unable to give up her drugs. But Jurgis has found his own new place, living and working among socialists. He hears various polemics—against the Roman Catholic Church, against "the stygian midnight of American evangelicalism"; yet an ex-preacher, also a socialist, claims that Jesus was "the world's first revolutionist, the true founder of the Socialist movement." Jurgis listens also to a man calling himself a "philosophic anarchist," espousing "communism in material production, anarchism in intellectual." The author closes the book with political discourse, giving the final words to an orator who declares that socialists will organize and take over Chicago: "Chicago will be ours!"

Critical Reception

The book became the sensation of the year. Novelist Jack LONDON, writing in *The Appeal to Reason,* compared it to Harriet Beecher Stowe's *Uncle Tom's Cabin,* the pre–CIVIL WAR abolitionist novel, calling it "the 'Uncle Tom's Cabin' of wage-slavery." From a literary point of view, critics pointed to the weakness of the ending, devolving into non-narrative polemics; they noted also the less-than-rounded characterization. Yet the work had one immediate effect: Later in the same year, Congress passed the Pure Food and Drug Act and the Meat Inspection Act, mandating stricter controls over food-producing and meatpacking procedures. Finley Peter DUNNE's Mr. Dooley, imagining the reaction of President Theodore ROOSEVELT, concluded: "Since thin th' Prisidint, like th' rest iv us, has become a viggytaryan."

Sinclair expressed disappointment in the reception of his work, regretting that his call to socialism was lost simply in a call for meat inspection; he wrote in his *Autobiography,* "I aimed at the public's heart, but by accident I hit it in the stomach." He acknowledged the weakness of the ending, claiming he had run out of funds to make a second trip to Chicago. Floyd DELL, a biographer of Sinclair and longtime friend, noted a further artistic problem: "Sinclair's characters, except when they suffered, were not human beings at all."

A silent movie adaptation of the novel was filmed in Chicago in 1914; Sinclair played the role of a socialist modeled on Eugene V. DEBS. A play by 20th-century German playwright Bertold Brecht, *St. Joan of the Stockyards,* set in Chicago in 1904, presents meatpackers making life miserable for the poor.

"A Jury of Her Peers"
Susan Glaspell
(1917)

First published in the periodical *Every Week,* the short story is drawn from a murder case that Susan GLASPELL covered while reporting for the *Des Moines Daily News.* A farm women is questioned in the death of her husband, who has been found murdered by a rope placed around his neck while he slept; the wife claims she heard nothing at all. Two women, the sheriff's wife and a neighbor, look on while an investigation of the home takes place; the men in charge—disparaging the wife's untidy housekeeping, making generally condescending remarks—cannot make sense of the case. The wife is the assumed suspect, and yet they can find no motive for murder; nor can they understand the unlikely method, since a gun is known to be in the house. While the men are upstairs, the neighbor, who knew the husband to be a hard man, discovers a bird, its neck wrung; she now knows the motive for the murder, as well as the reason for the particular method. The women hide the bird, keeping the clue a secret; they are forming their own jury, making their own decision. The story was recreated from Glaspell's play *Trifles,* performed in 1916 by the PROVINCETOWN PLAYERS. In 1999, its classic status was renewed by its inclusion in John Updike's *The Best American Short Stories of the Century.*

K

K.A.M. (Kehilath Anshe Mayriv)

The first Jewish congregation in Chicago was established in November 1847. The K.A.M., or Congregation of the Men of the West, built its first temple in the downtown area in 1851; it was destroyed in the GREAT FIRE 20 years later. The father of Dankmar ADLER became rabbi in the next decade; a new synagogue, designed by ADLER AND SULLIVAN, was built in 1891. K.A.M. by then had become the center of an established German-speaking Jewish community on the South Side; the congregation later moved farther south into the Hyde Park area. In 1921, the building became the African-American Pilgrim Baptist Church, known as the birthplace of gospel music through its choir director, Thomas A. DORSEY.

Kane, Lester

This character appears in Theodore DREISER's novel *JENNIE GERHARDT*. The second son of a wealthy carriage manufacturer in Cincinnati, Lester meets Jennie GERHARDT while visiting the house of friends in Cleveland, where she is employed as a maid. He achieves his conquest by making clear that he can help her impoverished family. Their relationship becomes domestic when Lester moves to Chicago to open a branch of the family business; he finally learns about Jennie's daughter, VESTA, whose existence Jennie had been afraid to mention. The daughter comes to live with them, as does Jennie's father, who believes they are legally married; the father subsequently dies. When Jennie learns that Lester will lose his inheritance from his disapproving family, she realizes that she must give him up—a conclusion with which he reluctantly agrees. Dreiser portrays Lester as a basically decent man who nevertheless must follow the decrees of society, especially the decree that economics is an all-important factor.

Kantor, MacKinlay
(1904–1977) *novelist*

Born in Webster City, Iowa, moving to Chicago as a young man, Kantor published his first novel, *DIVERSEY*, in 1928 at the age of 24. Two years later, he published *El Goes South*, the title referring to the elevated train line's southbound run from the city's North Side. Kantor's first commercial success came with *Long Remember*, appearing in 1934, a novel of the CIVIL WAR battle of Gettysburg. His 1945 *Glory for Me*, dealing with problems faced by soldiers returning from World War II, became the Academy Award–winning movie *The Best Years of Our Lives*. The 1955 Civil War novel *Andersonville*, focusing on the Confederate prison camp ANDERSONVILLE, won the Pulitzer Prize for fiction.

In a November 1960 issue of *Look* magazine, Kantor published one of his most famous tales—the "what if," or alternative history, story, "If the South Had Won the Civil War." In the fictional piece, the author reports that on May 12, 1863,

General Grant died in a fall from a horse; thereafter, the tide of war turned, and the Confederacy triumphed, leading to the dissolution of the Union. When readers suggested that killing off the Northern general made the case too easy, Kantor reminded them that Grant himself, in his *Personal Memoirs* of 1885, had recounted a serious fall from a horse, less than a month after the battle of Vicksburg.

Keene, Kinsey   *See* SPOON RIVER ANTHOLOGY.

Kelley, Florence
(1859–1932) *women's labor leader*

Daughter of a Pennsylvania congressman, a graduate of Cornell University, Kelly was refused, as a woman, admission for graduate study at the University of Pennsylvania. She instead entered the University of Zurich, receiving a doctorate in economics. There, in addition to marrying and bearing three children, she took up the cause of SOCIAL-ISM, translating Fredrick Engels's *Condition of the Working Class in England in 1844*; her translation became the first English edition of the work. Returning to America with her family in 1886, she studied the problems of "sweatshop" labor, typically women's labor in the garment industry. When her husband became abusive, she and her children fled in 1891 to Chicago, where she took up residence at HULL-HOUSE; she boarded her children in the home of writer and reformer Henry Demarest LLOYD. After John Peter ALTGELD became governor of Illinois in 1892, she and other labor organizers achieved passage of the Illinois Factory Law, mandating an eight-hour day for women in factories, also banning work for children under 14. Although the law was later overturned, the principles were established, leading ultimately to the establishment of state hourly laws for both men and women.

Kelley is credited also with making changes in Hull-House, persuading Jane ADDAMS to abandon her regular evening prayer sessions, to become less interested in moral uplift, to work more actively for broad social betterment. In 1895, Kelley published

the *Hull-House Maps and Papers*, attributing authorship to "the Residents of Hull-House"; the study was the first systematic survey of an American working-class neighborhood, the result of a house-to-house canvass of the area. Modeled on an 1889 London survey by Charles Booth, *Life and Labour of the People of London*, the work became a precedent-setting document for the new UNIVERSITY OF CHICAGO school of SOCIOLOGY. When Governor Altgeld's defeat for reelection caused her to lose her job as state factory inspector, she moved to New York, serving as head of the newly formed National Consumers' League, an organization advocating labor reform for women and children; she held that position more than 30 years, until her death at the age of 72.

Kenna, Michael "Hinky Dink"
(1857–1946) *alderman*

Along with fellow alderman John "Bathhouse" COUGHLIN, Kenna controlled the First Ward in the early years of the 20th century, an area including the LEVEE, the notorious vice district. First elected in 1897, he came to be known as the Levee's principal power, promising and delivering votes at election time, personally enriching himself along the way. His nickname came from his short stature. Along with Coughlin, Kenna receives several mentions as a notorious underworld character in Upton SINCLAIR's THE JUNGLE. In Theodore DREISER's THE TITAN, the two men are given fictitious names; they cannot be equaled, Dreiser writes, for their "sordidness of atmosphere."

Kennedy, Ray

This character appears in Willa CATHER's novel THE SONG OF THE LARK. A generous, uncomplicated railroad man living in a small Colorado town—who reads the work of Robert INGERSOLL—Kennedy plans to marry Thea KRONBORG when she comes of age. When he dies in an accident, his bequest gives Thea the money to go to Chicago, thus initiating her musical career.

Kent College of Law

Founded in 1887 as the Chicago College of Law, this evening law school followed the goal of giving opportunity to economically disadvantaged students; it enrolled minority students, as well as women. In 1902, it became the Chicago-Kent College of Law; in 1969, it joined the Illinois Institute of Technology. Robert S. ABBOTT, founder of the CHICAGO DEFENDER, received a degree from the Kent College of Law in 1899; Cyrus COLTER, a government official turned writer, received a degree from the Chicago-Kent College of Law in 1940.

Kerr, Charles H.
(1860–1944) *publisher*

The Charles H. Kerr Company is said to be the oldest continuing radical publishing house in the world. Kerr, born in Georgia, grew up in Rockford, Illinois, and graduated from the University of Wisconsin in 1881. He moved to Chicago for magazine work, establishing his own firm in 1886; in politics he supported first the POPULIST PARTY, then turned to SOCIALISM, launching the INTERNATIONAL SOCIALIST REVIEW in 1900. Carl SANDBURG became an early contributor. During WORLD WAR I, Kerr and the *International Socialist Review* opposed American military involvement; the periodical, banned from the U.S. mails, soon folded. Kerr left the company in 1928; it later became a nonprofit, employee-owned enterprise.

Kilmer, Joyce
(1886–1918) *poet*

Killed in action in WORLD WAR I, Kilmer is remembered as author of "Trees," the most popular poem published in POETRY magazine. Born in New Brunswick, New Jersey, Kilmer graduated from Columbia University and taught high school in Morristown, New Jersey, before moving to New York City. "Trees," appearing in the August 1913 issue of *Poetry*, was collected in the 1914 *Trees and Other Poems*. In 1917, when the United States entered the war, Kilmer enlisted in the army, dying in France the following year. On Armistice Day, 1918, Vachel LINDSAY wrote "In Memory of My Friend, Joyce Kilmer, Poet and Soldier," paying tribute to the man who "heard the hero-call."

Kinzie, John
(1763–1828) *trader, survivor of the Fort Dearborn massacre*

Born in Quebec, arriving in Chicago from Michigan in 1804, Kinzie bought the land that had once been part of Jean Baptiste DU SABLE's trading post. He became an important fur trader, prospering through ties with the local POTAWATOMI tribe. According to story, Kinzie and his family were saved after the FORT DEARBORN massacre by a half-Irish, half-Potawatomi, Jesuit-educated trader known as Billy Caldwell, also known as Sauganash, meaning Englishman; the family fled to Michigan, returning to Chicago after Fort Dearborn was rebuilt in 1816. Kinzie's version of the massacre, often doubted for its accuracy, became the standard account presented in history and fiction, starting with the novel by his daughter-in-law, Juliette KINZIE, the 1856 WAU-BUN: THE "EARLY DAY" IN THE NORTH-WEST.

Kinzie, Juliette M.
(1806–1870) *writer, daughter-in-law of John Kinzie*

Kinzie's WAU-BUN: THE "EARLY DAY" IN THE NORTH-WEST, published in 1856, has been acknowledged as an important historical document, providing an account of the FORT DEARBORN massacre; the work has also been called the first Chicago novel, although it is largely a memoir of the author's life on the frontier. In writing her Fort Dearborn account, Kinzie drew on the recollections of her father-in-law; John KINZIE—although historians now agree on its many inaccuracies. Born in Connecticut, Juliette Magill Kinzie came west upon her marriage in 1830 to John H. Kinzie, Indian agent at Fort Winnebago, Wisconsin; she remained at Fort Winnebago until 1833, when she returned with her husband to his home in Chicago. Prospering from the sale of family land, including property once owned by Jean Pointe Baptiste DU SABLE, the Kinzies settled into local prominence. Juliette Kinzie published *Wau-Bun* at the age of 50; her subsequent fiction provided further accounts of her frontier life in Wisconsin. She died in Chicago at the age of 64.

Kirkland, Joseph
(1830–1894) *novelist*

An early writer of rural western life, Kirkland was an influence on the work of Hamlin GARLAND. Born in New York State, living as a boy in rural Michigan, Kirkland eventually followed the precedent set by his mother, Caroline Kirkland, herself an author describing frontier existence. Caroline Kirkland had written three volumes on backwoods life in Michigan in the 1830s and 1840s; the best known is *A New Home—Who'll Follow?*, a pseudonomynous autobiographical novel appearing in 1839.

Joseph Kirkland moved to Illinois in 1856, working for the ILLINOIS CENTRAL RAILROAD; his living downstate, before finally settling in Chicago, provided the background for his best-known work, *ZURY: THE MEANEST MAN IN SPRING COUNTY*, published in 1887. In that novel, Kirkland looks back three-quarters of a century to a harsh pioneering life in fictional Spring County, Illinois; depicting severe rural conditions, he is challenging traditional picturesque views of rural life, as popularized in LOCAL COLOR writing. In 1891, Kirkland published *The Captain of Company K*, based on his experiences in the CIVIL WAR, and a year later *The Story of Chicago*, an early history of the city.

Knapp, Nancy   See SPOON RIVER ANTHOLOGY.

Knights of Labor

This early labor group began as a secret fraternity of garment workers in Philadelphia in 1869. Following the model of FREEMASONRY, it broadened in the 1880s into an organization of more than a half-million workers. In 1882, the group agitated for a national LABOR DAY holiday, naming the first Monday in September; the day was eventually adopted by Congress in 1894. The organization's policy was nonconfrontational, favoring negotiation and conciliation over striking and work stoppage, advocating cooperative schemes between producers and consumers. After the HAYMARKET AFFAIR of 1886—the same year in which the AMERICAN FEDERATION OF LABOR was founded—the group's influence declined.

Know-Nothing movement

This nativist, or antiforeign, movement, beginning in the 1840s, led to the formation in 1853 of the Native American Party, later named the American Party. The party's platform called for excluding nonnatives from public office and repealing naturalization laws; the organization was anti-Catholic as well as anti-immigrant. The Know-Nothing label came from the group's imitating the secrecy practices of FREEMASONRY, or Freemasonry-like organizations; members responded, when asked about the organization, that they knew nothing. Two years after its founding, the party split along antislavery and proslavery lines; antislavery advocates joined the new Republican Party, and the American Party soon dissolved. The CHICAGO TRIBUNE was founded in 1847 as a Know-Nothing newspaper.

"Knucks"   See CORNHUSKERS.

Kraft, James L.
(1874–1953) *entrepreneur*

Founder of one of the nation's largest food companies, Kraft represents the second generation of Chicago food entrepreneurs; he follows the post–CIVIL WAR generation of Philip D. ARMOUR and Gustavus F. SWIFT. Born in Fort Erie, Ontario, Canada, into a large Mennonite family, Kraft came to Chicago in 1903; making use of a rented horse and wagon, he began buying cheese wholesale from warehouses and distributing it to retail grocers. Six years later, joined by several of his brothers, he established the J. L. Kraft and Brothers Company; the firm made extensive use of advertising, including posters on elevated trains. In 1916, Kraft obtained a patent for processed cheese; in 1928, he introduced Velveeta, a pasteurized, processed loaf. Moving into a nationwide packaging and distributing operation, the company acquired other brands along the way. The Kraft company was bought by the Philip Morris Companies in 1988.

Kreymborg, Alfred
(1883–1966) *poet, editor*

Born in New York City, publishing in both POETRY and LITTLE REVIEW, Kreymborg founded in 1913 the short-lived periodical *Glebe;* it presented the imagist poetry that made up Ezra POUND's 1914 volume DES IMAGISTES. In July 1915, aiming to rival Harriet MONROE's *Poetry,* Kreymborg founded OTHERS, featuring work by T. S. ELIOT, William Carlos WILLIAMS, and Wallace STEVENS; *Others* published also a "Chicago issue," including pieces by Carl SANDBURG. The magazine discontinued in 1919. Kreymborg later edited a series of poetry anthologies, including *The American Caravan* series and *Lyric America;* his history of American poetry, *Our Singing Strength,* appeared in 1929. In Sherwood ANDERSON's short story "The Man Who Became a Woman," collected in HORSES AND MEN, the owner of a horse is given the name Alfred Kreymborg.

Kronborg, Thea

Thea is the principal character in Willa CATHER's novel THE SONG OF THE LARK. Raised in a small Colorado town, one of seven children of a Swedish minister, Thea is perceived as different by everyone around her. A German piano teacher proclaims her musical talent, and when a railroad worker who had hoped to marry her is killed, his $600 insurance policy sends her to Chicago for music lessons; eventually others—those few who see her superiority—help her as well. One of these admirers is Dr. Howard ARCHIE, whom she summons to New York to lend her money for further musical study in Germany; later, she returns to the country as an international opera star.

Thea's early life shows many parallels to Cather's; the author, too, sought to free herself from small-town convention. Cather drew also from the life of the Swedish-born, Minnesota-raised singer Olive FREMSTAD; like Thea, Fremstad supported lessons by playing piano accompaniment for other pupils. Critics have suggested that Thea is Cather's private dream as well—a dream of the powerful woman who rises above all that is trivial and inferior, whose only possible sin is weakness, or a lack of success.

Krupa, Gene
(1909–1973) *drummer*

Son of a Chicago alderman, Krupa studied for the priesthood until he became part of what was known as the Austin High Gang, young white aspiring JAZZ musicians from the West Side. The young men were seeking to follow the precedents set in Chicago by Joe "King" OLIVER and Louis ARMSTRONG. Krupa, going to New York along with fellow Chicagoan Benny GOODMAN, became part of Goodman's ensembles of the 1930s; he formed his own band in 1938. Known for his showmanship, for his flamboyant percussionism, he is credited with making the drum into a solo instrument; his performance at Goodman's famed Carnegie Hall concert in 1938, in the piece titled "Sing Sing Sing," is said to be the first extended drum solo in jazz. The 1959 film *The Gene Krupa Story* starred Sal Mineo.

L

Labor Day

This holiday honoring the worker is celebrated on the first Monday in September in the United States and Canada; the day was initially proposed by the KNIGHTS OF LABOR in 1882. In other parts of the world, the holiday has been designated as May 1, the day the HAYMARKET AFFAIR began in Chicago. After the 1886 Haymarket incident, labor organizations proposed the May 1 date; labor activist Mary Harris "Mother" JONES even claimed—falsely—to have been born on May Day. When Congress passed the Labor Day law in 1894, its naming of the September date was seen as a repudiation of organized labor.

Laemmle, Carl
(1867–1939) *early film producer*

Born in Laupheim, Germany, coming to America at the age of 17, Laemmle first found work at a dry-goods store in Oshkosh, Wisconsin. Moving to Chicago, he bought his first NICKELODEON— an early movie venue, charging five cents for admission—in 1906; he soon expanded his venture into a chain of nickelodeons. His next step was to produce movies for his showcases; founding the Independent Motion Picture Company in 1909, he produced as his first film a short version of the Henry Wadsworth Longfellow poem "Hiawatha." Undertaking the distribution of films, he founded the Universal Film Distribu-

tion Company; its location on South Wabash Avenue became part of what was known as Film Row, offices for distributors of movies throughout the Midwest. In 1910, Laemmle moved to New York, then finally to California; his Universal Pictures, established in California in 1915, became an important production studio, known for its horror films, including the 1925 *The Phantom of the Opera*. His nephew was the respected director William Wyler, maker of the 1952 *Carrie*, based on Theodore DREISER's *SISTER CARRIE*. Laemmle died in California at the age of 72.

Edna FERBER, in her autobiography *A PECULIAR TREASURE*, refers to Laemmle as a "gnomelike little Oshkosh storekeeper." As in a fairy tale, she writes, he became an overnight millionaire because he saw "the possibilities of a thing called the nickelodeon."

Lake Michigan

This freshwater body provides Chicago with 29 miles of lakefront. The remains of the Earth's Ice Age, along with the other Great Lakes, Lake Michigan is the largest freshwater lake entirely within United States territory. Serving as a waterway connecting to the East, it became also the corridor for bringing lumber and iron ore from northern areas to Chicago and Indiana mills. Efforts were made as early as the 1830s to keep the shores of the lake free from industry—unlike other city waterfronts, which became covered with factories and warehouses; in 1836, commissioners overseeing canal construction decreed that the lakefront should remain "forever open, clear and free." Daniel H. BURNHAM, presenting his *The Plan of Chicago* in 1909, declared that the lakefront "by right belongs to the people"; the ILLINOIS CENTRAL RAILROAD, earlier allowed to run a track along the lake on the city's South Side, agreed in 1912 to depress its tracks as part of a landfill project, extending parkland out into the lake. Because of various landfill projects—creating public parks, grassland, bicycle paths—much of the present shoreline is man-made. The efforts of Montgomery WARD ultimately guaranteed the open lakefront; Ward spent 20 years in litigation, spending his own money, to keep the shoreline free of encroachment.

Lakeside Press   *See* DONNELLEY, R. R.

Landis, Kenesaw Mountain
(1866–1944) *jurist, baseball commissioner*

Stepping in as baseball commissioner after the BLACK SOX SCANDAL of 1919, Landis is remembered as the man who restored the reputation of professional baseball. He was also the judge who sentenced William "Big Bill" HAYWOOD, leader of the INDUSTRIAL WORKERS OF THE WORLD, to a 20-year prison term; Haywood, awaiting retrial, jumped bail and escaped to the Soviet Union in 1921. Landis had earlier presided over a baseball ANTITRUST case, resulting in the dissolution of the Federal League in 1915. In 1921, banning eight Black Sox players from baseball for life, the new commissioner, who had been named after a CIVIL WAR battle, took the office he would hold until his death 24 years later. He served as one of the pallbearers at Billy SUNDAY's funeral in 1935.

Lardner, Ring W.
(1885–1933) *short-story writer*

Born in Niles, Michigan, Lardner briefly attended the ARMOUR INSTITUTE and obtained his first newspaper job in South Bend, Indiana. In 1908, he was hired as a baseball reporter for the CHICAGO TRIBUNE, participating in the era when sports writing was becoming a journalistic specialty; his "In the Wake of the News" column ran in the *Tribune* from 1913 until 1919, covering topics of general interest as well as sports. In 1914, his letters from a fictional semiliterate baseball player, Jack Keefe, appeared in the *Saturday Evening Post*; they formed the 1916 volume, YOU KNOW ME AL, which first brought Lardner national fame. In 1917, he published another series of stories, GULLIBLE'S TRAVELS, ETC., introducing a crude, uneducated man who tries to advance culturally and socially. Lardner moved to New York in 1919, wishing to work in the theater; his one successful drama, *June Moon*, cowritten with George S. Kaufman—a theatrical collaborator with Edna FERBER as well—was produced in New York in 1929. His first collection of individual short stories, HOW TO WRITE SHORT STORIES [WITH SAMPLES], appeared in 1924 to critical acclaim, followed by the 1926 THE LOVE NEST AND OTHER STORIES and the 1929 *Round Up*. Suffering from tuberculosis and alcoholism, Lardner died on Long Island, New York, at the age of 48. His son, Ring Jr., a Hollywood scriptwriter, produced scripts for *M*A*S*H* and other successful movies; he spent 10 months in prison in 1950–51 for refusing to name names to the Communist-hunting House Un-American Activities Committee.

Critical focus on Lardner's work first centered on his use of language. H. L. MENCKEN, in his revised 1921 edition of *The American Language: An Inquiry into the Development of English in the United States*, praised Lardner as a recorder of common speech, a writer rendering accurately the American vernacular; critics agreed that "the Lardner idiom" mirrored with precision the language of the unsophisticated speaker. In 1925, Virginia Woolf, responding to the *You Know Me Al* stories, praised "the quickest strokes" with which Lardner lets his baseball player reveal himself as vain and foolish.

By the mid-1920s, Lardner's stories were making less use of the first-person narration—and thus less of the Lardner idiom—and critics began to find an increasing bitterness and misanthropy.

Comparisons had long been made between Lardner's satirical portraits and those of Sinclair LEWIS, who had achieved fame in the early 1920s with *Main Street* and *Babbitt;* in 1929, critic Clifton Fadiman made a clear-cut distinction between the two authors, declaring that Lardner "really hates" his characters, that Lardner, unlike Lewis, "is without a soft streak." Another critical stance, taken in the 1930s after the author's death, declared that Lardner had never fulfilled his potential, that he had stayed within bounds that were too narrow; his work relied too directly on the vernacular of his day, on patterns of speech and culture that shifted rapidly, depriving his work of permanent value. Yet when contemporary readers place themselves imaginatively into his era—when they substitute emblems of current popular culture for those referenced in Lardner's tales—they find that his psychological insights ring true, that his often cruel portraits of fallible men and women demonstrate basic realities of human nature.

Further Reading

Patrick, Wilton R. *Ring Lardner.* New York: Twayne Publishers, 1963.

Yardley, Jonathan. *Ring: A Biography of Ring Lardner.* New York: Random House, 1977.

La Salle, René-Robert Cavelier, sieur de
(1643–1687) *explorer*

Arriving at the site of the future city of Chicago in late 1681, nearly two decades after Louis JOLIET and Jacques MARQUETTE, La Salle called the location "the gate of empire." He understood the importance of the short portage, over which canoes were carried, linking the Great Lakes and the Mississippi River systems. Continuing southward to the mouth of the Mississippi, he claimed for France the Mississippi Valley, including territory extending to Lake Michigan, naming it Louisiana after King Louis XIV. In 1684, setting out to govern the region, approaching from the Gulf of Mexico, he missed the mouth of the Mississippi, failing also to reach the river by land; he was murdered by his men in a mutiny.

Frank NORRIS, in THE PIT, is one of many who later echoed La Salle's words regarding Chicago: "It was Empire, the resistless subjugation of all this central world of lakes and prairies."

Lawrence, D. H.
(1885–1930) *English novelist*

Producing controversial novels in the early decades of the 20th century, including the 1913 *Sons and Lovers* and the 1921 *Women in Love,* Lawrence was hailed by many as a prophet of sexual fulfillment, erotic mysticism, "blood consciousness." He is cited as an influence on Sherwood ANDERSON, particularly on Anderson's long fiction of the 1920s; the novels DARK LAUGHTER and MANY MARRIAGES repudiate what is seen as overintellectualism, exalting states of bodily awareness. Critics have suggested a possible reverse influence as well, noting that *Dark Laughter,* in which a woman enters into a liaison with her gardener, predates Lawrence's *Lady Chatterley's Lover,* in which a woman enters into a liaison with her gamekeeper. Lawrence died of tuberculosis at a sanatorium in France at the age of 44.

Lawson, Victor F.
(1850–1925) *owner of the Chicago Daily News*

Son of the publisher of a Norwegian-language newspaper, Lawson bought the afternoon CHICAGO DAILY NEWS from its founder, Melville E. STONE, in 1876; he retained Stone as editor and general manager. Five years later, he launched a morning edition of the paper, first known as the *Chicago Morning News,* then the *Chicago Record.* In 1890, Lawson established the Chicago City Press Association, a news-gathering organization; in 1893, he oversaw the formation of the Associated Press as a cooperative enterprise, serving as president of the agency from 1894 until 1900.

"Lawyer"   See CORNHUSKERS.

Leander, Elsie

This character appears in Sherwood ANDERSON's story "The New Englander," collected in THE TRIUMPH OF THE EGG. Elsie, 35 years old, is one of many frustrated unmarried women in Anderson's fiction. That she is from New England signals that she is repressed; her sole memory of love comes from the time that her cousin, dying of tuberculosis, wished to kiss her. She has since moved with her parents to Apple Junction, Iowa, and the vast prairie and great expanses of cornfields awaken her once more; she watches a young farmhand working in the fields, but she sees unhappily that his interest is in a 16-year-old girl. The final scene shows her sobbing in the fields, her clothes torn, as a great storm breaks overhead.

Leblanc, Georgette
(1875–1941) *French actress and opera singer*

Previously the companion of Belgian playwright Maurice Maeterlinck, Leblanc became the companion of Margaret ANDERSON from 1923 until her death. The sister of writer Maurice Leblanc, creator of the famed fictional criminal, Arsène Lupin, Leblanc lived with Maeterlinck for 23 years. A professional reversal occurred in 1902, when she lost the leading role in the premiere of Claude Debussy's opera *Pelléas et Mélisande*—based on a play by Maeterlinck—to Scottish-American soprano Mary GARDEN. Later Leblanc and Anderson became disciples of occultist George GURDJIEFF.

Leiter, Levi Z.
(1834–1904) *businessman*

Born in Maryland, Leiter arrived in Chicago in 1854, and along with Marshall FIELD, bought controlling interest in Potter PALMER's dry-goods establishment in 1867. Four years later, the store burned to the ground in the GREAT FIRE. The rebuilt firm became Field, Leiter and Company until 1881, when Leiter retired and moved to Washington, D.C. In 1895, his daughter, Mary Leiter, married Englishman George Nathaniel Curzon, soon to be Lord Curzon, Viceroy of India.

Lemoyne, Arthur

A character in Henry B. FULLER's novel BERTRAM COPE'S YEAR, Lemoyne, the son of a Wisconsin businessman, joins Bertram COPE in suburban Churchton; they resume a relationship that is obliquely labeled as homosexual. Flaunting his femininity in a cross-dressing musical comedy, Lemoyne subsequently causes his exile from the drama club—and from the university and Churchton as well—by accosting a man afterward while still in female attire. He is presented as both musical and artistic; Mrs. Medora PHILLIPS, upon meeting him, feels certain that he will appreciate her ballroom and art gallery. Yet he is generally disliked, arousing jealousy in those who aspire to Cope's friendship; it is Cope, not Lemoyne, who is the object of desire for both men and women.

Leopold and Loeb   *See* CRIME OF THE CENTURY.

the Levee

This Chicago vice district, located on the near South Side, running along Clark and Dearborn Streets, was home to saloons, gambling halls, and brothels, including the famous mansion of the EVERLEIGH SISTERS on South Dearborn Street. The district began flourishing in the late 19th century; its name is said to have come from southern gamblers, who were accustomed to levees, or landings, along the Mississippi River. Its establishments were noted for paying protection to police and politicians, including notorious First Ward aldermen John COUGHLIN and Michael KENNA. Reform-minded figures shut the establishments down in 1911. In Edna FERBER's 1926 novel SHOW BOAT, the last portion set in Chicago, the heroine's husband spends his time in the gambling dens of the Levee.

Levin, Meyer
(1905–1981) *novelist*

Belonging to the generation of writers following the Chicago Renaissance, Levin is remembered for his 1956 novel *Compulsion,* a fictionalized account of the Leopold-Loeb murder case, called the CRIME OF THE CENTURY. Born in Chicago, Levin joined the staff of the CHICAGO DAILY NEWS in 1924 and published his first novel, *The Reporter,* based on his newspaper experiences, in 1929; the novel *The Old Bunch,* recounting the lives of West Side Jewish immigrants, appeared in 1937. Much of his subsequent work focuses on the Holocaust and Israel; he wrote the original stage version of *The Diary of Anne Frank.* His last novel, *The Architect,* is a fictionalized life of Frank Lloyd WRIGHT. The movie *Compulsion,* released in 1959, features Orson Welles as Clarence DARROW.

Lewis, Joe E.
(1902–1971) *singer, comedian*

Born in New York as Joseph Klewan, Lewis became a popular entertainer at the GREEN MILL GARDENS, a gangster-controlled nightclub serving illicit alcohol during the PROHIBITION era. In 1927, having defected from the Green Mill Gardens to a rival nightclub, he was beaten and left for dead by mob hirelings, his throat slit and his vocal cords damaged; at that time, the underworld controlled a club's entertainment as well as its flow of liquor. After years of recovery, never regaining his singing voice, he returned to the nightclub circuit as a comedian during the 1940s and 1950s. The 1957 movie *The Joker Is Wild,* starring Frank Sinatra, is based on his life.

Lewis, Sinclair
(1885–1951) *novelist*

Publishing his first important work in 1920, shortly after Edgar Lee MASTERS and Sherwood ANDERSON had achieved prominence, Lewis became another participant in the REVOLT FROM THE VILLAGE phenomenon. Born in Sauk Centre, Minnesota Lewis

graduated from Yale University and began his writing career as a journalist and editor. The novel that brought him fame was the best-selling *Main Street,* an exposé of the limitations and hypocrisies of small-town life; the work was considered feminist as well, in that its main character, a woman, is stifled not only by her small town, but also by broader assumptions about a woman's proper sphere of activity. Lewis's next novel, *Babbitt,* another best-seller, appearing in 1922, gave the name of its title character to the world—signifying a narrow, conventional businessman; Lewis was seen as a sharp satirist of provincial middle-class life. Anderson, whose revolt-from-the-village stance was less judgmental, criticized the writer's seeming contempt for his characters; he once wrote that Lewis "has never touched American life, except to make it uglier by his touch." In 1930, Lewis became the first American to win the Nobel Prize in literature; in his acceptance speech, paying tribute to Theodore DREISER—the novelist whom many observers thought should have won the award—Lewis lauded Dreiser for bringing to American fiction the qualities of "honesty, boldness, and passion of life."

Lewis Institute

Established in 1895, offering evening courses for men and women, the Lewis Institute pioneered in adult education for the working poor; it can also be called an early junior college. The school offered a four-year high school course in the arts and sciences, as well as a two-year college course; its curriculum included home economics, then called household management. In 1940, it merged with the ARMOUR INSTITUTE to become the Illinois Institute of Technology. Sherwood ANDERSON attended an evening class at the Lewis Institute in September 1897.

Leyendecker, Joseph C.
(1874–1951) *illustrator*

From his studio in the FINE ARTS BUILDING, Leyendecker launched a career that would make him a leading cover artist and illustrator for the *Saturday*

Evening Post and other mass-audience periodicals. Born in Germany, coming to Chicago at the age of seven, he studied at the ART INSTITUTE and in Paris; in 1898, he rented space in the building where Arthur W. W. DENSLOW, future illustrator of *THE WONDERFUL WIZARD OF OZ*, rented space as well. Leyendecker's first *Saturday Evening Post* cover appeared the following year. In 1901, turning also to commercial and advertising art, the illustrator moved to New York City; he produced more *Post* covers than later famed *Post* illustrator Norman Rockwell. Leyendecker is now understood as a pioneering homoerotic artist.

Liberty Life Insurance Company

The first African-American-owned insurance company in the North, located in BRONZEVILLE, the firm was founded by Frank L. Gillespie in 1919; three years later, merging with two other companies, it became the Supreme Life Insurance Company of America, one of the few major Bronzeville businesses to survive the GREAT DEPRESSION. The Supreme Life Insurance building was given Chicago landmark status in 1998.

"Limited"   *See* CHICAGO POEMS.

Lincoln, Abraham
(1809–1865) *16th president of the United States*

Leader of the nation during the CIVIL WAR, Lincoln was assassinated five days after the South's surrender at Appomattox Court House, Virginia. He soon became a mythologized figure, taken up with particular enthusiasm by Chicago Renaissance writers having roots in downstate Illinois. Born in Kentucky, growing up in rural Indiana and Illinois, Lincoln moved in 1837 to SPRINGFIELD, Illinois, the new state capital. He served in the state legislature and in Congress, moving into presidential politics after Illinois Senator Stephen A. DOUGLAS engineered the 1854 Kansas-Nebraska Act, allowing "popular sovereignty" to determine whether west-

ern territories permitted slavery. In 1858, running for the Senate, Lincoln entered into a series of debates against Douglas, losing the election but gaining national prominence. Supported by the influential CHICAGO TRIBUNE, he was nominated for president at the first convention of the new Republican Party, held in Chicago, in May 1860. His election in November, against candidates that included Douglas, was seen by the South as cause for secession; the firing by Confederates on the federal Fort Sumter in Charleston, South Carolina, in April 1861, began the four-year conflict. On September 22, 1862, Lincoln issued the Emancipation Proclamation, declaring slaves in rebel territories to be free at the start of the following year; the proclamation strengthened his stand—including among European nations, from whom the Confederacy had still hoped for recognition—in upholding and preserving the Union. Finding the right military commander in General Ulysses S. GRANT, Lincoln presided over the Union victory, accomplished after Southern General Robert E. Lee surrendered to Grant on April 9, 1865; the war cost more lives than any other war in American history.

Lincoln's assassin was John Wilkes BOOTH, a Southerner and member of a prominent acting family; he fired at the president in a theater box in Washington, D.C., on Good Friday evening, April 14, 1865. On May 1, Lincoln's funeral train arrived in Chicago, and 125,000 mourners poured into the city to view the body lying in state at the Court House. After a day and a half, the train continued on its way to Springfield, the president's final resting place.

Lincoln has long held a place in the history of American rhetoric, beginning with his biblically based statement—"a house divided against itself cannot stand"—in his speech in Springfield, accepting the Republican nomination for U.S. senator; he declared that "this government cannot endure permanently half slave and half free." Perhaps the most quoted of all American oratory is the Gettysburg Address, delivered on November 19, 1863, at the dedication of a cemetery on the battlefield in Gettysburg, Pennsylvania; the brief speech, beginning with the famous "Four score and seven years ago," ends with the resolve that "this government of the people, by the people, for the people, shall not perish from the earth." Lincoln's Second Inaugural Address, delivered on March 4, 1865, as the war was coming to a close, echoes also in the public consciousness; the president expresses hope that the work undertaken will be concluded "with malice toward none, with charity for all."

One of the great eulogies of the English language is Walt WHITMAN's "When Lilacs Last in the Door-yard Bloom'd," composed shortly after the president's death. The poet's "O Captain! My Captain!," the more immediately popular piece, casts the president as captain of the ship of state. Both poems inspired later Lincoln celebrators Vachel LINDSAY and Carl SANDBURG.

Among the outpouring of volumes on the martyred president were Francis Fisher BROWNE's *The Every-Day Life of Abraham Lincoln,* published in 1886, and Edward EGGLESTON's novel THE GRAYSONS: A STORY OF ABRAHAM LINCOLN, appearing the following year. An important early biography was compiled by Lincoln's former law partner in Springfield, Thomas H. HERNDON, whose three-volume publication of 1889 fostered the Ann RUTLEDGE legend, the tale of Lincoln's lost love, as well as the story of his presumably unhappy marriage and lifelong habits of melancholy. A massive 10-volume biography, published in 1890 by John G. Nicolay and John Hay, who had both served under the president, provided an understanding of his later years. Ida M. TARBELL's *Life of Abraham Lincoln,* appearing in 1900, inspired Theodore DREISER's favorable words about Lincoln in his novel THE FINANCIER.

In 1909, Francis GRIERSON, remembering his boyhood in rural Illinois, published *The Valley of Shadows: Sangamon Sketches;* writing as an expatriate in London, he makes the president into a Christ figure, bearing the nation's burden for God's judgment on slavery; Lincoln, he writes, was part of an 1850s spiritual awakening on the Illinois prairies. Grierson's 1918 volume, *Abraham Lincoln: The Practical Mystic,* continues the Christ evocation.

Dreiser's homage in *The Financier* appeared in 1912. His protagonist Frank COWPERWOOD, seeing the president as he comes out of Philadelphia's Independence Hall, watches the tall, impressive figure, who appears sad and meditative; Cowperwood realizes he has been allowed "to look upon one of the world's really great men." In Dreiser's 1915 THE "GENIUS," the mother of the protagonist was once privileged, as a young girl, to go to Springfield to see Lincoln buried.

In late 1914, at the beginning of WORLD WAR I, Lindsay's "Abraham Lincoln Walks at Midnight" was published in THE CONGO AND OTHER POEMS; it remains the poet's most frequently anthologized work. The following year, Edgar Lee MASTERS contributed to the Lincoln legend through his Ann Rutledge graveyard monologue, appearing in SPOON RIVER ANTHOLOGY; the poem has since been inscribed on Rutledge's gravestone in Petersburg, Illinois.

Sandburg's "Knucks," published in *Cornhuskers* in 1918, is one of the poet's first pieces to deal with Lincoln. In 1920, Masters speaks favorably of the president in his novel MITCH MILLER—and yet two years later, in CHILDREN OF THE MARKET PLACE, his fictional account of the life of Stephen A. Douglas, he begins his criticism, contrasting Lincoln to a now-idealized Douglas. The same year, African-American spokesman W. E. B. Du Bois, writing in *The Crisis,* the magazine of the National Association for the Advancement of Colored People, questions Lincoln's attitude toward African Americans, pointing out his lack of belief in the equality of the races. Masters's *Lincoln: The Man,* appearing in 1931, continues the Lincoln criticism, portraying the president as hypocritical and egotistical, as representative of the capitalist North; the book caused a hostile reaction toward the author, and some observers saw it as a petulant effort to compete with his fellow downstater Sandburg.

Sandburg's two-volume *Abraham Lincoln: The Prairie Years,* published in 1926, turned the poet-celebrator of Lincoln into the prose-celebrator; his *Abraham Lincoln: The War Years,* adding four more volumes, completed in 1939, strengthened his role as the principal modern purveyor of the ongoing Lincoln myth. Historians have questioned the accuracy of the Sandburg biography; critic Edmund Wilson, writing in 1962, called the work "a repository of Lincoln folk-lore." Robert Sherwood's play *Abe Lincoln in Illinois,* beginning a successful New York run in 1938, was followed two years later by a popular movie of the same name, starring Raymond Massey.

Gore Vidal's 1984 novel, *Lincoln,* returns to a less reverent attitude toward the president, portraying Lincoln as cunning and secretive. The play *Topdog/Underdog,* a 2001 work by black playwright Suzan Lori-Parks, features an arcade show in which two African-American brothers, named Lincoln and Booth, pantomime the shooting of the president; the play, later winning a Pulitzer Prize, explores a complex attitude toward the Great Emancipator.

Lincoln, Mary Todd
(1818–1882) *wife of Abraham Lincoln*

Born in Kentucky, Mary Todd married LINCOLN in SPRINGFIELD, Illinois, in 1842; the ceremony took place after a long broken engagement, a source of subsequent rumors about the marriage. Lincoln's law partner and early biographer, William H. HERNDON, declared the union to be unhappy, and he blamed the president's lifelong melancholia on the death of his true beloved, Ann RUTLEDGE—a legend of lost love that was later disproved. Mary Todd Lincoln, in her later years, showed signs of mental instability, often attributed to grief over the death of her husband and three of her four children. Her one surviving son, Robert Todd LINCOLN, initiated her commitment to a mental institution in 1875; the judgment was reversed a year later through the efforts of Myra BRADWELL and the *Chicago Legal News.*

Lincoln, Robert Todd
(1843–1926) *lawyer*

Born in SPRINGFIELD, Illinois, the only surviving child of Abraham LINCOLN and Mary Todd LINCOLN, Robert Todd Lincoln became legal counsel for the PULLMAN PALACE CAR COMPANY in 1893. Serving on the staff during the PULLMAN STRIKE the following year, he became president of the company after George M. PULLMAN's death in 1897; he remained in the position until 1911. He has been remembered for committing his mother to a mental institution in 1875, as well as for denying access to his father's papers, except to autho-

rized biographers John G. Nicolay and John Hay; the Lincoln documents were left sealed until 21 years after his death.

Lincoln Gardens *See* ROYAL GARDENS.

Lincoln Park

Located on the North Side and established in 1864 as Lake Park, the area was renamed when President Abraham LINCOLN was assassinated the following year. In 1867, the bodies of 6,000 Confederate soldiers who had died at CAMP DOUGLAS, who been had buried at the south end of the parkland, were reburied in the Confederate Mound in Oak Woods Cemetery on the South Side. The following year, crowds fleeing the GREAT FIRE took refuge along the Lincoln Park lakefront. Augustus SAINT-GAUDENS's admired statue of Lincoln was placed in the park in 1887; two other statues, of CIVIL WAR general Philip Sheridan and Illinois governor John Peter ALTGELD, were created by Gutzon Borglum, best known for his Mount Rushmore presidential sculptures. The largest park in Chicago, featuring a popular zoo, Lincoln Park eventually became a fashionable North Side location; Carrie MEEBER, of Theodore DREISER's *SISTER CARRIE,* enjoys a ride past the park and compares the luxurious homes with her own modest circumstances; Curtis JADWIN, of Frank NORRIS's *THE PIT,* builds a grand mansion facing the park.

Lindsay, Vachel
(1879–1931) *poet, public performer*

Born in SPRINGFIELD, Illinois, a doctor's son, Lindsay attended Hiram College in Ohio, a CAMPBELLITE institution; his family espoused strong religious convictions, creating in their son a visionary, a preacher of his own form of gospel. In 1901, Lindsay enrolled in the ART INSTITUTE in Chicago, hoping to earn his living by "Christian cartooning," as other artists practiced political cartooning. Two years later, studying art in New York City, he began peddling his poetry on the streets, selling leaflets of poems, illustrated by himself, for pennies. In 1904, he started experiencing religious visions, soon creating his own elaborate Map of the Universe, featuring such unorthodox items as the Jungles of Heaven and the Palace of Eve. Images from this Map recur in many of his poems.

A life of vagabonding began in 1906, when he boarded a boat from New York to Jacksonville, Florida, intending to walk northward. He carried with him copies of poems, bound and decorated, planning to exchange them for food and lodging along the way; hitching rides, he finally returned to his home in Springfield. In 1909, approaching the age of 30, he began working for the ANTI-SALOON LEAGUE, lecturing in support of legislation suppressing alcohol, speaking in small towns throughout central Illinois. In the same year, he sent a collection of pieces, *The Tramp's Excuse*, to Floyd DELL, associate literary editor at the *Chicago Evening Post*; the volume included, besides religious verse and a drawing of his Map of the Universe, "Why I Voted the Socialist Ticket." Dell reviewed the book, praising the unknown author as a socialist, a religious mystic, and a poet. In 1911, Lindsay's "THE EAGLE THAT IS FORGOTTEN," memorializing the poet's boyhood hero, John Peter ALTGELD, appeared in wide newspaper circulation; Harriet MONROE, planning her new literary venture, wrote to Lindsay, suggesting he contribute to her new POETRY magazine.

In 1912, Lindsay took to the road again with his pamphlets, including a collection titled *Rhymes to be Traded for Bread*. In Southern California, he wrote the poem he would send to Monroe, "GENERAL WILLIAM BOOTH ENTERS INTO HEAVEN," which brought him instant fame. Back in Springfield, he followed this success with another, "The Congo"—which he soon began declaiming in public, even at a Chicago banquet where Monroe was honoring William Butler YEATS, the Irish poet. Lindsay had developed an oratorical style by then—described as alternately bellowing, chanting, and whispering—which he used for the rest of his life; he termed it a "higher VAUDEVILLE," referring to the popular theater of the day. On occasion he incorporated dance and pantomime into his performances, once calling upon a young woman dancer to act out his visionary storytelling at Maurice BROWNE's LITTLE THEATRE.

With the publication of the volumes *General William Booth Enters into Heaven and Other Poems* and THE CONGO AND OTHER POEMS, appearing in 1913 and 1914, Lindsay was no longer traveling the open road but instead touring the lecture circuit; he gave recitations throughout the East, including Ivy League campuses. When travel restrictions were lifted after WORLD WAR I, he began touring England, including London, Oxford, and Cambridge—reciting such Americana as his poem "Bryan, Bryan, Bryan, Bryan," extolling the politician and orator William Jennings BRYAN.

As an edition of his *Collected Poems* was being prepared for publication in 1923, Lindsay realized that audiences wanted to hear only the old poems, mainly "General Booth" and "Congo"; he resented, too, that he was being seen as vulgar, as a mere vaudevillian—as opposed to the "higher vaude-ville" he once claimed to be practicing. In 1924, at the age of 45, he moved to Spokane, Washington, partly to be near Glacier Park, where he had once taken an extensive walking trip; in this new locale, he met the 23-year-old daughter of a Presbyterian clergyman, and they married the following year. Increasingly forgotten on the literary circuit, he began running out of funds to support his family, which soon included two young children. He returned to Springfield in 1929; two years later, he committed suicide by drinking a bottle of the disinfectant Lysol—a fact not generally known until Edgar Lee MASTERS's biography, *Vachel Lindsay: A Poet in America*, was published in 1935. After his many years of travel, he died in the same house in which he had been born.

In MacKinlay KANTOR's 1928 novel DIVERSEY, the protagonist, facing poverty and joblessness in Chicago, remembers a line of Lindsay's: "O broncho . . . would not be broken of dancing." Repeating the words to himself, the character feels renewed in spirit. The use of this line—from the poem "The Broncho That Would Not Be Broken," collected in THE CHINESE NIGHTINGALE AND OTHER POEMS—illustrates the poet's once-high reputation; its coming toward the climax of a novel would not be surprising in 1928. In more recent times, in part because of the racial stereotyping of the once-famous "The Congo," Lindsay's reputation has declined; his poems are available today mainly in anthologies. "The Eagle That Is Forgotten" remains an enduring piece, and "Abraham Lincoln Walks at Midnight," originally collected in *The Congo and Other Poems*, persists in the national consciousness as a poem capturing the sorrows of war.

Further Reading

Ruggles, Eleanor. *The West-Going Heart: A Life of Vachel Lindsay.* New York: Norton, 1959.

"Little Boy Blue"
Eugene Field
(1888)

Beginning with the words, "The little toy dog is covered with dust," Eugene Field's most famous poem laments the death of a child, describing the toys that have remained faithful through the years. Published in the Chicago periodical AMERICA, the work achieved mass popularity, at a time when childhood mortality rates continued high; three of Field's eight children, including his firstborn, had died young. The poem, until it faded from the public mind, became increasingly subject to parody.

Little Review

A literary magazine founded in Chicago by Margaret ANDERSON, *Little Review* followed mandates differing from those of Harriet MONROE's POETRY, established a year and a half earlier. The scope of this magazine was envisioned as broader, publishing fiction, poetry, and reviews, as well as personal commentary. The first issue, appearing in March 1914, included essays on Rupert BROOKE, Gertrude STEIN, and Rabindranath TAGORE, as well as a poem by Vachel LINDSAY; the third issue, dated May 1914, included Anderson's praise of anarchist Emma GOLDMAN, who had recently lectured in Chicago. Like Monroe's magazine, *Little Review* also published the poetry of IMAGISM in its early years, including the work of Amy LOWELL and Richard ALDINGTON; Lowell's best-known piece, "Patterns," appeared in the August 1915 issue.

In 1916, Anderson and her new associate, Jane HEAP, moved to California, hoping for patronage, settling near Mill Valley in the Bay Area. It was from California that they published the notorious September issue of 64 empty pages; only the two center pages contained material, consisting of drawings by Heap illustrating Anderson's recent activities, including her attending lectures on ANARCHISM by Goldman. Anderson declared that since no art was being produced they could not publish any. The patronage, meanwhile, failed to materialize, and in a few months the women returned briefly to Chicago, then moved on to New York City. At the same time, the expatriate American poet Ezra POUND offered his services as "foreign editor"—as he had done earlier with *Poetry*—and he brought in money from his backer, John Quinn, a New York lawyer and arts patron. Soon the *Little Review* was receiving the work of Pound, T. S. ELIOT, and William Butler YEATS, including "The Wild Swans at Coole."

In March 1918, the periodical achieved its most notable place in history, beginning the serialization of James JOYCE's *Ulysses*—received from Pound—and continuing the novel's publication on a monthly basis for three years. At the urging of the NEW YORK SOCIETY FOR THE SUPPRESSION OF VICE, the U.S. Post Office seized and burned four of the issues, deeming them obscene, not to be purveyed through the U.S. mails; in 1921, Anderson and Heap were brought before a court and fined. By then both women, having ended their relationship, had decided to leave the country; they moved eventually to Paris. Heap took over editorship of the magazine in 1922, publishing two early stories by Ernest HEMINGWAY, later collected in *In Our Time*; her editorial choices increasingly emphasized European work, focusing on avant-garde movements such as surrealism and dadaism. The magazine ceased publication in 1929; the final issue printed pieces by many of the writers who had contributed in the early days.

The *Little Review* never had a consistent editorial policy. Anderson was accused of having no clear idea as to what her magazine was, except that it embraced "beauty." One observer called it "a glittering, and occasionally silly, hodge-podge." Sherwood ANDERSON spoke of its "sledgehammer pronouncements," accompanied by a "flaunting joy of life."

Although first appearing in Chicago, the periodical refrained from publishing Chicago writers who championed REALISM; in its 15 years of existence, it published the major writers of the era—Eliot, Pound, Yeats, Joyce, Hemingway, Anderson—and yet it followed a policy of experimentalism, of internationalism, that only tangentially acknowledged its roots in the Midwest and in Chicago.

Further Reading

Anderson, Margaret, ed. *The Little Review Anthology.* New York: Horizon, 1953.

Little Room

In the early 1890s, during preparations for the WORLD'S COLUMBIAN EXPOSITION, artists and writers began meeting informally in the studio of sculptor Lorado TAFT. Later, the meetings became regularized, and a room on the top floor of the FINE ARTS BUILDING became the designated venue; the time was Friday afternoon, after matinees of the CHICAGO SYMPHONY ORCHESTRA. The name *Little Room* came from a short story by Madeline Yale Wynne, about a room that disappeared and reappeared, as the group itself had gathered in different locales. The circle included Henry B. FULLER, Harriet MONROE, Francis Fisher BROWNE, Floyd DELL, George Barr MCCUTCHEON, Hamlin GARLAND, Robert HERRICK, William Vaughn MOODY, Herbert S. STONE, and Howard Van Doren SHAW; under Little Room auspices, Anna MORGAN's school of elocution gave the first American performances of George Bernard Shaw's *Candida* and *Caesar and Cleopatra.* Unlike the men-only CLIFF-DWELLERS CLUB, the Little Room included women in its gatherings; it flourished through the first decade of the new century, finally dissolving by the early 1930s. Edgar Lee MASTERS, scorning the group and its "dilettanti," wrote later of its members' practicing "a haughty exclusiveness."

little theater movement

This movement sought to establish experimental, noncommercial theater. Rejecting the popular

stage, presenting drama that was not commercially viable, the little theater movement offered an outlet for the modernist and avant-garde; it was essentially—despite some populist roots—an elitist enterprise. Early forerunners were Chicago's LITTLE THEATRE and the HULL-HOUSE theater; both groups inspired the PROVINCETOWN PLAYERS, the East Coast progenitor of the movement. American playwright Eugene O'NEILL first gained recognition through the Provincetown Players.

Little Theatre

Although pioneering credit must be given to Anna MORGAN, who sponsored early performances of new playwrights—and to HULL-HOUSE, sponsoring a similar institution—the Little Theatre is often cited as the landmark institution in the LITTLE THEATER MOVEMENT. Established by Englishman Maurice BROWNE in 1912, it was part of an effort to find an alternative to the popular commercialized theater.

A converted storage room on the fourth floor of the FINE ARTS BUILDING, the Little Theatre held 91 seats; adjoining it was a tea room, offering catering by Harriet Brainerd MOODY's fashionable establishment. The first production presented two short plays, one of them William Butler YEATS's "On Baile's Strand." A later production of Euripides' *The Trojan Women,* viewed by Theodore DREISER, starred actress Elaine HYMAN, who later became Dreiser's companion. Jane HEAP, before going abroad to study art—and before meeting Margaret ANDERSON—acted in the original troupe. In 1913, the company made a tour of several cities in the East.

In 1915, as WORLD WAR I continued in Europe, *The Trojan Women* was revived as a pacifist play—a move that did not make Browne popular with some of his patrons. George Bernard Shaw's *Mrs. Warren's Profession* received a successful production, as well as works by August Strindberg and Arthur Schnitzler, writers seen at the time as avant-garde. In 1916, Vachel LINDSAY and a young female dancer, costumed as King Solomon and the Queen of Sheba, gave a recital-dance performance of his poem "King Solomon"; Lindsay sought audience participation in the chanted refrain. Decreasing support from patrons caused the theater to close in 1917.

Theodore DREISER, in THE TITAN of 1914, speaks of an amateur drama group, seeking "to elevate the stage"; he names the director Lane Cross, a public-deceiving artist, and the actress Stephanie PLATOW—versions of Browne and Hyman. Dreiser's character Frank COWPERWOOD becomes involved with the actress, as did Dreiser in real life. Floyd DELL's autobiographical novel of 1921, THE BRIARY-BUSH, presents the group as the Artists' Theatre, putting on Arthur Schnitzler's play Anatol; Dell's alter ego, too, becomes involved with the actress, here named Elva Macklin.

Livermore, Mary
(1820–1905) *social reformer, lecturer*

Born in Boston, Livermore moved to Chicago in 1857 and became active during the CIVIL WAR in soldiers' aid and relief societies. After the war, becoming involved in the advocacy of women's right to vote, she established an early periodical devoted to women's suffrage, the *Agitator*, in 1869; it later transferred to Boston as *Women's Journal*. Returning east, Livermore embarked on a career of public lecturing, speaking mainly on women's issues; she became one of the first women to succeed commercially in the male-dominated lecture circuit.

Lloyd, Henry Demarest
(1847–1903) *writer, muckraking pioneer*

Born in New York City, Lloyd graduated from Columbia University law school and came to Chicago in 1872; he joined the staff of the CHICAGO TRIBUNE, serving as financial editor from 1873 until 1885. Settling in the northern suburb of Winnetka, he and his wife made their home a gathering place for Jane ADDAMS, Eugene V. DEBS, Charlotte Perkins GILMAN, and others; the Lloyds took in Florence KELLEY's three children when Kelley, separated from her husband, moved into HULL-HOUSE in 1891. Lloyd's best-known work is WEALTH AGAINST COMMONWEALTH, published in

1894, an exposé of Standard Oil and other monopolies; the volume, making its author the first of the great MUCKRAKING writers, foreshadowed Ida TARBELL's 1904 HISTORY OF THE STANDARD OIL COMPANY. His son, William Bross Lloyd, became a founding member of the Communist Labor Party in Chicago in 1919; Clarence DARROW defended the younger Lloyd and 19 others unsuccessfully against sedition charges in 1920. Sentenced to one to five years in prison, Lloyd was pardoned by the governor after serving one month at the state penitentiary in Joliet.

local color

Local-color literature, flourishing in the 19th century, focused on regional rural settings, incorporating local mannerisms and vernacular. It traditionally emphasized the quaint and picturesque; it has been accused of substituting sentimentality for realistic depiction. Often associated with New England, local-color writing created also a romantic South and a romantic Far West—the latter as exemplified in the mining-camp stories of Bret Harte, achieving great popularity in the late 1860s. A more realistic regionalism, appearing in the 1870s and 1880s, came in the work of midwesterners—Edward EGGLESTON, Edgar Watson HOWE, Joseph KIRKLAND—who combined local-color elements with darker depictions of rural and agricultural life. Their successor, Hamlin GARLAND, wrote what some consider the ultimate anti-local-color fiction in his 1891 MAIN-TRAVELLED ROADS; these tales, far from picturesque, convey the unrelieved harshness of plains farm life during a time of agricultural depression.

The term *local color* continued to designate regional writing, whether realistic or geared to popular sentimental tastes. Garland wrote in his 1894 CRUMBLING IDOLS that local color is necessary to fiction; a native element is vital, he argued—as he downplayed the clear-cut distinctions between his own severe *Main-Travelled Roads* and the popular sentimental fiction of the day.

"Localities" *See* CORNHUSKERS.

London, Jack
(1876–1916) *novelist*

Born in California, best known for the Klondike tale, *The Call of the Wild*, London was one of many Americans influenced by the work of German philosopher Friedrich NIETZSCHE. London's idealizing of strong men, such as the ruthless sea captain in *The Sea Wolf* and the socialist revolutionary in THE IRON HEEL, is similar to Theodore DREISER's idealizing of his overreaching businessman in the Frank COWPERWOOD trilogy. *The Iron Heel*, published in 1907, is said to have influenced Sherwood ANDERSON's MARCHING MEN, a novel featuring a heroic man who rises up as a leader; Francis HACKETT, writing in *The New Republic* in 1917, draws a comparison between Anderson's *Marching Men* and London's tendency to "caveman piffle." The first social upheaval that London describes in *The Iron Heel*, set in the future, takes place in Chicago, the city most ripe for revolution.

"Loneliness"   See WINESBURG, OHIO.

the Loop

The central commercial district of Chicago, a one-half-square-mile area, the Loop was first outlined in 1882 by a cable-car system, run from central steam-powered plants. In 1897, an elevated railway, the Union Loop, powered by small steam engines, replaced the cable cars. *The Loop* soon became a standard term for downtown Chicago. Edna FERBER, in her 1917 story, "The Gay Old Dog," collected in CHEERFUL BY REQUEST, speaks of the Loop as "a clamorous, smoke-infested district embraced by the iron arms of the elevated tracks"; in a smaller city, she adds, it would be called downtown.

Lorimer, George Horace
(1867–1937) *editor, writer*

Known for making the *Saturday Evening Post* into a major mass-circulation magazine, Lorimer gained early experience at the Armour Packing Company in Chicago; he subsequently defended Philip D. ARMOUR and other meatpackers against criticism, including accusations leveled by Upton SINCLAIR. Born in Louisville, Kentucky, the son of a Baptist minister, Lorimer worked at the Armour company in Chicago from 1887 to 1895, rising from mailroom clerk to department head. Moving to Boston, then to Philadelphia, he became editor in 1899 of the *Post*, a periodical recently purchased by Cyrus H. Curtis, owner of *Ladies' Home Journal*. Lorimer published work by Frank NORRIS and Jack LONDON, running London's classic *Call of the Wild* in 1903; he later published stories by Ring LARDNER, starting with the 1914 pieces that became the YOU KNOW ME AL collection. Lorimer was noted for filling his pages with illustrations; an early cover for the magazine was drawn by Chicago artist Joseph C. LEYENDECKER, who went on to produce more covers than any other artist, including Norman Rockwell.

Wishing to foster the virtues of dutifulness and hard work, Lorimer began serializing in 1901 his "Letters from a Self-Made Merchant to His Son," following the model of the 18th-century *Letters to His Son* by Lord Chesterfield. While his English model had written to a real-life son, instructing him in manners and worldly advancement, Lorimer created a persona named John Graham, "Head of the House of Graham and Company, Pork-packers in Chicago," instructing his son in common sense, honesty, and dedication. The first collected volume, *Letters from a Self-Made Merchant to His Son*, appeared in 1902; the fictional John Graham defends big business and corporate capitalism, including Chicago's stockyards and meatpacking companies.

"Lost"   See CHICAGO POEMS.

The Love for Three Oranges
Sergei Prokofiev
(1921)

The opera by the Russian composer Sergei PROKOFIEV received its world premiere at the CHICAGO OPERA COMPANY in December 1921; the composer himself conducted. Prokofiev, newly arrived in America after the Russian revolution, wrote both the music and the libretto, basing his story on an 18th-century comedy by the Italian Carlo Gozzi; the fairy-tale plot revolves around the effort of the King of Clubs to cure his son of melancholia. Writing his libretto in Russian, Prokofiev approved a French translation for the Chicago production. Ben HECHT described a dress rehearsal in his CHICAGO DAILY NEWS column, "1001 Afternoons in Chicago," making gentle fun of the proceedings, as well as the modernist music—the sound, he wrote, of "street pianos, New Year's eve horns, harmonicas, and old-fashioned musical beer steins"; he ends up admitting that he likes the "hobgoblin extravaganza."

The Love Nest and Other Stories
Ring Lardner
(1926)

In these stories, published toward the end of his career, LARDNER moves beyond the world of sport, focusing instead on marital relationships, particularly those harmed by discord and misunderstanding. In the title story, a young movie actress marries a wealthy man, hoping he will promote her career; he refuses to let her continue acting professionally, forcing her to act instead the role of a happy wife—to the point that she loathes him. Lardner, in his tales of marital disharmony, makes clear that the fault lies with both husband and wife; critic Clifton Fadiman later referred to him as the "recorder of the Great American Bicker." H. L. MENCKEN, reviewing the volume in *The American Mercury*, found the stories "acid and appalling."

Lowell, Amy
(1874–1925) *poet*

Member of a prominent Massachusetts family, Lowell is best known today as an exponent of IMAGISM. Born in Brookline, near Boston, growing up among siblings who included astronomer Percival Lowell and Harvard president Abbot Lawrence Lowell, she first published in POETRY magazine in July 1913. Her

article "Vers Libre and Metrical Prose," promoting FREE VERSE, appeared in *Poetry* the next year; her best-known poem, "Patterns," went to Margaret ANDERSON's LITTLE REVIEW, published in August 1915. Known for her imperiousness, as well as her cigar-smoking, Lowell came into conflict with Ezra POUND when the London-based American expatriate, choosing the contents of his 1914 volume DES IMAGISTES, included only one of her poems. She counteracted with her own volume, *Some Imagist Poets*, published in 1915, featuring Richard ALDINGTON, Hilda DOOLITTLE, D. H. LAWRENCE, and herself and pointedly excluding Pound; imagism, Pound responded, had now become "Amygism." Lowell produced two further imagist anthologies in 1916 and 1917. Another poet interacting with Lowell was Carl SANDBURG; early in his career, Lowell had criticized Sandburg for sacrificing art to propaganda. Later, the poets became friends, sharing an interest in literary forms such as the HAIKU.

Lukoszaite, Elzbieta, or Teta "Aunt"

A character in Upton SINCLAIR's novel THE JUNGLE, Teta Elzbieta, the widowed stepmother of Ona RUDKUS, comes to Chicago from Lithuania with her own six young children. She watches as some of the children die, as others are led astray by the ways of the city. Yet she refuses to listen as Jurgis RUDKUS espouses SOCIALISM; her resistance to new ideas is strong because "her soul had been baked hard in the fire of adversity."

Lusitania

The sinking of this British ocean liner by a German submarine—the result of a torpedo attack near the Irish coast on May 7, 1915—spurred agitation for the United States to enter WORLD WAR I. Of the 1,200 dead, 128 were Americans, including Herbert S. Stone, cofounder of STONE AND KIMBALL, and Elbert HUBBARD. Vachel LINDSAY's "To Jane Addams at the Hague," collected in THE CHINESE NIGHTINGALE AND OTHER POEMS, was written in response to the sinking; it appeared in the *Chicago Herald* on May 11.

M

MacArthur, Charles
(1895–1956) *journalist, playwright, screenwriter*

MacArthur is remembered as the collaborator with Ben HECHT on the 1928 play THE FRONT PAGE, based on his and Hecht's journalism experiences in Chicago. Born in Scranton, Pennsylvania, the son of an evangelist, MacArthur came to Chicago for newspaper work in 1915; his service in WORLD WAR I led to his first volume, *A Bug's Eye View of the War*. After theatrical success with *The Front Page* and a subsequent play, *Twentieth Century*, he and Hecht turned to screenwriting, producing scripts for *Twentieth Century*, *Gunga Din*, *Wuthering Heights*, and other popular movies; MacArthur wrote the screenplay also for *The Sins of Madelon Claudet*, starring his wife, stage actress Helen Hayes, bringing her an Academy Award. Known for his hard-drinking habits, MacArthur died of alcoholism in New York City at the age of 60; Hecht memorialized him the following year in *Charlie: The Improbable Life and Times of Charles MacArthur*. MacArthur's younger brother, insurance executive John D. MacArthur, established the Chicago-based MacArthur Foundation, noted for its unsolicited "genius" grants.

Main-Travelled Roads
Hamlin Garland
(1891)

Recounting the hardships of prairie life, GARLAND makes clear in these stories that tilling the soil is not an ideal pastoral vocation. Despite the beauty of the natural settings—which he regularly describes—farming requires grueling physical work, and its toll is compounded by the severe economic problems the farmer faces. Garland himself, having escaped from his parents' agricultural life, returned to the plains for two summers in the late 1880s, reacquainting himself with the material that would go into *Main-Travelled Roads*. "Up the Coulé" is partly autobiographical, portraying the guilt felt by a son who has deserted his family; also drawn from personal history is "The Return of a Private," presenting a version of Garland's own father, who had returned to a harsh farm life after the CIVIL WAR. "Under the Lion's Paw" reflects the economic views of reformer Henry GEORGE, who declared that farmers must own the land they use, putting them no longer at the mercy of landlords or mortgage holders. "Mrs. Ripley's Trip" is a story that Garland heard from his mother during one of his return visits.

The harshness of these tales caused resistance from mainstream periodicals. *The Arena*, a radical Boston periodical, having run Garland's articles on the SINGLE TAX and other economic issues, published the story "The Return of the Private"; the magazine then undertook presenting the six-story volume *Main-Travelled Roads*.

Synopses

"AT THE BRANCH-ROAD"

In Iowa, in the year 1880, Will HANNON is on his way, at daybreak, to help with the threshing on the

Dingman farm; he is thinking happily of the under-standing that he and Agnes DINGMAN have reached. He meets a one-time rival for Agnes, Ed Kinney, as well as other men arriving for the day's work; Agnes and her mother will provide a hearty lunch and dinner. Will is upset by the coarseness of the men, including their jocularity at his perceived relationship with Agnes. As a result, he recoils when Agnes shows him special attention; confused by his reaction, she responds attentively to the other men. Will works in a fury till dusk, at which time he refuses dinner, saying he will eat at home.

Several days later, Will sets out in his rig to take Agnes to the county fair; he is certain she will be waiting for him, forgetting his petulant behavior. But the rig loses a wheel on the way, and he has to search along the road to find the nut for resecuring the wheel. By the time he arrives at Agnes's house, he finds it empty; Agnes has gone to the fair with Ed Kinney. In a fit of anger Will rushes back home, packs a trunk, and heads for the train station. He sends a letter saying he will never return.

Seven years later, Will returns from the South-west, observing changes that have come to his farmland home. Making inquiries, he learns that Agnes has married Ed and has a child, that she has been ill, and that Ed mistreats her. He comes to the Dingman property and finds that the house is boarded up.

Will goes to see Agnes, who is living with Ed and his parents. He notes right away that she seems wasted, that her beauty is gone. He under-stands, too, that she is imprisoned not only by her husband and her demanding in-laws, but also by her cooped-up existence within a shabby, isolated farm-shack in a land of failing farms and agricul-tural malaise. He apologizes for his past behavior and implores that she—and the child, too, he sud-denly remembers—come away with him. He real-izes that he does not love the woman he sees before him, but rather the girl she once was; yet he understands his responsibility for her present plight. Abandoning moral issues, she agrees to flee with him.

"UP THE COULE: A STORY OF WISCONSIN"
Howard MCLANE, a successful New York actor, returns after 10 years to the Wisconsin coolly, or

valley, where he was born. He learns that his brother, his brother's wife and child, and his mother no longer live on the family farm; it has been foreclosed, lost to unmet mortgage pay-ments. Howard had never received the letter telling of the family's desperate need for money. His brother, Grant, is angry and the bitter—to-ward the brother who has escaped the drudgery of farm life, and toward farm life itself, which re-quires unceasing, soul-killing work.

The next morning, Howard helps his brother pitch hay; Grant remarks that his clothes are too fine for such work. The two men argue, and Grant once more points out the disparity in their lifestyles. Howard decides to make inquiries of the German couple who have bought the family farm, to see if he can buy it back.

Neighbors drop by to visit the household, in-cluding Rose, an attractive woman of 25 who is considered an old maid; all the appropriate young men have gone west. A man takes up a fiddle and plays; the group grows sad, as the music brings out wistfulness and melancholy. Howard thinks of the tragedy of these forlorn lives, which the world, in its romantic ignorance, considers harmonious and pastoral.

Grant's wife, who had once been a teacher, admits to Howard that she was "a fool for ever marrying," for letting herself be tied down to a way of life that will never change. Howard contrasts the beauty of nature about them—the sky, the singing brook, the wild grapevines—and the be-numbing existence, burdened with toil and debt, that farmers are forced to lead. When he offers to buy back their old farm, to make up for his failure to help in the past, Grant refuses.

"AMONG THE CORN-ROWS"
Rob RODEMAKER, holder of a new land claim in the Dakota territory, travels back to the farm country of Wisconsin, where he was raised, to find a bride. He tells friends he will return in 10 days.

Julia PETERSON, daughter of Norwegian immi-grants, is plowing corn in the hot Wisconsin sum-mer sun. Her family is strict, insisting that she work as hard as the men; she resents their severity, as well as their stinginess. Rob renews a formerly casual acquaintance with her, and he is moved by her plight; he proposes that she come with him to his new land, where she need do no work but cook for him. Julia agrees, although she refuses to let him kiss her until he declares that he likes her. Late that night, she sneaks out from her parents' house and joins him.

Garland has been accused of heavy-handedness in his stories, and yet he leaves unsaid in this tale what he knows the reader will understand—that Julia will work as unceasingly on the Dakota farm as she worked on the farm she is escaping.

"THE RETURN OF A PRIVATE"
The train carrying returning Civil War veterans leaves off several men at a station in La Crosse, Wisconsin; from there they will walk home to their farms. The men, who have been gone for three years, are visibly emaciated; one man limps, another is scarred, another is debilitated by fever. The last is Ed SMITH, who left a wife, three children, and a farm that takes half its earnings to pay the mortgage.

It is Sunday, and Mrs. Smith, who has heard that her husband will be coming north from New Orleans, remembers how he answered the call for volunteers in unselfish patriotism—"while the millionaire," Garland notes, "sent his money to England for safe-keeping." She and her family gather for Sunday dinner at the home of the Widow Gray, the matriarch of a large family; the widow's kindly, if poverty-tinged, generosity shows the basic decency and hospitality of the western farmer. That afternoon they spot a lonely figure in a blue coat trudging up the road; the oldest boy—the stand-in for Garland—runs on ahead: "He will never forget that figure, that face." Edward Smith, army private, sick and gaunt, is returning home to his mortgaged farm; his war with the South is over, and he is resuming again his everyday fight—against nature, against the injustice of his fellow men.

"UNDER THE LION'S PAW"
Stephen Council is plowing his Iowa land one late autumn day, working into the darkness, when a stranger, along with his wife and three children, approaches in a wagon. The stranger,

Timothy HASKINS, has come from Kansas, where he has been driven from his farm by grasshoppers; he remarks that he passed good vacant land on his way—echoing Henry George's point that speculators are acquiring desirable land and driving farmers westward onto poorer land. Council and his wife take in the Haskins family for the night.

Jim BUTLER started a grocery business in town, but he found he could sell a piece of land for four times what he paid for it; he realized that land speculation was the way to become rich. He began buying land at forced sales, issuing mortgages; when the mortgage payments could not be met, the farmer remained as a tenant—although in the case of a property near the Councils', the farmer, cursing Butler, went off to Dakota. Haskins agrees to rent the property, assuming he will eventually be able to buy it.

The Haskins family, including the nine-year-old boy, work diligently to improve the derelict farm; child labor is not an issue in western agricultural life. Gradually, after a year's back-breaking toil, the farm seems tentatively prosperous. Haskins meets with Butler about buying the farm, but Butler, seeing its present condition, doubles his price because the worth of the farm has doubled. Haskins is furious; the farm's improvements were accomplished by his own labor. Yet Butler remains smug and implacable, and Haskins realizes he is "under the lion's paw." He seizes a pitchfork, ready to commit harm, but he lowers it at the sight of his small child nearby. He will meet the price; he instructs Butler to make out the deed and mortgage.

"MRS. RIPLEY'S TRIP"
Mrs. Jane RIPLEY, an aging Iowa farm wife, having spent 23 years on the prairie, decides to travel back to New York State to visit her family. Ethan Ripley is dumbfounded; he had no idea she wanted to do such a thing, and he cannot believe she has worked as hard as she claims for all those years. Moreover, they have no money for a trip. Yet Ethan decides she deserves the trip, and he sells some corn and two young hogs to raise the money. Mrs. Ripley herself has saved up over the years, mainly dimes and quarters, and she pays for the

journey on her own; she will take along a chicken and some hard-boiled eggs. One day, months later, a neighbor sees her returning. She settles back into cleaning the house, resuming her duties. Mrs. Ripley has taken her trip, and she is resuming her burdens once again.

The story, the earliest piece in the volume, first appeared in *Harper's Weekly*.

Critical Reception

The book did not sell well; William Dean HOWELLS reviewed it favorably in *Harper's Monthly*, although noting "a certain harshness and bluntness." The Chicago publisher STONE AND KIMBALL brought out a decorative edition in 1893, but sales continued to be poor—especially in "the West," or Midwest, where Garland was accused of disloyalty, of giving a one-sided picture of his native region. Later in his career, Garland added "softer," more nostalgic stories to subsequent editions; these pieces altered the starkness of the 1891 publication.

"At the Branch-Road," sympathetically describing an illicit elopement, appeared almost a decade before Theodore DREISER's *SISTER CARRIE*; yet Garland's tale deflected moral criticism by emphasizing the woman's economic hardship. Critics have noted a continuing theme of return in these stories; Will Hannan and Howard McLane return—although they escape again—while Private Smith and Mrs. Ripley return permanently to take up their labors. A difficulty for modern readers is presented by the DIALECT WRITING, a standard and accepted practice at the time.

Majestic Theatre

A popular VAUDEVILLE theater, opening on January 1, 1906, on Monroe Street in the LOOP, the Majestic was the first new theater since the tragic IROQUOIS THEATER fire of 1903. Housed in what was known as the Majestic Building, at that time the city's tallest structure, the theater presented vaudeville acts six days a week, afternoon and evenings. Ben HECHT, in his autobiography *A CHILD OF THE CENTURY*, speaks of buying an after-noon ticket in 1910, having come the day before, at the age of 16, from Wisconsin to Chicago. In 1945, the theater became the Shubert Theatre, part of the Shubert chain; it was sold to the Nederlander Organization in 1991.

"Mamie"   *See* CHICAGO POEMS.

manifest destiny

A doctrine exalting American expansionism, manifest destiny proclaimed that the nation must extend its boundaries westward, all the way to the Pacific Ocean. First set forth in 1845 regarding the annexation of Texas, the doctrine stated that the "manifest," or obvious, destiny of the nation is to cover the entire continent. The addition of Oregon in 1846, the acquisition of territory after the Mexican War in 1848, the purchase of Alaska in 1867—all were seen as inevitable, if not preordained, extensions of national sovereignty. In the SPANISH-AMERICAN WAR of 1898, the phrase was used to call for overseas colonization and to justify acquisition of the Philippines.

"A Man of Ideas"   *See* WINESBURG, OHIO.

"The Man's Story"   *See* HORSES AND MEN.

"The Man Who Became a Woman"   *See* HORSES AND MEN.

Many Marriages
Sherwood Anderson
(1923)

First appearing serially in abridged form in the *DIAL*, this novel received initial praise from critics; novelist F. Scott Fitzgerald declared its central character to be a "stupendous achievement." Yet as readers began focusing on the work's sexual content—a content not so much enacted as endlessly talked about—censorship forces began to gather; booksellers, worrying about obscenity prosecutions, removed the volume from their shelves. The protagonist, John Webster, is a middle-aged man in the process of leaving his wife for another woman; a large portion of the novel is devoted to his telling his nearly grown daughter, while he himself is in the nude, of his sexual experiences with his wife, the daughter's mother.

Contemporary readers find incestuous overtones in the passages—as they do in the scenes between Margaret ORMSBY and her father in ANDERSON'S MARCHING MEN. Yet when the novel is juxtaposed with the contemporaneous "The Man's Story," collected in HORSES AND MEN, the similarities between the novel and the short story suggest a different conclusion—that the protagonist's overwhelming characteristic is rather a total self-absorption; in the short story, the protagonist not only expresses concerns similar to Webster's, but also displays the same blindness and impersonal cruelty that Webster displays. *Many Marriages* was written in the period when Anderson was breaking up with his second wife, Tennessee MITCHELL; in the novel, Webster's wife commits suicide—as the real-life Mitchell was to do six years later. At the time of writing, ANDERSON claimed to be creating "something looser, more real, more true," and he continued defending the work, later declaring the similarly themed "The Man's Story" to be one of his finest pieces. Yet an important difference between the novel and the short story is the story's use of a narrator; the narrative voice provides distance and perspective. Upton SINCLAIR—a writer who would have censorship troubles as well—declared the novel to be "a sick book, written by a sick man about a sick world."

Marching Men
Sherwood Anderson
(1917)

Written in Ohio, brought as a manuscript to Chicago in 1913, *Marching Men* was published after WINDY MCPHERSON'S SON, although it was possibly the earlier manuscript. Both novels, as well as the later WINESBURG, OHIO, depict a small-town teenager leaving his rural area for the big city, as ANDERSON himself had done; in this particular work, the author draws as well on the military training he received in the Ohio National Guard during the 1898 SPANISH-AMERICAN WAR, after which he served briefly in Cuba. Like his protagonist Beaut MCGREGOR, Anderson also attended night school in Chicago, although not at the UNIVERSITY OF CHICAGO, but at the LEWIS INSTITUTE, now part of the Illinois Institute of Technology. The killing of a wealthy man's son in a Chicago brothel is reminiscent of rumors surrounding the death of Marshall FIELD's son in 1905, the subject also of the poem, "Rosie Roberts," in Edgar Lee MASTERS's SPOON RIVER ANTHOLOGY.

The dedication, "To American Workingmen," echoes Upton SINCLAIR's 1906 dedication in THE JUNGLE: "To the Workingmen of America." A literary influence is Jack LONDON's novel of 1907, THE IRON HEEL, depicting a strong man's assuming leadership during times of social upheaval.

Synopsis

BOOK I

Norman McGregor, nicknamed "Beaut," growing up in the mining town of Coal Creek, Pennsylvania, feels hatred for the town and its citizens; he despises the disorder and ineffectiveness he sees in the lives around him. He sneers also at the local socialist, who foresees the day when men will march shoulder to shoulder, when life will no longer be aimless but full of meaning. His one fond memory is of his father, "Cracked" McGregor, so-called because he, too, hated the men about him; once in a saloon, when a stranger offered a friendly drink, he knocked the man to the floor and kicked him. Yet "Cracked" dies trying to rescue men trapped in a mine fire.

When Beaut is a teenager, the undertaker's daughter, 10 years older than he—a character who is never named, referred to only as "the tall woman" or "the pale woman"—takes an interest in him. She understands also that Beaut will go away and make a place for himself in the world.

When strikes are called among the miners—and the socialist orator makes speeches about the coming brotherhood of man—troops of cavalry arrive on the scene, and the strikes subside. Beaut hates the soldiers who come to his town, and yet he sympathizes with them; he admires, too, the "order and decency" he sees among the ranks of uniformed men. Meanwhile, Beaut's mother, Nance McGregor, has bought a bakery with the money his father had saved; when another strike is called, the miners, although having no money, expect to receive bread from Nance on credit. Beaut, who has seen them reeling out of the saloon, declares that if they have enough money to get drunk, they can pay for their bread; he closes up the bakery. The undertaker's daughter, fearing for his safety, tells him to leave, saying the miners are coming to smash the shop. He arms himself with a hammer, planning to fight, but the soldiers arrive to disperse the miners. Beaut admires the orderly, trained men, moving shoulder to shoulder.

After the strike is over, Nance, having extended too much credit, is unable to reopen the bakery. Beaut gets a job in a livery stable, cleaning and feeding horses; the stable owner warns him that the undertaker's daughter has designs on him. Meanwhile, two boys at the stable conspire to get him drunk, mixing a potent drink that makes him ill; he falls and cuts himself, and the undertaker's daughter and Nance carry him home. That evening, Beaut climbs aboard a passenger train, heading west out of Coal Creek.

BOOK II

McGregor arrives in Chicago in 1893. He finds employment at a warehouse and attends school at night, studying law. A fellow boarder at his rooming house, a barber named Turner, has deserted a wife and four children in Ohio; McGregor asks Turner how to deal with women, and the barber responds that he pays money for their services. One day, when McGregor and Turner are in a park, two women look at them invitingly; Turner wants to go with them, but McGregor holds him back, telling the women to leave. He thinks later about the hidden power he has felt, the power to rise above the messiness and disruption of common life.

Yet McGregor decides to try Turner's advice about women; he walks along an appropriate street and sees a woman beckoning him from a window. He enters the house, and a man grabs him, while the woman empties his pockets. McGregor frees himself, felling the man with a blow, and he seizes the woman, demanding his money back. The woman, frightened, gives him the rest of her money; he ends up making a profit of $27. He is appalled that he could have been interested in such a woman.

Turner prevails on McGregor to go to a dance hall, and there McGregor meets a frail-looking woman, Edith CARSON, who reminds him of the undertaker's daughter in Coal Creek. Edith is a 34-year-old milliner, or hat-maker, who lives behind her store; not normally patronizing dance halls, she had decided that night to do something adventuresome. She even told herself that if she met a man, "he can have what he wants of me." McGregor comes back with her to her home, but to her surprise, he smokes a pipe and talks for two hours; she makes him tea.

McGregor continues a platonic relationship with Edith. He thinks of her sometimes with desire, but he fights against feelings that might upset his long-range purpose in life, which is to lead mankind into better ways. He remembers the soldiers coming into his mining town; they were ordinary men individually, but they became powerful when marching together. He himself is not sure what he will do, but he will keep himself ready.

BOOK III

McGregor's mother dies, and the son goes home for the funeral; he sees again the undertaker's daughter. She suffers from consumption, or tuberculosis, and she is dying. Meanwhile, a socialist orator speaks of voting for his party, and McGregor becomes furious; he looks at the blank faces and weak bodies around him, declaring that mankind should be "a great fist ready to smash and to strike." He decides that the men of the world—such as the Coal Creek miners, or the millions of workers in Chicago—have been betrayed by their leaders; he will become a leader of men, but he will serve their ends, not his own. He spends his last evening with the undertaker's daughter, sitting out on the hillside with the sick woman, gathering her into his arms, as he resolves to take appropriate actions in the future.

BOOK IV

Edith Carson offers McGregor funds from her savings so that he can go to school; he attends the University of Chicago. A professor speaks in class of how the world is full of unrest, and McGregor responds that men must be taught to march, that the world must become "a great camp"—and if men do not understand, they should be "knocked down." The professor is upset, dismissing the class, saying he rejects violence. McGregor quits the university.

He is admitted to the bar and begins practicing law. One night, the son of a wealthy citizen is found dead in an alley behind a well-known brothel; the newspapers have lately been campaigning against vice, and underworld figures want a murderer found quickly. A name is suggested arbitrarily—the name of an ordinary yeggman, or thief—and the man, Andy Brown, is arrested; Brown hires McGregor to defend him. McGregor wanders about the vice district, looking for information as to who the real murderer is. He goes to a woman he has seen working at a SETTLEMENT HOUSE, thinking she will be able to find out. The settlement-house worker is Margaret ORMSBY, a beautiful young woman who is the daughter of an important industrialist; Margaret is frightened by McGregor's strength and forthrightness, but she promises to help. It is revealed that a prostitute in the brothel had struck a blow to the young heir, and his body was thrown into the alley; McGregor brings witnesses to these events into court. After the defendant is acquitted, the lawyer becomes a hero in the city, having stood up to powerful men and achieved victory.

BOOK V

McGregor decides to marry Margaret Ormsby, and Margaret in turn is fascinated by this strong and forceful man. Yet Edith, six years older than he, also loves him, and McGregor understands that she has expectations of him. He tells Margaret about Edith, and he wants Margaret to agree to

marry him; he will then tell Edith that she must give him up. Margaret agrees to the marriage, but says she herself must first talk to Edith.

One evening, McGregor is standing on an elevated railroad platform. A teamsters' strike has been taking place, and a riot occurred that afternoon, injuring several people. Watching now from the platform, McGregor sees a regiment of troops begin marching through the streets; the uniformed soldiers march with measured steps past the disorderly mob. He goes to Edith's shop with new resolution.

Yet Edith has sold her shop; the new owner says she has just left, having waited several days for him to come. McGregor rushes off to the train station, finding her there before her departure. His next step is to bring her to Margaret's house; he will test them both, as well as himself. As David Ormsby, Margaret's father, looks on, McGregor tells Margaret that he wants her because she is beautiful and he wishes to have beautiful children—even though he loves Edith. Margaret, after hearing his words, says she cannot marry him. His response is that he wants offspring; referring to Edith and her seeming frailty, he asks rhetorically, "Do you think she could bear children?" Edith, asserting her new strength, replies that such is for her to decide; she challenges Margaret, asking her how she knows she could bear beautiful children. Margaret exclaims to her father that she did not know life could be like that; she knows she is defeated, and McGregor, recognizing her father's antagonism toward him, leaves with Edith.

BOOK VI

Marching companies are organized throughout the city. McGregor insists upon proper training; the men should march rhythmically, and they should sing a song carrying a message of brotherhood. Soon, he believes, hundreds of thousands of men will be marching, ceasing to be individuals, becoming an all-powerful mass. The marchers understand "the undercurrent of terror" they inspire, and they are glad to cause such feelings among the rich and comfortable.

David Ormsby speaks to McGregor, saying that capitalists like himself are not only after money; they have something larger in mind. Ormsby wants McGregor to join up with him, asserting that the younger man's power can be better used. The march of the world, he claims, is greater than the march of the workers. McGregor's answer is to point to the body of men swinging around a corner at that moment, moving as a rhythmic mass. Ormsby feels unmanned. He thinks, too, that if he had been Margaret, he would have held onto McGregor.

A first-person narrator appears for the first time in the novel. The new "I" persona assumes the stance of looking backward, referring to the past, to "the year of the Marching Men." During that time period, the narrator relates, McGregor was seen almost as a god, casting a long shadow over the thoughts of men. That was when working men, who now shuffle along ineffectively, had swung into a "world-wide rhythmical march"; that was a time of "world madness." One night, when McGregor was speaking to a gathering, a socialist got up on the platform to argue, but McGregor sprang at the man and spun him about, making him look small and comical. The socialist, McGregor declared, represented Old Labor, a personification that was being transformed.

The reader learns that on the great Labor Day celebration in Chicago, the marchers filled the streets and the ground trembled. Margaret Ormsby and her father sat in a carriage on Van Buren Street, watching the crowds. McGregor stood on a raised prominence in Grant Park, and the workingmen marched past him. He lifted his hands, and as a hush came over the crowd, he proclaimed: "We are at the beginning." The people fell silent, although Margaret Ormsby was weeping softly.

BOOK VII

The narrator is gone, and the reader is brought back to the time of the Marching Men. Margaret, having given up her work at the settlement house, is sitting in a carriage with her father on that Labor Day—the same day the narrator has described. Her father, believing that the Marching Men movement is simply an intoxication, seeks to counter McGregor's power over his daughter. As they ride through a workers' neighborhood, they

come across a crying child; the child is the daughter of the socialist who had once climbed onto the platform with McGregor, confronting him "with the propaganda of the Socialist Party." The girl screams for a banana. Father and daughter also ride by a saloon, where a drunkard is beating on a drum and discordantly trying to sing the song of the Marching Men; Ormsby points out that the movement is already beginning to disintegrate. He speaks of a labor leader in his own factory, whom he bought off with money. The passage of time, he declares, will bring about McGregor's destruction. Ormsby drives past another saloon, where a group of street urchins, led by a drunken man, do a grotesque imitation of the marchers. Margaret realizes, too, that the forces that will destroy the Marching Men are at work.

Late that night, Ormsby sits up reading, thinking again of McGregor. Margaret, unable to sleep, thinks of him as well. Yet at the same moment, both father and daughter wonder if perhaps Ormsby was wrong in what he said about McGregor. Perhaps McGregor knew all along that he would fail, and yet he kept on courageously anyway. Ormsby wonders to himself—what if McGregor and "his woman," Edith, knew what they were doing? What if they knowingly and bravely chose their path, even as they understood it would lead to failure?

Critical Reception

Marching Men sold poorly, in part because the dust jacket carried the disclaimer that the novel, despite its title—and despite publication after the United States had entered WORLD WAR I—was "not a war novel." Critics labeled it a proletarian novel; Francis HACKETT in *The New Republic*, although ridiculing the hero's scheme for labor solidarity, praised the work for expressing "the great fictional theme of our generation, industrial America."

Subsequent critics, watching the rise of fascism in Europe, called the novel totalitarian, not proletarian. Maxwell Geismar spoke of its "early American fascism," and Lionel Trilling noted its distasteful "political mysticism"; Irving Howe said it demonstrated "the asexual fanaticism of modern totalitarian leaders"—even though Beaut McGregor eventually marries. In the posthumously published *Sherwood Anderson's Memoirs*, Anderson wrote of the novel's foreshadowing fascism in Europe, acknowledging the dangers of the movement he describes: "I grew afraid of my dream." Yet the mass gatherings of Nazi Germany promoted racial ideology, whereas *Marching Men* promotes no ideology at all.

Critics have long pointed out that the novel offers no specific platform, no definite program. Although the reader might expect an espousal of SOCIALISM, Anderson makes clear that his hero's ideas have nothing to do with socialism or ANARCHISM or communism. At no time does McGregor call for strikes or labor action; when a strike occurs, he stands on the side of the troops that quell it. On several occasions, the rich are said to be fearful of his marching men, and yet it is never spelled out exactly what it is that they fear. McGregor once spots a businessman from Ohio and fulminates against his comfortable existence, but again, no political or economic conclusion is drawn; Anderson is perhaps criticizing his own earlier persona as a businessman in Elyria, Ohio. McGregor talks periodically of "brotherhood," and yet little meaning is given to the term; his character has been driven by hatred, a hatred that tends to be directed toward fellow workers—not toward the bosses, as would be advocated in socialism, nor toward those peoples deemed inferior, as would be advocated in fascism. Francis Hackett wrote in 1917 that *Marching Men* is "rhetorical"; it is "not a literal novel."

Markham, Kyrah   *See* ELAINE HYMAN.

Marquette, Jacques
(1637–1675) *French Jesuit priest, explorer*

Arriving in NEW FRANCE in 1666, Father Marquette accompanied Louis JOLIET in the exploration of the Mississippi River, searching for waterway connections between the Gulf of Mexico and the Great Lakes. In 1673, returning northward, the two men reached the CHICAGO RIVER by way of the Indian portage, carrying their canoes across the low-lying continental divide; Joliet and Marquette were the first Europeans to realize that only several miles separated the DES PLAINES RIVER, flowing into the Mississippi system, and the Chicago River, flowing into LAKE MICHIGAN. Because Joliet's records were lost, Marquette's account became the chief source of information on the journey. The following year, Marquette returned to Illinois, founding a mission in what is now Utica, Illinois; he died of dysentery at the age of 37 near present-day Ludington, Michigan. Chicago's Marquette Building, constructed in 1894 by Holabird and Roche, features bronze reliefs depicting incidents in the life of the explorer.

Marsellus, Louie

In 1916, Willa CATHER's close friend Isabelle McClung married Jan Hambourg, a violinist of Russian-Jewish extraction; Cather's character of Marsellus in the novel THE PROFESSOR'S HOUSE is based on Hambourg. Cather is known to have been upset by the marriage; she also produced writings that reflect the standard anti-Semitism of her day. Marsellus is the engineer who patents and develops the aeronautical device invented by Tom OUTLAND, a young man killed in WORLD WAR I; members of the family resent what they consider his financial exploitation of the device, put into his hands because he married the inventor's fiancée. Although depicted as thoughtful and generous toward the family, Marsellus is seen also as superficial, an unworthy upstart to be contrasted with the lost, heroic Outland.

Cather dedicated THE SONG OF THE LARK to McClung in 1915, a year before her friend's marriage. Ten years later, she dedicated *The Professor's House* to Hambourg: "For Jan, because he likes narrative"; critics have called the dedication purposefully insulting.

Marshall, David

This character appears in Henry B. FULLER's novel WITH THE PROCESSION. An "old settler," a man who helped build the city before the CIVIL WAR, Marshall is portrayed as losing his grip on his once-prosperous wholesale grocery business. After the GREAT FIRE, he was forced to take on a partner, Gilbert Belden, a less-than-scrupulous man who has been increasing his share of the business; the author is suggesting that greedy newcomers are taking over the city. Marshall dies soon after his daughter Jane MARSHALL insists, foolishly, that the family move out of the old house that is no longer fashionable, that has not kept up with the times.

The added dimension to his character is that he had once courted Susan BATES, the woman who went on to become the city's social leader, the head of the procession. Jane learns of his early courtship from Mrs. Bates, and she learns, too, that her father was once fond of poetry, that he read Shakespeare aloud to the young Sue Lathrop. Yet later in the novel, the author seems to forget that he once bestowed these traits on Marshall; the reader is told that art is inexplicable to Marshall, that the idea of a businessman's indulging in such trivia is inexplicable as well. The likely explanation for the inconsistency is that Fuller had been eager to idealize his character, bestowing multiple admirable qualities, while enveloping him in a wistful nostalgia for older, less cutthroat times.

Marshall, Jane

The principal character in Henry B. FULLER's novel WITH THE PROCESSION, Jane is the daughter of David MARSHALL, a businessman who is losing control of his once-successful enterprise. She becomes caught up in the wish to rejoin the "procession," to place her family once more among Chicago's elite. Her growing friendship with Susan BATES, the city's acknowledged social leader, takes her along this path, although it is not through Mrs. Bates's direct influence, but rather through her own blindness to the consequences of her actions. In pressuring her family to leave their old neighborhood, to build a new house in a more fashionable area, Jane hastens the death of her brokenhearted father.

Marshall, Truesdale

This character appears in Henry B. FULLER's novel WITH THE PROCESSION. The younger son of a once-successful businessman, David MARSHALL, Truesdale is portrayed as the artistic offspring, the son who goes off to Europe and studies subjects far removed from business and finance. The author is said to be reflecting himself in this character; Fuller had also traveled in Europe as a young man, and he, too, disliked the subsequent pressures put upon him to maintain the family finances—although the fictional Truesdale Marshall falls into affairs with women, as the undoubtedly homosexual Fuller did not. Truesdale is not a particularly sympathetic character; Fuller makes clear that he is a dilettante and ultimately a fraud. At the end of the novel, because of a scandal involving a woman, he is obliged to leave the city.

Susan BATES, the social leader of the day, discusses her own son with David Marshall; she had been worried over his showing "signs of cleverness," over his wanting to write or paint. She and her husband could not allow any such behavior, and so she adds happily—as Fuller continues in irony—that the boy is now working in business with his father.

The businessman's artist-son had already appeared in Fuller's earlier novel, THE CLIFF DWELLERS; Marcus BRAINARD demonstrates a taste for drawing, and he is contrasted, like Truesdale, with the conforming older brother. Another portrayal of the artistic son occurs in Frank NORRIS's novel of six years later, THE PIT; in this case, Sheldon CORTHELL, living on family capital, continues to function in society, although he loses out romantically to the nonartistic businessman.

Marshall Field and Company

This major department store grew out of the dry-goods establishment founded by Potter PALMER, situated in the then-principal shopping district on Lake Street. The company was taken over by employees Marshall FIELD and Levi Z. LEITER in 1867. When Palmer bought land on State Street, he persuaded Field and Leiter to move from Lake

Street to what would be the city's new commercial thoroughfare, State Street; the new store opened in 1868. After being destroyed in the GREAT FIRE, it was rebuilt, only to be razed by fire again in 1877 and rebuilt once more two years later. In 1881, Field bought out his partner and gave the store its present name; he also enunciated—as he strove to maintain the store's aura of courtesy and gentility—the widely quoted "Give the lady what she wants." By the 1890s, Marshall Field and Company was the world's largest department store.

In his 1903 novel THE PIT, Frank NORRIS describes "a vast dry goods house" on a late winter afternoon; its hundreds of windows are gleaming, and multitudes of fashionably dressed women pour from the doorways, looking for their waiting carriages. In Ring LARDNER's story "The Facts," collected in the 1924 HOW TO WRITE SHORT STORIES [WITH EXAMPLES], a character carries out his Christmas shopping at "Marsh's"—a large store, complete with floorwalkers, personnel who oversee sales and give assistance to customers.

Marx brothers

Originally VAUDEVILLE performers, later movie actors, the Marx brothers lived for a decade in the Chicago area before achieving stardom. In 1910, several vaudeville circuits were headquartered in Chicago, and the city offered a central location for touring performers. The Marx family, including matriarch and stage mother Minnie, moved to a house on the West Side; Minnie called herself Minnie Palmer, taking her name from Potter PALMER's prestigious hotel, the Palmer House. It was while performing in Galesburg, Illinois, Carl SANDBURG's hometown, that the names of Groucho, Chico, Harpo, and Gummo—for Julius, Leonard, Adolph, and Milton—were born; Zeppo, for Herbert, came later. Between theater performances Groucho explored Chicago's music and book stores, meeting and befriending the poet Sandburg at the COVICI-MCGEE COMPANY bookstore; Ben HECHT, frequenting the store as well, speaks of seeing the "perpetual Halloween called the Marx Brothers." During WORLD WAR I, Minnie

Marx bought a 27-acre farm in suburban La Grange, responding to reports that men engaged in agriculture would be exempt from the draft; the family made an effort to raise chickens, then abandoned the project. The Marxes returned to New York in 1920; their greatest fame came later from the classic movies of the 1930s, *Animal Crackers*, *Duck Soup*, *A Night at the Opera*, and *A Day at the Races*.

Mason, Warren

This character appears in Hamlin GARLAND's novel ROSE OF DUTCHER'S COOLLY. A newspaperman, a bachelor in his late 30s, Mason possesses intelligence, insight, and general superiority—as befitting a partner for the superior girl from Wisconsin, Rose DUTCHER. Although lonely in his book-filled rooms, he questions the institution of marriage and resists it—in part because he knows his own shortcomings, including the possibility that he may not remain faithful. He conducts a long discussion with a friend on the possible women he might marry, including a woman of wealth—reflecting a similar discussion in Henry B. FULLER's THE CLIFF-DWELLERS, published two years earlier. Yet Rose continues to intrigue him, and he writes a letter proposing marriage, spelling out his undesirable personal traits as well; she accepts the proposal, as they are two rational people entering into a partnership. The novel ends with his expressing satisfaction that he will never be lonely again—although it fails to indicate the benefits that Rose will derive from the marriage, besides the conventional blessings assumed in any Victorian novel.

The Masses

This monthly socialist magazine was first issued in January 1911 in New York City. In 1912, it was taken over by Max Eastman, a one-time Columbia University doctoral candidate and assistant to John DEWEY; his volume of literary criticism, *The Enjoyment of Poetry*, appeared the next year. Floyd DELL, arriving from Chicago, became an editor of the journal in 1913. Among financial supporters was the publisher E. W. Scripps, who had earlier sponsored the Chicago workingman's tabloid, the CHICAGO DAYBOOK. *The Masses,* unlike many political magazines, devoted a large number of pages to literature, including poetry by Carl SANDBURG; at that time, FREE VERSE and SOCIALISM were considered equally revolutionary. Sherwood ANDERSON's "The Book of the Grotesque" and "Hands" appeared in *The Masses* in 1916, later to be collected in WINESBURG, OHIO.

In 1917, after the United States entered WORLD WAR I, *The Masses,* like the *INTERNATIONAL SOCIALIST REVIEW* and other socialist publications, maintained a pacifist position. The July and August 1917 issues, featuring antiwar material, advocating resistance to the draft, were barred from the mails under the newly passed Espionage Act; the magazine folded by the end of the year. Eastman, Dell, and others were tried twice for antiwar activities; each time the case was dismissed because of a deadlocked jury. Early in 1918, the periodical was revived as *Liberator,* edited by Dell; in 1924, it merged with the Communist Worker's Party *Worker's Monthly. New Masses* was founded in 1926.

Although *The Masses* followed a socialist line, it promoted women's issues and women's suffrage as well; in doing so, it went against the socialist dogma still prevalent in some circles—as held, for instance, by labor activist Mary Harris "Mother" JONES—that class issues were of greater importance than feminist issues.

Masters, Edgar Lee
(1868–1950) *poet*

Masters is best known for the collection of poems SPOON RIVER ANTHOLOGY. This series of monologues, spoken from the graveyard, became a highlight of the new poetry appearing in the second decade of the 20th century. Describing dysfunctional small-town prairie lives, *Spoon River Anthology* also marked a milestone in what became known as the REVOLT FROM THE VILLAGE.

Born in Garnett, Kansas, Masters moved with his family as an infant to rural Illinois, the region where his father had grown up. His father, a lawyer, settled in Petersburg, one of two communities that make up the fictional Spoon River; it was also the home of William H. HERNDON, Abraham LINCOLN's one-time law partner, later his biographer. In 1880, the Masters family moved 40 miles north to Lewistown, the other model for Spoon River. From 1884 to 1889, the young man worked for the *Lewistown News;* at his father's insistence, he studied law, passing the Illinois bar in 1891. The following year, at the age of 23, he moved to Chicago.

Entering into a law partnership, Masters began pursuing the profession he claimed to dislike; in 1898, he married the daughter of a railroad executive. In 1903, replacing former governor John Peter ALTGELD, who had died the previous year, he joined the law firm of Clarence DARROW; both men were Democrats, advocates of labor and champions of the underdog. Yet they often quarreled over money, Masters contending that Darrow withheld fees that belonged to the firm. He resigned in 1911 to establish his own practice. He had entered, meanwhile, into a two-year relationship with music teacher Tennessee MITCHELL; Mitchell later married Sherwood ANDERSON. Another liaison involved Eunice TIETJENS, associate editor of POETRY magazine. A relationship with a young and wealthy widow, begun in 1919, caused the formal breakup of his marriage; his wife retained the legal services of Darrow. A trip abroad in 1921 is said to have included a brief affair in Paris with the American poet Edna St. Vincent Millay.

While continuing to practice law, Masters published, mostly privately, several volumes of poetry, plays, and essays. Some of the work was political, including the verse play *Maximilian,* the prose collection THE NEW STAR CHAMBER AND OTHER ESSAYS, and the poetry volume THE BLOOD OF THE PROPHETS; these works, published between 1902 and 1905, criticized the SPANISH-AMERICAN WAR, Theodore ROOSEVELT, and American postwar expansionism in the Philippines. Then, following the suggestion of William Marion REEDY, editor of the St. Louis magazine *Reedy's Mirror,* Masters began reading in the GREEK ANTHOLOGY, the collection of classical verse that includes first-person graveyard epitaphs; Masters soon began writing his own

FREE VERSE tombstone inscriptions, in which deceased villagers tersely sum up their lives.

Theodore DREISER influenced the poet at this time, especially with the candor of his novel SISTER CARRIE. Late in 1912, Dreiser came to Chicago to research the life of Charles T. YERKES for his novel THE TITAN; Masters helped provide information and legal documentation. The lawyer-poet also took Dreiser for a visit to Menard County, Illinois, the Spoon River locale; the novelist appears in Spoon River Anthology as "Theodore the Poet."

The first poem to become part of Spoon River, "The Hill," appeared in May 1914 in Reedy's Mirror; it was credited to "Webster Ford," a pseudonym combining the names of two 17th-century British dramatists, John Webster and John Ford. The graveyard monologues appeared regularly in the periodical through January 1915, by which time Reedy had revealed the poet's identity; the October 1914 issue of Poetry reprinted three of the pieces. In 1915, when Masters was 46, Spoon River became a noteworthy phenomenon—a best-selling poetry volume. Capturing the nation's imagination, the collection went through multiple editions. The poet published a revised version of Spoon River in 1916, adding 31 epitaphs that became part of the accepted canon.

This collection of verse was to be his only triumph. In 1916, Masters published two further volumes of poems, Songs and Satires and The Great Valley; they received little favor. By the end of the decade, he was spending less time practicing law, and money worries led him to write fiction; he published the autobiographical novel of his childhood, MITCH MILLER, in 1920. In 1923, his divorce finalized, causing him to lose money and property, he moved to New York; at age 55, he was dependent on writing for his income. Two follow-up autobiographical novels, SKEETERS KIRBY and Mirage, appeared in 1923 and 1924; neither were successful. The New Spoon River, an attempt to repeat his one great success, appeared also in 1924; it garnered scattered favorable reviews, but its reception was ultimately disappointing.

In 1926, Masters married his second wife, 31 years younger than he; their son, born in 1928 in Kansas City, continued living in the Midwest with his maternal grandparents. In 1930, Masters and his wife moved into New York's Chelsea Hotel, noted as an inexpensive haven for artists and writers; by the next year, they had begun to live increasingly separate lives.

As money continued to be a problem, Masters turned to writing a biography of Abraham LINCOLN, planning to capitalize on his childhood in Lincoln territory; he felt pique, too, that fellow Illinois poet Carl SANDBURG had published the 1926 best-selling biography, ABRAHAM LINCOLN: THE PRAIRIE YEARS. Masters's views on Lincoln had radically shifted since he wrote favorably on the president in the "Anne Rutledge" epitaph in Spoon River Anthology, as well as in the novel Mitch Miller. In the 1922 CHILDREN OF THE MARKET PLACE, a fictionalized account of the life of Stephen A. DOUGLAS, Masters began his denigration of Lincoln, claiming that his fellow downstater represented commercialism and fostered the decline of agrarian ideals. His biography of 1931, Lincoln: The Man, carried the animus further, branding the president as an egotist and a hypocrite. A lifelong Democrat, Masters blamed Lincoln for hastening the decline of the agrarian West, as well as the doctrine of states' rights. The book sold relatively well, but caused a public reaction against the author, alienating him further from readers who still found interest only in the volume published in 1915; it was now Sandburg's Lincoln that held the public's preference.

In 1932, Masters undertook to write a biography of another fellow Illinois poet, Vachel LINDSAY, who had died by suicide the previous year; the two men had lived as boys within 20 miles of each other. Yet Lindsay's reputation had declined even more than Masters's—the latter still had the recognition of Spoon River Anthology—and "The Congo" poet's life aroused little interest and brought little economic reward. In 1936, Masters published an autobiography, Across Spoon River; deleting the final third of the work, leaving out accounts of love affairs, he ended the story in 1917, the time of his greatest fame. He also misstated the year of his birth, making himself a year younger. The book sold poorly.

In 1943, as he became increasingly ill and impoverished, his second wife took over his care; he lived seven more years, dying in a Pennsylvania nursing home at the age of 81. He is buried next to his grandmother, the model for Lucinda Matlock of *Spoon River*, in Petersburg, Illinois.

Of the 53 books published in his lifetime, only one has endured; *Spoon River Anthology* has never been out of print. Sherwood Anderson, writing to a critic, summarized Masters's career as early as 1918; his success, Anderson observed, came from "a burning hatred," turning "his lackadaisical talent into something sharp and real"—but soon the fire went out, leaving the poet "empty." *Spoon River* was part of the new wave of poetic expression in the second decade of the century; Illinois poets Masters and Sandburg partook of that wave, as did the Missouri-born T. S. ELIOT and the Idaho-born Ezra POUND. Masters made use of new techniques and subject matter, but he never mastered, like Eliot and Pound, the wider, farther-ranging voice of MODERNISM.

Further Reading

Masters, Edgar Lee. *Spoon River Anthology: An Annotated Edition*. Edited and with an Introduction and Annotations by John E. Hallwas. Urbana: University of Illinois Press, 1992.

Russell, Herbert K. *Edgar Lee Masters: A Biography*. Urbana: University of Illinois Press, 2001.

Matlock, Lucinda   *See SPOON RIVER ANTHOLOGY.*

Maxwell Street

Chicago's great outdoor market, centered at Maxwell Street south of downtown, began in the 1880s; it was identified with Jewish merchants, mainly of eastern European origin, although Poles, Lithuanians, and others participated, later joined by African Americans, Latinos, and Asians. At its peak, the market covered six full blocks and displayed the wares of more than 2,000 vendors; the goods ranged from junk to live chickens, and bargaining was the accepted practice. By the 1950s, the market had declined, and much of the area has since been taken over by the University of Illinois at Chicago. Theater builder Barney BALABAN and musician Benny GOODMAN are among figures with roots in the Maxwell Street area.

McChesney, Emma

A character featured in stories by Edna FERBER, based on the author's mother, Emma McChesney is a successful businesswoman, an unprecedented figure in American literature. *Roast Beef Medium, Personality Plus,* and EMMA McCHESNEY & CO., published in three successive years, 1913–15, are collections featuring the dynamic divorcée who travels the Midwest, then moves on to New York as partner in the firm of T. A. Buck Featherloom Petticoat Company, a skirt manufacturer. Emma is hardworking, clear-thinking, energetic, and imaginative, and yet her success lies within a woman's domain; her business wiles revolve around a feminine fashion sense—an understanding of ruffles, scarves, the draping of silk, lace, crêpe de Chine, and taffeta.

Ferber, in her 1938 autobiography, *A Peculiar Treasure*, tells of meeting ex-President Theodore ROOSEVELT in Chicago—and being queried by him about the fate of Emma McChesney, a character with whom he was familiar. "He knew the character," Ferber writes, "as well as I did." Ferber abruptly gave up her Emma stories, although the saleswoman plays a brief role in the novel FANNY HERSELF.

McClure, S. S.
(1857–1949) *publisher, magazine founder*

Born in Ireland, coming as a young boy to northwest Indiana, Samuel Sidney McClure graduated from Knox College in Galesburg, Illinois, in 1882. Two years later, he established the country's first profitable journalistic syndicate, selling articles to newspapers and magazines. In 1893, he founded MCCLURE'S MAGAZINE, a monthly geared to popular appeal, making wide use of photographic material and soon establishing a reputation for MUCKRAKING. In 1906, McClure hired the then-unknown Willa CATHER, who became the magazine's managing editor two years later. The periodical flourished in the first years of the century, after which McClure lost financial control; he spent the last decades of his life in relative obscurity, dying at the age of 92.

McClure's Magazine

Founded by S. S. MCCLURE, published between 1893 and 1929, this monthly periodical noted for MUCKRAKING pioneered in the use of illustration as well as in journalistic exposé. Frank NORRIS was a correspondent from Cuba after the SPANISH-AMERICAN WAR; Ida M. TARBELL's biography of Abraham LINCOLN, offering to the public for the first time many now-familiar Lincoln pictures, was serialized in 1900. Lincoln STEFFENS's *THE SHAME OF THE CITIES* and Tarbell's *HISTORY OF THE STANDARD OIL COMPANY* both began appearing late in 1902, continuing throughout the following year. In 1906, a group of writers, including Tarbell, Steffens, and Ray Stannard BAKER, left *McClure's* to initiate their own periodical, *The American Magazine*; Willa CATHER came to *McClure's* as a replacement, becoming managing editor in 1908. McClure lost control of the magazine in 1912, and *McClure's* soon lost its importance in American journalism.

McCormick, Cyrus H.

(1809–1884) *inventor*

The McCormick harvester, manufactured in Chicago, revolutionized farming in the United States and throughout the world. As a young man, McCormick had watched his father, a blacksmith in rural Virginia, work to devise a mechanical harvesting device; he developed his own successful version in 1831, patenting it three years later. Realizing the value of proximity to the nation's farmlands, McCormick established his MCCORMICK REAPER WORKS in Chicago in 1847.

McCormick's son, Harold McCormick, married Edith Rockefeller, daughter of John D. ROCKEFELLER, not long after her father had provided funding for the UNIVERSITY OF CHICAGO; the Harold McCormicks, although eventually divorcing, acted as sponsors of the CHICAGO OPERA COMPANY. Another branch of the McCormick family became publishers of the *CHICAGO TRIBUNE*.

McCormick, Robert R.

(1880–1955) *owner of the* Chicago Tribune

Descending from two prominent families, the McCormick reaper family and the Medill newspaper family, Robert McCormick became one of the most powerful media figures of his era. After graduating from Yale University and NORTHWESTERN UNIVERSITY law school, then entering local politics, he served as alderman and sanitary commissioner in the first decade of the last century; in 1911, he took over the *CHICAGO TRIBUNE*, initially sharing duties with his cousin, Joseph Medill PATTERSON, later becoming sole editor and publisher. One of his innovations was acquiring timber lands and paper mills, increasing the range of company operations; McCormick is credited with making the *Tribune* the leading newspaper of the Midwest. Promoting politically conservative, antiunion views, he became known also for his isolationist stance in foreign policy.

McCormick Reaper Works

Chicago's first major industrial firm, established in 1847 by Cyrus MCCORMICK, the company changed the face of agriculture at home and abroad. Its machinery, cutting and gathering hay with unprecedented speed, made large-scale wheat farming possible for the first time. The McCormick company was also the first manufacturing firm to guarantee its product, as well as to let customers pay in installments; McCormick understood the seasonal nature of agriculture. The original factory was built on the north bank of the CHICAGO RIVER near the lake; it was destroyed in the GREAT FIRE of 1871. The subsequent plant, spreading over 23 acres on the Southwest Side, was at one time the largest manufacturing facility in the world. A major event in American labor history, the HAYMARKET AFFAIR, arose from a strike at the McCormick plant; repercussions from the strike and its aftermath were felt worldwide for years to come. In 1902, the McCormick Reaper Works, combining with other machinery makers, formed International Harvester; in 1986, the firm became Navistar.

In his 1917 *A SON OF THE MIDDLE BORDER*, Hamlin GARLAND, recalling the strenuous life on his boyhood Iowa farm—including the physical toil of harvesting wheat—speaks of his family's buying a McCormick "self-rake" in 1874, marveling over its ingenuity. The machine, requiring four horses, cut and raked the grain into bunches, or sheaves, although the sheaves, he notes, still had to be tied by hand. Yet he was already hearing improbable tales of a more advanced machine, one that would actually bind the sheaves as well.

McCutcheon, George Barr
(1866–1928) *novelist*

Born in Indiana McCutcheon moved to Chicago for newspaper work. He achieved popular success with his 1901 novel *GRAUSTARK*. Set in a mythical Balkan country, depicting a virtuous American who enlightens decadent old-world specimens, the novel became a best-seller, later a popular Broadway play. In the next dozen years McCutcheon produced best-selling volumes nearly every year, including the 1902 *Brewster's Millions*. Moving to New York, he continued making use of Chicago settings; his 1906 *Jane Cable* features the adopted daughter of a Chicago railroad magnate, who becomes a nurse in the Philippines during the SPANISH-AMERICAN WAR.

Brewster's Millions has persisted in a long film tradition; telling of a young man forced to spend a million dollars in a short period of time, the novel became six successive movies. A silent feminine version, *Miss Brewster's Millions*, appeared in 1926; the film starring comedian Richard Pryor, reinstating the original title, appeared in 1985.

McCutcheon's brother was cartoonist John T. MCCUTCHEON.

McCutcheon, John T.
(1870–1949) *political cartoonist*

Born in Tippecanoe County, Indiana, brother of novelist George Barr MCCUTCHEON, lifelong friend of George ADE, McCutcheon became a nationally known newspaper cartoonist. His first drawings were for the CHICAGO RECORD; at a time when line drawings were standard newspaper fare, he drew daily illustrations for Ade's "STORIES OF THE STREETS AND OF THE TOWN" column. During the SPANISH-AMERICAN WAR. McCutcheon served as war correspondent in the Philippines; Ade, visiting him in Manila, gathered material there for his first playwriting success, *THE SULTAN OF SULU*. In 1903, McCutcheon joined the staff of the *CHICAGO TRIBUNE*, where he remained until 1946; he won a Pulitzer Prize in 1931. The drawing of a hound dog, inserted originally to fill out space in a cartoon, became his signature emblem.

McDowell, Eugene

This character appears in Henry B. FULLER's novel *THE CLIFF-DWELLERS*. A real-estate developer and brother-in-law of George OGDEN, McDowell cheats Ogden out of a large portion of his inheritance; his actions exacerbate the latter's financial troubles. Ogden physically assaults McDowell, although the matter is hushed up; the particular drama takes place as does much of the action—in the CLIFTON, Fuller's microcosm for the business world at large.

McDowell, Rutherford   *See SPOON RIVER ANTHOLOGY.*

McGee, Ollie; McGee, Fletcher   *See SPOON RIVER ANTHOLOGY.*

McGregor, Norman "Beaut"

A principal character in Sherwood ANDERSON's novel *MARCHING MEN*, Beaut is raised in the mining town of Coal Creek, Pennsylvania. He rejects and scorns his fellow townsmen, comes to Chicago, and finds work in a warehouse. He studies law at night and is admitted to the bar; his first major case acquits a defendant who had been framed by political manipulators. Yet he is not interested in such matters, immersed rather in his dream of "Marching Men"—his founding of a movement in which working men march shoulder to shoulder, stepping rhythmically, chanting, demonstrating a collective will. That these are working men suggests labor agitation, as well as the socialist doctrines of his day; yet at no time are labor grievances cited or bosses reviled. Those who are reviled are the socialist leaders and orators, standing on their soapboxes.

After leading a sexless life, Beaut chooses to marry, declaring his wish for children. Torn between the beautiful industrialist's daughter, Margaret ORMSBY, and the frail, older milliner, Edith CARSON, he ends up with Edith—although after that point, no more is heard of her, nor of any children.

Through a suddenly appearing narrator, speaking retrospectively, the reader learns that "The madness of the Marching Men" did not last. The movement deteriorated, and the workmen began shuffling again in their old disorder and ineffectiveness. How this change occurred, how the marching men stopped marching, the reader is never told. It is suggested that McGregor chose his path courageously, knowing his movement would ultimately fail. Yet the actual content of his movement—its ideology, its goal—is never spelled out.

McKinley, William S.
(1843–1901) *25th president of the United States*

McKinley was the last CIVIL WAR veteran to serve as U.S. president. Defeating William Jennings BRYAN in 1896, he presided over the SPANISH-AMERICAN WAR of 1898, leading to the nation's emergence as a world power and its acquisition of possessions outside of its continental area. Despite opposition by the ANTI-IMPERIALIST LEAGUE and other groups, McKinley was reelected by a large margin in 1900, defeating Bryan once again. In September 1901, he was shot by an anarchist in Buffalo, New York, after opening the Pan-American Exposition; he died eight days later. He was succeeded in office by his vice president, Theodore ROOSEVELT.

McLane, Howard

A character in Hamlin GARLAND's story "Up the Coule," from MAIN-TRAVELLED ROADS, Howard is the brother who has escaped a grueling farm life by traveling East and becoming a successful actor. Returning to find the family farm foreclosed, he offers to buy back the farm, but his brother refuses. The outlines of the plot, telling of a son's escape from his family and temporary return, are autobiographical. In real life, Garland relocated his parents from the Dakota territory back to Wisconsin.

McNabb, Cornelia

Like Theodore DREISER's Carrie MEEBER of a few years later, this character in Henry B. FULLER's novel THE CLIFF-DWELLERS is from a small Wisconsin town, coming to Chicago to make her way in the world. Like Carrie, she succeeds, although her path is smoother in that she legally marries the older son of the tycoon Erastus BRAINARD. The protagonist of the novel, George OGDEN, observes her at various stages of her rise in status, mainly in the world-within-a-world of the CLIFTON building.

McPherson, John "Windy"

A character in Sherwood ANDERSON's novel WINDY MCPHERSON'S SON, once a sergeant in the infantry during the CIVIL WAR, Windy has been unable to cope with postwar life in the town of Caxton, Iowa. Like many men who spent four years walking "across the smoking embers of a burning land," he cannot return home and fit into a peaceful life. Windy is an inept housepainter and a drunk, boasting and blustering; he has become the town laughingstock, much to the embarrassment of his son, Sam MCPHERSON. A painful moment occurs when Windy takes on the role of bugler in a Fourth of July celebration; mounted on a white horse, he produces only a piercing squawk, disrupting the solemn occasion. Meanwhile, Windy's wife, forced to take in laundry to support the family, becomes fatally ill. As she lies on her deathbed, Sam, angry at his father for disturbing her, chokes him into silence; he carries Windy's unconscious body outside and dumps it—and yet Windy is seen later that evening on the town's main street: "Nothing could kill that old war horse," remarks townsman John TELFER. After his wife's death, Windy marries a farmer's widow and fathers four more children.

McPherson, Sam

The principal character in Sherwood ANDERSON's novel WINDY MCPHERSON'S SON, Sam is first seen as a 13-year-old boy selling newspapers in Caxton, Iowa; he shrewdly beats out a railroad merchant in selling to passengers on a train passing through town. In his enterprise, he is different from his father, Windy MCPHERSON, a drunken housepainter who has never adjusted to life after the CIVIL WAR; Sam resents his father's incompetence which forces his sickly mother to take in laundry. At the time of his mother's death, he chokes his father with near-murderous intent; his two friends in town, the artist-intellectual, John TELFER, and the schoolteacher, Mary UNDERWOOD, come to his aid.

Sam moves to Chicago, where his industry and cleverness bring him increasing wealth. He marries Sue RAINEY, the daughter of an arms manufacturer. After bearing several stillborn children, Sue turns to social causes; she leaves her husband when he forces her father out of the company. Yet Sam finds his success meaningless, and he takes to the road, wandering about the country; eventually he adopts three neglected children and returns with them to his wife—in an ambiguous ending, in which he accepts the confinement of marriage and home.

The autobiographical material in the novel begins with Anderson's portrayal of the parents—the father as ineffectual, the mother as overwhelmed and suffering. The autobiography continues as Sam leaves his small town in Iowa after his mother dies; Anderson himself left his small town in Ohio after his mother's death—as George WILLARD, too, leaves his town in WINESBURG, OHIO. The later Sam McPherson, alternat-

ing between loving and hating mankind, results from the imagination of a writer who has not yet left—but will soon do so—his job and his wife.

M'Cumber, Daniel   *See* SPOON RIVER ANTHOLOGY.

McVey, Hugh

The principal character in Sherwood ANDERSON's novel POOR WHITE, Hugh, the unschooled son of a Missouri town drunkard, is taken in as a boy by the local telegraph operator's wife. Moving eastward, he begins tinkering and inventing; in Ohio, he falls into the hands of a new capitalist class of men, who begin manufacturing his inventions, making him wealthy. Yet his personal relationships are still burdened by what he sees as his "white trash" heritage; he impulsively marries the daughter of the town's richest farmer-turned-capitalist, eventually feeling secure enough to rise beyond his outsider status. He begins also to understand the power of machines to transform society, for good and for bad, and he loses interest in the process of inventing, in the abilities that had once led him to prominence.

McVicker's Theatre

This Chicago theater, built in 1857 by one-time actor James H. McVicker, became an early first-ranking showcase. Among the actors presented was John Wilkes BOOTH, of the famed Booth acting family; he played Shakespeare on its stage in 1862, three years before assassinating President Abraham LINCOLN. Frank NORRIS's mother, an actress before she married in 1867, made her debut at the McVicker's, playing Emilia in Shakespeare's *Othello*. The building burned down in the GREAT FIRE of 1871—as did every other theater and concert hall in the city—and was rebuilt in 1872; it was remodeled in 1885 by ADLER AND SULLIVAN, and again after another fire in the 1890s. Rebuilt yet again in 1925, the theater became part of the BALABAN AND KATZ chain,

The McVicker's Theatre, destroyed in the Great Fire of 1871, was soon rebuilt; this picture dates from the late 1870s. *(Chicago Historical Society)*

presenting movies and VAUDEVILLE. It was demolished, as have been most Balaban and Katz theaters, in 1985.

Means, Tom

This character in Sherwood ANDERSON's story "The Man Who Became a Woman," collected in *HORSES AND MEN*, is a would-be writer who works as a groom at a racetrack. He is a surrogate for Anderson himself, as less directly is the narrator, Herman DUDLEY. Five years older than Herman, Tom is a constant talker, entrancing the younger man with his words about both horses and writing. At one point, describing the beauty of racing, Tom weeps with emotion; he claims that a woman could never understand such feelings. Later, the narrator reports, Tom becomes "a writer of some prominence."

Medill, Joseph
(1823–1899) *editor of the* Chicago Tribune

Born in New Brunswick, Canada, moving as a boy to Massillon, Ohio, Medill established the *Cleveland Leader* in 1852. He came to Chicago in 1854, buying into the CHICAGO TRIBUNE the next year; he controlled the newspaper from 1874 until his death. Tempering the paper's support of the anti-immigrant KNOW-NOTHING MOVEMENT, he took an antislavery stance and became an early member of the Republican Party; he was instrumental in securing Abraham LINCOLN's nomination for president in 1860. Medill was noted for antialcohol, antigambling, antilabor views. His daughter married Robert Sanderson McCormick, nephew of reaper manufacturer Cyrus MCCORMICK; their son, Robert Rutherford MCCORMICK, took over the *Tribune* in 1911. Another of Medill's grandsons, Joseph Medill PATTERSON, moving to the East Coast, established the *New York Daily News* in 1919.

Meeber, Carrie

The principal character in Theodore DREISER's novel *SISTER CARRIE*, Carrie leaves her hometown of Columbia City, Wisconsin, at the age of 18, boarding a train for Chicago. On that train she meets Charles DROUET, the man who will first help her succeed in the world. Later, meeting a new lover, Charles HURSTWOOD, she continues her rise in the world, while Hurstwood's life begins a parallel decline. Carrie triumphs in part because men with resources help her; her sexual liaisons are consistent with the conventions of NATURALISM, suggesting that she is giving in to larger forces that shape her life—although in her case, becoming an actress gives her the means to be independent, no longer reliant on men.

"A Meeting South"   *See* DEATH IN THE WOODS.

"Memoir of a Proud Boy"   *See* CORNHUSKERS.

The Memoirs of an American Citizen
Robert Herrick
(1905)

First serialized in the *Saturday Evening Post*, this fictional autobiography tells of the rise of an Indiana farm boy, Van HARRINGTON, who arrives penniless in Chicago and eventually makes his way to great fortune, using bribery and other illegal means. HERRICK presents events from Harrington's point of view; he assumes the reader will see that this view is morally wrong, that Harrington is reprehensible in both his attitude and his actions. Yet the author keeps his protagonist's immorality within the realm of business; unlike Theodore DREISER's later tycoon, Frank COWPERWOOD, Harrington leads an unassailable family life.

At the time of writing, Herrick assumed his readers would respond readily to contemporary references. When his narrator studies the works of English naturalist Charles Darwin and English philosopher Herbert SPENCER, readers know he is taking up SOCIAL DARWINISM, the belief in the survival of the "fittest" in social and economic realms. When the narrator recounts the HAY-MARKET AFFAIR and its subsequent trial, readers remember the events that had occurred less than two decades previously. When Harrington and his family visit "the beautiful city of white palaces," readers understand the reference to the WORLD'S COLUMBIAN EXPOSITION of 1893. When he predicts that someday a canal will be dug, they know that construction began on the PANAMA CANAL the year before the novel appeared. When he is accused of selling spoiled meat to the army during the SPANISH-AMERICAN WAR, they recall the charges made against Philip D. ARMOUR.

Synopsis

CHAPTERS I–III: "THE LAKE FRONT IN CHICAGO," "THE HARRISON STREET POLICE COURT," "JASONVILLE, INDIANA"

The first-person narrator, the 20-year-old Van Harrington, arrives in Chicago, having tramped from Indiana with only a few cents in his pocket. He falls in with another young homeless man, Ed Hostetter, who is coming from a farm in Michigan. In a downtown store, Harrington is accused of stealing a young woman's purse; he is freed when the woman admits she did not see him actually take the purse. The narrator recounts his small-town Indiana background, focusing on his confrontations with the local judge, owner of the land on which his father's general store stands; when the narrator was accused of burning down the judge's barn, the woman he had hoped to marry rejected him, even though he was later proven innocent. The woman, May, took up instead with his quiet and churchgoing brother, Will. Harrington headed north for Chicago, resolving that he would conquer the world.

CHAPTERS IV–VI: "THE PIERSONS," "A MAN'S BUSINESS," "FIRST BLOOD"

Harrington's friend Ed finds his aunt, who runs a boardinghouse, and she takes in the two of them. Among the other boarders are Hillary Cox, a cashier at a nearby market, and Jaffrey Slocum, a law student; Hillary finds Harrington a job at the market. One day he catches a glimpse of Strauss, the meatpacking king, and vows again that he will live for success.

Realizing that the market is not being properly run, Hillary suggests that she and Harrington, both of whom have been saving money, buy out the business and form a joint enterprise; the implication is that they join in other ways as well. Harrington realizes that a man like himself, "hard and selfish," travels best alone. A large wholesale packer, Henry I. DROUND, buys the market, and Harrington talks his way into a job as a driver with the Dround firm. Surveying the stockyards, a one-time prairie that has turned ugly and filthy, he decides that his future lies there; meatpacking is a basic human industry, one that feeds the people of the Earth.

Harrington discusses history and politics with Slocum, learning about Charles Darwin and Herbert Spencer. He begins to have ideas about improving his new company's business, such as packaging sausage in special boxes so that it seems less suspect, or providing kosher meat for the Jewish West Side—although such ideas are turned down by the conservative Dround. Yet Harrington is learning about the packing business, including its many secret deals and illegal actions; getting hold of inside information, he brings his own money, the thousand dollars he has saved, to a friend who is a clerk at the CHICAGO BOARD OF TRADE. The sum soon multiplies into a total of $5,000, and Harrington understands that he can be a success.

CHAPTERS VII–VIII: "THE BOMB," "THE TRIAL OF THE ANARCHISTS"

Following Slocum's legal advice, Harrington schemes to gain control of a small packing firm outside the city; he begins pushing his special sausage and kosher meats. He ignores the labor strife taking place around him, although one evening Slocum and others return to the boarding-house to tell of a horrifying scene at the Haymarket—an explosion, followed by shots from the police. Hillary, he learns, has been disfigured by a bomb fragment. The morning after the event, Harrington, who has now advanced within the Dround organization, happens to be standing in front of the office, watching a carriage drive up; he feels spellbound by the woman he sees sitting within the carriage. Their eyes meet, and she gives him the sharpest look he has ever received from a woman; her face is strange, dark, yet pale. Going on into the office, he wonders who she is.

At the subsequent trial of the anarchists, it becomes clear that the city's prominent citizens want a jury that will do their bidding; the jury list includes names of small manufacturers or upper-level clerks, excluding laborers and workingmen. Harrington is among those chosen. Throughout the trial, he watches the eight defendants; he decides that two are "stupid," three are "shifty," and three have "a kind of wild enthusiasm"; they are dreamers, not thugs. The prosecutors cannot prove who made the bomb or who threw it, and yet the jury decides that these men must suffer for their subversive ideology; Harrington and the others have performed their civic duty. He refuses to go to a celebration dinner afterward, but he overcomes his misgivings, understanding that he has acted for the good of society; he understands that the strong are the ones who rule, that the world is made for the strong.

CHAPTERS IX–X: "ANOTHER BOOST," "LOVE"

Harrington plays a bluffing game with Strauss, and the old tycoon expends a large sum of money for the sausage business that Harrington has been running on the side; this is a triumph, since Harrington knows that his firm, squeezed by larger interests, had been in financial trouble. Meanwhile, a new stenographer begins working for him, and she turns out to be the woman whose purse he had once been accused of stealing. She is a woman of social graces, whose family has left her in unfortunate circumstances; Dround, an old acquaintance, has taken pity on her. Yet Sarah is a poor stenographer, unfit for the competitive business world. Harrington feels the need to protect her, to counter her weaknesses with his own strength, and he promises to marry her.

The Drounds invite Harrington to dinner, and to his surprise he is greeted by the woman he had seen in the carriage that morning after the bombing. This beautiful, foreign-looking woman is Jane DROUND herself. The dinner guests include the city's important businessmen, and afterward they attend the opera; Harrington is in a sphere he has never inhabited before. During intermission, he and Mrs. Dround talk about Strauss, the packer whose business seems to be expanding—to the point, Harrington warns, that Strauss will soon swallow up all competitors, including Dround. Sarah later speaks of Jane Dround, saying that the woman's father was a legendary half-breed who made a fortune by trading with the Indians and acquiring government lands. Sarah says she is afraid of her—because she is so strong.

CHAPTERS XI–XIII: "MARRIAGE," "AN HONORABLE MERCHANT," "THE WILL OF A WOMAN"

Before their marriage, Sarah insists that she and Harrington visit his home in Indiana, believing that he should reconcile with his parents. His father is dead, and his brother Will, married to May and the father of children, has been running the family store. Yet business is poor; the growing mail-order business has cut into the rural trade. Harrington offers Will a job in the Dround company, and Will and May accept gratefully.

Dround has been accused by competitors of bribery, of paying for special privileges from the city. He denies the charge, but Harrington knows that Dround's manager has been making such deals, following the only way that business can be accomplished. Yet Dround, priding himself on the integrity of his firm, fires the manager. He asks Harrington to take over, although Harrington explains that he would have to follow the same methods the previous manager followed, or else the firm would face ruin.

The fired manager joins the Strauss firm, trying to persuade Harrington to join as well; he talks about Strauss's developing control of a vast food empire, including railroads and steamship lines to transport the products. Harrington tells Mrs. Dround that her husband's business is doomed to fail, but she disagrees; her face glowing with enthusiasm, she inspires Harrington to begin making plans, to begin scheming of ways to make the company strong again—allowing, to be sure, no impediment of scruples. He feels nothing but admiration for this woman; she should have headed a regiment or run a railroad, he realizes. Later that evening, Will arrives from Texas, where he has been scouting the territory; he speaks of the promise of that part of the country.

CHAPTERS XIV–XVI: "THE FIRST MOVE," "THE ATLAS ON THE FLOOR," "THE STRUGGLE"

As his first move, Harrington bribes a company to sell its assets to Dround, rather than to Strauss; his next step is to begin taking over other plants, then incorporating them into a holding company. Speaking to Jane Dround—whose aging husband has become increasingly irrelevant to the business—he takes an atlas down from the shelf, pointing to lands toward the south and west. Settlers are pouring into the territory, he says, and the railroads are following; soon meat and grain will flow toward the Gulf and outward to Europe and Asia, and someday a canal will be dug. He feels inspiration once more as the two of them go over their far-reaching plans.

Yet the depression of 1893–94—obscured temporarily by the glamour of the world's fair, which Harrington and his family visit—makes the necessary financing hard to acquire. Jane Dround says mysteriously that if a time of need arises he should turn to her; she sends him an envelope, in

which lies another envelope, to be opened in a time of crisis. He tosses the envelope into a drawer.

CHAPTERS XVII–XXII: "NO GOSPEL GAME," "THE STRIKE," "DENOUNCED," "TREACHERY," "A SQUEEZE," "JUDGMENTS"

When a fraud case is brought against the Dround company, the judge is bribed into dismissing it. A newspaper gets hold of the story and publicizes it, and yet no political consequences ensue. Harrington discovers that his old friend in homelessness, Ed Hostetter, who has been working for him—and who feels jealous of his success—is the one who turned him in; a formerly upstanding man, he has become, as a result of crooked dealings, a rascal. In a different milieu, at a company plant in Indiana, Harrington is threatened by a striker, who accuses him of murdering his friends at the Haymarket trial; Harrington gives the man "a good sermon," the gospel "of man against man." Yet his wife has been listening in church to the Reverend Mr. Hardman, an exponent of CHRISTIAN SOCIALISM; one Sunday morning, when Harrington accompanies her to church, the minister accuses him directly of defying the laws of man and God. Harrington leaves angrily, taking his wife with him.

A personal confrontation with Strauss follows, in which Harrington threatens to do his own exposing—of Strauss's illegal dealings; he achieves a temporary victory. Yet Henry Dround, outraged at the scandal, plans to divest himself of his stock; Harrington's concern now is to keep the stock out of the wrong hands. His brother Will, urged on by May, quits the Texas branch of the company, upset at the bribing of state legislators to build a railroad through to the Gulf. Harrington, depressed at his brother's defection, feels that the only person who understands him now is Jane Dround.

CHAPTERS XXIII–XXV: "HAPPINESS," "WAR," "THE LAST DITCH"

Jane says she must go away. A separation will make no difference, she insists; the two of them still think the same thoughts. As they sit silently, Sarah comes upon them and cries out in jealousy; she accuses Jane of taking her husband from her, as well as exerting an evil influence over him. Jane replies that she could take her husband, but for his sake, she will not.

The Spanish-American War erupts, and financial markets slide; Harrington feels the downturn as well. One day the Reverend Hardman comes to see him, hoping that he will buy some bonds bought with his wife's inheritance; Harrington sends him away, pleased to see that the Christian socialist is as greedy as anyone else. Then, feeling again the hardship of his own situation, he receives a telegram from Jane Dround, reminding him of the envelope she had given him long ago. He opens the envelope and sees a name and address; the address leads him to an unlikely warehouse area, and there he finds a short, swarthy man, "some sort of foreigner." The man says he himself has the Dround stock, meaning that Strauss cannot get hold of it; the man also gives Harrington a note to take to a banker—to access, Harrington is sure, Jane Dround's private fortune.

CHAPTERS XXVI–XXXII: "VICTORY," "DOUBTS," "A NEW AMBITION," "THE SENATORSHIP," "THE COST," "FURTHER COST," "THE END"

As a result of Harrington's manipulations, Strauss is forced to offer an exorbitant sum for his company; bankers begin conferring with Harrington about his vast railroad properties in the Southwest. The Drounds return from abroad, and Harrington understands that the power he has achieved is because of her. She tells him that an Illinois senator is ill, that he should think of taking a seat in Washington; the senator dies, and Harrington decides that politics is the new challenge in his life. Chicago newspapers denounce him, saying he will represent only the corrupt interests; at a political rally, he sees his brother Will speaking out against him, telling the crowd of his misdeeds—not only his bribing the Texas legislature, but also his selling tainted beef to the army during the Spanish-American War. Talking later to Will, Harrington realizes that his brother, despite his obvious impoverishment, will accept no help from him. The state legislature, meanwhile, elects him to fill the unexpired senatorial term. Saddened that Will's wife, May, also rejects his help, Harrington revives

his spirits as he gazes at the factories and railroad yards of the city. They are a part of him, he knows; the work of the world is going forward, and his soul has gone into its making. Later, in Washington, arriving in the senate chamber, he sees an arrangement of American Beauty roses on his desk; without looking at the card, he knows they are from Jane Dround.

Critical Response

A reviewer in *The Nation* claimed that the novel seemed "cynical," that it provided too much of an apology for the businessman's actions. Such an apology was far from Herrick's intention—as other critics understood, including William Dean HOWELLS, who applauded the work's moral insight. Yet Howells recognized also that the first-person narrative is problematic, requiring that the meaning be suggested rather than expressed directly. The reader is often drawn into Harrington's point of view, at which time he finds it difficult to detach himself from the character and pass judgment on him.

Jane Dround, on whom the reader is expected to pass judgment as well, is also a figure whom contemporary readers are likely to admire. She is forced to work through a man to accomplish her ends, and yet she is a strong woman; readers do not wish to condemn her, even though they know they are supposed to do so. Herrick's admiration of Jane Dround seems to stand behind Harrington's, and to the degree that the author admires her, the social criticism in the story is muted.

Memorial Day

This holiday was initiated to honor the Union soldiers who died in the CIVIL WAR. Originally called Decoration Day, for the purpose of decorating the graves of veterans, the holiday began in 1868 under the leadership of Illinois-born John A. Logan, former Union general and commander of the veterans' organization, the GRAND ARMY OF THE REPUBLIC. First designated as May 30, Memorial Day subsequently became the last Monday in May, honoring the dead of all American wars.

Mencken, H. L.
(1880–1956) *writer, literary critic*

Coeditor of the magazine *Smart Set,* cofounder and editor in 1924 of the prestigious *American Mercury,* Mencken became an influential figure in the first half of the 20th century. As a social critic, he is famed for his attacks on the middle class—calling it the "booboisie," a version of *bourgeoisie*—and on middle-class complacency and presumed tasteless-ness. His stance made him a foe of censorship; he attacked what he saw as a lingering American puritanism, defined in his well-known phrase as "the haunting fear that someone, somewhere, may be happy." A friend of Theodore DREISER, he supported the novelist when he was accused of immorality; a 1917 piece in the magazine *Seven Arts,* titled "The Dreiser Bugaboo," attacked Dreiser's critics, claiming that the author's novels represented a worthy tradition of REALISM.

An admirer of German culture, Mencken had earlier helped popularize the ideas of German philosopher Friedrich NIETZSCHE; Mencken's *The Philosophy of Friedrich Nietzsche,* appearing in 1907, described such Nietzschean concepts as the glorifying of the strong, willful man, concepts that would influence Dreiser and other novelists. In 1919, Mencken published the first of several editions of *The American Language: An Inquiry into the Development of English in the United States;* the much-admired work, becoming an important linguistic resource, defined the distinguishing characteristics of American English as opposed to British English, in terms of usage, idiom, and vernacular. The 1921 edition gave special credit to Ring LARDNER for his rendering of common American speech.

In 1917, Mencken published an article in the CHICAGO TRIBUNE in praise of Chicago literature, declaring that writers with something new to say are likely to be connected with "the abbatoir by the lake"—a reference to Chicago's slaughterhouses and stockyards; the midwestern city, he adds, is not Europe or the East Coast, but rather "American in every chitling and sparerib." Three years later, in a piece in the London *Nation* titled "The Literary Capital of the U.S.," Mencken repeated his declaration, saying that Chicago, drawing authors from "remote wheat-towns and far-flung railway junc-tions," gave writers an independence and honesty that could not be matched in the East; he singled out Sherwood ANDERSON, Dreiser, Edgar Lee MASTERS, Carl SANDBURG, and George ADE, concluding that in the last several decades, one could hardly find an important literary trend "that did not originate under the shadow of the stockyards."

Micheaux, Oscar
(1884–1951) *African-American filmmaker*

Raised in the southern Illinois town of Metropolis—famed later as the birthplace of the *Superman* comic strip—Micheaux moved to Chicago in 1900. He worked as a Pullman porter, then bought homesteading land in South Dakota, where he farmed for several years; returning to the city, he wrote a series of autobiographical novels, including *The Homesteader,* published in 1917. The following year he founded the Micheaux Film and Book Company, for the purpose of making a movie from the novel; the film, first shown at the Eighth Regiment Armory in BRONZEVILLE in 1919, was a success among African-American audiences.

After the RACE RIOTS of the same year, Micheaux produced "Within Our Gates," a movie showing a graphic mob lynching; praised by the CHICAGO DEFENDER, it opened at the VENDOME THEATRE on South State Street in 1920. Micheaux presented himself as the adversary of D. W. GRIFFITH, whose 1915 *The Birth of a Nation,* glorifying the Ku Klux Klan, had been a source of racist propaganda. Micheaux's *Symbol of the Unconquered,* produced also in 1920, presented the Klan as the villain. In 1921, the filmmaker transferred his operations to New York City, where he created his best-known silent film, *Body and Soul,* the 1924 movie debut of actor and singer Paul Robeson; in 1931, his *The Exile* became the first black sound film. In a career of three decades, Micheaux wrote, directed, and produced more than 40 feature movies. Although criticized for casting his heroes as lighter skinned than his villains, for indulging at times in minstrel-show stereotypes, he has been recognized as an important figure in black cultural history, as well as the forebear of American independent filmmaking.

Michigan Avenue

Chicago's historic north-south avenue, once called Michigan Boulevard, showcases major cultural institutions, including the ART INSTITUTE, the AUDITORIUM BUILDING, the FINE ARTS BUILDING, and ORCHESTRA HALL, since renamed Symphony Center. Sherwood ANDERSON, first coming to Chicago in 1896, wrote that occasionally on Sunday afternoons he walked along Michigan Boulevard, "a noble and beautiful street," seeing the "beautifully dressed women" and the "faultlessly dressed men." In the 1920s, North Michigan Avenue, where the pre-GREAT FIRE structures of the WATER TOWER AND PUMPING STATION stand, was developed as the upscale shopping mecca called the Magnificent Mile.

Mid-American Chants
Sherwood Anderson
(1918)

A collection of FREE VERSE, portions of which had appeared in POETRY and Seven Arts magazines, the work by Sherwood ANDERSON was seen as following in the path of Carl SANDBURG's CHICAGO POEMS; titles of individual poems ranged from "Song of Industrial America" to "Song of the Soul of Chicago." Reviews were mixed, and Anderson's friend Floyd DELL, who had been instrumental in the publication of the novel WINDY MCPHERSON'S SON two years earlier, found a falling off in what he referred to as "a semi-mystical prose-poem about himself." When Anderson's gathering of short fiction, WINESBURG, OHIO, appeared the following year, his poetry was immediately forgotten.

Midway Plaisance

This stretch of green parkland on the South Side of Chicago, one mile long and 600 feet wide, connects JACKSON PARK and Washington Park. Named by designer Frederick Law OLMSTED, the Midway Plaisance became the amusement strip for the WORLD'S COLUMBIAN EXPOSITION of 1893. A major attraction of the fair, the Ferris wheel, invented by George Washington FERRIS, stood centrally located on the Midway. Because of its proximity to the UNIVERSITY OF CHICAGO, the green strip has subsequently been associated with that institution. At the west end stands the massive 1922 Lorado TAFT sculpture, "Fountain of Time," consisting of a 127-foot-long grouping of statuary, a large reflecting pool, and a 26-foot-high statue of Father Time.

"Milk Bottles"   *See* HORSES AND MEN.

Miller, Julia   *See* SPOON RIVER ANTHOLOGY.

"A Million Young Workmen, 1915"   *See* CORNHUSKERS.

Miner, Georgine Sand   *See* SPOON RIVER ANTHOLOGY.

Mitchell, Tennessee
(1874–1929) *music teacher, sculptor*

Mitchell is remembered today for her associations—as mistress to Edgar Lee MASTERS, as wife to Sherwood ANDERSON. Born in Jackson, Michigan, named after Tennessee Claflin, suffragist and women's rights advocate, Mitchell arrived in Chicago at the age of 17; she became music teacher to the nieces of Masters, entering into a relationship with the poet in 1909. In 1916, she married Sherwood Anderson; Anderson's 1921 volume, THE TRIUMPH OF THE EGG, features black-and-white photographs of her "Impressions in Clay," sculptures representing characters in the stories. The couple separated in 1922 and divorced in 1924; Mitchell continued her sculpting, holding exhibits in Chicago and New York. In 1929, she was found dead in her Chicago apartment, said to be from an overdose of sleeping pills.

In Masters's SPOON RIVER ANTHOLOGY, the title character of "Georgine Sand Miner"—who appears also in the previous poem, "Daniel M'Cumber"—has been identified as Mitchell. Masters's autobiography of 1936, *Across Spoon River,* gives Mitchell the name of Dierdre; the poet, known for his cantankerousness, declares that "Deirdre's poison" lasted in his blood for years.

Mitch Miller
Edgar Lee Masters
(1920)

Beginning a trilogy featuring the autobiographical Skeeters Kirby, the novel is set in the first 12 years of the boy's life in rural Illinois; it focuses on Kirby's friend Mitch—the actual name of MASTERS's real-life friend—who was killed trying to hitch a ride on a moving train. Mitch's story was previously presented in the "Johnnie Sayre" epitaph in SPOON RIVER ANTHOLOGY. Abraham LINCOLN is represented positively in this work, as he is in *Spoon River;* Masters's debunking of the president would not appear until two years later, in CHILDREN OF THE MARKET PLACE.

modernism

The literature of modernism, flourishing in the first half of the 20th century, has been characterized as complex, allusive, replete with ambiguity—and most tellingly, elitist; the modernist movement was never concerned with art for the masses. While using such unorthodox techniques as FREE VERSE and stream-of-consciousness narrative, modernist writers, in a seeming paradox, invoked history and tradition—although the tradition was classical, Renaissance, 17th-century; the break with orthodoxy was a break with Victorianism and the 19th century. Exponents of modernism included Ezra POUND, T. S. ELIOT, James JOYCE, and Wallace STEVENS; similar movements in other arts, including painting and music, flourished at the same time. Modernist writing led to an academic industry of explication, explanation, and allusion-hunting; works that proved the most intractable were labeled "high modernism." The ascendancy of modernism damaged the reputation of writers

working in a more broadly based, "democratic" tradition; figures such as Carl SANDBURG or Theodore DREISER lost status in the triumph of modernism's patrician sensibilities.

Monadnock Building

The tallest of the major load-bearing buildings, still standing at Jackson Boulevard and Dearborn Street, the Monadnock, named after the New Hampshire mountain, was built in 1891 by the firm of BURNHAM AND ROOT. Its weight borne by its walls, the 16-story structure required six-feet-thick masonry at the base. Despite the conservative engineering, the Monadnock foreshadows the high-rise structures to come—in its lack of ornamentation and in its narrow rectangular shape that allows natural light into interior spaces. The architect, John Wellborn ROOT, died the same year the building was completed, at the age of 41. Two years later, in 1893, the structure served as the likely model for the CLIFTON BUILDING, the central symbol in Henry B. FULLER's novel THE CLIFF-DWELLERS. As late as 1928, when high-rises had long soared to greater heights, a character in MacKinlay KANTOR's novel DIVERSEY boasts that she is a telephone operator in the Monadnock Building.

Monahan, Ella

This character in Edna FERBER's novel FANNY HERSELF is a successful businesswoman, secondary only to the young Fanny BRANDEIS. Ella is a woman who would like to have married but is content pursuing her career; she is a glove buyer for the Haynes-Cooper mail-order firm. The manager has made clear that he never hires a woman if he can hire a man instead, but he acknowledges Ella's superior capabilities; Ella learned her knowledge of leather in her father's tannery business in Racine, Wisconsin. She represents another of the successful businesswomen that Ferber introduced into popular American literature—although, in accordance to the convention of the day, none of these women is married; Emma MCCHESNEY is divorced,

Fanny Brandeis will marry and give up her career, and Ella Monahan is permanently single.

Monroe, Harriet
(1860–1936) *founder of* Poetry *magazine*

Daughter of a once-prominent lawyer, Monroe was acquainted early in childhood with the families that would eventually provide funding for her literary venture. Her formal education ended with finishing-school instruction at the Visitation Convent in Georgetown, Washington, D.C. Writing art and drama reviews for the *Chicago Tribune*, publishing poetry in various periodicals, Monroe was commissioned to write the words for a cantata dedicating ADLER AND SULLIVAN's new AUDITORIUM BUILDING in 1889; another celebratory effort was "The Columbian Ode," a poem recited at the October 1892 dedication ceremonies for the WORLD'S COLUMBIAN EXPOSITION. In 1896, she published a biography of her late brother-in-law, architect John Wellborn ROOT.

After the turn of the century—having been born the same year as activist Jane ADDAMS and seeking, like Addams, a sense of purpose and achievement—Monroe decided to devote herself to furthering the cause of poetry; she began soliciting funds, aiming to establish the nation's first magazine devoted solely to verse. Like Addams, she received funding from the city's industrial, retail, and banking elite, as well as from clergymen, academics at the new UNIVERSITY OF CHICAGO, and lawyers such as Clarence DARROW. Reading current English and American literary magazines, she began compiling a list of poets to ask for submissions to her new periodical, POETRY magazine. Poet Ezra POUND, living in London, volunteered to be a "foreign correspondent."

In September 1912, at the age of 51, Monroe sent out the first issue, dated October, of the periodical that continues to the present day. For the next 22 years, she edited the magazine, publishing almost all the important American and English poets of her era. Her aesthetic limitations have been duly noted by critics; she has been accused of harboring tastes that were conventional, and she was slow to recognize the talents of such figures as T. S. ELIOT and Wallace STEVENS. She and her coeditor, Alice Corbin HENDERSON, published an anthology, *The New Poetry*, in 1917, consisting of material from the magazine. During the GREAT DEPRESSION, her efforts were sustained by a grant from the Carnegie Foundation.

In 1935, Monroe published her own collected *Chosen Poems*. A year later, after attending a convention of P.E.N., the writers' organization, in Buenos Aires, she traveled to Machu Picchu in Peru, where she died of a brain hemorrhage at the age of 75. Her autobiography, *A Poet's Life: Seventy Years in a Changing World*, was published posthumously in 1938. Monroe's place in literary history lies in her vision, in her encouraging and

Harriet Monroe posed for a "Streets of Paris" amateur performance in 1906, six years before launching *Poetry* magazine. *(Chicago Historical Society)*

promoting poetry during the great modernist surge in the early decades of the century. While carrying out such mundane tasks as fund-raising and looking after business details, her vision led her to reach out internationally, to find the best poetry of the era in the English-speaking literary world.

Further Reading

Williams, Ella. *Harriet Monroe and the Poetry Renaissance: The First Ten Years of Poetry, 1912–1922.* Urbana: University of Illinois Press, 1977.

Montgomery Ward and Company

The first major mail-order company was founded by Montgomery WARD in 1872. As farmers were seeking to break the monopoly held by rural merchants, Ward claimed that his catalogue operation, selling directly to the customer by mail, eliminated the merchant and the middleman; the company had no store and no salesmen, thus imposed no retailer's mark-up. The catalogue business was further advanced by the establishment in 1896 of the United States Post Office's rural free delivery; the 500-page catalogue reached the farmer in his own mailbox.

In 1907, the company constructed a nine-story, 2.2 million-square-foot catalogue building along the north branch of the CHICAGO RIVER—at the time the world's largest reinforced-concrete building; although Montgomery Ward personally fought to keep the lakefront free of commercial enterprises, his concern for open land never extended to the riverfront. The building housed 24 railroad cars, loading and unloading mail-order products; staff members traversed the long halls on roller skates. Yet competition from SEARS, ROEBUCK AND COMPANY, led by Julius ROSENWALD, steadily increased, and after the turn of the last century, the upstart firm surpassed the pioneer in the mail-order business. In 1999, the Montgomery Ward company filed for bankruptcy; the riverside catalogue building later became a massive condominium development.

Robert HERRICK, in his 1905 novel, *THE MEMOIRS OF AN AMERICAN CITIZEN,* speaks of a failing general store in a small Indiana town; the mail-

order business has cut into its trade. Edna FERBER's 1917 novel, *FANNY HERSELF,* raises the same issue, in that catalogue firms are said to "eat a small-town merchant every morning for breakfast." The heroine of that novel goes to Chicago to work for a firm that resembles Montgomery Ward—to the point that she is credited with instigating the staff's use of roller skates; the company reaches out, she notes, to "the remotest dugout in the Yukon, the most isolated cabin in the Rockies, the loneliest ranch-house in Wyoming."

Moody, Dwight L.
(1837–1899) *evangelist*

Born in Massachusetts, Moody moved to Chicago in 1856 and, after working as a shoe salesman, dedicated his life to religious teaching in 1860. He served as president of the Chicago Young Men's Christian Association from 1866 to 1869, then undertook a series of extended revivalist tours in the early 1870s, including overseas destinations in England and Scotland. In 1889, for the purpose of training evangelists, he founded the Chicago Bible Institute, later the Moody Bible Institute. During the WORLD'S COLUMBIAN EXPOSITION of 1893, Moody set up tents outside the fair, inveighing against its evils, as well as the city's general licentiousness. In Frank NORRIS's novel *THE PIT,* businessman Curtis JADWIN is shown as being persuaded by Moody to sponsor Sunday schools for the poor—as Norris's own father had been persuaded, under Moody's influence, to take up Sunday school teaching. In Nelson ALGREN's latter-day screed, *Chicago: City on the Make,* the author titles a chapter "Are you a Christian?"—referring to Moody's walking about the streets of Chicago, asking that question of strangers.

Moody, Harriet Brainerd
(1857–1932) *patron of poets*

Having started a catering business at MARSHALL FIELD AND COMPANY, which expanded to include service on Pullman cars and elsewhere, Harriet Brainerd was a successful businesswoman when she

This engraving, dating from 1899, advertises the efficient activity taking place in the Montgomery Ward building on Michigan Avenue. *(Chicago Historical Society)*

met poet William Vaughn MOODY in 1899; they married a decade later, when he was already fatally ill. After her husband's death, she turned their house into a literary salon, accommodating visiting writers and poets, ranging from Robert FROST to Rabindranath TAGORE; acting as a financial backer of *POETRY* and other projects, she was known for her limitless generosity. She also traveled twice to Hollywood, first in 1920 to consult on the filming of her husband's play *The Faith Healer,* then in 1924 to consult on *THE GREAT DIVIDE.*

Moody, William Vaughn
(1869–1910) *poet, dramatist*

Born in Spencer, Indiana, educated at Harvard University, Moody was recruited in 1895 to teach at the UNIVERSITY OF CHICAGO. Already a respected poet in literary circles, he received broader public attention for his poem "ODE IN TIME OF HESITATION," published in the *Atlantic Monthly* in 1900, attacking President William MCKINLEY's foreign policy and U.S. territorial annexation after the SPANISH-AMERICAN WAR. The ANTI-IMPERIALIST LEAGUE collected the work in its volume, *Liberty Poems Inspired by the Crisis of 1898–1900.* Another political poem, "ON A SOLDIER FALLEN IN THE PHILIPPINES," published in the *Atlantic* in 1901, was a likely influence on Edgar Lee MASTERS's "Harry Wilmans," appearing 14 years later in *SPOON RIVER ANTHOLOGY.*

In 1906, turning from verse drama to prose drama, Moody achieved popular success with a play, THE GREAT DIVIDE, set in the American Southwest. Featuring an uncultivated miner who wins an eastern woman by physical force, the drama celebrates masculine strength, advocating a character's rising above social conventions. Although it would be called melodrama today, the play was considered a step toward promoting REALISM on the American stage; after its initial success in Chicago, it ran in New York for two years. Later, it became a hit on the London stage. His next play, *The Faith Healer*—at one time scheduled to star Tyrone Power Sr., father of the later-to-be movie idol—opened in 1909; in that drama, a faith-healer fulfills his spiritual vision through the earthly love of a "wicked" woman.

In 1909, Moody married Harriet Brainerd, owner of a successful catering business. He was already ill at the time, suffering from a brain tumor; he died the next year at age 41. In 1912, Harriet MONROE, seeking to fill out the first issue of POETRY magazine, turned to Moody's widow, who provided the feminist poem, "I Am the Woman."

Although he gained notice as an antiwar poet and then, several years later, gained popularity as a dramatist, Moody is generally, if perhaps unjustly, forgotten today. His plays were adapted several times into silent movies—*The Faith Healer* of 1920 included Adolphe Menjou in the cast—but faded quickly from public awareness; the arrival of Eugene O'NEILL a decade later resulted in the neglect of Moody and other earlier American dramatists.

Further Reading
Brown, Maurice F. *Estranging Dawn: The Life and Works of William Vaughn Moody.* Carbondale: Southern Illinois University Press, 1973.

Moon-Calf
Floyd Dell
(1920)

The title of this autobiographical novel indicates a dreamy, moonstruck young man. Describing a childhood of increasing poverty in southwestern Illinois, recounting the family's move across the Mississippi River to Port Royal—DELL's name for Davenport, Iowa—the novel focuses on the protagonist's continuing self-education. As a teenager, Felix Fay works in factory jobs, at the same time frequenting the public library, joining socialist and FREE THOUGHT organizations; the young man eventually obtains work as a newspaper reporter. After a romantic breakup, after losing his job, Felix eyes a map on the wall of the railway station—and sees "the iron roads from all over the Middle West centering in a dark blotch in the corner." That dark blotch is Chicago, and he realizes he must go there. The final paragraph of the novel consists of two words: "Chicago! Chicago!"

The work achieved considerable success, although it was outsold by two popular books of the same year, Sinclair LEWIS's *Main Street* and Zona

GALE's *Miss Lulu Bett*. As those volumes were viewed as exposés of small-town America, *Moon-Calf* was seen in a similar light—although the work, Dell insisted later, was an exposé of nothing more than his own autobiographical character. Sherwood ANDERSON's *POOR WHITE*, another novel using a small-town setting, appeared also in that significant postwar year.

Moore, Marianne
(1887–1972) *poet*

One of the modernists emerging in the second decade of the 20th century, Moore first published in POETRY in May 1915. Born in Kirkwood, Missouri, moving with her family to Carlisle, Pennsylvania, she graduated from Bryn Mawr College in 1909. Objecting to what she considered Harriet MONROE's editorial intrusions, she turned instead to Alfred KREYMBORG's *OTHERS*, which published five of her poems in December 1915. Her most quoted piece, "Poetry," appearing in *Others* in 1919, begins, "I, too, dislike it"; the work goes on to assert that poetry is "imaginary gardens with real toads in them." Moving to New York City, working for the New York Public Library, Moore served as editor of *DIAL* from 1926 to 1919; her 1951 *Collected Poems* won the Pulitzer Prize for poetry.

Morgan, Anna
(1851–1936) *early figure in the little theater movement*

Born in Auburn, New York, Morgan came to Chicago in 1876 and became a monologist, or performer of one-person dramatic recitals. Dramatic monologues were a standard theater form of the day, ranging from Shakespeare recitations to oral interpretations of poetry. Turning to teaching, Morgan began to direct plays for her students; she produced the first American performances of Henrik Ibsen's *The Master Builder* in 1895, as well as George Bernard Shaw's *Candida* and *Caesar and Cleopatra* in 1899 and 1902. Her studio in the FINE ARTS BUILDING

became an attraction for visiting actors and critics. Relying on simple staging, maintaining her and performers' amateur status, Morgan provided an early example of the experimental, noncommercial theater that would lead to the LITTLE THEATER MOVEMENT, Maurice BROWNE's LITTLE THEATER, and the PROVINCETOWN PLAYERS.

Morris, William
(1834–1896) *English writer, craftsman, social reformer*

Reacting against industrialism and mass production, Morris was an instigator of the ARTS AND CRAFTS MOVEMENT, idealizing medieval guilds, lauding the concept of workmanship, and advocating the making of handcrafted objects—as opposed to products of the industrial production line. He espoused as well a communal SOCIALISM, in which the worker-artist, unexploited by CAPITALISM, pursues his unique craft. His Kelmscott Press, producing books to be seen as objects of art, emphasized fine paper, premodern type styles, and fine binding; its work influenced the Chicago firms of STONE AND KIMBALL and WAY AND WILLIAMS. Morris's utopian novel, the 1891 *News from Nowhere*, followed American Edward BELLAMY's 1888 *Looking Backward*—although Morris rejects the machines and industrial organization that Bellamy had accepted. His American disciple, Illinois-born Elbert HUBBARD, founded the Kelmscott-inspired Roycroft Press in New York in 1893, similarly emphasizing the virtues of workmanship.

Sandburg's early antiwar poem "Salvage," appearing in CHICAGO POEMS, addresses Morris, finding comfort that the earlier writer did not live to see the destruction of medieval buildings during WORLD WAR I.

Morton, Ferdinand "Jelly Roll"
(1890–1941) *jazz pianist and composer*

Born in Gulfport, Louisiana, Morton is regarded as one of the founders of JAZZ, as well as a popularizer of the form. Originally performing in the Storyville district of New Orleans, he first came to Chicago in 1905; other New Orleans figures, including Louis ARMSTRONG, began following after 1917, when Storyville was closed down by the United States Navy. Between 1923 and 1928, Morton made a series of classic recordings in Chicago, including the "Original Jelly Roll Blues" and "Doctor Jazz." Considered the first important musical arranger in jazz, he is seen as presenting a contrast to Armstrong's improvisatory style.

Most, Johann
(1846–1906) *anarchist leader*

Born in Germany, Most arrived in the United States in 1882, having served a prison sentence in England for an article applauding the assassination of Russian Czar Alexander II; the article was titled "At Last!" Visiting Chicago the following year, he advocated violent revolution and the use of that new weapon, DYNAMITE. His slogan was "propaganda by deed," as opposed to words. In 1883, he was among the founders of the INTERNATIONAL WORKING PEOPLE'S ASSOCIATION, an organization promoting a mix of anarchist and socialist goals. He died in Cincinnati at the age of 60.

"The Mother"   *See* WINESBURG, OHIO.

Motley, Willard
(1912–1965) *novelist*

Nephew of painter Archibald Motley, Willard Motley is a member of the first post–Chicago Renaissance generation; he achieved fame with his best-selling first novel, *Knock on Any Door,* published in 1947. An African American, Motley created as his protagonist an Italian American, a young criminal who is executed at the age of 21; the character's credo is the oft-quoted "Live fast,

die young, and leave a good-looking corpse." The 1958 sequel, *Let No Man Write My Epitaph,* tells the story of the criminal's illegitimate son; the setting of both works is the MAXWELL STREET area. Motley, who spent his last years in Mexico, has been called the progenitor of "the modern black queer novel." The movie *Knock on Any Door,* starring Humphrey Bogart and John Derek, appeared in 1949.

"Mrs. Ripley's Trip"   *See* MAIN-TRAVELLED ROADS.

muckraking

President Theodore ROOSEVELT initiated the modern use of *muckraking*—applying it to exposés of scandals and corruption—in a 1906 speech, evoking a character in the English Puritan John Bunyan's *The Pilgrim's Progress.* In that work of 1678, the Man with the Muckrake is the man who looks only downward, raking muck, or manure. Roosevelt's immediate target was David Graham Phillips, whose articles in *Cosmopolitan* magazine had exposed corruption in the United States Senate. Other muckraking magazines included McCLURE'S MAGAZINE and *The American Magazine;* among prominent muckrakers were Lincoln STEFFENS, Ida TARBELL, Upton SINCLAIR, and Ray Stannard BAKER. The classic muckraking novel is Upton Sinclair's THE JUNGLE, originally published in periodical form in THE APPEAL TO REASON. Muckraking journalism flourished in the first decade of the 20th century as part of the PROGRESSIVE movement, declining with the beginning of WORLD WAR I.

Muni, Paul
(1895–1967) *actor*

Born in Austria as Meshilem Weisenfreund, Muni came with his family to Chicago in 1902. The son of a Yiddish theater owner, he performed regularly in his father's theater, as well as at HULL-HOUSE. Joining a Yiddish theater group in New York, later appearing on the Broadway stage, he became a movie star in the title role of *Scarface,* the 1932 gangster film evoking the career of Al CAPONE; the script was written by ex-Chicagoan Ben HECHT. Other films included *The Story of Louis Pasteur,* for which he won an Academy Award, *The Good Earth,* in which he played a Chinese peasant, and *The Life of Emile Zola.* Returning to the New York stage in 1955, Muni won a Tony Award for playing the Clarence DARROW character in *Inherit the Wind,* a drama based on the Scopes trial.

"Murmurings in a Field Hospital"   *See* CHICAGO POEMS.

Museum of Science and Industry

A technology-oriented museum located on the South Side near the UNIVERSITY OF CHICAGO, the Museum of Science and Industry is the one major Chicago museum not located near the downtown area. Originally the Palace of Fine Arts at the 1893 WORLD'S COLUMBIAN EXPOSITION, the building subsequently housed the collection that went to the FIELD MUSEUM OF NATURAL HISTORY. A 1933 gift from Julius ROSENWALD funded reconstruction of the building, maintaining its original classical style, turning it into a showcase for scientific and technological achievement. The first exhibit was a replica of a southern Illinois coal mine, including a cage to lower visitors to the bottom of a mineshaft, 50 feet down; it remains one of the museum's most popular exhibits.

N

"Nancy Knapp"   *See SPOON RIVER ANTHOLOGY.*

National American Woman Suffrage Association

This organization, dedicated to giving women the vote, was founded in 1890. Combining two previous suffrage groups, the NAWSA was led in its first decade by long-time feminist Elizabeth Cady Stanton; Jane ADDAMS later served as vice president. Alice HENRY, arriving in the United States in 1906, met Addams at an NAWSA convention in Baltimore and was invited to HULL-HOUSE; she stayed in Chicago for the next 20 years. With the enactment of the NINETEENTH AMENDMENT in 1920, NAWSA leaders initiated the League of Women Voters.

National Women's Trade Union League

This labor organization, originally known as the Woman's Trade Union League, formed in 1903 at the AMERICAN FEDERATION OF LABOR convention in Boston. The National Women's Trade Union League sought to encourage women to form unions or to join existing locals; Jane ADDAMS served as the first vice president. The league arose at a time when women had little awareness of unionization—and when union meetings might be held in saloons, thus effectively barring women. The Chicago branch, founded in 1904, employed Australian feminists Alice HENRY and Miles FRANKLIN, who also edited its periodical, *Life and Labor.* Franklin—later to resume her career as the celebrated Australian novelist—served as secretary, then secretary-treasurer, of the national organization. To the reported disgruntlement of Samuel GOMPERS, head of the AFL, the league is said to have been as important to women's suffrage as to labor causes; the right to vote was often uppermost in the minds of the middle-class women who were its leaders.

naturalism

A late 19th-century literary mode, demonstrated in works of both fiction and drama, naturalism has been called the next step beyond REALISM; it goes beyond realism's chronicling of the details of everyday life. According to the naturalist's view, realism adheres to middle-class standards of gentility, overlooking the harsh, brutal elements that are part of human life as well. Naturalism historically has focused on the lower classes, on sex, drunkenness, and vice; it presents human specimens as defeated by forces they cannot resist—overwhelming compulsions, social and economic laws, the implacable laws of heredity. The naturalist writer adopts the stance of the detached observer, watching as his characters go through the inevitable steps that bring them to their destiny. The principal exponent of this view was the 19th-century French writer Émile ZOLA, whose novel *L'Assomoir,* or *The Drunkard,* has been considered the prime model for naturalism.

English philosopher Herbert SPENCER, drawing on the work of naturalist Charles Darwin, espoused a cosmic determinism as well, denying man's control over his fate; Spencer, although not a literary figure, was read by American followers who were immersed also in the tenets of naturalism. Turn-of-the-last-century works by Theodore DREISER and Frank NORRIS exemplify these combined world views; Dreiser's 1900 novel SISTER CARRIE and Norris's 1903 novel THE PIT present protagonists who are swept along—and in the case of *The Pit*, crushed—by seemingly inexorable forces.

Newberry Library

Established by the will of businessman Walter Loomis Newberry, this independent research library, built in 1893, is noted for its collections in history, literature, anthropology, music, and Americana. The building was designed by Henry Ives COBB, architect of the gothic structures of the UNIVERSITY OF CHICAGO campus. In Hamlin GARLAND's novel of 1895, ROSE OF DUTCHER'S COOLLY, the Wisconsin farm girl, newly arrived in the city, finds herself frequenting the library's "beautiful reading-room."

New France

By the mid-17th century, French adventurers, traders, and missionaries had traversed land that included eastern Canada, the Great Lakes, and the Mississippi Valley. The Company of New France, established by Cardinal Richelieu in 1627, pioneered in fur trading and settlement; in 1663, its territory became a colony administered by the French government. Among explorers were Louis JOLIET and Jesuit Father Jacques MAR-QUETTE, who first came to the site of Chicago and the CHICAGO RIVER in 1673. Robert Cavelier de LA SALLE, arriving at the site late in 1681, claimed the entire Mississippi Valley for France the following year, naming it Louisiana after King Louis XIV. New France, never gathering the numbers of settlers that came to the English colonies, lost to Great Britain in the French and Indian War; the decisive battle took place at the Plains of Abraham outside of Quebec in 1759—in which both the English and French generals, James Wolfe and the Marquis de Montcalm, were mortally wounded; France surrendered to Britain the following year. Concluding what was known in Europe as the Seven Years War, the Treaty of Paris of 1763 placed all land east of the Mississippi River under English rule. New England historian Francis Parkman, writing in the last half of the 19th century, produced a series of volumes on the French in North America; Illinois novelist Mary Hartwell CATHERWOOD, following Parkman's lead, wrote historical novels using the New France setting.

The New Spoon River
Edgar Lee Masters
(1924)

Attempting to recapture the success of his 1915 SPOON RIVER ANTHOLOGY, Edgar Lee MASTERS produced a new series of poems, containing 318 new epitaphs; the magazine *Vanity Fair* began serial publication in 1923. Receiving little acclaim, the volume sold poorly; Masters's moment in literary history had passed. The poems were judged simpler, demonstrating less subtlety than those of the original volume, and the public was looking elsewhere—for a new direction, even for the rigors of MODERNISM.

The New Star Chamber and Other Essays
Edgar Lee Masters
(1904)

The original Star Chamber was a meeting place of councilors to English kings in the 15th and 16th centuries—so called because of stars painted on the ceiling—in which proceedings were said to defy the law. The term came to suggest unjust legal actions. The prose collection, written when Edgar Lee MASTERS was a law partner of Clarence DARROW, presents essays opposing the SPANISH-AMERICAN WAR, President Theodore ROOSEVELT, and American expansionism.

A New Testament
Sherwood Anderson
(1927)

A collection of prose poems by Sherwood ANDER-SON, begun in 1919, appearing partially in LITTLE REVIEW, these "testaments," or poetic aphorisms, were gathered and published after Anderson became a newspaper editor in rural Virginia; the author called them experiments in thought and emotion. By the time the volume appeared, reviewers were considering Anderson a writer in decline; *The New Republic* wrote that "the author of 'Winesburg, Ohio,' is dying before our eyes."

New York Society for the Suppression of Vice

This censorship organization, founded in 1873 by Anthony COMSTOCK, was taken over after Comstock's death in 1915 by John S. Sumner. Among Sumner's acts were the banning of Theodore DREISER's THE "GENIUS" and the suppression of LITTLE REVIEW's publication of James JOYCE's *Ulysses.* Floyd DELL's 1923 novel *Janet March* was another target, as well as Maxwell BODENHEIM's 1925 *Replenishing Jessica* and Upton SINCLAIR's 1927 *Oil!*; the latter was banned for its references to birth control. Margaret Sanger, pioneer in the birth-control movement, had long been one of Sumner's targets.

nickelodeon

These early motion-picture showplaces, created in the early years of the 20th century, were located mainly in storefronts in working-class city neighborhoods. Nickelodeons proliferated initially in Chicago and the Midwest. The name *nickelodeon* indicated the price for a show, usually five cents; *odeon* is the Greek word for indoor theater. Depending on the number of reels offered, a show lasted from 10 minutes to an hour, accompanied by piano, organ, or accordion; lantern slides were sometimes alternated with moving pictures. Crucial to the nickelodeon owner was a continuing supply of films, resulting in the next step, the production of motion pictures. Two Chicago nickelodeon owners, Adolph ZUKOR and Carl LAEMMLE, went on to found distribution and production companies; Zukor became president of Paramount Pictures, Laemmle of Universal Pictures. The era of the nickelodeon was over by 1915, as producers began making longer films, as motion picture venues became larger and more palatial.

Nietzsche, Friedrich
(1844–1900) *German philosopher*

Nietzsche's influence was strongest on American writers in the early years of the 20th century—including Jack LONDON, Sherwood ANDERSON, and Willa CATHER—before the nation became involved in military conflict with Germany. Born in Prussia, the son of a Lutheran clergyman, professor of classical philology at the University of Basel, Nietzsche was declared insane and institutionalized in 1889; he died years later. After his death, his writings became influential in many contexts, and yet he is often seen as a photo-fascist, the result of his appropriation by the National Socialist, or Nazi, Party in Germany before and during World War II. Long dead before the rise of Nazism, Nietzsche became associated, falsely, with anti-Semitism and doctrines of racial superiority.

A contributing factor was his own terminology, which proved particularly subject to adaptation; concepts such as the "superman" and the "will to power"—targeting Christian morality and middle-class convention—were readily misinterpreted. Assuming a confrontational stance, asserting that religion imposed shackles on the strong, Nietzsche called for the naturally strong hero to reject the "slave" virtues of humility and altruism, to opt instead for a life-affirming pride and power.

Among American writers influenced by Nietzsche was the novelist Jack London, a writer who was seen as influencing, in turn, Sherwood Anderson's 1917 novel MARCHING MEN. London's polemic of a decade earlier, THE IRON HEEL, describes the leader of a future socialist revolution as a superman, "a blond beast such as Nietzsche has described";

Anderson's counterpart leader—although less specifically Nietzschean and less specifically ideological—appears similarly conceived. Although London links his superman to left-wing politics, he has been accused of right-wing notions as well.

In his 1905 MEMOIRS OF AN AMERICAN CITIZEN, Robert HERRICK presents a protagonist who, while reading works of SOCIAL DARWINISM, blends the doctrines of Herbert SPENCER with those of Nietzsche; after the sentencing of the HAYMARKET AFFAIR anarchists, Herrick's narrator declares that the world is made for the strong, "and I am one of them." William Vaughn MOODY's play of 1906, THE GREAT DIVIDE, presents another reflection of the Nietzschean hero, triumphing over convention by his superior strength of will. Theodore DREISER's Frank COWPERWOOD, appearing in THE FINANCIER and THE TITAN, published in 1912 and 1914, exemplifies similar traits; he is depicted as a superior man brought down by the pettiness of others, by the lack of vision of those inferior to him. In Willa Cather's novel of 1915, THE SONG OF THE LARK, the gender of the superior character is switched, making her into a woman; singer Thea KRONBORG triumphs in the works of Richard WAGNER, the composer whom Nietzsche, and later the Nazis, most favored. Cather received criticism for her seemingly pro-German work published during WORLD WAR I. The term neo-Nietzschean has been applied to the Russian-American writer Ayn Rand, whose 1943 novel, The Fountainhead, is said to be based in part on the career of architect Frank Lloyd WRIGHT.

Nineteenth Amendment

The constitutional amendment granting women's suffrage, or the right to vote, was passed by Congress in 1919, and a campaign followed for the necessary two-thirds state ratification. President Woodrow WILSON supported the measure. Political radicals and long-standing union leaders, deeming economic issues more crucial than gender issues, were not consistently enthusiastic; some felt, too, that women might vote for conservative candidates. The Nineteenth Amendment, although it became law in 1920, was not enforced

in regard to African-American women in the South. Republican Warren G. HARDING became the first president elected with the help of women's votes.

"Nobody Knows" See WINESBURG, OHIO.

Norris, Frank
(1870–1902) *novelist*

Previously known for his western locales, Norris set THE PIT, his final work, in Chicago, the city of his birth. Living in Chicago until the age of 14, growing up in financial privilege—the mansion described in *The Pit* is said to be a recreation of his early home—Norris moved with his family to Oakland, California, in 1884. Studying art in Paris, he returned to attend the University of California, embracing there the theories of literary NATURALISM as espoused by the French novelist Émile ZOLA. In 1896, Norris traveled to South Africa to write dispatches for the *San Francisco Chronicle*; in 1898, he served as a war correspondent in Cuba for MCCLURE'S MAGAZINE during the SPANISH-AMERICAN WAR.

In 1899, Norris produced his first major novel, *McTeague*, a tale of sex and murder, often considered America's first naturalistic novel; the final scene leaves the protagonist stranded in California's Death Valley, handcuffed to a corpse, viewing the vast desert about him. Reviewers found the work unpleasant and brutal; William Dean HOWELLS, although deeming it "a remarkable book," found it overly dwelling upon the "squalid and cruel and vile and hateful."

Norris's next work, *The Octopus*, appearing in 1901, was the first of a projected trilogy, "The Epic of Wheat." The author planned three volumes to tell of the production, distribution, and consumption of grain, a basic human food staple. The first volume, set in California, describes the growing of wheat and the harm done to ranchers by the railroads; the latter are the "octopus," a term applied at the time to business monopolies. Although often interpreted as a social polemic, the novel is also a depiction of deterministic forces, of an indifferent world that crushes those who try to assert themselves against it; the railroad is one such unstoppable force. The second volume, *The Pit,* focusing on speculation and manipulation on the CHICAGO BOARD OF TRADE, depicts once more the forces that destroy men, over which they have no control; the projected third volume, *The Wolf,* dealing with famine in Europe, remained unwritten. Norris died suddenly of peritonitis at the age of 32. In 1906, his letters and papers were destroyed in the San Francisco fire, an event that has subsequently handicapped biographers.

Contemporary readers often find Norris's overwhelming forces—railroads, grain, the grain market—somewhat less than overwhelming today; the exigencies of life have altered during the last century. Critics have also redefined Norris's naturalism, branding it instead as a type of romanticism; the naturalism of *The Octopus* and *The Pit* exaggerates "realism," they claim, to the point that it loses its basis in the recognizable, the ordinary. In Norris's rendering, the railroad of *The Octopus* becomes "the soulless force, the ironhearted power"; the BOARD OF TRADE BUILDING of *The Pit* becomes "black, grave, monolithic, crouching on its foundations." The author, forgoing the everyday for the grandiose, reaching for heightened effects, is said to be rendering his destructive forces as mythic, beyond recognizable reality, thus partaking of a once-rejected romanticism.

Further Reading

Graham, Don, ed. *Critical Essays on Frank Norris.* Boston: G. K. Hall, 1980.

———. *Frank Norris Revisited.* New York: Twayne Publishers, 1992.

Hochman, Barbara. *The Art of Frank Norris, Storyteller.* Columbia: University of Missouri Press, 1988.

McElrath, Joseph R., Jr., and Katherine Knight. *Frank Norris: The Critical Reception.* New York: Burt Franklin, 1981.

Northwestern University

A university in suburban EVANSTON, Illinois, founded by Methodists, opening in 1855, Northwestern was long noted for its charter banning "spirituous, vinous, or fermented liquors" within a four-mile radius of campus. Near the campus later stood the home of Frances E. WILLARD, head of the WOMEN'S CHRISTIAN TEMPERANCE UNION. Henry B. FULLER's novel of 1919, BERTRAM COPE'S YEAR, and Willa CATHER's novel of 1925, THE PROFESSOR'S HOUSE, feature instructors at an unnamed university, set in a renamed Evanston. Cather, undoubtedly thinking of her own University of Nebraska, makes the school a state-supported institution, while yet adding a gibe about "the Methodists."

Northwest Territory

First explored in the 17th century as part of NEW FRANCE, this region, south and west of the Great Lakes, included Ohio, Indiana, Illinois, Michigan, Wisconsin, and part of Minnesota. The area was valued for its furs. In 1763, Great Britain obtained the territory from France, and 20 years later, at the end of the Revolutionary War, it became part of the United States—although not irrevocably so until after the British defeat in the WAR OF 1812. The loss by the British in that war forced Native Americans, their sometime allies, to sign treaties and make way for U.S. expansion.

Not Without Laughter
Langston Hughes
(1930)

At the end of this novel by Langston HUGHES, the protagonist, having grown up poor in a Kansas town—his family presided over by a pious, hardworking grandmother—joins his mother in Chicago, where she is waiting to hear news of her husband who is fighting overseas in WORLD WAR I. Having been warned that Chicago is a "wicked city," the young man finds himself accosted in turn by a gay man, a girl who wants him to buy her a theater ticket, and a prostitute; the el train rumbling by his apartment keeps him from sleeping at night. Determined to further his education, he takes a job as an elevator operator in a LOOP hotel.

O

Oak Park

A suburb immediately west of Chicago with an upper-middle-class demographic, Oak Park is known as the birthplace of writer Ernest HEMINGWAY and the home of architect Frank Lloyd WRIGHT. The city is also the seat of many of Wright's early buildings, exemplifying the PRAIRIE SCHOOL OF ARCHITECTURE. Hemingway's mother and Wright's wife were both at one time members of the Nineteenth Century Women's Club; Hemingway would later describe the suburb as a place of "broad lawns and narrow minds."

"Ode in a Time of Hesitation"
William Vaughn Moody
(1900)

Referring to the continuing conflict in the Philippines after the SPANISH-AMERICAN WAR, the poem, appearing in the *Atlantic Monthly*, brought MOODY to national attention. The poet initially evokes a CIVIL WAR monument, commemorating those who died saving their country from shame; yet currently, he declares, the nation is fighting an "ignoble battle." He asks for some "elder singer," such as Walt WHITMAN, to arise and give voice to mourning, to lament that the nation is now casting away its spiritual righteousness. The poem was reprinted in *Liberty Poems Inspired by the Crisis of 1898–1900*, published by the ANTI-IMPERIALIST LEAGUE.

Ogden, George

This principal character in Henry B. FULLER's novel *THE CLIFF-DWELLERS*, Ogden, an ambitious young man comes to Chicago from the East; he achieves a measure of success, although it is viewed against the pervasive greed of the burgeoning city about him. He marries a woman whose personal extravagance brings him to the edge of financial disaster; feeling desperation, he tries to enrich himself illegally—and loses everything as a result. When his wife dies, he marries his former employer's daughter, now impoverished herself, and they are content to live an ordinary, obscure existence.

O. Henry   *See* PORTER, WILLIAM SYDNEY.

"An Ohio Pagan"   *See* HORSES AND MEN.

"Old Timers"   *See* CORNHUSKERS.

Oliver, Joe "King"
(1885–1938) *jazz musician, cornetist*

Born in Abend, Louisiana, Oliver began playing in New Orleans's Storyville red-light district in 1904. After the United States Navy closed down Storyville, Oliver came north to Chicago in

1918, bringing the music called Dixieland; he formed his Creole JAZZ Band, playing at the ROYAL GARDENS nightclub and other venues. In 1922, he coaxed Louis ARMSTRONG from New Orleans; the next year, the two men began making a series of historically important acoustical recordings, using studios in Chicago and Richmond, Indiana. Oliver is reputed to have banned alcohol on stage during performances, restricting his musicians to ladling from a bucket of sugar water. When Armstrong left for New York in 1924, the ensemble dissolved; Oliver began a new band, the Dixie Syncopators, playing between 1925 and 1927, but his career never fully revived. He died in obscurity in Savannah, Georgia.

Olmsted, Frederick Law
(1822–1903) *landscape architect*

Born in Connecticut, achieving initial recognition as a travel writer, Olmsted designed and supervised the creation of Central Park in New York City. In 1869, he and William Le Baron JENNEY developed the Chicago suburb of Riverside, west of the city on the DES PLAINES RIVER. Called the nation's first planned "railroad suburb," Riverside was designated as a place for the middle class to escape urban ills. In the same year Olmsted, along with his partner Calvert Vaux, initiated designs for a park system in Chicago, including JACKSON PARK, Washington Park, and the MIDWAY PLAISANCE. For the 1893 WORLD'S COLUMBIAN EXPOSITION, Olmsted supervised landscaping for the still undeveloped Jackson Park, dredging marshland, deepening the lagoon, and creating bridges, terraces, and walkways.

"On a Soldier Fallen in the Philippines"
William Vaughn Moody
(1901)

Appearing in the *Atlantic Monthly*, following up on his earlier "ODE IN A TIME OF HESITATION," the piece reflects MOODY's continuing opposition to the nation's Philippines venture after the SPANISH-AMERICAN WAR. The poet asks that the fallen soldier never know that the blood he shed was his country's blood—that what he did, that "what we bade him do," was wrong. Edgar Lee MASTERS's later poem, "Harry Wilmans," appearing in the 1915 *SPOON RIVER ANTHOLOGY*, also depicts a soldier fallen in the Philippines—although this man has learned the truth, realizing that his death was a waste.

O'Neill, Eugene
(1888–1953) *major playwright*

O'Neill came to prominence through presentations by the PROVINCETOWN PLAYERS, the theatrical group founded in 1915 by George Cram COOK and Susan GLASPELL. Born in New York City, the son of popular actor James O'Neill, he briefly attended Princeton University before setting off as a merchant seaman to South America and South Africa; he began writing plays when confined to a tuberculosis sanatorium in 1912. After his early one-act pieces, including *Bound East for Cardiff* and *The Moon of the Caribbees*, were performed by the Provincetown Players, he turned to professional theater productions with his full-length dramas of 1920, *Beyond the Horizon* and *The Emperor Jones*; the star of the latter drama, Charles S. Gilpin, had previously been a member of the Chicago PEKIN THEATER players. Other plays of the early 1920s were *Anna Christie*, *The Hairy Ape*, and *Desire Under the Elms*. O'Neill subsequently became influenced by the stream-of-consciousness narrative technique of MODERNISM—as practiced by James JOYCE, as emulated by Sherwood ANDERSON in the 1925 *DARK LAUGHTER*—and his 1928 play, *Strange Interlude*, using spoken asides, attempted to transform a prose fiction technique into a dramatic technique. His 1946 *The Iceman Cometh* and his autobiographical *Long Day's Journey into Night*, produced posthumously in 1957, confirmed his status as one of the important dramatists of the 20th century. His daughter, Oona, married actor Charlie CHAPLIN in 1943.

1001 Afternoons in Chicago
Ben Hecht
(1922)

HECHT's daily sketches and anecdotes, running for nearly two years under the "1001 Afternoons in Chicago" heading in the CHICAGO DAILY NEWS, became one of the paper's most popular features. The column ended when Hecht was fired from the paper, the result of obscenity charges leveled against his novel, FANTAZIUS MALLARE—a work that had been published three months earlier by the same Chicago firm, COVICI-McGEE, that published *1001 Afternoons*. In his memoirs Sherwood ANDERSON writes that he was "a little sore" at Hecht for telling in his column—under the title "Don Quixote and His Last Windmill"—of a failed businessman who, after promising a party, commits suicide; Anderson had wished to tell the tale himself. The story was included in the book collection, then transformed into a successful 1940 movie, *Angels Over Broadway*, written by Hecht and starring Douglas Fairbanks Jr.

"On the Banks of the Wabash"
Paul Dresser
(1897)

Said to be written with the help of DRESSER's brother, Theodore DREISER, the song celebrates the brothers' native Indiana; first published in 1897, it became a sheet-music best-seller. The original full title, "On the Banks of the Wabash, Far Away," indicates the era's fondness for nostalgia; the final stanza, lamenting the death of a loved one, indicates the era's popular sentimentality. The Wabash River is located in western Indiana; the song was adopted as the Indiana state song in 1913.

Orchestra Hall

The home of the CHICAGO SYMPHONY ORCHESTRA, built in 1904 on South MICHIGAN AVENUE by Daniel H. BURNHAM, the structure replaced the AUDITORIUM BUILDING as the orchestra's concert hall. Conductor Theodore THOMAS had long wished for a venue more intimate than the 4,000-seat Auditorium theater; Orchestra Hall seated 2,500. On the top floor the building housed the CLIFF-DWELLERS' CLUB, the men-only artistic and literary society established by Hamlin GARLAND; the club maintained quarters there from 1909 until 1995. A massive renovation in 1997 turned Orchestra Hall into the renamed Symphony Center.

Oriental Theatre

This movie theater in the LOOP Randolph Street theater district opened in 1926 and replaced the demolished Colonial Theater. The Oriental stood on the site of the original IROQUOIS THEATER, notorious for the deadly fire that occurred in 1903. The Oriental Theatre, part of the BALABAN AND KATZ chain, designed by movie-palace architects Cornelius and George Rapp, took its name from the then-fashionable Far East décor. Offering both films and live performance—the Three Stooges were among those who played onstage in the 1920s—the theater maintained its popularity until after World War II, finally closing in 1981. It was restored and reopened as a stage venue in 1998, renamed the Ford Center for the Performing Arts.

Ormsby, Margaret

A character in Sherwood ANDERSON's novel MARCHING MEN, the daughter of an industrialist, Margaret is first seen as a SETTLEMENT HOUSE worker. Yet she is never shown as an advocate of social causes; Anderson's purpose is to make her the upper-class admirer of the masculine, working-class leader, Beaut MCGREGOR. When McGregor asks her to marry him, while telling her also of his long friendship with Edith CARSON, Margaret insists on talking to Edith; she realizes Edith's superior claim and relinquishes McGregor, although continuing to be obsessed by him. Her father, trying to win her over from McGregor, trying to make her renounce him—in scenes that a modern reader finds incestuous in tone—convinces her that McGregor's ideas are ephemeral, that his movement will not last. Yet she finds herself doubting her father's precepts and continues to think longingly of the leader of men.

Orpheum Circuit

A VAUDEVILLE theater chain that started on the West Coast in 1887, the organization eventually established theaters in every major city in the country. Its East Coast rival was the Keith-Albee circuit, which ultimately absorbed the Orpheum theaters; the black vaudeville circuit was the Theater Owners Booking Agency, or TOBA. Chicago's MAJESTIC THEATER, built in 1906, was part of the Orpheum chain, as was the flagship PALACE THEATER, also in the LOOP, opening in 1926. As motion pictures became popular as sound was introduced to film, live vaudeville acts gave way—first partially, then completely—to the movies. The combined Radio-Keith-Orpheum circuit became the RKO movie studio.

Others

Founded by Alfred KREYMBORG at an artists' community in Ridgefield, New Jersey, this literary magazine began publication in July 1915. Attempting to compete with Harriet MONROE's Chicago-based *POETRY*, the periodical presented works by Amy LOWELL, William Carlos WILLIAMS, Wallace STEVENS; Stevens's "Peter Quince at the Clavier" had previously been rejected by *Poetry*. Ezra POUND, another figure feeling disaffected from Monroe—angered by her delayed publication of T. S. ELIOT's "The Love Song of J. Alfred Prufrock"—sent Eliot's "Portrait of a Lady" to Kreymborg; the piece appeared in September 1915. A June 1917 "Chicago number" included work by Carl SANDBURG, and a later Chicago-edited issue, appearing in December 1917, presented Stevens's "Thirteen Ways of Looking at a Blackbird." The last issue was published in July 1919. Three volumes of *Others* anthologies appeared in 1916, 1917, and 1920.

"The Other Woman"   *See THE TRIUMPH OF THE EGG.*

Ottenburg, Fred

A character in Willa CATHER's novel *THE SONG OF THE LARK*, Fred is the man whom Thea KRONBORG eventually marries, although readers do not learn that fact until the Epilogue; throughout the course of the novel, he is presented as already married. At the age of 20, Fred married the woman from whom he has since separated; as evidence of her indiscretions, she is revealed as suffering from general paresis, the dementia and paralysis that follow syphilitic infection. Fred, the son of a wealthy family, is an accomplished amateur musician, and he is also Thea's seeming soul mate. He helps the young woman awaken from her depression by sending her to his father's ranch in Arizona; there she lives among the cliff-dwellings of ancient peoples, finding renewed connections with life and a renewed determination in her art. Fred's devotion is similar to that of Dr. Howard ARCHIE, the other figure who recognizes Thea's superiority and who is unhappily married as well—although Archie always defers to the more sophisticated Fred, who has a greater understanding of the world into which Thea is moving.

Our Penal Machinery and Its Victims
John Peter Altgeld
(1884)

Written as ALTGELD was entering Chicago politics, this treatise criticizes the criminal justice system as favoring the rich and victimizing the poor; it urges society to eliminate the causes of crime, rather than focus on punishing the criminal. Altgeld calls also for a humane treatment of convicts, arguing that cruel treatment does not bring about reformation; he is critical of brutal police tactics. The book has been called the beginning of prison reform. Clarence DARROW, reading the volume in Ashtabula, Ohio, is said to have been inspired to come to Chicago.

Outland, Tom

This character appears in Willa CATHER's novel *THE PROFESSOR'S HOUSE*. A scientist and inventor,

Tom is engaged to the professor's daughter. When Tom is killed in WORLD WAR I, the daughter then marries Louie MARSELLUS, who patents the aeronautical invention that Outland had bequeathed to her. The invention enables Marsellus and his wife to live in wealth. Tom's earlier days, spent in New Mexico, are told in the novel's story-within-a-story; the first-person account tells of Tom's discovering a hidden city of abandoned cliff dwellings on a New Mexico mesa. The tale serves as a background for the malaise that the professor, Godfrey ST. PETER, is currently experiencing; his friendship with Tom, his traveling with Tom to the Blue Mesa, had brought moments of joy to St. Peter's life. Cather first traveled to the Southwest in 1912, although she drew portions of Outland's story from Gustaf Nordenskiold's 1893 volume, *The Cliff-Dwellers of the Mesa Verde*—the likely source for the title of Henry B. FULLER's novel, THE CLIFF-DWELLERS.

"Out of Nowhere into Nothing" See THE TRIUMPH OF THE EGG.

Owen, Chandler
(1889–1967) *journalist*

Born in Warrenton, North Carolina, Owen graduated from Virginia Union University in 1913 and came to New York City soon afterward, cofounding with A. Philip RANDOLPH the socialist magazine *Messenger* in 1917. In 1923, he moved to Chicago, becoming editor of the African-American newspaper the *Chicago Bee*; he continued aiding Randolph's efforts to unionize service employees of the PULLMAN PALACE CAR COMPANY. During WORLD WAR I, taking a stance opposite to that of the *Messenger*, he supported African-American participation in the war effort. He became increasingly involved in Republican Party politics, serving as speechwriter for Republican presidential candidates Wendell Wilkie, Thomas E. Dewey, and Dwight Eisenhower, as well as for Illinois senator Everett Dirkson.

P

Packingtown

This name was given to the UNION STOCK YARDS district. The area where the workers lived was called also the Back of the Yards, a place noted for its deplorable housing and permanent stench. Defenders of the town of PULLMAN, the planned company town criticized for its paternalism and social control, pointed to the Back of the Yards as the dismal alternative for workers' housing. Upton SINCLAIR's 1906 novel, THE JUNGLE, noting that the area housed a quarter of a million inhabitants, brought Packingtown's substandard sanitary and living conditions to national attention. During the RACE RIOTS of 1919, many of the white rioters came from Packingtown.

Palace Theatre

The Chicago flagship of the ORPHEUM CIRCUIT, the major VAUDEVILLE chain, the Palace Theatre opened in the LOOP's Randolph Street theater district in 1926. Designed by the renowned team of theater architects, the Rapp brothers, the theater took its name from interior scenes of the French palaces of Fontainebleau and Versailles. In 1931, the showcase began presenting movies along with stage shows, then solely movies. After a 1999 renovation, the renamed Cadillac Palace Theatre became a venue once more for stage productions.

Palmer, Bertha Honoré

(1849–1918) *social leader, wife of Potter Palmer*

Born in Louisville, Kentucky, the daughter of a hardware merchant, Bertha Honoré moved with her family to Chicago in 1855. At the age of 21, in 1870, she married the 44-year-old bachelor Potter PALMER, already wealthy from his dry-goods store, recently embarked on a new career in real estate development. While maintaining a luxurious lifestyle, Bertha Palmer also engaged in social causes, including championing the rights of working women. As chairman of the Board of Lady Managers for the WORLD'S COLUMBIAN EXPOSITION, she was instrumental in the planning and development of the fair's Women's Building. A major portion of her extensive art collection, including work of the French Impressionists, was bequeathed to the ART INSTITUTE. In the final chapter of W. T. STEAD's 1894 IF CHRIST CAME TO CHICAGO!, presenting Chicago as a 20th-century utopia, Bertha Palmer has become the city's reform-minded mayor. In Henry B. FULLER's novel of the next year, WITH THE PROCESSION, the sympathetic character of Susan Lathrop BATES is modeled in part on Palmer.

The parapeted Potter Palmer mansion, built in 1882 as the largest private residence in Chicago, was demolished in 1950. *(Chicago Historical Society)*

Palmer, Potter

(1826–1902) *entrepreneur, husband of Bertha Honoré Palmer*

Born to Quaker parents in upstate New York, Palmer came to Chicago in 1852 at the age of 26. His first enterprise was a dry-goods store, selling fabric and clothing; his employees included Levi Z. LEITER and Marshall FIELD, who later bought out the establishment. Among his innovations in retail policy were allowing the return of goods, holding special sales, and delivering free of charge; he made a particular point of catering to women. His next venture was in real estate; purchasing land along State Street, persuading the city council to widen the narrow road, he created the city's new main commercial thoroughfare. In 1868, the store that would become MARSHALL FIELD AND COMPANY moved from Lake Street—the previous commercial thoroughfare, subject to odors as it neared a branch of the CHICAGO RIVER—to State Street, and in 1870, the elegant Palmer House Hotel was completed, serving as a wedding present to his new bride, Bertha Honoré PALMER.

In the GREAT FIRE of 1871, Palmer lost 95 buildings, including his hotel; he rebuilt the Palmer House in 1873, decreeing new standards for fireproofing. His 1882 mansion on Lake Shore Drive, complete with turreted towers, designed by Henry Ives COBB, stood at the time as the largest house in Chicago; it was demolished in 1950 to make way for high-rise construction.

The millionaire of Frank NORRIS's novel *THE PIT*, Curtis JADWIN, making his fortune in real estate, is modeled in part on Palmer.

Palmer raids

The term was applied to the arrests of alleged subversives after WORLD WAR I. In 1919–20, following the instructions of U.S. Attorney General A. Mitchell Palmer, federal agents raided socialist, communist, anarchist, and union offices, rounding up thousands of radical leaders and spokesmen. The arrests concentrated on the foreign-born; 250 aliens were subsequently deported, including Emma GOLDMAN and her one-time lover Alexander Berkman. The term *red scare* came into use; Palmer's article "The Case Against the 'Reds'" appeared in 1920 in the periodical *Forum,* making special mention of the Chicago-based Communist Party. In the same year, 20 members of the newly formed Communist Labor Party, including the son of Henry Demarest LLOYD, were tried and convicted in Chicago, despite a defense by Clarence DARROW. A follow-up on the Palmer raids was the Immigration Act of 1924, the nation's first broadly restrictive immigrant legislation, imposing quotas according to national origins.

Panama Canal

This waterway across the isthmus of Panama, built by the United States government in the decade 1904–14, connects the Atlantic and Pacific Oceans. After the canal was built, vessels no longer had to take the route around Cape Horn in South America. As early as the 1500s, the Spanish had conceived the idea of a canal; a French company began work on a waterway in 1881 but went bankrupt eight years later. After an insurrection in 1903 established Panama as independent of the country of Colombia—an insurrection encouraged by the U.S. government—the United States began construction under the leadership of Theodore ROOSEVELT. The protagonist in Robert HERRICK's 1905 novel, *THE MEMOIRS OF AN AMERICAN CITIZEN,* envisions, from his 1890s vantage point, a vast future business empire; one day, he predicts, a canal will be dug, giving him access to the ports of the world.

Panic of 1873

This financial depression was triggered by the fall of the Philadelphia banking house of JAY COOKE, the firm that had financed the CIVIL WAR. The resulting unemployment and poverty marked the most severe downturn up to that time in U.S. history. Agricultural prices began to decline during this period, leading to rural discontent; labor unrest led to the GREAT STRIKE of June 1877. In Theodore DREISER's novel *THE FINANCIER,* protagonist Frank COWPERWOOD profits from the Panic of 1873; recently released from prison, having little to lose, he sells "short" in the market, profiting from borrowed stock, and soon regains his fortune.

Panic of 1893

This financial depression began with a decline in railroad fortunes, followed by bank failures, the nationwide economic downtown led to a high rate of joblessness by the end of 1893. One result was COXEY'S ARMY, a group of unemployed men who trekked to Washington the following spring, asking the federal government to provide jobs; the PULLMAN STRIKE began soon afterward in Chicago. In the agricultural Midwest, economic discontent fueled the call for FREE SILVER, for abandoning the GOLD STANDARD and increasing the money supply, leading to the presidential candidacy of William Jennings BRYAN in 1896. Robert HERRICK's novel of 1900, the Chicago-based *THE WEB OF LIFE,* covers the period's economic woes from an urban vantage point.

Pantier, Benjamin; Mrs. Benjamin; Reuben
See SPOON RIVER ANTHOLOGY.

"Paper Pills"   *See* WINESBURG, OHIO.

Parcival, Doctor   *See under* WINESBURG, OHIO: "The Philosopher."

Parsons, Albert
(1848–1887) *anarchist executed after the Haymarket Affair*

Born in Montgomery, Alabama, serving in the Confederate Army during the CIVIL WAR, Parsons moved to Texas after the conflict; he and his African-American wife, Lucy PARSONS, came to Chicago in 1873. First a socialist activist, participating in the GREAT STRIKE OF 1877, Parsons turned to ANARCHISM, becoming an associate of August SPIES. He was the only native-born American involved in the HAYMARKET AFFAIR, remembered particularly as an effective and poetic orator. Frank HARRIS, in his novel THE BOMB, notes that Parsons was neither rebellious nor revolutionary by nature; he displayed "a gift of speech, but not of thought." After the bombing, Parsons fled Chicago, but returned to face trial along with his fellow anarchists; refusing to request leniency—a stance supported by his wife—he was hanged with Spies and two others.

Parsons, Louella
(1881–1972) *movie columnist*

Known for initiating the world's first movie column, Parsons began writing for the CHICAGO RECORD in 1914. Born in Freeport, Illinois, she grew up in Dixon, Illinois, then spent four years in Chicago working for the *Record* and the ESSANAY FILM MANUFACTURING COMPANY. Moving to New York, then California, she became a national columnist for the Hearst newspaper chain, establishing herself as one of the most powerful figures in Hollywood.

Parsons, Lucy
(1853–1942) *anarchist, activist, wife of Haymarket Affair martyr Albert Parsons*

Claiming Mexican and Indian parentage, Parsons is believed to have been born into slavery in Texas; she is also likely never to have officially married Albert PARSONS. The couple moved from Texas to Chicago in 1873, where Lucy Parsons opened a dress shop; becoming active in radical causes, she wrote for THE ALARM, the weekly paper edited by her husband, sponsored by the anarchist-influenced INTERNATIONAL WORKING PEOPLE'S ASSOCIATION. Her famous piece, "TO TRAMPS," advocating violence, was reprinted and distributed as a pamphlet; it was later used by the prosecution in the HAYMARKET AFFAIR trial, bolstering the case

Lucy Parsons, shown in a 1903 photograph, continued her life of social activism long after the 1887 execution of her husband. (*Chicago Historical Society*)

against the anarchists. Albert Parsons was hanged in 1887; Lucy Parsons made no move to seek clemency, believing that his martyrdom would further the cause of overthrowing CAPITALISM. She was seen as the more militant of the couple, as well as the more dogmatic; she claimed that the plight of African Americans came from their being poor, not from their race—consistent with radical doctrine of the time, viewing the world's problems in terms of social class and economics. In 1905, along with Eugene DEBS, Mary "Mother" JONES, and William "Big Bill" HAYWOOD, she was a founding member in Chicago of the INDUSTRIAL WORKERS OF THE WORLD. Continuing for nearly four more decades as a speaker and activist, Parsons died in a fire in her home at the age of 89; her ashes were buried at the Haymarket Martyrs' Monument in WALDHEIM CEMETERY.

Patterson, Joseph Medill
(1879–1946) *writer, editor*

Born in Chicago, grandson of the first CHICAGO TRIBUNE editor, Joseph Medill, Patterson as a young man espoused socialist views and directed the presidential campaign of socialist candidate Eugene V. DEBS in 1908. His novel, *A Little Brother of the Rich*, published the same year, presented a vigorous attack on the leisure class. When his father died in 1910, Patterson returned to serve as editor of the *Tribune*, sharing duties with his cousin Robert R. MCCORMICK; he introduced the comic strip *The Gumps* in 1917. In 1919, founding the tabloid New York newspaper, the *Daily News*—and introducing further comic strips, *Little Orphan Annie* and *Dick Tracy*—Patterson created a paper that soon boasted the largest circulation in the United States.

Patti, Adelina
(1843–1919) *coloratura soprano*

Enjoying an international operatic career, Patti was a particular favorite of Chicago audiences. Born in Madrid of Italian parents, moving to the

Soprano Adelina Patti sang her standard encore song, "Home Sweet Home," at the dedication of the Auditorium Building in 1889. *(Chicago Historical Society)*

United States at an early age, she toured the country as a child prodigy; she made her operatic debut in New York City in 1859. Thirty years later, after a long career, she was invited to sing at the dedication of the theater of the AUDITORIUM BUILDING in 1889; she pleased the audience with her signature "Home, Sweet Home." Given to making farewell tours, the first in 1887—two years before the Auditorium dedication—she continued making farewell tours as late as 1906. In Hamlin GARLAND's 1895 novel, *ROSE OF DUTCHER'S COOLLY*, Rose, newly arrived in Chicago, finds herself admiring "Patti and Edwin Booth"; no first name is necessary to identify the singer.

Pearson, Ray   *See under* WINESBURG, OHIO: "The Untold Lie."

Peet, Rev. Abner   *See* SPOON RIVER ANTHOLOGY.

Peggy from Paris
George Ade, William Lorraine
(1903)

Repeating the success of his previous year's musical comedy THE SULTAN OF SULU, George ADE—although working with a different composer—saw the work staged first in Chicago before it moved on to New York. The plot centers on a girl from a small Illinois town who goes to France to take singing lessons; six years later she comes to Chicago as the Parisian singer Mademoiselle Fleurette Caramelle. Her father, fresh off the farm and not knowing any better, exposes her identity on opening night. The musical continued to prove that the one-time popular journalist could write successfully for the popular theater.

Pekin Theater

This African-American musical and VAUDEVILLE theater, claimed as the first black-owned theater in the United States, opened in BRONZEVILLE in 1905. It is credited also with establishing the first African-American acting company, as well as providing the site of the first African-American film production company. The Pekin acting company included Charles S. Gilpin, subsequently renowned for playing the title role in Eugene O'NEILL's *The Emperor Jones*; it inspired the later founding, under Gilpin's leadership, of the Lafayette Players in New York City. As motion pictures became a new medium, William Foster, using Pekin actors, established the Foster Photoplay Company, the nation's first black film company; his initial production, the two-reel comedy *The Railroad Porter*, appeared in 1912. Foster later moved to Los Angeles; as with most early silent cinema, his films have been lost.

Peterson, Julia

A character in Hamlin GARLAND's story "Among the Corn Rows," collected in MAIN-TRAVELLED ROADS, Julia, the daughter of a Norwegian farmer in Wisconsin, is forced into the exhausting drudgery of farm labor. Toiling in the corn rows, she dreams of marrying a Yankee, not a Norwegian, since a Yankee would never ask his wife to work in the fields. Rob RODEMAKER, one-time schoolmate now homesteading in the Dakota territory, reappears at her family farm; he is looking for a wife to bring back to his land—although he is not thinking specifically of Julia, whom he has known only casually. Yet he is touched by seeing her life of toil, and he impulsively asks her to become his wife on his new homestead; she will need only to cook for him, he promises. Agreeing, she sneaks out of her family home that night—never thinking of the undoubtedly greater toil she will soon be facing.

Petit, the Poet   *See* SPOON RIVER ANTHOLOGY.

Phillips, Medora

This character appears in Henry B. FULLER's novel *BERTRAM COPE'S YEAR*. Like Mrs. Susan BATES in Fuller's WITH THE PROCESSION, Mrs. Phillips is a woman of wealth, a socially prominent figure; yet her domain, the university suburb of Churchton, is smaller than Mrs. Bates's domain, and she is less broadly philanthropic and civic-minded. A childless widow in her mid-40s, she entertains lavishly at her mansion, giving accommodation to visiting luminaries at the university; she hosts further activities at her summer house on the INDIANA DUNES. She also adopts young protégés, male and female, to add to her entourage. When they leave—as Bertram COPE does eventually—she feels their loss; she is paired in this respect with Basil RANDOLPH, another collector who mourns when the young depart.

"The Philosopher"   *See* WINESBURG, OHIO.

Pinkerton, Allan
(1819–1884) *detective agency founder*

Born in Glasgow, Scotland, Pinkerton came to West Dundee, Illinois, outside of Chicago, in 1842 and worked as a cooper, or barrel-maker. His shop became a station on the Underground Railway, the escape route for slaves into Canada. Later becoming county deputy sheriff, then the first detective on the Chicago police force, he established the private Pinkerton National Detective Agency in 1850, specializing in railroad theft cases. In 1861, hearing rumors of an assassination attempt on the newly elected President Abraham LINCOLN, he secretly conducted the president into Washington on the eve of his inauguration; during the CIVIL WAR, under an assumed name, he organized a spy network behind Confederate lines. In the aftermath of the GREAT FIRE of 1871, his agents guarded ruined stores and other buildings; in the following years, Pinkerton agents, hired by management, became involved in strike-breaking activities, for which they were soon considered notorious. Among the company's involvements was the 1892 HOMESTEAD STRIKE against the Carnegie Steel Company in Pennsylvania, in which 300 armed Pinkerton agents engaged in lethal conflict with strikers. Pinkerton is credited with inventing the mug shot—establishing, via photography, a new sort of database. His motto, "The Eye That Never Sleeps," gave birth to the term *private eye.*

In Jack LONDON's socialist vision of the future, *THE IRON HEEL*, Pinkerton agents are described as private detectives who become the "hired fighting men of the capitalists."

Pink Marsh: A Story of the Streets and the Town
George Ade
(1897)

After the success of earlier recurring characters, Artie Blanchard and Doc' Horne, in his popular newspaper column, "STORIES OF THE STREETS AND OF THE TOWN," ADE created Pink Marsh, an African-American bootblack, in 1896. Using the accepted DIALECT WRITING of the era, the tales were popular, and the firm of STONE AND KIMBALL published a collection of the columns the following year. The volume was illustrated—as the newspaper columns had been—by John T. MCCUTCHEON. Among professed admirers of Pink Marsh was the writer Mark Twain.

The Pit
Frank Norris
(1903)

This novel, subtitled *A Story of Chicago,* is the second of NORRIS's projected trilogy, *The Epic of Wheat.* The first novel, *The Octopus,* published in 1901, focused on the struggle between farmers and railroads in California's San Joaquin Valley; the third, *The Wolf,* unwritten at Norris's death, was to depict "the relieving of a famine in an Old World community." The title *The Pit* refers to the trading floor of the CHICAGO BOARD OF TRADE, occupying the second floor of the 1885 CHICAGO BOARD OF TRADE BUILDING. The main event in the novel, an attempt to corner the international wheat market, comes from a real-life episode of 1897–98, involving a failed attempt by the speculator Joseph Leiter; another real-life figure provides the basis for the character HARGUS, the old ruined trader who continues to haunt the building. Among other players at the time was Philip D. ARMOUR, commodities speculator and grain-elevator owner, as well as one of the city's major meatpackers.

Influenced by the NATURALISM of French novelist Émile ZOLA, Norris depicts wheat as a force of nature, greater than the men who seek to control it, inevitably triumphing over human institutions and human effort. The city also is an indomitable force, crushing and annihilating men "with a horrible indifference." Norris anticipates the work of Carl SANDBURG, describing the city—a dozen years before *CHICAGO POEMS*—as crude, vigorous, brutal, "arrogant in the new-found knowledge of its giant strength."

Curtis JADWIN and Laura DEARBORN are modeled in part on Norris's father and mother, a self-made businessman and a former actress—although

Jadwin, wealthy from real estate, bears a resemblance as well to the real-life Potter PALMER; Palmer had also long remained a bachelor before marrying a younger woman of non-Chicago origins, and he also, after his marriage, lived in an extravagant mansion on the North Side. An additional parallel with Norris's father lies in the depiction of Jadwin as a supporter of evangelist Dwight L. MOODY; the novelist's father similarly supported the man who had found business and religion compatible.

Before book publication, the work was serialized in abridged form in the *Saturday Evening Post*, running from September 1902 through January 1903; Norris died on October 25, a month after the serialization began.

Synopsis

CHAPTER I

The young Laura Dearborn, newly arrived in Chicago, is awaiting the rest of her operagoing party at the AUDITORIUM BUILDING theater. She hears two men nearby speaking of "corners" and "margins" and learns that their topic is the recent Helmick failure, a notable loss in corn speculation. A member of her own party, Charles CRESSLER, is known to deplore such commodities speculation—not only, he believes, because one can never truly corner a market, but also because it is wrong to try; the world's food should not be at the mercy of the Chicago wheat pit. Another member of the party, Curtis Jadwin, a man grown wealthy in real estate, talks briefly to Laura, impressing her with his quiet strength. Also in the party is Sheldon CORTHELL, an artist with a studio in the FINE ARTS BUILDING, who has hopes of marrying Laura. During the performance, she hears once again the men discussing "shortages" and "bushels," instead of heeding the musical drama onstage. On the way home, from her carriage window, she is amazed to see office buildings still glowing, their lights burning at one o'clock in the morning, activity visible from every window; here, she realizes, is another kind of drama. She is in the "commission district," viewing the Board of Trade building, the site of the wheat and corn pits, the arena of flourishing grain speculation.

CHAPTER II

Laura and her sister move into a new home. Landry COURT, a young broker's clerk, helps in the procedure, expressing hopes, too, of marrying Laura. The sisters, along with Aunt Wess' and Court, take a streetcar downtown, where Laura sees ships and trains—"a vast, cruel machinery" of pistons leaping, engines throbbing—and realizes that she is at the center of Empire, of a realm of immeasurable power. She realizes, too, that it is a man's, not a woman's, world: "a life in which women had no part." She sees Landry as representing "the Battle of the Street"—that is, La Salle Street, where the Board of Trade stands—and she realizes that under his pleasant exterior there must exist a coarseness, a callousness; by contrast, her other wooer, Corthell, lives a calm, gentle life, cultivating beauty and tranquility. She wonders which existence she prefers.

Passing "a vast dry goods house"—to be identified as MARSHALL FIELD AND COMPANY—the group runs into Mrs. Cressler, who invites the women to her home. Laura learns she has impressed Jadwin, the Michigan farmer's son who has risen to wealth and prominence in real estate. He is also a philanthropist, sponsoring a Sunday-school mission for poor children; Mrs. Cressler emphasizes the man's good-heartedness. Laura thinks of her two suitors, Corthell and Court, but now she contemplates a new figure, older, stronger, more successful, more formidable.

CHAPTERS III–IV

Jadwin, approaching the Board of Trade building, near his own ROOKERY building office, feels the seemingly irresistible force of that structure; like a whirlpool, it draws men toward it, sucking them in. Entering, he views the Western Union Telegraph installation, buzzing and clicking, as well as a group of derelict men gathered around the chalkboard; one of them, he learns, is a well-known former millionaire, now ruined in wheat speculation.

Against his better judgment, Jadwin lets himself be talked into speculating in May wheat. Selling wheat "short" means that one sells wheat he does not own, charging the current price; the wheat is to be delivered at a later date, at which time the price is anticipated to be lower—and as a result one pays less to buy and deliver the wheat, resulting in a profit. Jadwin is assured by his broker that the price of wheat will go down. Yet rumors of a possible war between England and Turkey spread, as the Higgins-Pasha incident—pasha being a title in Turkish officialdom—is cited; war would increase the demand for wheat, causing prices to rise. Landry is among those trading in the Pit, carrying out his commissions; amid hectic activity, the war rumors are suddenly discounted, and prices begin to fall, favoring speculators who sell short.

Jadwin has triumphed, making a small fortune; others have lost. Cressler expresses regret, fearing that his friend will continue gambling—using a word that disturbs Laura. Gambling in the Pit, he warns, is "worse than liquor, worse than morphine." Jadwin and Corthell both propose marriage to Laura; her response is that she has no intention of marrying. When her third suitor, Court, impulsively kisses her, she decides she has been too encouraging of these men; she writes notes to each, stating her position once more. The one man who responds by calling in person is Jadwin.

CHAPTER V

Corthell, disappointed in love, has gone abroad. Cressler believes that Jadwin is speculating again, bargaining in both wheat and corn. Laura announces that she and Jadwin will marry, even though she has told him she does not love him. She is moved by the fact that he loves her, that his wealth is impressive; he is buying an extravagant mansion for them to live in after their marriage. He has also bought and remodeled a home in Lake Geneva, Wisconsin, where they will spend their honeymoon; his only wish, he tells her, is for her to kiss him spontaneously, showing him an instinctive affection.

They marry in a quiet ceremony. Laura returns briefly to her home, bidding farewell to her old life; Jadwin comes to her, saying he understands her feeling—and she realizes she has been stubborn and unyielding; she kisses him, telling him she loves him.

CHAPTER VI

It is three years since the wedding, and Jadwin is continuing his speculation in wheat. Prices have been going down, accruing great profits to those, like him, who are selling short—although farmers are being impoverished—but now he senses an impending change; prices are going to rise, he believes, and he tells his broker to buy. Laura, meanwhile, is exulting in her perfect happiness; she knows that love is "less a victory than a capitulation." She reads to her husband in the evening, although the only author he cares for is HOWELLS, whose everyday characters he understands. Yet he cannot keep himself away from La Salle Street and the Wheat Pit. Realizing that the demand for wheat is growing, he commits himself more deeply; prices continue to rise, and he buys his own seat on the Board of Trade.

CHAPTER VII

Laura sees that Jadwin is changing, spending more time away from her. When she reminds him that they have more money than they can spend, he admits that it is the excitement, the thrill, that drives him on. He shows her a cable he has just received, indicating that Argentine shipments have been curtailed, that European demand is growing; he goes off at once to the Board of Trade. Later in the day, while riding in LINCOLN PARK, Laura meets Sheldon Corthell, who has returned from his four-year sojourn in Europe. She invites him to join her and Jadwin for dinner; Jadwin fails to appear, and she and Corthell go to the art gallery and pipe-organ room, where Corthell schools her in his superior knowledge of painting and music; he plays music, too, that is chosen for its seductive qualities. When Jadwin finally arrives home, he excitedly exclaims that he has just made $500,000—an astounding sum in that era.

Jadwin stays briefly out of the market, promising Laura he will no longer speculate. Yet impatience overcomes him, and he is soon back at the Board of Trade, where rumors abound that an "Unknown Bull" has entered the market, buying steadily, gathering up wheat from the bins and elevators of the West. Putting together information from various sources, Jadwin comes to believe he can corner the market on wheat—meaning he can purchase all or most of the supply, thereby being able to name his price.

CHAPTER VIII

The Unknown Bull has taken control of the Pit, driving out everyone else, while Europe clamors for the grain that would feed its "crowded streets and barren farms." The price of wheat rises to a full dollar a bushel: "Dollar wheat," is the cry. A rival broker privately realizes that the Bull is Jadwin himself, and he enlists others, including Jadwin's friend Cressler, to band together to defeat this figure who is cornering the market. Cressler, although disapproving of speculating—and unaware that he is working against Jadwin—finally agrees. Jadwin, meanwhile, becomes all the more absorbed in his project; as his team of horses carries him along La Salle Street, he hears in the rhythm of the hoofs only "Wheat—wheat—wheat, wheat—wheat—wheat." He is staying increasingly away from home, and Laura feels angry and hurt, although she understands, too, that he is not entirely to blame, that he is caught up in something larger than any one man.

Corthell reenters Laura's life, calling on her when Jadwin is away. One evening she invites him into her private sitting room, asking his advice on a picture; he lights a cigarette, showing her his antique matchbox. "An hour later," Norris writes, he leaves—and some readers choose to think that sexual intimacy has taken place. Yet her sister Page's vague accusations, after Corthell's matchbox has been found, can cover either psychological or physical infidelity.

Laura tells Corthell that he must never see her again. She insists that Jadwin stay home one evening; planning a surprise for him, she dresses up to play various roles from the theater and opera. After she presents a dance from the opera *Carmen*, complete with castanets, Jadwin finally makes clear that he cares little for such "overwrought" and "unnatural" performing; he would rather she play for him the familiar songs of the day. They share a moment of happiness, claiming that perhaps they do not need the wealth and goods they have acquired—when his broker breaks in on the scene, announcing that a show-

down will take place in the Pit the next day; they must plan a strategy. Jadwin leaves at once, and Laura is alone again.

CHAPTER IX

Jadwin resolves to bankrupt one of his adversaries, Dave Scannel, once instrumental in the ruin of a man named Hargus, now the derelict who habituates the Board of Trade building. Cressler, meanwhile, loses heavily, finally learning that it is Jadwin who is cornering the market. Jadwin's triumph, putting wheat at high prices, is helping farmers, who can now pay off mortgages and buy farm equipment, but it is harming others—those who need bread to eat. Jadwin arranges for Hargus to receive payments from Scannel, and yet he himself is bringing others to ruin; the number of "broken speculators" is increasing. Yet he decides he has only just begun; he will keep up his corner, continuing to raise prices—even though he is reminded that farmers, enjoying the high prices, will plant even more grain; an oversupply will result. "You're fighting against the earth itself," he is warned.

Laura, seeing little of her husband, feels abandoned. In a moment of recklessness, she writes a letter to Corthell, knowing she is taking a great leap, approaching "a new and terrible country." Yet at the last minute she retrieves the letter, vowing to remain faithful to her absent husband. She hears that Charles Cressler is ill, worrying too much about business matters; when she goes to his house, she discovers him dead of a gunshot.

CHAPTER X: CONCLUSION

Wheat acreage has increased because of the high prices farmers are receiving, and Jadwin finds that controlling the supply is becoming more difficult. To raise funds to keep buying, he mortgages his real estate, including the mansion he and his wife live in; he writes promissory notes as well. At the Board of Trade building, spectators fill the gallery overlooking the Pit, anticipating an unfolding drama; among them is Page, now engaged to Landry Court. The latter is representing Jadwin on the floor—until the Bull himself emerges, crying out his bids. But the inevitable happens; trading is closed, and Jadwin goes to defeat and financial ruin.

Laura is waiting at home, anticipating her husband's arrival and the celebration of her birthday. Page returns from the Board of Trade, not fully understanding what has happened; yet she accuses Laura of selfishness, of not properly appreciating her husband's business interests. Corthell comes to wish Laura a happy birthday, and she gives in to his entreaties, agreeing to go away with him—except that Jadwin returns home, a broken man, and husband and wife once more cling to each other.

In the novel's concluding section, Jadwin has been ill for weeks, and Laura has devotedly nursed him; they are planning to move west, where they will start afresh. A string of other brokerage failures has followed Jadwin's collapse, and a large bank has toppled, taking away the savings of many depositors. As Laura and Jadwin leave the city, she catches a glimpse once more of the Board of Trade building, standing dark and monolithic, representing the forces that had overwhelmed them.

Critical Reception

Since Norris died between the time the novel appeared serially and in book form, the news of his death helped the book achieve best-seller status. Lamenting the author's passing, reviewers found the work a worthy successor to his previous volumes, most notably *The Octopus*; the *New York Times* noted that the novel displayed "all the small faults as well as all of the large virtues of its predecessors." Floyd DELL mourned the end of a career that could have made the author "a towering figure among the great masters of literature." Dell later praised Norris's, recreation of the city, calling *The Pit* "the best fictional guidebook to Chicago in existence."

Critics have suggested that *The Pit* suffers in that the major force, the wheat, is not seen, as it is in *The Octopus*, where it teems from the earth or flows voluminously into grain elevators; speculators are buying and selling commodities they do not physically possess, or even see. On the other hand, the novel has been called the rare work of

fiction that shows the excitement of business activity; Jadwin's gambling compulsion creates a figure of new romantic proportions. The character who often troubles contemporary readers is Laura; she is presented as a strong, up-to-date woman who nevertheless subordinates herself to a yet-stronger man.

A play was made from the novel in 1904, followed by a D. W. GRIFFITH movie in 1909, the one-reel *A Corner in Wheat*. In the movie, the villain is trapped in a grain elevator and drowns in wheat—the fate met by the railroad representative in Norris's previous novel, *The Octopus*.

Platow, Stephanie

This character appears in Theodore DREISER's novel THE TITAN. The daughter of a wealthy Jewish Chicago furrier and a Texas woman who was once his bookkeeper, Stephanie is a young actress connected to a local theatrical group, the Garrick Players; she becomes the mistress of Frank COWPERWOOD after the departure of Rita SOHLBERG. Yet she is not Cowperwood's mistress exclusively, continuing her affairs with various artistic and literary figures. Cowperwood becomes suspicious, thinking of the "bland way in which she could lie"—which reminds him of himself. He has her followed, then bursts in on her when she is with another man; he abruptly ends the relationship. Although Charles T. YERKES, the basis for Cowperwood's character, was known for his liaisons with women, Stephanie is based on a woman with whom Dreiser himself had a relationship, the actress Elaine HYMAN.

Poetry: A Magazine of Verse

This innovative magazine, the only periodical of the era devoted exclusively to poetry, was founded by Harriet MONROE in 1912. Its motto came from Walt WHITMAN: "To have great poets there must be great audiences too"; she was going to bring new audiences and new poets together. She was also going to publish midwestern poets, American poets—to "break the chains which enslave Chicago to New York, America to Europe." The first issue, dated October 1912, included two poems by the expatriate American Ezra POUND, as well as pieces by Chicagoans Sherwood ANDERSON, Floyd DELL, Margery CURREY, Eunice TIETJENS, Arthur Davison FICKE, and the late William Vaughn MOODY. The January 1913 issue featured Vachel LINDSAY's "GENERAL WILLIAM BOOTH ENTERS INTO HEAVEN," an immediately popular piece. Soon Pound, designated as "foreign correspondent," was sending the work of William Butler YEATS, Richard ALDINGTON, H. D. (Hilda DOOLITTLE), William Carlos WILLIAMS, Rabindranath TAGORE, D. H. LAWRENCE, Robert FROST, and T. S. ELIOT. Carl SANDBURG's "Chicago" and other "Chicago Poems" appeared in March 1914.

The reaction was not always favorable. A long-standing major literary periodical of the time, the DIAL, railed not only against the magazine's publishing of FREE VERSE, or nonmetrical verse—which "acknowledges subordination to no kind of law"—but also of poetry employing inappropriate subject matter; the stockyards and railroads were not seen as fit subjects for verse. The magazine, it declared, in its abandonment of Parnassian heights, was a "futile little periodical."

Poetry also took up the cause of what Pound labeled "Imagisme," or IMAGISM. Describing this poetic movement in one of his "London Letters," Pound pushed Aldington and H.D. as major Imagiste poets; their work involved *vers libre,* or free verse, as well. Sandburg, too, was seen as a disciple of Pound because of his use of free verse. In October 1914, *Poetry* published the first Edgar Lee MASTERS pieces, reprinting items from a serial installment in a St. Louis publication, to be collected in *SPOON RIVER ANTHOLOGY;* Masters, a Chicago lawyer, was using a pseudonym at the time, "Webster Ford." In November of that year, *Poetry* published the results of its War Poem Contest, thereby printing the first pieces by Wallace STEVENS.

The June 1915 issue achieved a new high point, presenting T. S. Eliot's "The Love Song of J. Alfred Prufrock"—although Monroe included it only reluctantly, upon Pound's insistence. Stevens's

"Sunday Morning" appeared in November of that year; in that case, Monroe had insisted that the poet make cuts in his poem. Pound was now seeing the editor as essentially conservative, and he turned instead to the LITTLE REVIEW, setting himself up as foreign correspondent for that periodical as well. Yet he sent Monroe pieces by Eliot and himself for 1916, as well as lyrics by James JOYCE for 1917. Monroe also continued to acquire work from Stevens, publishing in 1919, among other pieces, his much-anthologized "Anecdote of the Jar." Other writers presented in the early years of *Poetry* include Amy LOWELL, Edward Arlington ROBINSON, Sara TEASDALE, Marianne MOORE, and Ernest HEMINGWAY. The most quoted of all poems ever published in the periodical was Joyce KILMER's "Trees," appearing in the July 1913 issue; Kilmer was killed in action in WORLD WAR I.

Yet critics agree that the magazine was in decline after its first few years; poets had found other outlets, as other periodicals were flourishing, if only briefly. Monroe was facing financial constraints as well; the original five-year pledges from her contributors, gathered from the ranks of Chicago's elite, were up for renewal in 1917, and the gift-giving climate seemed different in the years of the war. Another of Monroe's problems was that her assistant editor from the beginning, Alice Corbin HENDERSON, was now ill and living in New Mexico; although less international-minded than Monroe, Henderson was the one who came upon Sandburg and Masters—and even some early poetry of Sherwood Anderson—and many have said she played an important role in the early years of *Poetry.* Henry B. FULLER acted as proofreader for the first issues.

Monroe remained at the helm of *Poetry* for nearly a quarter of a century. During the GREAT DEPRESSION, a grant from the Carnegie Foundation helped the magazine survive. As other periodicals fell along the way—and as yet other periodicals took away many of her poets—Monroe remained an able and astute editor, keeping the magazine going through aesthetic and financial adversity; it continues to the present day. In 2002, *Poetry* received an endowment of $100 million from the Lilly pharmaceutical fortune, making it one of the world's wealthiest publications.

Poor White
Sherwood Anderson
(1920)

Appearing a year after the acclaimed collection of his stories, WINESBURG, OHIO, Sherwood ANDER-SON's *Poor White* takes on larger, more sustained themes than the previous work. Although the title refers to the principal character, Hugh MCVEY, the work is ultimately about the industrialization of a midwestern town, the transformation of a once-rural area and its people; the real-life parallel is to Anderson's hometown of Clyde, Ohio, the site of new factories built in the 1880s. The opening section owes its setting in a Missouri town along the Mississippi River, as well as the father-son duo, to Mark Twain's *Adventures of Huckleberry Finn*. The character Joseph WAINSWORTH, the harness-maker who scorns machine-made items, parallels Anderson's father, a harness-maker achieving little success in several small Ohio towns.

Synopsis

CHAPTERS I–II
Hugh McVey lives with his widowed father, an unemployed drunkard, in a fishing shack on the banks of the Mississippi River in a Missouri town; he has never gone to school. When he is 14, the railroad comes to town, and he begins working for the station master and his wife, Sarah Shepard. Sarah takes the boy in, teaching him how to sit at a table, how to use a fork, how to talk to people. Eventually, she teaches him reading and arithmetic, exhorting him, too, to avoid the laziness that she considers his heritage—his "poor white trash" background.

Five years later, the Shepards move to Michigan, and Hugh takes over as station master. His father is killed in a drunken quarrel, and he decides to move on, seeking something better in life. In 1886, at the age of 20, he heads eastward. For the next three years, he works as a farm laborer in Illinois, Indiana, and Ohio; he stops briefly in Chicago, but the crowds frighten him. Employed on an Indiana farm, he is intrigued by the farmer's daughter, who is engaged to a bank clerk; one night he watches in the shadows as they embrace,

having never before seen a man express affection for a woman. He moves on the next day. As he travels to various towns, he finds himself hearing serious discussions—of better ways to cultivate corn or build a barn, of religious beliefs, of the nation's political destiny; he hears men having earnest, even spiritual, things to say. He remembers the words of Sarah Shepard, realizing that he must better himself. Taking long walks at night, he begins making mathematical calculations; one night he counts the pickets in fences, calculating the number of pickets in all the fences in town. He buys a ruler at the hardware store and measures the pickets, estimating the number that could be cut from a single tree of a certain size. Soon he is counting the trees in the streets, then building imaginary houses from them.

CHAPTERS III–IV
Arriving at the age of 23 in Bidwell, Ohio, an established farming community, Hugh takes over the job of telegraph operator at a railroad station. Discussion of new forces, of a new industrialization, is in the air all about him. Farmers will increasingly be using machinery, people say, and factories will be built to produce that machinery; then the character of the town will change. No longer will the craftsman be respected; the merchant and the capitalist will replace him as the leading figures of the community. Nor will serious-minded men talk anymore of God and spiritual matters; they will become awakened to a new way of life, to a new understanding of earthly life and its possibilities.

The townspeople see Hugh as somewhat strange; he speaks little and is seen to take long walks at night. When thinking about the corn he once cut on an Illinois farm, he wonders if a machine might not do the same work. He sends away for textbooks on mechanics; he enrolls in a correspondence school. Yet wishing also to become part of the life of the town, he watches again as men court women; then his early sense of inferiority returns to him, and he goes back to his books and diagrams.

CHAPTERS V–VI
The townspeople begin to talk about this telegraph operator and his books. Steve HUNTER, the jeweler's

son, having returned from a business college in Buffalo, hears about Hugh, who seems to be busy studying and inventing things; Steve decides that if the telegraph operator has made some sort of invention, he will raise money and start a factory.

The farms around Bidwell practice cabbage cultivation—growing a crop that involves the tedious task of transplanting seedlings one by one into the ground. One night Hugh sees a farm family laboriously planting seedlings by moonlight; he thinks of a machine that might accomplish the same work.

Steve Hunter, meanwhile, is walking about town, hinting with an air of superiority that important things are about to happen; when challenged, he impulsively declares that he has made a deal with the telegraph operator to manufacture an important new invention. Worrying about his boast, he goes to see Hugh at the railroad station, and finds that the young man indeed is working on a planting machine; he is ready to make a trial model. Steve writes out a contract on the spot. The next step is to get financing from the town's leading citizens; these men, including Thomas BUTTERWORTH, a wealthy farmer, envision great rewards, realizing that the new era of industrialization is coming.

CHAPTER VII

The year is now 1892. A model of Hugh's machine is set to work, planting seedlings in a showcase field; when the seedlings show signs of dying, Steve sneaks out at night and replaces them. He also begins soliciting investments from the townspeople, in addition to the money put up by his original backers; establishing the Bidwell Plant-Setting Machine Company, he initiates construction of a factory. Yet gradually it becomes clear that the machine is a failure; it is too heavy to handle, and it works only in certain types of soil. Steve proposes to his principal backers that when the company fails—and when the small stockholders lose their money—they should buy up the factory at a low price; they would then use it to make another product.

Hugh comes up with another invention, a device for lifting a coal car and dumping its contents into a chute—a chute that leads to the hold of a

ship or to the engine room of a factory. Steve sells the patent in New York and receives a large sum of money, sharing it with Hugh; construction on the new factory continues. Hugh is developing also a corn-cutting machine.

As the new spirit of industry takes over the region, craftsmen like Joseph Wainsworth, the town's harness maker, become disturbed by the events. Wainsworth has already told Tom Butterworth that he will not repair any factory-made harnesses. Yet he has put his life savings, a total of $1,200, into the Bidwell Plant-Setting Company. Although holding misgivings, he assumes his investment is sound—but doubts arise again when he hears his neighbor praying in his bedroom, before an open window, for the success of the plant-setting machine. The neighbor, a devout Methodist, is praying for worldly goods.

CHAPTERS VIII–IX

Tom Butterworth, a widower, the richest man in the area, lives with his sister and his daughter, Clara BUTTERWORTH, who has just graduated from high school. Having grown up with her father's farmhands, Clara is used to dealing with men in a casual way, but when she playfully tosses an ear of corn at one of the farmhands, the man thinks she is making an invitation; he makes a forcible attempt on her, which she repulses. Yet the farmhand keeps coming around, and Tom, noting the man's leering confidence, decides that Clara has been offering encouragement; she and her father quarrel. She is beginning now to learn about grown-up matters; she stays out late with the new young schoolteacher and quarrels again with her father.

Clara leaves the farm to attend the state university at Columbus; she will live in the city with relatives. She meets various young men at the university, but she meets also a woman, Kate CHANCELLER, whom she feels she does not totally understand; Kate, thrusting her hands into skirt pockets as if they were trousers pockets, is "in her nature a man." Kate is also a bold thinker, and she claims revulsion at the rules by which society restricts women; she is also a socialist, explaining to Clara the meaning of capital and labor.

CHAPTERS X–XI

The plant-setting machine company goes into receivership, losing the townspeople's money. Steve Hunter and Tom Butterworth buy the factory and start manufacturing Hugh's corn-cutting machine, which is a success from the beginning. Soon the factory is too small for the corn-cutter manufacturing, and a new building is constructed; the old building will be used to manufacture bicycles. The town is booming. Hunter and Butterworth see themselves as men of the future, as strong men whose actions are for the good of the community.

When Clara returns from Columbus, Tom tells her it is time for her to marry, although it cannot be to an ordinary man; her father is now a leading citizen in town. Clara remembers that Kate Chanceller, who scorns marriage, is planning to become a doctor, but Clara knows that her own father would never support such an effort on her part. Meanwhile, she sees how the town is prospering; the local carpenter, once taking personal care in his projects, now has many men working for him; he has not driven a nail himself for several years. Joe Wainsworth has had plenty of harness business as well; he has taken on an assistant, Jim Gibson, and in the last year, he has made more money than he lost in the plant-setting machine company. Yet Gibson is gradually taking over the business operation, charging the customers higher prices than what Wainsworth suggests; the old harness-maker seems helpless in this new competitive era.

CHAPTERS XII–XV

Hugh McVey has become a respected man throughout the Midwest because of his inventing the coal-loading apparatus and the corn-cutting machine; he has also become rich. Yet he still feels personally isolated, continuing to live as a boarder in a widow's house, along with Rose, a schoolteacher. He tries to establish a relationship with Rose, but his awkwardness, as well as her reticence, keeps them apart. Their rooms in the house are adjoining; one night they both sit at their open windows, and he almost reaches across to her, but then draws back. He decides he has no right to impose himself; he should be thinking instead about the problems of his new hay-loading device.

A man named Alfred Buckley comes to Bidwell from New York City; Buckley has long talks about future industrial development with Tom Butterworth, and he wants to marry Tom's daughter. Clara has no interest in him; she is beginning to think more about Hugh McVey, the untutored boy from Missouri who has become a hero because of his cleverness and ingenuity. Meanwhile, Hugh, whom the governor of Ohio has publicly praised, decides that maybe he is worthy of a woman.

A federal officer comes to arrest Buckley for various swindling schemes, as well as bigamy, and the town is shocked; Tom Butterworth had hinted that Buckley and his daughter were engaged. The townpeople begin talking about Clara, and Hugh thinks his chance has come; he can rescue her from gossipers. He comes to her house that evening, saying he wants to marry her, and she accepts, saying they should go at once to the county seat and get married. She hitches up a horse and buggy, telling a farmhand that she and Hugh are getting married; they will be back by midnight.

CHAPTERS XVI–XX

Tom Butterworth, hearing the news of his daughter's elopement, wakes up the town to provide a wedding dinner at his house. The old days when Tom was a simple farmer are gone; a grand banquet will be prepared for the couple's return. When Clara arrives and sees the celebration, she feels overwhelmed; she wishes she had a woman to talk to, to help her understand her new state of matrimony. She will have a life of submission now; Kate Chanceller had said that is how married women live. When the guests leave, Clara and Hugh go upstairs, but Hugh gives in to his awkwardness once more; deciding that he cannot impose himself, he crawls out the window onto the kitchen roof. He escapes into the darkness and walks across the fields, lamenting now that he has had his chance and missed it.

Tom brings Hugh back to the house the next day. Clara and Hugh continue to sleep in different bedrooms, and Clara, like Rose before her, awaits him expectantly. It is only after a week that Clara becomes bold enough to make clear that she wants him to come to her.

CHAPTERS XXI–XXIII

It is three years since Hugh and Clara have married. She still feels emotional barriers between them, and she blames the barriers on machines—the machines that Hugh is constantly pondering. Her father, meanwhile, has bought a motorcar.

The first industrial strike in the town of Bidwell takes place in the corn-cutting machine plant; the foreman, once a carpenter's apprentice, makes unreasonable demands on his workers. A labor organizer from Cleveland comes to town, then others as well; soon the workingmen of Bidwell are hearing foreigners speaking of ANARCHISM and SOCIALISM. A Swede, a socialist, reminds the townsmen of the money they have lost in the plant-setting machine company; the capitalist class has robbed them.

Jim Gibson is running Joe Wainsworth's harness shop, even placing an order for machine-made harnesses; he considers Wainsworth a fool who, all his life, has made harnesses by hand, thinking that is the only way. In the evening, when the two men are still working in the shop, Wainsworth takes his circular harness-maker's knife and approaches Gibson—and attacks him, nearly severing his head from his body. Sitting now in the darkened shop, Wainsworth takes the factory-made harnesses and cuts them one by one into small pieces. Then he takes a revolver and leaves the shop; he intends to kill himself but does not want to die in the same room with Gibson. Out on the street, he sees Steve Hunter, the man who had lost his $1,200, the man who has been bringing machine-made innovations to Bidwell. He nervously takes out the revolver, shoots, but drops the gun and runs away.

That evening, Clara and Hugh are out riding with Tom Butterworth in his motorcar; Tom talks about the new plant he is starting in Bidwell for making automobile tires, and he speaks angrily about the labor unrest in town. He recounts the story about how Jim Gibson made Joe Wainsworth buy factory-made harnesses to sell; no one can stop the machines, he declares. Then the car's headlights catch three figures struggling

in the darkness; two men have apprehended Wainsworth, who has not only shot Steve Hunter but also killed his employee, Gibson. As they take Wainsworth to the police station—and after Clara, taking Wainsworth's side, has warned them fiercely not to harm the man—the harness-maker lunges at Hugh, saying that he, the inventor, is the real murderer.

From that moment on, Hugh is a changed man; he is now reflective about the consequences of what he has done. Clara is changed, too; whereas she once thought hostilely about machines, hating what they did, she rose to Hugh's defense on that particular night. It was she who pulled the crazed harness-maker off her husband, who threw the man to the floor of the car. She had once defended the past, the old ways, but when the past rose up against her husband, she reacted against it; she had already borne Hugh a daughter and was soon to bear him another child. So, as a wife and mother, she has stopped thinking about larger issues—and it is now Hugh who does the thinking; he thinks about other inventors working as he had once done, about the concerns of the next generation that will be following. The poor white boy, who had once tinkered and invented, is now a thoughtful man who will no longer strive heedlessly or blindly.

Critical Reception

Reviewers were predisposed to favor the novel, coming just a year after *Winesburg, Ohio.* H. L. MENCKEN praised the volume in his *Smart Set,* and the *DIAL,* having recently moved to New York and shifted its once-conservative stance, also lauded the novel, although complaining about its abrupt ending. Francis HACKETT, writing in *The New Republic,* found fault with the ending as well, although appreciating the work's "large, loose sense of life." Reviewers began stating what would become the received wisdom about Anderson's work—that his long fiction is not as successful as his short fiction; one critic complained that *Poor White* contains "twenty-nine distinct stories," which sometimes join with the whole and sometimes do not. A handicap to commercial success was that Sinclair LEWIS's *Main Street* appeared the same year, and comparisons generally favored the younger writer.

Critics have since dwelled on the inconsistent characterization of Clara, as well as the unconvincing relationship between her and Hugh; improbable behavior patterns have been analyzed. As with WINDY McPHERSON'S SON, the first portions of the work, depicting the young man's growing up in rural surroundings, have been declared superior to the rest. *Poor White* nevertheless retains its appraisal as the best of Anderson's novels. It was reprinted in a Modern Library edition in 1926.

Populist Party

This political party, also known as the People's Party, hold its first national convention in Omaha in 1892. The Populist Party consisted mainly of midwestern farmers who opposed what they considered predatory eastern interests and practices. Although the word *populism* suggests an appeal to common people in general, the movement labeled as populism remained regional and agricultural; the farmer rarely felt in accord with the urban worker. The agenda of the Populist Party included FREE SILVER—to increase the money supply, putting it beyond the control of eastern banks—as well as government ownership of railroads and utilities. James B. Weaver of Iowa became the first Populist candidate for president, drawing nearly a million votes and carrying six farm states in the 1892 election. In 1896, the Populist Party allied with the Democratic Party to nominate William Jennings BRYAN for president; after Bryan's defeat, the party maintained little influence and was ultimately absorbed by the Democrats.

Porter, William Sydney

(1862–1910) *short-story writer*

Known for his sentimentality, plot twists, and tidy endings, Porter, writing under the pen name of O. Henry, became the foil for writers seeking to update and modernize the short story. Born in North Carolina, moving to Texas, Porter worked as a bank teller in Austin until convicted, in 1898, of embezzling funds; he spent three years in prison. While serving his term, Porter began writing stories, using the pseudonym to hide his identity. Moving to New York, he continued writing tales of simple, common people; his collection *The Four Million*, published in 1906, ironically refers to the "Four Hundred," the list of New York City's social elite. Porter died an alcoholic at the age of 47.

Much of the magazine short fiction of the era is traceable to the influence of O. Henry. Edna FERBER writes of searching through periodicals in her Appleton, Wisconsin, public library, looking for examples of his work; her tales demonstrate a use of his techniques and patterns of plotting. Sherwood ANDERSON, wishing to discredit Porter, later referred to popular magazine fiction as "nice little packages, wrapped and labeled in the O. Henry manner"; Anderson himself ignored plotting, time-bound narrative, and other standard story-telling devices.

"Portrait of a Motorcar"   *See* CORNHUSKERS.

Potawatomi

A Native American group of the Algonquian branch, living in Michigan in the early 17th century, the Potawatomi were driven west by the Iroquois and settled in southeastern Wisconsin. By 1800, they were living around LAKE MICHIGAN, including northern Illinois and Indiana. Originally siding with the French against the English, they allied with the English against the Americans in the WAR OF 1812, hoping to defeat the new country and halt its westward expansion; along with Chippewa and Ottawa allies, the Potawatomi carried out the FORT DEARBORN massacre. Yet settlers continued advancing westward, and in 1833, the leaders of the Potawatomi, Chippewa, and Ottawa nations, meeting in Chicago, formally ceded land east of the Mississippi, moving on to Iowa and eventually to Kansas.

Pound, Ezra
(1885–1972) *poet*

Idaho-born, Pennsylvania-raised, an expatriate all his adult life, Pound is one of the founders of MODERNISM. In 1906, he became briefly engaged to future poet Hilda DOOLITTLE, whom he later renamed "H.D." Moving to London in 1908, he became known for his verse and for his championing of other writers, including Robert FROST and T. S. ELIOT; his editorial trimming of Eliot's "The Waste Land" helped make that poem a milestone of modernism.

In 1912, responding to Harriet MONROE's request for contributions to her new magazine, POETRY, Pound sent some of his own work, offering to serve also as overseas correspondent and send along the work of others; he later undertook the same role for Margaret ANDERSON's LITTLE MAGAZINE. He became known for his hectoring and quarreling with editors, particularly Monroe, although he convinced the *Poetry* founder, whose tastes tended to the conservative, to publish such ground-breaking poetry as Eliot's "Love Song of J. Alfred Prufrock." In his own writing, he led the IMAGIST movement, experimenting also with the HAIKU, rendering translations from Anglo-Saxon, Latin, Chinese, and Japanese; his literary advocacies broadened the domain of poetry, diminishing the sway of conventional poetics and sentimental Victorianism. His epic collections of *Cantos*, appearing over a 50-year period, combine a spectrum of images and allusions, ranging from ancient myth to contemporary economic theory. In the 1930s, living in Italy, Pound gave support to the fascism of Benito Mussolini; his radio broadcasts during World War II led to his arrest by Allied troops after the war. Confined for 12 years to a mental institution in Washington, D.C., he died in Venice at the age of 87.

prairie

The first Europeans to see the treeless grassland of the central United States were the French, bestowing on it a word for meadow; the American poet William Cullen BRYANT lamented that "the speech of England has no name." Travelers, viewing the open sky and endless horizons, compared journeying across the grassland to voyaging across the ocean. In some locales, the grasses rose over six feet in height; the artist George Catlin spoke of having to stand high in his stirrups to look out over them. In the area's later agricultural development, the black-soil prairie of the upper Mississippi Valley, formed by the growth and decay of vegetation, became one of the world's most fertile farmlands; settlers readily converted the prairie to fields of wheat and corn.

New York novelist James Fenimore Cooper published his best-selling novel *The Prairie* in 1827, sending his protagonist, journeying beyond the bounds of white settlement, into a new form of wilderness. In 1832, New Englander Bryant toured westward, describing the region's vastness in his poem "The Prairies"; he evoked the ocean and its "rounded billows"—as did Herman Melville, comparing the Atlantic Ocean to the "Illinois prairie" in the 1851 *Moby-Dick*. Carl SANDBURG's "Prairie," collected in CORNHUSKERS in 1918, updated Bryant's loosely metrical verse with his own strictly nonmetrical FREE VERSE.

"Prairie" See CORNHUSKERS.

Prairie School of Architecture

This architectural style and practice is associated with Frank Lloyd WRIGHT. Leaving the firm of ADLER AND SULLIVAN in 1893, establishing himself in OAK PARK, a Chicago suburb, Wright began specializing in residential structures, developing what became known as the Prairie Style. The style advocates that the architect open up interior space, eliminate extraneous detail, and create a unity of design; the last precept meant creating a home's furnishings and accessories as well. Wright decreed that a building must fit its site; the low-lying prairie, embodying horizontal lines, requires a horizontal building design, including low terraces, low and wide doors, and broad roofs extending outward. Influenced by the ARTS AND CRAFTS MOVEMENT, the

Prairie School advocated also the use of natural materials, including indigenous wood and stone.

An admired example of the style is Wright's 1910 Robie House on South Woodlawn Avenue in Chicago; its broad overhanging roof extends 20 feet beyond the masonry. The Robie House came close to demolition in 1941 and again in 1957; it was eventually acquired by the UNIVERSITY OF CHICAGO. The dominance of the Prairie School waned after WORLD WAR I, and yet its principles—even though originally developed as appropriate to a local terrain—have been imitated in other parts of the country.

"Prayers of Steel"   *See* CORNHUSKERS.

primitivism

When writers and artists make use of premodern, non-Western material in their work, they are dealing in primitivism. Current concepts of primitivism began in France and England in the 18th century—in the belief that natural man is good, that contemporary man has been corrupted by a debased society and by his alienation from nature. The vaunted "noble savage" remains free of these impurities. The idealized person has sometimes been deemed to live communally, sometimes to be sexually unrestrained—qualities depending on the agenda of the idealizer; primitivism has often been a platform for criticism of one's own culture.

Primitivist art is far from "genuine," in that the sensibility remains modern; it tends also to be condescending, in that it involves no dialogue, no equal interchange between cultures. An example is VACHEL LINDSAY's poem "The Congo," collected in *THE CONGO AND OTHER POEMS;* it presents images of African peoples that are stereotypical, including references to indigenous religion. Lindsay's primitivism paved the way for Eugene O'NEILL's drama *The Emperor Jones,* first performed in 1920, in which a former Pullman porter turned Caribbean-isle dictator returns in racial memory to a Congo riverbank, facing a witch doctor and ritual sacrifice. Both "The Congo" and *The Emperor Jones* present a Western-conceived version of a non-Western milieu. Although neither of these works engages in self-criticism, the oft-found self-criticism and social criticism occurs in Sherwood ANDERSON's novel of 1925, *DARK LAUGHTER;* the work introduces a standard primitivist agenda, celebrating a presumed African-American sensuality, attacking European-American intellectualism and sterility.

The Professor's House
Willa Cather
(1925)

This novel has been called the most personal of CATHER's works, depicting her own feelings of depression at that time in her life. Her professor, Godfrey ST. PETER, is 52 years old, Cather's own age, and he is weary, living "without delight." He is loath to leave the attic sewing room he has long used as a study, and biographers note the room's resemblance to Cather's own room at the house of Isabelle McClung—and the fact that Isabelle, said to have been the most important person in her life, had just taken the step of marrying; the man Isabelle married is the basis of the character of Louie MARSELLUS. At the end of the novel, St. Peter thinks briefly of his childhood on the PRAIRIE, where he had been brought at the age of eight—as Cather herself had been brought at a young age. Yet St. Peter's most transcendent memories are of his journeying to the Southwest—where Cather, too, found transformation, as did the semiautobiographical Thea KRONBORG of *THE SONG OF THE LARK.*

The setting of the novel is Hamilton, a university town in a lakeside Chicago suburb, a renamed EVANSTON, home of NORTHWESTERN UNIVERSITY. The academic institution is described as state-supported, suggesting that Cather is thinking of her own University of Nebraska as well—although when the professor suggests that art and religion are the same thing, a listener jokingly wonders how he gets by the Methodists; the reference is to Northwestern, founded as a Methodist institution.

Ranging between suburban Chicago and the Southwest, the novel takes a brief trip also to Washington, D.C., where Tom OUTLAND tries to interest government officials in his archaeological findings; Cather herself briefly held a translating job in Washington. Viewing the capital, Tom describes government workers as "hundreds of little black-coated men" emerging from their buildings at the end of the day; "how much more depressing," he muses, "they are than workmen coming out of a factory." Cather grew up in times of labor strife, and yet she is dismissing here the image of the exploited worker—more evidence leading to her being branded as unsympathetic to social causes.

Synopsis

BOOK ONE: THE FAMILY

Professor Godfrey St. Peter has let his family talk him into building a new house in their university town. He has sufficient funds now, provided by the prize awarded to his eight-volume work, *The Spanish Adventurers in North America;* as a result, family members can move from the old, creaking house they have lived in for more than 20 years. Yet St. Peter does not want to leave that house, particularly the third-floor study, where he wrote his opus—despite the room's shabbiness, despite the gas stove with no flue, requiring that he keep the window open even in the coldest winter. The old sewing woman, Augusta, with whom he feels a special affinity, often used the room for her dressmaking. St. Peter tells Augusta he has arranged with the landlord to keep using the house, although people might think, he acknowledges, that he and his wife have separated.

The professor has two daughters and two sons-in-law. The elder daughter, Rosamond, was once engaged to a student, Tom Outland, who was killed in WORLD WAR I; Outland, the inventor of an important aeronautical device—although he never patented it or developed it—had named Rosamond in his will. She since married an engineer, Louie Marsellus, who has taken over the device and marketed it; the two of them have become wealthy as a result. St. Peter feels resentment against Marsellus, since he exploited the invention of the dead man; his and Rosamond's displays of wealth are considered excessive. The professor also finds Marsellus shallow and trivial,

although the man is pleasant and generous; his "Semitic" appearance is noted by the author. The professor's wife, Lillian, still handsome and charming—although no longer interested in her husband's doings—has taken up, almost flirtatiously, with her sons-in-law; she defends them against all criticism.

On Christmas morning, months after the family moves to the new house, St. Peter is still inhabiting his private refuge. He joins the family for dinner; Marsellus, amidst banter about the baleful effects of PROHIBITION, announces that he is taking the family to France the next summer, where they can drink Burgundy. St. Peter thinks once more of the dead Tom Outland, whose ingenuity has bestowed so much fortune on his daughter—although he recognizes, as always, that it was Marsellus's efforts that made the fortune possible. He recalls how he first met Outland when the young man had come to see him about getting into the university without proper prerequisites. Outland had grown up in New Mexico, adopted by a family after his parents had died crossing the prairie; his education had been mainly from the tutoring of a priest. When asked about money, Tom acknowledged a bank account in New Mexico, although he said it was money he could not touch. Gradually, Outland became almost a member of the family.

Meanwhile, as Marsellus describes his plans for their summer holiday in France, St. Peter knows he is not going to go. Just as his wife and daughters used to spend their summers in Colorado, leaving him behind to work, so they, along with his sons-in-law, will now go to Europe, again leaving him behind. St. Peter muses that sons-in-law were ordained to take the husbands' place when the husbands were no longer lovers. He is planning to spend part of the summer editing Tom Outland's diary; Lillian had always been suspicious of Outland, particularly about a mysterious friend named Rodney, as well as about his untouchable bank account. Now comes the story that Tom once told St. Peter.

BOOK TWO: TOM OUTLAND'S STORY

Tom, working as a messenger for the railroad, sees a fireman, Rodney Blake, winning a large sum of money in a poker game; understanding that the man is intoxicated, he follows him home to protect him. The next morning Tom persuades Rodney to put the money in a bank; soon the two men become friends. Later, they find jobs with a cattle company, engaging to ride the range during the summer, then to take the cattle to a winter camp. The camp is near a mesa, an isolated plateau, to which cattle sometimes escape by crossing a dangerous river; yet no man, the foreman tells them, has ever made it to the mesa. The next spring, Roddy and Tom make their way there and find a city of ruins, abandoned dwellings where Native Americans once lived; this civilization had been wiped out, perhaps by an epidemic, perhaps by enemies. Tom knows he must go to Washington, to the Smithsonian Institution, to report these findings; archaeologists must come to this city and study it. Roddy gives him money to cover the trip. Yet when Tom gets to Washington, he meets only frustration; museum officials and government officials are not interested. But on his return to New Mexico, he finds a new problem; Roddy has brought a German collector to the mesa and sold him all its treasures, receiving a large amount of money. Furious, Tom exclaims that their findings were never to be tainted by commerce; Roddy says the money is in the bank under Tom's name for the purpose of his going to college, of his making his way in the world. The men quarrel, and Roddy stalks off—never to be seen again; Tom's efforts to find him are to no avail. The next year, Tom shows up at the professor's university.

BOOK THREE: THE PROFESSOR

St. Peter recalls the trip he made with Tom to the Southwest, a journey that brought immediacy to his ongoing research on the Spanish adventurers. But then the war came, and Tom was dead. St. Peter understands that the young inventor escaped the legal tangles and complexities that commercializing his device would have entailed, complexities that his son-in-law Marsellus undertook, reaping the rewards as well.

His family away in Europe, the professor spends his summer in the attic room in the old house, realizing that he must be alone, that he cannot live with his family again; he is drifting away from all domestic and social relations. On an autumn afternoon, just before his family returns, he lights the stove and lies down—and awakes to realize that the window has fallen shut and the room is full of gas. He lies still: What if he fails to get up to open the window?

Awaking again, he finds that Augusta, the sewing woman, is sitting by his couch. She has pulled him out of the room and saved his life. As he lies there, knowing that his family will be arriving shortly, he feels no obligation toward them; moreover, they have no need of him, preoccupied as they are with their own affairs. Life is possible without delight, he realizes, and he will learn to live that way.

Critical Reception

Although generally receptive, reviewers found problems with the structure of the novel, objecting to the story-within-a-story, finding a severe disconnect between the separate narratives. The novel was accused of leaving too many loose ends, demonstrating an "odd episodic brusqueness"—although reviewers expressed admiration for the character of St. Peter, for novel's basic core of human truth. *The Nation* reviewer concluded reluctantly that the book was a disappointment; the professor, he wrote, is admirably conceived, but Outland is an unconvincing character, "almost an abstraction." Critic Stuart Sherman, focusing on St. Peter, bolstered the view of Cather as a writer with a conservative agenda; Sherman, who had once found the work of Theodore DREISER immoral, described St. Peter as lamenting the passing of a way of life, saying a reluctant farewell "to a vanishing order of civilization."

Critics have since attempted to reconcile the disparate sections of the novel, noting that St. Peter's long-term scholarly subject matter, the Spanish explorers of North America, provides the link between his genteel existence in a university town and Outland's adventure in New Mexico. A more difficult task is to reconcile the abrupt switch between the omniscient narration of Books One and Three and the first-person narration of Book Two. Yet critics have spoken of Cather's purposeful ironic contrast—between two segments of the professor's life, between two civilizations, between the idealistic Outland and the materialistic Marsellus. The professor once rejoiced in the creativity and high-mindedness of his young student; yet the student's invention is now exploited, providing prosperity to family members whose interests are petty, whose existence no longer seems compatible with that of the professor.

progressive movement

A variety of early-20th-century reform groups can be placed under the "progressive" heading. Their efforts, ranging from charitable uplift to ANTITRUST activities to women's suffrage agitation, were reformist rather than revolutionary. The movement has been called the result of a leftover Protestant zeal, in that the nation's middle class, although increasingly secular, was said to have retained remnants of its original religious ardor. A more immediate spur was the MUCKRAKING journalism of the day, serving to counteract the SOCIAL DARWINISM that continued to flourish in some quarters. The progressive movement came to an end after WORLD WAR I; two of its outcomes were a moralistic, Protestant-inspired PROHIBITION and a democratically inspired women's suffrage.

Progressive Party

The first Progressive Party, popularly called the Bull Moose Party, was established in 1911 by Republican Party dissidents; it took its name from the PROGRESSIVE MOVEMENT of the era. Denouncing the renomination of William Howard TAFT at the Republican convention in Chicago in June of 1912, supporters of Theodore ROOSEVELT gathered in August of that year at the Chicago Coliseum, nominating the former president to run against Taft and Democrat Woodrow WILSON. Women's suffrage and other social reforms were on the platform, and Jane ADDAMS seconded Roosevelt's nomination, becoming the first woman to take on that political role. Addams also led a suffrage parade, starting at the ART INSTITUTE and marching

southward toward the Coliseum; others in the parade included Margery CURREY and Tennessee MITCHELL. As a result of the split in Republican vote, Wilson won the presidency.

In 1924, the SOCIALIST PARTY OF AMERICA, the AMERICAN FEDERATION OF LABOR, and other groups sponsored a new Progressive Party, naming Senator Robert La Follette of Wisconsin as presidential candidate; farmers and organized labor supported the ticket, which advocated—as had previous nonmainstream platforms—public ownership of railroads and utilities. La Follette won 5 million votes but lost to Republican Calvin COOLIDGE.

A third Progressive Party, challenging the reelection of Democrat Harry Truman, was formed in 1948.

Prohibition

The period in United States history known as Prohibition began January 16, 1920; the Eighteenth Amendment, ratified the previous year, outlawed the manufacture, sale, and transportation of alcoholic beverages. Enforcement measures were provided by the Volstead Act, passed by Congress over the veto of President Woodrow WILSON, in 1919; the law empowered federal agents to investigate and prosecute violators. The enactment of such a far-reaching measure has been attributed to a backlash against immigrants and Catholics; 27 states, including most of the South, had already passed antiliquor legislation. Further antialcohol sentiment arose during WORLD WAR I, since most of the nation's brewers were understood to be of German origin.

The forerunner of Prohibition was the 19th-century temperance movement, represented by such organizations as the PROHIBITION PARTY and the ANTI-SALOON LEAGUE; Vachel LINDSAY spoke for the Anti-Saloon League in downstate Illinois early in the 20th century. On the other side, Edgar Lee MASTERS's father, a lawyer, fought temperance agitation in the 1880s in his small town of Lewiston, Illinois; Clarence DARROW spoke against Prohibition throughout the Midwest in the early 1900s.

The law, once passed, could never be successfully implemented. It gave rise to organized crime on an unprecedented scale; underworld figures became entangled with political figures, and a new criminal culture, cutting across many levels of society, appeared in the nation's cities. Chicago was unique in its competitive bootlegging activities and, as a result, hosted the highest number of gangland murders; the Thompson submachine gun, or tommy gun, invented during WORLD WAR I, is said to have found its first underworld use by a South Side Chicago gang in 1923. A member of the Chicago Crime Commission, a private group organized to fight mob activities, coined the phrase *public enemies* in 1930; the gangster movie *The Public Enemy*, starring James Cagney, appeared the following year. As public sentiment turned against the law, as even one-time supporters such as John D. ROCKEFELLER deserted the antialcohol cause—and as the GREAT DEPRESSION changed American priorities to economic issues, such as unemployment—Prohibition ended late in 1933 with the passage of the Twenty-first Amendment; the repeal of Prohibition was the only instance in which a constitutional amendment was overturned by another amendment.

Prohibition forms a backdrop, in varying degrees, to fiction written during the 1920s. In Willa CATHER's 1925 novel, THE PROFESSOR'S HOUSE, a character at a Christmas dinner begins "the usual Prohibition lament," although he acknowledges that he can get hard liquor; it is those who like fine wines who have problems. At the very end of the novel, the professor, resigned to a diminished life, supposes he must also be resigned, "in a Prohibition country," to live without sherry.

In a Sherwood ANDERSON story published the same year, "The Return," collected in DEATH IN THE WOODS, a small-town doctor obtains liquor by writing prescriptions for a medicinal tonic; the characters later go to a roadhouse where "drinks could be had if you knew the ropes." Another story in the collection, "A Meeting South," tells of a southerner whose father employs a man to make whisky for the family; the father never sells the liquor, thus remaining, he believes, within a reasonable application of the law.

Prohibition also presented an entire new subject matter for fiction—the world of crime and bootlegging, along with the violence that goes with it. MacKinlay KANTOR's 1928 novel, DIVERSEY, offers an early version of gangland activity; it was followed the next year by W. R. BURNETT's *Little Caesar*. Soon the new genre of gangster cinema would arise as well in Hollywood, as Burnett and Ben HECHT went west to impart their Chicago-based crime knowledge to screenwriting.

Prohibition Party

Gathering delegates from 20 states, this antialcohol political party was founded in Chicago in 1869. Initially entering state elections, it ran its first presidential candidate in 1872. Although never achieving the effectiveness of the ANTI-SALOON LEAGUE—an organization working within existing political groups, supporting antialcohol candidates of either party—the Prohibition Party is said to have cost the Republicans the presidency in 1884; in the state of New York, the party took sufficient votes from the Republican candidate to throw the state to Democrat Grover CLEVELAND, giving Democrats the national election. In the 1880s, Frances E. WILLARD, president of the WOMAN'S CHRISTIAN TEMPERANCE UNION, persuaded her organization to support the Prohibition Party, believing that neither Republicans nor Democrats would endorse a temperance platform.

Prokofiev, Sergei
(1891–1953) *20th-century Russian composer*

Prokofiev came to Chicago in 1921, overseeing and conducting the world premiere of his opera THE LOVE FOR THREE ORANGES, commissioned by the CHICAGO OPERA COMPANY. Born in the Ukraine, he left Russia in 1918 after the revolution and arrived in America as an established composer; the premiere of *The Love for Three Oranges* was a triumph for then–company manager Mary GARDEN. Spending most of the next decade in Paris, he returned to the Soviet Union in 1936, where he composed some of his best-known pieces, including *Peter and the Wolf,* the ballet *Romeo and Juliet,* and movie scores, working for the director Sergei Eisenstein. In 1948, along with fellow composer Dmitri Shostakovich, he was denounced for producing subversive music, and his work was banned. He died at the age of 61, on the same day as his denouncer, Soviet ruler Joseph Stalin.

Provident Hospital

An African-American hospital founded in 1891 by Daniel Hale WILLIAMS, the Provident Hospital and Training School became the first black-owned hospital in the country. Offering previously unavailable opportunities for black physicians and staff, it provided also at the instigation of Fannie B. WILLIAMS, the city's first nursing school for African-American women. As the black population in Chicago expanded, the facility, which originally had room for 12 beds, moved twice to larger quarters. By the 1950s, as other hospitals opened their doors to African-American doctors and patients, Provident became a less important institution in the black community. Closing as a private facility in 1987, it reopened under Cook County auspices in 1993.

Provincetown Players

Two of the founders of this important group within the LITTLE THEATRE MOVEMENT were Susan GLASPELL and George Cram COOK. Both were from Iowa and lived in Chicago before moving on to New York. Another founding member was Chicago-born Hutchins HAPGOOD. First performing in Provincetown, on Massachusetts's Cape Cod, the Players made use of a home rented by Hapgood in July 1915; the productions included a short comedy, *Suppressed Desire,* by Glaspell and Cook, satirizing psychoanalysis. In July 1916, the Players, putting together a makeshift playhouse called the Wharf Theater, staged Eugene O'NEILL's one-act *Bound East for Cardiff;* the production, presenting the newly discovered playwright, made the group's reputation. The Players also staged Glaspell's Iowa-based play *Trifles,* later to become the story, "A JURY OF HER

PEERS." In the fall of 1916, the group moved to New York City, producing its first plays in November of that year. Among the productions were works by Floyd DELL, as well as by Glaspell and Cook; among the cast members was the Chicago actress Elaine HYMAN. Joining the group a year later, playing the female lead in a play by Dell, was the already recognized poet Edna St. Vincent Millay. When O'Neill chose other organizations to present his work, the Players temporarily suspended operations; Glaspell and Cook left for Greece in 1922.

Puckett, Lydia   *See SPOON RIVER ANTHOLOGY.*

Pullman

The country's first planned industrial town was built for workers at the PULLMAN PALACE CAR COMPANY. The town of Pullman, located south of Chicago but later incorporated within its limits, received its first residents in 1881. As the population grew to about 8,000, the community included a hotel, shops, churches, parks, a school, a library, a theater, and recreational facilities. George M. PULLMAN saw himself as progressive for building homes for his workers, which contrasted with the chaotic, unsanitary slum housing of PACKINGTOWN, where the stockyard workers lived. His infrastructure included paved streets and sewer lines, and brick houses featured indoor plumbing and indoor gas—although a hierarchy prevailed; the company's skilled craftsmen lived in large, comfortable structures, while the semiskilled workers were housed in multiple-flat buildings. Many residents resented what they saw as paternalism, accusing Pullman of using the town as a means of social control. No workingman's saloon existed; the luxurious Florence Hotel, named for the owner's daughter, provided a bar for wealthy visitors, but was not considered appropriate for laborers. Union organizers and political speakers were not welcome. Labor unrest flared up during the PULLMAN STRIKE of 1894, exacerbated by the company's lowering of the workers' wages, but not their rents. In 1898, a year after Pullman died, the Illinois Supreme Court ordered the divestiture of the town from company control, and the houses were eventually sold to individual owners. Today, more than 800 homes remain; the area was listed as a National Landmark District in 1971.

Pullman, George M.

(1831–1897) *inventor of the railroad sleeping car, creator of the planned industrial town of Pullman*

Born in upstate New York, Pullman started as a woodworker, then moved to Chicago to engage in the building-raising program of the late 1850s. The purpose of the program was to rid streets of swampy conditions and make way for the construction of sewers. His next project was converting old passenger coaches into sleeping cars, making rail travel comfortable for the first time, eventually revolutionizing travel worldwide. In 1865, he built the *Pioneer*, a luxuriously upholstered and ornamented railroad sleeping car; his public-relations coup was to have the car convey the body of President Abraham LINCOLN, assassinated in April of that year, on the last leg of its journey, from Chicago to SPRINGFIELD, Illinois. The PULLMAN PALACE CAR COMPANY was soon prospering, later followed by PULLMAN, Illinois, the planned workers' town.

After the 1894 PULLMAN STRIKE, a presidential commission condemned Pullman for unfair policies against his workers; in the midst of a suit forcing his company to divest itself of ownership of the town, he died of heart failure. Robert Todd LINCOLN assumed presidency of the company.

Pullman Palace Car Company

A manufacturer of railroad sleeping and dining cars, this pioneering company was established by Chicago builder George M. PULLMAN in 1867. Two years previously, after the assassination of President Abraham LINCOLN, Pullman had convinced a Chicago committee that the car he was developing should carry the president's body to its final resting place in SPRINGFIELD, Illinois. Pullman subsequently put his car on display, reaping wide public-

ity. Later, in the 1880s, he developed the company town of PULLMAN for his workers.

At a time when rail travel was uncomfortable by modern standards—and as rail travel was becoming transcontinental—Pullman advertised the comfort and luxury of his sleeping-car accommodations. His firm developed not only sleeping berths, but also vestibules between cars, allowing passengers to move readily from one car to another—including the Pullman-built dining cars, observation cars, and private cars; the company also manufactured freight cars, refrigerator cars, and urban streetcars. The firm did not sell its products, but leased them to the railroads. When Pullman died in 1897, Robert Todd LINCOLN, the son of the president, an attorney for the company, became the firm's president.

Historically, the porters, or service workers, on the Pullman cars were African American; by the 1920s, the firm was the largest private employer of black workers in the country. For decades the Pullman company resisted attempts by the porters to unionize; in 1925, A. Philip RANDOLPH organized the BROTHERHOOD OF SLEEPING CAR PORTERS, winning concessions from the company 12 years later, in 1937. The factory closed in 1958.

Whenever rail travel is mentioned in the fiction of the era, Pullman cars, often named specifically, become a generic term. In Theodore DREISER's 1900 novel, *SISTER CARRIE*, George HURSTWOOD reads in the paper about old acquaintances, noting that "Pullmans were hauling them to and fro about the land." The reference implies opulence or luxury; in Dreiser's *THE TITAN*, Frank COWPERWOOD, traveling to Chicago from Philadelphia, spends two nights "in the gaudy Pullman," featuring "an over-elaboration of plush and tortured glass." An Edna FERBER story from the early 1920s, "Not a Day over Twenty-One," collected in *GIGOLO*, features a New York actress invited to Hollywood, all expenses paid, finding herself traveling luxuriously in a Pullman drawing room.

Pullman strike

Taking place in the aftermath of the PANIC OF 1893, the nation's worst economic downturn up to that time, this labor struggle involved both factory and railroad workers. The immediate cause was wage cuts at the PULLMAN PALACE CAR COMPANY, reducing salaries of workers by 25 percent—while yet failing to lower the rents charged for those living in the town of PULLMAN; rents continued to be deducted from the employees' paychecks. The workers struck in May, having recently joined the new AMERICAN RAILWAY UNION, led by Eugene V. DEBS; the strike spread, tying up railroads across the country and interrupting mail service. George M. PULLMAN refused to negotiate—refusing, too, an offer of mediation from social activist Jane ADDAMS—and hired scabs, or nonunion members, to take over the work; the resulting riots burned trains and destroyed rail yards. As a result, President Grover CLEVELAND, overriding the wishes of Illinois Governor John Peter ALTGELD, sent in federal troops from FORT SHERIDAN, north of the city, to break the strike; he declared that rail service must resume and the United States mail be delivered. The union conceded defeat early in July, having gained no concessions from Pullman; more than 30 people were killed in what remains Chicago's deadliest labor action. Robert Todd LINCOLN, lawyer and son of the martyred president, served at the time on the Pullman company's board of directors, supporting Pullman throughout. Debs went to jail for six months in Woodstock, northwest of Chicago, despite a defense by Clarence DARROW. The strike and its aftermath led ultimately to the founding of the SOCIALIST PARTY OF AMERICA.

Putt, Hod   *See SPOON RIVER ANTHOLOGY.*

Q

"Queer"   *See* WINESBURG, OHIO.

Quinn Chapel A.M.E. Church

The first African-American church in Chicago, named after Paul Quinn, an early bishop of the African Methodist Episcopal Church, the congregation officially organized in July 1847. In its early years, the church served as a station on the Underground Railroad, helping slaves to escape to Canada. The small African-American settlement in Chicago at the time consisted of both freemen and fugitive slaves; by 1860, the black population reached close to a thousand.

R

race riots

Defined historically as conflicts instigated by whites against blacks, race riots occurred in many areas of the country during the summer of 1919. In Chicago several days of strife began on July 27, 1919, when a black child swimming in LAKE MICHIGAN was said to have encroached on a "white" beach. Thirty-eight lives were lost over a period of several days. Many of the white rioters came from PACKINGTOWN, home of the stockyard workers; a continuing issue was the packers' bringing in black workers to work more cheaply than white workers—an issue foreshadowed in Upton SINCLAIR's THE JUNGLE, the 1906 novel that depicts black workers being brought in as scabs, or strike breakers.

Carl SANDBURG, who had interviewed residents of BRONZEVILLE shortly before the event, wrote a series of articles collected as THE CHICAGO RACE RIOTS, JULY 1919. His poem "Hoodlums," dated July 29, 1919, appearing in SMOKE AND STEEL the following year, sets forth the rioters' chant, "let us kill, kill, kill." James T. FARRELL gives a young white man's view of the riots in The Young Manhood of Studs Lonigan, published in 1934.

Radical Republicans

This segment of the early Republican Party was primarily led by easterners. Before the CIVIL WAR, the Radical Republicans formed the most fervently abolitionist, or antislavery, faction; afterward, they were the most zealous in pushing RECONSTRUCTION legislation, granting legal rights to African Americans. In 1868, Radical Republicans impeached Abraham LINCOLN's successor in the presidency, Andrew Johnson of Tennessee, accusing Johnson of pursuing conciliatory policies toward the South; Johnson remained in office by the margin of only one Senate vote. Active in the impeachment process was Illinois Radical Republican John A. Logan, former Union army general, founder of the veterans' organization, the GRAND ARMY OF THE REPUBLIC.

Rainey, Gertrude "Ma"
(1886–1939) *singer*

Born in Georgia, Rainey toured on the black VAUDEVILLE circuit in the 1920s and was signed to a contract with Paramount Records after appearing at the Monogram Theater in BRONZEVILLE. Paramount was a white-owned company producing "race" records, recordings by and marketed to African Americans. Rainey, dubbed "the mother of the blues," recorded nearly 100 songs for Paramount in Chicago between 1923 and 1928, among them "Ma Rainey's Black Bottom" and "See See Rider," also known as "C.C. Rider"; Joe OLIVER and Jelly Roll MORTON recorded for the company as well. The drama by August Wilson, *Ma Rainey's Black Bottom*, opening in New York in

1984, is set in a Chicago recording studio in 1927. Rainey was inducted into the Rock and Roll Hall of Fame in 1990.

Rainey, Sue

A character in Sherwood ANDERSON's novel WINDY McPHERSON'S SON, Sue, heir of an arms manufacturing company, rejects any flaunting of her wealth, believing instead in giving service to mankind. She marries Chicago businessman Sam McPHERSON, and they agree to produce children who will in turn render service to mankind. After several stillbirths, Sue turns increasingly to social causes, and the rift between her and Sam continues to widen; she leaves him when he expands his business empire and forces her father out of the firm. Sam later leaves the moneymaking world, turning to a life of vagabonding. When he comes upon a woman who is neglecting her three children, he takes the children to Sue, who accepts them as her own; she accepts Sam's return as well. Sue is not portrayed as a sympathetic character; Sam's return to her is presented as a heroic act on his part, as a surrender, as an acceptance of confinement.

Raisa, Rosa
(1893–1963) *soprano*

An international star, singing the lead in the premiere of Giacomo Puccini's posthumous opera *Turandot* in 1926, Raisa spent many years with the CHICAGO OPERA COMPANY. Born Rose Burschstein in Bialystok, Poland, making her American debut in 1913, she first came to Chicago later that year; she sang regularly with the Chicago Opera Company, later the Chicago Civic Opera, between 1916 and 1932. Raisa was an early opera singer to make recordings, recreating her roles in Giuseppe Verdi's *Aida* and *Il Trovatore* and other popular operas. After her retirement, she and her husband, baritone Giacomo Rimini, established a vocal training school in Chicago, housed in the 1950s in the FINE ARTS BUILDING. Raisa died in California at the age of 70.

Rand McNally and Company

In 1856, William Rand opened a print shop in the area that was to become the LOOP. First producing railroad tickets, he was joined by Andrew McNally; they soon began printing railroad timetables and railroad maps. In the late 1880s, the growing Rand McNally company engaged the firm of BURNHAM AND ROOT to design its headquarters; the building became the world's first all-steel-frame structure, completed in 1890. With the development of the automobile, Rand McNally produced the first road map in 1904 and the first road atlas in 1924; the company soon became the world's leading producer of maps and cartographic materials. In 1952, the firm relocated to the northern suburb of Skokie.

Randolph, A. Phillip
(1889–1979) *social activist, founder of the Brotherhood of Sleeping Car Porters*

Born in Crescent City, Florida, the son of a minister, Randolph grew up in Jacksonville, then moved to New York City in 1911 at the age of 22. In November 1917, he and Chandler OWEN founded the monthly magazine *Messenger*, which would become a voice of black SOCIALISM. Addressing the recent American entry into WORLD WAR I, the periodical claimed that blacks should not fight in the conflict; it opposed the war also in principle, as did other socialist publications, claiming that it was a capitalists' war, fought for the benefit of profiteers. In 1925, Randolph established the BROTHERHOOD OF SLEEPING CAR PORTERS, unionizing African-American workers who had been excluded from other labor organizations; Chicago, home of the PULLMAN PALACE CAR COMPANY, boasted the largest union chapter. During World War II, Randolph mounted a campaign to end discrimination in the war industries; in 1963, he was one of the organizers of the March on Washington, introducing Martin Luther King Jr. Still affirming the socialist belief that issues of race were subsumed under issues of economics, he met criticism during rise of black nationalism. Randolph died in 1979 at the age of 90.

Randolph, Basil

This character appears in Henry B. FULLER's novel BERTRAM COPE'S YEAR. A gentleman stockbroker in his mid-50s, holding a position gained through family inheritance, Randolph is the polar opposite of Fuller's striving businessmen. His sensibilities are artistic, and he spends little time with his firm, whose partners are said to prefer his nonparticipation. As a result, he is free to cultivate young men— although they often seem ungrateful and treat their elders carelessly. Randolph's interest in Bertram COPE is complicated by Cope's involvement with another man, the young Arthur LEMOYNE, who, although living at the time in Wisconsin, dictates that Cope break off a weekend trip with the man he considers a rival. Randolph later finds employment for Lemoyne as a favor for Cope, knowing that he will get little in return. When Cope leaves for the East, the older man ends up in his usual solitary state, understanding that as he ages the young will be increasingly uninterested in him.

"Ready to Kill"   See CHICAGO POEMS.

realism

This style of literary expression, associated with both fiction and drama, realism became the advanced literary mode of late 19th-century America. Focusing on the details of everyday life, rejecting the past for the present, realism superseded the often-exotic romantic fiction—exotic in both place and time—of mid-19th-century writers Nathaniel Hawthorne and Herman Melville. The first major exponents of realism were William Dean HOWELLS and Henry James; Howells, serving as editor of two influential journals, *Atlantic Monthly* and *Harper's Magazine*, became an outspoken advocate of fiction dealing with the details of daily life—business matters, social arrangements, day-to-day concerns. Unlike the more dogma-driven NATURALISM, realism avoided the pessimistic assumption that man is helpless in the face of social or economic forces; it avoided also the naturalistic emphasis on the sordid or brutal, maintaining a middle-class perspective. In the Midwest, Hamlin GARLAND, a sometime disciple of Howells, chose the term VERITISM, rejecting what he considered the timid and genteel realism of the East.

By the third decade of the 20th century, the issue of realism no longer seemed vital or significant. Its underlying tenets had been accepted, and the issue now turned into a straightforward matter of censorship—the matter of how explicitly the details of daily life could be set forth; the NEW YORK SOCIETY FOR THE SUPPRESSION OF VICE continued its zealous overseeing of literature and its sales. Yet because realism had been accepted, it also, as a result, came to be rejected; among the voices repudiating realism was that of Sherwood ANDERSON, insisting that his fiction, although condemned by moralists and would-be censors, was far from "realistic." In his 1924 "A Note on Realism," collected in *SHERWOOD ANDERSON'S NOTEBOOK*, Anderson declares that a writer holding a notebook—that is, a writer faithfully transcribing the life he sees around him—is "a bad workman"; his work is flawed because he distrusts his imagination. Denying that *WINESBURG, OHIO* presents an exact portrait of small-town life, Anderson insists on his own imaginative re-creation: "A stroke of my pen saves me from realism."

Reconstruction

This post–CIVIL WAR period in the South began when Congress, led by RADICAL REPUBLICANS, passed the Reconstruction Acts of 1867. The acts mandated new state constitutions and required ratification by states of the Fourteenth Amendment, which gave legal protection to African Americans. Southern states were divided into military districts, commanded by officers supervising the carrying out of the legislation. In Congress, conflict arose when the successor to the assassinated President Abraham LINCOLN, Andrew Johnson, took a lenient stance toward the South; he was brought to impeachment by Radical Republicans in 1868, barely avoiding removal from office. In 1870, the Fifteenth Amendment was enacted, giving African Americans the right to vote. Resentment among ex-Confederates over these measures led to resistance, including the formation of the secret white-supremacy organization the Ku Klux Klan. When the last federal troops left the South in 1877, Jim Crow laws, mandating restriction and segregation, were put into place; lynching and terrorism went unpunished. Soon-to-be-Chicagoan Ida B. WELLS became a national crusader against lynching, and early in the 20th century the CHICAGO DEFENDER began advocating that African Americans move north.

Reed, John
(1887–1920) *writer, activist*

A founder of the Communist Labor Party in America, Reed is the only American buried in the Kremlin, the central area of Moscow. Born in Portland, Oregon, graduating from Harvard University in 1910, he moved to New York the following year, writing for the journal THE MASSES. Harriet MONROE published his poem "Sangar," honoring the MUCKRAKING journalist Lincoln STEFFENS, in POETRY in December 1912. His long poem, *The Day in Bohemia, or Life Among the Artists,* appeared in 1913.

Reed subsequently served as a journalist reporting on the Mexican revolution, WORLD WAR I, and the Russian revolution; his *Ten Days That Shook the World,* an eyewitness account of events in Russia, became a best-seller in 1919. He died of typhus in Moscow the following year. In 1929, the American Communist Party named its network of writers' organizations the John Reed Clubs; Richard WRIGHT and Nelson ALGREN were among members of the Chicago chapter.

Reedy, William Marion
(1862–1920) *publisher of* Reedy's Mirror *of St. Louis*

Initiating his periodical as the *Sunday Mirror* in 1891, later changing the name to *Reedy's Mirror,* Reedy became a crucial figure in the career of poet Edgar Lee MASTERS. Reedy's weekly literary magazine gave first publication to poems that later appeared in SPOON RIVER ANTHOLOGY. Reedy and Masters had begun to correspond in 1907, when the poet had submitted work to the periodical; at the time Masters was practicing law in Chicago. Reedy suggested that he look into the GREEK ANTHOLOGY, the collection of epigrammatic classical verse. *Reedy's Mirror* also published work by Vachel LINDSAY and Carl SANDBURG, as well as St. Louis-born poet Sarah TEASDALE. Masters, becoming a personal friend of the editor, called Reedy "the Literary Boss of the Middle West." The periodical folded after Reedy died suddenly at the Democratic National Convention in San Francisco.

Reefy, Doctor   *See* WINESBURG, OHIO: "Paper Pills" *and* "Death."

regionalism

Fiction that makes use of local materials has been called regionalism; the term is often given negative connotations, implying a lack of universal values or broadly based appeal. Many midwestern writers have been labeled, to their discredit, as regional writers, including Edward EGGLESTON, Hamlin GARLAND, Zona GALE—and even Carl SANDBURG, once he became more the poet of the PRAIRIE than the city. In contemporary times writers are less likely to be labeled, and denigrated, as regionalists; a writer's grounding in a particular locale—in an era of mass-media penetration—is no longer considered disadvantageous.

Remington, Frederic
(1861–1909) *artist*

Known today as a western artist, Remington served also as a journalist; his reporting on labor agitation included the 1892 HOMESTEAD STRIKE and the 1894 PULLMAN STRIKE. Born in upstate New York, after traveling west as a young man, he illustrated the serialization in *Century Magazine* of Theodore ROOSEVELT's *Ranch Life and the Hunting Trail,* appearing in 1888. During the Homestead Strike, Remington published sketches of the conflict in

Frank Leslie's Illustrated Weekly, depicting strikers unsympathetically, as disorderly rioters. During the Pullman Strike, his illustrations for *Harper's Weekly* were accompanied by a description of workers as a "malodorous crowd of foreign trash." In 1897, sent to Cuba by William Randolph Hearts's *New York Journal*—and requesting permission to leave, finding the city of Havana peaceful—Remington received the famous, perhaps apocryphal, telegram in reply: "You furnish the pictures, I'll furnish the war"; Hearst's sensationalistic journalism has been accused of fomenting the SPANISH-AMERICAN WAR. Remington died suddenly of appendicitis at the age of 48. His western material, celebrated for action scenes—depicting Indians, soldiers, and cowboys, riding on spirited horses—portrays Indians as following a noble but doomed way of life; Remington's sympathies with Native Americans contrasted with his hostility to immigrant groups. Hamlin GARLAND's 1923 collection of western fiction, *The Book of the American Indian*, featured Remington illustrations.

"Respectability"   See WINESBURG, OHIO.

"The Return"   See DEATH IN THE WOODS.

"The Return of a Private"   See MAIN-TRAV-ELLED ROADS.

revolt from the village

This phrase applies to critical writing about small-town America. As Chicago and other cities drew migrants from rural areas, writers turned against their native towns, finding them to be places of repression, narrow-mindedness, and hypocrisy. The small town or village no longer represented to the world, as it once had, community or togetherness, but rather isolation and despair. Edgar Watson HOWE's THE STORY OF A COUNTRY TOWN, published in 1883, provided an early example; Hamlin GARLAND's MAIN-TRAVELLED ROADS, published eight years later, presented a

harsher, more devastating scene. Edgar Lee MAS-TERS's *SPOON RIVER ANTHOLOGY*, reaching a large readership in 1915, became a prime force in the phenomenon—even as it rendered village disharmony in poetic form. Influenced by *Spoon River*, Sherwood ANDERSON's 1919 collection of stories, WINESBURG, OHIO, portrayed an oppressive village from which its young man must escape; the next year, Sinclair LEWIS published MAIN STREET, the first of the Minnesotan's best-selling savage portraits of small-town life. Critic Carl Van Doren provided a name for the movement in 1921; his article, "The Revolt from the Village: 1920," appearing in *The Nation*, declared Masters as initiator, Anderson and Lewis as followers, of a movement in which writers turned, often vengefully, against their origins.

Rhodes, Thomas   See SPOON RIVER ANTHOLOGY.

Richardson, Henry Hobson
(1838–1886) *architect*

Working mainly in the East, Richardson was known for his Romanesque style, featuring thick walls, stone arches, and grand proportions. Toward the end of his life, he designed several Chicago buildings, creating what many observers considered his greatest work, the massive Wholesale Store for MARSHALL FIELD AND COMPANY; completed in 1887, extending a full city block, the structure was seen as an influence on ADLER AND SULLIVAN's AUDITORIUM BUILDING, built two years later. Yet by the 1920s, the Field wholesale division, selling to merchants throughout the Midwest, had become unprofitable, and the Wholesale Store was demolished in 1930. One of Richardson's last commissions was the 1887 John J. Glessner house on Prairie Avenue, his only surviving Midwest structure.

Richmond, Seth   See WINESBURG, OHIO: "The Thinker."

"The Right to Grief"   See CHICAGO POEMS.

Riley, James Whitcomb
(1849–1916) *poet*

Known for folksy humor and sentimental evocations of youth, Riley, "the Hoosier poet," was the most popular American versifier of the late 19th century. Born in Greenfield, Indiana, making use of DIALECT WRITING, he evoked old swimming holes, barefoot boys, and the Indiana countryside. His children's poems, "Little Orphant Annie" and "The Raggedy Man," made him a rival of his contemporary, Eugene FIELD; like Field, he wrote much of his verse for newspapers, including the oft-quoted "When the Frost is on the Punkin." His best-known collection is *"The Old Swimmin' Hole" and 'Leven More Poems*, published in 1883.

Hamlin GARLAND, in his 1921 autobiography, A DAUGHTER OF THE MIDDLE BORDER, speaks of Riley's Indiana country as commonplace, as "flat, unkempt"—and yet declares that the poet drew from it "the sweetest honey of song." Harriet MONROE, in her posthumous autobiography of 1938, recalls Riley as a reminder of a past era; comparing his rural Indiana to Edgar Lee MASTERS's rural Illinois, she finds Riley's region smaller, more restricted, less universal.

Ripley, Jane

This character appears in Hamlin GARLAND's story "Mrs. Ripley's Trip," collected in MAIN-TRAVELLED ROADS, Mrs. Ripley is the Iowa farm wife who decides, after nearly a quarter of a century on the plains, to undertake a visit to her family in New York State. She becomes a determined woman who carries out her plan, allowing no opposition; when the trip is over, she calmly resumes her duties on the Iowa farm. Mrs. Ripley is the figure in this volume who approaches LOCAL COLOR status; that is, although working in harsh farm conditions all her life, she appears sentimentalized when compared with Garland's devastated Agnes DINGMAN in "At the Branch Road" or the sickly wife of Timothy HASKINS in "Under the Lion's Paw."

Roberts, Rosie   *See* SPOON RIVER ANTHOLOGY.

Robinson, Edward Arlington
(1869–1935) *poet*

Although considered the first important American poet of the 20th century, Robinson followed conservative poetic practices, employing conventional rhyme and meter. Born in Maine, Robinson attended Harvard University, then published the collection *Children of the Night* in 1897, presenting characters from a fictional Tilbury Town, a stand-in for Gardiner, Maine. The Tilbury characters, including Luke Havergal and Richard Cory—the latter "went home and put a bullet through his head"—are the figures for whom Robinson is remembered today; other noted inhabitants of his town are Miniver Cheevy and Eben Flood of "Mr. Flood's Party." President Theodore ROOSEVELT, an admirer of Robinson's work, gave the poet the once-common writer's sinecure, a New York City Customs House position, which he held between 1905 and 1909. POETRY magazine published his "Eros Turannos" in March 1914. Robinson's *Collected Poems*, appearing in 1921, received a Pulitzer Prize, the first of three that the poet won in the 1920s.

Robinson, Enoch   *See* WINESBURG, OHIO: "Loneliness."

Rockefeller, John D.
(1839–1937) *American industrialist*

Born in New York State, Rockefeller moved with his family to a farm near Cleveland, Ohio, in 1853. He and his partners established an oil refinery 10 years later, partaking in the new growing industry. In 1870, he organized the Standard Oil Company of Ohio, soon to dominate the petroleum business, eventually to become part of the Standard Oil TRUST. The company become a favorite MUCKRAKING subject, beginning with Henry Demarest LLOYD's 1894 WEALTH AGAINST COMMONWEALTH, and subsequently a target of ANTITRUST activity, resulting in a Supreme Court decision that broke up the trust in 1911. Rockefeller, a lifelong Baptist, a contributor to the ANTI-SALOON LEAGUE, supplied funds for the founding of the originally Baptist UNIVERSITY OF CHICAGO in 1892.

Rodemaker, Rob

A character in Hamlin GARLAND's story "Among the Corn Rows," collected in MAIN-TRAVELLED ROADS, Rob has followed a pioneering spirit by moving from Wisconsin to a new claim in the Dakota territory. Having built his own shanty, he is pleased at is independence, feeling that he is subservient to no one. Yet he needs a wife, and he announces that he is going back to Wisconsin; he will return with a bride in 10 days. The rest of the story belongs to Julia PETERSON, the overworked Norwegian farm girl who agrees to come back to the Dakotas with him. Neither Rob nor Julia realizes the drudgery that is awaiting them.

Roe, E. P.
(1838–1888) *author*

Edward Payson Roe is the author of BARRIERS BURNED AWAY, a popular novel set during the time of the GREAT FIRE. A New York Presbyterian minister and former CIVIL WAR chaplain, Roe traveled to Chicago upon hearing news of the fire; he spent several weeks gathering on-the-spot detail. Using this background, providing a description of the devastating course of the conflagration, he fashioned a tale of moral regeneration as well; the city and its inhabitants become morally regenerated in the wake of the disaster. The novel, appearing in 1872, became a bestseller. Roe retired from the ministry two years later, believing he could evangelize more widely through his fiction; his tales of religious enlightenment made him one of the most popular writers of his day.

the Rookery

Designed by John Wellborn ROOT of BURNHAM AND ROOT, the Rookery is considered one of the most noteworthy examples of Chicago architecture. The 11-story office building, completed in 1888, continues to stand in the financial district on South LaSalle Street. Combining load-bearing exterior walls and steel-skeleton interior walls, the structure is praised for its elegant windows, spiral staircase, and two-story inner courtyard, covered with a glass roof; this "light well" provides natural light to the lobby and upper floors. The name of the building refers to a nesting place for birds; the name was inspired by pigeons living near the previous building, a temporary city hall—although it is said to come also from the word *rook*, meaning swindler, a reference to corrupt municipal politicians. Famed lawyer Clarence DARROW kept offices in this building; the fictional Curtis JADWIN, in Frank NORRIS's THE PIT, holds offices there as well.

Roosevelt, Theodore
(1858–1919) *26th president of the United States*

Roosevelt has been called the father of American imperialism, as well as the father of the conservation movement; he is known also for his pursuit of ANTITRUST actions, targeting "malefactors of great wealth." Another designation has been as the first "modern" president, in that he played to the media, achieving an international celebrity; Ben HECHT, although a longtime admirer, labeled him "a ham actor and a grandstand player." Appointed in 1897 as assistant secretary to the navy under Republican president William MCKINLEY, he became a national hero by resigning his post during the SPANISH-AMERICAN WAR and fighting in Cuba with a volunteer regiment known as the Rough Riders. Elected vice president in 1900, he came to the presidency after McKinley's assassination in 1901; at age 42, he was the youngest president up to that time. Roosevelt continued, as had McKinley, to push the country into the role of major world power; the building of the PANAMA CANAL was initiated during his time in office. In 1906, he won Nobel Peace Prize for mediating the end of the Russo-Japanese War. Among his domestic achievements was the creation of the national park system, as well as the initiating of antitrust activity. In response to the publication of Upton SINCLAIR's THE JUNGLE, exposing the meatpacking industry, he supported passage of the Pure Food and Drug Act in 1906.

Having served nearly two terms, Roosevelt declined to run for reelection in 1908, recommending William Howard TAFT for the nomination; Taft readily defeated William Jennings BRYAN. In 1912, when Taft received the Republican nomination once more, Roosevelt, deeming Taft's policies too conservative, led his followers into the newly formed PROGRESSIVE PARTY. Although supported by Jane ADDAMS at the party convention in Chicago that year, he lost the resulting three-way race to Democrat Woodrow WILSON. Touted as a possible Republican nominee again in 1920, he died in 1919 at the age of 60, his death said to be hastened by the loss of his son in WORLD WAR I.

In Sherwood ANDERSON's novel DARK LAUGH-TER, published in 1925, a soon-to-be-cuckolded husband, losing his wife to a more virile man, regrets that Roosevelt was not president during World War I; if "Teddy," he declares, had been in office at the beginning of the conflict, "we would have got in quicker—smashed 'em." The image of Roosevelt continued as the Rough Rider, as the man who popularized the adage "Speak softly and carry a big stick."

Root, George Frederick
(1820–1895) *songwriter*

Born in Massachusetts, Root moved to Chicago in 1859 and joined the music-publishing firm of Root and Cady, which was founded by his brother. In the era before recordings, sheet music was the means for the distribution of music, as well as a source of income for songwriters; Root became a well-known writer of popular songs. When the CIVIL WAR began, he produced celebrated Union Army songs, including "Tramp, Tramp, Tramp" and "Marching Through Georgia." His 1862 "The Battle Cry of Freedom"—"we'll rally round the flag, boys"—became a Union marching song. When the body of assassinated President

Abraham LINCOLN came to Chicago, Root wrote a new song for the occasion, "Farewell, Father, Friend and Guardian."

Root, John Wellborn
(1850–1891) *architect*

Born in Lumpkin, Georgia, Root spent the latter years of the CIVIL WAR studying in England and received an engineering degree from New York University. In 1872, he moved to Chicago; a year later, at the age of 23, he formed a partnership with Daniel H. BURNHAM. Root is credited with the structural innovation that made possible Chicago's first SKYSCRAPER, the Montauk Building; he helped create the "floating foundation," a platform of concrete and steel, sustaining and distributing a structure's weight in the swampy soil of the city. Viewed as the creative partner in the firm of BURNHAM AND ROOT, Root designed the acclaimed 1888 building, THE ROOKERY, considered one of Chicago's finest structures; lawyer Clarence DARROW housed his office in the Rookery. Another celebrated Root structure is the historically important MONADNOCK BUILDING, completed in 1891; it continues to stand as the world's tallest wall-bearing building. In the midst of making plans for the WORLD'S COLUMBIAN EXPOSITION along with partner Daniel H. Burnham, Root died suddenly of pneumonia at the age of 41. Harriet MONROE, his sister-in-law, published an admiring biography in 1896. His son, John Wellborn Root Jr., aided in his education by Burnham, later joined William HOLABIRD's firm of Holabird and Roche, eventually to become Holabird and Root.

Rosenwald, Julius
(1862–1932) *businessman, philanthropist*

Taking over the business operations of SEARS, ROEBUCK AND COMPANY, Rosenwald led the mail-order firm to its status as a major corporation. Born to German-Jewish immigrants in SPRINGFIELD, Illinois, engaging first in clothing manufacture, he bought an interest in Sears, Roebuck in 1895; he was soon overseeing the company's rapid growth. By 1900, Sears had surpassed the pioneering firm of MONTGOMERY WARD AND COMPANY.

A member of the congregation of Rabbi Emil HIRSCH, Rosenwald was influenced by Hirsch's advocacy of philanthropic activity. Among his projects was providing seed funding for over 5,000 black schools in the rural South; recipients of Rosenwald Fellowships, aiding African Americans in higher education, included future statesman Ralph Bunche and singer Marian Anderson. Another project, completed after his death, was the rebuilding and developing of the MUSEUM OF SCIENCE AND INDUSTRY, opening in 1933. Rosenwald died in Chicago at the age of 69.

Rose of Dutcher's Coolly
Hamlin Garland
(1895)

The story of a young woman who grows up in rural Wisconsin and escapes to Chicago, *Rose of Dutcher's Coolly* can be considered a forerunner of Theodore DREISER's *SISTER CARRIE*. Yet Rose DUTCHER, enjoying economic support from her father, having no need to find work, never faces the vicissitudes that Carrie faces; she finds an elite circle of friends and maintains a genteel lifestyle, never subjected to the social and economic forces detailed by Dreiser in his novel of REALISM-verging-into-NATURALISM. Hamlin GARLAND, who had pursued his own brand of realism four years earlier in the grim tales of *MAIN-TRAVELLED ROADS*, is here following a different agenda; he is introducing several "advanced" cultural issues of his day—sexuality, feminism, marital free-thinking—and yet these issues are introduced in theory only. In each case Garland hedges, drawing back, as the times required, into an acceptance of convention. When Rose is growing up in rural Wisconsin, the author suggests that sexuality is a part of the natural setting—and yet his frankness is undermined by the implacable virtue he imparts to his heroine. When Rose makes her way to Chicago, she meets a successful professional woman—and yet the woman insists that marriage and children are

necessary to her life, as they are to any woman's life. When Rose agrees finally to marry, her husband-to-be insists on viewing marriage as a nonbinding contract—and yet no suggestion is made that such freedom will be put into practice. The author of *Sister Carrie* presents no such hedging; Dreiser, avoiding theory, offers a heroine who is swept along in life, who unreflectingly commits those acts labeled as immoral.

A "coolly," or "coulee," is a dry ravine, a common phenomenon in southern Wisconsin.

Synopsis

CHAPTERS I–V: HER CHILDHOOD; CHILD-LIFE, PAGAN-FREE; DANGEROUS DAYS; AN OPENING CLOVER BLOOM; HER FIRST PERIL
Rose Dutcher is five years old when her mother dies; she grows up with her father, John DUTCHER, on an isolated Wisconsin farm. Dutcher worries about his daughter, about the many questions she is asking, about what seem to be the coming dangers of womanhood; he sends for his widowed sister to live with them. Rose is a quick student in school, learning and reciting poetry, and yet she lives a "pagan" life in the fields, acting no differently from the boys, swinging on trees and slipping off her clothes to run amid the cornstalks. Observing "episodes of the barn-yard," she knows, too, what no city girl knows; yet she is instinctively refined and virtuous, even refraining from speaking of such matters to her aunt, whom she has heard use coarse words. Meanwhile, she is becoming a young woman, joining her contemporaries on picnics, and they frolic wholesomely in nature; a boy named Carl is attentive to her, and she feels the allure of his youth.

One winter, the local schoolteacher is a young woman whose beauty stirs the older boys; they begin feeling a rivalry over her, and she responds flirtatiously—to the point that students, including Carl and Rose, become involved in feelings of passion as well. They are allowing "something feverish and unwholesome" into their lives. The fathers of the community realize what is happening, and they send the teacher away. John Dutcher tells Carl that he has done wrong, that he will be allowed to see Rose again only when he is truly sorry; after a few weeks, the young people's innocent companionship is restored. Contemporary readers, puzzled by the chapter's veiled language, are left to decide the specifics of the offending behavior; it is likely to be considered mild by modern standards.

CHAPTERS VI–IX: HER FIRST IDEAL; ROSE MEETS DR. THATCHER; LEAVING HOME; ROSE ENTERS MADISON

A traveling circus comes to the nearby town, bringing glamour and excitement; Rose eagerly attends with Carl. One performer stands out, a handsome acrobat of grace and style, and she sets him up as her ideal. Ambitions begin to flourish within her; she feels that she will achieve something great for his sake.

A former pupil at her school, Dr. Thatcher, now living in Madison, the state capital, pays a visit to the old schoolhouse; he is impressed by the accomplishments of the young scholar, Rose. She tells him she wants to go to the university and be a writer; he agrees to arrange for her attendance at a preparatory school and then the university.

Carl is unhappy at Rose's leaving, assuming they were engaged; she makes clear that they will never marry. Her own unhappiness comes from her leaving her father. On the train ride to Madison she experiences what today would be considered sexual harassment on the part of the conductor and the brakeman; both men, realizing she is a naïve country girl, turn their tormenting attentions on her. She is rescued by a well-dressed woman, who tells the conductor she will have him fired; the woman is identified as a well-known lawyer in Milwaukee—and thus an early example of a professional woman in American fiction. She will soon be followed by another example, the physician Isabel HERRICK, whom Rose will meet in Chicago.

Rose stays in Madison at the house of Dr. and Mrs. Thatcher; she worries about proper knives and forks, as well as proper clothing, but soon adjusts—and everyone, as always, finds her admirable.

CHAPTERS X–XIV: QUIET YEARS OF GROWTH; STUDY OF THE STARS; THE GATES OPEN WIDE; THE WOMAN'S PART; AGAIN THE QUESTION OF HOME-LEAVING

At the university, Rose reads the standard English novelists—Walter Scott, Charles Dickens, William Makepeace Thackeray—and discovers as well the American Nathaniel Hawthorne, author of *Twice-Told Tales, Mosses from an Old Manse,* and the novel *The Scarlet Letter.* The last, featuring the adulterous Hester Prynne, telling of "woman's sin and man's injustice," causes Rose to question the laws of men; the one-time farm girl wonders why men are not as free as the animals. Yet her unorthodoxies are strictly intellectual; on the personal level, she avoids passion and maintains virtue. Moreover, the two young men she has taken note of in Madison prove unworthy; the handsome one is revealed as shallow and vain, and the older one, a law student, proves his unacceptability when, after seeing a stage play, he agrees with the character who shuns his wife over a lapse of virtue.

Yet Rose finds Dr. Thatcher becoming seemingly distant; she never realizes he has felt so intensely involved with her that he knows he must avoid her. Graduation day comes, and yet another young admirer approaches her, offering his hand in marriage; she responds that she cannot marry him or anyone else, that she is going to Chicago, that she is going to see the world. Dr. Thatcher, in parting, tells her she can accomplish anything—as long as she does not marry.

When she returns home, she sees the new house her father has built for her; she is to live in it when she marries a local young man. Rose is torn by love and loyalty to her father, but she eventually makes clear that she is not staying, that she is leaving for the city.

CHAPTERS XV–XIX: CHICAGO; HER FIRST CONQUEST; HER FIRST DINNER OUT; MASON TALKS ON MARRIAGE; IN THE BLAZE OF A THOUSAND EYES

The train takes her into the loud, frightening city; a friend from the university has found her a room in a boardinghouse. Rose gradually takes in the sights, including the mansions of the wealthy; she feels she belongs among such people. Bearing an introduction from Dr. Thatcher, she calls on Isabel Herrick, who is won over by her forthrightness and superior bearing; Isabel invites her for dinner.

Rose continues to explore the city, including immigrant neighborhoods; she visits the ART

INSTITUTE, the "Wheat Exchange"—the CHICAGO BOARD OF TRADE BUILDING—and the Masonic Temple, the BURNHAM AND ROOT building that is the tallest in the city. Going to Isabel's flat for dinner, she meets her hostess's fiancé, Dr. Sanborn, and the prominent journalist Warren MASON. Rose is asked to read some of her poetry; Garland describes it as derivative of the work of Alfred Tennyson and Elizabeth Barrett Browning. The listeners are pleased, although Mason says nothing. Later, Mason discusses the issue of marriage with Sanborn, saying that he cannot marry because he is conscious of the flaws in women, because he loses interest once the flaws are manifest—and because, too, he is not prepared to swear eternal fidelity.

Rose continues to explore the city; she has $300 from her father, which will last her through June. Isabel invites her to a CHICAGO SYMPHONY ORCHESTRA concert at the AUDITORIUM BUILDING; her front-row seating in a box makes her visible to the audience, and all admire her beauty—including Mason, sitting with a group of newspaper critics. Mason regrets that he had already put in the post a forthright critique of her poetry. Rose is enraptured by the music of Richard WAGNER, which she is hearing for the first time. After the concert, Mason tells her she must burn his packet when it arrives, including her manuscript as well as his letter. She agrees, realizing that she must start anew.

CHAPTERS XX–CONCLUSION: ROSE SETS FACE TOWARD THE OPEN ROAD; MASON TALKS AGAIN; SOCIAL QUESTIONS; A STORM AND A HELMSMAN; MASON TAKES A VACATION; ROSE RECEIVES A LETTER; MASON AS A LOVER; THE WIND IN THE TREE-TOPS

Rose feels disturbed by Mason; she thinks she cannot understand him, and sometimes he frightens her. Meanwhile, a pleasant, handsome young rich man is showing an interest in her, and Rose knows he could offer relief from financial worry; yet she knows, too, that liking a man is not the same as loving him. Mason talks again with Sanborn, this time on whether a man should marry a rich girl, thus escaping work, or a poor girl, thus having to work yet harder—or whether he

should marry at all. Isabel talks to Rose, telling her that she must marry—"the world must have its wives and mothers"—but that she must marry well.

Rose and Mason witness a winter storm on LAKE MICHIGAN, in which several men in boats perish after a heroic struggle. Mason, inspired, says that the men have taught him a lesson; previously he had been drifting, but now he will sail. He tells Rose he has something to say to her; since she will be visiting home shortly, he will write to her.

Isabel and Sanborn marry. Mason visits their vacation spot and discusses with Isabel the idea of marrying Rose; Isabel declares that the two of them would be good for each other. Rose, now at her father's farm, receives the marriage proposal. Mason states that he cannot promise her great material comfort, nor cordial relations with her relatives, nor even permanent fidelity—although he will always be honest, he adds, about any change in heart; he will never lead a double life. Moreover, she, too, will be free to leave him whenever she wishes, whenever another man pleases her more than he. Rose telegraphs her affirmative reply, and Mason comes to the farm, meeting her father; Dutcher weeps for his lost daughter. The couple are married by a judge, and Rose enters Mason's apartment, feeling comfortable and at home. Yet the final words, readers have noted, are her husband's, not hers: Mason says he will never be lonely again.

Critical Response

The novel was not well reviewed, particularly by western critics sensitive to implied aspersions on their region. The work was also branded in some quarters as indecent; its depiction of a nature-inspired, or "natural," sexuality, although far from explicit, was recognizable as such. Garland toned the element down in a later edition. Yet since Rose, whether on the farm or in the city, maintains her virtue throughout, the work was not so scandalous as Dreiser's *Sister Carrie*, appearing five years later, in which Carrie MEEBER placidly engages in sexual liaisons. The episode of the wayward woman schoolteacher, disrupting the small town, is echoed 25 years later in Sinclair LEWIS's *MAIN STREET*; Lewis's young woman, too, finds her employment terminated. Biographically oriented critics have found a direct link between Rose and Garland himself, declaring that Rose's rise from rural beginnings to intellectual elitism is really Garland's rise; the author is telling his own story.

Royal Gardens

This popular BRONZEVILLE nightclub, located at Thirty-first Street and Cottage Grove Avenue, became Lincoln Gardens in 1921. Joe "King" OLIVER played at the Royal Gardens beginning in 1918; he was joined in 1922 by JAZZ innovator and trumpeter Louis ARMSTRONG. The Royal Gardens Motion Picture Company, an early African-American foray into cinema, operated briefly in 1919–20.

Rudkus, Jurgis

The principal character in Upton SINCLAIR's novel *THE JUNGLE*, Jurgis, an uneducated Lithuanian immigrant, comes to Chicago with his fiancée and her family. Suffering brutal working conditions in the meatpacking industry, as well as being forced to live in appallingly substandard housing in PACKINGTOWN, he loses his wife and son; he further experiences crime, political corruption, and beggary—before seeing salvation as offered by the doctrines of SOCIALISM.

Rudkus, Ona

This character appears in Upton SINCLAIR's novel *THE JUNGLE*. Married, at not quite 16, to Jurgis RUDKUS, Ona had come with her husband from Lithuania; she is forced by financial necessity to go to work in the packing plant. One of her roles in the novel is to exemplify the issue of sexual exploitation in the workplace; she accedes to her boss's demands in order to keep her job. After giving birth to a son, she dies in a second childbirth. Jurgis exacerbates his own problems by assaulting her boss and going to jail; he is told he should have gone along with his wife's exploitation.

"Rutherford McDowell"   *See* SPOON RIVER ANTHOLOGY.

Rutledge, Ann
(1813–1835) *figure in the Abraham Lincoln story*

Dying in her early 20s, Rutledge has been claimed as the fiancée of the future president; her death, according to legend, left him grief stricken. She was the daughter of an innkeeper in New Salem, Illinois, where LINCOLN lived from 1831 to 1837; the story of their relationship was told in William H. HERNDON's 1889 biography of Lincoln. Partly as a result of the Herndon story, her remains were removed in 1890 from a country graveyard to the new Oakland Cemetery near Petersburg, Illinois. Edgar Lee MASTERS paid tribute to Rutledge in 1915 in *SPOON RIVER ANTHOLOGY*—using Herndon's spelling of the first name—and the poem was placed, slightly altered, on a monument to her in 1921. Carl SANDBURG kept the story alive in his 1926 biography *ABRAHAM LINCOLN: THE PRAIRIE YEARS*. In 1931, Masters, in a reversal of sentiment, chose to take a debunking attitude toward the president, repudiating the story in his biography *Lincoln: The Man*. Scholars have since discounted the relationship between Rutledge and Lincoln.

S

"The Sad Horn Blowers"   *See HORSES AND MEN.*

Saint-Gaudens, Augustus
(1848–1907) *sculptor*

Born in Dublin, Ireland, Saint-Gaudens moved with his family to New York City and eventually became known for public statuary and monuments, including two statues of Abraham LINCOLN in Chicago parks. "Standing Lincoln," located at the south end of LINCOLN PARK, dedicated in 1887, is considered one of the best likenesses of the president, portraying Lincoln as an orator, his head slightly bowed, about to address the audience. "Seated Lincoln," depicting the president sitting in a chair atop a granite pedestal, is located in downtown Grant Park. For the WORLD'S COLUMBIAN EXPOSITION of 1893, Saint-Gaudens created the 18-foot-tall "Diana of the Tower," poised with bow and arrow, topping the dome of the Agricultural Building. In Edna FERBER's story "Home Girl," collected in the 1922 *GIGOLO*, a character is compared to the Lincoln Park Lincoln, in that he is "kindly, thoughtful, harried."

St. Peter, Godfrey

The principal character in Willa CATHER's novel *THE PROFESSOR'S HOUSE*, St. Peter, feeling estranged

Augustus Saint-Gaudens's "Standing Lincoln" in Lincoln Park is considered one of the finest representations of the president; selections from Lincoln's speeches are carved on a low surrounding wall. *(Chicago Historical Society)*

from his family, persists in staying in the attic study of the house he has lived in for more than 20 years. He has no wish to move to the new house built with prize money from his eight-volume history, *The Spanish Adventurers in North America.* In an autobiographical expression on Cather's part, the professor recalls a time of great joy in his life when he journeyed to the cliff-dwellings of New Mexico, accompanied by his friend Tom OUTLAND. Cather concludes the novel as St. Peter realizes that his life must now be lived without joy.

St. Peter, Lillian

A character in Willa CATHER's novel THE PROFESSOR'S HOUSE, Lillian is partner in a marriage that has become a matter of convenience; her husband pursues interests far removed from her own. Yet she is not depicted unsympathetically, and her husband, the reader is told, once loved her; he hastily accepted his professorship so that the two could marry. Readers have suggested that Cather, in her depiction of Lillian, is addressing the issue of women's exclusion from the professions; university professors, being men, have wives who are encouraged by society to become mere accouterments, not intellectual companions—and thus social conventions have dictated Lillian's estrangement from her husband's life.

St. Valentine's Day Massacre
(1929)

This famed gangland slaying has been attributed to Al CAPONE. According to the oft-told story, seven men, attached to the rival gang of George "Bugs" Moran, were lured into a garage for a liquor deal, then lined up against a wall and mowed down by a thousand bullets. The Thompson submachine gun, invented during WORLD WAR I, had become the gangland weapon of choice. No trial took place, because no witnesses could be found to testify; the general agreement is that Capone, vacationing in Florida at the time, hired out-of-town gangsters to carry out the killings. Yet the massacre was the beginning of the

end for Capone; the high-profile case aroused public opinion and led federal agents to begin to look for ways to bring him down; they succeeded—using income tax evasion charges—just two years later. The site of the killings, a building on North Clark Street, was demolished in the late 1960s. The 1959 movie classic *Some Like It Hot,* starring Jack Lemmon, Tony Curtis, and Marilyn Monroe, uses the St. Valentine's Day Massacre as a backdrop.

"Salvage"   See CHICAGO POEMS.

Salvation Army

This evangelical and philanthropic organization was founded in England and came to America in 1880. The Salvation Army inspired the poem that brought fame to Illinois poet Vachel LINDSAY. Established in London by William BOOTH, originally a Methodist minister, the movement began in the 1860s as the East London Revival Society; it became the Salvation Army in 1878, taking on a military-style structure and adopting uniforms. After 1884, the organization broadened its policy to provide social services along with its evangelical work, establishing orphanages, shelters, and food depots. Lindsay, recalling Salvationists he had seen in his native SPRINGFIELD, wrote the poem "GENERAL WILLIAM BOOTH ENTERS INTO HEAVEN" to be accompanied by drums, tambourines, flutes, and banjos.

Sandburg, Carl
(1878–1967) *poet*

Coming to fame in the second decade of the 20th century, Sandburg remains the best-known poet of the Chicago Renaissance. Born in Galesburg, Illinois, the son of a Swedish immigrant, he held a variety of laboring jobs as a young man, first visiting Chicago at the age of 18. At the beginning of the SPANISH-AMERICAN WAR in 1898, he enlisted in the Sixth Illinois Division, serving eight months of noncombat duty in Puerto Rico. On his return he

This 1918 portrait shows Carl Sandburg four years after his first appearance in *Poetry* magazine, two years after the publication of *Chicago Poems*. *(Chicago Historical Society)*

enrolled in Galesburg's Lombard College, subsequently Knox College, graduating in 1902.

In 1907, Sandburg became an organizer in rural Wisconsin for the SOCIALIST PARTY OF AMERICA; there he met and married Lilian Steichen, sister of the photographer Edward Steichen. He wrote for two Milwaukee socialist papers, the *Social-Democratic Herald* and the *Milwaukee Leader,* and served as a delegate to the 1908 Socialist Party convention in Chicago, which nominated Eugene V. DEBS for the presidency. Campaigning to elect Emil Seidel as mayor in Milwaukee—who became the first socialist mayor of an American city— Sandburg later worked as Seidel's private secretary. In 1912, he moved to Chicago; between 1913 and 1917, he wrote for the CHICAGO DAY BOOK, a tabloid paper aimed at the working man.

In March 1914, POETRY published nine poems by Sandburg, including the key work, "Chicago"; it won the Helen Levinson Prize, awarded for the best poetry published in that magazine during the year. *Poetry* published his further work in May and November of the same year. While continuing to write for the *Day Book,* Sandburg was writing as well for the Chicago-based INTERNATIONAL SOCIALIST REVIEW, a magazine increasingly radicalized as it supported the unionism of the INDUSTRIAL WORKERS OF THE WORLD; many of his pieces were published anonymously or under a pseudonym. When the *Day Book* folded in 1917, he went to work at the CHICAGO DAILY NEWS.

Sandburg's CHICAGO POEMS, published in 1916, established his reputation as an urban poet, a celebrator of the working man. CORNHUSKERS, appearing two years later, draws in contrast on his rural roots; in the long initial poem, "Prairie," reminiscent of the work of Walt WHITMAN, the poet sings of the prairie that nurtured him. The volume also brings Abraham LINCOLN within his focus, beginning his fashioning of Lincoln into an American folk hero. The "Shenandoah" section, evoking both the CIVIL WAR and WORLD WAR I, shows Sandburg's rejecting the antiwar stance of many of his labor and socialist associates; he supported America's entrance into the conflict. His next two collections, SMOKE AND STEEL and SLABS OF THE SUNBURNT WEST, appearing in 1920 and 1922, feature both industrial and natural landscapes.

By the 1920s, Sandburg was taking to the lecture circuit; like his predecessor Vachel LINDSAY, he began touring the country, reciting his poetry—although, unlike Lindsay, he brought along a guitar as well. Ben HECHT later wrote that Sandburg had a fine voice for reading, better than that of actors Paul MUNI or John Barrymore. Along with poetry recitations, Sandburg accompanied himself, singing folk songs and ballads; this activity is the origin of THE AMERICAN SONG-BAG, published in 1927. Between 1920 and 1928, he also wrote film criticism for the *Daily News,* creating a firsthand history of the silent film era; his work is of particular importance since the majority of silent films have been lost. He expressed a continuing admiration for Charlie CHAPLIN, and an interview with the actor was transformed into his poem "Without the Cane and Derby," appearing in *Slabs of the Sunburnt West.* Sandburg has also been lauded as an early proponent of the 1950s auteur, or author, theory, in which credit for a film is given ultimately to the director; writing in 1922, he dismissed actors as secondary, declaring that "in all pictures the big main star is the director." In 1924, he reviewed a filmed life of Abraham Lincoln, publishing views that would surface two years later in his biography ABRAHAM LINCOLN: THE PRAIRIE YEARS.

In the late 1920s, Sandburg bought a house near Harbert, Michigan, a small Chicago-accessible summer community on the eastern shore of LAKE MICHIGAN; he moved there permanently when he left the *Daily News* in 1932. By the 1930s, having muted his social criticism, he was identifying himself with "the people" as a whole, with the American mainstream; he was no longer raising a workingman's voice of protest. Pulitzer Prizes came from the 1939 ABRAHAM LINCOLN: THE WAR YEARS and the 1950 *The Complete Poems.* His only novel, *Remembrance Rock,* appeared in 1948, and his autobiography, *Always the Young Strangers,* appeared in 1953; in that same year, his 75th birthday was celebrated at a gathering at the BLACKSTONE HOTEL. Looking for milder winters, he moved to Flat Rock, North Carolina, dying there at the age of 89.

Sandburg has never been popular in academic circles. His earliest achievements, most notably *Chicago Poems,* appeared at a time when academics paid little attention to contemporary poetry; in the first quarter of the 20th century, a major gap existed between the avant-garde and academia, and periodicals such as *Poetry* and LITTLE REVIEW went generally unnoticed in scholarly institutions. When MODERNISM, as practiced By Ezra POUND and T. S. ELIOT, took over the avant-garde—and finally academia—Sandburg came to be considered "popular," a term of opprobrium. His career shows parallels to that of Robert FROST; the New England poet had also become publicly adulated, although retaining a respectability among academics and intellectuals, perhaps because he displayed a stubborn regional toughness that the expansive prairie poet seemed to lack. Yet

Sandburg continues as a figure venerated by the American public, and his early innovative poetry remains one of the indisputable fonts of 20th-century modernism.

A 1960 stage show by Norman Corwin, *The World of Carl Sandburg,* presenting stories, poems, songs, and excerpts from the Lincoln biography, starred actress Bette Davis.

Further Reading
Bernstein, Arnie, ed. *"The Movies Are": Carl Sandburg's Film Reviews and Essays, 1920–1928.* Chicago: Lake Claremont Press, 2000.
Niven, Penelope. *Carl Sandburg: A Biography.* New York: Charles Scribner's Sons, 1991.
Yanella, Philip R. *The Other Carl Sandburg.* Jackson: University Press of Mississippi, 1996.

Sayers, Walter

This character appears in Sherwood ANDERSON's story "Out of Nowhere into Nothing," collected in THE TRIUMPH OF THE EGG. Sayers is a frustrated businessman, owing his job, which he despises, to his wife's investment in the company; he had wanted to be a singer, although he knew his voice was not large enough. He can sing when he is out on the open road with his secretary, Rosalind WESCOTT, and they discuss becoming lovers, although he warns her that unhappiness may result. Rosalind will ultimately give herself to him, it is understood—although she, too, has been warned by her mother, who has spoken in dire terms against men and against sex.

Sayre, Johnnie   *See* SPOON RIVER ANTHOLOGY.

Sears, Roebuck and Company

This mail-order company and retailer, established in 1886, surpassed the original mail-order firm, MONTGOMERY WARD AND COMPANY, within two decades. The enterprise began when Sears, working as a railroad station agent in Minnesota, took over a shipment of watches that had been refused by a retailer, then sold the watches at a profit. Moving to Chicago in 1887, he teamed with Alvah C. Roebuck, a watch repairer, issuing his first catalogue that year; Sears, Roebuck and Company was formed in 1893. Two years later, Roebuck sold his interest in the company, and clothier Julius ROSENWALD bought into the firm; the first general Sears, Roebuck catalogue appeared in 1896. Rosenwald, taking over business operations, put in place a new organizational efficiency—as well as eliminated some of the deceptive claims made in the early Sears catalogues—and led the company to become one of the nation's major retail corporations. In 1920, the firm bought the *Encyclopedia Britannica*, bringing it to Chicago; it later gave the publication to the UNIVERSITY OF CHICAGO.

"Seeds"   *See THE TRIUMPH OF THE EGG.*

Selig, William N.
(1864–1948) *early motion-picture producer*

Born in Chicago, operating a minstrel show—and claiming to have discovered performer Bert WILLIAMS—Selig founded the Selig Polyscope Company in 1896. A decade later, he brought to Chicago William G. ANDERSON, star of the The *Great Train Robbery,* the pioneering movie made in 1903 at the East Coast Edison studios; Anderson, after acting and directing for the Selig company, went on to cofound his own Chicago firm, the ES-SANAY FILM MANUFACTURING COMPANY. In 1910, Selig collaborated with writer L. Frank BAUM, author of THE WONDERFUL WIZARD OF OZ, to produce the first of many Oz movies. The following year, using replicas of Christopher Columbus's ships—sent to Chicago by the Spanish government for the WORLD'S COLUMBIAN EXPOSITION of 1893—Selig photographed the vessels sailing into the JACKSON PARK yacht harbor; the resulting movie, *The Coming of Columbus,* was an international success. In 1914, Selig joined with newspaper magnate William Randolph Hearst to distribute silent newsreels, a medium soon to become a staple of movie theater programming. In

1918, his last production in Chicago, *Pioneer Days,* a recreation of the FORT DEARBORN massacre, was shot in the north-suburban village of Wilmette. Yet, the weather of Southern California was proving increasingly enticing, and the company left Chicago in 1919.

settlement house

Established to benefit the urban poor, settlement houses flourished from the 1880s through the 1920s. The guiding concept was that educated people lived in a settlement, or community, along with the poor in order to share with them and help them better their lives. The movement began in 1884 with the establishment of Toynbee Hall in London's East End, an institution housing male university graduates. Jane ADDAMS, visiting in 1888, found inspiration for her own future settlement house, to be an institution housing college-educated women. Lillian Wald founded a similar Henry Street Settlement in New York City. The establishments typically included residential housing, meeting halls, and classrooms.

The standard charge against settlement houses was paternalism and cultural imposition—foisting middle-class standards and modes of thought on the poor and working class. UNIVERSITY OF CHICAGO economist Thorstein VEBLEN castigated settlement houses in his 1899 THE THEORY OF THE LEISURE CLASS, calling them instruments of propaganda. Many have noted that the American institutions were dominated by women; the standard explanation was that society denied educated women a role in the professions or in business, giving them no other appropriate outlet.

In Upton SINCLAIR's novel of 1906, THE JUNGLE, a settlement worker, "a real fine lady," uses her contacts to get the protagonist a job in the steel mills; yet the immigrant family is suspicious, distrustful of "rich people" who come to live in their neighborhood "to find out about poor people." The local priest discourages the family from having anything to do with strange religions.

The Shame of the Cities
Lincoln Steffens
(1904)

This MUCKRAKING exposé by Lincoln STEFFENS, collected from articles in MCCLURE'S MAGAZINE, presents six pieces on six cities and finds corruption in city governments as well as in big business. The initial article, "Tweed Days in St. Louis," appearing in *McClure's* in October 1902, was followed by articles on Minneapolis, Pittsburgh, Philadelphia, Chicago, and New York. The Chicago piece finds police graft, as well as a general profligacy, permeating both business and labor; Steffens accuses corporations of undermining reform in city government.

Shaw, Howard Van Doren
(1869–1926) *architect*

Born in Chicago, working in the office of William Le Baron JENNEY, Shaw became a favored residential architect for the wealthy. Influenced by the ARTS AND CRAFTS MOVEMENT, he was known for valuing workmanship, for incorporating crafted detail into his homes. His first nonresidential work was the 1897 Lakeside Press Building, followed in 1912 by a structure for another R. R. DONNELLEY-founded company, the massive printing plant for R. R. Donnelley and Sons on the Near South Side. On the MIDWAY PLAISANCE, Shaw designed the base and reflecting pool for the 127-foot-long sculpture by Lorado TAFT, "Fountain of Time," dedicated in 1922. His last work was the Goodman Theater, completed in 1925, memorializing the young playwright Kenneth Sawyer GOODMAN. His own estate, named Ragdale, built in 1894 in the northern suburb of Lake Forest, has subsequently become a writer's colony.

Shedd Aquarium

The first aquarium of its kind in America, built in 1929 on the lakefront, the Shedd Aquarium was founded with a gift from John G. Shedd, president of MARSHALL FIELD AND COMPANY from 1909 to 1926. Its classical-inspired architecture blends with that of with the nearby ADLER PLANETARIUM, FIELD MUSEUM OF NATURAL HISTORY, and SOLDIER FIELD. A 1991 glass-fronted addition is the oceanarium, accommodating dolphins and whales.

"Shenandoah"   *See* CORNHUSKERS.

Sherwood Anderson's Notebook
Sherwood Anderson
(1926)

The volume collects notes and essays by Sherwood ANDERSON. One piece, "A Meeting South," published in the DIAL in 1925, reappeared as a short story in the 1933 DEATH IN THE WOODS; it presents a version of the author's encounter with the writer William FAULKNER in New Orleans in 1924. "Four American Impressions" briefly discusses four writers: Gertrude STEIN, Ring LARDNER, Paul Rosenfeld, and Sinclair LEWIS. Stein and Lardner are praised for their use of language, and Rosenfeld—who subsidized Anderson on his first European trip, when he first met Stein—is lauded for his critical sensibility; Lewis, on the other hand, is accused of writing dull prose, of conveying a "sense of dreary spiritual death."

In "An Apology for Crudity," first appearing in the DIAL in 1916, Anderson argues that American writing must be crude and ugly because current American life demonstrates those qualities. Seemingly espousing REALISM, he notes that factories and industrialism have replaced the forests and rivers of Mark Twain and Walt WHITMAN. Yet the essay is in large part a plea for an American—more specifically, a midwestern—grounding for literature. Perhaps our grandchildren, Anderson suggests, can "produce a school of American writing that has more delicacy," but for now the writer must produce crudity and ugliness.

Another essay in the volume, "A Note on Realism," published eight years after "An Apology for Crudity," argues specifically against the doctrine of realism. Reminding readers that the life of the imagination is separate from the life of reality, Anderson declares that even "the so-called great realists were not realists at all." Referring to a character created by the 19th-century French novelist Gustave Flaubert, he notes that Madame Bovary did not exist in fact, but rather in the imagination of her creator; it was her creator who placed her into "the imaginative life of his readers." The argument is in part a matter of rhetoric—*Madame Bovary* is undeniably more "realistic" than the romances of an earlier era—and yet Anderson is signaling a change in the direction of literary discourse. Realism is no longer the byword; the battle for its acceptance has been won, and other literary modes, deeming realism to be limited, have found expression as well.

The Sho-Gun
George Ade, Gustav Luders
(1904)

Following up on his popular THE SULTAN OF SULU, ADE provided the book and lyrics for this musical comedy, while Luders supplied the music. The work opened in Chicago, before going on to popular success on the New York stage. As in the earlier musical, the plot features a supposed comedic encounter between Americans and peoples overseas—a newly popular story line, resulting in part from the SPANISH-AMERICAN WAR and its aftermath. This time an American finds himself in Korea, where a palace revolution is threatening, and he becomes a candidate either for the throne or for a beheading; the United States Navy arrives to restore order. The passages of pseudo-oriental music recall Gilbert and Sullivan's 1885 The Mikado, the English comic operetta set in a fantasy Japan—the popular work that Theodore DREISER's characters view in SISTER CARRIE. Gustav Luders subsequently teamed up with Ade for further successful musicals.

Shope, Tennessee Claflin   *See* SPOON RIVER
ANTHOLOGY.

Show Boat
Edna Ferber
(1926)

A best-seller, serialized first in the *Women's Home Companion,* this book held an exotic appeal for Americans in the 1920s, both in its locale and its characters. Featuring a Mississippi River showboat, a vessel that docks at small towns along the Mississippi and its tributaries, the work presented sympathetic—although today seen as stereotyped—portrayals of African Americans. In a key incident in the novel, a Mississippi sheriff boards the boat, saying he has heard of an interracial marriage on board, which would violate the state's antimiscegenation laws; the white husband of the mixed-race actress quickly cuts the actress's finger and sucks her blood, claiming that he has African blood in him. The couple leave the boat, and the woman turns up years later as the assistant to a brothel madam in Chicago. The last portion of the novel, set in Chicago, depicts the heroine, married to a gambler, shuttling between luxury hotels and rooming houses, eventually resuming the theatrical career she had begun on the riverboat.

The work pays tribute to the theater, which Edna FERBER always claimed as her first love. The Cotton Blossom Floating Palace Theater Company provides entertainment and escape to a town's hardworking citizens, presenting "warmth, enchantment, laughter, music," Referring to the classical river of forgetfulness, Ferber adds, "It was Lethe. It was Escape. It was the Theatre."

Show Boat was turned into a musical, produced by Florenz ZIEGFELD Jr. in 1927, featuring music by Jerome Kern, book and lyrics by Oscar Hammerstein II—although the lyrics of one song, "Bill," had been written earlier by the English novelist P. G. Wodehouse. The stage production, treating the topic of miscegenation, became the first American musical to deal seriously with social issues; it provided also an early instance of stage interaction between white and black actors. Various revivals over the years included a successful New York production in 1993—despite protests that out-of-date racial themes were being sanctioned—leading to several years of national touring. Of the three movies made of the musical, the

1936 version casts the African-American actor and singer Paul Robeson, rendering the by-then well-known "Ol' Man River"; the director is the latter-day cult figure James Whale. In the 1951 film version, the Robeson role is taken by William Warfield.

Sibley, Amos; Mrs. Sibley   *See* SPOON RIVER ANTHOLOGY.

Sinclair, Upton
(1878–1968) *writer*

Born in Baltimore, shuttled as a boy between rich and poor relatives, Sinclair grew up knowing the worlds of both wealth and poverty. An early novel, *Manassas,* dealing with slavery and the CIVIL WAR, appeared in 1904; among its characters is a German refugee who introduces the hero to SOCIALISM. As a result of this work, the Kansas-based socialist weekly, THE APPEAL TO REASON, sent the author to Chicago to write about the UNION STOCK YARDS. Spending seven weeks in Chicago in 1904, Sinclair published the first installment of his exposé of stockyard conditions in *Appeal* early the next year. The completed novel, THE JUNGLE, appeared in 1906, when the author was 27 years old; the work shocked the nation and led to the passage of the Pure Food and Drug Act the same year.

Later in 1906, using money earned from his best-seller, Sinclair established a cooperative community near Englewood, New Jersey. Called Helicon Hall, housed in a former private school, complete with swimming pool and tennis court, the community was inspired by the writings of Charlotte Perkins GILMAN; its founding principles were communal living and communal child care—although servants were soon hired for cooking, laundering, and taking care of the children. Yale University dropout Sinclair LEWIS was employed as a janitor. Forty adults and 14 children participated in the experiment, visited by John DEWEY, Emma GOLDMAN, and other notables. The community came to an end after four and a half months, when a fire—believed by some to be the result of capitalist arson—destroyed the premises.

An outspoken socialist, Sinclair was caught up in the SOCIALIST PARTY OF AMERICA's divided reaction to WORLD WAR I. Like Carl SANDBURG, he broke with party ranks and supported the war, claiming that German militarism had to be stopped. The MUCKRAKING movement essentially ended with the war, although Sinclair continued what he called his "Dead Hand" series, a set of volumes exposing institutions he claimed to be stifling American freedoms. In 1918, he published *The Profits of Religion: An Essay in Economic Interpretation*, attacking the greed of religious leaders throughout the ages, excoriating modern organized religion as being corrupted by CAPITALISM. He cites as an example the Baptists, the religious group claiming as a member John D. ROCKEFELLER of the Standard Oil Company; Baptist preachers, Sinclair declares, believers in baptism by immersion, "practice total immersion in Standard Oil." A novel, *Oil!*, published in 1927, deals with the corruption of oil companies, although it was banned in Boston for references to contraception; the same year, Floyd DELL wrote a flattering biography of the author. Later in life, Sinclair turned to writing popular fiction, winning a Pulitzer Prize in 1943. Living the last half of his life in Southern California—and running unsuccessfully as Democratic candidate for governor in 1934—he died at the age of 90.

Further Reading
Harris, Leon. *Upton Sinclair: American Rebel.* New York: Thomas Y. Crowell, 1975.

single tax

Amateur economist Henry GEORGE used this phrase to designate his economic theory. A single tax is a tax levied on land, which would be sufficient, George argued, to cover all the needs of government. The problem is that economic prosperity makes land more valuable, and as a result, the landowner, while expending no personal effort, receives ever greater returns; the wages of workers are correspondingly depressed. The appeal of George's theory lay in its suggestions of egalitarianism, of a redistribution of wealth. In Theodore DREISER's SISTER CARRIE, a man in a soup kitchen remarks, "This here Single Tax is the thing"—meaning that the single tax is the answer to the nation's social and economic problems.

Sister Carrie
Theodore Dreiser
(1900)

This novel is Theodore DREISER's groundbreaking work. When Dreiser submitted the manuscript to the Doubleday firm, Frank NORRIS, acting as reader, recommended the book, and it was officially accepted. Then the publisher, returning from abroad, read the novel and found it immoral; he honored the acceptance reluctantly, allowing a few copies to be printed. The charge of immorality lay in the fact that the heroine enters into illicit liaisons and yet remains unpunished; at the end of the novel, Carrie, still dreaming of her future, meets no appropriately tragic end.

Carrie's desperate search for a job at the outset is a mirroring of Dreiser's own experiences in Chicago in 1887, when he arrived at the age of 15 from Warsaw, Indiana; he, too walked the streets for miles, receiving rejections, finding himself fired, enduring difficult work. For Carrie's later life, Dreiser drew from the experience of his sister Emma, eloping with a married man who had stolen money from his employer's safe; the couple fled from Chicago to Montreal, ultimately moving to New York City. For Carrie's acting career, Dreiser had been introduced to the theatrical world by his actor-songwriter brother, Paul DRESSER; one model might have been Louise Dresser, née Kerlin, a protégée of his brother, who claimed Louise as his sister and launched her in a successful theater career. Another inspiration might have been the public scandal involving an actress, Mrs. Leslie Carter, whose wealthy husband sued for divorce in 1889, naming five corespondents; Mrs. Carter's stage career later flourished, while her ex-husband, after losing his fortune, killed himself, turning on the gas in a stove, the same method used by George W. HURSTWOOD in

the novel. In his description of Hurstwood's decline, Dreiser drew in part from own experiences in Toledo and New York in 1894. Briefly covering a streetcar strike for the *Toledo Blade,* he rode in a car operated by a strikebreaker, facing the same angry crowd that Hurstwood faces; going on to New York in the wintertime, finding no employment, he wandered the streets and slept in flophouses. The influence of NATURALISM, as well as the philosophy of Herbert SPENCER, is pervasive in the novel, beginning with the subtitle of the initial chapter, "A Waif Amid Forces." Suggesting that Carrie is helpless against the tides of fate—"a lone figure in a tossing, thoughtless sea"—Dreiser is saying that she is not the master of her fate, that she is prey to larger forces about her.

Synopsis

CHAPTERS 1–4: THE MAGNET ATTRACTING: A WAIF AMID FORCES; WHAT POVERTY THREATENED: OF GRANITE AND BRASS; WE QUESTION OF FORTUNE: FOUR-FIFTY A WEEK; THE SPENDING OF FANCY: FACTS ANSWER WITH SNEERS

In August 1889, 18-year-old Caroline MEEBER, having grown up in the small town of Columbia City, Wisconsin, boards a train for Chicago. A traveling salesman, or "drummer," Charles DROUET, begins talking to her, offering to show her around when they arrive in the city. Carrie says she will be living with her sister, and Drouet obtains the address, giving her his card as well. At the train station, her sister, Minnie Hanson, meets her; Minnie and her husband and baby live in a small, drab apartment in a working-class area. The Hansons are eager for Carrie to find work; it is understood that she will be paying for her board. She sees at once how their lives are narrowed by their efforts to survive; Hanson works in the UNION STOCK YARDS, cleaning refrigerator cars. Carrie realizes that Drouet could never call on her there; her sister and brother-in-law understand only a daily round of toil. She writes Drouet, saying he will have to wait to hear from her.

Carrie sets out to look for employment, but having no experience or skills, she meets constant rebuffs. Finally, the manager of a shoe factory offers her work; she had been expecting a salary of six dollars a week, but she is forced to accept four-fifty a week. The assembly-line work, she soon learns, consisting of punching eyeholes in shoe leather, is difficult and tiring, and the working conditions are unpleasant.

CHAPTERS 5–8: A GLITTERING NIGHT FLOWER: THE USE OF A NAME; THE MACHINE AND THE MAIDEN: A KNIGHT OF TODAY; THE LURE OF THE MATERIAL: BEAUTY SPEAKS FOR ITSELF; INTIMATIONS BY WINTER: AN AMBASSADOR SUMMONED

Drouet stops at the bar of Fitzgerald and Moy's, an elegant establishment managed by George W. HURSTWOOD, whom Drouet cultivates as a man worth knowing. Hurstwood, a clever, prosperous-looking man of 40, is successful in his stewardship of the popular gathering place.

Carrie comes home discouraged from her first day of work, although finding little sympathy from the Hansons. She realizes she is supposed to work and not complain, as well as pay four dollars a week for her room and board; she will have to walk to and from work, as she will not be able to afford a streetcar. Meanwhile, winter is coming, and she has no appropriate clothes; she becomes ill and misses work, and her job is gone. Finally, looking once more for employment, she runs into Drouet; she is relieved, feeling that he will help her. He buys her a meal and gives her money for clothes, telling her to meet him the next day.

The Hansons want Carrie to go back home to Wisconsin if she is unable to find work; they are not willing to keep her. When she meets Drouet the next day, she says she is unable to spend the money he has given her because she can never explain the clothes to her sister; she announces that she is going home. Drouet says he will rent her a room, insisting that she buy the clothes; she is persuaded to come away from her sister's and go to a rooming house. After the purchase of more clothes on several occasions—and after seeing the popular operetta *The Mikado* one evening, then enjoying a fine after-theater meal—Carrie joins Drouet in his rooms.

CHAPTERS 9–13: CONVENTION'S OWN TINDERBOX: THE EYE THAT IS GREEN; THE COUNSEL OF WINTER: FORTUNE'S AMBASSADOR CALLS; THE PERSUASION OF FASHION: FEELING GUARDS O'ER ITS OWN; OF THE LAMPS OF THE MANSIONS: THE AMBASSADOR'S PLEA; HIS CREDENTIALS ACCEPTED: A BABEL OF TONGUES

Hurstwood lives discontentedly with his wife and two nearly grown children. Drouet invites him over one evening for cards, telling Carrie he will introduce her as Mrs. Drouet, although he knows that Hurstwood knows he is unmarried. Carrie, meeting Hurstwood, realizes at once that he is superior to Drouet; he is more clever, more polished, less obviously egotistical. Since Carrie herself has become more sophisticated and fashionable than she once was, Hurstwood immediately sees that she is superior to Drouet. He invites Carrie and Drouet to the theater.

Carrie has been out driving in a buggy with the woman who lives on the floor above her, and they pass the elegant mansions of the North Side. She realizes that her circumstances are still modest; she and Drouet occupy only three rooms in a boardinghouse. She feels sadness and longing. Then, when Drouet is away on his business traveling, Hurstwood comes to call; he sees Carrie's unhappiness and speaks to her of it—and sees that he has made an impression. He calls again in Drouet's absence, and he and Carrie take a buggy ride on what he hopes is an isolated road; he declares his love for her.

CHAPTERS 14–19: WITH EYES AND NOT SEEING: ONE INFLUENCE WANES; THE IRK OF THE OLD TIES: THE MAGIC OF YOUTH; A WITLESS ALADDIN: THE GATE TO THE WORLD; A GLIMPSE THROUGH THE GATEWAY: HOPE LIGHTENS THE EYE; JUST OVER THE BORDER: A HAIL AND FAREWELL; AN HOUR IN ELF LAND: A CLAMOR HALF HEARD

Others in the boardinghouse, including the housemaids, have noticed Hurstwood's calling on Carrie in Drouet's absence. She and Hurstwood agree to correspond, using the services of a post office branch. Drouet returns, suspecting nothing, telling Carrie, as he has done before, that they will marry as soon as he completes a real estate deal. She understands that he is not serious—and yet she has no knowledge that Hurstwood is himself married. Drouet, Carrie, and Hurstwood attend a play; on the way out, as a homeless man accosts them, Hurstwood does not notice, although Drouet, feeling pity, hands over a coin.

Hurstwood wants Carrie to leave Drouet; he says he will be coming for her, and she assumes he means marriage. Meanwhile, Drouet's Elks lodge is planning to put on a theatrical, and Drouet suggests Carrie as an actress. Taking the name of Carrie Madenda, she proves her talent, triumphing in front of a large audience. She is now beginning to realize the independence that success bestows, and she seems to be looking down on Drouet, condescending to him.

CHAPTERS 20–25: THE LURE OF THE SPIRIT: THE FLESH IN PURSUIT; THE LURE OF THE SPIRIT: THE FLESH IN PURSUIT [SAME TITLE FOR CHAPTERS 20 AND 21]; THE BLAZE OF THE TINDER; FLESH WARS WITH THE FLESH; A SPIRIT IN TRAVAIL: ONE RUNG PUT BEHIND; ASHES OF TINDER: A FACE AT THE WINDOW; ASHES OF TINDER: THE LOOSING OF STAYS

Drouet, returning home unexpectedly, learns that Carrie has gone out with Hurstwood; he learns, too, from the boardinghouse maid, that Hurstwood has called on her more times than he had been led to believe. Carrie agrees to go away with Hurstwood; she assumes they will marry. Yet Hurstwood's wife has heard of his driving in a buggy with another woman; she and Hurstwood argue, and he realizes that she has the advantage because she has their property, including their house, in her name.

Drouet confronts Carrie, telling her that Hurstwood is married. Carrie feels the blow, then accuses Drouet of deception in not telling her. Their quarrel ends with Drouet's packing a bag and leaving. Hurstwood waits for Carrie at the usual spot, and he cannot understand why she fails to come; in the following days he hopes for a message, but hears nothing.

CHAPTERS 26–27: THE AMBASSADOR FALLEN: A SEARCH FOR THE GATE; WHEN WATERS ENGULF US WE REACH FOR A STAR

Carrie decides she wants nothing more to do with either man, and so she must earn her living; she

thinks of her recent success in acting. Going to a popular theater and making inquiries, she finds herself talking to a man who invites her to go out with him; she realizes his intentions and leaves. She finally sends a note to Hurstwood, castigating him for deceiving her, saying they must no longer meet.

Hurstwood thrills to get the note, believing it means that Carrie still loves him. He is staying now at the Palmer House hotel, and he catches a glimpse of Drouet there as well; he realizes that Drouet and Carrie have quarreled. That night, closing up Fitzgerald and Moy's, he sees that the safe has not been properly shut by the cashier; pulling the door open, he sees the money inside. He knows he should shut the door properly, and yet he feels a fascination; he counts the money, finding that it totals more than $10,000. Finally putting the money back, he realizes he has put the sums in the wrong boxes; he takes it out again, and the lock springs shut on the door. He can no longer open the safe and return the money. A combination of fate and personal foible has marked out the next step in his life.

Hurstwood walks out into the street, knowing he must quickly leave the city; he takes a cab to Carrie's place, telling her that Drouet is in the hospital, injured, and wants to see her. She believes Hurstwood and goes with him, as he quietly instructs the driver to go to the train station.

CHAPTERS 28–32: A PILGRIM, AN OUTLAW: THE SPIRIT DETAINED; THE SOLACE OF TRAVEL: THE BOATS OF THE SEA; THE KINGDOM OF GREATNESS: THE PILGRIM ADREAM; A PET OF GOOD FORTUNE: BROADWAY FLAUNTS ITS JOYS; THE FEAST OF BELSHAZZAR: A SEER TO TRANSLATE

Hurstwood maintains the ruse by telling Carrie that Drouet is on the South Side, where a train can take them the most quickly. As Carrie gradually realizes his falsehood, he tells her they are going to Montreal; he assumes the police are already on his track. Reaching the Canadian city, he decides he has to give the money back; he returns most of it to Fitzgerald and Moy, promising the rest, and they agree not to pursue the matter. Using an assumed name, he finds a minister to marry him and Carrie—a ceremony he knows is not legal—and they go on to New York City.

Hurstwood finds a bar to buy into and manage; since he has little capital, it has far less elegance than Fitzgerald and Moy's. Moreover, business turns out to be less than expected, and he tells Carrie she has to be careful with expenses; she is seeing him now in a new light. She becomes acquainted with neighbors, the Vances, and she understands her situation more clearly; not only is she not as well dressed as Mrs. Vance, but her life is lacking in interest. Going to a theater matinee, she sees the glamour of Broadway, and her old longing and melancholy return. On another occasion, the Vances invite her to dinner and the theater, along with a young man named Bob AMES, a cousin of Mrs. Vance's from Indianapolis. While Carrie exults in the luxury of the dinner surroundings, Ames remarks that it is a shame for people to spend so much money. Such a thought had never occurred to her, and she finds Ames interesting. He criticizes a popular best-selling novel, although not sarcastically or superciliously; he simply thinks at a higher level, Carrie decides. He seems wiser than Hurstwood, smarter than Drouet; he also praises the theater. She is disappointed when he leaves the party.

CHAPTERS 33–40: WITHOUT THE WALLED CITY: THE SLOPE OF THE YEARS; THE GRIND OF THE MILLSTONES: A SAMPLE OF CHAFF; THE PASSING OF EFFORT: THE VISAGE OF CARE; A GRIM RETROGRESSION: THE PHANTOM OF CHANCE; THE SPIRIT AWAKENS: NEW SEARCH FOR THE GATE; IN ELF LAND DISPORTING: THE GRIM WORLD WITHOUT; OF LIGHTS AND OF SHADOWS: THE PARTING OF WORLDS; A PUBLIC DISSENSION: A FINAL APPEAL

Hurstwood is not the same man he was in Chicago, not the successful, confident, buoyant figure. He and Carrie move to a smaller, cheaper flat. The bar he co-owns is losing its lease, and since his partner has no interest in moving, he will lose his investment. He looks for other investment opportunities, but finds nothing; he learns, too, that he can sit in a hotel lobby undisturbed, reading a newspaper. He begins asking for jobs, but he soon gives up and goes back to sitting in a hotel lobby; excuses such as bad weather keep him

inside. Carrie keeps asking him for money to pay the landlord or the grocer; his store of money is dwindling. Claiming a headache, she begins sleeping in the front room.

Carrie thinks of the stage again; she follows up a lead to find a theatrical agent, then makes a round of theaters. Finally, a manager gives her a job in a chorus line; she is Carrie Madenda again. She still performs her domestic duties, even as Hurstwood continues to stay at home, but when she gets promoted to a larger role, she decides to stop giving him money. She socializes with new friends as well, although she thinks of Ames again, a man of superior taste and education, and breaks off with these friends. Hurstwood reads about a coming trolley strike in Brooklyn, including an appeal for workers to take the place of striking men; he decides to become a scab.

CHAPTERS 41–47: THE STRIKE; A TOUCH OF SPRING: THE EMPTY SHELL; THE WORLD TURNS FLATTERER: AN EYE IN THE DARK; AND THIS IS NOT ELF LAND: WHAT GOLD WILL NOT BUY; CURIOUS SHIFTS OF THE POOR; STIRRING TROUBLED WATERS; THE WAY OF THE BEATEN: A HARP IN THE WIND

Hurstwood is employed as a motorman and given police protection. He manages several trips, but a final trip draws a mob; a shot from a pistol grazes his shoulder, and he goes home. Carrie, meanwhile, has gained a speaking role in her production, and a fellow actress, not realizing her domestic situation, invites her to share a room with her; Carrie accepts. Hurstwood is now on his own.

Carrie is receiving favorable notices in the newspapers; she has money to spend on clothes, as well as on carriage rides. The manager of a new hotel on Broadway approaches her, asking her to occupy one of the apartments; her name will be worthwhile for the hotel. One afternoon, after a matinee, Mrs. Vance comes to see her, inviting her out again—assuming, too, that she has left Hurstwood.

Hurstwood now has no source of income, and he is living in a cheap lodging house. He manages to get a job doing scrub work at a hotel, but he comes down with pneumonia and spends three weeks in a hospital. He is now begging on the streets.

One evening, Drouet, having been transferred to New York, comes to Carrie's dressing room. He asks after Hurstwood, and Carrie says she has not seen him; Drouet makes reference to Hurstwood's "mistake"—and Carrie finally learns about his taking the money. She encounters Hurstwood, looking thin and shabby, in front of the theater one night; he asks for money, and she gives him all she has at the moment. She makes clear she has no interest in seeing him anymore.

Bob Ames is back in town, and he seems less than impressed by her success, since it is in comedy. She should go into drama, he says, which is more serious, which will draw on her sympathetic nature. He urges her to make use of her natural gifts, to make them valuable to others. She is stirred, challenged.

Hurstwood realizes he is viewed now as just another beggar. The police hustle him along, and pedestrians avoid him. Seeing Carrie's name blazing on a Broadway marquee, he tries unsuccessfully to get into the theater. Carrie is staying at the Waldorf now, reading Balzac's novel *Père Goriot*, which Ames has recommended to her. Drouet, at the same moment, is meeting friends, including some young women, for dinner. Meanwhile, an incoming Pullman train is bringing Mrs. Hurstwood and her daughter and rich son-in-law into the city, on their way to Rome. Hurstwood finds a room near the Bowery; turning on the gas, applying no match, he lies down, stretching out to rest.

Carrie, having let Ames point the way, still yearns for more, for further steps in life. She dreams of a happiness she may never feel.

Critical Response

As the publisher expected, some reviewers voiced censure over the book's immorality, or at least over its general disagreeableness—"a most unpleasant tale"—and yet others expressed mixed judgments, some even praise. William Marion REEDY, the St. Louis journalist who was to become important to the career of Edgar Lee MASTERS, lauded the work, finding it moral and truthful; he declared that "its veritism out-Howells Mr. Howells and out-Garlands Mr. Hamlin Garland"—a reference to the REALISM espoused by William Dean HOWELLS and

Hamlin GARLAND. Howells, editor of the influential *Harper's* magazine, never reviewed the novel; Dreiser later claimed that the critic had personally expressed disapproval. Garland—who, a decade earlier, had made his name by portraying a harsh rural life—wrote that the novel lacked grace and cultivation, although it offered "verity."

An English publication of *Sister Carrie* appeared in 1901; the first portion of the work was condensed, fitting the length restrictions of a uniform series, and as a result, the emphasis shifted from Carrie to Hurstwood. The reviews were favorable, praising the novel for its strength and power. The *Manchester Guardian* declared it among "the veritable documents of American history"; another critic suggested that *Sister Carrie* belongs on a shelf next to Émile ZOLA's *Nana*.

In 1907, the firm of B. W. Dodge and Company republished the novel; by then, social attitudes had changed, at least sufficiently to allow the important reviews to be favorable. The volume sold relatively well, and the following year a reprint house brought out a cheap edition. Gradually, *Sister Carrie* became recognized as a milestone in American literature, the touchstone for realistic presentations of urban life.

The 1952 film *Carrie*, starring Jennifer Jones, appeared in 1952; producers dropped "Sister" from the title to avoid suggesting that the movie was about a nun. Laurence Olivier, playing Hurstwood, received the British Film Academy award for Best Actor.

Skeeters Kirby
Edgar Lee Masters
(1923)

This autobiographical novel by Edgar Lee MASTERS, the second of a trilogy, follows the title character as he studies law at his father's insistence; going to Chicago, becoming a lawyer, he writes successful poetry as well. He also finds a variety of women, based on the many women with whom Masters himself became involved. When Kirby's marriage fails, his former law partner causes him to lose his fortune; Masters is portraying negatively his own former law partner,

Clarence DARROW. The third novel in the trilogy, *Mirage,* published in 1924, follows up on these themes of victimization; the hero suffers because of women, including his wife and mistress, and because of a fickle public.

skyscraper

The term *skyscraper* first denoted a structure of 10 stories or more, accessed by an elevator. The 16-story MONADNOCK BUILDING, completed in 1891, was designated a skyscraper, although it rested on six-foot-thick load-bearing masonry walls. Later, by the end of the century, the term came to mean a structure built around a steel skeleton. The HOME INSURANCE BUILDING, completed in 1885, was partially supported by a steel frame; the Rand McNally Building, completed five years later, made first full use of steel-frame construction. The new construction allowed for thin walls, as well as large expanses of glass; it increased the building's interior room, in that supporting columns were no longer required. A necessary precondition for the skyscraper was the invention of the elevator—first steam-powered, then hydraulic, then electric. A further precondition was the development of the Bessemer process, used for manufacturing high-strength steel. Tall-building construction required also a new type of architectural firm, relying on engineers to design plumbing, heating, fireproofing, elevator technology, and communications technology.

A major objection to skyscrapers was the "canyons" they created, making streets dark, blocking out sunlight, blocking light from neighboring structures; zoning laws soon appeared to regulate the height of buildings. ADLER AND SULLIVAN, constructing the Schiller Building in 1894, pioneered in the "setback," placing upper stories back from the street, preventing the overpowering frontal wall. In human terms, the upper floors of the tall buildings were only gradually deemed desirable, even prestigious; in pre-elevator days, the panoramic views offered by upper floors could not compensate for the task of stair climbing. In Henry B. FULLER's novel of 1895, *WITH THE PROCESSION,* a benefactress, providing a lunchroom

for working girls, apologizes for the high floor on which the facilities are located; she acknowledges that the building has elevators, and yet in those days, the luxury of the penthouse had not been fully felt.

"Skyscraper"   *See* CHICAGO POEMS.

Slabs of the Sunburnt West
Carl Sandburg
(1922)

In the fourth volume of poetry, Carl SANDBURG moves away from the urban settings of his earlier work. The first piece, "The Windy City," returns to the theme of CHICAGO POEMS, and yet the title poem, placed last, goes far afield, evoking the Grand Canyon. The volume received a favorable review in the DIAL, marking the first time that the periodical, having embraced new editorial policies, had fully approved of his poetry. Yet the same issue showcased T. S. ELIOT's "The Waste Land"—and as a result, Sandburg's one-time role as innovator was doomed. The poet had been broadening his vistas to celebrate America as a whole, relinquishing social criticism to become an exponent of mainstream populism, and yet the ascendancy of the essentially undemocratic MODERNISM, embodied in Eliot and his mentor Ezra POUND, soon left him behind, deeming him irrelevant to the modern literary, academic, and intellectual world.

Slack, Margaret Fuller   *See* SPOON RIVER ANTHOLOGY.

Small, Albion W.
(1854–1926) *founder of the sociology department at the University of Chicago*

Born in Maine, Small trained as a Baptist minister, studied at Johns Hopkins University and in Germany, then became president of Colby College in 1889. Three years later, he came to the new UNIVERSITY OF CHICAGO to establish the new academic field of SOCIOLOGY. His influential text-book, *An Introduction to the Study of Society*, coauthored with colleague George E. Vincent, appeared in 1894; the following year, Small founded and edited the first sociology journal in the United States, the *American Journal of Sociology*. Despite his pioneering efforts, the criticism of Small has been that he relegated women researchers to social work, insisting that men and women have separate academic realms. Claiming, too, that politics is a man's domain, he never supported women's suffrage.

Smith, Private Edward

This character appears in Hamlin GARLAND's story "Return of a Private," from *MAIN-TRAVELLED ROADS*. After serving three years in the Union army during the CIVIL WAR, Wisconsin farmer Ed Smith, emaciated and feverish, returns to his family, children, and land—and to the toil that will once more be his lot. His nine-year-old son soberly watches his return. In real-life, the son was Garland himself, who tells the tale again in his autobiography, *A SON OF THE MIDDLE BORDER*.

Smoke and Steel
Carl Sandburg
(1920)

In his third book of poetry, a volume twice the size of his previous two volumes together, SANDBURG returns in part to the social commentary of *CHICAGO POEMS*; he returns also to an urban industrial landscape. The title poem grew out of a steel strike in 1919 in South Chicago and Gary, Indiana; it includes a depiction of five men fallen into a vat of molten steel, "their bones kneaded into the bread of steel." Yet with the rise of the literary MODERNISM in the postwar world—an elitist movement, lacking in concern for the masses—Sandburg's revisiting of social issues aroused decreasing interest.

So Big
Edna Ferber
(1924)

A best-seller, based on a short story from 1919, "Farmer in the Dell," the novel won the Pulitzer Prize in 1925. A plucky woman schoolteacher marries a vegetable farmer in a Dutch community south of Chicago; after her husband's early death, she takes over the farm, running her rickety wagon and horses into Haymarket Square to sell her produce, and the enterprise becomes successful for the first time. FERBER is once more presenting a woman who retains a generous heart while yet succeeding in the economic world. Film actresses playing the heroine included Colleen Moore in 1925, Barbara Stanwyck in 1932, and Jane Wyman in 1953.

Social Darwinism

A theory of society deriving from the work of English naturalist Charles Darwin, Social Darwinism was first propounded by the late 19th-century English philosopher Herbert SPENCER, who coined the phrase "survival of the fittest." In America, Yale University professor William Graham Sumner applied Spencerian doctrines to issues of political and economic reform, asserting that attempts to improve social conditions interfere with mankind's natural evolutionary course. The human race, Sumner declared, like the rest of the animal kingdom, competes for survival, and those who survive—the rich and the powerful—are the most fit; the poor are those who are unfit, and their natural condition must not be artificially altered. The doctrines of Social Darwinism proved compatible with those of German philosopher Friedrich NIETZSCHE, who declared also that the superior strong man must ignore the weaklings beneath him. The overweening businessmen of Robert HERRICK's *MEMOIRS OF AN AMERICAN CITIZEN* and Theodore DREISER's Frank COWPERWOOD trilogy reflect both views.

socialism

In broadest terms, socialism is a political and economic system in which goods-producing facilities, as well as transportation and utilities, are publicly owned. The modern call for socialism arose with the growth of industrialism and the resulting disparity between the owners' rewards and the workers' rewards. The leading theorist in the 19th century was the German Karl Marx, supporting the call for class conflict between owners and workers, leading to revolution and the establishment of a new society. Other varieties of socialism ranged from experiments in communalism—disavowing private property, practicing collective sharing—to utopian visions of nonviolent progress in which CAPITALISM is gradually superseded.

In Chicago, the exponents of socialism were largely foreign-born, incorporating doctrines of ANARCHISM into their views. Their militancy, combined with their nonnative status, placed limits on their public effectiveness—although after the PULLMAN STRIKE of 1894, the labor movement as a whole spoke increasingly of working-class solidarity, opposing what was called the capitalist class. The SOCIALIST PARTY OF AMERICA, founded in 1901, led by Indiana-born Eugene V. DEBS, received nearly a million votes in the presidential elections of 1912 and 1920.

Upton SINCLAIR's novel of 1906, THE JUNGLE, ends with a didactic presentation of socialist doctrine; the immigrant protagonist is portrayed as readily converted. Carl SANDBURG, while writing his best-known poetry, was writing at the same time for the INTERNATIONAL SOCIALIST REVIEW. Sherwood ANDERSON's 1920 novel, POOR WHITE, presents a man who has lived through the CIVIL WAR, who declares now that a new war is coming—between social classes, "between those who have and those who can't get"; Anderson, along with Theodore DREISER, supported labor actions and socialist causes in the 1930s.

Socialist Labor Party

One of several parties in the United States espousing SOCIALISM, the Socialist Labor Party was founded in New York City in 1877. Growing out of the earlier Workingmen's Association, the party became identified with its large numbers of German immigrant members. In 1890, the organization came under the leadership of Daniel DeLeon, author of *Socialist Reconstruction of Society*; less

than a decade later, dissident members defected to the less militant Socialist Democratic Party, soon to become the SOCIALIST PARTY OF AMERICA. In 1905, DeLeon became one of the founders in Chicago of the INDUSTRIAL WORKERS OF THE WORLD.

Socialist Party of America

The principal organization espousing SOCIALISM in the United States, the Socialist Party of America was founded in Indianapolis in 1901. It combined the Social Democratic Party, formed in 1898 by Eugene V. DEBS and Victor Berger, with a moderate branch of the SOCIALIST LABOR PARTY. It was less doctrinaire, less Marxist, than the earlier Socialist Labor Party, considering its basic agenda to be the public ownership of the means of production. During the 1912 presidential campaign, the party divided over its association with the violence-condoning INDUSTRIAL WORKERS OF THE WORLD; despite IWW defections, candidate Debs won a nearly million votes for president that year.

In April 1917, when America entered WORLD WAR I, the party opposed the war, branding it a capitalist conflict; Debs, speaking against the military draft, went to prison under the Espionage Act. Other prominent socialists, including Carl SANDBURG and Upton SINCLAIR, supported the war, declaring that German militarism must be suppressed. Another split occurred in 1919, when dissidents from the Socialist Party, meeting in Chicago, formed the Communist Party of America and the Communist Labor Party. In the 1920 election, Debs, still imprisoned, running for president from his prison cell, again received nearly a million votes. In 1924, the party joined the AMERICAN FEDERATION OF LABOR and other union organizations to support the unsuccessful presidential candidacy of Wisconsin Senator Robert La Follette in a new Progressive Party; in 1928, the Socialist Party ran as its candidate Norman Thomas, one of the founders of the American Civil Liberties Union.

Floyd DELL, in his autobiographical novel MOON-CALF, writes of his membership in the Socialist Party in Port Royal—his name for Davenport, Iowa—in the early years of the 20th century.

He speaks of the schism in American socialism, between his group and the Socialist Labor Party, although in Port Royal, he writes, "the thunderings of DeLeon were now forgotten." He refers to relatively mild activities, such as putting up candidates for local elections and competing in street meetings with the SALVATION ARMY.

sociology

This modern-era academic discipline, this field of study came first to America at the UNIVERSITY OF CHICAGO. The new university, founded in 1892, created the nation's first sociology department in the same year. As formulated in Chicago, the discipline followed a methodology that had already been employed by researchers at HULL-HOUSE, producing what became known as "Chicago sociology." In the *Hull-House Maps and Papers,* published by Florence KELLEY in 1895, the women of Hull-House, using detailed maps and analyzing social and economic patterns, provided the first thorough study of an American working-class neighborhood, establishing methods employed by university sociologists for decades following. Department members began turning to the city as a laboratory, conducting field studies of urban life, tracing residential patterns, studying immigrant and racial-group clustering; a division of sanitary science studied residential sanitary conditions. Albion W. SMALL, chairman of the department from 1892 until 1926, founded the *American Journal of Sociology,* soon to become a major journal in the field.

After WORLD WAR I, sociology became increasingly segregated by gender; the academic ranks were filled by men, taking on greater intellectual respectability, while the women increasingly became social workers—and social work, even in academia, was the less prestigious field. Sociology split also on "theory" versus "practice"; the male academic department became increasing apolitical, employing terms such as "objective" and "scientific," while social reform was left to women and nonacademics.

In Edna FERBER's novel of 1917, *FANNY HERSELF,* the founder of a mail-order firm initiates a

profit-sharing plan among his employees—the result, says a disgruntled executive, of his "milling around with a herd of sociologists, philanthropists, and students of economics." Sinclair LEWIS's *Main Street,* appearing three years later, presents a sociology instructor at a college in Minneapolis, a young man who "had lived among poets and socialists and Jews" in New York; he now leads his "giggling" students through prisons and charity agencies in the upper Midwest.

Sohlberg, Rita

This character appears in Theodore DREISER's novel THE TITAN. After the marriage of protagonist Frank COWPERWOOD to Aileen BUTLER, Rita is Cowperwood's first significant mistress. Married to a Danish violinist living in Chicago, Rita receives income from her father, thereby keeping her husband unsuspicious when Cowperwood buys her gifts and fine clothes. Her character is not drawn clearly, her main distinction being that she is six years younger than Aileen; at one point, Cowperwood finds her "much richer spiritually"—a quality remaining unexplained—and yet she is also "a pagan," feeling no qualms about the affair. Rita is the mistress whom Aileen attacks physically, in the presence of both Cowperwood and Harold Sohlberg, thereby ending the relationship; Rita leaves both men and goes off to Europe.

"Soiled Dove"   *See* CHICAGO POEMS.

Soldier Field

This sports stadium, designed by the firm of Holabird and Roche, features classical columns fitting in with those of the neighboring FIELD MUSEUM and SHEDD AQUARIUM. Opening in 1924 as the Municipal Grant Park Stadium, Soldier Field was renamed and dedicated the following year on Armistice Day, November 11, 1925 to memorialize Americans killed in WORLD WAR I. In September 1927, accommodating 100,000 spectators, it was the site of the celebrated heavyweight championship fight between

Jack Dempsey and Gene Tunney, in which Dempsey lost in the controversial "long count" decision. A renovation project, controversial because of its tampering with the structures classic lines, was completed in 2003.

The Song of the Lark
Willa Cather
(1915)

Set partially in Chicago, the work portrays the development of a woman artist, an opera singer. CATHER, recreating her childhood home in Red Cloud, Nebraska—changed here to Moonstone, Colorado—makes the early portion of the work autobiographical; as in the case of the novel's heroine, she herself was treated for pneumonia as a young girl, and an itinerant German musician, noted for his tendency to drink, gave her piano lessons. Yet much of Thea KRONBORG's career parallels that of the Swedish-born, Minnesota-raised opera singer Olive FREMSTAD; Cather was an admirer and a personal friend of Fremstad, a singer who helped popularize in America the operas of Richard WAGNER. Another influence on the novel is the trip that Cather made to the Southwest in 1912; her heroine's visit to the ancient cliff dwellings is depicted as an overwhelming experience, setting Thea on the road to greatness.

Cather has said that her purpose in *The Song of the Lark* was to tell of a woman's striving, against difficult circumstances, to achieve an artistic career. The novel presents Cather's only portrait of a woman artist whose ambition is fulfilled; it is considered the first extended treatment in fiction of the growth and development of a woman artist.

Synopsis

PART I: FRIENDS OF CHILDHOOD
In the 1890s, Dr. Howard ARCHIE, the young doctor in the small town of Moonstone, Colorado, attends the birth of the seventh child of Peter Kronborg, a local minister of Swedish origin. While at the house, Dr. Archie sees that the 11-year-old Thea Kronborg is ill; he diagnoses pneu-

monia and treats her. He sees also that the girl is different from the rest, more clever, more determined; he notices the upright piano in the parlor. Thea has been pronounced a talented musician by her piano teacher, Professor Wunsch, an erudite German alcoholic boarding nearby. Her main allies within her own family are her mother, whom she most resembles, and her aunt Tillie Kronborg, her father's sister, who lives with the family, grateful for no longer being cruelly overworked on her father's farm in Minnesota. Thea becomes attached to Dr. Archie, an unhappily married man who takes her on his rounds to see his patients; among these patients are Spanish Johnny, a singer and mandolin-player living in the Mexican quarter, who suffers bouts of fever and madness. Another friend of Thea's childhood is Ray KENNEDY, a railroad man in his 30s who hopes to marry the girl when she comes of age. Yet among her peers Thea has no friends; she finds most of the people in Moonstone, including her siblings, trivial, conventional, and jealous.

Thea loses her piano teacher when Wunsch goes on a drunken binge and his pupils desert him; he has to leave town and establish himself elsewhere. She herself becomes the town's music teacher. She wants to study further, but she has no money for traveling. A turning point in her life comes when Ray Kennedy dies in a railroad accident; Thea, now 17, learns that he has left a $600 insurance policy in her name, instructing that she use the money to go to Chicago for further study. Dr. Archie agrees to accompany her, to help her find appropriate lodging and an appropriate teacher.

PART II: THE SONG OF THE LARK
After staying briefly at the Young Women's Christian Association in Chicago, Thea finds lodging with two widows; she is promised income by the pastor of a Swedish Reform Church, who hires her for his choir and for singing at funerals. Dr. Archie has determined that she will study with the best teacher available, a pianist named Andor Harsanyi. By big-city standards, Thea turns out to be untutored, unsophisticated—"the savage blonde," one of Harsanyi's students calls her—but she displays intelligence, determination, and

discipline. Dropping by the ART INSTITUTE one day, she is enthralled by Jules BRETON's "The Song of the Lark," portraying a peasant girl, scythe in hand, to the bird's song in the early morning light; she sees herself as the listening girl, standing in the countryside at dawn. Thea attends her first symphony concert, going to a matinee in the AUDITORIUM BUILDING—and resolves at once that such ecstasy, such triumph, will one day be hers. Harsanyi, hearing her sing, realizes that her greatest talent is not in the piano but in her voice. Knowing he will miss her as a student, he persuades her to take up with the best vocal teacher in Chicago, Madison Bowers; she will also have to study French, German, and Italian. That summer she goes home for a visit to Colorado, but soon feels alienation from most of her family and those around her—except for her mother, Spanish Johnny, and her old friend, Dr. Archie. As she sits on the train returning to Chicago, she knows she will not return; she is going away forever.

PART III: STUPID FACES

Thea is taking singing lessons now from Bowers, earning money by playing accompaniment for his other pupils. She likes neither Bowers nor his students—the title of the section refers to those she finds irritating—including the mediocre concert singers to whom he gives lessons. She moves her lodgings frequently, unable to get along with either her landladies or her housemates; she is intolerant of the commonplace. Then a new, interesting figure enters her life, Phillip Frederick OTTENBURG, scion of a St. Louis brewery family; Fred Ottenburg runs the Chicago branch of the business, although he is also an accomplished musician and an opera connoisseur. Meeting her through Bowers, Fred takes up Thea as his special cause; he introduces her to the Henry Nathanmeyers, a wealthy and cultivated couple who appreciate good music and are happy to have her sing at their social gatherings. He also brings about a significant change in her life—the result of his persuading her to spend time at his father's Arizona ranch, where the twisting canyon walls are marked by the cliff dwellings of ancient peoples.

PART IV: THE ANCIENT PEOPLE

Sleeping now in a rock room she has lined with Navaho blankets, feeling the heat of the sun, sensing the aroma of the cedars, Thea hears music in a new and sensuous form. The world seems older and richer to her; the ancient cliff-dwellers have lengthened her past, given her older and higher obligations. When Fred arrives, the two of them spend their time exploring and adventuring; when they finally board an eastbound train, they have not yet decided where they are going. Fred suggests heading south to Albuquerque, to El Paso, to Mexico; Thea, broaching a new subject, suggests they get married in Chicago. At this point, Fred resolves to help her to get on in life—because he knows he is already married; he has been married since he was 20 years old. His estranged wife lives in Santa Barbara, California. He had always thought that Thea was not the marrying kind, since she often antagonized people rather than conciliated them. Yet on that train she opts to go to Mexico—and as he looks into her expectant face, he realizes he can do better by her than any other man.

PART V: DR. ARCHIE'S VENTURE

Dr. Archie, having begun to invest in a silver mine, receives a letter from Thea—unexpectedly, since she has not written in a long time. She explains that she is in difficulty, that she is in New York; she needs his advice and friendship, and she also needs money. She is going to Germany to study, since her voice is now ready; she asks Archie to come to her hotel in New York. Archie has never been that far east, but he borrows money and leaves at once. Meanwhile, Fred is upset that Thea is not taking money from him to finance her study; she says that doing so would mean he is "keeping" her. Fred and Thea meet with Dr. Archie, and after an initial awkwardness, the two men find a mutual interest—in Thea—and they find friendship with each other as well. Thea sails for Germany.

PART VI: KRONBORG: TEN YEARS LATER

Dr. Archie is now the prosperous owner of a silver mine, living in Denver; his wife has died. When Fred visits him, he announces he is going to New

York to hear Thea sing; she has been establishing herself as an international star. When Archie notes that she did not return to Colorado when her mother was dying, Fred reminds him that doing so would have meant giving up a chance to sing at the Dresden Opera; her staying abroad was necessary for her career. Arriving in New York, Archie goes to see Thea in Wagner's *Lohengrin*. When she appears onstage, he feels both admiration and estrangement; she is no longer the girl he once knew, but rather a beautiful and radiant woman who seems to chill his affection. Thea meets with Archie and Ottenburg, and they are joined by an effete young man named Landry, a fellow student of Thea's in Germany; Landry seems now a fixture in her life. Archie learns also about a married singer named Nordquist, who wanted Thea to pay his wife to divorce him; Thea scornfully refused. In a triumphant performance as Wagner's Sieglinde, Thea is applauded by Archie, Ottenburg, Harsanyi, and—unknown to her—Spanish Johnny, brought to New York by Barnum and Bailey's circus, which featured a Mexican band that year.

EPILOGUE

In the year 1909, Thea's eccentric aunt Tillie is the last Kronborg remaining in Moonstone; she lives in her own world, proudly keeping newspaper clippings of her niece's artistic triumphs. It has been announced that Thea has married Fred Ottenburg. When the Metropolitan Opera last came to Kansas City, Thea sent for Tillie and brought her to every performance. Now a New York paper arrives in the mail, and Tillie sees that Madame Kronborg is performing Wagner's Isolde in London, also singing for the king at Buckingham Palace. The townspeople have grown tired of Tillie's stories, and yet in the east part of town, where the humbler folks live, people still listen and marvel that dreams can come true.

Critical Reception

The *New York Times Book Review* found Cather's heroine unsympathetic, pursuing her career with a "steady, calm ruthlessness"; *The New Republic* spoke of her self-centeredness. Feminist critics

have since pointed out a double standard in such comments, noting that a greater degree of ruthlessness is tolerated in male than in female protagonists. Cather herself made revisions in subsequent editions, softening Thea's seeming callousness as she achieves greatness in her career.

The novel has also been accused of a pro-German bias, particularly noticeable in its publication date of 1915, in the midst of WORLD WAR I. The work has been charged as Nietzschean as well, supporting the precepts of German philosopher Friedrich NIETZSCHE; Thea often scorns "stupid" and untalented people, disdaining timidity and weakness. Nietzsche's praise of the "superman," rising above restraining conventions, had struck a response in the early decades of the 20th century; Cather's attitude seems to be that Thea suffers an emotional toll—but such is required for the truly great soul, particularly the great woman's soul.

Another criticism has focused on the novel's PRIMITIVISM, its suggestion that Thea's sojourn among the ancient peoples of the canyon is for the purpose of personal rejuvenation; the role of the ancient culture is simply to fulfill her needs. More favorable commentary has lauded Cather's portrait of a small prairie town, a rendering of her own childhood town; here she joins in the REVOLT FROM THE VILLAGE movement.

A Son of the Middle Border
Hamlin Garland
(1917)

In this autobiographical work by Hamlin GARLAND, the Middle Border is the Great Plains, the land between the older border states of Indiana and Illinois and the Rocky Mountains. Garland begins his volume with the return of his father to a bleak Wisconsin farm after the CIVIL WAR—an event previously fictionalized in "The Return of a Private" in MAIN-TRAVELLED ROADS. Subsequently, the family moves farther west, to farmland in Iowa. Garland gives an account of his boyhood reading, much of it from McGuffey's Readers, the basic school text of the era, particularly popular in the

Midwest; his poetry selections match those he depicts Rose DUTCHER as reading in ROSE OF DUTCHER'S COOLLY. Garland tells also of following the serialization of Edward EGGLESTON's THE HOOSIER SCHOOLMASTER in the magazine *Hearth and Home*; he notes that the "Moody and Sankey Song Book," containing familiar hymns—mentioned also in *Rose of Dutcher's Coolly*—is in every farmer's home. His own home also gives sitting-room honor to a steel engraving of the family hero, General Ulysses S. GRANT. When the family moves again, to the Dakota territory, Garland chooses not to go, eventually making his way to Boston.

"Sophistication"   See WINESBURG, OHIO.

"Southern Pacific"   See CORNHUSKERS.

Spalding, Albert G.
(1850–1915) *baseball player, team owner; sporting goods manufacturer*

An early figure in the development of baseball, Spalding became an important manufacturer of sporting equipment. Born in Byron, Illinois, becoming a major-league pitcher, then owner of a Chicago team, Spalding is credited with innovations in the game's increasing professionalization. He established spring training and minor-league farm clubs; his *Score Book* and annual *Spalding's Official Baseball Guide,* the latter first appearing in the 1880s, became essential baseball publications. In 1876, he opened a sporting goods store in Chicago, A. G. Spalding and Brothers, soon turning to manufacturing as well; he developed the baseball glove and catcher's mask, producing also the first regulation balls and bats. Spalding died in California at the age of 65, lauded as "the Father of Baseball."

Spanish-American War

As a result of this brief conflict between Spain and the United States of 1898, the Spanish Empire was dissolved, Cuba became independent, and former possessions of Spain—Puerto Rico, the Philippines, and Guam—became U.S. territories. Starting with the desire of Cubans to rid themselves of Spanish control, the conflict came to involve the United States partly through efforts of expansionists, inflamed by the "yellow journalism" of papers owned by William Randolph Hearst and Joseph Pulitzer. The key event was the explosion and sinking of the battleship *Maine* in the Havana harbor in February 1898; no perpetrator was positively identified, nor blame proved, but declarations of war followed. In May of that year, Admiral George Dewey defeated the Spanish fleet in the harbor of Manila, the Philippines, and in July, Theodore ROOSEVELT led his famed Rough Riders up San Juan Hill in Cuba, resulting in the surrender of the city of Santiago. The war itself—a "splendid little war," according to Secretary of State John Hay—lasted only a few months. During that period, Sherwood ANDERSON served in the military occupation of Cuba, and Carl SANDBURG was stationed in Puerto Rico.

Efforts to crush subsequent guerrilla uprisings in the Philippines continued for years. The official justification was that if America relinquished that Pacific nation, another country, such as Japan or Germany, would intervene. Public opinion became divided; the ANTI-IMPERIALIST LEAGUE arose to decry American expansion, supported by William Jennings BRYAN, writer Mark Train, and industrialist Andrew Carnegie. William Vaughn MOODY's antiwar poems, "ODE IN A TIME OF HESITATION" and "ON A SOLDIER FALLEN IN THE PHILIPPINES," published in the *Atlantic Monthly,* received national attention. Henry B. FULLER published a privately printed *The New Flag* in 1899, critical of the war and the administration of President William MCKINLEY; another opponent of expansionism, Edgar Lee MASTERS, published a series of articles, THE NEW STAR CHAMBER AND OTHER ESSAYS, in 1904. Later, in 1915, Masters's SPOON RIVER ANTHOLOGY presented to a vast audience the bitter epitaph of Harry Wilmans, dead in the Philippines, buried in Spoon River with a flag over his grave.

Sparks, Emily   See SPOON RIVER ANTHOLOGY.

Spencer, Herbert
(1820–1903) *English philosopher*

Coiner of the phrase "survival of the fittest," Spencer is known as the expositor of SOCIAL DARWINISM. Rejecting supernaturalism, advocating a scientific examination of social phenomena, he applied to society the evolutionary doctrines of naturalist Charles Darwin. The result was a belief in evolutionary human progress— a progress developing automatically, collectively; individual men were deemed unable to control their destiny. In these views, Spencer's vision complemented that of literary NATURALISM. Theodore DREISER was influenced by Spencer's rejection of religion, as well as by his essentially mechanistic view of the universe. Dreiser's play *The Hand of the Potter,* presenting a child molester and murderer, takes its title from a line in Edward FitzGerald's translation of *The Rubáiyát of Omar Khayyám,* declaring that humans are shaped by a potter's hand, having no control over their nature; Dreiser is heeding Spencerian as well as naturalistic principles—as he would in AN AMERICAN TRAGEDY, presenting a character following a course seemingly determined by his nature.

Spies, August
(1855–1887) *editor of* Arbeiter Zeitung

Born in Germany, Spies came to the United States in 1872, gaining employment as an upholsterer. He joined the Socialist Labor Party, then turned to ANARCHISM, espousing in the *Arbeiter Zeitung* violence and the use of DYNAMITE. At the HAYMARKET AFFAIR rally, Spies was the first to speak, subsequently leaving the assembly; yet he was among the men arrested after the bombing. His speech at the trial—declaring, among other points, that the barbaric state is doomed to die— is often quoted, as are his final words, "The day will come when our silence will be more powerful than the voices you are throttling today." The Martyrs' Monument at WALDHEIM CEMETERY, where Spies and four others are buried, was dedicated in 1895.

The Spirit of an Illinois Town
Mary Hartwell Catherwood
(1897)

The title refers to the spirit of an orphaned young woman, harshly treated as a servant, whom the first-person narrator has loved; she dies in a PRAIRIE tornado. The narrator subsequently idealizes her, seeing her aura in the town of Trail City, Illinois— and as a moral guiding spirit in his own life. The narrator had previously spent several years abroad, eager to leave the Midwest; now, because of this idealized woman, because of her continuing influence, he is reconnected with uprightness and virtue.

Under the subtitle "Two Stories of Illinois: At Different Periods," the novel was published along with another short work, "The Little Renault." Set in 1680, the latter tale returns to CATHERWOOD's NEW FRANCE milieu, the scene of her earlier romances. "The Little Renault" is an exercise in gender-bending, as the title character is a young orphan girl, dressed as a boy to survive in the rugged world of French explorers and Indians. Conveniently, she dies before having to face the issue of puberty and gender identity. Both stories, although set 200 years apart, deal with the death of an innocent young woman; their sentimentality often amazes the modern reader.

The Spirit of Youth and the City Streets
Jane Addams
(1909)

Drawing in part from juvenile court cases, ADDAMS details the restless lives of young people in the neighborhood around HULL-HOUSE; the youth are discontented because they have no appropriate outlets for their energy. The city overstimulates the young person, Addams declares, even its "brightly colored theater posters," advertising the popular VAUDEVILLE and burlesque theaters of the day; those institutions teach false values—as opposed to the theater of Shakespeare and Molière. Addams encourages urban governments to provide more recreation centers, parks, and playgrounds;

she advocates industrial training for young men and women. Philosopher William James reviewed the volume favorably in the *American Journal of Sociology*. More than a half-century later, Edna FERBER, noting that the book comes to mind whenever she sees a group of idle youths, suggested a comparison between its portrait of youthful disaffection and that depicted in the stage musical *West Side Story*.

"The Spooniad" *See SPOON RIVER ANTHOLOGY.*

Spoon River Anthology
Edgar Lee Masters
(1915)

One of the most influential volumes of poetry written in America, the work consists of nearly 250 monologues spoken by the dead, small-town inhabitants buried in the local cemetery. Masters uses FREE VERSE, a technique not generally accepted at the time, and he presents a frankness not generally found in poetic subject matter. *Spoon River Anthology* is a document in the REVOLT FROM THE VILLAGE movement, demonstrating that the small town is not to be idealized for its benevolent pastoral qualities. The real-world Spoon River is a small stream flowing into the Illinois River; the fictional town of Spoon River is a composite of two Illinois communities in which the poet lived as a boy and young man—Petersburg, not far from SPRINGFIELD, and Lewistown, 40 miles to the north. In contradiction to what the poet Amy LOWELL wrote in her *Tendencies in Modern American Poetry*, the village of Hanover, Illinois, was never Masters's model.

The immediate literary model is the collection of poems known as the GREEK ANTHOLOGY, a gathering of verse that includes gravestone epitaphs. A further antecedent is the poem "Earth," by the mid-19th-century American poet William Cullen BRYANT, presenting voices from the graveyard, telling about unhappy lives. The 19th-century English poet Robert Browning, celebrated for his character-revealing dramatic monologues, is also

seen as an influence; Masters read a paper on Browning before a literary gathering several years before *Spoon River* appeared.

The *Spoon River* poems first ran as a series for eight months during 1914–15 in *Reedy's Mirror*, a weekly magazine published in St. Louis by William Marion REEDY. The pieces appeared originally under the pen name of Webster Ford, although Reedy revealed the poet's identity while the series was still running. The collected volume was published in 1915, and an expanded volume, containing additional pieces, which are now part of the accepted body of poems, appeared the following year.

Synopses of Selected Poems

"THE HILL"
This opening poem follows the UBI SUNT, or "Where are?" formula, a traditional rhetorical query; its purpose is to suggest the transience of human life. Masters begins his poem with "Where are . . .," naming a variety of townspeople, representing a variety of human types. He concludes, "All, all are sleeping on the hill"—a reference to the Oak Hill Cemetery in Lewiston, Illinois. The poet reviews the various ways in which these people met their deaths—by mine accident, by brawling, by fever, by war. As is common in the *ubi sunt* tradition, the query is repeated throughout the poem; the answer echoes in the refrain, "All, all are sleeping."

Yet the final query, "Where is Old Fiddler Jones . . .?" brings a different response. Jones, although his "ninety years" are complete—although he, too, sleeps on the hill—continues to sing of long-ago events, such as fish-frys and horse-races, such as what favorite son Abraham LINCOLN said in Springfield. Jones, in other words, is the Homer, the bard, remaining to sing the tales, to tell of figures and events so that they become part of history.

"HOD PUTT"
Hod lies in his grave next to a man who grew rich by manipulating the bankruptcy law. Yet when he, Hod, tried to grow rich by robbing a traveler, he accidentally killed the man, and he was tried and

hanged for his act. Now the two of them, having dealt with bankruptcy in their own ways, sleep side by side in peace. "The bankrupt law" that Hod speaks of refers also to the larger criminal justice system.

Many poems later, a character known only as the Circuit Judge recalls sentencing Hod to hang; he realizes that Hod was more innocent of soul than he.

"OLLIE MCGEE"; "FLETCHER MCGEE"

The second and third monologues present a bitter pairing of husband and wife. Ollie McGee, the first to die, claims that her husband broke her spirit and shamed her with a secret cruelty, robbing her of youth and beauty. His knowledge that he did so— that he made her what she was—gnaws at him, she says, and that knowledge is bringing him to his grave. Fletcher McGee, meanwhile, claiming that his wife drained him and sapped his strength, admits that he turned on her and manipulated her pitilessly; he gave her the face that she hated and that he himself ended up fearing. Then she died, haunting him.

The two poems set forth stories that correlate with each other; the husband adds the motive that explains his cruelty. Yet what he actually did is unspecified; the terse format that Masters adopts precludes details. The couple have simply been long locked in mutual destructiveness.

"AMANDA BARKER"

The people of the village do not understand that Henry purposely impregnated his wife, knowing she would die in childbirth; they always assumed he was a loving husband. The address to the "traveler" is a common device in the Greek Anthology; the most famous of all epitaphs, in which Spartan soldiers explain their stand to the death at the pass of Themopylae, makes a similar address to a "traveler"—translated also as "friend," "stranger," or "passerby." In the classical poem the fallen soldiers ask the traveler to bring back the news that they died obedient to the laws of their land; in Masters's poem Amanda makes a simple proclamation to the traveler, telling him what the village does not know, that her husband hated her and caused her death.

"CONSTANCE HATELY"

The name is obvious, but the last two lines of the poem illustrate a standard device in epigrammatic poetry—a final twist, a punchline that clarifies, even reverses, the meaning of the rest of the poem. The citizens of Spoon River have praised Constance for raising her sister's orphans, and they have condemned the girls for their subsequent contempt of her—but it is true, she acknowledges: She poisoned her good deed by constantly reminding the girls of their dependence on her.

"KINSEY KEENE"

The figure is based in part on Masters's father, who opposed the growing temperance movement in the town of Lewiston, Illinois. Keene addresses various civic leaders, as well as the Social Purity Club, suggesting that they remember what the French general Count Cambronne said after the defeat of his army at Waterloo, Belgium, when asked to surrender to the English. What Cambronne replied, he declares, is what he says to them now, and he wants it carved upon his headstone. That reply, fabled in history—although unspecified in the poem—is the word for excrement.

Thomas Rhodes, Editor Whedon, Rev. Abner Peet, and A. D. Blood all have their say later in the volume.

"BENJAMIN PANTIER"; "MRS. BENJAMIN PANTIER"; "REUBEN PANTIER"

Benjamin Pantier, attorney at law, found solace in life finally only with his dog, Nig, who is now buried with him. His wife survived him, but she had broken his will and "bled" him; he who had once looked forward to life had lost all hope. He went to live with Nig in the back room of the office. Now his and Nig's bones join in the grave.

Mrs. Pantier, meanwhile, knows that the town loved him, but she, who heard the poetry of Wordsworth in her ears, hated his smell of whiskey and onions. As a man, he filled her with disgust.

Reuben Pantier, the son, escaped from Spoon River after getting the milliner's daughter in trouble; he traveled as far as Paris. Yet one day, thousands of miles away, tears came to his eyes as he thought of his schoolteacher, Emily Sparks, who had prayed for him, who had refused to give up her hopes for him. Whatever he finally became in life, he says, was because of her.

Emily Sparks's monologue follows; later, A. D. Blood decries that Reuben Pantier and Dora, the milliner's daughter, are nightly making his grave an "unholy pillow." Dora Williams and her mother, the milliner, make explanations from their own graves.

It has long been assumed that Mr. and Mrs. Pantier reflect the poet's own parents and Reuben the poet himself—although the Pantiers are said to reflect also Masters's own unhappy first marriage.

"EMILY SPARKS"

The self-described old maid teacher still thinks of her favorite pupil, Reuben Pantier, for whom she has constantly prayed, to whom she once wrote a letter. Her hope is that Reuben accepts the love of Christ. Yet the reader, seeing Reuben as Masters's stand-in, understands that Reuben's own undoubted wish is to achieve poetic greatness. Emily speaks of fire burning out the dross, yielding "nothing but light," but that desired light is for the sake of his soul; she gives no thought to his creativity or literary expression.

Emily shares similarities with another unmarried schoolteacher caring especially for a student, Kate Swift of Sherwood ANDERSON's *WINESBURG, OHIO*—although their expressed goals for their students differ radically.

"DAISY FRASER"

Daisy Fraser, the town prostitute, wonders why the leaders of the community never contributed money to the public good, while she, when taken to Justice Arnett's courtroom, always had to come up with $10. Editor Whedon, she knows, received money for printing favorable stories and suppressing others; the Circuit Judge issued rulings that helped no one but the railroad and the bankers; the clergy kept their salaries while keeping quiet about municipal corruption.

Whedon, the Circuit Judge, the two clergymen, and Justice Arnett all speak their pieces later on.

"KNOWLT HOHEIMER"; "LYDIA PUCKETT"

A bullet entered Knowlt Hoheimer's heart at Missionary Ridge, the CIVIL WAR battleground in Tennessee. Knowlt was serving with the Union Army, having run away from home and joined up after being caught stealing hogs. Back now in Spoon River, he lies under a war hero's grave marker—a winged marble figure on a granite pedestal, inscribed "Pro Patria." He wonders what the words mean. Lydia Puckett, meanwhile, describes the real reason for his joining the army. Knowlt caught her with another man, and after they quarreled, he stole the hogs and ran away. She adds: Behind every soldier is a woman. Masters chose Missionary Ridge perhaps because the poet had an uncle who was wounded there.

"JULIA MILLER"

Married to a man 35 years older than she, pregnant with a child not her husband's, Julia thought of the last letter written by her lover—and then took morphine and began reading the Bible. She still sees the words on the page as darkness came over her, promising that she will dwell in paradise.

Because of Christian proscriptions against suicide, the implication exists that Julia is deluded in thinking she will be in paradise—although, as readers have suggested, she is speaking to the passerby from the cold ground, implying that no special afterlife abode exists at all.

"JOHNNIE SAYRE"

After the train wheel sank into his body, Johnnie hoped to live long enough to ask forgiveness from his father for playing truant, for stealing rides on trains. The poem refers to a boyhood friend of the poet, killed at the age of 10; the words chiseled on the gravestone, "Taken from the evil to come," are those on the real gravestone. Masters's first novel, *MITCH MILLER*, published five years later, in 1920—using the friend's actual name—tells the same story.

"THEODORE THE POET"

Breaking the precedent of monologues from the grave, this poem addresses a man who once, as a boy, spent hours waiting for a crawfish to appear from its burrow on the riverbank. Now this man has turned his eyes to the city, watching for men and women to appear from their "burrows of fate" so that he can watch them, study them. This poem, likely the first written of the *Spoon River Anthology* collection, is Masters's tribute to his friend—and exponent of REALISM—Theodore DREISER.

"MARGARET FULLER SLACK"

Named after the 19th-century American writer Margaret Fuller, Margaret says she would have been as great as George Eliot, the English woman novelist. Yet she faced the long-standing problem: Can a woman achieve her ambition if she marries, or must she remain unencumbered and free? The wealthy John Slack gave her an answer, promising that she would have the leisure to write, and so she married him—and bore eight children. Then, while following her housewifely role, she jabbed her hand with a needle and died from lockjaw. She issues a warning to the ambitious: Sex is a curse.

"GEORGE TRIMBLE"

In the political polarizations of the day, Trimble supported the FREE SILVER, or anti-GOLD STANDARD, platform of William Jennings BRYAN, the "peerless leader," as well as the single-tax plan of Henry GEORGE. Yet when Bryan was defeated, Trimble's wife urged her husband to support instead the movement to ban alcohol. So his former radical friends—followers of Bryan and George—grew suspicious of him, and the antiliquor conservatives in town felt unsure of him; as a result, he ended up with no friends at all.

"JUSTICE ARNETT"

The judge died when the old docket, a book containing court entries, fell from a shelf above his head. As a lawmaker, he wants to provide a rational explanation of his death, but then gives in to what frightened him as he lay dying—his understanding that the leaves of the book were the days of his life. Fate seemed to be torturing him, scattering those leaves filled with insignificant entries—because what was falling about him were his full 70 years of days.

In this poem Masters has chosen to not to follow his frequent course of finding flaws in public officials. Justice Arnett instead is presented at a moment of personal epiphany, when he sees that his life is ending—and when he sees, too, that his life was one of accumulated detail, of aggregated matters of little importance.

The gasoline tank explosion, burning Butch Weldy, involves a separate thread of characters and events; Weldy, a one-time rapist, later serves as foreman of a jury that falsely convicts another man of rape.

"DEACON TAYLOR"

This advocate of PROHIBITION, whom the town thought died of eating watermelon, actually died of cirrhosis of the liver; he had long been a secret drinker. Deacon Taylor is one of many portraits based on a Lewistown editor who was a political enemy of the poet's father—Editor Whedon is another—although the specific allegation in the poem is untrue. The piece is often quoted because of its succinct exposé of hypocrisy.

"A. D. BLOOD"

A. D. Blood, Spoon River's moralistic, self-righteous mayor, applauds himself for closing saloons, banning card playing, and bringing Daisy Fraser before the judge. The irony lies in his knowledge that Reuben Pantier and Dora Williams once made love every night on his grave.

A. D. Blood is a recurring villain among Masters's townspeople.

"DORA WILLIAMS"

Abandoned by Reuben Pantier, Dora, the milliner's daughter, went off to the state capital of SPRINGFIELD, where she took advantage of a drunken rich man and married him; stuck in a miserable life, she became free when her husband was one day found dead. She moved on to Chicago, then to New York, marrying another rich man; when this man died in her arms, his purple face haunted her, and a scandal almost arose—the poet's hint that she herself had a part in his death. When she moved on once more, this time to a cosmopolitan life in Paris, she met and married an Italian count from Genoa; the count was the cause of her death, by poisoning. The implication is that Dora poisoned her first two husbands, finally receiving her own just reward in return.

The tombstone reads, "Countess Navigato asks for eternal peace"—an irony, in that few of Masters's graveyard speakers have achieved peace; readers note that the grave of this townsperson lies far from Spoon River.

"MRS. WILLIAMS"

When her daughter Dora disappeared, the townspeople said it was because of the girl's faulty upbringing. Yet Mrs. Williams, a milliner dealing with hats and trimmings, as well as with matters of beauty in general, has seen that women who steal husbands wear such decorations; her suggestion is that wives wear them as well. In regard to her daughter, she wonders if Spoon River would have been worse if its children had been raised in public facilities, if their parents had been given the freedom to change mates. The implied answer is negative; it would have made no difference, she is saying—especially since parents already change mates, anyway—and Dora would have been no different.

The line "To set off sweet faces" appears in the song "Little Buttercup," from the late 19th-century operetta *H.M.S. Pinafore*, by Gilbert and Sullivan. Biographers have noted that Masters's parents once performed in the operetta in Lewistown, his mother singing the Buttercup role.

"THE CIRCUIT JUDGE"

The judge asks passersby to take note of the physical erosion of his headstone; it seems as if the wind and rain—or Nemesis herself, the goddess of retribution—are marking scores against him. He himself, he acknowledges, decided cases on the points that lawyers scored, not on what was right and just. Even the murderer Hod Putt, whom he sentenced to be hanged, was far more innocent of soul than he.

"NANCY KNAPP"

Nancy, addressing the passerby, wants to explain her side of the story. The money with which she and her husband bought the farm came from his father's will—the result, according to her husband's disinherited siblings, of his poisoning their father's mind against them. Thereafter, calamities befell the cattle and the crops, and the farm, failing to prosper, had to be mortgaged. Her husband grew silent, the neighbors turned against them—and at some point, in her case, madness set in. She set fire to the house, dancing about the flames.

"BARRY HOLDEN"

At the same time that his sister set fire to her house, Barry sat in on the trial of a man who had killed a woman who was pregnant by him. Barry listened to the testimony for two weeks. Then, when he came home to his pregnant wife and eight children—and his wife started to talk about the mortgage on the farm—he picked up a hatchet and killed her.

Banker Thomas Rhodes is the most frequently mentioned of Masters's villains.

"BARNEY HAINSFEATHER"

Since the fatal train to Peoria was not only wrecked, but also burned, Hainsfeather was misidentified. So here he lies in Spoon River—a town where running a clothing store was bad enough—while John Allen lies in the Hebrew Cemetery at Chicago. The poet is suggesting anti-Semitic prejudice against the merchant expressed by the citizens of Spoon River.

"PETIT, THE POET"

The name is French for "small" and for "minor" or "lesser." Petit's derivative verse forms, such as the French triolet or villanelle, are like seeds in a pod, making a dry, ticking sound—not vibrant, stirring poetry. Moreover, the poetic conventions of an earlier era, like the snows of yesterday—an oblique reference to the *ubi sunt* theme of "The Hill"—have vanished. So the poet must look around him, even in his own village, and see tragedy and comedy, heroism and failure; these are what the Greek bard Homer and the American bard Walt WHITMAN used for their poetry, and instead of ticking in metrical forms, they roared in the tall pines.

Petit can be compared to Archibald Higbie, speaking later, who fled overseas and tried to root out Spoon River from his soul; the impulse in both figures is said to be autobiographical.

"REV. ABNER PEET"

Scorned earlier by Daisy Fraser for not speaking out against political malfeasance, Peet is shown now as obsessed with the disposal of his estate. Assuming his importance to his congregation, he believes that its members were happy to have his personal effects as a memorial. Yet what upsets him is that a local saloon owner bought his trunk and burned its contents, which were the manuscripts of his sermons; he burned the sermons as waste paper.

Tennessee Claflin Shope later speaks of Peet as a learned man, reading Greek, yet laughing at her Eastern mysticism.

"JEFFERSON HOWARD"

Like Kinsey Keene, Howard is based on the poet's father, and once more the man's combative qualities are made clear; Howard is proud of the spirited battles he has fought. His foes were the puritanical and repressive; the church proved life-denying, while he himself was a friend of the humanity-affirming tavern. Yet as he grew older, he felt deserted; his children went away from him, no longer witnessing his valiant fights.

"DANIEL M'CUMBER"

Daniel addresses a woman from Spoon River, Mary McNeely, whom he once loved. He tells of going to the city, Chicago, and becoming involved with the landlady's daughter. Then he met Georgine Miner, a woman representing Fourierist free love, or sexual license, as espoused in the radical communes that flourished before the CIVIL WAR. Georgine, after turning to him for comfort from a lost love, bit his hand and befouled him. Now he is bleeding and malodorous, unworthy of his early Spoon River love.

Georgine has been identified as Tennessee MITCHELL, the poet's mistress in the years 1909–10. She speaks in her own voice in the next poem, although it is an unsympathetic voice that Masters gives her.

"GEORGINE SAND MINER"

Georgine was long the secret mistress of an effeminate loafer and dabbler in the arts, then of others as well, including Daniel M'Cumber. When Daniel's sister accused her of being his mistress, Daniel wrote to Georgine, decrying that "shameful word," while declaring the beauty of their love. Then a lesbian friend intervened, influencing Georgine to complain to Daniel's wife, saying that Daniel had been pursuing her.

Georgine would rather have escaped with Daniel to London, but he chose to stay in Chicago, presumably to maintain his marriage. She attempted revenge, not only by returning to her old lover, but by showing Daniel's wife the letter in which Daniel proclaimed his love, yet in such gallant wording that Georgine seemed to have maintained her virtue. Thereupon, Daniel denounced her, finally revealing the full extent of her lying and sexual misconduct.

Georgine's first two names form a version of the pen name, George Sand, of the 19th-century French writer Amandine Aurore Lucile Dudevant, known in America more for her love affairs than for her novels.

"THOMAS RHODES"

Rhodes, the town banker, addresses scornfully all those who soared to intellectual or imaginative heights, such as Margaret Fuller Slack, Petit the Poet, and the still-to-be-heard-from Tennessee Claflin Shope. They found it hard, he declares, to keep a rein on their souls, to keep their souls from fragmenting. On the other hand, those who sought and hoarded physical treasure, such as himself, were able to maintain their firm, compact selves.

"AMOS SIBLEY"; "MRS. SIBLEY"

Sibley, the clergyman, says that the townspeople thought he put up patiently with his wife's adulteries, but he did not. He restrained himself, he says, so that he could continue doing God's work; a divorce would have required his giving up the ministry. Yet he admits to seeking other occupations to earn a salary—implying that his reason for not seeking a divorce was that he could find no other way to make a living.

In Mrs. Sibley's response, the mound suggests the burial of a baby or a fetus; Editor Whedon later mentions a dump where abortions are hidden. The word *mound* suggests also the Latin *mons veneris*—

the mountain, or mound, of Venus—designating the female genitalia, a common reference in Renaissance literature.

"THE UNKNOWN"

The speaker is a villager who has no gravestone to mark his burial. His status in Spoon River had always always lowly; he once wandered as a boy "near the mansion of Aaron Hatfield"—indicating his position as an outsider to the town's elite. Then he became a criminal, or was seen by Spoon River as a criminal, and was imprisoned. When young, he had shot and wounded a hawk, which he put in a cage; the bird cawed at him angrily. Now dead, he searches for the soul of the hawk, to offer comradeship; both souls were wounded and caged in life.

"CARL HAMBLIN"

On the day that the HAYMARKET AFFAIR anarchists were hanged, Hamblin, editor of the Spoon River *Clarion,* wrote in his paper about a vision that came to him. He describes the vision now, a perverted representation of the Roman goddess of Justice. The woman's eyes, he declares, were covered by a bandage, as opposed to the traditional blindfold, which allows her to dispense justice without personal consideration. Moreover, as she wielded her sword, she struck not the evildoer, but the defenseless child and the mistreated laborer. In her other hand she held scales for weighing, and yet these scales weighed not the merit of a case, but the gold coins that had been dropped into it, given in bribery. Then someone removed the bandage, and her eyes were revealed as diseased and abscessed, her face marked by madness. Hamblin, because he published an editorial describing this vision, was tarred and feathered, and his office was wrecked.

"EDITOR WHEDON"

This editor, unlike the righteous Hamblin, was able to see every side of a question—because his opinion was for sale. Ancient Greek actors wore masks, he notes, indicating roles, hiding themselves; his mask was his newspaper. If bribed, he covered up scandal; if seeking revenge, he dug up scandal. He exulted in this power to crush

others—as a mentally disordered boy exults in derailing a speeding train. Now he lies where sewage flows, where garbage is dumped, where aborted fetuses lie.

"ROSIE ROBERTS"

Rosie, returning in illness to her childhood home in Spoon River, wrote about what had happened that night at Madam Lou's—although no one, she says, wanted to hear it. What happened was that she shot the son of the merchant prince because he knocked her down when she scorned his money and said she would see her lover instead. The papers lied when they said he accidentally killed himself cleaning a gun.

The merchant prince is retailer Marshall FIELD, whose son died of a gunshot wound in 1905. Although the shooting was ruled accidental, rumors pointed to murder or suicide in a Chicago brothel, and the family was suspected of orchestrating a cover-up. Masters is providing a fictional version of the rumors, as would Sherwood ANDERSON two years later in MARCHING MEN.

"MAGRADY GRAHAM"

Graham asks the passerby, was Altgeld elected governor? And if elected, was he triumphant in the cause of the people, or was he brought down? Graham's heart gave out as the election returns were coming in; his yearning was too great. The ardent Democrat remembers once taking Altgeld's hand and looking into his eyes, being moved by his "air of eternity."

John Peter ALTGELD was elected governor of Illinois in 1892; Grover CLEVELAND won his second presidential term that year. The biblical Salome requested the head of John the Baptist; Graham is asking whether Altgeld was destroyed by those aligned against him—as would be the case later, after he pardoned the remaining HAYMARKET AFFAIR anarchists.

"ARCHIBALD HIGBIE"

Higbie always tried to rise above the confining atmosphere of Spoon River. In Rome, living among artists, he thought he might finally break free of his origins. Yet in the faces he drew, onlookers would sometimes find a trace—not of Apollo, the Greek god of art and music, but of Abraham Lincoln. Feeling shamed, he would pray for another birth, in another place, carrying no more Spoon River in his soul.

"HARRY WILMANS"
At the time of the SPANISH-AMERICAN WAR, the Sunday school superintendent made a speech about how the flag must be upheld, and everyone cheered; Wilmans went off to war. In the Philippines, following that flag, he found degradation and disease; then he was shot dead, falling with a scream. Now there is a flag over his grave in Spoon River.

This grave marking can be compared to that of Knowlt Hoheimer, who died at Missionary Ridge in the Civil War; the two memorials reveal different attitudes toward the two wars. Hoheimer went to war in a far less noble spirit than Wilmans, and yet as one of the Civil War dead, he is honored grandly in marble.

Wilmans's "I fell with a scream" is reminiscent of a line in William Vaughn MOODY's much-quoted anti-Spanish-American War poem, "ON A SOLDIER FALLEN IN THE PHILIPPINES," in which the poet refers to "his bullet's scream."

"ANNE RUTLEDGE"
From the inspiration of this unknown woman, the poet says, came the spirit of forgiveness after the Civil War. From Ann RUTLEDGE—the beloved of Abraham Lincoln, dying young—came the president's deathless words, "With malice toward none, with charity for all," and the ideals of the Republic.

This poem helped make permanent one aspect of the Lincoln myth, the set of stories that permeated Masters's boyhood in downstate Illinois; among them was the tale of Lincoln's lost great love, as told by William HERNDON, Lincoln's law partner and early biographer. In 1921, a granite headstone, carved with Masters's poem, was placed on Rutledge's headstone in Petersburg. The words quoted in the poem come from Lincoln's Second Inaugural Address of 1865.

Later, the story of Rutledge and Lincoln's relationship was discredited, and Masters made clear he no longer believed the tale. In 1931, reversing his earlier stance, he wrote his debunking biography of Lincoln.

"WILLIAM H. HERNDON"
William H. Herndon, whom Masters recalled seeing as a boy downstate, is the former Lincoln law partner who began fostering the tale of Ann Rutledge soon after the president's death; he repeated it in his 1889 biography, dwelling also on Lincoln's melancholia, attributing it to Rutledge's death. When Herndon says, "I saw a man arise from the soil," Masters is crediting him with promulgating the Lincoln myth.

"RUTHERFORD MCDOWELL"
McDowell has enlarged the old-fashioned photographs of pioneering farmers, and he has photographed them in person as well—those sturdy men who participated in life at the time of the American Revolution. McDowell saw and appreciated their depth and strength. Yet these men are now forgotten; his camera records instead the faces of their grandchildren and great-grandchildren, and the strength and faith and courage are gone.

As in the subsequent monologue of the patriarch Aaron Hatfield, the poet is paying tribute to an earlier generation, from whom, he says, there can be only a falling off in the less virtuous present. Readers have long noted that the characters become more admirable toward the end of the volume; Masters later cited as his example Dante's *Divine Comedy,* in which the "heroic and enlightened spirits" are to be found at the end of the journey.

"HANNAH ARMSTRONG"
Hannah, who had once been Abraham Lincoln's landlady in small-town Illinois, had a letter written and sent to the president, asking for her son's compassionate discharge from the army. Receiving no reply, she herself went to Washington, and the president, greeting Aunt Hannah, talked of the old days as he wrote the discharge.

Hannah Armstrong is a historical figure. When Lincoln lived in New Salem, Illinois, he successfully defended Hannah's son in a murder trial in 1857; later, during the Civil War, in which another of Hannah's sons was killed, a mutual friend secured from Lincoln the discharge of the son that Lincoln, in the role of a lawyer, had defended earlier. Masters embellishes the story, in that the real-life Hannah did not personally go to Washington;

the James Garber he names as the letter writer is not the character whose monologue appears later in the volume.

"LUCINDA MATLOCK"

Lucinda speaks more positively of her life than most Spoon River women. She was courted in her youth, married, and raised 12 children, although she eventually lost eight of them. She worked hard in her long life, keeping house, nursing the sick. Then, at age 96, it was time to go. She asks, showing a touch of scorn, what is this I hear of weariness? Of anger and discontent? The younger generation fails to measure up to old standards.

The poem is based on the life of Masters's admired grandmother.

"TENNESSEE CLAFLIN SHOPE"

Tennessee is considered strange by the villagers, because her ideas differ from theirs. Among those who laugh at her is Rev. Peet, a learned man who reads Greek. Instead of talking of economic issues, such as free trade, or preaching baptism, or indulging in superstitions—activities of the other townspeople—Tennessee has read Hindu mysticism and thereby cured her soul, even before Mary Baker Eddy founded Christian Science. She has read the *Bhagavad Gita*, and she ends by quoting its benediction, Peace to all worlds.

Rev. Peet has been heard from earlier, lamenting the posthumous burning of his sermons.

"AARON HATFIELD"

The poet's grandfather, here renamed, represents the virtues of the nation's pioneering stock. On one Communion Sunday at church, Hatfield spoke of the peasant of Galilee, killed by the bankers and lawyers of the city. He spoke also of the sorrows felt by the pioneers gathered before him—as they grieved for sons killed in battle, for daughters and children dying young. Then the wine and the bread were passed, and reconciliation came; those gathered became brothers of the peasant of Galilee, and the descending Holy Spirit brought comfort and consolation.

Referring twice to the peasant of Galilee, Hatfield is linking Christ to his agrarian congregation;

these rural Presbyterians possess greater virtue, he is saying, than the city-dwellers.

"THE SPOONIAD"

The poem, in its invocation of the muse and in its depiction of warfare, makes reference to Homer's *Iliad*, and yet the warfare is mock warfare, and the heroics are mock heroics; Masters is drawing upon the mock-epic work of 18th-century English poet Alexander Pope. Treating trivial subject matter with grandiose descriptions, the genre ridicules the subject matter and its cast of characters. A further reference to Pope—known also for his translations of Homer—is in the title itself, evoking his satiric poem *The Dunciad*. The first two names of the attributed author, Jonathan Swift Somers, are those of another great 18th-century satirist.

Masters's work depicts a village at war over moral issues, including whether or not liquor should be banned; many characters who have already spoken from the graveyard appear in this poem. To the modern reader the absurd and exaggerated actions are inappropriate to the tone and content of the rest of the volume.

Critical Reception

Critics and readers responded favorably, although some objected to the work's abandoning of poetic conventions, as well as its seemingly unpleasant subject matter. William Marion Reedy wrote the first critical praise of the poet, hailing "a new light and a new voice in letters"; Ezra POUND declared that "at last America has discovered a poet." The DIAL reviewer protested the nontraditional practices, finding fault with *Spoon River's* "scrutiny of disagreeable matters," labeling the volume as "deliberately unlovely." William Dean HOWELLS claimed that the work was not poetry at all, but "shredded prose," unlikely to last. Other readers linked Masters with New Englanders Edward Arlington ROBINSON and Robert FROST, declaring that these three regional poets are creating a new indigenous American verse. The book became an improbable best-seller.

Masters never achieved that level of popularity again. His *New Spoon River* of 1924, one of 22 subsequent publications, achieved only moderate success. The trends in poetry were heading in new directions, toward the MODERNISM of Ezra Pound, T. S. ELIOT, and James JOYCE. A stage adaptation of *Spoon River Anthology* was produced in Los Angeles, then New York, in 1963; presenting nearly 50 characters in story and song, the work ends with the voice of "The Unknown."

Springfield, Illinois

The capital of Illinois, home of President Abraham LINCOLN, and birthplace and home of poet Vachel LINDSAY, the city of Springfield was settled in 1818 and served as the center of an agricultural and coal-mining region. Lincoln practiced law in the city from 1837 to 1861; his famous "house divided" speech, accepting the Republican nomination for the United States Senate, was delivered at the capitol in 1858. Seven years later, in 1865, his body was brought to Springfield for burial. Carl SANDBURG's poem "Knucks" begins with a description of "Abraham Lincoln's city," foreshadowing the poet's elevation of Lincoln into a major American folk hero.

"States Attorney Fallas"   *See SPOON RIVER ANTHOLOGY.*

Stead, William T.
(1849–1912) *English journalist and reformer*

Son of a clergyman, Stead is best known in America for his polemic IF CHRIST CAME TO CHICAGO!, published in 1894. Arriving in Chicago at the closing of the WORLD'S COLUMBIAN EXPOSITION, he claimed to see intemperance and vice all about him, deploring the city's brothels, saloons, and gambling parlors, as well as its political corruption. He had previously published crusading articles in the London periodical the *Pall Mall Gazette*, including a series on child prostitution, "The Maiden Tribute of Modern Babylon"; he would later take on corruption in New York City, publishing

Satan's Invisible World in 1897. As the Boer War commenced in South Africa in 1899, he denounced militarism and Britain's involvement in the conflict. Invited to speak at a peace symposium in New York City, he died in the sinking of the *Titanic*.

Steffens, Lincoln
(1866–1936) *writer*

Born in San Francisco, Steffens graduated from the University of California, then became editor of MCCLURE'S MAGAZINE in 1901. The periodical became known for its MUCKRAKING, or exposing of corporate and governmental corruption. In 1902, he began his THE SHAME OF THE CITIES series for the magazine, aiming first at St. Louis; he came to Chicago the following year, researching the city's municipal and corporate corruption. The collection of six articles on six cities was published in 1904. His next work, *The Struggle for Self-Government*, appearing in 1906, detailed malfeasance at the state level. In 1912, the then-unknown writer John REED honored Steffens in a poem, "Sangar," published in the December issue of the new POETRY magazine. Visiting Russia in 1919, Steffens is famed for his comment, "I have seen the future, and it works." His *Autobiography*, published in 1931, has been widely read for its depiction of an era of political dissension and upheaval.

Stein, Gertrude
(1874–1946) *writer, patron of the arts*

A friend and longtime correspondent of Sherwood ANDERSON, Stein and her experimental writings have been credited with influencing Anderson's prose style. Born in Allegheny, Pennsylvania, Stein attended Radcliffe College and studied medicine briefly at Johns Hopkins University. She settled in Paris in 1903. Her experiments in stream-of-consciousness writing include her best-known work, *Three Lives*, published in 1909; *Tender Buttons*, a series of "cubist" portraits in verse—inspired by paintings she had bought from

Pablo Picasso—appeared in 1914. Anderson later wrote of the excitement he had felt on reading *Tender Buttons,* vowing to make a similar effort himself, "dealing in words separated from sense"; he credited Stein with helping free him from the strictures of REALISM, providing him with new verbal tools, showing him new stylistic possibilities. The imagery in the story "Hands," written in 1915, later collected in WINESBURG, OHIO, is said to derive from her work.

By the 1920s, Stein had established a literary salon in her Paris home; Anderson, who was almost her exact contemporary, visited in 1921, as did Ernest HEMINGWAY later, bearing the older writer's introduction. Anderson wrote a laudatory preface to Stein's *Geography and Plays,* published in 1922, and his further appreciation of her work appeared in "Four American Impressions," collected in SHERWOOD ANDERSON'S NOTEBOOKS; he wrote that her "feeling for the taste, the smell, the rhythm of the individual word" is more important to writers than the work of artists more readily accepted and understood. Stein's "Idem the Same—A Valentine to Sherwood Anderson" appeared in LITTLE REVIEW in 1923. The two writers remained friends and correspondents until Anderson's death; they last met when Stein made an American tour in 1935.

Two posthumously appearing Stein works deal with Ulysses S. GRANT—her collection *Four in America,* praising the prose of Grant's *Personal Memoirs,* and her libretto for American composer Virgil Thomson's opera *The Mother of Us All.* The opera, premiering in 1947, focusing on women's suffrage leader Susan B. Anthony, includes Grant—speaking anachronistically of the World War II general Dwight D. Eisenhower—among a series of historical figures.

Stener, George W.

This character appears in Theodore DREISER's novel THE FINANCIER. Serving as the Philadelphia city treasurer, Stener owes his position to the powerful men who run the city, including the contractor Edward Malia BUTLER. With the help of financier Frank COWPERWOOD, Stener continues the practice of letting banks use city funds

for their own purposes. When markets fail, as a result of unrelated external circumstances, both Stener and Cowperwood are exposed for their misappropriations and subject to criminal charges. Stener is portrayed as the foil to Cowperwood—weak, fearful, foolish—but both men are charged and convicted because of the animosity of Butler toward Cowperwood. Stener is the hapless political tool; Dreiser uses him for contrast with his strong hero, whose downfall is only temporary.

Stevens, Wallace
(1879–1955) *major modern poet*

Born in Pennsylvania, Stevens attended Harvard University and New York Law School. He worked as a successful businessman throughout his life; during his spare time he produced some of the important poetry of the 20th century, including "Peter Quince at the Clavier," "The Emperor of Ice-Cream," and "The Idea of Order at Key West." His first major poem, "Sunday Morning," appeared in POETRY in November 1915—although only after Harriet MONROE had asked him to make alterations and deletions; Stevens complied, but restored the original for the collected 1923 volume, *Harmonium.* Monroe had already rejected "Peter Quince at the Clavier," which Alfred KREYMBORG published in his magazine OTHERS in August 1915; another major piece, "Thirteen Ways of Looking at a Blackbird," appeared in *Others* in December 1917. Becoming vice president of the Hartford Accident and Indemnity Company in 1934, a position he held until his death, Stevens produced the classic volumes *The Idea of Order at Key West* and *The Man with the Blue Guitar* during the same decade; his *Collected Poems,* published in 1954, won the Pulitzer Prize for poetry.

The Stoic
Theodore Dreiser
(1947)

The last volume of the Frank COWPERWOOD trilogy, fictionalizing the final phase of the life of magnate Charles T. YERKES, *The Stoic* was published three decades after the second volume, THE TITAN. The novel is briefer, less complete in its financial detailing than its predecessor; it is considered the weakest of the three volumes. DREISER had put it aside after *The Titan* appeared in 1914, in part because he needed further research into Yerkes's London career, in part because sales of *The Titan* had been disappointing. He feared also a libel suit from Emilie Grigsby, the model for the character Berenice FLEMING.

At the close of *The Titan*, Cowperwood has been denied an extension on his transportation franchises in Chicago, and now, nearing the age of 60, he seeks opportunities in the expanding London Underground system. First transferring his American base to New York City, he then moves on to England—keeping two households there, one for the socially acceptable maintenance of his wife, Aileen BUTLER Cowperwood, the other for his "ward," Berenice Fleming, his young mistress. He secretly hires a penniless social hanger-on, Bruce Tollifer, to distract Aileen, to keep her from finding out about Berenice's presence in England; Aileen discovers the plot and angrily breaks off with Tollifer. Meanwhile, the London Underground is in the process of modernization and electrification, including the building of the largest electrical power plant in the world. Yet the magnate's health problems arise; suffering from kidney disease, Cowperwood returns to New York, where he is placed under nursing care. He soon dies, and his financial empire disintegrates, assailed by litigation; the charities he had envisioned, including a hospital for the poor, are no longer possible, and his widow is left with few resources. Yet Berenice, for whom he had provided separately and clandestinely, maintains her affluence—although she now feels the pull of spiritual matters; she sails to India, where she spends four years under the tutorship of a guru, advising her on matters of transcendence. Returning to New York, she vows to establish the charitable hospital her lover had once dreamed of establishing. The penultimate chapters of the novel—which remained incomplete at Dreiser's death in 1945—present a lengthy screed of the guru's teachings; they resemble the penultimate chapters of Dreiser's other posthumous novel, THE BULWARK, published a year earlier, which sets forth a series of Quaker teachings.

Stone, Melville E.

(1848–1929) *founder of the* Chicago Daily News

Born in Hudson, Illinois, Stone came to Chicago in 1860; at the age of 27, he started a newspaper that would become a major force in Chicago journalism. Charging a penny a copy, publishing a demonstration issue on Christmas Day, 1875, he inaugurated the afternoon CHICAGO DAILY NEWS in January 1876. Several months later, short of funds, he sold the enterprise to the more affluent Victor F. LAWSON; he himself stayed on as editor. In 1893, combining a group of news-gathering organizations, he became Associated Press manager, a position he held for 30 years. Stone was the father of Herbert S. Stone, cofounder of STONE AND KIMBALL.

Stone and Kimball

This publishing firm was established in 1893 by Herbert S. Stone, son of CHICAGO DAILY NEWS founder Melville E. STONE, and fellow Harvard University undergraduate Hannibal Ingalls Kimball. The company was short-lived but prestigious, publishing fine books in the tradition of William MORRIS and his Kelmscott Press. The chief editor was Lucy Monroe, sister of POETRY founder Harriet MONROE. In 1894, the firm launched THE CHAP-BOOK, a literary magazine influenced by the English ARTS AND CRAFT MOVEMENT; it also began publication of the periodical HOUSE BEAUTIFUL. Producing editions of Edgar Allan Poe, Robert Louis Stevenson, Henrik Ibsen, Maurice Maeterlinck, and others, the company turned to local authors as well, presenting Hamlin GARLAND's CRUMBLING IDOLS in 1894 and ROSE OF DUTCHER'S COOLLY in 1895; George Barr McCUTCHEON's GRAUSTARK and *Brewster's Millions* also appeared under its imprint. The firm closed in 1897; its successor, Herbert S. Stone and Company, continued issuing *The Chap-Book* for another year, presenting the serial publication of Henry James's *What Maisie Knew*. Herbert Stone died in the sinking of the LUSITANIA in 1915.

Stoner, Melville

A character in Sherwood ANDERSON's story "Out of Nowhere into Nothing," collected in THE TRIUMPH OF THE EGG, Stoner, a bachelor in his 40s, lives next door to the family home of Rosalind WESCOTT in Willow Springs, Iowa. Possessing an independent income, he does not work, but chooses to spend his time alone in his house. He closely observes his neighbors, knowing about their ways, and Rosalind fears that he is vulturelike, living too much off them. Yet Stoner gives Rosalind a sense of fellowship and understanding, even though he himself is lonely—perhaps "to the door of insanity," she realizes. When she suggests that he come away from Willow Springs, he says his time for leaving has long passed.

"Stories of the Streets and of the Town"

This newspaper column by George ADE began in 1893 and ran next to Eugene FIELD's "Sharps and Flats" in the CHICAGO RECORD. The pieces ranged from narrative to verse to dialogue, and subjects ranged from Polish immigrants to Pullman porters to Jewish junk dealers; accompanying the columns were the line drawings by Ade's longtime friend John T. MCCUTCHEON. The newspaper published eight paperback collections of Ade's columns and McCutcheon's illustrations between 1894 and 1900.

The Story of a Country Town
E. W. Howe
(1883)

A document in what would be called the REVOLT FROM THE VILLAGE, *The Story of a Country Town* appeared a dozen years after the groundbreaking regional novel, Edward EGGLESTON's 1871 THE HOOSIER SCHOOLMASTER. E. W. HOWE's novel presented characters more severely flawed than its predecessor, as well as provided a generally bleak depiction of rural life. In the community of Fairview, Missouri, the farmers face overwork and hard times; in the larger town of Twin Mounds,

Missouri, the citizens are narrow, jealous, and malicious. The rural Protestantism of the region, as exemplified by the Rev. John Westlock, the bitter, punitive preacher—modeled on the author's father—is joyless and hard. William Dean HOWELLS noted that the book "does not flatter the West."

A Story Teller's Story
Sherwood Anderson
(1924)

Containing autobiographical notes and sketches written in Reno, Nevada, where ANDERSON was staying to obtain a divorce from Tennessee MITCHELL, the volume presents the author's account of his becoming a storyteller, an American artist. During a visit to Chartres Cathedral in 1921, Anderson writes, he concluded that Americans have spent too much time with the past, that "the future of the western world" lies with America. Although he called the volume one of his best, readers have considered it valuable mainly for the background it gives on his fiction; Anderson is more sympathetic to his father than in previous depictions, declaring him "made for romance" and unfit for a money-grubbing Ohio village. Gertrude STEIN reviewed the book favorably; William FAULKNER, while appreciating the portrait of the author's father, found in the rest of the volume the author's inability "to write successfully of himself."

"The Strength of God"   *See* WINESBURG, OHIO.

"The Strength of the Lonely"   *See* THE CONGO AND OTHER POEMS.

Sullivan, Louis
(1856–1924) *architect*

Considered the greatest figure of the CHICAGO SCHOOL OF ARCHITECTURE, Sullivan is mostly remembered today for two still-standing structures, the AUDITORIUM BUILDING and the Carson, Pirie,

Scott and Company store. Born in Boston, Sullivan studied architecture at the Massachusetts Institute of Technology. He moved to Chicago in 1873 and found employment as a draftsman in the firm of William Le Baron JENNEY, builder of the first steel-frame structure. Briefly enrolled at the ÉCOLE DES BEAUX-ARTS in Paris, Sullivan came in contact with neoclassicism, the revival of Greek and Renaissance styles, a style he would deplore when it prevailed in

the design of the WORLD'S COLUMBIAN EXPOSITION, the ART INSTITUTE, and other buildings of the era. In 1881, he formed a partnership with Dankmar ADLER, and the firm of ADLER AND SULLIVAN created the Auditorium Building of 1889, the Schiller Building of 1892, and CHICAGO STOCK EXCHANGE BUILDING of 1894; Sullivan is credited with the vision that gave these buildings their strength and beauty. The Schiller Building, home of the GARRICK

The Carson, Pirie, Scott and Company department store, designed by Louis Sullivan, was built in several phases early in the 20th century; this photograph dates from 1912. *(Chicago Historical Society)*

THEATRE, was razed in 1960, the Chicago Stock Exchange Building in 1972. Sullivan also designed the much-admired Wainwright Building in St. Louis and the Guaranty Building in Buffalo.

His famous dictum was "form follows function," suggesting that the outward form must express the required function, that the solution to a problem comes from the nature of the problem; if needs are met, the resulting art grows and unfolds naturally. A predecessor in this idea was the American sculptor Horatio Greenough, arguing in the 1840s against classical forms in favor of naturally developing structures. Another favorite Sullivan term was *organic,* emphasizing again the natural development of art from its particular circumstances; in the use of this term he was preceded by the English writer and art historian John Ruskin, who had spoken of "organic architecture," and the English writer Owen Jones, who, in his *The Grammar of Ornament,* had advocated following "organic and natural laws."

Yet the derivative architecture that Sullivan deplored came to dominate the plans for the 1893 world's fair. Calling its classical buildings "a parade of white elephants," Sullivan designed his nonconforming Transportation Building—a structure relegated to the side, noted for its multicolored décor and arched golden doorway. After the fair his career began a slow decline, exacerbated by his break with Adler in 1895; he had failed to appreciate the value of his partner's practical talents. His major postfair project was the 12-story 1904 Schlesinger and Mayer department store, now Carson, Pirie, Scott and Company, in the LOOP. The Carson building is noted for its lavish wrought-iron ornamentation on the first two floors, a decorative botanical motif reflecting Sullivan's concern with nature as well as the ART NOUVEAU style of the time.

His final commissions were mainly banks in small towns. The National Farmer's Bank in Owatanna, Minnesota, has been called his last masterpiece. Sullivan was increasingly seen as a man turning inward, rejecting what his protégé Frank Lloyd WRIGHT, writing an admiring biography, called the "mobocracy." He spent his final years in a room in a shabby hotel, despondent, alcoholic, dependent on financial help from others. His *Autobiography of an Idea,* articulating many of his concepts, was completed just before his death at the age of 67. Wright's biography appeared in 1949.

The Sultan of Sulu
George Ade, Alfred G. Wathall
(1902)

This musical comedy, book and lyrics by George ADE, music by Alfred G. Wathall, opened in March 1902 at the Studebaker Theater in the FINE ARTS BUILDING. The show went on to a successful run in New York. The plot derives from events following the SPANISH-AMERICAN WAR, involving a treaty negotiated between the United States government and the Muslim sultan of the Sulu Archipelago, an area in the southern Philippines. Ade had heard about the negotiations while visiting in Manila with his friend John T. McCUTCHEON, serving as a war correspondent. In a libretto that today would be considered insensitive, Ade depicts the U.S. Navy as encountering a sultan with multiple wives; an American woman, offended by the sultan's marital state, strives for his reform—although the ruler thinks that he should add her to his collection. In terms of Ade's career, the play signaled a turn toward the stage, leading the one-time newspaper columnist away from journalism and the Chicago settings that had once been his base.

Sunday, William Ashley "Billy"
(1862–1935) *Chicago-based evangelist*

Born in Iowa, Sunday became a professional baseball player for the original Chicago White Stockings team; he began working for the Young Men's Christian Association in Chicago in 1891. Five years later, he turned to full-time evangelism, first drawing crowds in midwestern towns, then staging extensive revivals in major American cities. Among his causes was PROHIBITION.

Sunday drew criticism for what was considered his overwrought emotionalism and VAUDEVILLE-like antics; labor leaders denounced him for declaring religion to be the answer to the workingman's problems. Carl SANDBURG, attacking him in the poem "Billy Sunday," called him a hypocrite and fraud; later, the publisher of Sandburg's CHICAGO POEMS, wishing to avoid a libel suit, persuaded the poet to change the title to "To a Contemporary Bunkshooter," as well as to soften some of the perceived antireligious sentiments.

Sinclair LEWIS's novel of 1922, *Babbitt*, includes references to Mike Monday, described as a well-known evangelist; the city's Chamber of Commerce learns that wherever he appears, he turns the minds of workingmen "from wages and hours to higher things"—thus deflecting the demands of labor—and he is promptly invited to speak.

Swanson, Gloria
(1899–1983) *film actress*

First working at the ESSANAY FILM MANUFACTURING COMPANY, Swanson became a major star of the silent era. Born in Chicago, living in the neighborhood of the studio, she debuted as a teenager in the 1915 *The Fable of Elvira and Farina and the Meal Ticket*, a rendition of a fable by George ADE. In the same year she took a small role in *His New Job*, the one film that Charlie CHAPLIN made for the Chicago branch of the company; she played a "typewriter," as a typist was then called. She was subsequently cast with Wallace BEERY in *Sweedy Goes to College*; she married Beery, the first of six husbands, and went with him to California. Swanson won two Academy Award nominations in the late 1920s, one for *Sadie Thompson*, based on a then-scandalous story and play by Somerset Maugham. In 1950, after a long retirement, she returned to the screen, receiving an Academy Award nomination for *Sunset Boulevard*.

Swift, Gustavus F.
(1839–1903) *meatpacker, developer of railroad refrigerator cars*

Born on a farm on Cape Cod, Massachusetts, Swift settled in Chicago in 1875 after first establishing butcher shops in the Boston area. At the time, the principal method of preserving meat was by salting or smoking, a process used mainly for pork. Although the refrigerator car had been patented earlier, Swift's major achievement was the development of a refrigerated transportation system in the late 1870s, setting up icing stations along the railroad tracks, continuing all the way to the East Coast. As a result, fresh beef could be shipped to the rest of the country in every season of the year. Swift was an early developer of what has been called the vertically integrated company, controlling both the producing and the distribution of goods. He died in suburban Lake Forest at the age of 63.

Swift, Kate   See WINESBURG, OHIO: "The Strength of God" and "The Teacher."

T

Taft, Lorado
(1860–1936) *sculptor*

Establishing himself as an artist at the 1893 WORLD'S COLUMBIAN EXPOSITION, Taft began to undertake commissions for statues, monuments, memorials, and fountains; his complex of studios, maintained near the UNIVERSITY OF CHICAGO, became known as the sculpture capital of the world. Born in Elmwood, Illinois, studying at the University of Illinois and the ÉCOLE DES BEAUX-ARTS in Paris, Taft become an instructor at the ART INSTITUTE, a position he held from 1886 through 1907; his *The History of American Sculpture,* published in 1903, gave the first comprehensive overview of a new subject in American art history. In 1907, he began his "Fountain of Time" sculpture, consisting of 100 cast-concrete figures, extending 127 feet, depicting human progression from birth to death—and watched over by a cloaked, 26-feet-tall Father Time; the monument was dedicated in 1922 on the MIDWAY PLAISANCE. For economic and practical reasons, concrete was used instead of the more durable granite; as a result, the sculpture has suffered over the years from weather erosion, requiring ongoing repairs and renovation. Another work by Taft is the 50-foot-tall statue of BLACK HAWK, the Sauk warrior, overlooking the Rock River in Oregon, Illinois, completed in 1911 as a tribute to Native Americans; a year later, his statue of Christopher Columbus was erected in Washington, D.C. In 1913, Taft's "The Fountain of the

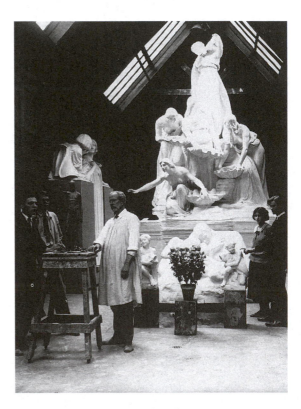

Lorado Taft, shown in his studio in 1912, specialized in heroic sculptures and monuments. *(Chicago Historical Society)*

Great Lakes" was placed at the Art Institute, now standing outside the south wing; in that grouping,

328

five female figures hold shells, from which water flows in the same course as it flows in the Great Lakes system, from Lake Superior to Lake Ontario. The marriage in 1899 of Taft's sister to Hamlin GARLAND led to the writer's founding of the artist-and-writer-oriented CLIFF DWELLERS CLUB. Three weeks before his death, Taft traveled to Quincy, Illinois, to dedicate his sculpture commemorating the historic debates between Abraham LINCOLN and Stephen A. DOUGLAS. He died in Chicago at the age of 76.

By the time of his death, Taft's reputation had already begun its decline. Beaux-Arts ideals of a classical tradition, of allegorical interpretation, had long given away to modernist tenets of art and sculpture. Taft today holds only a small place—except for conscious attempts at historical appreciation and revival—in the records of 20th-century sculpture. Nelson ALGREN, in his 1951 *Chicago: City on the Make*, refers to "the acres of Lorado Taft's deadly handiwork."

Taft, William Howard
(1857–1930) *27th president of the United States*

A Cincinnati lawyer, serving as President Theodore ROOSEVELT's secretary of war, Taft was chosen by Roosevelt to be his Republican successor in the 1908 presidential election; he defeated Democrat William Jennings BRYAN, who was running for president for the third and last time. The conservative Taft became increasingly alienated from the progressive wing of the Republican Party, which supported reforms such as the lowering of tariffs, or duties imposed on imports; running again in 1912, he was opposed by Roosevelt, who had left the Republicans and joined the new PROGRESSIVE PARTY. The resulting split in the vote defeated both Taft and Roosevelt, bringing Democrat Woodrow WILSON to the presidency. In 1921, Taft was appointed chief justice of the Supreme Court by President Warren G. HARDING, becoming the only figure in American history to hold the highest office in both the executive and judicial branches of government.

Tagore, Rabindranath
(1861–1941) *Indian poet*

Born in Calcutta into the Brahmin caste, Tagore wrote poetry showing a sympathy for the village poor and a love of the Bengali countryside. As arranged by Ezra POUND, several of his poems appeared in the December 1912 issue of POETRY magazine, translated from the Bengali by Tagore himself; these were his first publications in English. Early in 1913, visiting his son, a student at the University of Illinois in downstate Urbana, Tagore came to Chicago, staying at the home of Harriet Brainerd MOODY, patron of artists and widow of poet William Vaughn MOODY. In that year he won the Nobel Prize in literature.

"Tandy"   See WINESBURG, OHIO.

Tar: A Midwest Childhood
Sherwood Anderson
(1926)

This fictionalized autobiography by Sherwood ANDERSON features the character Tar Moorehead. Switching during the course of the writing from first person to third person, Anderson called the work his "childhood dramatized." A version of the story "Death in the Woods," the names of the characters changed, appears in the volume. James T. FARRELL read the book as a young man, claiming it as an inspiration for writing his own childhood memories in *Young Lonigan*.

Tarbell, Ida M.
(1857–1944) *writer*

Tarbell is remembered today as author of HISTORY OF THE STANDARD OIL COMPANY, the classic corporate exposé published in 1904. Born in Pennsylvania, near the site of the nation's first oil gusher, she had seen her father's business, an independent oil-producing company, ruined as John D. ROCKEFELLER put together his Standard Oil Company monopoly.

She first gained note as a writer for McCLURE'S MAGAZINE in 1900, serializing what turned out to be an important biography of Abraham LINCOLN, involving original research in Virginia, Kentucky, Ohio, and Illinois, collecting letters, court records, and other basic material. Her MUCKRAKING *History of the Standard Oil Company* was serialized in *McClure's* as well, consisting of 19 installments starting in November 1902. Tarbell's work was a follow-up on Henry Demarest LLOYD's groundbreaking WEALTH AGAINST COMMONWEALTH, published in 1894.

Taylor, Deacon   *See SPOON RIVER ANTHOLOGY.*

"The Teacher"   *See WINESBURG, OHIO.*

Teasdale, Sara
(1884–1933) *poet*

Born in St. Louis, first publishing in POETRY in 1914, Teasdale gained celebrity for her collection *Love Songs*, which appeared in 1917, winning the first Poetry Society of America prize. Earlier, corresponding with Vachel LINDSAY after her *Poetry* publication, she met the Illinois poet the same year—and received a marriage proposal as well; she married instead a wealthy St. Louis shoe manufacturer, moving to New York soon afterward. Divorced from her husband in 1929, Teasdale died of an overdose of sleeping pills at the age of 48.

Telfer, John

This character appears in Sherwood ANDERSON's novel *WINDY McPHERSON'S SON*. Living on inherited income and his wife's millinary, or hat-making, business, Telfer is the town's man of leisure and self-proclaimed artist. Once studying art in New York and Paris, he returned to Caxton, Iowa, after failing to achieve success. He says now that he is devoting himself to that most difficult of arts, the art of living, as well as teaching wisdom and judgment to the townspeople. Yet he admits a flaw to his protégé,

Sam McPHERSON—namely, that he has let himself be satisfied with small successes; he acquired this flaw from women, he declares, and he warns Sam against letting women keep him from his proper path in life. At the end of Book I, as Sam prepares to leave Caxton, Telfer finds a new protégé, "a new son," the boy who has bought Sam's newspaper business. Based on a real-life citizen of Anderson's hometown of Clyde, Ohio, Telfer is briefly mentioned again in "An Ohio Pagan," collected in *HORSES AND MEN*, referred to as "our town poetry lover."

Thanet, Octave
(1850–1934) *writer*

Thanet was the pen name of Alice French, author of the best-selling novel *The Man of the Hour*, published in 1905. The work is said to be the first fiction to deal with the PULLMAN STRIKE. Born in Andover, Massachusetts, moving as a child to Davenport, Iowa, Thanet became known principally as a LOCAL COLOR writer, making use of Iowa locales, drawing also on settings in Arkansas, where she maintained a winter home. In *The Man of the Hour*, she takes an antilabor stance; her protagonist, coming from Iowa to Chicago to support the striking workers, realizes that he cannot win the workers' confidence, and he eventually switches sides. He returns home, becomes a factory manager, and takes the lead in local strikebreaking and union-busting.

That Royle Girl

Shot partially in Chicago and starring the comedian W. C. Fields in a dramatic role, the 1925 silent film is one of the American Film Institute's "ten most wanted" lost films. Based on a novel by Chicago newspaperman Edwin BALMER, the movie was directed by D. W. GRIFFITH and featured scenes at the Augustus SAINT-GAUDENS statue of Abraham LINCOLN in LINCOLN PARK; the producing studio was Adolph ZUKOR's Famous Players-Lasky Company. Carl SANDBURG, reviewing the film in the *CHICAGO DAILY NEWS*, found that the audience was held by its humor and melodrama, watching the story of a young girl who rises wholesomely out of a "sodden environment" of a drunken father, W. C. Fields, and a drug-addicted mother.

Theodore the Poet   *See SPOON RIVER ANTHOLOGY.*

The Theory of the Leisure Class: An Economic Study of the Evolution of Institutions
Thorstein Veblen
(1899)

In his most famous work, Thorstein VEBLEN castigates the accumulators of capital, declaring that the acquisition of property beyond necessity becomes not a matter of survival, but rather a matter of status. The result is a competitive CONSPICUOUS CONSUMPTION, as shown in women's fashion and other displays of luxury. Veblen's analysis of excess is so thorough that some readers assumed the volume to be satire; Charlotte Perkins GILMAN, who would later add her feminist perspective to the issue of women's clothing, declared the work "the most brilliant penetrating satire I ever saw." Nearly two decades later, Floyd DELL, writing in *THE MASSES,* was still praising Veblen for "that masterpiece of analytical satire." Another target in the volume is the SETTLEMENT HOUSE movement; Veblen saw Chicago's HULL-HOUSE as a propaganda tool for the rich.

"These Mountaineers"   *See DEATH IN THE WOODS.*

"The Thinker"   *See WINESBURG, OHIO.*

Thomas, Theodore
(1835–1905) *founder of the Chicago Symphony Orchestra*

Born in Germany, Thomas came to New York as a child; in 1862, he created the Theodore Thomas Orchestra, which toured throughout the country, seeking to increase interest in classical music. In 1891, a group of Chicago businessmen asked him to establish the permanent CHICAGO SYMPHONY ORCHESTRA, making use of the AUDITORIUM BUILDING theater. Finding the hall cavernous, as well as hard to fill for classical music concerts, Thomas campaigned for a new, more intimate hall; he died just after ORCHESTRA HALL was completed in 1904. In Willa CATHER's *THE SONG OF THE LARK,* Thomas is presented as an orchestra conductor who is particularly sympathetic to vocal music; he tells of his days as a young violinist, when he received his greatest inspiration from women singers, including the Swedish soprano Jenny Lind.

"Three Balls"   *See CORNHUSKERS.*

Tietjens, Eunice
(1884–1944) *poet, associate editor of* Poetry *magazine*

Born in Chicago, moving as a teenager to Geneva, Switzerland, the 19-year-old Eunice Hammond met and married composer Paul Tietjens in 1904; he had already written the score for the popular stage version of L. Frank BAUM's *THE WONDERFUL WIZARD OF OZ.* The couple divorced 10 years later. In 1913, Tietjens joined the staff of Harriet MONROE's *POETRY* magazine; in 1917, when America entered WORLD WAR I, she went to France as a correspondent for the *CHICAGO DAILY NEWS.* Returning to *Poetry* after the war, she served as associate editor, replacing Alice Corbin HENDERSON, who had moved to New Mexico for health reasons. In addition to her own work, Tietjens published translations from the French poet Charles Baudelaire, as well as from the Japanese; Ben HECHT once spoke of her being "abubble with Japanese mysticism." In his autobiography, *Homecoming,* Floyd DELL singles out Tietjens's "The Drug Clerk" as one of his favorite poems; first published in *The Masses,* the work presents a drugstore clerk, presiding over shelves containing sleeping potions, painkillers, and aphrodisiacs, who scornfully denies that he has pomade, or hair oil, insisting that his store caters only to an upscale trade. The poem was anthologized in Louis Untermeyer's *Modern American Poetry*, published in 1919.

Tillford, Jerry

This character is featured in Sherwood ANDERSON's story "I Want to Know Why," collected in *THE TRIUMPH OF THE EGG*. Trainer of the racehorse Sunstreak, Jerry is a man whom the teenage narrator admires; the older man understands horses, and an unspoken bond exists between him and the stallion Sunstreak. Before a race, the narrator sees the shine in Jerry's eyes; the trainer is sensing what the horse senses. That evening, the boy follows Jerry to a farmhouse, which turns out to be a brothel; hiding by a window, he hears Jerry bragging, saying that he himself has made the horse a champion. The boy sees Jerry looking at a woman with the same shine in his eyes, kissing her. He runs off in anger and disillusionment. The narrator has been initiated into an adult world, which is far from the purity of an innocent life with horses and men.

The Titan
Theodore Dreiser
(1914)

The Titan is the second novel in the Frank COWPERWOOD trilogy, based on the life of transportation magnate Charles T. YERKES. The work begins as the financier Cowperwood, released from prison, leaves Philadelphia for Chicago. DREISER is now in familiar territory—as opposed to the Philadelphia of *THE FINANCIER*—as he analyzes Chicago society in its various strata, as he describes the city's challenges and opportunities for a businessman. Aileen BUTLER, having become Aileen Cowperwood, becomes Dreiser's guide to society, as she tries to gain ascendency in her new environment; in these passages the novel resembles the work of Henry B. FULLER, whom Dreiser once credited with setting forth the truth about the city. The opening of Fuller's *WITH THE PROCESSION* points to one of Cowperwood's business challenges as well; describing a long line of vehicles, including a streetcar held up by a drawbridge over the CHICAGO RIVER, Fuller sets forth a problem that Cowperwood will solve by putting public transportation into tunnels under the river.

Many real-life counterparts are identifiable in the novel. The Garrick Players are the figures associated with LITTLE THEATRE; the actress Stephanie PLATOW is Elaine HYMAN; the critic Gardner Knowles is Floyd DELL; the director Lane Cross is Maurice BROWNE. The "tall, melancholy" poet, Forbes Gurney—whose relationship with Stephanie is discovered by a jealous Cowperwood—is Dreiser himself; the author has arranged events so that his own fictional counterpart triumphs over his fictionalized Titan. In these theater chapters he is drawing on his personal experience, not that of his subject, Yerkes; Stephanie has no direct parallel in the magnate's life. On the other hand, Berenice FLEMING is based on a real-life counterpart in Yerkes's life, including the fact that her mother ran an upscale brothel in Louisville, Kentucky.

In other real-life identifications, the retailer Anson Merrill is Marshall FIELD; the university's Dr. Hooper is William Rainey HARPER; the idealistic Governor Swanson is Governor John Peter ALTGELD; the politicians Patrick "Emerald Pat" Kerrigan and Michael "Smiling Mike" Tiernan are John "Bathhouse" COUGHLIN and Michael "Hinky Dink" KENNA.

Synopsis

CHAPTERS I–VI: THE NEW CITY; A RECONNOITER; A CHICAGO EVENING; PETER LAUGHLIN & CO.; CONCERNING A WIFE AND FAMILY; THE NEW QUEEN OF THE HOME

Leaving the penitentiary in Philadelphia in 1873, where he has served 13 months for embezzlement of city funds, Frank Cowperwood decides to investigate opportunities in the West. Boarding a train for Chicago, he promises his mistress, Aileen Butler, that he will be back for her shortly. He sees at once that the new, young city is the place for him; he understands, too, that streetcar transportation, which will grow as the city grows, offers economic possibilities.

Holding letters of introduction, Cowperwood calls on a bank president, who is impressed by his visitor and invites him to lunch at the Union Club; there Cowperwood meets some of the leading businessmen of the day. Aileen soon joins him in Chicago, and Cowperwood forms a partnership with an older man, a CHICAGO BOARD OF TRADE operator. Lillian COWPERWOOD, meanwhile, has been persuaded to divorce her husband, and so Aileen becomes his new wife. The couple rent a furnished house in a fashionable area and acquire appropriate servants; they invite various luminaries and their wives for dinner. Aileen makes an attractive hostess, although she worries about fitting in conversationally with these sophisticated people.

CHAPTERS VII–X: CHICAGO GAS; NOW THIS IS FIGHTING; IN SEARCH OF VICTORY; A TEST

Cowperwood becomes interested in Chicago gas companies, firms that provide the natural gas that is used for lighting. Three separate companies have divided up the city, and his project is to buy them and combine them. Yet none are for sale, and since he himself knows nothing about the gas business— about machinery, mains, franchising contracts—he finds a man who is knowledgeable, who will help in starting up franchises in the suburbs.

Cowperwood is building a new mansion on South MICHIGAN AVENUE, and Aileen hopes for social success. She worries when people ask about her Philadelphia acquaintances, feeling nervous about her past and her years as Cowperwood's mistress. In the fall of 1878, the couple hold an opening for their new house, lavishly furnished and decorated; one guest, surveying the scene, remarks that Cowperwood might be able to enter into society if he were on his own, but that he needs a different woman, one who can play her cards better than Aileen. Cowperwood's wife is almost too good-looking, he suggests—and she is not cold enough, not clever enough.

CHAPTERS XI–XVII: THE FRUITS OF DARING; A NEW RETAINER; THE DIE IS CAST; UNDERCURRENTS; A NEW AFFECTION; A FATEFUL INTERLUDE; AN OVERTURE TO CONFLICT

The "gas war" is waging. Cowperwood's new companies are seen as threatening the exclusive terri-

tory of the long-standing firms; charges of conspiracy and bribery are leveled. Another businessman, Schryhart, moves to buy up the old companies himself, but Cowperwood arranges with the city council—through a political fixer named McKenty—to obtain, through bribery, a blanket franchise for himself.

Cowperwood's business dealings attract scrutiny from Chicago society, and his and his wife's past in Philadelphia is revealed—to the horror of everyone who is respectable. The doors of society are no longer open to Mr. and Mrs. Cowperwood; Aileen feels the slight in particular. Yet Cowperwood himself gets along well with the outstanding men of the community, and he wonders if another type of woman would be more appropriate for him.

He begins to conduct casual affairs, until he meets someone about whom he does not feel casual, Rita SOHLBERG. Rita is the wife of a Danish violinist living in Chicago; at 27, she is six years younger than Aileen. Receiving funds from her prosperous father in Wichita, Kansas, she can easily explain to her husband the extra money she is receiving; Sohlberg does not know that Cowperwood is paying for his wife's fine new clothes.

Yet another woman exists in Cowperwood's life as well—his stenographer, a young woman of Polish immigrant parents named Minka Nowak, who has already changed her name to Antoinette. Cowperwood takes Antoinette less seriously than Rita, and yet she is the one who first arouses Aileen's suspicions of her husband—when Aileen sees him talking to her at his office, when she catches a glimpse of him in a carriage at a time he is supposedly out of town. Cowperwood has also seemed remote, alienated of late.

CHAPTERS XVIII–XX: THE CLASH; HELL HATH NO FURY—; MAN AND SUPERMAN

Aileen hires a private detective to follow her husband, and not only are her suspicions of Antoinette confirmed, but she learns about Rita Sohlberg as well—a particular shock, since the Cowperwoods and the Sohlbergs have been on friendly terms socially. When the Sohlbergs pay a call one afternoon, Aileen asks Rita to come upstairs—at which point she physically attacks the woman, scratching, choking, tearing, beating her fiercely. Rita screams loudly, and Cowperwood, arriving home, rescues her, reproving his wife for starting a brawl in their own house. Later, he tells Sohlberg that Aileen is unbalanced, that her accusations are false; at the same time he offers Sohlberg $5,000 annually to stay away from Chicago for at least three years. The violinist returns to Denmark, and Rita, deserting both men, goes off to Europe.

The chapter title "Hell Hath No Fury—"—to be completed by the words, "like a woman scorned"—is a version of a quote from the English Restoration playwright William Congreve. The succeeding chapter title, "Man and Superman," is from the 1905 play by George Bernard Shaw, in which "Superman" suggests the writings of Friedrich NIETZSCHE, the German philosopher who lauded the strong man's rising above the constraints of bourgeois morality.

CHAPTERS XXI–XXIII: A MATTER OF TUNNELS; STREET-RAILWAYS AT LAST; THE POWER OF THE PRESS

Cowperwood, having won the gas wars, is now looking at the street-railway lines; he dreams of combining them, forming a citywide network that he controls. As with the gas companies, three separate street-railway companies are currently operating in the south, north, and west sides of the city. The streetcars themselves, horse-drawn, are flimsy and old-fashioned, providing no stoves for winter heat; passengers are protected from the cold by a layer of straw on the floors. Moreover, the lines are held up by traffic congestion at the bridges spanning the Chicago River; every time a bridge is opened, or turned—a frequent occurrence, since commerce on the river is heavy—the traffic on either side, including streetcar traffic, is tied up for inconvenient periods of time. Cowperwood learns that two tunnels were built years earlier beneath the river but were abandoned because their grades were too steep for public conveyances; the city now owns the tunnels. Cowperwood has also learned of a new concept in public transportation—cable cars, already introduced in San Francisco; a cable, attached to a car and driven by engines at powerhouses, can move a heavy vehicle

up and down steep grades. Cowperwood makes arrangements with the politician McKenty, gaining assurance that the city will not sell the tunnels to anyone else, nor help existing street-railway companies to extend their lines. Soon Cowperwood is taking his first step, wresting control of the North Side line; his next step is to acquire the tunnels under the river for his new cable cars. He speaks to the city's newspaper owners, whose support he hopes to cultivate; one newspaperman suggests obliquely that he himself could be bribed.

CHAPTERS XXIV–XXVIII: THE COMING OF STEPHANIE PLATOW; AIRS FROM THE ORIENT; LOVE AND WAR; A FINANCIER BEWITCHED; THE EXPOSURE OF STEPHANIE

Although managing to soothe Aileen, Cowperwood feels a continued longing for youth and beauty. He meets Stephanie Platow, a "Russian Jewess" on one side of her family; Stephanie is a 20-year-old actress with an amateur theater group, the Garrick Players, who, unknown to him, has been carrying on an affair with the director of the group. As she begins her affair with Cowperwood, she admits only a brief episode with a drama critic.

To the dismay of rival businessmen, Cowperwood wins use of the tunnels from the city council. Adding the West Side street-railway to his system, he has once again defeated Schryhart and the others. Soon the tunnels under the river are refurbished, glowing with electric lights, and cable lines and powerhouses are constructed. The man whom longtime Chicago businessmen consider an upstart, a jail bird, is flourishing politically and financially.

Stephanie takes up with yet another artistic figure, a poet named Forbes Gurney. Although not knowing specific details, Cowperwood feels jealous over this actress who seems to engage herself freely with the city's artistic figures; he has always thought he could bind a woman to him, and yet Stephanie, young and poetic, seems elusive. He employs a man to check up on her at a studio in the New Arts Building—Dreiser's version of the FINE ARTS BUILDING—and learns that Stephanie is meeting Gurney there. Cowperwood breaks in on them one evening, discovering them together, and announces that her days of lying to him are over, that they will not meet again.

CHAPTERS XXIX–XXXIII: A FAMILY QUARREL; OBSTACLES; UNTOWARD DISCLOSURES; A SUPPER PARTY; MR. LYNDE TO THE RESCUE

Aileen learns about her husband's relationship with Stephanie and also, from overhearing servants' gossip, about his involvements with other women; she learns about the daughter of a street-railway executive, as well as the daughter of a newspaper owner, a man who had previously been sympathetic to Cowperwood. She confronts her husband, who denies everything. He realizes that he must continue as he is, that he is "too radiant, too individual and complex" to belong to just one woman.

Cowperwood requires a third tunnel now for expanding his street-railway system; he needs to buy land for the digging. When a man whose building is in the way refuses to sell, Cowperwood chooses a weekend to send over laborers with picks, shovels, and dynamite sticks—a time when no courts are open to issue an injunction. The building is conveniently razed, and the matter is settled out of court. Yet public sentiment against Cowperwood is growing, and when the newspaper owner learns about the seduction of his daughter, the paper turns against him. Further serious consequences arise when a powerful businessman, Hosmer Hand, learns that his young wife, too, has been seduced by Cowperwood; enraged, the husband determines to rid Chicago of this man.

Aileen herself is thinking about other men. Polk Lynde, whose father owns a reaper works, is a clever and charming man who pursues her. She maintains her resistance, even as she reads in a gossip sheet that a prominent businessman is engaging in notable liaisons—a man whose wife was herself once caught up in scandal in the East. She knows the reference is to her and her husband.

CHAPTERS XXXIV–XXXIX: ENTER HOSMER HAND; A POLITICAL AGREEMENT; AN ELECTION DRAWS NEAR; AILEEN'S REVENGE; AN HOUR OF DEFEAT; THE NEW ADMINISTRATION

Hosmer Hand is rallying his forces. An election is coming, and he will change the makeup of the city council, putting in place a municipal government that will refuse to do Cowperwood's bidding. Hand approaches a political figure, Patrick Gilgan, and offers funds for a citywide campaign to oust the current Democratic majority. Gilgan's job is to see that every ward picks a strong anti-Cowperwood candidate, that these candidates are then elected. Gilgan must be particularly persuasive with two ward bosses who control a large floating vote population, whose wards have long been noted for ballot-box stuffing and vote-repeating.

Polk Lynde finally succeeds in winning Aileen, and Cowperwood is upset by that development more than by the defeat of the city government that had favored him. He feels the loss of the love that Aileen once held for him—and as for the city council, he knows he still has various courses of action. He learns, for instance, that the new Republican mayor has weaknesses that might be exploited; a young woman with a shady past, but an innocent manner, is sent as a stenographer to the mayor, and she does her job well, acquiring incriminating evidence against him. Then Cowperwood deals with Patrick Gilgan, convincing the politician that his interests lie with Cowperwood's; the votes against Cowperwood's interests are not so numerous as expected.

CHAPTERS XL–XLVI: A TRIP TO LOUISVILLE; THE DAUGHTER OF MRS. FLEMING; F. A. COWPERWOOD, GUARDIAN; THE PLANET MARS; A FRANCHISE OBTAINED; CHANGING HORIZONS; DEPTHS AND HEIGHTS

On a trip to Louisville, Kentucky, Cowperwood meets a Mrs. Carter, a woman who runs a socially exclusive house of prostitution. Mrs. Carter has a daughter attending an expensive boarding school in New York, and financial setbacks force her to seek help from her new friend, Cowperwood; he is interested in her, but yet more interested in her daughter, Berenice Fleming, who is 17 years old. Cowperwood is 52 years old.

Public transportation is demanding new elevated tracks, as well as electricity to replace the cable, but local opposition to Cowperwood makes it difficult for him to get financing. Yet the great new university in the city, donated by the Standard Oil millionaire, is seeking to build a giant telescope and observatory; Cowperwood, who has been interested in the heavens since his days at the penitentiary in Philadelphia—where, taking advantage of his special privileges, he sat out in a prison garden at night—pledges $300,000 to build the lens, the telescope, the machinery, and the building for the observatory. He is lauded internationally as a patron of science, and funds become available for his railway lines. Further opposition is kept at bay when he threatens to expose the indiscreet letters written by the mayor, letters which he now has in his possession.

His thoughts turn to New York City, where Mrs. Carter has been established in an apartment near her daughter's school. Cowperwood begins to contemplate building a mansion there; he would house in it his growing art collection, and he would be closer to Berenice. He suggests to Aileen that they move to New York, where Aileen might, he says, have a chance of being accepted socially, although he knows she has no such chance. In regard to Berenice, Cowperwood is still playing the role of family friend; he realizes that she does not take him as seriously as he takes her.

The new university is the UNIVERSITY OF CHICAGO, donated by John D. ROCKEFELLER. Dreiser titles his chapter. "The Planet Mars," knowing that readers are aware of recent claims made by the astronomer Percival Lowell, brother of poet Amy LOWELL, that canals can be viewed on Mars, that life exists on the red planet.

CHAPTERS XLVII–XLIX: AMERICAN MATCH; PANIC; MOUNT OLYMPUS

Dreiser, speaking for public opinion in the late 1890s, describes a set of contemporary Titans; like the giants of ancient times, living "without heart or soul," they wish only to keep the rank and file in chains. Cowperwood is one of them. Yet a prophet rises up in the West—Dreiser is referring to William Jennings BRYAN—who calls for the free coinage of silver, who argues for the abandonment of the GOLD STANDARD and an increase in the money supply. The Titans see this prophet as a threat, an orator calling for the confiscation of their wealth, and because of his agitation, stocks are weakened, and financial unrest increases.

Thus "silver agitation" provides the background for Cowperwood's next coup. Two Chicago businessmen, Phineas Hull and Benoni Stackpole, have created a monopoly company, American Match, but they lack adequate capital and have been forced to receive backing from a group of prominent Chicago businessmen. Yet with the nomination of the "Apostle of Free Silver" for president, the market has slackened, and their stock has declined. Hull and Stackpole try to support the price of their stock by purchasing additional shares, but reaching their financial limits, they approach Cowperwood, a financier who has had nothing to do with the firm; they suggest that he buy shares at what would be a discount price, thereby helping to support the market. Fully understanding the situation, Cowperwood refuses and sends them away. Then he secretly negotiates with bankers to lend sums of money to Hull and Stackpole, who are to use the shares they attempted to sell to Cowperwood as collateral; the sums to be lent are smaller than the worth of the shares at the time. Thus Cowperwood, who reimburses the bankers, now owns the shares; he is free to sell them at the current price, still far in excess of the loan. Therefore, in the weeks following, the additional shares appear on the market, and the value of the stocks collapses. Hull and Stackpole face bankruptcy; their investors are losing large sums as well.

Concluding that Cowperwood is behind the influx of additional shares, these investors plot their next move. They learn that Cowperwood himself has outstanding loans, and they decide that his creditors should call them in. Holding a nighttime conference in one of their stately homes, they invite Cowperwood to come and talk to them. They indicate that his loans will be called, and he replies that he can meet them—he has millions of dollars in government bonds in safety vaults—but adds that if even a single one of his loans is called, he will "gut" every bank in Chicago. That is, he is telling the businessmen that he controls loans they do not even know about. He warns that panic, "all the panic you want," will result if they make any move against him. He takes his leave, knowing that he has triumphed.

CHAPTERS L–LIII: A NEW YORK MANSION; THE REVIVAL OF HATTIE STARR; BEHIND THE ARRAS; A DECLARATION OF LOVE

Cowperwood's loans are not called, and American Match collapses. The businessmen, losing their investment, vow that they will break Cowperwood, although they agree it will have to be done through politics, not finance.

Meanwhile, building a splendid mansion in New York City, Cowperwood and Aileen are planning their move; he continues to support Mrs. Carter and her daughter, Berenice, although Berenice is not aware of such arrangements. The daughter is interested in a Lieutenant Braxmar, handsome and well positioned socially; her mother pushes his case, hoping that her daughter marries well, not understanding Cowperwood's intentions of himself marrying her daughter. One evening in a hotel dining room, where Cowperwood, Mrs. Carter, Berenice, and Lieutenant Braxmar have gathered after the opera, a drunken man approaches Mrs. Carter, recognizing her from her less-respectable days in Louisville. He reveals enough information, before being hastened away, to make Braxmar realize that the man is speaking the truth; the lieutenant nevertheless declares his love for Berenice and asks her to marry him. Berenice, feeling shame, sends him away. She also forces her mother to admit the truth about her past, as well as the fact that the family has no money, that Cowperwood has been supporting them. Berenice now knows, although her mother still does not, why Cowperwood is supporting them. He soon makes a declaration of his love, and she responds enigmatically, saying she must think about what he has said.

The chapter title, "Behind the Arras," is a reference to Shakespeare's *Hamlet*, in which the character Polonius hides behind a tapestry to gain intelligence about his daughter; in this chapter, the daughter, Berenice, learns truths from her mother.

CHAPTERS LIV–LVII: WANTED—FIFTY-YEAR FRANCHISES; COWPERWOOD AND THE GOVERNOR; THE ORDEAL OF BERENICE; AILEEN'S LAST CARD

Cowperwood allies himself financially with the prominent New York firm of Haeckellheimer, Gotloeb and Company; Dreiser, following the then-ac-

cepted practice of DIALECT WRITING, gives Gotloeb a "semi-German, semi-Hebraic dialect." What Cowperwood needs now is a renewal of his Chicago street-railway franchises, preferably for a period of 50 years—and any renewal at all is problematic, since so much local animosity, on the part of both businessmen and newspapers, is being held against him. Yet the idea of public ownership has entered into the national consciousness, and businessmen are conflicted about denying Cowperwood his franchises—if, as a result, such a "socialistic" idea is promoted.

Cowperwood learns that in New York the state legislature has dealt with local transit issues, and he resolves to take his own problem to the Illinois state legislature—even though such dealings are forbidden by the Illinois state constitution. He sets his standard bribery procedures in motion, and his measure seems to gain merit, except that the newspapers get hold of the story and the governor says he will veto the legislation; the Swedish-born Governor Swanson is depicted as a thoughtful, idealistic man. Cowperwood knows that the governor has suffered financial setbacks and needs the money offered to him; out of respect he promises to loan the governor money even if he vetoes the bill. Swanson vetoes the bill, and Cowperwood loans him $100,000.

Berenice first sees Aileen in an opera box in New York. She understands her position fully now; at age 22 she enjoys only a precarious social position, and her wealth is solely dependent on a benefactor who wants to marry her—except that he himself is married. Aileen herself finally learns about Berenice; she sees the young woman and her husband together and follows them into a hotel dining room. When she upbraids her husband, he takes the opportunity to ask for a divorce. Her reaction is a halfhearted suicide attempt.

CHAPTERS LVIII–LXII: A MARAUDER UPON THE COMMONWEALTH; CAPITAL AND PUBLIC RIGHTS; THE NET; THE CATACLYSM; THE RECOMPENSE

Cowperwood renews his efforts to bribe the Illinois state legislature, but by now the newspapers are vigorously against him. The legislature gives the right to decide franchises back to the Chicago city council, and Cowperwood has yet another battle to fight. By this time the political climate has shifted, giving voice to "anarchists, socialists, single-taxers, and public-ownership advocates." Moreover, a better life for the rank and file means not only an eight-hour day, but also public, not private, ownership of franchises serving the public good. Cowperwood, the papers declare, must no longer be allowed to bribe his way into denying the common man his rights.

Berenice reads the New York papers and decides that this man, seemingly "a superman, a half-god," should not be subject to the ordinary rules of mankind. She realizes, too, that New York society is learning about her mother's past and therefore rejecting her.

Back in Chicago, the city council is under pressure to defeat Cowperwood's franchise extensions. The outcry is against "boodle," or bribe money, and the consensus is that "boodlers" and "boodleism" must be defeated. When the roll call is taken, Cowperwood loses by 16 votes; he will never have extensions on his franchises. In this depth of defeat, Berenice appears at his home, coming to him from New York. She cannot stay away any longer, she declares—and perhaps, she adds, they should go somewhere else, such as London or Paris.

Critical Reception

The novel was not well received. The CHICAGO TRIBUNE found it "sordid, disagreeable"; the University of Illinois critic Stuart P. Sherman, summing up the two Cowperwood works so far, likened the novels to a sandwich, "composed of slices of business alternating with erotic episodes." Other reviewers found the fiction too reportorial, consisting of piles of facts and proceedings—although another declared that the novel failed to exemplify REALISM because Cowperwood was too abnormal. William Marion REEDY found the novel to be elitist, arguing that it ignored the workingmen on whom Cowperwood's ascendancy depended.

Subsequent critics noted that Dreiser had come a long way from the NATURALISM that

governed his first work of fiction, SISTER CARRIE. His characters are no longer buffeted by the forces of life, but are instead making their own way, bringing about their own destiny. The Titan reflects less the views of Émile ZOLA than those of Friedrich Nietzsche; the setbacks that Cowperwood, the superior strong man, faces are not the result of fate, but of petty human machinations. The great man is brought down not by inevitable forces, but by vindictive and jealous human beings.

"To a Contemporary Bunkshooter" See CHICAGO POEMS.

Tolstoy, Leo
(1828–1910) Russian novelist

Author of classics such as War and Peace and Anna Karenina, Tolstoy in the last decades of his life devoted himself to a philosophy of nonviolence and rural simplicity. As a result, he became a cult figure in Russia and abroad, inspiring others to try for an unworldly agricultural life. One such figure was George Cram COOK, who, returning from Harvard University to his native Davenport, Iowa, temporarily established a Tolstoyan farming life; he later moved to Chicago and ultimately to the East. Jane ADDAMS visited Tolstoy in Russia in 1896—in a seemingly unsatisfactory encounter; Tolstoy is said to have criticized her clothing, complaining of the extravagant amount of material in her sleeves.

In Upton SINCLAIR's THE JUNGLE, the protagonist hears about Tolstoy at a socialist rally; this new figure becomes part of his political awareness. In 1915, after the sinking of the British ocean liner LUSITANIA during WORLD WAR I, Vachel LINDSAY published two poems in the Chicago Herald, one addressing Jane Addams, attending a peace-seeking International Congress of Women at The Hague, Netherlands, and the other, "Tolstoi Is Plowing Yet," evoking the spirit of the recently deceased pacifist writer; both were collected in THE CHINESE NIGHTENGALE AND OTHER POEMS in 1917.

Toomer, Jean
(1894–1967) *African-American writer*

Toomer's novel *Cane* has been seen as an influence on Sherwood ANDERSON's DARK LAUGHTER, as *Cane* itself is said to have been influenced by Anderson's WINESBURG, OHIO. Born in Washington, D.C., Toomer enrolled at the University of Wisconsin in 1914. Often passing as white, he came to Chicago in 1916, briefly attending the UNIVERSITY OF CHICAGO. He began a correspondence with Anderson in 1922; at one point the older writer offered to write an introduction to Toomer's forthcoming volume. *Cane,* a miscellany of verse, sketches, and a play, focusing on the lives of black Americans in the rural South, appeared in 1923; like *Winesburg,* it presents portraits of twisted characters, in this case, twisted by the heritage of slavery. As opposed to Anderson's *Cane*-influenced *Dark Laughter,* the volume was not commercially successful; critics today, comparing the two books, declare that Anderson's African Americans are simply stereotyped versions of Toomer's African Americans. In the early 1920s, Toomer became interested—as did Margaret ANDERSON and Jane HEAP—in the teachings of the mystic and occultist George GURDJIEFF; in 1924, Toomer made his first visit to Fontainebleau, outside of Paris, home of Gurdjieff's Institute for the Harmonious Development of Man. In 1926, he returned to the Chicago, leading a Gurdjieff center for the next five years; he later headed a Gurdjieff-inspired commune in Portage, Wisconsin, birthplace and continuing part-time home of writer Zona GALE. He spent his last years participating in the Society of Friends, or Quakers.

The Torrents of Spring
Ernest Hemingway
(1926)

For this parody of Sherwood ANDERSON's DARK LAUGHTER, HEMINGWAY takes his title from the Russian author Ivan Turgenev, adding as a subtitle, "A Romantic Novel in Honor of the Passing of a Great Race." Hemingway's protagonist embarks on travels northward instead of southward—

Anderson's character had headed toward New Orleans—and he finds Native Americans instead of African Americans. The author mocks Anderson's creation of a chorus of African-American "dark laughter"; he claims that the sounds of "an Indian war-whoop" can be heard, and Indians also hum "old tribal chanties." The white characters, by contrast, continually recite extended literary references, indulging also in a heightened rhetoric that can be considered reminiscent of WINESBURG, OHIO. References to horses and stables are also purposeful on the author's part, evoking Anderson's well-known stories set at livery stables and racing tracks.

"To Tramps"

This article by Lucy PARSONS appeared in the October 4, 1884, issue of ALARM, the publication of the anarchist INTERNATIONAL WORKING PEOPLE'S ASSOCIATION. The article exhorts the hungry and unemployed to resort to violence against the wealthy. Referring to the new weapon, DYNAMITE, Parsons concludes, *"Learn the Use of Explosives!"* The article was later circulated in leaflet form, and one of the leaflets was introduced at the trial of her husband, Albert PARSONS, and eight other defendants after the HAYMARKET AFFAIR bombing.

"Trifles"   *See* "A JURY OF HER PEERS."

Triggs, Oscar Lovell
(1865–1930) *writer, follower of William Morris*

An English instructor at the UNIVERSITY OF CHICAGO, Triggs published *Chapters in the History of the Arts and Craft Movement* in 1902, promoting the ideals of handicraft that MORRIS and the ARTS AND CRAFT MOVEMENT espoused. He became editor of the Bulletin of the Morris Society of Chicago, which evolved into the "free-thinking" periodical, *To-Morrow;* Carl SANDBURG contributed to the magazine in 1905–06. Offering opposition to Triggs was his economist colleague Thorstein VEBLEN; the machine-endorsing Veblen declared Triggs's handicraft-endorsing efforts to be antiquated and obsolete. Known for his socialist interpretations of literature, Triggs eventually lost his position at the University of Chicago, achieving notoriety for advocating "free love, free verse, and socialism."

Trimble, George   *See* SPOON RIVER ANTHOLOGY.

"The Triumph of a Modern or, Send for the Lawyer"   *See* HORSES AND MEN.

The Triumph of the Egg
Sherwood Anderson
(1921)

This collection of stories by Sherwood ANDERSON, subtitled *A Book of Impressions from American Life in Tales and Poems*, is illustrated by photographs of sculptures by Tennessee MITCHELL, Anderson's wife at the time. The first story, "I Want to Know Why," derives from Anderson's work in a livery stable in his hometown of Clyde, Ohio, as well as his traveling on a local horse-racing circuit; these experiences recur in stories of the subsequent collection, HORSES AND MEN. In "The Egg," Clyde becomes Bidwell, Ohio, as it does in the novel POOR WHITE and in other tales from *Horses and Men*. In "Brothers," the unnamed setting is Palos Park, Illinois, a town southwest of Chicago, where Anderson lived in 1920. "Seeds" gives a portrait of a psychoanalyst Anderson met while camping in upstate New York. Two stories, "Unlighted Lamps" and "The Door of the Trap," focusing on a character named Mary Cochrane, are part of an uncompleted novel Anderson worked on while living as a businessman in Ohio. The longest piece in the collection, "Out of Nowhere into Nothing," makes use of a story line that Theodore DREISER employed two decades previously in SISTER CARRIE—telling of a small-town woman, coming to work in Chicago, who finds illicit sexual entanglement. Yet unlike Dreiser, Anderson shows no interest in economic issues; his character, receiving money from her father, is never confronted by poverty, and the quandaries she faces are sexual, not monetary.

As with early-20th-century work by Anderson, Carl SANDBURG, and others, modern readers must recognize that language sensibilities have changed over the decades. Words now considered to be racial slurs had fewer negative connotations—or at least greater mainstream acceptance—in the first years of the 20th century.

Synopses of Selected Stories

"I WANT TO KNOW WHY"
The unnamed first-person narrator, a 15-year old Kentucky boy, rides the rails to Saratoga, New York, during the horse-racing season. Middlestride and Sunstreak, two thoroughbreds from his hometown, are running in the events. The narrator loves horses and instinctively understands them; Sunstreak's trainer, Jerry TILLFORD, lets him visit Sunstreak in his stall before a race. Intuiting how the horse feels, the narrator understands that Sunstreak, although outwardly calm, is inwardly "a raging torrent." He looks at Jerry and recognizes that the trainer, too, understands the horse's feelings; he feels love for Jerry, as they both know what the horse knows. Tears coming to his eyes, he sees a shine in Jerry's eyes as well.

That night, the narrator follows along a road where Jerry has gone. Coming to a farmhouse, he approaches the windows and sees women in loose dresses; he realizes it is a place for "bad women." He hears bad language, and then he hears Jerry boasting about Sunstreak, claiming that he himself made the horse; the boy is upset at his bragging. Then he sees Jerry look at one of the women—in the same way he had looked at Sunstreak, his eyes shining; Jerry kisses the woman.

The boy creeps away in anger. Ever since that evening, he has been thinking about what he saw, and he still cannot understand how Jerry can watch a horse like Sunstreak running a race—and then, on the same day, kiss such a woman. Thinking about the scene now spoils everything he does at the track. He wants to know what made Jerry do it. He wants to know why.

"I Want to Know Why" was first published in the November 1919 *Smart Set,* a periodical coedited by H. L. MENCKEN; it appeared six months after the publication of *WINESBURG, OHIO.*

"SEEDS"

The psychoanalyst claims that in his work he has entered into people's lives, including the lives of women. The first-person narrator tells him that he cannot enter into the lives of others; moreover, the illness he pretends to cure is the universal illness, which is incurable. The analyst, sneering, responds in sarcasm: "How smart we are—how aptly we put things!" He says that lives are like trees in a forest, which are being choked by vines; he himself is being choked, and he wants to run freely like a leaf blown by the wind.

A young woman from Iowa has come to the narrator's rooming house in Chicago. The men in the house note that she acts seductively, even standing naked in the bathroom and leaving the door slightly ajar; yet she repels any advance they make toward her. The landlady, hearing complaints, orders her to leave. The woman enters the room of LeRoy, a painter, and kneels at his feet, pleading, "Take me." The landlady, having followed her, confronts her, and LeRoy, thinking quickly, tells the landlady that he and the woman are engaged; she has been unwell, and he will take her away. LeRoy finds a new rooming house for the woman, and then he sits with her on a park bench, talking to her; nothing more happens.

The narrator later tells him that he could have been her lover. LeRoy grows angry, and words come to him that were said by the other man: "How smart we are. How aptly we put things." He declares that the woman was like a tree choked by vines; she needed a lover, but she also needed to be loved. Her disease is universal. He himself is covered by vines, and he cannot be a lover; he would like to be a leaf blown by the wind.

The story first appeared in the July 1918 LIT-TLE REVIEW.

"THE OTHER WOMAN"

A first-person narrator tells a tale that another man, who is about to be married, tells about him-self. Although a prospective bridegroom, the man admits that he has been obsessed with another woman, the wife of the owner of a nearby tobacco shop. The obsession persists even though the woman is ordinary, as well as 10 years older than he. On the morning before his wedding, he stops by the shop, asking the woman to meet him in his apartment that evening. That same morning, he receives a letter from his fiancée, saying that she is feeling nervous, that she knows nothing about life—the implicit reference is to sex—and that he must be patient and kind with her; she will repay him with love and tenderness.

The man is moved by the beauty of his fiancée's character, vowing that he "will take care of the dear little woman." He decides to send away the tobaccanist's wife when she arrives that evening, and yet he does not. He opens the door and takes her into his arms.

The marriage has now taken place, and the man claims never to think about the other woman, although he immediately contradicts himself, telling his listener that sometimes when his wife is asleep, he awakes at midnight and thinks of the other woman and "the most notable experience of my life." But when he awakes the next morning, he insists, the other woman is gone.

The story first appeared in the May-June 1920 issue of *Little Review.* It serves as the Anderson selection in the 1999 *The Best American Short Stories of the Century.*

"THE EGG"

The father of the unnamed first-person narrator had been an ordinary farmhand near Bidwell, Ohio, harboring no ambition to rise in the world, until the age of 34. Then, marrying the narrator's mother, a schoolteacher, he finds that everything has changed. The couple, along with their new child, become eager to get ahead, and the mother talks the father into renting land and raising chickens. Yet the chickens become ill and die, and after struggling for 10 years, the couple give up their efforts. Abandoning farming, they move into Bidwell, where their next project is to open a restaurant; they will live in rooms above the business.

The father brings to the restaurant his collection of deformed chicks, preserved in alcohol; the bottles go on a shelf in back of the counter. The couple decide to keep the restaurant open at night, since trains come by during the late hours; the night switching crews partake of their fare. The father tends the business during the late hours, while the mother and son sleep in the rooms above.

The father decides that trade would improve if he tried to be more cheerful, even if he provided entertainment for his customers. One evening his efforts prove disastrous—as he wakes his wife and son with a "roar of anger"; tramping upstairs, holding an egg in his hand, he falls to weeping. The boy reconstructs the events that occurred downstairs.

The son of a Bidwell merchant is sitting in the restaurant, waiting for the 10 o'clock train; the train is three hours late, and the customer and the proprietor are alone on the premises. The father decides it is time to provide entertainment. Taking an egg from a basket on the counter, he talks about making it stand on end. He is referring to the famous story about Christopher Columbus, when the navigator demonstrated to the Spanish court his method of solving a problem; to make an egg stand on end, he simply cracked the end. The father has missed the point of the story, which is to show a straightforward, can-do philosophy; he calls Columbus a cheat. His egg will stand on end, he claims, after he rolls it back and forth between his hands; the warmth of his hands will create a new center of gravity. After half an hour of trying, the egg stands on its end, although only for a moment, and the customer is not even watching.

Desperate to keep up the performance, the father starts bringing bottles of deformed chicks down from their shelf; the customer is made ill by the sight of them. Then the father heats an egg in a pan of vinegar, saying that the shell will be softened and he can put the egg through the neck of a bottle—after which it will return to its normal shape; people will wonder how it got there. After many tries, he still cannot get the egg into the bottle. Meanwhile, the delayed train arrives, and the customer heads for the door. The father, making one last effort to get the egg into the bottle, breaks the shell; the customer, looking back, laughs.

The father grabs an egg from the basket and throws it angrily at the customer, just missing his head. Then, grasping another egg, he goes upstairs, where his anger turns to total collapse. The next morning, the boy sees the egg on the table, and he understands what has happened—that hens and eggs have triumphed in his father's life.

Originally titled "The Triumph of the Egg," the story was published in the March 1920 DIAL. A stage adaptation was performed by the PROVINCETOWN PLAYERS in New York in 1925; the play is included in the 1937 volume *Plays: Winesburg and Others*.

"UNLIGHTED LAMPS"

Mary COCHRAN, 18 years old, has gone for a walk on a Sunday evening in the small town of Huntersburg, Illinois. She must think about what her father, Dr. Lester COCHRAN, has just told her—that he has heart disease, that he might die at any moment, that he will leave her little money and she must make plans for her future. The doctor, when telling her this news, had wanted to put his arm on her shoulder, but he could not bring himself to make the gesture.

Mary walks in an area of laboring men's houses, where the men live who have come to work in the town's new factory. She feels comfortable there because the workers and their wives do not know her family history; they do not know the town gossip about her mother and father's unhappy marriage. Yet she realizes she must soon be setting out in the world; she has been to Chicago several times and knows she might soon be living there.

During her walk she is accosted by Duke Yetter, a brash young man who has been following her. She slaps him on the cheek, shouting that if he follows her she will get someone to kill him. The gossip is that her mother ran off with some young tough—and here is another young tough. She adds angrily that her father wants to kill someone like him. Yetter claims he meant no harm.

Mary watches two boys fishing in a creek, and the boys' father recognizes her as Dr. Cochran's daughter. He tells her how her father once gave medical aid to his son, charging no fee and giving money to the family for groceries and medicines. He tells Mary that her father is a good man.

Dr. Cochran is sitting alone in his office, thinking of his marriage. His wife had been an actress with a traveling company, stranded in town because of illness; he had paid her hotel bill and attended to her needs, and she had decided that living in a quiet town might be appealing. But soon she could no longer live with a cold-seeming man. Dr. Cochran took her to Chicago, where she found work with a theatrical company; he gave her money and turned away, deeply stirred by the occasion, although he remained quiet on the surface.

A farmer calls for the doctor to attend his wife's childbirth. The delivery is difficult, and it is 11 o'clock before the doctor returns to the livery barn to put up his horse and buggy. Mary is sitting by the window of her father's office, awaiting his return. In front of the barn Duke Yetter and several other men are lounging; the night watchman tells of a CIVIL WAR experience, and the younger man laughingly challenges him. Mary hears her father saying good night to the men; she hears him coming upstairs, speaking to himself about the child that has been born—at a time when death is standing at his elbow. She hears a shout of laughter outside from Duke Yetter. Then the doctor falls backward down the stairs; Mary hears the clattering sound. It is Yetter who carries the dead man up the stairs and lays him on a bed.

The story first appeared in the July 1921 *Smart Set*.

"BROTHERS"

The nameless first-person narrator lives in a house in the country, 20 miles outside of Chicago. An old man, whom people call "cracked," lives by himself in the neighboring woods; the narrator often sees him walking down the road, carrying a small dog in his arms. The old man speaks of his relatives, except that he has none; he takes names from the newspapers and claims them as his kin. Enrico Caruso, the singer, for instance, has married his wife's sister; the narrator knows that the old man never married. At one time the Chicago papers are telling of a millionaire caught up in a scandal with an actress. The old man, who is 60 years old,

claims that the young actress is his sister; he speaks of their childhood together.

Then the papers begin telling the story of a murder. The accused man, a foreman in a bicycle factory, loves a girl working in the factory office. The foreman watches her, becomes obsessed with her. In his mind he takes her home with him, even though he lives with a wife, two children, and a mother-in-law; his wife is expecting their third child. Although the man means nothing to her, the girl in the factory realizes his feelings. In her own mind she replaces him with an attractive young man, imagining this young man looking at her with the same eager eyes as the foreman. Sometimes she purposely stays late, knowing that the foreman will walk her home. He is humble and deferential, and she knows she is safe with him.

One evening the man kills his wife. In the hallway of their apartment building, he takes a knife out of his pocket and stabs her a dozen times. Running upstairs, he washes the knife, then claims that his wife was killed in a holdup. Yet after a day or two, the police begin questioning him closely, and he confesses right away. He says he does not know why he killed his wife.

The narrator meets the old man, still holding the dog in his arms. The man says the murderer is his brother. They have different names, he explains, because their father went away to sea; yet they played together as boys in the barn behind their house. The narrator sees that the man is telling a tale of loneliness—perhaps of all men's loneliness.

The man's arms wrap tightly around the dog, and the creature cries out in pain. The narrator reaches forward and pulls the arms away, and the dog falls, whining, to the ground; it is injured, its ribs perhaps broken. Later, the narrator sees the old man go past his house, and the dog is not with him. Perhaps the man has crushed its life out; perhaps it is dead, just like the foreman's wife and the unborn child.

The story was first published in the April 1921 *Bookman*.

"THE DOOR OF THE TRAP"

Hugh WALKER, a professor of mathematics in a small college in Union Valley, Illinois, married with three young children, feels imprisoned; he sees himself as living inside a shell, trying to break out. He feels a connection only to the old black woman who takes care of the children; she sings soft songs that take him far away. Unlike his wife and children, she is outside his life, having no hold on him.

One day in class, Hugh takes notice of one of his students, a young woman named Mary COCHRAN; he knows her father is dead, perhaps her mother as well. He begins talking to her, and soon she is coming to his house, playing with his children, joining the family for meals; his wife accepts her presence. Hugh understands that Mary does not belong to him, that she has no necessary connection to him; she has brought him back from his withdrawal from life, and yet she herself remains free. He muses that she will eventually make her own prison, but it will have nothing to do with him.

One day Hugh comes home to find his family in the living room, as well as the black woman and Mary Cochran; Mary is reading a book. He snatches the book from her and throws it into the fire, exclaiming that people should live their lives, instead of reading about life in books. Everyone is startled, and Hugh apologizes. For two weeks Mary does not come to the house. Seeing her on campus, he pleads with her not to desert him. That evening she is at the house again, and he realizes she is beginning to look like a person who belongs there.

Yet soon her visits come to an end. One evening, when Mary is putting the children to bed, Hugh takes her by the hand and leads her to his room. She looks frightened. He says he will kiss her—and then he will ask her to leave and never come back. He holds her and kisses her, and she stumbles out of the house. He feels proud of himself. She will someday be imprisoned, but it will not be he who builds the prison for her.

"THE NEW ENGLANDER"

Elsie Leander, an unmarried woman in her mid-30s, comes west with her parents from their New England farm. They are joining her brother, Tom, who owns a grocery store in Apple Junction, Iowa. Elsie feels excited and awakened by the long rail

journey from her native hills and valleys to the vast and broad PRAIRIE. Her new home is a large brick house that her brother has bought, rising out of the flat fields. From the steps she begins watching a young farmhand driving a team of horses; throughout the plowing and planting season, she keeps watching him in the fields.

That night, unable to sleep, Elsie thinks of a cousin who had died at the age of 23, a young man who had visited her from New York City the year before he died. He had said to her tearfully that he wanted to grow strong; the assumption is that he suffered from tuberculosis. He then declared that he wanted her to kiss him, and when she hesitated, he repeated, as before, that he wished he were strong. In her new house in Iowa, Elsie hears again his request for a kiss.

Tom Leander and his family, including his 16-year-old daughter, Elizabeth, come to visit Elsie and her parents every Sunday. At the same time, the young farmhand whom Elsie has been watching, who turns out to be interested in Elizabeth, makes a point of being around as well. One Sunday afternoon Elizabeth runs out as usual with her brothers and their dogs between the tall rows of corn. The dogs kill a rabbit, and she tears the bleeding animal away from them. As Elsie walks along the corn rows, she sees Elizabeth with the farmhand, still holding the rabbit. When Elizabeth comes into the house, encountering Elsie, she throws the rabbit on the table in the parlor, the blood running onto the white crocheted table cover.

After dinner Elsie runs out into the cornfields again. Crawling over a wire fence, she tears her dress, exposing her breasts; she clutches at her dress. In the distance she hears the children and the dogs; black clouds, meanwhile, are threatening a storm. She lies for a long while on her back, no longer holding the dress over her breasts, certain that something is about to happen.

She hears her brother calling to his children. She sees Elizabeth and the farmhand kissing, then going on their way. Creeping toward the farmhouse on her hands and knees, she sees her brother and his family driving away in the wagon. Her mother is calling to her, but the voice seems to have nothing to do with her. The threatening storm finally breaks, sending sheets of rain over her. The storm within her breaks as well, and she abandons herself to sobbing. The thin voices of her mother and father continue calling to her.

"OUT OF NOWHERE INTO NOTHING"

I: Rosalind WESCOTT has come home briefly to Willow Springs, Iowa, from her employment in Chicago; her purpose is to talk to her mother about a particular issue. Yet it is hard for her to say anything; she keeps walking out of town along the railroad tracks. She had continued living in Willow Springs for three years after graduating from high school; she had then gone to live with her brother in Chicago, finding employment as a stenographer. She has been in Chicago now for six years.

As she lies in bed in her father's house, she hears noises that she has heard since she was a girl, noises that have always seemed terrible to her—her father's nightly ritual of pumping a pail of water by the kitchen door, bringing the pail into the house, winding the clock, then climbing the stairs with heavy feet.

The house next door in Willow Springs has long been occupied by Melville STONER, a bachelor in his 40s. Rosalind watches Stoner bantering with the widow down the street, whose hens get into his yard. She thinks, meanwhile, of the man she has been seeing in Chicago, with whom she has spent many hours during the last two years. Now she is home in Willow Springs, hoping to be able to talk to her mother, hoping to share something that must be buried deep, she feels, within all women.

Walking along the railroad track, she sees the body of a man, whom she thinks has been struck by a train—but then Melville Stoner sits up, laughing. The two of them walk back to town, and he tells her he has watched her grow up; he tells of her father's pumping the pail of water in the evening and bringing it indoors, and Rosalind feels frightened; Melville Stoner seems able to invade her privacy. Yet he has shown her, too, that human beings can understand each other.

Ma Wescott is making gooseberry jam, and the sounds of housekeeping come from the kitchen.

Rosalind hopes she can talk to her mother, walk into her mother's life and establish a sense of sisterhood.

II–V: Rosalind is glad she has escaped to Chicago; she thinks of how the city spreads out before her, as she walks up and down its streets, as she visits its parks and lakeshore. She feels alive in the city—and thinks obliquely of sex. She has become secretary to a man in his late 30s, Walter SAYERS, who is married with two children. Sayers had once wanted to be a singer, not a businessman, but his voice is not large enough; his present position has been secured by his wife's investments. Frustrated and angry in his job, Sayers has taken up photography as a hobby. One Sunday afternoon, while his wife is at home gardening, he takes his camera out to the countryside. Yet he does not want to be a photographer; he wanted to be a singer. He takes the camera and swings it against a tree trunk; the breaking sound is like a song he might have sung.

One evening, coming home from work to his wife's garden, Sayers, thinking about Rosalind, wants to sing there in the garden, just as he had once taken Rosalind out into the country and suddenly had begun to sing; he had sung one song over and over. Sitting in the garden now, he tries to sing, but he cannot; his wife has started talking, and he has lost his wish to sing. His wife is talking to the young black man who helps her with the gardening. Sayers thinks of Rosalind, of their speaking of becoming lovers.

He remembers now the history of the young black man. The man had educated himself, going to law school, and he had opened a law office; yet he had been falsely accused of a murder and, although acquitted, had lost his chance of a legal career. Sayers's wife has taken him in, giving him lodging in a house at the foot of the garden; the two of them seem bound to each other. The wife goes indoors, and the black man, retreating to his own small house, begins to sing; he sings softly a song from the South, a sad song.

Sayers walks out past the gate and finally into the open country. He begins to sing, but it is not the song he had sung with Rosalind; it is the song of the black man. It has lost its sadness now, becoming a kind of challenge to the world.

VI: Rosalind recalls her earlier life in Willow Springs, including the day, after graduating from high school, when she went to the house of a friend who was to be married. Several girls had come to see the bride's trousseau, spread out on a bed, and one girl fell to her knees, pleading with her friend, "Don't do it!"

During dinner at the Wescott house, Rosalind looks at her mother, seeing that her face is heavy and her eyes dull. After the meal her father, noting that his daughter seems alive and radiant, remarks on how pretty she looks. He leaves the house, as he does every evening, to join the men who gather at the town's hardware store, escaping their houses and their wives, enjoying male companionship.

Rosalind is certain that Melville Stoner is sitting in his house within the sound of her voice. She wonders if she has begun to love two men; she feels both men coming toward her, ready to give her a knowledge of life. Yet she loves Walter Sayers and wants to offer herself to him; she had thought she should tell her mother and hear what the older woman had to say. She puts the image of Melville Stoner out of her mind.

Her mother is sitting on the front porch, and Melville Stoner is sitting on his. Rosalind finally begins speaking to her mother, saying she has fallen in love with a man she cannot marry; they love each other, but he is married with two children. She has come home to speak of this matter before she gives herself to him. She wonders if Melville Stoner can hear what she is saying.

Her mother says nothing. Rosalind waits, thinking about the day that Walter Sayers drove her into the country and suddenly began to sing. He sang softly, then more boldly, singing the song over and over. Rosalind realized he was able to sing because of her. Yet the spirits of Melville Stoner and Walter Sayer both seem still to be hovering over her. She wants her mother to save her from men, to have something true to say. She forces Melville Stoner out of her mind, and Walter Sayers enters instead. She will express her love for him physically and find the wonder of life.

Rosalind's mother breaks her silence. She knows she must save her daughter from the conspiracies of men, which lead them to write books and sing songs about love, causing young girls to believe in love; she must make clear to her daughter the terrible fate of all women. "Don't do it, don't do it," she mutters over and over. She herself had been a farmer's daughter who had married without thinking, and ever since she has worked for a man like a beast. She has thought that perhaps a world might exist where there is no marriage—a quiet, blissful place, without sex. "Men only hurt women," she says, and love does not exist. Rosalind hears her mother going indoors in the darkness, weeping. She thinks again of the girl in the bride's room, sobbing, "Don't do it." Rosalind goes to bed, while Melville Stoner continues to sit outside, knowing all that has passed between mother and daughter. Rosalind's father comes home, starting his nightly ritual at the pump outside the door.

Rosalind gets up, taking her bag out of the closet. She knows that an eastbound train toward Chicago passes through Willow Springs at two in the morning—although she will not wait for it, but walk the eight miles to the next town. She runs out of the house, past where Melville Stoner is waiting; he says he thought he might have another chance to walk with her. Rosalind feels grateful to him now, realizing that they have established a living fellowship. She invites him to walk with her beyond the edge of town, but he says his time for leaving has passed. Rosalind begins to run, finding joy in the running, knowing that she is driving darkness away.

The story first appeared serially in the 1921 *Dial*.

Critical Reception

Praise was high for this first collection of stories since *Winesburg, Ohio*. Besides laudatory remarks from H. L. MENCKEN and other American critics—"an American masterwork," wrote a reviewer in *North American Review*—the English writer Rebecca West singled out Anderson as the young American writer "we have most reason to envy." The *Dial*, recently establishing a prize for young writers, named the author as the first recipient of a lucrative award.

A theme that critics often find in these stories—and in 19th-century and early 20th-century

American literature generally—is that of innocence, of awakening from innocence, even of a refusal to awaken from innocence. In "I Want to Know Why," the teenage boy learns about the grown-up world, receiving what might be called a vicarious sexual initiation; yet he rejects this awakening, feeling angry, wishing a return to the Eden-like world of animals and racing and uncomplicated male companionship. Leslie Fiedler, Leo Marx, and R. W. B. Lewis are among critics who have focused on this motif of innocence in American literary expression.

Much has been written also about Anderson's methods of tale-telling, as exemplified in this volume. One of his favored devices is the unnamed first-person narrator, whose storytelling allows the reader to draw conclusions beyond those explicitly expressed; the reader uses his own knowledge to add to the interpretation. In "The Other Woman," Anderson takes the further step of using two narrators; the first nameless narrator tells of listening to a story told by the second nameless narrator. This double tale-telling leaves room for different degrees of understanding, not only between the two narrators, but, as always in Anderson, between the narrator and the reader. The reader, perhaps along with the first narrator, understands the self-deception and hypocrisy of the second narrator.

In the same story, modern readers take offense at the second narrator's reference to the "dear little woman"; the wife has already been called a "glad child." A debatable issue is the degree of irony intended in these references; an author understands that he cannot use irony effectively if his readers fail to grasp it, if they fail to see the further levels of meaning. Sophisticated readers in 1920, having been exposed to Freudian theory, might focus on the issue of male sexuality vis-à-vis female sexuality, on the gap in knowledge and practice between the sexes; yet being less exposed to feminist theory than today's readers, they might be less likely to focus on issues of paternalism and patriarchalism.

Trunnion, Louise   See WINESBURG, OHIO: "Nobody Knows."

trust

This term refers to a business combination that eliminates competition and controls prices. A trust is a private—as opposed to public—monopoly; in the 1880s, the number of trusts in America rapidly increased, resulting in an unprecedented concentration of economic power. A standard metaphor was "octopus," as used by Frank NORRIS in his novel *The Octopus;* in that 1901 work, the octopus is the railroad—although a character notes that "if it is not a railroad trust, it is a sugar trust, or an oil trust, or an industrial trust that exploits the people." In Upton SINCLAIR's 1906 novel, THE JUNGLE, the focus is on "the Great Butcher," or the beef trust—"the spirit of Capitalism made flesh." The ANTITRUST movement began with the Sherman Antitrust Act of 1890, later spurred by President Theodore ROOSEVELT's railing against "malefactors of great wealth."

Turner, Frederick Jackson

(1861–1932) *historian, enunciator of the Turner thesis*

Born in Portage, Wisconsin, receiving a Ph.D. from Johns Hopkins University, Turner taught at the University of Wisconsin from 1889 until 1910, then moved east to Harvard University. In July 1893 he delivered his landmark address, "The Significance of the Frontier in American History," at the Historical Congress of the WORLD'S COLUMBIAN EXPOSITION. He spent the next two decades of his life further elaborating on the TURNER THESIS; a collection of essays, *The Frontier in American History,* appeared in 1920, followed by *Significance of Sections in American History* in 1932. His last years were spent as a research associate at the Huntington Library in San Marino, California.

Turner thesis

An interpretation of the role of the West in American history, the thesis was first set forth in a paper read by Frederick Jackson TURNER in July 1893 at the Historical Congress of the WORLD'S COLUMBIAN EXPOSITION. Titled "The Significance of the Frontier in American History," the paper was responding to the theme of European arrival in the New World. Turner's claim was that the frontier, ever moving westward, was the ultimate source of American character, of American democracy and individualism; the frontiersman, interacting with the wilderness, became a new man, independent of European ideas. That land was readily available to him offered also a continuing economic opportunity, as well as a "safety valve"; it prevented the development of a hierarchical class system. The closing of the frontier, which Turner pronounced as currently taking place, meant that the first period in American history had closed, that the nation faced a less certain future.

In presenting his thesis, a historian from a western state was seeking to counteract the work of eastern scholars, who still looked to the East and to Europe as the source of American culture and society. Turner's reinterpretation of history gave significance to the rest of the nation, as its population moved steadily westward. For the next three-quarters of a century, the Turner thesis became accepted doctrine.

In more recent times, the thesis has been denigrated as ethnocentric and imperialist, ignoring genocide and celebrating conquest. Another criticism has been that it pays too little attention to the cultural memories that frontier settlers brought with them; it downplays the fact that pioneers continued to hold onto the beliefs and assumptions of the past. As Joseph KIRKLAND, in his novel published six years earlier, ZURY: THE MEANEST MAN IN SPRING COUNTY, had written, the westward-moving wagons were "carriers of virtue, honesty, intelligence, and freedom"; he labeled them the "Mayflowers of the West," suggesting their continued conveyance of a specific, identifiable culture.

Turpin, Ben
(1874–1940) *movie comedian*

First filming at the ESSANAY FILM MANUFACTURING COMPANY in 1907, Turpin became a popular movie star in the 1920s. Born in New Orleans, he played on stage and in VAUDEVILLE, before achieving his breakthrough film role in the Essanay Charlie CHAPLIN vehicle, *His First Job,* released in 1915. Turpin went on to work in Hollywood with Mack Sennett, an early producer of comedies, including the Keystone cops series. Famously cross-eyed, he was known also for his falls, including spectacular backward tumbles.

U

ubi sunt

The Latin phrase translates as "where are?" A traditional formula, it has served as a reminder of the transience of human life. The famous example comes from the 15th-century French poet, François Villon: "But where are the snows of yesteryear?"

Edgar Lee MASTERS draws on the formula for his opening poem, "The Hill," in SPOON RIVER ANTHOLOGY. The Hill is the graveyard, the plot of ground answering the "where are?" question; his townspeople are in the graveyard, having reached their inevitable destination. Vachel LINDSAY uses the *ubi sunt* formula in his 1919 poem, "Bryan, Bryan, Bryan, Bryan"; in the last section, he asks rhetorically where various famous men are—and repeats the unvaried response: "Gone."

"Under a Hat Rim"   *See* CHICAGO POEMS.

"Under the Lion's Paw"   *See* MAIN-TRAVELLED ROADS.

Under the Skylights
Henry Blake Fuller
(1901)

In this collection, the best known story, "The Downfall of Abner Joyce," is an obvious portrait of Hamlin GARLAND, depicting the artistic affecta-

tions assumed by a one-time western farmboy. The protagonist, having made his name with harsh descriptions of rural life, supporting the tax-reform doctrines of Henry GEORGE, is gradually corrupted by money and ambition. Garland apparently took little offense at the portrayal, writing later of FULLER's "shrewd and laughing eyes," declaring that the older writer "measured us and weighed us."

Underwood, Mary

A character in Sherwood ANDERSON's novel WINDY MCPHERSON'S SON, Mary is the unmarried schoolteacher, the woman whom the townspeople do not understand; she is silent and reticent, avoiding church suppers, walking alone on country roads. She is one of the two people in Caxton, Iowa—the other being John TELFER—who can talk to the young Sam MCPHERSON about books and ideas; like Telfer, she has lived elsewhere, beyond the confines of Caxton. She has also been the subject of town gossip, involving a married man; the gossip arises again when she tries to help Sam on the night of his mother's death, going with him to his house after he claims to have killed his father, bringing John Telfer to the house as well. She understands, too, that Telfer is her rival for the soul of the boy.

When Sam, approaching her house, sees her standing on the veranda in the rain, singing about a lover riding through the storm, he realizes that Telfer, who had discounted her, had judged her wrongly; Anderson is implying that she once had a secret life. Sam suggests that they marry, but Mary insists that she sees him as a son; he must go on to the city and make his way in the world. Later, Telfer, who has reconciled with her, writes Sam of her death; she had been ill and without income, and he criticizes Sam for never answering her letters. In WINESBURG, OHIO, the same character—the loving, stifled, misunderstood schoolteacher—will be reincarnated as Kate Swift.

Union Stock Yards

An area for animal-slaughtering and meat-processing, originally covering 345 acres, located four miles southwest of the LOOP, the yards were established in December 1865 as a joint venture by nine railroad lines. The railroads profited as providers of transportation for the burgeoning meatpacking industry. Because of the distance from the central city, the stockyards survived the GREAT FIRE of 1871. By the 1870s, refrigerator cars, innovated by Gustavus SWIFT, were adding to the importance of the yards and their parent railroads; fresh beef was now shipped out to the rest of the nation regardless of the season, in addition to the standard salted pork and smoked ham. The area became a tourist attraction as well, facilitated by a commuter rail line from downtown. It is said that Henry Ford, visiting the stockyards in 1905, observing what has been called their "synchronized killing machine," first envisioned there his own automobile assembly line. The identification of Chicago with the yards—"Porkopolis," in Eugene FIELD's term—continued for years. In the 1950s, as the meatpacking industry decentralized, as railroad transportation

The Union Stock Yards, here photographed in the 1920s, covered at their greatest reach a full square mile. *(Chicago Historical Society)*

became less crucial, the facility declined in importance; it closed in 1971. Remaining today is the triple-arched limestone entrance gateway, built by BURNHAM AND ROOT in the 1870s.

The Union Stock Yards became a standard topic for fiction. In Clarence DARROW's novel of 1905, AN EYE FOR AN EYE, a character begins work in the yards at age 14; he remarks how one quickly gets used to seeing throats cut and blood shed. A year later, the ultimate horror-novel of the stockyards appeared, Upton SINCLAIR's THE JUNGLE; this volume details the brutality of animal slaughter, as well as the use of diseased animals and the lack of minimal hygienic controls.

Willa CATHER's 1915 novel, THE SONG OF THE LARK, depicts its heroine, a newcomer to Chicago, expressing interest in seeing the packinghouses; all the hogs and cattle she once saw going through her native Colorado town were bound for that destination. Floyd DELL's 1921 novel, THE BRIARY-BUSH, tells of his hero's visiting the stockyards on first coming to Chicago; the protagonist joins a long line of visitors, led by a guide from building to building, although he leaves before coming to "the great scene," the cattle killing.

Other fiction notes the environmental effect of the yards on surrounding areas. In Theodore DREISER's 1910 novel, JENNIE GERHARDT, an investor loses money on a tract of residential real estate, the result of a rumor that a packing company is taking over a nearby area; the land would be good only for "a foreign population neighborhood." At issue is the pervasive odor coming from the yards, which depends on which way the wind is blowing; in Edna FERBER's 1922 story, "Old Man Minick," a South Side couple, opening the window at night, perceive the stench at once—"Just smell the Yards"—telling them that the wind is from the west. In MacKinlay KANTOR's 1928 novel, DIVERSEY, a North Sider recalls spring seasons when the wind came from the northeast and "you couldn't smell a bit of the Yards," an ideal condition that might last for several days.

University of Chicago

Founded in 1892, financed by John D. ROCKEFELLER, and promoted by a visionary president, the university became an institution of instant prestige. An earlier University of Chicago, a Baptist school, had gone bankrupt, and Rockefeller, a lifelong Baptist, had been persuaded to finance a new institution that would include a Baptist divinity school; Marshall FIELD donated the South Side land. Architect Henry Ives COBB designed a campus of Gothic limestone buildings; when the nearby WORLD'S COLUMBIAN EXPOSITION became the WHITE CITY, the university campus was titled the Gray City.

The first president, William Rainey HARPER, a biblical scholar from Yale University, gathered a faculty of high repute from campuses across the country, including John DEWEY, Robert HERRICK, Thorstein VEBLEN, and Albion W. SMALL. The mandate was to enroll both men and women students. Among prestigious periodicals issued by the University of Chicago Press were the *Journal of Political Economy* and the *American Journal of Sociology*; the new academic subject of SOCIOLOGY found a home in the nation's first sociology department.

In his 1914 novel, THE TITAN, Theodore DREISER refers to "a humble Baptist college of the cheapest character" that suddenly becomes a great university; his protagonist donates a giant telescope and an observatory—as did his real-life counterpart, Charles T. YERKES. Beaut McGREGOR, the principal character of Sherwood ANDERSON's 1917 novel, MARCHING MEN, briefly attends the University of Chicago, upsetting a professor with his talk of violence and advocacy of proto-fascism.

"The Unknown"   *See* SPOON RIVER ANTHOLOGY.

"Unlighted Lamps"   *See* THE TRIUMPH OF THE EGG.

"The Untold Lie"   *See* WINESBURG, OHIO.

"Up the Coule: A Story of Wisconsin"   *See* MAIN-TRAVELLED ROADS.

Uptown Theater

This opulent movie theater was built in 1925 in the North Side community of Uptown, then a predominantly Swedish area. As part of the BALABAN AND KATZ chain, it was designed for movies and VAUDEVILLE. The 4,400-seat venue, featuring a palatial lobby and grand circular staircases, was built as the largest free-standing theater in the country—a designation that still holds today; it stands a half-block north of the GREEN MILL GARDENS. The theater closed in 1981. In MacKinlay KANTOR's 1928 novel, *DIVERSEY*, the protagonist and his companion spend a night out at the Uptown Theater, considered a memorable occasion.

urbs in horto

The Chicago city motto, adopted in 1854, translates literally as "the city in the garden"; the phrase became simply "Garden City." Louis SULLIVAN, arriving in Chicago in 1873, noted that the Garden City had vanished as a result of the GREAT FIRE; after that event Chicago became the city of monumental buildings and skyscrapers.

The Uptown Theater, built in 1925 for the Balaban and Katz organization, was the premier luxury theater on Chicago's North Side. *(Chicago Historical Society)*

V

Van Volkenburg, Ellen
(1882–1979) *actress, theater founder*

Along with her husband Maurice BROWNE, Van Volkenburg was the guiding force behind the LITTLE THEATRE, a progenitor of the LITTLE THEATER MOVEMENT. Born in Battle Creek, Michigan, she moved to Chicago with her family, she graduated from the University of Michigan in 1904. She met Browne, an Englishman, while traveling in Florence, Italy; he came to Chicago to marry her in 1912, after which they opened the Little Theatre in the FINE ARTS BUILDING. The theater presented noncommercial productions, dedicated to new and experimental drama, relying on the city's elite for financial backing. Van Volkenburg became known for her role of Hecuba in a recent translation of Euripides' antiwar play, *The Trojan Women*. In 1915, as WORLD WAR I continued in Europe, she and the Little Theatre company presented the play on tour throughout the country; when the United States entered the war in 1917, the theater lost its financial support and was forced to close. In 1918, Browne and Van Volkenburg took up teaching in an arts school in Seattle, Washington; in 1927, after they divorced, Browne returned to England, where he revived a successful theater career. Van Volkenburg pursued projects in London, Seattle, and Los Angeles, dying in Los Angeles at the age of 97.

vaudeville

Descended from the English music hall, popular from the 1880s until the 1930s, vaudeville consisted of varied stage acts, ranging from singing and dancing to comedy, acrobatics, magic, juggling, and trained animals; the acts often continued in rotation throughout the afternoon and evening. Iowa-born Lillian Russell, growing up in Chicago, became a renowned vaudeville and music-hall singer at Tony Pastor's New York theater in the 1880s; Indiana-born Paul DRESSER performed at that venue as well. Theater impresario Florenz ZIEGFELD Jr. began his career with a Chicago vaudeville act, presenting acrobat and weightlifter Eugen Sandow, "the strongest man in the world," at his father's Trocadero Theater in 1893. The MARX BROTHERS, later famed for movie comedy, lived in Chicago from 1910 until 1920, traveling on a midwestern vaudeville circuit. This form of entertainment declined when movies became the preferred diversion of the masses.

In Edna FERBER's 1918 collection, CHEERFUL BY REQUEST, the story "That's Marriage" presents a brief picture of traveling vaudeville performers in a small midwestern town; the Bijou Theater of Wetona, Wisconsin, hosts a troupe of acrobats, bicyclists, trained seals, and coquettish young women "in slightly soiled pink."

Veblen, Thorstein
(1857–1929) *economist, social critic*

Born in Manitowoc County, Wisconsin, Veblen received a doctorate from Yale University, then served as professor at the UNIVERSITY OF CHICAGO for 14 years, from 1892 to 1906. THE THEORY OF THE LEISURE CLASS, published in 1899, became a social-science classic, adding the phrase CONSPICUOUS CONSUMPTION—the competitive flaunting of material opulence—to common parlance. Although targeting what was then called the capitalist class, Veblen, unlike many of his contemporaries, never embraced SOCIALISM; the flaw of the capitalist class, he argued, was its losing the principles of workmanship, its ignoring the input of engineers and technocrats. His *The Instinct of Workmanship and the State of the Industrial Arts,* published in 1914, elaborated on the harm caused by business practices on man's instinct for workmanship; this instinct, he maintained, is the source of human welfare. As readers of the day were aware, Veblen took the term *workmanship* from the ARTS AND CRAFTS MOVEMENT, a view promoting the ideals of handicraft against the encroaching machine; Veblen consciously broadened the term *workmanship* to include the machine process, the machinery of modern industry. The engineer, he believed, is a positive force in society, as opposed to the parasitic, nonproducing leisure class.

Forced out of his university position because of an extramarital liaison, Veblen went on to Stanford University, from which he was also forced to leave. His 1918 *The Higher Learning in America: A Memorandum on the Conduct of Universities by Business Men* argues that university administrators, as businessmen, have little real interest in higher education; he criticizes the college athlete as well. In 1919, Veblen was one of the founders of the New School for Social Research in New York City. He died in California at the age of 72.

Vendome

A theater in BRONZEVILLE, opening in 1919 on South State Street, the Vendome was one of a chain of theaters catering to African-American audiences. It showed both Hollywood-produced movies and "race" movies, films aimed at black audiences; in 1920, it presented Oscar MICHEAUX's controversial *Within Our Gates.* Live JAZZ concerts formed part of its programming, presenting Louis ARMSTRONG, pianist Earl Hines, Lillian "Lil" HARDIN, and others. Audiences began declining during the 1930s, and the theater was demolished in 1949.

veritism

This term, defined by Hamlin GARLAND in the 1890s, came to indicate Garland's espoused mode of writing—a REALISM rooted in the rural Midwest. Drawing upon the realism of William Dean HOWELLS, Garland adds a western bias, rejecting what he considers received content—from Boston, New York, Europe—as well as received literary forms. His veritism is nativist, populist.

Yet his formula, like that of Howells, specifically avoids the more radical NATURALISM; the new literature, according to Garland's 1894 CRUMBLING IDOLS, will deal not with "crime and abnormalities," but with "the wholesome love of honest men for honest women." Garland acknowledges that the veritist must write stories that are not always pleasant, but that unpleasantness will change as times change; the veritist is "an optimist, a dreamer." The author had already moved away from the bitterness and despair—seemingly an authentic veritism, or rural realism—of his work of three years previously, MAIN-TRAVELLED ROADS.

Vesta

This character appears in Theodore DREISER's novel JENNIE GERHARDT. Eventually given the surname of Stover, the maiden name of Jennie's mother, Vesta is the illegitimate daughter of Jennie and Senator George S. BRANDER, who dies before knowing of her existence. Vesta is hidden for several years from Jennie's longtime lover, Lester KANE, although he eventually takes her in. When Jennie and Lester separate, Vesta grows into the ideal loving daughter, appropriate for the idealized, loving mother; she dies of typhoid at the age of 15.

Volstead Act *See* PROHIBITION.

W

Wagner, Richard
(1813–1883) *German composer*

Although associated in the 20th century with anti-Semitism and the rise of Nazi Germany, Wagner, at the end of the 19th century, represented to Americans a pinnacle of European culture. German-American conductors Theodore THOMAS and Walter Damrosch had helped spread his prestige and popularity through their widely touring orchestras, beginning with Thomas's orchestra as early as the 1860s. In 1898, famed Austrian-American contralto Ernestine Schumann-Heink made her United States debut in Chicago, singing in Wagner's opera *Lohengrin*; shortly after the turn of the century, Swedish-American soprano Olive FREMSTAD appeared in Wagner-ian performances in New York City. In Hamlin GARLAND's 1895 novel, *ROSE OF DUTCHER'S COOLLY*, the Wisconsin farm girl, gaining exposure to the city's high culture, attends a CHICAGO SYMPHONY ORCHESTRA concert; the music means little to her at first, but then "the voice of Wagner came to her for the first time," and she is exalted to a new level of consciousness. Willa CATHER's heroine in the 1915 *THE SONG OF THE LARK*, modeled in part on Fremstad, becomes a great international singer, which to Cather means that she is a Wagnerian singer.

Wainsworth, Joseph

A character in Sherwood ANDERSON's novel, *POOR WHITE*, Wainsworth is a skilled craftsman, the town's harness-maker. He scorns harnesses that are made in factories, refusing even to repair such machine-made items. Driven mad by a competitive employee who orders factory-made goods, Wainsworth murders the employee, nearly decapitating him with a harness knife. Wainsworth shoots and wounds Steve HUNTER as well, the man he considers responsible for the industrialization that has changed his town for the worse. Anderson's father had unsuccessfully practiced the trade of harness-making.

Waldheim Cemetery

This cemetery in Forest Park, Illinois, outside of Chicago, is the resting place of five HAYMARKET AFFAIR anarchists—the four men hanged on November 11, 1887, plus the man who committed suicide in prison the day before. A Haymarket Martyrs' Monument was dedicated in June 1895, in a ceremony attended by thousands of sympathizers, brought to the cemetery by special trains; the next day, Governor John Peter ALTGELD pardoned the three remaining prisoners. In 1928, half the ashes of labor leader William "Big Bill" HAYWOOD were scattered at the Monument—the other half were buried near John REED in the Kremlin—and in 1940, anarchist Emma GOLDMAN was laid to rest nearby. The cemetery, established by a German order of FREEMASONRY in 1873, had once been a POTAWATAMI burial ground; it has subsequently become known—translating its German name—as Forest Home Cemetery. Evangelist Billy SUNDAY was buried there in 1935.

Walker, Hugh

A character in Sherwood ANDERSON's story "The Door of the Trap," collected in THE TRIUMPH OF THE EGG, Hugh is a professor of mathematics at a college in Union Valley, Illinois. Hugh—like many depressive Anderson characters of the early 1920s—feels detached from life and yet imprisoned by it as well. He is married and has three young children; his wife and children are "facts" that bind him because they belong to him.

He befriends a young woman student, Mary COCHRAN, apparently without family; she joins his own family, helping to care for his children. When he realizes that she is beginning to belong to him, he says he will kiss her and then she must leave, never to come back; like many Anderson male characters, he seems capable of acting cruelly. Yet he credits himself with a noble gesture, keeping her from being trapped by him—although he is keeping himself free from further entrapment as well.

Ward, Montgomery
(1844–1913) *founder of first major mail-order business*

Born in New Jersey, Ward moved with his family to Niles, Michigan, then came to Chicago in 1865; he worked as a clerk at the Field and Leiter store, the forerunner of MARSHALL FIELD AND COMPANY. Starting his own mail-order business, taking advantage of the GRANGERS movement—in which farmers sought merchandise for cooperative stores without going through middlemen—Ward planned on an 1871 opening for his enterprise, but lost his stock in the GREAT FIRE; he began operations in the spring of 1872. Soon MONTGOMERY WARD AND COMPANY became an instrument for farmers not only to avoid local high prices, but also to overcome rural isolation; after two decades, the Montgomery Ward catalogue was reaching a quarter of a million people.

Ward's great civic crusade, fought in the courts for 20 years, was to maintain an open, unobstructed lakefront. Hoping to keep Chicago different from other cities, in which waterfront property was dominated by industry, Ward declared that the lakefront must feature only parks and beaches, available to all the citizenry: "I fought for the poor people of Chicago, not the millionaires." He filed the first of four lawsuits in 1890; the Illinois Supreme Court's final ruling, upholding his case, appeared in 1909. The ART INSTITUTE already stood on the lakefront at the time; Ward consented to allow also the construction of the FIELD MUSEUM OF NATURAL HISTORY, the SHEDD AQUARIUM, and the ADLER PLANETARIUM. He died in 1913 at the age of 69.

War of 1812

Among the causes of this conflict between the United States and Great Britain was the American desire for continuing expansion across the continent; westward movement was seen as hampered by the British in alliance with Indian confederates. Declared in June 1812, the war officially ended with the Treaty of Ghent late in 1814, although the final battle, the defeat of the British at New Orleans, took place early in 1815. The destruction of FORT DEARBORN by the POTOWATAMI in August 1812 was an early repercussion of the war; the later routing of the Indians westward opened up lands for further American expansion. In Joseph KIRKLAND's 1887 novel of the Illinois frontier, ZURY: THE MEANEST MAN IN SPRING COUNTY, the family patriarch gains his tract of land as a reward for service during the War of 1812.

"Wars"   *See* CHICAGO POEMS.

"Washerwoman"   *See* CORNHUSKERS.

Water Tower and Pumping Station

These stone structures, designed by William W. BOYINGTON, completed in 1869, were built to distribute fresh lake water into the city's water mains; they were among the few buildings that remained standing after the GREAT FIRE of 1871. They continue to attract tourists to North MICHIGAN AVENUE, where a vertical shopping mall, Water Tower Place, was constructed in 1976. In 2003, a home for the Lookingglass Theater Company was constructed within the Pumping Station.

Watkins, Maurine
(1896–1969) *playwright*

Born in Louisville, Kentucky, Watkins grew up in Crawfordville, Indiana; he became a crime reporter for the CHICAGO TRIBUNE in 1924. Her witty newspaper coverage of two murder trials in 1924—in both cases of women accused of murdering their lovers—is said to have contributed to their acquittal. Leaving the *Tribune,* Watkins enrolled in the Yale University School of Drama, where she wrote the play CHICAGO, first performed on Broadway in 1926; she later moved to Hollywood to pursue screenwriting. Two movies were made from the play, including the Ginger Rogers vehicle *Roxie Hart,* and yet she refused permission for a stage musical; her death in Florida at the age of 73 allowed purchase of the rights for a stage production, and the 1975 Broadway musical *Chicago* and the 2002 movie *Chicago* followed.

Wau-bun: The "Early Day" in the North-West
Juliette Kinzie
(1856)

Although sometimes called the first Chicago novel, *Wau-bun* is in large part an autobiographical depiction of KINZIE's life on the northwestern frontier; it is best known for its description of the FORT DEARBORN massacre, taken from the account of her father-in-law, John KINZIE. The first portion of the work tells of Kinzie's living from 1830 to 1833 at Fort Winnebago, Wisconsin, where her husband served as Indian agent; it subsequently recounts tales told by her husband's family, including the story of the massacre, although the account of that event is now recog-

nized as containing inaccuracies. Kinzie also describes from her vantage point the BLACK HAWK war of 1832, indicating sympathy for Native Americans driven from their lands. The work is in the tradition of romance, anticipating the historical fiction of Mary CATHERWOOD in its evocation of a land "with its vast lakes, its boundless prairies, and its mighty forests." *Wau-bun* is a Winnebago Indian word for "early day."

Way and Williams

This publishing firm, influenced by William MORRIS's Kelmscott Press and the ARTS AND CRAFTS MOVEMENT, following the local example of STONE AND KIMBALL, was established in Chicago in 1895 by W. Irving Way and Chauncy L. Williams. Way had previously designed a souvenir edition—using handmade paper and pen-and-ink drawings—of Harriet MONROE's "Columbian Ode," the poem recited at dedication ceremonies for the WORLD'S COLUMBIAN EXPOSITION. The firm produced fine books for three years, including the 1897 *Mother Goose in Prose,* the first children's book by L. Frank BAUM and first volume illustrated by artist Maxfield Parrish. Another notable production was Stanley Waterloo's early science-fiction novel, *The Story of Ab: A Tale of the Time of the Caveman.*

The Web of Life
Robert Herrick
(1900)

In this novel, a young doctor, witnessing the severe economic effects of the PANIC OF 1893, as well as violent labor strife, decides to sacrifice material prosperity for a career of service. HERRICK's novel is set in the aftermath of the WORLD'S COLUMBIAN EXPOSITION, which had presented to the world its gleaming white buildings; the doctor watches as the structures—once signifying opulence, now abandoned and deteriorating—go up in flames. The PULLMAN STRIKE, soon to be suppressed by federal troops, begins at the same time.

Weissmuller, Johnny
(1904–1984) *Olympic swimming champion, movie star*

Born Peter Jonas Weismüller in what is now Hungary, Weissmuller came to Chicago with his family as a child. Dropping out of school, taking up swimming at the age of 16, he set the hundred-meter world swimming record two years later in 1922. Using his younger brother's American birth certificate, he competed in the 1924 and 1928 Olympic games, winning five gold medals. Film stardom came with the role of Tarzan, created by fellow Chicagoan Edgar Rice BURROUGHS; *Tarzan the Ape Man*, the first of his 12 Tarzan movies, appeared in 1932. Although Weissmuller performed his own swimming feats, stuntmen were engaged for other displays of athleticism. His last Tarzan movie, *Tarzan and the Mermaids*, appeared in 1948.

Welling, Joe   *See* WINESBURG, OHIO: "A Man of Ideas."

Wells, Ida B.
(1862–1931) *African-American social activist*

Spending the last half of her life in Chicago, Wells became nationally known as a leader of antilynching and antidiscrimination campaigns. Born in Holly Springs, Mississippi, Wells moved to Memphis and wrote for a black-owned Memphis paper, drawing attention to the lynchings of African Americans; in 1892, the newspaper's office was destroyed. She moved to New York, writing for the *New York Age*, continuing her campaign against lynching and related terrorism, publishing a pamphlet titled "Southern Horrors." In 1893, she joined Frederick DOUGLASS in Chicago, protesting the exclusion of African-American achievement from the WORLD'S COLUMBIAN EXPOSITION. Her 80-page booklet, *The Reason Why the Colored American Is Not in the World's Columbian Exposition*, was published and distributed with Douglass's assistance. In 1895, Wells married Chicago lawyer Ferdinand L.

Barnett, the first black Cook County assistant state's attorney, founder of the pioneering black weekly, the *Conservator;* the militant stance taken by Wells and Barnett kept them critical of the accommodationist policies of black leader Booker T. Washington. In 1908, Wells founded the Negro Fellowship League on the South Side, giving aid to African Americans arriving from the South; in 1913, after the state of Illinois had granted women the right to vote in municipal contests, she established the black Alpha Suffrage Club, becoming instrumental in Oscar DE PRIEST's 1915 election as Chicago's first black alderman. In the mid-1920s, Wells supported A. Phillip RANDOLPH's targeting of the PULLMAN PALACE CAR COMPANY in his efforts to unionize Pullman service workers. She began her autobiography, *Crusade for Justice*, in 1928; it remained incomplete before her death, finally appearing in 1970.

Wescott, Glenway
(1901–1987) *writer*

Born in Kewaskum, Wisconsin, Wescott moved to Chicago at the age of 13 and later attended the UNIVERSITY OF CHICAGO. He worked for a short time in Harriet MONROE's office at POETRY, publishing early pieces in *Poetry* and the DIAL. His first novel, *The Apple of the Eye*, appeared in 1924, when he was 23 years old, recounting a boyhood on a Wisconsin farm. Moving to France, Wescott wrote the successful novel *The Grandmothers*, published in 1927, a family chronicle of three generations, detailing the effects of the CIVIL WAR and the poverty and hardships of frontier life; the book was seen as part of the REVOLT FROM THE VILLAGE movement, bringing comparisons with the work of fellow Wisconsin native Zona GALE. His short-story collection, *Goodbye, Wisconsin*, appeared in 1928. Living to the age of 85, publishing no fiction after the age of 45, Wescott became a figure in the New York City gay community. He served as the model for the character Robert Prentiss in Ernest HEMINGWAY's novel *The Sun Also Rises*.

Wescott, Rosalind

This character appears in Sherwood ANDERSON's story "Out of Nowhere into Nothing," collected in THE TRIUMPH OF THE EGG. Growing up in Iowa, Rosalind spends three years after high school simply "waiting"; she then goes to Chicago, living with her brother and sister-in-law, and taking up stenography. Falling in love with her employer, Walter SAYERS, a married man with two children, she comes home to Willow Springs for a few days, hoping to talk to her mother, telling her mother that she is about to give herself to the man she loves, a man she cannot marry. Back in her hometown, she feels again its deadness, its killing spirit; the city had excited her, made her think about vitality and sex. Her mother speaks bitterly about sex; she had hoped her daughter would be above giving in to men, who "can't help wanting to hurt women." Rosalind leaves the house that night, taking the train back to Chicago, feeling that she is leaving the life-destroying small town.

Whedon, Editor   *See* SPOON RIVER ANTHOLOGY.

White, Helen   *See* WINESBURG, OHIO: "The Thinker" and "Sophistication."

White City   *See* WORLD'S COLUMBIAN EXPOSITION.

Whitman, Walt
(1819–1892) *major poet*

Considered today the most important American poet of the 19th century, Whitman exerted particular influence on writers of the Chicago Renaissance. His reputation, not always high in his own century, had revived by the time Carl SANDBURG and others began absorbing their early poetic influences. Born on Long Island, living much of his life in New York, Whitman came to be viewed as the celebrator of democracy and brotherhood, expressing sympathy and concern for humankind. His

nonmetrical lines, following the cadence of the human voice, were seen as a rejection of literary tradition—and a loosening, critics declared, of social constraints as well. His early collection, *Leaves of Grass*, first published in 1855, included "Song of Myself," a work proclaiming the poet as representative of the common man, singing in a voice outside the received tradition. His influence was greatest on male poets, including Vachel LINDSAY and Carl SANDBURG; women of the era could not follow him into realms of moral expansiveness and sexual freedom.

Sandburg's first collection of verse, the 1916 CHICAGO POEMS, celebrating the workingman, drew the same criticism as Whitman's verse had drawn—for unpoetically discarding meter and rhyme. The Illinois poet's "Prairie," published in the 1918 CORNHUSKERS, continued a conscious Whitmanesque influence, including long listings of people and places, a device used by the earlier poet to indicate an all-embracing vision.

Another Whitman influence comes from his celebrations of the martyred President Abraham LINCOLN. His elegy "When Lilacs Last in the Dooryard Bloom'd" has long resonated in the minds of Illinois poets; Lindsay wrote his "ABRAHAM LINCOLN WALKS AT MIDNIGHT" at the same time that Sandburg began writing his own poetry about the 16th president.

Whitman's "Pioneers! O Pioneers!" is echoed in the title of Willa CATHER's 1913 novel, *O Pioneers!* Edgar Lee MASTERS's poem "Aaron Hatfield," in the 1915 SPOON RIVER ANTHOLOGY, makes use of the same phrase; Masters published a biography of Whitman in 1937.

"Who Am I?"   *See* CHICAGO POEMS.

Willard, Elizabeth

This character appears in Sherwood ANDERSON's WINESBURG, OHIO. The mother of the main figure, George WILLARD, Elizabeth Willard is based in part on Anderson's own mother, who died in 1895 in Clyde, Ohio. The death of Anderson's mother is said to have freed the writer-to-be to leave the small town of Clyde—as the fictional Elizabeth Willard's death frees George Willard to leave Winesburg. The character is featured in the stories "Mother" and "Death."

Willard, Frances E.
(1839–1898) *temperance leader, president of the Women's Christian Temperance Union*

Born in Churchville, New York, Willard settled with her family in EVANSTON, Illinois, home of several Methodist institutions. In 1872, she became the first dean of women at the Methodist NORTHWESTERN UNIVERSITY, resigning two years later to become a leader in the WOMEN'S CHRISTIAN TEMPERANCE UNION. She worked briefly with Dwight L. MOODY, passing out temperance pamphlets at revival meetings, although soon breaking with the evangelist, whom she found unappreciative of women's issues. In 1879, she was elected president of the WCTU, and under her Chicago-based leadership, the organization gained in range and influence, supporting women's rights and women's suffrage along with temperance. On economic matters Willard often held views more radical than those of many of the WCTU members, including support for CHRISTIAN SOCIALISM—and yet, as African-American spokesman Frederick DOUGLASS pointed out, she was guilty also of a seeming racism, of making statements that appeared to condone lynching; her genteel white woman's perspective proved narrow and limited. Willard died in New York City at the age of 58; thousands of mourners gathered at railroad stations to see her funeral train, returning her to Chicago.

Willard, George

A character in Sherwood ANDERSON's *WINESBURG, OHIO*, George is a reporter for the *Winesburg Eagle*, as well as an aspiring writer; he is based on Anderson himself. In many of the stories George acts as a sounding board for the tales of others; some characters actively seek him out to explain themselves

to him—although in some cases, as in "The Strength of God" and "The Teacher," he is depicted as not really understanding them or their stories. In the final tale, after his mother's death, he takes leave of Winesburg.

Williams, Bert
(1874–1922) *African-American performer*

The first black entertainer on Broadway to play in an otherwise all-white production, Williams became a major performer in Florenz ZIEGFELD Jr.'s *Ziegfeld Follies*, beginning in 1910. Born in Antigua, West Indies, said at one time to have been a member of Chicagoan William N. SELIG's minstrel show, Williams throughout his career performed in blackface, continuing the long-standing minstrel tradition. In the *Follies of 1916*, a show focusing on Shakespearean themes, he played a version of Othello in blackface; in the *Follies of 1917*, he was cast as a railroad porter opposite Eddie Cantor, the white comedian, playing his son in blackface. In 1922, while performing in Chicago, he collapsed suddenly and died from pneumonia; he was 47 years old. Ben HECHT paid tribute to Williams in a "1001 Afternoons in Chicago" column; referring to the dwelling place of heroic souls in Norse mythology, Hecht imagines Williams entering the Valhalla of Great Actors. Invoking the entertainer's trademark gesture, Hecht imagines that the audience sees first only a white-gloved hand, visible at the side of the stage, and then the actor himself makes his entrance.

Williams, Daniel Hale
(1858–1931) *African-American surgeon*

Born in Hollidaysburg, Pennsylvania, Williams graduated from Chicago Medical School in 1883; he founded PROVIDENT HOSPITAL, the nation's first black-owned hospital, In 1891. Two years later, he is credited with performing the world's first successful open-heart surgery, operating on a man brought to the hospital with a knife wound. In

1912, Williams joined the staff of St. Luke's Hospital, subsequently the Rush-Presbyterian St. Luke's Medical Center; he was among the original members of the American College of Surgery, founded in Chicago in 1913. Living his last years at Idlewild, Michigan, a popular African-American resort, he died at the age of 75.

Williams, Mrs. Dora   *See SPOON RIVER ANTHOLOGY.*

Williams, Fannie B.
(1855–1944) *African-American civic leader*

Born in Brockport, New York, Williams moved to Chicago in 1887 and pioneered in Chicago society as a clubwoman and lecturer. She also helped found a training school for African-American nurses. Her husband, lawyer S. Laing Williams, was a partner of Ida WELLS's husband, Ferdinand L. Barnett. She is said to have been light skinned and "stunningly beautiful"—and to declare *je suis française*, "I am French," to avoid segregationist practices. In 1891, she participated in the establishment of PROVIDENT HOSPITAL, which included, at her insistence, a training school for African-American nurses. In 1895, Williams became the first black member of the Chicago Woman's Club, a social organization, founded in the 1870s, consisting mainly of the wives of businessmen.

Williams, Wash   *See WINESBURG, OHIO: "Respectability."*

Williams, William Carlos
(1883–1963) *poet, physician*

Born in Rutherford, New Jersey, Williams practiced medicine throughout his life but came gradually to be recognized as a major American poet. Ezra POUND provided early encouragement, sending his work to *POETRY* magazine, where it first appeared in June 1913; Pound also included his verse in the *Des Imagistes* anthology of 1914. Reacting against *Poetry* editor Harriet MONROE's suggestion of editorial changes, Williams soon turned to other periodicals, including *LITTLE REVIEW* and *OTHERS*. His best-known work is the long poem *Paterson*, named after the New Jersey town, published between 1946 and 1958. He won a posthumously awarded Pulitzer Prize for poetry in 1963.

Wilmans, Harry   *See SPOON RIVER ANTHOLOGY; also* ANTI-IMPERIALIST LEAGUE.

Wilson, Carlotta

This character appears in Theodore DREISER's novel THE "GENIUS." As one of many women in protagonist Eugene WITLA's life, Carlotta, married and separated from her husband, differs in that she is an experienced woman who initiates the relationship; the other, often younger, women are pursued by Eugene. Carlotta expresses opinions on matters of morality, saying that religion is a lie, that a morbid conscience must be suppressed. Eugene knows that society would condemn Carlotta—while praising his wife, Angela, as a "thoroughly good woman"—and yet he prefers Carlotta. The novel's portrayal of casual sexual alliances brought threats from the NEW YORK SOCIETY FOR THE SUPPRESSION OF VICE, and the volume was withdrawn from bookstores for almost a decade.

Wilson, Edgar

This character appears in Sherwood ANDERSON's "The Man's Story," collected in HORSES AND MEN. Having run away with a druggist's wife in Kansas City, Wilson lives with the woman in a Chicago boardinghouse. She supports the two of them by working with wardrobes in a theater; Wilson sits at a table and writes poetry. The woman, the narrator surmises, has selflessly lent herself to him, and as a result he can access life and express himself—although his poetry is still about building walls, about standing behind high walls. When the woman is shot by a deranged man, Wilson is so absorbed in himself that he fails to notice; he steps over the body, realizing only later what has happened. He is arrested and tried for murder, although he seems uninterested in the outcome, even when the real murderer confesses; he no longer has his passive, obedient catalyst for expression. As an artist, Wilson possesses tenderness and sensitivity—and yet, also as an artist, he is "casual and brutal."

Wilson, Woodrow
(1856–1924) *28th president of the United States*

Elected in 1912, after Theodore ROOSEVELT's candidacy split the Republican Party, Wilson was the second Democrat to hold the office since the CIVIL WAR. The most significant event of his presidency was America's entry in April 1917 into WORLD WAR I, two and a half years after the start of the conflict in Europe. Reactions ranged from the pacifism of Jane ADDAMS—for which she received her first long-lasting criticism—to the pro-American response of Carl SANDBURG, modifying his loyalties to antiwar SOCIALISM; Sandburg had previously published strong antiwar poetry in his 1916 collection, CHICAGO POEMS. Chicago-related repercussions from the 1917 Espionage Act, criminalizing draft obstruction and other disloyalties to the war effort, included the trial of former Chicagoan Floyd DELL, the conviction in Chicago of 100 members of the INDUSTRIAL WORKERS OF THE WORLD, and the deportation of popular-in-Chicago anarchist Emma GOLDMAN. Also taking place during the Wilson presidency—spanning the years 1913 to 1921—were the Clayton Antitrust Act, instituting proceedings in 92 ANTITRUST cases; the EIGHTEENTH AMENDMENT, ushering in PROHIBITION; and the NINETEENTH AMENDMENT, giving women the right to vote.

Windy City

A nickname that has nothing to do with the weather, the term was applied to Chicago by sup-

porters of New York City's bid to host the WORLD'S COLUMBIAN EXPOSITION of 1893. When the eastern city lost to the western city, New York newspapers accused Chicago lobbyists of excessive boasting; a writer on the *New York Sun* advised, "Pay no attention to the claims of the Windy City."

Windy McPherson's Son
Sherwood Anderson
(1916)

This first novel was written in Elyria, Ohio, when ANDERSON was still pursuing a business career; the unpublished manuscript came with him to Chicago in 1913. The early material in the novel—the family dynamics, the small-town setting—is autobiographical. John "Windy" McPHERSON is a portrait of Anderson's father, a CIVIL WAR veteran given to telling tall tales of battle, a failed harness-maker who became a housepainter; Mrs. McPherson, taking in washing, is modeled on Anderson's mother. Both fictional and real-life mothers are dead at a relatively young age, and both fathers remarry. The boy, Sam McPHERSON, industriously selling newspapers in Caxton, Iowa, is Anderson himself in Clyde, Ohio; the later Sam, taking up a nomadic life, is a projection of the existence Anderson would follow in later years. The portion of the novel that critics praise is Book I, containing the seeds of the later WINESBURG, OHIO.

Synopsis

BOOK I: CHAPTER I
Thirteen-year-old Sam McPherson, holding a bundle of newspapers under his arm, offers a cigar to the baggage man at the railroad station in Caxton, Iowa. Accepting the cigar, the baggage man follows Sam's instructions; he takes a wrapped pack of newspapers, lying against the building, and brings them into the seclusion of the baggage room. Sam then returns to the town's Main Street and joins the men lounging in front of the drug store; they include Freedom Smith, a buyer of farm products, and John TELFER, the local dandy who lives on an inheritance and his wife's milliner's shop. Telfer had once studied art in New

York and Paris, returning to Caxton after he failed to make a success; he reminds his listeners that he is an artist, practicing the art of living, setting an example to others and teaching them judgment and wisdom.

When the train from Des Moines arrives, Sam runs back to the station with his papers. The train news merchant, descending to the platform, looks for the papers he plans to sell; by the time he retrieves them from the baggage room, Sam has already gone through the cars, selling his own papers. The boy jumps off the last car, his papers sold, coins jingling in his pocket. The ambitious young man has triumphed once again.

BOOK I: CHAPTER II

Sam's father is Windy McPherson, a man who has never recovered from the effects of the Civil War. He was once an infantry sergeant, commanding a company in Virginia; now he is a drunken house-painter, boastfully reliving battle scenes to all who will listen. He came briefly to prominence by founding a local branch of the A.P.A., the American Protective Association, a secret anti-Catholic society growing out of the KNOW-NOTHING MOVEMENT. Yet most of the time he brags and blusters about his role in the war; he is one of many who spent four years of their lives in the great struggle—until, as Anderson relates, "something snapped in their brains." These men now attend meetings of the G.A.R., the GRAND ARMY OF THE REPUBLIC, a veterans' organization, in which men come together to tell and retell their stories of war.

Sam is embarrassed by his father, as he sees other men laughing at him. The townspeople begin planning a Fourth of July celebration; convening at a meeting hall, they seek contributions toward a brass-band carnival and a Civil War battle reenactment. Windy walks to the front of the hall and gives $17—"From one of the boys of '61," he announces. Sam resents his father's contribution, knowing that his mother, at that very moment, is at home doing washing for the town's shoe merchant—who has just given $5. Another citizen suggests that a bugler, mounted on a white horse, should ride through town at dawn on the Fourth, blowing reveille. Windy McPherson, saying he was

once a regimental bugler, volunteers for the assignment. Sam is upset, believing that his father cannot play the bugle, that the family will be embarrassed again. He confronts his father, who expresses amazement that anyone could doubt him; Windy launches into another war story, about a surprise nighttime attack by the enemy, about his rallying the regiment to fight while personally facing a hail of bullets. Sam is convinced, and he uses his newspaper money to send to Chicago for a shiny new bugle.

On the day of the celebration, the townspeople arrive on Main Street at dawn. They see a figure riding into view, wearing the blue uniform of the Union, sitting on a white horse; Sam looks on proudly. Then the figure raises the bugle to his lips—and produces piercing squawks. The crowd shouts with laughter, and John Telfer comes to lead Windy and his horse away. Sam weeps in humiliation; he resolves he will never be a fool like his father.

BOOK I: CHAPTER III

An evangelist comes to Caxton, and Sam is expected to attend meetings with his mother. He has always gone to church on Sunday, although regularly falling asleep, worn out from selling papers on the street late Saturday night. At a meeting the evangelist proclaims that the town is a cesspool of vice, that the devil is finding it a suburb of hell; Sam is frightened. He has thought about religion, and he has worried about death, since his mother is becoming ill. Sam has also had thoughts about sex.

When the evangelist asks the people to stand up for Jesus, Sam's mother stands, but Sam does not. A man sitting behind begins praying loudly for Sam's soul, asking God to help this boy who keeps company with sinners and publicans; he is referring to Sam's going into saloons to sell his newspapers. Although angered, Sam stands up, and the evangelist calls on him to testify, asking what he as to say for the Lord. Not knowing how to respond, Sam blurts out, "The Lord maketh me to lie out in green pastures"—misquoting the Twenty-third Psalm, substituting "lie out" for "lie down." Members of the congregation begin laughing, and Sam walks out of the church, vowing never to return.

People in the town, he is sure, will be asking taunting questions, such as, "Do you sleep out alone in them green pastures?"

Mike McCarthy, the town idler, assaults a man with a knife and leaves him bleeding; the man had accused Mike of having an affair with his wife. Mike is a self-declared socialist, anarchist, and atheist, having been heard praising free love as well; Sam has long admired the man, thinking of him as brave and liberated. The town marshal arrests Mike, bringing him to the jail; the prisoner begins ranting to those standing by, calling the town by the term the evangelist had used, a "cesspool"—except that in this version the town is a cesspool of respectability. Its people negate life, Mike claims, for he has seen men and women living in the town year after year without producing children, denying new life—a veiled reference to nonreproductive sexual practices or forms of birth control. Yet he himself, the prisoner adds, has been with these women, and he proceeds to call out the names of 11 women; Sam is pleased that one of those named was at the evangelist's meeting, urging others to stand up and be counted. Mike declares that the people of Caxton must understand that there is no afterlife, that they must live their current lives and make new lives. Sam feels cleansed after hearing these declarations—unlike how he felt after the evangelist's meeting—and he vows to live well, to live according to his new appreciation of life.

BOOK I: CHAPTERS IV–VI

John Telfer is one of the few men in Caxton to whom Sam can talk; Telfer quotes to him the poetry of Edgar Allan Poe and Robert Browning. Sam can also talk to the schoolteacher, Mary UNDERWOOD. Like Telfer, Mary has seen the world beyond Caxton, having attended school in Massachusetts. Yet the local people do not understand her, distrusting her silence and her independence; at one time she was the subject of gossip involving a married man. Mary has tried to influence Sam, suggesting books for him to read, but Telfer convinces him that women know little; Telfer himself prefers Edward BELLAMY's *Looking Backward*, the 1888 novel depicting a future socialist utopia. Telfer warns Sam about the attractions of women, saying that they will keep a man from his greater purpose in life. Sam has the genius to be a man of finance, he says, and he should let nothing stand in his way.

Freedom Smith takes Sam into partnership, and the young man, buying produce from local farmers and selling it to a Chicago firm, doubles Freedom's business within a year. Acting from generosity, Freedom recommends Sam to the Chicago firm, and the young man, now 18 years old, knows that he will leave Caxton. He knows, too, that his mother is terminally ill; he will leave when she dies. He carries with him a picture of George Eliot, the English woman novelist, finding that the image resembles his mother before her illness. Mrs. McPherson, lying on her sickbed, tells Sam of her former life—that of a bound servant in Ohio, struggling to become a schoolteacher, marrying the dashing ex-soldier, John McPherson, coming with McPherson from Ohio to Iowa, then watching him buy a store that soon went into the sheriff's hands. Sam knows that as a result she became the town laundress.

Once when Windy wakes up after a drunken sleep, starting to talk loudly about how old soldiers are cheated, Sam angrily tells him to be silent, to stop disturbing his mother. He feels an urge to kill his father—who, he believes, has brought his mother to her death. Sam puts his hands around his father's throat, choking the man until he is silent; he carries the unconscious Windy outside into a rainstorm, throwing him onto a grassy bank. He rushes off to find Mary Underwood.

BOOK I: CHAPTERS VII–VIII

Approaching the schoolteacher's house, Sam sees Mary on the veranda, singing as the rain is falling on her, singing of a lover riding through the storm. John Telfer was wrong, he realizes, in disparaging her. Mary invites Sam inside, and the young man has the sudden idea that he should marry her; he says he needs a woman in the house, and he has come to marry her. But when he announces, too, that he has just killed his father, Mary reacts at once, grabbing some outer clothes and leaving the house with him. Accompanying Sam to his door, she goes on to John Telfer's house, bringing Telfer back with her—until Telfer remembers that he has seen Windy in town that night, covered with mud, saying he had been in a fight with the saloon keeper. Mary and Telfer go into the McPherson house and find Sam sitting by his mother's bed, holding her cold hand.

At his mother's funeral Sam receives a note from Telfer, saying he will not attend but will hold a ceremony in his heart; he will also take flowers as an appreciation to Mary Underwood. When Mary arrives at the service, Sam disrupts the proceedings to show her the note. At once, whispers start among the congregation; Mary realizes that people are talking about her, as they did in the days of the old scandal. She gets up and leaves.

At the railroad station Sam hears two women talking about Mary, saying that a neighbor saw her come to Sam's house one evening, carelessly dressed; she went out again and returned with John Telfer. The woman wonders how many other men is she seeing? Sam, furious, rushes at the women and grabs their hair, knocking their heads together; he shouts at them to stop their lies. He tells Mary once more that they must marry, but she responds that she has in Sam a son, not a husband or lover. Sam writes s statement about what happened that night at his house—how he tried to kill his father, how Mary, then Telfer, came to his house to give aid—and he gives the statement to the editor of the local newspaper. The editor's wife remarks that the men of the town should have finished the job of choking Windy McPherson.

BOOK II: CHAPTERS I–IV

During his first year in Chicago, Sam lives with a family from Caxton; he is working hard to make a success. One evening he finds himself walking in the red-light district, but remembers John Telfer's telling him about the disease and death that lurk in such places; he flees to a park at the edge of the lake. Meanwhile, he is working on South Water Street, where produce is sold; he is accumulating money, as well as acquiring investments from others. This is the era, Anderson notes, when the whole nation has been "seized with a blind grappling for gain." Sam begins working for Colonel Tom Rainey, owner of the Rainey Arms Company, a maker of firearms; the company had made great profits during the Civil War with an innovative

breech-loading gun. Sam sees that the firm has not been properly run in this postwar period, and he puts himself increasingly in charge.

Sam has made the acquaintance of a young woman, Janet Eberly, who, having fallen from a barn loft in her youth, is bound to a wheelchair; she lives in the city with her sister. Janet is an intellect, a reader of books, disregarding "all the usual womanly points of view"; Sam would marry her, he knows, if she were able-bodied. She dies suddenly, leaving him desolate.

Colonel Rainey, a widower whose daughter is his sole heir, has taken up with an actress, Luella London, whom he plans to marry. His daughter, Sue RAINEY, calls on Sam, insisting that the wedding be stopped, that Luella is a crude, scheming woman. Sam meets with Luella, bluffing that he knows the man she used to live with, that he will get the man's aid in stopping the marriage. Luella falls into his trap; she names a man and agrees to break off with Colonel Rainey, although she also reminds Sam how hard it is for a woman to make it alone in the world. Sam gives her a paper to sign, and yet, admiring her drive—and knowing, too, that many people have tried to attach themselves to the Rainey fortune—he promises to invest money in her name; he persuades Sue Rainey to write a check for $20,000. Luella does her part, telling the colonel that she has an incurable disease and will soon be bedridden; Rainey—as she knows he will do—buys her off with money, and she gives half of the sum to Sam.

BOOK II: CHAPTERS V–IX

Sue Rainey, heiress of a fortune, has many suitors, but she has been indifferent to them. After Janet Eberly's death, Sam begins to talk with her, and she questions him about his views on the world; Sam decides he should read a book on SOCIALISM. Sue tells him about hearing a lecturer on William MORRIS, the English artist and social reformer. As they talk about marriage, Sue says she wants to serve mankind, to avoid the frivolous life that wealth bestows; her wealth, she adds, combined with his ability, should lead them to produce children who will also serve mankind.

They marry, and Sue becomes pregnant; this child is to be the first of a brood that will grow into responsible men and women. Yet Sue is becoming less stable mentally, showing a temper, lashing out at servants; she herself suggests that she is growing insane. The child is born dead, as Sam overhears a doctor saying she is unfit. A second child dies as well.

Sue turns to social causes. Sam sees that earnest, ardent people, advocating social uplift, are appearing at their house. He is persuaded to teach a class at a SETTLEMENT HOUSE, but he finds that the men, factory laborers during the day, are uninterested in what he has to say; they fall asleep or wander outside to smoke. He finds himself drifting further from Sue and her point of view. One evening he brings to dinner an acquaintance who decides to outdo her friends in his fervor; he excoriates the rich, calling for the masses to arise, urging revolution. Sam knows he is shamming, but Sue and her guests are delighted. When Sam tells her later that it was all an act, she calls him hard and cynical, insisting that the man spoke from his heart. Sam reveals that he is an advertising man, that he could have made a convincing case for cannibalism—and she is appalled. The two of them no longer share common ground.

For the next two years Sam throws himself into his work. The consolidation of industry, forming ever-growing monopolies, is taking place throughout the nation. Sam, gaining control of rival companies, is himself creating a vast new organization, although in the process he is forcing out his father-in-law. Sue begs him not to push the old man aside, but he is determined, and he knows now that the two of them must part. She takes her father away to the East, and Sam, sitting in his new offices in THE ROOKERY, knows he has become one of the giants of American industry.

Yet it is all becoming meaningless to him. He hears of the death of Mary Underwood, and he hears that a despondent Colonel Rainey has shot himself in a New York hotel room. He decides he will change his life; he will walk out on everything he has, and he will seek truth.

BOOK III: CHAPTERS I–II

Standing at a railroad ticket window, Sam sees a man carrying a box of carpenter tools; he buys a ticket to the same Illinois town the man is head-ing for. Using an assumed name, he gets a job working for a builder. Yet labor strife is brewing; a fellow worker gives him a pamphlet attacking rich men and corporations. Another worker, Jake, enlists his aid in raising wages, and Sam offers to write a pamphlet exposing management's illegal scheming, frightening management into give the workers what they want. Sam pays to print the pamphlet, contributing money for other matters as well; he feels he is doing something for the people. A speaker appears in town, holding forth nightly in front of the drugstore, declaring himself a follower of Karl Marx, exhorting support for the workers' cause. One day the builder, Sam's employer, attacks Sam, beating him and throwing him onto the street. Yet Sam realizes that he has never seen a printed copy of his pamphlet, that Jake has been keeping the money for himself. He talks to the socialist speaker, revealing his true identity—"I am McPherson, Sam McPherson of Chicago"—and offers to pay for a public rally that will set forth the facts of management's illegalities. The socialist is astonished, saying he must call headquarters in Chicago, and he does so—after which Sam's offer is turned down; Sam later hears the socialist speaking on the street, proclaiming that McPherson of Chicago has tried to make a fool out of him, that a "capitalist king" has tried to bribe him and his party. Jake apologizes to Sam for his beating, admitting that he and the builder have been in collusion all along—and assuming that Sam, too, has been working under cover. Sam realizes that his attempt to do good has come to nothing.

He turns to a vagabond life. The working man, he decides, does not want real social reform, only a 10 percent raise in his wages. Sam talks to his fellow vagabonds, finding them generally foolish—as they condemn the rich and steal from the poor. Meeting a woman at a railroad station and riding with her, he listens to her talk of life in the West, of the loneliness on the plains; he decides that her experience provides him no guidance. A young minister gives him a ride and takes him to his home, where they talk about God; the minister turns out to be dissatisfied with his congregation and his existence, and his wife asks Sam to leave, as he is making her husband unhappy.

BOOK II: CHAPTERS III–VI

Sam continues his wanderings. He works briefly as a bartender, selling whiskey that the proprietor himself has made; he wonders why his customers turn to drink, and he asks them—then is fired for his impertinence. Coming to a manufacturing town in Pennsylvania, he meets a young man who lives on an inheritance and devotes himself to socialism; he tells Sam of a strike among women employees at a Jewish shirtwaist factory, which has brought in nonunion replacement, or "scab," labor. Sam talks to one of the strikers, who is identified as "the Jewish woman"—she is never named—and suggests a campaign of letter writing, appealing to the strikebreaking women, explaining that they are hurting the original workers; he will provide the funds for the mailing. The union leader in Pittsburgh, hearing about the scheme, arrives and accuses Sam of being paid by capitalists to break the union; he stops the letter-writing campaign, although it had been achieving success. The Jewish woman comes to Sam as he is leaving town and says she is going with him; although feeling a moment of desire, he sends her back to town.

Sam, continuing his traveling, reflects on the coarseness of the people he meets; he muses that American forests and plains are noble, and yet American men and women are not. Once he meets a prostitute and offers to buy her dinner, making clear that dinner is the extent of the engagement; the woman, telling Sam her hard-luck story, says that such an evening makes her feel clean. One afternoon Sam goes to the village on the Hudson River where his wife, Sue, now lives; he has not seen her in two years. He spies on her for an hour, but realizing that he cannot face her, he leaves. At that point he turns to drinking and carousing, knowing that he is not living in the right way but feeling unable to change.

BOOK IV

Coming to St. Louis, Sam rents a steamboat, planning to entertain a group of companions on board. He drunkenly orders a young man to dance, then asks to see a woman who is also a mother, who has borne children. A woman, Belle, steps up, claiming to have three children; she points to a row of houses on the river bluff, saying that her children are getting supper there now. Sam orders the boat to turn back, and he accompanies the woman around town; he learns she plans to sell her home and buy a saloon, letting her children fend for themselves. When they arrive at her house, Sam sees two boys, aged 14 and 10, and a girl of seven. The woman strikes the older boy, accusing him of not washing the dishes; Sam orders the woman to bed, and he himself begins washing the dishes. He eventually sleeps on the couch.

Sam stays in the city for a week, coming to the house every day; the mother continues to leave in the evening. A new purpose is growing within him; he goes into the city and buys clothes, toys, and books. He tells the mother that a woman in the East would take the children in and raise them; the mother is happy to sign the paper he offers her. Sam brings the children to Sue, and she accepts them. Standing within her house, feeling the urge to flee, he resolves nevertheless to stay and enter once more into life; he will try to face life and understand it.

Critical Reception

Floyd DELL, who had been instrumental in finding a publisher for the novel, reviewed the work favorably, speaking of its resemblance to the fiction of Dostoevsky and recent Russian writers. Ben HECHT, writing in the *FRIDAY LITERARY REVIEW,* called it a "literary miracle"; *The Nation* decreed it "perhaps the most remarkable" book of the year. Yet the novel by this unknown author sold poorly; Dell wrote later that it was published too soon, that it would have found greater favor if it had appeared after WORLD WAR I; "it was the true pioneer of all the newer Middle-Western realism."

The immediate point of comparison became the celebrated book of poetry published the previous year, Edgar Lee MASTERS's *SPOON RIVER ANTHOLOGY.* The resemblance of the fictional Caxton, Iowa, to the fictional Spoon River, Illinois, was noted—although the portrait of Caxton, declared a *Nation* critic, is truer to life than that of Spoon River; Caxton is unmarred by Masters's "relish for evil." As always when comparisons are made between Anderson and Masters, the latter's greater emphasis on malice and malfeasance is underscored.

Waldo Frank, writing in *Seven Arts* magazine, focused on the non-Caxton scenes of the novel; the work's importance lies in its second portion, he suggested, when the hero abandons materialism and begins searching for truth. Later critics, although approving the hero's rejection of business values, reversed the judgment, dismissing the last two-thirds of the novel; that segment, they claim, presents merely Anderson's wishful-thinking version of himself, depicting a pretentious and self-congratulatory hero. Critics have noted also that Theodore DREISER, by the time *Windy McPherson's Son* appeared, had already published two novels featuring his own business magnate, Frank COWPERWOOD; comparisons between Cowperwood and Sam McPherson have always been to the detriment of McPherson. Meanwhile, critical appreciation of the Caxton portion of the book accelerated after the publication four years later of WINESBURG, OHIO.

A common complaint about Anderson's long fiction has been his weakness in portraying women; Sue Rainey has seemed unconvincing to readers, finally reduced to a maternal figure—as Clara BUTTERWORTH in *POOR WHITE* becomes ultimately a maternal figure as well.

Winesburg, Ohio
Sherwood Anderson
(1919)

Although he published two previous novels, AN-DERSON first gained fame with this collection of stories. He was living in Chicago at the time of its writing, working as an advertising copywriter; he had left his business in Ohio, as well as his wife and family. Edgar Lee MASTERS's *SPOON RIVER ANTHOLOGY* had already burst onto the scene, a bestseller and an early document in the REVOLT FROM THE VILLAGE movement; the *Spoon River* tales of small-town unhappiness and repression, contradicting notions of pastoralism and rural harmony, influenced Anderson to set down his own tales of small-town unhappiness and repression. Using Masters's device of interconnecting characters, he

differed from the poet in organizing his characters around a central figure, George WILLARD, a stand-in for the author himself. As Masters had drawn from his two childhood towns in downstate Illinois, Anderson drew from his hometown of Clyde, Ohio—although he claimed, too, that "the hint for almost every character" came from fellow boarders in his Chicago rooming house, many of whom had never lived in a small town.

Synopsis

"THE BOOK OF THE GROTESQUE"

An aging writer is depicted as retiring into bed, letting the images of men and women he has known —who are now "grotesques"—run through his mind. They have taken up a particular truth to live by, but in their adherence to that truth, they have become grotesque; their truth, being distorted, has become falsehood instead. Although Anderson suggests that this idea is the basis for the stories that follow, the author ranges far wider than such a narrow scheme would have allowed.

The story first appeared in THE MASSES in February 1916.

"HANDS"

Wing Biddlebaum, a day laborer who lives in the house of his deceased aunt, talks one evening to George Willard, the son of the local hotel proprietor, who is a reporter for the *Winesburg Eagle*. Biddlebaum tells the young man that he must have dreams, that he must not be like the others in town; to emphasize the point, he lays his hands on the young man's shoulder—and then withdraws them in horror. He tells Willard he cannot talk anymore, saying he must be getting home. The young man, understanding that something is wrong, suspects that the man's hands are related to his fears of people.

The reader learns about the one-time schoolteacher in Pennsylvania, who was driven out of town by an angry mob who had listened to tales told by "a half-witted boy." Bringing a rope to hang him, the townspeople had ended up merely throwing mud after the pitiful figure escaping into the night. Since that time, Biddlebaum, coming to live with an aunt in Winesburg, has never fully understood how his hands once brought him trouble; he had merely used them to caress shoulders, to tousle hair, to bring dreams into young boys' minds. The final scene shows him kneeling like a priest as he picks up crumbs from his meal; his hands—"the medium through which he expressed his love of man"—are moving as if telling devotions on a rosary.

The story first appeared in *The Masses* in March 1916.

"PAPER PILLS"

Doctor Reefy, an old man whom Winesburg has forgotten, has had the habit of sitting in his office and writing down thoughts on pieces of paper; he puts the scraps of paper into his pockets, where they become hard, round balls. Years before, at the age of 45, Doctor Reefy married a rich girl whose parents had died and left her money. The girl had many suitors, and finally she came to Doctor Reefy because she was pregnant, a fact he seemed to understand at once. Her condition passed in an illness, but Doctor Reefy married her, reading to her everything he had scribbled on the bits of paper; then the following spring she died.

Titled "The Philosopher," this story appeared in the June 1916 issue of *LITTLE REVIEW*; the story in *Winesburg, Ohio* titled "The Philosopher" is a different piece.

"THE MOTHER"

George Willard's mother Elizabeth WILLARD still owns the hotel that had been her father's; her husband, Tom, now manages it. Over the years the property has lost patronage and has become increasingly shabby. Tom Willard sees both the hotel and his wife as drab, even embarrassing; he escapes when he goes out into the street, swaggering and walking with a military step. Elizabeth—who once dreamed of being an actress, who once walked out romantically with the traveling men who stayed at the hotel—focuses now only on George, with whom she feels a special bond. When she hears Tom talking to the boy, she resolves suddenly to kill her husband; Tom can bring only evil to her son. She retrieves from a closet the makeup kit left by a theater troupe; she will make herself beautiful and then stab the man she hates. But George comes to her

room and tells her he is planning to leave Winesburg; his father has said something that made up his mind. Elizabeth feels joy, realizing that George will not be defeated, that he feels the need to escape his father.

The story first appeared in *Seven Arts* in March 1917.

"THE PHILOSOPHER"

Doctor Parcival has been in town about five years, having come to Winesburg from Chicago. He has few patients, although he seems to have sufficient money. He suggests to his frequent listener, George Willard, that he has had an adventurous past; he tells tales that make humanity seem contemptible. In a street accident he refuses to come to the aid of a girl; the townspeople do not realize that he has refused, and yet he thinks that they do—and he claims now that they will be coming with a rope to hang him. That is the point, he declares: "everyone in the world is Christ and they are all crucified." Do not forget that, he concludes to Willard.

"NOBODY KNOWS"

George Willard has received a note at the office of the *Winesburg Eagle* from Louise Trunnion, a young woman about whom the town has been whispering. "I'm yours if you want me," the note says. When George meets Louise in the darkness to walk out into the countryside, she seems determined to resist, or at least to pretend to resist; he assures her that everything will be all right, that no one will know anything. Later in the evening, as he heads back home, he stops to buy a cigar at a drug store that is still open; he is happy to talk to the clerk, to speak for a few moments to another man. He reminds himself that she has nothing on him: "Nobody knows," he tells himself.

"GODLINESS"

Jesse Bentley's sole ownership of the family farm is decided when his four older brothers are killed in the CIVIL WAR. Jesse has been away, studying to become a Presbyterian minister, but his aging father calls him back to take charge of the farm. The neighbors, seeing the small and slender young man, are amused at his seeming unsuitability. Yet they soon realize that he is fierce and driven; he drives his new, delicate wife in ceaseless toil. As his wife is about to give birth, Jesse remembers the men of the Old Testament, whom God noticed and spoke to; he prays that God will speak to him. God sent the biblical Jesse a son called David, and he prays that God will send him, too, a son called David, who will pluck these godless lands from the grasp of the Philistines. His overworked wife dies in childbirth, bearing a girl.

Many years later, David Hardy, the grandson of Jesse Bentley, has been living with his mother, Louise, and her husband in Winesburg. Louise is considered troublesome, having once threatened her husband with a knife, having deliberately set fire to the house; it was said that she drank. When David is 12, he goes to the Bentley farm to live with his grandfather; the old man hopes that God at last is favoring him. When the two go out riding in a buggy, Jesse stops among the trees and falls to his knees, asking God for a sign, asking Him to make His presence known. David is terrified at the sight of the terrible old man, who seems not to be his grandfather, but someone who might hurt him; he runs in fright, sobbing, falling over the roots of a tree. He wakes up in the buggy, bleeding, and the old man is stroking his head, crying out to God: "What have I done that Thou dost not approve of me?"

Louise Bentley, as a young woman, moved into Winesburg to go to the high school. Staying at the house of a banker, she has focused her attention on the banker's son, writing him notes, telling him she will meet him in the orchard at night. When John Hardy responds, they become lovers, although she knows that this is not what she really wanted; when they marry and David is born, she is ambivalent, even cruel, toward the child.

When David is 15, he goes riding with his grandfather again. They come across a lamb born out of season, which David picks up and holds in his arms; Jesse decides he can connect with God again by building a fire and offering the lamb as a burnt offering. As they arrive at the spot they had stopped at before, David is once more frightened; when the old man, taking a long knife from his pocket, turns toward the boy and the lamb, the boy springs to his feet, releasing the

lamb and racing down the hill. As he sees his grandfather still coming, he takes the sling used for shooting squirrels, picks up a rock, and hits the old man squarely in the head. The man falls, lying still on the ground. David starts running again; he will never go back to the Bentley farm or to Winesburg. Later, when people ask Jesse Bentley about his grandson's disappearance, the old man says that a messenger from God took the boy away.

"A MAN OF IDEAS"

Joe Welling is a man prone to fits—mental fits, not physical fits; he suddenly corners passersby on the street and assaults them with a torrent of words. His topic can be simple, such as the water level in Wine Creek, and yet he delivers his ideas in excitement and passion. Welling starts courting Sarah, the unhappy-seeming woman who lives with her father, Edward King, an old man who has come to Winesburg from the South, and her brother, Tom, who is said to have killed a man; Tom was once fined $10 in Winesburg for killing a dog with a stick. Everyone expects trouble between the King family, who are seen as dangerous, and Welling, who is seen as strange. Late one afternoon the Kings are waiting for Welling in his room at the New Willard House. As George Willard looks on, Welling arrives carrying a bundle of weeds and grasses—and plunges at once into a verbal barrage, a description of a possible apocalypse. Suppose, he suggests, that the produce of the Earth is destroyed, leaving only wild grasses to remain. The Kings become caught up in his flow of words, and they listen as Welling goes on to outline the remedies, including the breeding of new fruits and vegetables. He says he has wanted to come to their house and explain his ideas, but Sarah was afraid that he and her family would quarrel. Yet that is foolish, he concludes, suggesting that they go to the King house now and talk further. George, looking out the window, sees the men walking along the street. Welling continues talking, declaring that milkwood has possibilities for starting a new vegetable kingdom: "Wait till you see Sarah," he adds, "she'll get the idea." Through sheer force of enthusiasm, he has triumphed.

The story appeared in *Little Review* in June 1918.

"ADVENTURE"

When Alice Hindman was 16, she walked out almost every evening with Ned Currie, a young man who planned to go to Cleveland and get a newspaper job. Alice said she wanted to go with him, even without their getting married; yet Ned, responding protectively, said he would get a job and then come back for her, although that night they became lovers. Ned failed to find a job in Cleveland, going on west to Chicago.

Alice is now 27 years old and working at a dry-goods store; she has not heard from Ned for years, although she still saves money in order to join him. In her loneliness she realizes that life is passing her by; she sometimes lets a drugstore clerk walk her home from church, although she sends him away when she cannot bear his presence. One night, as the rain beats against her window, she feels the urge to leave the house and run naked through the streets; she dashes down the stairs and out into the rain. Seeing a man stumbling homeward, she calls out to him, but he is deaf. Dropping to the ground, she crawls on hands and knees through the grass and returns to the house. She weeps as she gets into bed, forcing herself to face the realization that people often live and die alone.

"RESPECTABILITY"

Wash Williams, the Winesburg telegraph operator, is the ugliest man in town. Fat and dirty, he drinks great quantities of beer every night at the saloon on Main Street—and rails against women, calling them "bitches"; he pities men for being managed by women. One night, having seen George Willard walk out with Belle Carpenter, Wash tells George his own story, prefacing it as a warning against getting involved with a woman. Wash had once loved and married a woman, he relates, buying a house and cultivating a garden; yet after two years of happiness, he found that his wife had already acquired three lovers, who visited her while he was at work. He sent his wife home to her mother, giving her the money he had saved; he sold the house and gave her that money as well. Then her mother asked him to visit; the family, living in a stylish house, appeared respectable. Her mother took him into the parlor and left him there—and soon his wife appeared in the parlor naked; her mother had taken off her daughter's clothes and pushed the daughter into the room. Wash struck the mother with a chair; when she screamed, the neighbors intervened.

"THE THINKER"

Seth Richmond, whose father was killed in a street fight, is a quiet young man; the townspeople consider him a thinker. Yet his silence is really the result of his having nothing to say; he is not interested in much, and he has no great plan or purpose in life. One day, his friend, George Willard, says he is trying to write a love story, and he has decided to fall in love with Helen White, the banker's daughter, the richest and most attractive girl in town. George asks Seth to tell Helen that he, George, loves her. Unsettled, Seth goes to see her, but resolves to say instead that he is leaving town, that he is going to a city to find work. Helen is pleased to see him; she has always, ever since they were children, felt close to him. She admires Seth now, since his resolution shows him to be strong and purposeful; she assumes he has truly made up his mind, and she offers no objections to his leaving. Seth walks home slowly, feeling loneliness—and thinking that someone who talks a lot, someone like George, is the one who wins.

The story first appeared in *Seven Arts* in September 1917.

"TANDY"

Tom Hard pays little attention to his five-year-old daughter, whose mother is dead; he spends most of his time thinking and talking about religion, proclaiming himself an agnostic. A stranger, the son of a rich Cleveland merchant, comes to Winesburg, saying that his purpose is to cure himself of drink. Yet he continues drinking, and as he sits with others at the New Willard House, he explains why he still drinks; he is addicted not only to alcohol, but to love. A woman is coming, he declares, but he has missed her because she did not come in his time. Eyeing the five-year-old girl, he says that she may be that woman—and yet he must continue destroying himself with drink because she is still only a child. This woman, he adds, has met with struggles and defeats, but from these defeats has arisen a new quality; he has named that quality Tandy. He drops to his knees before the girl: "Be Tandy," he implores. He pleads drunkenly: "Be brave enough to dare to be loved." A few days later, he boards a train and returns to Cleveland. One evening, when the father addresses the girl by name, she cries out that she wants to be Tandy. Sobbing bitterly, she repeats: "I want to be Tandy."

"THE STRENGTH OF GOD"

The Reverend Curtis Hartman is pastor of the Presbyterian Church, the largest church in Winesburg. He laments that he lacks charisma, that he fails to arouse enthusiasm among his worshipers; he wishes to cry aloud the word of God, to make people tremble before the voice of God speaking through him. On Sunday mornings, his regular habit is to go to the small room in the church bell tower, praying for strength before delivering his sermon. One summer Sunday morning, as the stained-glass window in the tower is open, he sees the woman in the house next door, lying on a bed, smoking a cigarette; her bare shoulders are visible. Hartman is horrified, and his sermon that Sunday is unusually impassioned; he hopes his message is carrying into the woman's undoubtedly sinful soul.

The woman is Kate Swift, a 30-year-old schoolteacher. Hartman, recalling that she has lived in New York City, even traveled to Europe, realizes that maybe her smoking does not mean much. Yet early one Sunday morning, when he is unable to sleep, he walks through the streets—and picks up a stone, which he takes back to the bell tower and uses to break out a corner of the stained-glass window. But Kate Swift is not in her bed; the pastor rejoices at his deliverance from carnal desires. Yet his visits to the bell tower increase, and he finds himself coming there in the evenings. He gazes at the woman lying in bed as she reads; the light from her lamp streams down on her bare neck and shoulders. Hartman's next step is to walk through the streets of the town for hours, praying to God, asking God to return his servant to the path of righteousness.

One night, waiting in his tower, Hartman sees the woman suddenly appear in her room; she is naked and weeping, and she throws herself on the bed—then kneels in prayer. The pastor stumbles down the stairway, running into the street; he finds the office of the *Winesburg Eagle*, where the young George Willard is working late. Speaking incoherently to Willard about the ways of God, claiming he has found the light, he declares: "God has manifested himself to me in the body of a woman." Kate Swift is an instrument of God, he proclaims, bearing God's message to him. Hartman shows Willard his bleeding fist; he has smashed the window, and it will have to be replaced. The strength of God was in him, he explains, and he broke the window.

"THE TEACHER"

One night, after a lengthy snowfall, only three people are still awake in Winesburg. One is George Willard, sitting in the office of the *Eagle*; another is the Reverend Curtis Hartman, waiting in the bell tower for the woman to appear in her room; the third is Kate Swift, the schoolteacher, walking through the wintry streets. Her mood is excited because she is thinking of her one-time pupil, George Willard. Wishing to encourage his talent, she has often spoken to him; once she found him in his office and took him out to the fair ground, where she lectured him passionately on how he must take his abilities seriously. On another occasion, when he had come to her house to borrow a book, she spoke again to him fervently, even letting her lips brush his cheek. Now, on this snowy night, she is unable to sleep, and she comes again to the *Eagle* office, speaking once more to the young man; finally, she says she must be going, or else, she adds, "I'll be wanting to kiss you." George takes her into his arms at once and embraces her; she yields for a moment, then suddenly breaks loose and runs away. It is minutes later that the Reverend Curtis Hartman sees her from his bell tower, naked and weeping, then praying—and just another few minutes after that Hartman bursts in upon George in the *Eagle* office, holding his bloody fist, proclaiming that Kate Swift is the instrument of God. Later that night, when George goes to bed, he thinks of the schoolteacher, then of the minister—who seems suddenly to have gone insane—and can figure nothing out. He is the last person to go to sleep in Winesburg that night.

"LONELINESS"

Years ago, Enoch Robinson went from Winesburg to New York City to study art. But nothing turned out well for him. When he was a student there, other students would drop by his room, discussing his pictures, but they never saw what he had put into his work; they never understood what he had intended, and he found it impossible to explain to them. So he stopped inviting people over and locked the door—and soon he was inventing people with whom he talked, to whom he could explain his work. Yet, feeling lonely, he married the girl who sat next to him in art school; he got a job, moved into an apartment, and had two children. But he felt hemmed in by life, and when his mother in Winesburg died, leaving him $18,000, he gave the money to his wife and told her he could not live with her anymore. He returned to the rented room—and to the people he had invented there—and felt happy again.

Enoch is living now in Winesburg, where he appears on the streets as an obscure, strange personage. One day he decides that George Willard seems sympathetic; he will tell the young man his story. A woman, he says, who lived in the same boardinghouse, came into his room every now and then; yet she was too big for the room. He tried to tell her, in response, how big and important he himself was. But then she wanted to leave, and so he locked the door, swearing at her, stamping his foot, screaming, saying vile things. Finally, she got out the door—but she took all his people with her; all the life in the room followed her out. He was alone again. That is when he returned to Winesburg. "I'm alone," he laments to George, "all alone here."

"AN AWAKENING"

Belle Carpenter lives with her father, whom she hates, because he had treated her mother brutally. She walks out occasionally with George Willard, but her real love is Ed Handby, a bartender in the town saloon; Handby is known to have a violent past.

One evening George is walking by himself through town, coming to the shabby wooden houses where the day laborers live. He is thinking of the reading he has done lately, and deep but inexpressible thoughts are overwhelming him; all the people on this street, he feels, must be brothers and sisters. Soon he finds himself walking toward Belle Carpenter's house; he does not know that Handby has just been there, warning Belle to stay away from "that kid." Yet Belle walks out with George, pleased to make Handby jealous, and George tells her how new and powerful thoughts have come to him, how he is a new, strong man. They approach the fair grounds, and he kisses her passionately. Handby appears, grasping George by the shoulder and hurling him to the grass; he realizes that beating the boy is not necessary. Yet the young man keeps lunging at Handby, and each time he is sent sprawling into the bushes; the last time he strikes his head on the roof of a tree. As he creeps home, retracing his steps through the shantytown—and trying to summon up once again his powerful thoughts—he sees the street now as disreputable and squalid.

The story first appeared in *Little Review* in December 1918.

"QUEER"

Elmer Cowley, son of the less-than-successful merchant Ebenezer Cowley, watches a traveling salesman try to sell his father collar fasteners; the salesman promises exclusive rights if the father buys 20 dozen fasteners. At the same time, Elmer realizes that George Willard is standing at the back door of the newspaper office, listening to the transaction. Furious, Elmer rushes to a glass showcase, takes out a revolver, and waves the gun at the salesman; he exclaims that they are not going to buy any more goods until they begin selling them—and they are not going to keep on being queer and having folks staring at them. The salesman flees, and Ebenezer Cowley can only say, "I'll be washed and ironed and starched!"

Elmer tramps into the farmland outside of town, vowing that he will not be queer, that he will not be stared at. He returns to the farm his father once owned and finds there the half-witted man, Mook, whom he had known as a boy; it was Mook who had kept using the "laundered" saying. Elmer explains to the uncomprehending man that he is tired of being queer, that he is tired of his whole family's being queer. That night, he enters the store and finds his father's tin cash box. Taking $20, he resolves to steal a ride that night on the freight train to Cleveland; there he will get a job and make friends and no longer be queer. Deciding to tell this news to George Willard, he gets the night clerk at the New Willard House to wake up the young man and tell him to come to the train depot. George appears, and Elmer tries to explain, but he can only mutter incoherently: "I'll be washed and ironed and starched." Enraged, he thrusts the money at George—and then strikes the reporter fiercely, pummeling him with blow after blow; George falls half-conscious to the platform. As the train pulls out of the station, Elmer springs onto a flat car, crying out proudly that he showed him: "I ain't so queer. I guess I showed him I ain't so queer."

The story first appeared in *Seven Arts* in December 1916.

"THE UNTOLD LIE"

Ray Pearson and Hal Winters are farm laborers near Winesburg. Ray, a quiet man of 50, lives with his wife and half a dozen children in a run-down house; Hal, a younger man, is known for getting into "women scrapes." One October afternoon, as the two men are husking corn, Ray looks around at the beauty of the countryside and recalls the afternoon, years ago, when he walked into the woods with a girl—and his life, as a result, was changed. He was tricked, he tells himself.

As the men continue working, Hal starts talking about his own problems; he has got a girl in trouble, he says. Should he marry her? Should he put himself "into the harness"? Ray is unable to answer; tears come to his eyes, and he walks away, knowing there is only one right thing to say—but he cannot make himself say it. When he goes home, his wife is scolding him, saying he must go to town for groceries and the children will be crying. Ray races across the countryside, trying to catch up with Hal, remembering the dreams he himself once

had—to go west, to go to sea. But when he finds Hal, he loses his nerve; he is unable to speak. The younger man announces happily that he has made up his mind, that he wants to marry, settle down, have children. Watching him go off into the dusk, Ray walks slowly across the fields; he is thinking perhaps of pleasant evenings he has spent with his children, because he decides it is just as well he failed to speak. Whatever he might have said, he tells himself, would have been a lie.

The story first appeared in *Seven Arts* in January 1917.

"DRINK"

Tom Foster comes to Winesburg from Cincinnati at the age of 16, brought by his grandmother. He gets a job as a stable boy for the Whites, the banking family, but loses it because he hangs around with the other young men of the town instead of doing errands at the store or the post office; yet he is not a troublemaker, but rather a quiet young man whom everyone likes. Then one spring night he gets drunk for the first time, buying a bottle of whiskey and sitting down on the grass. Later that night, inebriated, he runs into George Willard—and starts talking about Helen White, the banker's daughter; he says he has been with her that evening. George knows differently because he has seen Helen with her father; he is angry at the young man for his fantasizing. Yet the two of them continue talking. Finally, somewhat recovered, Tom announces that it was good to be drunk; he will not have to do it again. It made him happy, and it made everything strange; he is glad he did it.

"DEATH"

Elizabeth Willard, tired and ill at the age of 41, sometimes comes to talk to Doctor Reefy in his office. They talk less about her health than about the thoughts they share, the ideas they seem to have in common. After Elizabeth sees the doctor, her step is always more lively, until she returns to the shabby New Willard House and her long-term sickroom. There she thinks of the lovers she once knew, although they never gave her the adventure she had yearned for; she thinks also of her decision, when her father lay dying, to marry Tom

Willard. Her father warned her not to marry Tom, telling her about the $800 he had hidden away in a box in his trunk; she should take the money and go away from Winesburg, although if she insisted on marrying, she should promise never to tell Tom about the money.

One afternoon, as Elizabeth sits talking in the chair in Doctor Reefy's office, the doctor sees her becoming younger and stronger. She is telling of a wild buggy ride she took not long after her marriage, plunging into a storm. As she kneels beside the doctor's chair, Reefy takes her into his arms and kisses her. Yet their lovemaking is interrupted by an intruder on the stairs outside, and Elizabeth leaves, rushing hysterically into the street. That will be the last time the doctor sees her alive.

Elizabeth dies the same year that her son, George, reaches the age of 18; she had been quiet and bedridden for a month. Dr. Reefy, called to the New Willard Hotel, stops the young man in the hallway and tells him the final news about his mother. Later, going to her room, George sees the doctor sitting at the dead woman's bedside; the doctor leaves in an awkward silence. Then, as reality of his mother's death takes hold, George, sobbing, leaves the room as well. He will go away to some city, perhaps get a job on a newspaper. The son never learns about the box containing the money—the box his mother had hidden for years behind the plaster at the foot of her bed.

"SOPHISTICATION"

The banker's daughter, Helen White, has returned from Cleveland, where she is attending college, to spend the day at the Winesburg County Fair. George Willard hopes to talk to her, explaining to her his new sophistication, his new understanding of life; he wants her to see that he is no longer boastful, as he once was. He sees that Helen is sitting in the grandstand with a young man, one of her instructors in college, who is staying in Winesburg as a guest of her mother. Yet Helen has grown tired of the pedantic young man, and she thinks of George, with whom she walked out once on a summer evening. During her months in the city, she, too, has grown in sophistication, and she wants George to understand this change in her.

In the evening, as the instructor talks pompously on the veranda of Banker White's house, Helen goes into the house—then runs out the back door, into the night, looking for George; her mother has been saying that no one in town is fit for a girl of her breeding. Helen finds George, and they walk together up the hill toward the fair ground; they sit in the grandstand, which earlier in the day had been overflowing with life; they feel now its almost terrifying silence. As they remain in the darkness, they kiss, and yet they draw back from each other. Returning to town, they embrace again—and once more draw back. Suddenly, they begin tumbling down the hill, acting like children, tripping, shouting, laughing. When they reach the bottom, Helen takes George's arm, and the two young people walk home in silence. From this evening, they have each received what they needed for their future life.

"DEPARTURE"

George Willard has been awake since two o'clock in the morning, thinking of the journey he is about to take. The westbound train leaves Winesburg at 7:45. After taking an early morning stroll, he goes with his father to the train station; he is taller now than his father. Various people on the platform wish him luck. When Helen White comes running along Main Street, hoping for parting word with him, he has already found a seat on the train and fails to see her. He surreptitiously counts his money, since his father has told him to keep track of his money and not look like a greenhorn. Thinking of the uncertainty of his coming life, he looks again out of the window, and the town of Winesburg has disappeared—only a background now for his future.

Critical Reception

Winesburg, Ohio received generally favorable reviews. *The New Republic* declared that "nothing better has come out of America"; the poet Hart Crane called the book "a living monument" in the American consciousness. Yet charges of indecency were heard; one critic spoke of its "gutter" material, and another called the stories "the picture of a maggoty mind." Comparisons were made as well with *Spoon River Anthology*; H. L. MENCKEN wrote that *Winesburg* achieved the goal that *Spoon River* had tried for but "missed by half a mile." The *CHICAGO TRIBUNE* noted that the reader finds reproach and bitterness in Masters, but in Anderson he finds instead "a homely tender feeling of participation in human destiny." The comparison between the writers continued as a standard critical theme, returning always to the idea that Anderson's emotional cripples are never as reprehensible as the figures who people Masters's town.

Critics have noted the moments of intense emotional experience captured in these stories—briefly described, because the moments themselves are brief. The effect differs from that of the cumulative REALISM found in the work of Anderson's best-known contemporary, Theodore DREISER. Dreiser's prose has been called slow and lumbering, while Anderson's has been labeled overwrought; readers have noted how many times the characters in *Winesburg* "tremble" or are found "trembling."

By the time of his death, Anderson's reputation had waned, although it revived in the following decade; critics of the 1950s began attaching to his work the then-favored themes of alienation and estrangement. These traits were found particularly in the *Winesburg* stories, proving that Anderson understood, even in his lifetime, that alienation is inevitably the modern condition. His characters' isolation, their inability to communicate, especially at moments of climactic feeling, fit well into the era's critical schema. As an example, critics cited the three figures in "The Teacher"—George Willard, Kate Swift, and the Reverend Curtis Hartman—who come together one night, yet whose juxtaposition underlines their basic solitude and isolation.

A Modern Library edition of the work was published in 1922, ensuring its classic status. A stage adaptation was produced by a Pennsylvania company in 1934 and published in *Plays: Winesburg and Others* in 1937. Another staging of *Winesburg* was presented in New York in 1958.

Winters, Hal　*See* WINESBURG, OHIO: "The Untold Lie."

With the Procession
Henry Blake Fuller
(1895)

The author, himself descended from "old settlers," portrays an old Chicago family, wealthy from the wholesale grocery business, whose fortunes are in decline. The title refers to the precession—of wealth, of achievement—that marches on in society; some people join the procession, some people try to join but fail, and others choose to drop out. The character of Mrs. Susan BATES, who had been mentioned in FULLER's previous novel, *THE CLIFF-DWELLERS*, is modeled on Bertha PALMER, although background details differ. Also in the earlier novel is the pervasive but unseen—until the very end—Mrs. Cecilia Ingles, who in the present work is depicted as a frivolous trophy wife. Theodore Brower appears in the earlier novel, although he is presented simply as an insurance adjuster, not as a man who serves high-end clientele and yet has lived in a SETTLEMENT HOUSE. Fuller seems to be making purposeful connections between his two works, published two years apart, ensuring that together they present a full portrait of upper-class Chicago at the end of the 19th century. The architect in the novel, Tom Bingham, resembles Daniel H. BURNHAM.

Synopsis

CHAPTERS I–III

Twenty-three-year-old Truesdale MARSHALL returns to Chicago and his family after four years abroad; his funds are being withdrawn due to straitened family circumstances. His father, David MARSHALL, founder of a once-prosperous wholesale grocery company, wonders if his son's travels have been worth the expenditure—although, as a simple man, he has never understood the benefits of studying art and music in Europe. His firm, formerly Marshall and Company, is now Marshall and Belden; the name change indicates his loss of control. Moreover, the family home is no longer fashionable, nor is it located in a fashionable area. Jane MARSHALL, the eldest daughter, senses that the family's standing has fallen, that the procession has passed them by. Yet she herself continues her involvement in social causes, seeking donations to her particular charity, a working-girls' lunchroom downtown. In the process she has struck up an acquaintance with Mrs. Granger Bates, one of Chicago's wealthiest women and a generally well-meaning philanthropist.

The Marshalls are no longer receiving the social invitations they once received, although the ambitious Gilbert Belden, Marshall's business partner, and his wife are invited to the elite functions. Belden is also trying, and seemingly succeeding, to wrest control of the business that Marshall started more than 35 years earlier. Yet Marshall smiles quietly when Mrs. Bates's name is mentioned; his thoughts return to the time, long ago, when he sat in a concert hall with the former Sue Lathrop and listened to the "Nightingale Serenaders."

CHAPTERS IV–V

Jane is making her first call upon Mrs. Bates. The sumptuousness of the home impresses her. Mrs. Bates, after an initial coolness, warms to Jane when she learns she is David Marshall's daughter; Jane is offended at first, but gradually finds herself liking the woman. When Mrs. Bates leads her to a small, cramped room filled with worn furniture, Jane realizes that this is where her hostess preserves her past, her roots. Mrs. Bates speaks of those earlier days, telling how she and her husband rose from obscurity to join "the procession." She speaks also of David Marshall, once one of her suitors; she shows Jane a daguerreotype, or early photograph, of her father as a young man. That is how he looked, she says, the last time they danced together; she begins playing on the piano the tune they danced to, and Jane joins in, singing. When Jane leaves, the two women have become friends.

CHAPTERS VI–VIII

Truesdale Marshall makes clear that he is not interested in his father's business, preferring a life of leisure and artistic pursuit. Among his friends are Theodore Brower, the Marshall insurance agent, who calls at the home frequently, and Arthus Paston, an Englishman whose family connections have secured him a job in the Chicago office of a London-based investment company. Truesdale and Arthur regularly free themselves from family and business restraints, preferring "Bohemia," the

Bertha Palmer, reincarnated as Susan Bates in Henry B. Fuller's *With the Procession,* led the social procession in Chicago for decades. *(Chicago Historical Society)*

realm of those who disregard social expectations and conventional lifestyles. Truesdale also meets Bertie Patterson, a young girl from Madison, Wisconsin, whom his aunt has taken under her wing.

Mrs. Bates visits David Marshall at work, deciding, because of her new acquaintance with Jane, that she should reacquaint herself with the man she had known decades before; she sees at once that he appears older, less effective. She reminds him that they are "old settlers," those who helped build the city. She suggests he leave his mark on the community by means of a charitable gift; she herself has donated a woman's dormitory to the UNIVERSITY OF CHICAGO. She encounters Tom Bingham, the architect, as well as Gilbert Belden, Marshall's partner. She invites Bingham for dinner, although she will never invite Belden, whose wife was acquired after a divorce.

The Marshalls, influenced by Jane—who in turn has been influenced by Mrs. Bates—prepare a coming-out party for Rosamund, the younger sister; she is now officially presented to society. This is a social occasion new to the Marshalls, one that was never offered for Jane.

CHAPTERS IX–XII

The major event of the year is the Charity Ball, and Jane brings with her Theodore Brower, who usually avoids social functions; he once lived in a settlement house. Mrs. Bates, meanwhile, undertaking Jane's social improvement, supervises her hairdressing, manicuring, and fashion-updating; Jane is becoming less like the earnest young woman who once lectured on the Russian novel at HULL-HOUSE. At the Charity Ball Mrs. Bates takes Brower in hand, pointing out her fellow workers for charitable causes, trying to convince him that her kind are not simply frivolous. Rosamund dances with Arthur Paston, dreaming now of Buckingham Palace and the English gentry. Yet Truesdale, although a friend of Paston's, does not approve of the Englishman's attentions to his sister; Paston is too much like himself.

The Bateses invite the Marshalls for dinner; Mrs. Bates tries to downplay their opulent lifestyle, and yet the Marshalls see the contrast with their own plain and out-of-date home. Mrs. Bates speaks of her plans for her girls' dormitory at the University of Chicago; another guest, the architect Bingham, speaks of the civic projects that public-spirited men should underwrite. Family pressure, meanwhile, is mounting on David Marshall to build a new house in a more fashionable neighborhood, leaving the area that now seems threatened by encroaching urban blight.

CHAPTERS XIII–XV

The Marshall family is reluctantly agreeing to build a new home in a more desirable area; its construction is to be supervised by Bingham. Truesdale, charmed by Bertie Patterson, agrees to paint the girl's portrait; his aunt, looking on, fails to understand his use of the latest techniques of French impressionism. Jane gives Truesdale and Bertie a tour of the new lunchroom for working girls that she has established. She apologizes that the facilities are on a high floor, although she notes that because of elevators no rent is saved; she is living in an era when tenants are still used to going up and down stairs, when high floors had not yet achieved high status. Truesdale sees one of the Jane's charitable beneficiaries, Sophie, a Swiss or Alsatian girl, and he turns away, trying to conceal his face; as he leaves the room, he purposely drops a glove, stooping for it, continuing to hide his presence.

Truesdale, Jane, their aunt, and Bertie stop by the Marshall and Belden Company, visiting David Marshall and the family's older son, Roger, a lawyer working for the firm. A clerk working for Belden, seemingly Swiss or Alsatian, catches sight of Truesdale, learning that this man is David Marshall's son; the clerk's smile is "slow and sinister."

CHAPTERS XVI–XXI

As Jane works with Bingham on plans for the new house, the family learns that Truesdale has been caught up in a scandal; Sophie's father is exerting financial leverage over the family. Using a counterploy, Truesdale suggests that Roger look into the existence of other men in Sophie's life. David Marshall feels discouraged and depressed, not only about his younger son, but about the family business and his partner, Belden, who is pursuing speculative business practices.

Bertie Patterson has been recalled to her home in Madison, to keep her away from the errant Truesdale; the latter travels to see her but is rebuffed by her mother. A wedding is arranged between Sophie and a young man, and cash changes hands; scandal is thereby averted, although Belden's wife makes sure that Mrs. Bates knows about it. Rosamund, meanwhile, rejecting one of the Bates sons, who is solid and unromantic, announces her engagement to Arthur Paston; Paston is fortuneless, but Rosy is dreaming of his roots in aristocratic England. The new Marshall house nears completion, and David Marshall becomes increasingly tired and ill; his firm is in receivership, and his children, except for Jane, seem estranged and remote.

Jane blames herself for what has happened; it was she who became involved in keeping up with the procession, who let her head be turned by Mrs. Bates—a woman who was well-meaning and sympathetic, yet led Jane and her family along paths they were not equipped to follow. David Marshall dies not long after moving into the new home. Truesdale leaves for Japan; Rosamund, to her surprise, finds that her husband's family in England is sober and sensible, not at all like her husband—a family that reminds her, in fact, of her sister, Jane. Jane marries Brower, and Marshall's estate allows her to bequeath a building to the new University of Chicago in her father's name.

Critical Response

The book achieved a brief best-selling status. Critic James Huneker wrote that *With the Procession* is less forceful than *The Cliff-Dwellers*, and yet it is "finer in its art, its characterization and development." William Dean HOWELLS noted its REALISM, claiming never to have read a book "more intensely localized"; he approved of Fuller's "fealty to Chicago," adding that no eastern writer is comparable at the moment. In a volume published later, the 1901 *Heroines of Fiction*, Howells singles out Mrs. Bates as a praiseworthy fictional character.

Modern readers are often surprised at the novel's complexity, its density of presentation. The narrative is relayed in irony, revealing the work of an ambitious stylist; Fuller takes a less straightforward path than might be expected from a follower of the tenets of realism. The University of Chicago Press issued a reprint edition in 1965—although only the author's subtly gay-themed novel of a quarter of a century later, BERTRAM COPE'S YEAR, continues to receive modern attention.

Witla, Angela *See* BLUE, ANGELA.

Witla, Eugene

The principal character in Theodore DREISER's novel THE "GENIUS," Eugene is Dreiser's most au-

tobiographical figure, although he is a visual artist instead of a writer. He travels the same geographical path as his creator, coming from a small midwestern town to Chicago and then to New York, and he follows a similar career course, from semisuccess to nervous exhaustion, and then finally to commercial success. His romantic life and marital history show close parallels as well. Floyd DELL, generally an admirer of Dreiser, found the character problematic because the author was "too immersed" in his creation.

As a young man, Eugene is already skeptical of morality and convention. He seeks feminine sympathy and kindness, although an early love, Ruby Kenny, tells him he cannot love any woman for long; another young woman, Christina CHANNING, says he cannot be happy married. When he finally—and reluctantly—marries Angela BLUE, he cannot accept that the tie is for life, nor can he act accordingly. As Angela confronts him in outbursts of jealousy, he feels sorry for her, yet never sufficiently sorry to curb his desire for beauty and love; he separates from Angela when the allure of the young Suzanne DALE overwhelms him. Yet as in the case of the other 18-year-old who infatuates him, Frieda Roth, he never consummates the relationship; Dreiser, aware of censorship issues, never allows his protagonist to cross a particular line.

The parallels between Eugene's and Dreiser's artistic endeavors are clear throughout. Rejecting traditional forms of beauty, Eugene draws factories, tugboats, and engines; he focuses on the grim and the shabby. "Thank God for a realist," a gallery owner muses. Viewers at the gallery are described as amazed at scenes considered outside the realm of art; one critic accuses the painter of wishing only to shock the public. Dreiser is repeating reactions to his own work, particularly SISTER CARRIE, a novel considered not fitting for the realm of literature.

The Wizard of Oz
(1902)

This musical stage production, based on L. Frank BAUM's children's book, THE WONDERFUL WIZARD

OF OZ, used music provided by Paul Tietjens, the future husband of poet Eunice TIETJENS. The show opened at the Grand Opera House in Chicago in 1902. The book's illustrator, Arthur W. W. DENSLOW, designed costumes and scenery. Although reducing the tale to a VAUDEVILLE-like review, adding new characters and sketches, the production was a success; the small dog, Toto, became a large cow, Imogene, so that an actor could play the animal part. Moving on to New York in 1903, *The Wizard of Oz* became one of the most popular musicals of the era. Like the movies that would follow, the stage show dropped the word *Wonderful* from the original title.

Wobblies   *See* INDUSTRIAL WORKERS OF THE WORLD.

A Woman of Genius
Mary Austin
(1912)

An early REVOLT FROM THE VILLAGE work, *A Woman of Genius* foreshadows Sinclair LEWIS's *Main Street* in its depiction of a woman tied down by small-town constraints. AUSTIN was acquainted with Lewis in New York City while writing the novel. The moral and social code of Taylorville, Ohianna—in reality, Austin's hometown of Carlinville, Illinois—is presented as exerting a particular hold on women, who are expected to marry, who are allowed no life apart from those of their husbands. Olivia Lattimore, growing up in Taylorville, marrying a local man, struggles to escape her town's narrowness and constriction. She is finally able to flee because she has what Austin calls the "Gift"—an acting ability, a talent to express herself artistically; she can earn a living and make her way in the world. Yet in doing so, she loses the love of her life, a man also from Taylorville, who has gone out into the world—and yet still holds to the belief that a married woman cannot have a life of her own. Olivia concludes, "the social idea, in which I was bred, is the villain of my plot."

Woman's Christian Temperance Union

An antiliquor organization established in 1874 in Cleveland, the WCTU became the largest women's organization of the era. Frances WILLARD, a resident of EVANSTON, Illinois, became the second president in 1879; her Chicago WCTU headquarters, first housed in the Young Men's Christian Association, transferred in 1892 to a WCTU-funded BURNHAM AND ROOT building, popularly known as the Women's Temple. Under Willard's leadership, the organization broadened its goals to include women's suffrage; Willard believed that if women had the vote, they would abolish the sale of liquor. Women's suffrage and PROHIBITION both became law by the end of the second decade of the new century. The Women's Temple was demolished in 1926.

The headquarters for the Woman's Christian Temperance Union, built through WCTU funding efforts, was designed by John Wellborn Root and completed in 1892. *(Chicago Historical Society)*

Women's International League for Peace and Freedom

This peace organization was established in 1919 in reaction to WORLD WAR I. The WILPF was preceded by the Woman's Peace Party, formed early in 1915 and led by Jane ADDAMS, Charlotte Perkins GILMAN, and others, who sought to end the war and keep America out of the war. In April 1915, at The Hague, Netherlands, Addams chaired the International Congress of Women, adopting a platform similar to that of the Woman's Peace Party. The WILPF became a permanent organization in 1919, headquartered in Geneva; Addams served as the first president. Vachel LINDSAY's poem, "To Jane Addams at the Hague," collected in THE CHINESE NIGHTINGALE AND OTHER POEMS, appeared in a Chicago newspaper after the German sinking of the British ocean liner LUSITANIA in May 1915.

The Wonderful Wizard of Oz
L. Frank Baum
(1900)

Considered the only fantasy tale that can match Lewis Carroll's *Alice's Adventures in Wonderland* and *Through the Looking Glass, The Wonderful Wizard of Oz* was inspired in part by the WHITE CITY of the WORLD'S COLUMBIAN EXPOSITION. The tale presents a version of the quest motif—although the wizard the characters seek turns out to be a con man and the EMERALD CITY is an illusion; it is emeraldlike because everyone wears green spectacles. BAUM, who came to Chicago as a journalist in 1891, was capitalizing on the fact that the gleaming buildings on the exposition grounds were made of plaster and fiberboard, built to last no longer than the fair itself. His characters, including the Scarecrow, the Tin Woodman, and the Cowardly Lion—known to children and adults alike through the 1939 Hollywood movie—set out on their journey, ultimately learning the truths that lie behind illusion, including truths about themselves.

The book's immediate popularity led to spin-offs long before the famous film version. A stage musical, THE WIZARD OF OZ—the word *Wonderful* dropped from the title, as it would be in future movies—was presented in Chicago two years after the book appeared. In 1910, the Selig Polyscope Company produced the first brief Oz movie, and Baum moved to California that same year. In 1925, a silent *Wizard of Oz* appeared, including the comedian Oliver Hardy as the Tin Woodman. Carl SANDBURG, reviewing the film in the CHICAGO DAILY NEWS, found it a "poor picture"—not a proper equivalent, he wrote, for "that odd and strange children's book." The classic movie is the 1939 Technicolor version starring Judy Garland; an African-American *The Wiz*, starring Diana Ross, Michael Jackson, and Richard Pryor, is based on a stage version dating from 1975.

Focusing on the era's debates over the GOLD STANDARD and FREE SILVER, critics have claimed to see a subtext in *The Wonderful Wizard of Oz*—a subtext relating to the western economic crisis of the 1890s. The silver shoes—ruby slippers in the movie—represent the espousal of silver coinage, and the yellow brick road represents the gold standard; *oz.* is the abbreviation for ounce, the measure of gold. The Scarecrow is the midwestern farmer, the Tin Woodman is the industrial worker, the travelers are COXEY'S ARMY, and the Emerald City is Washington, D.C., where the government is a charade, perpetuated through deception. Supporters of the populist interpretation note that Baum lived in South Dakota in the late 1880s—the journey begins with a plains twister—when the woes of the farmers were being publicized, when agitation was high to promote free silver and eliminate the gold standard. Other meanings found in this children's work include allegories of occultism and of SOCIALISM.

World's Columbian Exposition

This world's fair, held May 1–October 30, 1893, was the most renowned exposition on American soil. The fair heralded Chicago as the vibrant new city of the West, as the thriving upstart metropolis worthy of the world's attention. The year 1893 saw also the publication of the first Chicago-based novel, Henry B. FULLER's *THE CLIFF-DWELLERS*, one of the two Fuller works that would inspire Theodore DREISER to turn his own hand to urban fiction. The fair was attended by as many as 27 million visitors, at a time when the U.S. population was approximately 66 million; many of the visitors came from overseas. The burgeoning railroads, making transportation easy, facilitated attendance at the inland site. The purpose of the fair was to celebrate the 400th anniversary—one year late, because of the length of time needed for preparation—of Columbus's landing in the New World. Frederick Law OLMSTED, designer of New York's Central Park, was commissioned to choose and prepare a site, and architects Daniel BURN-

HAM and John Wellborn ROOT were delegated to oversee the design and construction of the grounds and buildings; the previous world's fair, the Paris Universal Exposition of 1889, had presented the Eiffel Tower to the world, and the mandate was to surpass that feat. When Root died suddenly in 1891, Burnham became the sole Director of Works, carrying out a vast and complex planning operation.

Because of the availability of transportation and the waterfront location, JACKSON PARK, a swampy area eight miles south of downtown, was selected as the fair site. The area was landscaped with fountains, statuary, canals, lagoons, and a wooded island; a low, horizontal Japanese pavilion

Louis Sullivan's Transportation Building at the 1893 World's Columbian Exposition stood as an anomaly among the white classical structures; the walls were multicolored, the doorway golden and silver. *(Chicago Historical Society)*

was placed on the island, inspiring architect Frank Lloyd WRIGHT in his interest in Japanese art. The dominant structures were 14 white-columned neoclassical buildings, erected around a lagoon, illuminated at night by thousands of lightbulbs; the name White City was soon applied. The buildings were designed to be temporary; only the Memorial Art Palace, constructed downtown as a meeting and lecture center—now housing the ART INSTITUTE—was built to be permanent. Louis SULLIVAN designed the Transportation Building, one of only two principal structures not following established neoclassical design. Sullivan said later that the fair's buildings set American architecture back 25 years; he blamed Daniel Burnham, claiming that the Director of Works sold out to commercial interests. Critics agree that the backward-looking architecture, as espoused by the Parisian ÉCOLE DES BEAUX-ARTS, constrained progress in American art and design; derivative classical and Renaissance styles continued long to be accepted for the nation's public buildings.

A Women's Building was designed by Sophia G. Hayden, the first woman graduate of the architecture school of the Massachusetts Institute of Technology. The exhibits in the building, chosen by Bertha PALMER and her Board of Lady Managers, were geared to demonstrate women's achievements. The Paris-based American Impressionist Mary CASSATT was commissioned to paint a mural depicting "Modern Woman." The huge painting, when completed and shipped to Chicago, was not considered a success; elevated 50 feet and attached beneath the glass roof, the work was not easily viewed from a distance. The mural on the opposite wall, "Primitive Woman," also commissioned from an expatriate American painter, Mary Fairchild McMonnies—and designed to show female servitude, including the carrying of burdens—was considered more successful. Both murals were placed in storage at the end of the fair, and they have never been recovered.

The Electricity Building presented the most wonders to fairgoers, its 120,000 incandescent lamps providing the first public electric lighting. Additional exhibits included Thomas A. Edison's Kinetoscope, a device for viewing motion pictures,

as well as the new "humane" execution device, the electric chair; the HAYMARKET AFFAIR anarchists had recently been hanged. Other buildings displayed achievements in mining, manufacturing, railroading, and agriculture; the *Pioneer*, the small steam engine that made the first railroad run in Chicago in 1848, was displayed in Sullivan's Transportation Building. Also on view were less-than-historically accurate replicas of Columbus's three ships, sailed from Spain the previous year; they would end up being used in a silent movie, *The Coming of Columbus*, in 1910.

In a separate entertainment area, a one-mile strip known as the MIDWAY PLAISANCE, stood the world's first Ferris wheel, invented by downstate native George Washington FERRIS; more than 250 feet in diameter, the wheel shone with 3,000 electric lightbulbs. Nearby, ragtime pianist Scott Joplin played his new music, and escape artist Harry Houdini and boxer Gentleman Jim Corbett exhibited their talents; a living Dahomey Village presented a condescending anthropological exhibit, and North African belly dancers created a sensation among fairgoers. One of the carpenters for the building projects was Elias Disney, father of movie-animator and theme-park-builder Walt Disney, who was born in Chicago in 1901; the Midway Plaisance has been called the world's first amusement park.

Seventy-five-year-old African-American leader Frederick DOUGLASS served as commissioner of the Republic of Haiti pavilion; he was joined at the fair by antilynching spokeswoman Ida B. WELLS, who circulated a pamphlet titled *The Reason Why the Colored American Is Not in the World's Columbian Exposition*. Prepared in part for foreign visitors, the pages protested that black achievement and progress had not been honored at the exposition. In a speech, "The Race Problem in America," Douglass protested also the government's failure to protect blacks from lynching and discrimination. The young poet Paul Laurence DUNBAR read a poem written for the occasion.

Another notable address was delivered at the Memorial Art Palace by University of Wisconsin history professor Frederick Jackson TURNER, setting forth what became known as the TURNER THESIS. Addressing the American Historical Association, Turner delineated the significance of the frontier in American history, adding that the frontier was now closed, that the first chapter in the nation's history had been completed.

At the end of the fair, on October 28, 1893, the mayor of Chicago, Carter Harrison Sr., was killed in the doorway of his home by a disappointed office seeker; his son would later become mayor.

The buildings of the White City, constructed of plasterboard over metal skeletons, began to deteriorate after the fair closed. As a result of the PANIC OF 1893—the effects of which the fair had temporarily masked in Chicago—the national economic depression deepened as winter came on, and the unemployed and homeless moved into the buildings. The following July, a fire destroyed the structures—the "rotting buildings of the play city," Robert HERRICK called them—at the same time that the PULLMAN STRIKE was bringing federal troops into the city.

L. Frank BAUM, writing his THE WONDERFUL WIZARD OF OZ nearby, is said to have created his falsely wondrous Emerald City of Oz from the inspiration of the White City; Arthur W. W. DENSLOW's illustrations bear a resemblance to the fair's buildings. Katherine Lee Bates, author of the words to the song "America the Beautiful," traveling to Colorado in 1893, stopped in Chicago to see the fair; it is believed that the White City inspired the line, "thine alabaster cities gleam."

Edna FERBER's story of the early 1920s, "The Afternoon of a Faun," collected in GIGOLO, presents a character going to Jackson Park on a Sunday afternoon, finding there "a rustic bridge" leading to a "fragrant, golden, green" island; the retreat is the Wooded Island, left over from the days of the world fair, nearly three decades in the past.

World War I

The European conflagration of 1914–18, pitting Germany and Austria-Hungary against France, Britain, and Russia—and the United States after April 1917—the Great War, as it became known, featured brutal, devastating carnage. American entrance into the conflict caused repercussions among politically minded writers, particularly those advocating anarchist or socialist causes; both ideologies opposed what was considered a capitalist conflict. The Selective Service Act, or draft, was passed in May 1917; the Espionage Act, enacted the following month, criminalized speaking against the draft or advocating resistance to the war—acts considered evidence of pro-German sympathies. As a result, anarchist Emma GOLDMAN was jailed and later deported to Russia; labor leader and socialist Eugene V. DEBS was imprisoned as well. The socialist periodicals THE MASSES and INTERNATIONAL SOCIALIST REVIEW were suppressed.

The Ferris wheel at the World's Columbian Exposition of 1893 stood at a height of 26 stories, taller than the tallest building in the world at the time. *(Chicago Historical Society)*

Clarence DARROW supported American entrance into the war, as did THE APPEAL TO REASON, the socialist magazine that had first published Upton SINCLAIR's THE JUNGLE a decade earlier. Carl SANDBURG, who had been writing articles for antiwar socialist journals, as well as publishing antiwar poetry, was caught up in the issue; he reversed his position once the United States entered the conflict, even publishing a jingoistic piece in POETRY magazine in 1917. The response of African-American leadership was equally mixed; spokesman and intellectual W. E. B. Du Bois called for all Americans to close ranks during the conflict, while A. Phillip RANDOLPH, later to found the BROTHERHOOD OF SLEEPING CAR PORTERS, argued in his black-oriented socialist monthly, *Messenger,* that blacks and socialists must both oppose the war. In the last phases of the war, after revolutionary Bolsheviks seized power in Russia and ended that nation's participation in the war—and when its socialist victory seemed threatened by German forces—many critics of the conflict began quietly to support it.

By the time the United States entered the war, poets had already described its horrors, and some had lost their lives. The English poet Rupert BROOKE, who had visited Chicago in 1914, published a group of sonnets in *Poetry* magazine in 1915; they appeared not long after his death had been reported. The American poet Alan Seeger, joining the French Foreign Legion, was killed in 1916, before U.S. entry into the war; his "I Have a Rendezvous with Death" remains well known. Another American, Joyce KILMER, whose "Trees" had appeared in *Poetry* in 1913, was killed in 1918. The playwright Kenneth Sawyer GOODMAN died the same year.

Vachel LINDSAY's well-known 1914 poem, "Abraham Lincoln Walks at Midnight," brought an American viewpoint to the as-yet European Great War; Lindsay invokes the CIVIL WAR president, imagining the American war leader's response to the new conflict. Sandburg's "Shenandoah" poems, published in CORNHUSKERS in 1918—after the United States had joined hostilities—also yoked together the two wars. Fresh in the minds of both Lindsay and Sandburg were images of the earlier strife, the greatest slaughter in American history—the ordeal that had not yet faded from national memory.

Wright, Frank Lloyd
(1867–1959) *architect*

Achieving international fame throughout his long career, Wright first came to prominence in creating what became known as the PRAIRIE SCHOOL OF ARCHITECTURE. Born in Richland Center, Wisconsin, Wright studied briefly at the University of Wisconsin, then arrived in Chicago in 1887 at the age of 19; a year later, he joined the firm of ADLER AND SULLIVAN, working on the interior of the massive AUDITORIUM BUILDING. Starting out on his own in 1893, working on residential structures in the suburb of OAK PARK, Wright became known for his low-lying architecture, including open interiors and continuous spaces—as dictated by the endless horizons of the midwestern PRAIRIE; these buildings arose from the "organic" dictum of Louis SULLIVAN and others, calling for buildings to grow naturally from their sites. In 1906, Wright built the famous Unity Temple, a Unitarian church, in Oak Park, and the suburb became home to more than two dozen of his early buildings; he is remembered also for the 1910 Robie house, built on South Woodlawn Avenue in Chicago, considered the ultimate expression of Prairie Style. A scandal in 1909, involving his leaving his wife and six children for another woman, caused him to move from the Chicago area; five years later, the other woman, along with her own children, was murdered by a deranged servant at Wright's home in Spring Green, Wisconsin. Between the years 1916 and 1922, Wright was involved in his important project in Japan, the Imperial Hotel in Tokyo; he had seen the Japanese pavilion at the WORLD'S COLUMBIAN EXPOSITION of 1893 and begun collecting Japanese prints before first visiting the nation in 1905. The Imperial Hotel withstood the severe earthquake of 1923, the result of his using the floating foundations developed by Chicago architects for their city's swampy soil; the hotel was demolished in the 1960s. Wright subsequently undertook multiple projects in California, Arizona,

Wrigley Field, shown here in 1915, was built the previous year as Weeghman Field; it became home of the Chicago Cubs baseball team in 1916 and was renamed Wrigley Field in 1926. *(Chicago Historical Society)*

Wisconsin, and Pennsylvania; one of his final works was the Solomon R. Guggenheim Museum in New York City, completed in 1959, the year of his death. His *Autobiography* appeared in 1932, then in revised form in 1943; a study of his mentor Louis Sullivan, *Genius and Mobocracy*—excoriating those who failed to appreciate Sullivan's genius—appeared in 1949. Wright died in Phoenix, Arizona, at the age of 91. His oldest son, Frank Lloyd Wright Jr., also an architect, working in California, married the actress Kyrah Markham, formerly Elaine HYMAN, formerly a companion of Theodore DREISER. His daughter, Catherine, was the mother of Hollywood actress Anne Baxter. A popular

novel of 1943, Ayn Rand's *The Fountainhead*, features an architect said to be based on Wright; Gary Cooper played the role in the movie of 1949.

Wright, Richard
(1908–1960) *African-American writer*

Born in Mississippi, Wright moved with his family to Memphis in 1911, then came to Chicago in 1927 at the age of 19. His subsequent employment included post office work, reflected in the novel *Lawd Today!*, a volume covering a 24-hour period in the life of four postal workers on the South Side;

written in the mid-1930s, unpublished until after his death, the novel has often been called his best fiction. In 1933, Wright joined the Chicago John Reed Club, part of a national organization of writers and artists, named for John REED, the American writer who had died a hero in the Soviet Union. A fellow club member was Nelson ALGREN, whose portrait of Wright appears in his novel of 1935, *Somebody in Boots;* the Wright character, named Dill Doak, is presented as serious and articulate, speaking confidently of the welcome changes taking place in Russian Soviet society. In 1937, Wright moved to New York City, where he wrote his best-known work, *Native Son,* published in 1940; set in Chicago's South Side, the novel features a bitter, defeated protagonist, Bigger Thomas. Wright spent the last 13 years of his life in Paris, dying at the age of 52.

Wrigley, William, Jr.
(1861–1932) *businessman*

Born in Philadelphia, Wrigley arrived in Chicago in 1891 and began developing the new concept of chewing gum made from Mexican-imported chicle; he pioneered the use of mass advertising to promote his product. In 1919, he bought control of the CHICAGO CUBS; in 1925, deciding to devote himself to baseball, he turned over the chewing gum business to his son, P. K. Wrigley. His Wrigley Building, a Spanish-influenced, white terra-cotta-clad structure erected in 1921, was the first SKYSCRAPER to be built in the area of MICHIGAN AVENUE and the CHICAGO RIVER; its derivative styling was criticized by architects such as Louis SULLIVAN. Wrigley died in Phoenix, Arizona, at the age of 70.

Wrigley Field

The home of the CHICAGO CUBS was built in 1914 for a Federal League team, the Chicago Whales. The stadium was named Weeghman Park after the Whales' owner Charles Weeghman. Located in a North Side residential area, it was designed by the architect who had previously designed the South Side Comiskey Park, home of the CHICAGO WHITE SOX. In 1915, the Whales merged with the Cubs, who were then playing on the West Side; Weeghman Park became the Cubs venue. William WRIGLEY Jr. took full ownership of the team in 1921; the field was renamed in 1926. The 1980 movie *The Blues Brothers* immortalized the Wrigley Field address, 1060 West Addison Street.

Y

Yeats, William Butler
(1865–1939) *Irish poet and playwright*

Leading figure of the Irish Renaissance, winner of the Nobel Prize in literature in 1923, Yeats is one of the major writers of the 20th century. Harriet MONROE first published his work in POETRY in December 1912, having received it from Ezra POUND; his "The Grey Rock" won the magazine's special prize in 1913—although Monroe's choice, overridden by Pound, had been Vachel LINDSAY's "GENERAL WILLIAM BOOTH ENTERS INTO HEAVEN." Yeats visited Chicago in 1914 at Monroe's invitation, staying as her house guest; he was honored at a banquet held on March 1 at the CLIFF-DWELLERS CLUB. In the course of the evening, he read a few of his poems, as well as praised Lindsay's "General William Booth Enters into Heaven." In 1917, Margaret ANDERSON, newly favored by Pound to receive poems sent from abroad, published a group of Yeats's poems, including "The Wild Swans at Coole," in the June and August issues of LITTLE REVIEW.

Yerkes, Charles T.
(1837–1905) *builder of Chicago's transportation system*

Born in Philadelphia, the son of a Quaker banker, Yerkes served a prison sentence for financial irregularities before coming to Chicago in 1881. Buying control of several railways, he expanded the city's cable-car system and built the elevated Union Loop rail line, developing also an encompassing electric trolley network; he is credited with making Chicago's transit system faster and cheaper than that of any other large American city. In 1892, Yerkes donated funds to the UNIVERSITY OF CHICAGO, establishing the Yerkes Observatory at Williams Bay, Wisconsin; the telescope, completed in 1897, was the largest of its type in the world. His business and financial problems arose when the press began divulging his use of "boodle," or bribery; exposure of his methods and his subsequent political defeat caused him to leave Chicago in 1901. Selling his holdings and moving to New York, then to London, Yerkes became involved in the development of London's Underground subway system, including its conversion from steam to electricity. His estate, after his death, became subject to legal wrangling, and much of his fortune was dissipated.

On the pictorial cover of W. T. STEAD's 1894 exposé of Chicago vice, IF CHRIST CAME TO CHICAGO!, Yerkes is portrayed as a money-changer whom Jesus drives from the temple. The previous year, in THE CLIFF-DWELLERS, Henry B. FULLER created the character Erastus BRAINARD, modeled in part on Yerkes. A more complete recreation is the COWPERWOOD character in DREISER's trilogy—THE FINANCIER, THE TITAN, and THE STOIC. The three novels, extensively researched, delve into details of Yerkes's financial and political manipulations. In a newspaper interview Yerkes once gave, Dreiser found the motto that Cowperwood proclaims throughout the three volumes: "I satisfy myself."

"Yet Gentle Will the Griffin Be" *See* THE CONGO AND OTHER POEMS.

You Know Me Al
Ring Lardner
(1916)

This collection of interconnected stories by Ring LARDNER is cast as a series of letters from a "busher," or minor league baseball player. The stories first ran in the *Saturday Evening Post* in 1914. Jack Keefe is a pitcher who writes misspelled, ungrammatical letters home to a friend, revealing, unconsciously, his stinginess, ignorance, vanity, defensiveness, and general imperception; describing events, telling what others have said to him, he relays meanings that he himself fails to understand. A player of major league promise, Keefe is brought up from the minors to the CHICAGO WHITE SOX; lacking discipline, he is sent back, although he later returns to the majors. He is pursued, meanwhile, by women who appear, as he describes them, to be shallow and calculating; he marries one of them. Relating a particular thought or event, Keefe occasionally adds the comma-less confidence to his friend, "You know me Al."

The vernacular style that Lardner gives to his semiliterate character is traceable to the DIALECT WRITING of his earlier newspaper colleagues, although the lapses from standard English are mild by comparison; the work is accessible to the modern reader in a way that the writing of Finlay Peter DUNNE is not. The correspondence in *You Know Me Al,* is one-sided—Al's responses are inferred by the reader—although in other tales, as in "Some Like Them Cold," collected in HOW TO WRITE SHORT STORIES [WITH SAMPLES], Lardner presents both sides of the exchange.

Published two years after the stories' magazine appearance, the volume brought Lardner immediate fame; beginning in 1923, he wrote the text for a comic strip version. In 1925, critical praise came from an unexpected source; Virginia Woolf, claiming a complete lack of knowledge of baseball, singled out Lardner's baseball stories for commendation. Citing his technique of letting Keefe innocently draw his own foolish portrait, Woolf declared that Lardner "writes the best prose that has come our way."

Z

Ziegfeld, Florenz, Jr.
(1869–1932) *theatrical impresario*

Born in Chicago, the son of a German immigrant, Ziegfeld grew up in an environment of classical music; his father was founder of the Chicago Musical College, a prominent institution located in the FINE ARTS BUILDING. Ziegfeld Sr., appointed director of musical events for the WORLD'S COLUMBIAN EXPOSITION of 1893, sent his son to Europe to hire classical musicians; the son returned instead with VAUDEVILLE and circus acts. His father, meanwhile, having converted an armory building on the North Side into a theater, naming it the Trocadero, Florenz Jr. took advantage of the new venue; he introduced a performer calling himself Sandow, the European strong man, at the Trocadero in August 1893. Eugen Sandow would become recognized as the originator of modern bodybuilding and physical culture. After touring with Sandow, Ziegfeld turned to producing stage shows in New York, instituting the *Ziegfeld Follies* in 1907. The *Follies* were variety presentations, featuring dancers, musicians, and comedians; an early routine was a parody of soprano Mary GARDEN's Dance of the Seven Veils in Richard Strauss's opera *Salomé*. For the *Follies of 1910*, Ziegfeld brought in the African-American singer and comedian, Bert WILLIAMS, using a black entertainer for the first time in an otherwise all-white show. In the *Follies of 1922*, he presented a skit, "The Bull Pen," written by Ring LARDNER, the former Chicagoan who had moved to New York in the hopes of writing for the theater.

In 1927, Ziegfeld produced the musical version of Edna FERBER's novel SHOW BOAT, bringing together composer Jerome Kern, who had earlier written music for work by George ADE, and lyricist Oscar Hammerstein II; included in the production was a scene set at the world's fair, as well as another at a theater called the Trocadero. The *Show Boat* production has been called the highpoint of Ziegfeld's career. Losing a fortune in the stock market crash of 1929, the impresario staged one last *Follies* show in 1931 and a revival of *Show Boat* in 1932; the latter brought African-American actor-singer Paul Robeson to the cast. Ziegfeld died not long afterward at the age of 63.

Zola, Émile
(1840–1902) *French novelist, polemicist*

Founder of the school of NATURALISM, Zola first gained fame in 1877 with *L'Assommoir*, or *The Drunkard*, a study of alcoholism, set in the slums of Paris. Another admired work is the 1885 *Germinal*, the tale of a coal mine strike. Zola's theories of naturalism in fiction proclaimed that the novelist must be a scientific observer, watching his characters as they follow fates already determined by heredity and environment. In 1898, Zola took up a political cause, championing Captain Alfred Dreyfus, falsely accused of treason in the era's climate of anti-Semitism; Dreyfus had been court-martialed in 1894 and sentenced to life in solitary confinement at Devil's Island, the penal colony off the coast of

French Guiana. In his open letter *J'accuse*, Zola accused the military court of suppressing evidence exonerating Dreyfus—and was himself prosecuted for libel, after which he fled for a year to England. Dreyfus was later pardoned and the verdict against him annulled. In 1902, Zola died accidentally from carbon monoxide poisoning, caused by a blocked stove chimney. The American novelist Frank NORRIS, first reading Zola at the University of California in the 1890s, strove for the naturalistic mode in his own fiction, including his novels *McTeague, The Octopus,* and *THE PIT.* In Edna FERBER's 1917 novel *FANNY HERSELF,* the protagonist excitedly reads Zola's 1883 novel *The Ladies' Paradise,* describing the coming of the modern department store to late 19th-century Paris.

Zukor, Adolph
(1873–1976) *movie executive*

Born in Hungary, Zukor came to New York City at the age of 16 and established a fur business in Chicago in 1892. He bought his first NICKELODEON, or early movie venue, in the city in 1903; two years later, he and Marcus Loew began purchasing theaters that would lead to a chain of motion-picture showcases. Acting on the increasing demand for movies, Zukor initiated the Famous Players Film Company in 1912; the company, following a series of mergers, became Paramount Pictures, one of the major Hollywood studios. In 1925, the BALABAN AND KATZ theater chain merged with Paramount; a decade later, Barney BALABAN succeeded Zukor as head of Paramount Pictures. Publishing his autobiography, *The Public Is Never Wrong,* in 1953, Zukor lived to the age of 103.

Zury: The Meanest Man in Spring County
Joseph Kirkland
(1887)

KIRKLAND's novel has been called the first realistic portrait of an American farmer, although it ul-

timately moves from frontier REALISM into the sentimentality of LOCAL COLOR. Unlike the depictions of rural midwestern life in Edward EGGLESTON's *THE HOOSIER SCHOOLMASTER* and E. W. HOWE's *THE STORY OF A COUNTRY TOWN,* *Zury* gives a strictly agricultural perspective, showing the toil and hardship in creating and maintaining a frontier farm; the setting is central Illinois in the early years of the 19th century. In its subject matter the novel anticipated—and influenced—the work of Hamlin GARLAND. Yet while Garland emphasized the economic issues of the day, portraying his farmers as defeated not only by the land but by landowning economic policies, Kirkland focused on the harshness of the land itself; his protagonist, toiling endlessly, ultimately triumphs.

Zury Prouder comes as a boy to central Illinois, where his father received a tract of land for service in the WAR OF 1812. His parents—for no clearly specified reason—have named him Usury, calling him Zury for short. He soon surpasses his father in hard work and agricultural know-how, rising to prosperity and local prominence. Yet he is "the meanest man" in the county, building his success not only through hard labor, but also through shrewdness and tight-fistedness; he continues, even after achieving prosperity, to practice parsimony and hard bargaining.

Like Eggleston before him, Kirkland makes use of DIALECT WRITING—so extreme, in this case, that the work becomes difficult for modern readers. The novel can ultimately be placed in the local-color category, although the traditionally picturesque characters—except for the New England schoolteacher—have been pre-empted by characters who are crude and blunt, often narrow-minded, possessing limited understanding. Yet a sentimentality emerges after the harsh portrait of farm life is completed; the widowed schoolteacher comes to look kindly on the twice-widowed Zury Prouder, and Zury himself lapses into kindness and generosity.

MAJOR AUTHORS AND WORKS DISCUSSED

MAJOR AUTHORS DISCUSSED

Addams, Jane
Austin, Mary
Ade, George
Anderson, Sherwood
Baum, L. Frank
Cather, Willa
Dreiser, Theodore
Field, Eugene
Ferber, Edna
Fuller, Henry B.
Garland, Hamlin
Hecht, Ben
Herrick, Robert
Lardner, Ring
Lindsay, Vachel
Masters, Edgar Lee
Moody, William Vaughn
Norris, Frank
Sandburg, Carl
Sinclair, Upton
Veblen, Thorstein

MAJOR WORKS DISCUSSED

Note: Works in **boldface** are given a complete synopsis in the text.

Addams, Jane
    Democracy and Social Ethics (1902)
    The Spirit of Youth and the City Streets (1909)

Ade, George
    "Effie Whittlesey" (1886)
    "Fables in Slang" (1897–1920)

    Peggy from Paris (1903)
    Pink Marsh: A Story of the Streets and of the Town (1897)
    The Sho-Gun (1904)
    "Stories of the Streets and of the Town" (1893–1900)
    The Sultan of Sulu (1902)

Anderson, Sherwood
    Dark Laughter (1925)
    Death in the Woods (1933)
    Horses and Men (1923)
    Many Marriages (1923)
    Marching Men (1917)
    Mid-American Chants (1918)
    A New Testament (1927)
    Poor White (1920)
    Sherwood Anderson's Notebook (1926)
    A Story Teller's Story (1924)
    Tar: A Midwest Childhood (1926)
    The Triumph of the Egg (1921)
    Windy McPherson's Son (1916)
    Winesburg, Ohio (1919)

Austin, Mary
    A Woman of Genius (1912)

Baum, L. Frank
    The Wonderful Wizard of Oz (1900)

Cather, Willa
    The Professor's House (1925)
    The Song of the Lark (1915)

Dreiser, Theodore
    An American Tragedy (1925)

The Bulwark (1946)
The Financier (1912)
The "Genius" (1915)
Jennie Gerhardt (1911)
Sister Carrie (1900)
The Stoic (1947)
The Titan (1914)

Ferber, Edna
Buttered Side Down (1912)
Cheerful by Request (1918)
Dawn O'Hara: The Girl Who Laughed (1911)
Emma McChesney & Company (1915)
Fanny Herself (1917)
Gigolo (1922)
Show Boat (1926)
So Big (1924)

Field, Eugene
"Little Boy Blue" (1888)

Fuller, Henry B.
Bertram Cope's Year (1919)
The Cliff-Dwellers (1893)
Under the Skylights (1901)
With the Procession (1895)

Garland, Hamlin
Crumbling Idols (1894)
A Daughter of the Middle Border (1921)
Main-Travelled Roads (1891)
Rose of Dutcher's Coolly (1895)
A Son of the Middle Border (1917)

Hecht, Ben
Erik Dom (1921)
Fantazius Mallare (1922)
The Front Page (1928)
1001 Afternoons in Chicago (1922)

Herrick, Robert
The Gospel of Freedom (1898)
Memoirs of an American Citizen (1905)
The Web of Life (1900)

Lardner, Ring
Gullible's Travels, Etc. (1917)
How to Write Short Stories [With Samples] (1924)

The Love Nest and Other Stories (1926)
You Know Me Al (1916)

Lindsay, Vachel
The Chinese Nightingale and Other Poems (1917)
The Congo and Other Poems (1914)
"The Eagle That Is Forgotten" (1911)
"General William Booth Enters into Heaven" (1913)
Johnny Appleseed and Other Poems (1928)

Masters, Edgar Lee
The Blood of the Prophets (1905)
Children of the Market Place (1922)
Mitch Miller (1920)
The New Spoon River (1924)
The New Star Chamber and Other Essays (1904)
Skeeters Kirby (1923)
Spoon River Anthology (1915)

Moody, William Vaughn
The Great Divide (1906)
"Ode in a Time of Hesitation" (1900)
"On a Soldier Fallen in the Philippines" (1901)

Norris, Frank
The Pit (1903)

Sandburg, Carl
Abraham Lincoln: The Prairie Years (1926)
The American Songbag (1927)
Chicago Poems (1916)
The Chicago Race Riots, July 1919 (1920)
Cornhuskers (1918)
Good Morning, America (1928)
Slabs of the Sunburnt West (1922)
Smoke and Steel (1920)

Sinclair, Upton
The Jungle (1906)

Veblen, Thorstein
The Theory of the Leisure Class: An Economic Study of the Evolution of Institutions (1899)

CHRONOLOGY

1673
French explorers Father Jacques Marquette and Louis Joliet, traveling northward in the Mississippi River system, carry their canoes for several miles across the low continental divide to the Chicago River, flowing into Lake Michigan. They envision a canal covering this portage route, connecting the Great Lakes and the Gulf of Mexico.

1682
Rene-Robert Cavelier, sieur de La Salle, traverses the same portage, having proclaimed the site at the mouth of the river as "the gate of empire."

1745
Jean Baptiste Pointe du Sable is born in Haiti.

1763
By the Treaty of Paris, France cedes North America east of the Mississippi to Britain.

John Kinzie is born in Quebec.

1767
Sauk warrior Black Hawk is born near what is now Rock Island, Illinois.

1784
Jean Baptiste Pointe du Sable builds a fur-trading post near the mouth of the Chicago River, becoming Chicago's first permanent non-Indian settler; he will leave in 1800.

1803
The United States completes the Louisiana Purchase, gaining control of the Mississippi River and increasing the importance of the Great Lakes, only a brief portage away from the river's tributaries.

Fort Dearborn is erected on the south bank of the Chicago River for the purpose of protecting the new land acquisition.

1804
John Kinzie arrives in Chicago from St. Joseph, Michigan.

1806
Juliette Kinzie is born in Middletown, Connecticut, September 11.

1809
Abraham Lincoln is born in Hardin County, Kentucky, February 12.

Cyrus McCormick is born in Rockbridge County, Virginia, February 15.

1812
The War of 1812 is declared, June 18.

On August 15, residents of Fort Dearborn, advised to evacuate and seek safety eastward, are attacked and killed a mile south of the fort by the Potawatomi allies of the British during the War of 1812. The area is abandoned by settlers.

1813
Stephen A. Douglas is born in Brandon, Vermont, April 23.

1815
Migration into the potential farmlands of Illinois accelerates at the end of the War of 1812. Between

1810 and 1850, the state's population grows from 12,000 to 850,000.

1816

Fort Dearborn is rebuilt, settlers return to the area, and trading activity resumes.

1818

Illinois becomes the nation's 21st state on December 3.

Jean Baptiste Pointe du Sable dies in St. Charles, Missouri.

1819

Allan Pinkerton is born in Glasgow, Scotland, August 25.

1822

Ulysses S. Grant is born in Point Pleasant, Ohio, April 27.

1825

On October 26, the Erie Canal in New York State opens, connecting Lake Erie to the Hudson River and the port of New York; the Great Lakes are now accessible to the Atlantic Ocean.

1826

Potter Palmer is born in Albany County, New York, May 20.

1828

John Kinzie, refugee from the Fort Dearborn massacre, dies in Chicago, January 6.

1830

A settlement of traders and adventurers, numbering about 50, lives at Wolf Point on the Chicago River.

On July 15, Sauk and Fox Indians cede lands in southern Wisconsin and northern Illinois, settling mainly in Iowa.

1831

George M. Pullman is born in Brocton, New York, March 3.

1832

On April 5, Sauk warrior Black Hawk leads Sauk and Fox Indians across the Mississippi River from Iowa in an attempt to regain Illinois lands; he is defeated at Bad Axe River, Wisconsin, August 2.

Philip D. Armour is born in Stockbridge, New York, May 16.

William Le Baron Jenney is born in Fairhaven, Massachusetts, September 25.

1833

Chicago, named from the Potawatomi word for wild onion, having grown to a population of 350, incorporates as a village, August 5.

Potawatomi, Chippewa, and Ottawa tribes, gathering in Chicago, sign away rights to land east of the Mississippi River, September 26–27.

Juliette Kinzie arrives in Chicago from Fort Winnebago, Wisconsin.

1834

Government engineers, cutting through a sandbar and deepening the channel, complete a harbor to bring large ships into the Chicago River.

Marshall Field is born in Conway, Massachusetts, August 18.

1836

On July 4, work begins on the Illinois and Michigan Canal, undertaken to connect the Great Lakes and the Mississippi River.

Lake Michigan lakefront is declared to remain public ground, "forever open, clear and free."

1837

The city of Chicago, its population more than 4,000, officially incorporates on March 4.

John Deere makes his first steel plow.

Dwight L. Moody is born in East Northfield, Massachusetts, February 7.

Mary Harris "Mother" Jones is born in County Cork, Ireland, July.

Charles T. Yerkes is born in Philadelphia, June 25.

Edward Eggleston is born in Vevay, Indiana, on December 10.

1838

Black Hawk, Sauk warrior, dies in Iowa, October 3.

1839

Gustavus F. Swift is born near Sandwich, Massachusetts, June 24.

Frances E. Willard is born in Churchville, New York, September 28.

1842

Allan Pinkerton arrives in West Dundee, outside of Chicago, to open a cooper's, or barrel-maker's, shop, which becomes a station on the Underground Railroad.

1843

Francis Fisher Browne is born in South Halifax, Vermont, December 1.

1844

Montgomery Ward is born in Chatham, New Jersey, February 17.

Dankmar Adler is born in Saxe-Weimar, Germany, July 3.

1846

Daniel H. Burnham is born in Henderson, New York, September 4.

1847

The *Chicago Tribune* begins publication, initially supporting the anti-immigration, anti-Roman Catholic "Know Nothing" movement June.

Cyrus McCormick moves his reaper manufacturing operation from Virginia to Chicago, forming the company that will revolutionize farming; it is the city's first great industrial firm.

Henry Demarest Lloyd is born in New York City, May 1.

The first African-American church, the Quinn Chapel A. M. E. Church, is organized in Chicago on July 22.

The first Jewish congregation, K. A. M., is established in Chicago, November 3.

John Peter Altgeld is born in Hesse, Germany, December 30.

Mary Hartwell Catherwood is born in Luray, Ohio, December 16.

1848

The first telegraph line reaches Chicago, instrumental in establishing the city's prominence in the world's grain market (January).

The Chicago Board of Trade opens, the world's first options and futures exchange, trading principally in grain and livestock (March).

The Illinois-Michigan Canal opens on April 16, making Chicago the inland port between the Atlantic Ocean and the Gulf of Mexico; the canal will soon be superseded in importance by the railroads.

On November 20, the first railroad, the Galena and Chicago Union Railroad, makes a 10-mile run between Chicago and the Des Plaines River, transporting wheat into the city.

The first steam-powered grain elevator is built in Chicago, accelerating the business of grain marketing.

1850

The city's population reaches 30,000, 3 percent of the state total; the region is still overwhelmingly agrarian, its population centers clustering in small towns and villages.

The Chicago City Council announces that police will not enforce the new fugitive slave law, requiring the return of escaped slaves, passed that year in Congress.

Allan Pinkerton founds the Pinkerton National Detective Agency.

John Wellborn Root is born in Lumpkin, Georgia, January 10.

Albert G. Spalding is born in Byron, Illinois, September 2.

Eugene Field is born in St. Louis, Missouri, September 2.

1852

Potter Palmer arrives in Chicago from Lockport, New York, and opens a dry-goods store, later to become Marshall Field's.

1853

Edgar Watson Howe is born in Wabash County, Indiana, May 3.

1854

On May 30, the Kansas-Nebraska Act is passed, leading to the organization of the antislavery Republican Party.

Joseph Medill arrives in Chicago from Cleveland; the next year he will buy into the *Chicago Tribune*.

1855

Northwestern University, founded by Methodists, enrolls its first students in the new suburb of Evanston, north of the city.

Eugene V. Debs is born in Terre Haute, Indiana, Nov. 5.

1856

Marshall Field arrives in Chicago from Pittsfield, Massachusetts.

Rand McNally and Company is founded to print railroad tickets and schedules.

Daniel Hale Williams is born in Hollidaysburg, Pennsylvania, January 18.

Louis Sullivan is born in Boston, September 3.

William Rainey Harper is born in New Concord, Ohio, July 26.

L. Frank Baum is born in Chittenango, New York, May 15.

Juliette Kinzie publishes *Wau-Bun: The "Early Day" in the North-West.*

1857

The first of several McVickers Theaters is built on Madison Street.

Clarence Darrow is born in Kinsman, Ohio, April 18.

Thorstein Veblen is born in Manitowoc County, Wisconsin, July 30.

Henry Blake Fuller is born in Chicago, January 9.

1858

Abraham Lincoln, accepting the Republican nomination for the U.S. Senate, makes his "house divided" speech in Springfield, Illinois, June 16.

Between August 21 and October 15, Lincoln and Stephen A. Douglas engage in a series of debates across the state, bringing Lincoln to national prominence.

Theodore Roosevelt is born in New York City, October 27.

Paul Dresser is born in Terre Haute, Indiana, as Johann Paul Dreiser, April 22.

1859

George M. Pullman moves to Chicago from Albion, New York.

Charles A. Comiskey is born in Chicago, August 15.

John Dewey is born in Burlington, Vermont, October 20.

Samuel Insull is born in London, November 11.

1860

Chicago becomes the center of the largest railroad network in the world.

Abraham Lincoln is nominated for president by the Republican Party at Chicago's first national political convention on May 16; Lincoln wins the presidential election over Stephen A. Douglas and two other candidates on November 6.

William Jennings Bryan is born in Salem, Illinois, March 19.

Lorado Taft is born in Elmwood, Illinois, April 29.

Jane Addams is born in Cedarville, Illinois, September 6.

Hamlin Garland is born near West Salem, Wisconsin, September 14.

Harriet Monroe is born in Chicago, December 23.

1861

In February, Allan Pinkerton foils a plot to assassinate the newly elected Pesident Lincoln.

Fort Sumter, a federal military post in South Carolina, is attacked by Confederate forces on April 12, initiating the Civil War.

Stephen A. Douglas dies in Chicago, June 3.

William Wrigley Jr. is born in Philadelphia, September 30.

Frederick Jackson Turner is born in Portage, Wisconsin, November 14.

Dankmar Adler arrives in Chicago from Detroit.

1862

John Wilkes Booth receives acclaim for his performance in Shakespeare's *Richard III* at the McVicker's Theatre in Chicago (January).

On May 20, the Homestead Act is signed into law by President Lincoln, fostering westward expansion, accounting for 10 percent of U.S. land's being claimed and settled.

Ida B. Wells is born in Holly Springs, Mississippi, July 16.

President Lincoln announces the Emancipation Proclamation on September 22 to take effect the following January 1.

William "Billy" Sunday is born in Ames, Iowa, November 19.

Julius Rosenwald is born in Springfield, Illinois, August 12.

Carrie Jacobs Bond is born in Janesville, Wisconsin, August 11.

1863

On November 19, Abraham Lincoln delivers the Gettysburg Address on the battlefield at Gettysburg, Pennsylvania, dedicating a national cemetery.

1864

R. R. Donnelley arrives in Chicago from Hamilton, Ontario.

William Nicholas Selig, pioneering filmmaker, is born in Chicago, March 14.

1865

On April 9, Confederate general Robert E. Lee surrenders to Union general Ulysses S. Grant at Appomattox Courthouse, Virginia, ending the Civil War.

President Abraham Lincoln is assassinated five days after the end of the war, at a theater in Washington, D.C., on April 14.

Lincoln's funeral train arrives in Chicago (May 1). Mourners pour into the city, viewing the body lying in state at the Court House; after a day and a half, the train continues to Springfield, the final resting place for the 16th president.

Montgomery Ward arrives in Chicago from St. Joseph, Michigan.

The Union Stock Yard and Transit Company opens on December 25, created by the railroads to bring live animals into the city and carry out meat products.

1866

First post of the Grand Army of the Republic, Civil War veterans' organization, is founded in Decatur, Illinois, April 6.

George Ade is born in Kentland, Indiana, February 9.

1867

The Chicago Water Tower and Pumping Station, one of the few structures that will survive the fire, is erected to distribute lake water to the city.

George M. Pullman establishes the Pullman Palace Car Company.

Frank Lloyd Wright is born in Richland Center, Wisconsin, June 8.

Peter Finley Dunne is born in Chicago, July 10.

Mary Harris Jones, later "Mother" Jones, moves to Chicago, establishing a dressmaking shop.

1868

Civil War hero General Ulysses S. Grant is nominated for president by the Republican Party in Chicago on May 21, winning the November election.

Marshall Field and Levi Leiter open their emporium on State Street on October 12.

Robert S. Abbott is born on St. Simon's Island, Georgia, November 24.

Robert Herrick is born in Cambridge, Massachusetts, April 26.

Edgar Lee Masters is born in Garnett, Kansas, August 23.

Mary Austin is born in Carlinville, Illinois, September 9.

1869

On May 10, the Union Pacific Railroad, its eastern terminus in Chicago, meets the Central Pacific Railroad in Utah as the "golden spike" is driven.

The first planned "railroad suburb" of Riverdale, Illinois, is designed by Frederick Law Olmsted and William Le Baron Jenney.

The Prohibition Party is founded in Chicago, September 1.

Florenz Ziegfeld Jr. is born in Chicago, March 15.

Howard Van Doren Shaw is born in Chicago, May 7.

William Vaughn Moody is born in Spencer, Indiana, July 8.

1870

The city population grows to 300,000; half of this population is foreign-born. In addition to railroads and meatpacking, the city is becoming a major manufacturing center, due to its access to lumber, coal, and iron ore.

Juliette Kinzie dies in Chicago, September 15.

Frank Norris is born in Chicago, March 5.

1871

The Great Fire, covering more than 2,000 acres, destroys the city's commercial district and leaves a third of the population homeless, October 8–10.

Oscar DePriest is born in Florence, Alabama, March 9.

Theodore Dreiser is born in Terre Haute, Indiana, August 27.

Edward Eggleston publishes *The Hoosier Schoolmaster.*

1872

Montgomery Ward starts the world's first general mail-order business, promising farmers to save money by eliminating the middleman.

John Wellborn Root arrives in Chicago from New York City.

E. P. Roe publishes *Barriers Burned Away.*

1873

The banking house of Jay Cooke and Company fails on September 18, leading to the Panic of 1873, the severest depression up to that time in American history; the event figures in Theodore Dreiser's *The Financier.*

The rebuilt Palmer House hotel opens in January, guaranteed to be fireproof.

Louis Sullivan arrives in Chicago from Philadelphia.

The architectural firm of Burnham and Root is established.

The Comstock Act is passed, enabling the federal government to prosecute disseminators of material considered obscene. The New York Society for the Suppression of Vice, established by Anthony Comstock the same year, will cause the suppression of Theodore Dreiser's *The Genius* and the conviction of Margaret Anderson for publishing *Ulysses.*

Willa Cather is born near Winchester, Virginia, December 7.

1874

The Woman's Christian Temperance Union, instrumental in the enactment of Prohibition, is established in Cleveland (November).

James L. Kraft is born in Fort Erie, Ontario, Canada, December 11.

Mary Garden is born in Aberdeen, Scotland, February 20.

Tennessee Mitchell is born in Jackson, Michigan, April 18.

Zona Gale is born in Portage, Wisconsin, August 26.

1875

The *Chicago Daily News* is founded on December 25, soon to become a major newspaper featuring legendary writers.

Philip D. Armour and Gustavus F. Swift, both originally from East Coast farms, arrive in Chicago to begin their meatpacking empires.

John Peter Altgeld moves to Chicago from Savannah, Missouri.

Edgar Rice Burroughs is born in Chicago, February 23.

1876

The Working-Man's Party is established in Chicago, combining unionism and political radicalism; it will become the Socialist Labor Party.

Albert G. Spalding opens a sporting goods store in the Loop, soon to expand into manufacturing.

Susan Glaspell is born in Davenport, Iowa, July 1.

Sherwood Anderson is born in Camden, Ohio, September 13.

1877

The Great Strike, involving rioting in Chicago and other cities, marks the beginning of labor violence in the United States (June).

The Newberry Library, a private facility holding important scholarly collections, is established.

1878

Carl Sandburg is born in Galesburg, Illinois, January 6.

Upton Sinclair is born in Baltimore, September 20.

1879

John D. Hertz is born in what will become Czechoslovakia, April 10.

The Salvation Army arrives from England, introduced first in Philadelphia.

Frances Willard, living in Evanston, Illinois, becomes president of the Woman's Christian Temperance Union.

Vachel Lindsay is born in Springfield, Illinois, November 10.

1880

Chicago's population is now half a million, making it the third-largest city in the country.

Robert Rutherford McCormick is born in Chicago, July 30.

The first issue of the *Dial* appears, soon to become the nation's foremost literary review (May).

1881

President James A. Garfield is shot and wounded on July 2, dying several months later, September 19. The architectural firm of Adler and Sullivan is founded (May).

In June, residents begin moving into Pullman, south of the city limits, the country's first planned industrial town.

Marshall Field buys out his partner, Levi L. Leiter, establishing the business in his own name. By the end of the century, Marshall Field's is the largest retail store in the world.

Charles T. Yerkes moves to Chicago from Philadelphia.

Louella Parsons is born in Freeport, Illinois, August 6.

1882

The Chicago Academy of Design changes its name to the Art Institute of Chicago.

1883

Anarchist Johann Most visits Chicago, advocating revolutionary violence and the use of dynamite.

On November 18, railroad officials meeting in Chicago establish a national time zone system.

Eugene Field begins his "Sharps and Flats" column for the morning edition of the *Chicago Daily News*, August 31.

Jane Heap is born in Topeka, Kansas, November 1.

Alfred Kreymborg is born in New York City, December 10.

Edgar Watson Howe publishes *The Story of a Country Town*.

1884

Toynbee Hall, pioneering London settlement house, is founded in the slums of the city's East End. Jane Addams and Ellen Gates Starr, visiting the establishment, are inspired to found Hull-House in Chicago.

Cyrus McCormick dies in Chicago, May 13.

Allan Pinkerton dies in Chicago, July 1.

Oscar Micheaux is born near Metropolis, Illinois, January 2.

Lucy Parsons publishes "To Tramps" in the October 4 *Alarm*, later distributed as a leaflet.

John Peter Altgeld publishes *Our Penal Machinery and Its Victims*.

1885

Construction is completed on the Home Insurance Building, the original skyscraper, the world's first structure to use a metal frame.

The Chicago Board of Trade Building is completed; dominating the financial district, it will be the setting of Frank Norris's *The Pit*.

The Studebaker Building, soon to become the Fine Arts Building, is built on South Michigan Avenue.

Ring Lardner is born in Niles, Michigan, March 6.

Edna Ferber is born in Kalamazoo, Michigan, August 15.

1886

Charles H. Kerr and Company is founded, later to publish the *International Socialist Review*.

On May 4, the Haymarket Affair brings anarchism and bomb throwing to the nation's consciousness.

Richard W. Sears begins a mail-order watch company in Minnesota.

Margaret Anderson is born in Indianapolis, November 24.

1887

On November 8, federal troops arrive at the outpost that will become Fort Sheridan, north of the city, established to counteract perceived civil threats.

Albert Parsons, August Spies, and two other men are hanged on November 11 in the aftermath of the Haymarket Affair.

Augustus Saint-Gaudens' "Standing Lincoln" is unveiled in Lincoln Park, October 23.

Peter Finley Dunne becomes the country's first full-time sports columnist, writing for the *Chicago Daily News*.

Floyd Dell is born in Barry, Illinois, June 28.

Frank Lloyd Wright arrives in Chicago from Madison, Wisconsin.

Clarence Darrow arrives in Chicago from Ashtabula, Ohio.

Theodore Dreiser arrives in Chicago from Warsaw, Indiana.

Joseph Kirkland publishes *Zury: The Meanest Man in Spring County*.

1888

Fenton Johnson is born in Chicago, May 7.

1889

Jane Addams and Ellen Gates Starr open Hull-House on September 18, seeking to benefit the city's disadvantaged.

Adler and Sullivan's Auditorium Building is officially opened by President Benjamin Harrison, December 9.

1890

Chicago becomes the nation's second-largest city, approaching a population of one and a half million; at least half the population is foreign-born.

On October 16, Montgomery Ward files the first of a series of lawsuits to clear the lakefront of all structures.

Reginald De Koven's operetta *Robin Hood,* featuring the wedding favorite "Oh Promise Me," premieres in Chicago, June 9.

George Ade arrives in Chicago from Indiana (June).

1891

Daniel Hale Williams is among the founders of the African-American Provident Hospital.

William Wrigley Jr. arrives in Chicago from Philadelphia.

John Wellborn Root dies in Chicago, January 15.

The Monadnock Building, the world's tallest wall-bearing building, is completed.

The massive landscaping and construction project for the World's Columbian Exposition begins. Elias Disney, father of Walt Disney, is one of the thousands of workers.

Rabbi Emil G. Hirsch edits the first issue of *Reform Advocate,* published on February 1.

Florence Kelley, fleeing her husband in New York City, arrives with her children at Hull-House (December).

L. Frank Baum arrives in Chicago from Aberdeen, South Dakota.

Theodore Thomas conducts the first concert by the Chicago Symphony Orchestra in the Auditorium Theater, October 16.

Hamlin Garland publishes *Main-Travelled Roads.*

1892

Elevated rapid-transit service begins, using small steam engines, running between the south Loop and Thirty-ninth Street.

Work begins on the Chicago Sanitary and Ship Canal, the greatest earth-moving project in urban history, the first step in the reversal of the flow of the Chicago River, September 3.

The University of Chicago opens on October 1; its first president, William Rainey Harper, spending Rockefeller money, has brought in a distinguished faculty.

Harriet Monroe's "The Columbian Ode" is recited at dedication ceremonies on October 21 for the upcoming world's fair; the date is believed to be the exact 400th anniversary of Columbus's landing in the New World.

The Masonic Temple Building, 21 stories, designed by Burnham and Root, becomes the world's tallest building.

Samuel Insull moves to Chicago as president of the Chicago Edison Company.

Maxwell Bodenheim is born in Hermanville, Mississippi, May 26.

Edgar Lee Masters arrives in Chicago from Lewistown, Illinois, July 21.

1893

Severe economic depression begins, lasting four years; it is counteracted temporarily in Chicago by the world's fair.

World's Columbian Exposition commemorates Columbus's arrival in the New World, May 1–October 30.

A permanent building connected with the exposition, the Memorial Art Palace, is opened in May on the lakefront downtown, to become the Art Institute of Chicago.

Ferris Wheel takes its first riders at the world's fair, June 11.

Governor John Peter Altgeld pardons the remaining Haymarket prisoners on June 26, sealing his own political fate.

On July 12, Frederick Jackson Turner delivers his address, "The Significance of the Frontier in American History," to be known as the Turner thesis.

Daniel Hale Williams performs the first open-heart surgery at Provident Hospital on July 22.

Florenz Ziegfeld Jr. begins his theatrical career, presenting European strongman Eugen Sandow at the Trocadero Theater, August 1.

Ida B. Wells arrives in Chicago from New York.

On August 25, Frederick Douglass speaks on "The Race Problem in America" at the World's Columbian Exposition, followed by a recitation by Paul Laurence Dunbar.

The Armour Institute opens in September, later to become the Illinois Institute of Technology.

Mayor Carter Harrison is assassinated, October 28.

Sears, Roebuck and Company is established.

The publishing firm of Stone and Kimball is founded.

Finley Peter Dunne writes his first "Mr. Dooley" column for the *Chicago Evening Post*, October 7.

George Ade writes his first "Stories of the Streets and Town" column, illustrated by William T. McCutcheon, for the November 20 *Chicago Record*.

Henry Blake Fuller publishes *The Cliff-Dwellers*.

1894

Three thousand employees of the Pullman Palace Car Company go on strike, May 11.

President Grover Cleveland sends federal troops from Fort Sheridan to break up the Pullman strike. The union concedes defeat six days later, July 3.

A fire destroys the remaining abandoned structures of the World's Columbian Exposition, July 5.

Joseph Kirkland dies in Chicago.

The first issue of *The Chap-Book* is published by Stone and Kimball, May 15.

Ben Hecht is born in New York City, February 28.

W. T. Stead publishes *If Christ Came to Chicago!*

Henry Demarest Lloyd publishes *Wealth Against Commonwealth*.

Hamlin Garland publishes *Crumbling Idols*.

1895

The Martyrs' Monument to the Haymarket Affair anarchists is dedicated at Waldheim Cemetery, outside of Chicago.

Louis Sullivan severs his partnership with Dankmar Adler, hastening the decline of his career.

The Little Room literary society informally begins.

In March, Willa Cather comes to Chicago for the first time, seeing the touring Metropolitan Opera performances.

Paul Muni is born in Bamberg, Austria, September 22.

Eugene Field dies in Chicago, November 4.

Henry Blake Fuller publishes *With the Procession*.

Hamlin Garland publishes *Rose of Dutcher's Coolly*.

1896

William Jennings Bryan delivers his "Cross of Gold" speech at the Democratic National Convention in Chicago on July 9, winning him the presidential nomination.

The socialist periodical *The Appeal to Reason* is founded in Kansas City; eight years later it will send Upton Sinclair to Chicago to study the abuses of the meatpacking industry.

The inauguration of rural free delivery by the U.S. Post Office on October 1 boosts the catalogue businesses of the Montgomery Ward and Sears, Roebuck companies.

John Dewey establishes the Laboratory School at the University of Chicago, aiming to follow progressive educational principles (May).

William N. Selig opens his Selig Polyscope Company.

Sherwood Anderson moves to Chicago for the first time from Clyde, Ohio.

George Ade publishes *Artie: A Story of the Streets and the Town*.

1897

George M. Pullman dies in Chicago, October 19.

George Ade publishes *Pink Marsh: A Story of the Streets and the Town*.

Mary Hartwell Catherwood publishes *The Spirit of an Illinois Town*.

L. Frank Baum publishes *Mother Goose in Prose*, illustrated by Maxfield Parrish.

1898

The battleship *Maine* is blown up in Havana harbor on February 15, leading to the Spanish-American War, fought between April–August.

Sherwood Anderson and Carl Sandburg join Ohio and Illinois militias, respectively, to serve in the Spanish-American War.

Joseph Leiter fails in an attempt to corner the wheat market on the Chicago Board of Trade, providing the basic episode for Frank Norris's *The Pit*.

Frances E. Willard dies in New York City, February 17.

Hamlin Garland publishes *Ulysses S. Grant: His Life and Character.*

Robert Herrick publishes *The Gospel of Freedom.*

Finley Peter Dunne publishes *Mr. Dooley in Peace and War.*

1899

Gloria Swanson is born in Chicago, March 27.

Joseph C. Leyendecker's first *Saturday Evening Post* cover appears, May 20.

Thomas A. Dorsey is born in Villa Rica, Georgia, July 1.

Dwight L. Moody dies in Northfield, Massachusetts, December 22.

Ernest Hemingway is born in Oak Park, a Chicago suburb, July 21.

W. R. Burnett is born in Springfield, Ohio, November 25.

Thorstein Veblen publishes *The Theory of the Leisure Class.*

Finley Peter Dunne publishes *Mr. Dooley in the Hearts of His Countrymen.*

George Ade publishes *Fables in Slang.*

1900

The reversal of the Chicago River is completed on January 2, a massive project to stop contamination of the city's water supply; for the first time in history, a river flows away from its mouth.

The luxurious Everleigh Club opens, February 1.

Charles A. Comiskey moves a baseball team from St. Paul to Chicago, naming it the Chicago White Stockings.

Maxwell Bodenheim arrives in Chicago from Hermanville, Mississippi.

The first issue of *International Socialist Review,* to become an outlet for Carl Sandburg, is published, July 1.

Dankmar Adler dies in Chicago, April 16.

L. Frank Baum publishes *The Wonderful Wizard of Oz.*

Theodore Dreiser publishes *Sister Carrie.*

Robert Herrick publishes *The Web of Life.*

1901

The Socialist Party of America is formed in Indianapolis, July.

President William McKinley is shot on September 6 and dies September 14; Theodore Roosevelt becomes president.

Philip D. Armour dies in Chicago, January 29.

Moviemaker Walt Disney is born in Chicago, December 5.

Glenway Wescott is born in Kewaskum, Wisconsin, April 11.

Henry Blake Fuller publishes *Under the Skylights.*

George Barr McCutcheon publishes *Graustark.*

1902

John Peter Altgeld dies in Joliet, Illinois, March 12.

Potter Palmer dies in Chicago, May 4.

Joe Tinker, John Evers, and Frank Chance, forming a new baseball infield for the Chicago Cubs, complete the first of their legendary double plays, September 15.

The musical comedy *The Sultan of Sulu,* book and lyrics by George Ade, opens on March 11 at the Studebaker Theater, before becoming a New York hit.

Mary Garden, soon to become reigning diva of the Chicago Opera Company, sings the leading role in the Paris debut of Claude Debussy's *Pelléas et Mélisande,* April 30.

The Wizard of Oz, a musical review based on the L. Frank Baum work, opens at the Grand Opera House, June 16; it will go on to long-term national success.

An abridged serialization of Frank Norris's *The Pit* begins in the *Saturday Evening Post,* September 20, continuing through January of the next year.

Langston Hughes is born in Joplin, Missouri, February 1.

Frank Norris dies in San Francisco, October 25.

Mary Hartwell Catherwood dies in Chicago, December 26.

Jane Addams publishes *Democracy and Social Ethics.*

1903

The Women's National Trade Union League is formed in Boston, later the National Women's Trade Union League; Jane Addams is vice president.

James L. Kraft, renting a horse and wagon, begins distributing cheese from wholesalers to retail grocers.

Bix Beiderbecke is born in Davenport, Iowa, March 10.

Gustavus F. Swift dies in Lake Forest, Illinois, March 29.

Frederick Law Olmsted dies in Brookline, Massachusetts, August 28.

Henry Demarest Lloyd dies in Winnetka, Illinois, September 27.

The Iroquois Theater burns, resulting in 600 deaths, December 30; Frank Lloyd Wright's sons escape.

Edgar Lee Masters joins Clarence Darrow's law firm (April).

William Dean Howells names the "Chicago School of Fiction."

Frank Norris publishes *The Pit*.

George Ade publishes *In Babel: Stories of Chicago*.

1904

Orchestra Hall, built by Daniel Burnham, opens, December 14.

Johnny Weissmuller is born in what is now Hungary, June 2, soon moving with his family to Chicago.

Upton Sinclair arrives in Chicago to study packinghouse conditions.

MacKinlay Kantor is born in Webster City, Iowa, February 4.

Lincoln Steffans publishes *The Shame of the Cities*.

Robert Herrick publishes *The Common Lot*.

Edgar Lee Masters publishes *The New Star Chamber and Other Essays*.

James T. Farrell is born in Chicago, February 27.

1905

The Industrial Workers of the World, "Wobblies," a radical labor organization, is organized in Chicago in July.

The first issue of *Chicago Defender* appears on May 5, soon to become a nationally influential African-American newspaper.

On November 27, Marshall Field's son dies of a gunshot, rumored to have been fired at the Everleigh Club, providing material for Edgar Lee Masters's *Spoon River Anthology* and Sherwood Anderson's *Marching Men*.

Charles T. Yerkes dies in New York City, December 29.

The Pekin Theater opens on June 18, soon to sponsor the nation's first African-American acting company and make the first African-American film.

Meyer Levin is born in Chicago, October 8.

Robert Herrick publishes *The Memoirs of an American Citizen*.

Clarence Darrow publishes *An Eye for an Eye*.

1906

The Majestic Theater opens as a popular vaudeville house, January 1, later to become the Shubert Theater.

The Cubs and the White Sox participate in Chicago's only intracity World Series; the White Sox win in six games.

William Rainey Harper dies in Chicago, January 10.

Paul Dresser, songwriter brother of Theodore Dreiser, dies in New York City, January 29.

President Theodore Roosevelt coins the term *muckraker*, March 17.

Marshall Field dies in Chicago, January 16.

Willa Cather is hired by *McClure's Magazine*.

Miles Franklin arrives in Chicago from Australia, October.

Upton Sinclair publishes *The Jungle*.

1907

Essanay Film Manufacturing Company is founded, filming its first movie with ex-vaudevillian Ben Turpin.

Montgomery Ward's Catalogue Building, providing the setting a decade later for Edna Ferber's *Fanny Herself*, is constructed along the Chicago River.

Donald J. Bell and Albert S. Howell form the motion-picture equipment company Bell and Howell, February 17.

William Le Baron Jenney dies in Los Angeles, California, June 15.

The Cliff-Dwellers' Club is established for writers and artists.

Carl Sandburg moves to Wisconsin to organize for the Socialist Party of America.

Theodore Dreiser's *Sister Carrie* is published in a new edition.

1908

The Blackstone Hotel, favored by presidents and celebrities, opens.

Barney Balaban purchases his first theater.

Margaret Anderson arrives in Chicago from Columbus, Indiana.

Lionel Hampton is born in Louisville, Kentucky, April 20.

Richard Wright is born in Adams County, Mississippi, September 4.

Floyd Dell arrives in Chicago from Davenport, Iowa, November.

1909

Daniel H. Burnham presents his Chicago Plan for the city's parks and boulevards, keeping the lakefront clear of development (July 4).

Gene Krupa is born in Chicago, January 15.

Benny Goodman is born in Chicago, March 30.

Friday Literary Review begins publication, March 5.

Frank Harris publishes *The Bomb*.

Jane Addams publishes *The Spirit of Youth and the City Streets*.

1910

The black population of Chicago is now 45,000; it will burgeon to 235,000 in the next two decades.

Julius Rosenwald joins Sears, Roebuck, soon overseeing its rapid expansion.

Comiskey Park, new home of the Chicago White Sox, opens, July 1.

Strike begins on September 22 at Hart, Schaffner, and Marx plant, involving, among others, Miles Franklin and Sidney Hillman.

Chicago Opera Company opens in Auditorium theater, November 3.

Edna Ferber arrives in Chicago from Milwaukee.

Ben Hecht arrives in Chicago from Racine, Wisconsin.

William Vaughn Moody dies in Colorado Springs, October 17.

Jane Addams publishes *Twenty Years at Hull-House*.

1911

Montgomery Ward wins final lawsuit to keep the lakefront clear of development.

Life and Labor, magazine of the National Women's Trade Union League, begins publication in January, edited by Alice Henry and Miles Franklin.

Vice crackdown in the Levee district forces the Everleigh Club to close, October 24.

Great Lakes Naval Training Station, north of the city, is dedicated, October 28.

Robert McCormick, grandson of Joseph Medill, takes over the *Chicago Tribune.*

The *Chicago Day Book,* a tabloid targeting the working man, is introduced by newspaper owner E. W. Scripps.

Francis X. Bushman, working for Essanay Studios, makes his first film.

Theodore Dreiser publishes *Jennie Gerhardt.*

Edna Ferber publishes *Dawn O'Hara: The Girl Who Laughed.*

1912

Jane Addams seconds the nomination of Theodore Roosevelt for president on the Progressive ticket at the Chicago Coliseum on August 7, the first woman taking on such a role at a presidential convention.

Eugene V. Debs receives nearly a million votes as Socialist Party of America candidate for president.

Daniel H. Burnham dies in Heidelberg, Germany, June 1.

The Little Theater is established, for the purpose of promoting avant-garde, noncommercial theater.

Willard Motley is born in Chicago, July 14.

Carl Sandburg returns to Chicago from Milwaukee in September.

The first issue of *Poetry,* dated October, appears, September 23.

Edgar Rice Burroughs's *Tarzan of the Apes* first appears in the pulp magazine *The All-Story* in October.

Sherwood Anderson suffers a nervous breakdown in Elyria, Ohio, November 28, returning to Chicago early the following year.

Theodore Dreiser publishes *The Financier.*

Edna Ferber publishes *Buttered Side Down.*

Mary Austin publishes *A Woman of Genius.*

1913

Northwestern University professor Arthur Andersen establishes accounting firm Andersen, DeLaney & Company.

Vachel Lindsay's "General William Booth Enters Heaven" appears as the lead poem in *Poetry* in January.

Ring Lardner begins his "In the Wake of the News" column for the *Chicago Tribune,* June 3.

1914

The baseball stadium Weeghman Park is constructed; it will be renamed Wrigley Field in 1926.

Charlie Chaplin is signed by Essanay studios for a record-breaking salary; Gloria Swanson is hired as an extra.

In March, Carl Sandburg's poems are first published in *Poetry,* including "Chicago."

Harriet Monroe hosts a dinner on March 1 for William Butler Yeats; Carl Sandburg recites "Limited," and Vachel Lindsay declaims "The Congo."

The first issue of *Little Review* appears, March.

Ring Lardner's "You Know Me Al" stories appear in *Saturday Evening Post,* March 7–November 7.

Edgar Lee Masters's first Spoon River poem, "The Hill," appears in *Reedy's Mirror,* May 29.

Theodore Dreiser publishes *The Titan.*

Edgar Rice Burroughs publishes *Tarzan of the Apes.*

1915

Oscar DePriest becomes the first African American to serve in the Chicago City Council, elected alderman from the Second Ward.

Jane Addams chairs the International Congress of Women in The Hague, Netherlands, adopting a pacifist and women's suffrage platform (April).

In August, John D. Hertz inaugurates a fleet of taxicabs, Yellow Cabs, painted yellow for easy recognition.

Albert G. Spalding dies in California, September 9.

Charlie Chaplin makes "His New Job" for the Chicago Essanay studios, costarring Ben Turpin; Gloria Swanson plays a bit part.

Herbert S. Stone and Elbert Hubbard die in the sinking of the ocean liner *Lusitania,* May 7.

The excursion ship *Eastland* sinks at its Chicago dock, resulting in more than 800 deaths, July 24.

Arthur W. W. Denslow dies in New York City, March 29.

Edward Eggleston dies in Lake George, New York, September 2.

Poetry publishes "The Love Song of J. Alfred Prufrock" by the unknown T. S. Eliot (June); later in the year, the magazine publishes "Sunday Morning" by Wallace Stevens, cut and edited by Harriet Monroe (November).

Alice Henry publishes *The Trade Union Woman.*

Edgar Lee Masters publishes *Spoon River Anthology.*

Willa Cather publishes *The Song of the Lark.*

Theodore Dreiser publishes *The "Genius."*

Edna Ferber publishes *Emma McChesney & Co.*

1916

James L. Kraft receives a patent for processing cheese, a significant step toward creating a major national food company.

Sherwood Anderson's "The Book of the Grotesque," later to become the prologue to *Winesburg, Ohio,* is published in *Masses* in February; "Hands" appears in the next issue.

In June, *Little Review* publishes Sherwood Anderson's "The Philosopher"; later, when published in *Winesburg, Ohio,* it will become "Paper Pills."

Seven Arts magazine publishes Sherwood Anderson's "Queer," December.

Jane Heap joins *Little Review.*

Carl Sandburg publishes *Chicago Poems.*

Sherwood Anderson publishes *Windy McPherson's Son.*

Ring Lardner publishes *You Know Me Al.*

1917

The United States enters World War I, April 6.

The Espionage Act, criminalizing speaking against the draft or the conduct of the war, is passed, June 15, leading to the imprisonment of Eugene Debs, Emma Goldman, and others.

Bolsheviks seize power in Russia, November 7.

The U.S. Navy forces closing of the Storyville section of New Orleans, sending jazz musicians Joe "King" Oliver and Louis Armstrong north to Chicago, November 12.

The Little Theatre closes in February.

H. L. Mencken publishes an article in the October 28 *Chicago Tribune,* proclaiming Chicago as the nation's literary center.

Hamlin Garland publishes *A Son of the Middle Border.*

Sherwood Anderson publishes *Marching Men.*

Edna Ferber publishes *Fanny Herself.*

Vachel Lindsay publishes *The Chinese Nightingale and Other Poems.*

Ring Lardner publishes *Gullible's Travels, Etc.*

1918

Floyd Dell and others from the magazine, *The Masses* go on trial under the Espionage Act in April; they are freed several weeks later by a hung jury.

World War I ends, November 11.

Joe "King" Oliver, New Orleans jazz cornetist, arrives in Chicago in June.

Little Review publishes Sherwood Anderson's "A Man of Ideas" in June and "An Awakening" in December, both stories to become part of *Winesburg, Ohio.*

Walter L. Jacobs opens pioneering car-rental operation in September, later sold to John D. Hertz, owner of Yellow Cab Company.

Oscar Micheaux founds the Micheaux Film and Book Company.

The Birth of a Race, a response to the anti-black *The Birth of a Nation,* opens at the Blackstone Theater in November.

Margaret Anderson and Jane Heap begin publishing James Joyce's *Ulysses* in *Little Review,* March.

Carl Sandburg, publishes *Cornhuskers.*

Edna Ferber publishes *Cheerful by Request.*

1919

Oscar Micheaux debuts *The Homesteader,* beginning his success as the first major African-American filmmaker, February 20.

Eugene V. Debs is convicted of sedition and sent to federal prison in April.

Race riots on the South Side begin over black and white "territory" on a Lake Michigan beach; after four days 38 people are dead and more than are 500 injured, July 27–30.

The Communist Party and the Communist Labor Party are founded in Chicago (September).

William Wrigley purchases the Chicago Cubs.

The Chicago White Sox throw the World Series in October, creating what will be known as the Black Sox scandal.

Emma Goldman is deported to Russia on December 21 under the Anarchist Exclusion Act.

L. Frank Baum dies in Hollywood, California, May 6.

Sherwood Anderson publishes *Winesburg, Ohio.*

Henry Blake Fuller publishes *Bertram Cope's Year.*

1920

The Volstead Act, enforcing Prohibition, becomes law, January 16; the city's profitable bootlegging enterprises begin.

Republican Party leaders choose Warren G. Harding as presidential nominee on June 11, meeting in secret deliberations at the Blackstone Hotel; the term *smoke-filled room* is born.

The Nineteenth Amendment, granting women's suffrage, becomes law, August 26; unlike Prohibition, it will be enforced—except for African-American women in the South.

Chicago judge Kenesaw Mountain Landis is named baseball's first commissioner, November 12.

Oscar Micheaux's response to the 1919 race riot, the film *Within Our Gates,* depicting a mob lynching, opens to a large audience, January 12.

H. L. Mencken names Chicago the "Literary Capital of the United States" in the London *Nation,* April 17, a recapping of his *Chicago Tribune* article published three years earlier.

Margaret Anderson and Jane Heap are charged with obscenity in their continuing serialization of James Joyce's *Ulysses* in *Little Review.*

Carl Sandburg writes his first movie review for the *Chicago Daily News,* September 27.

Carl Sandburg publishes *Smoke and Steel; The Chicago Race Riots, July 1919.*

Sherwood Anderson publishes *Poor White.*

Edgar Lee Masters publishes *Mitch Miller.*

Zona Gale publishes *Miss Lulu Bett.*

Floyd Dell publishes *Moon-Calf.*

1921

The Field Museum of Natural History opens, May 23.

The Chicago Theater, the prestige theater in the expanding Balaban and Katz chain, opens on October 26; silent-film and live entertainment are provided.

President Warren G. Harding commutes the prison sentence of Eugene Debs, December 25.

The Chicago Opera Company performs the world premiere of Serge Prokofiev's *The Love for Three Oranges*, December 30.

Sherwood Anderson and Ernest Hemingway meet for the first time in Chicago.

Ben Hecht begins his column, "One Thousand and One Afternoons in Chicago" for the *Chicago Daily News* in June.

Sherwood Anderson publishes *The Triumph of the Egg.*

Hamlin Garland publishes *A Daughter of the Middle Border.*

1922

Louis Armstrong arrives in Chicago from New Orleans in August, initiating a creative period in American jazz.

Lorado Taft's massive statuary grouping, "Fountain of Time," is dedicated on the Midway Plaisance, November 15.

Carl Sandburg publishes *Slabs of the Sunburnt West.*

Ben Hecht publishes *1001 Afternoons in Chicago.*

Edgar Lee Masters publishes *Children of the Market Place.*

Edna Ferber publishes *Gigolo.*

1923

The Thompson submachine gun, or tommy gun, developed for military use during World War I, is first used by a South Side underworld gang.

Gertrude "Ma" Rainey makes her first blues recording in Chicago for Paramount Records.

Ben Hecht and Maxwell Bodenheim begin publication of their short-lived *Chicago Literary Times*, March 1; it will last till June 1 of the following year.

Edgar Lee Masters publishes *Skeeters Kirby.*

Sherwood Anderson publishes *Many Marriages; Horses and Men.*

1924

In July, Richard Loeb and Nathan Leopold, murderers of a 14-year-old boy in "the crime of the century," are defended by Clarence Darrow and saved from the death penalty.

Louis Sullivan dies in Chicago, April 14.

Edgar Lee Masters publishes *The New Spoon River.*

Sherwood Anderson publishes *A Story-Teller's Story.*

Edna Ferber publishes *So Big.*

Ring Lardner publishes *How to Write Short Stories [With Examples].*

1925

Clarence Darrow defends John T. Scopes, schoolteacher accused of teaching Darwinian evolution, in Dayton, Tennessee, July 10–21; prosecutor is William Jennings Bryan. Bryan dies five days later in Dayton, July 26.

The Brotherhood of Sleeping Car Porters is founded in New York City by A. Philip Randolph, August 25; Chicago, home of the Pullman company, soon claims the chapter with the largest membership.

The largest free-standing theater in the nation, the opulent Uptown Theater, opens, August 18.

Soldier Field is dedicated as a World War I memorial, November 11.

Mary Harris Jones publishes *The Autobiography of Mother Jones.*

Theodore Dreiser publishes *An American Tragedy.*

Sherwood Anderson publishes *Dark Laughter.*

Willa Cather publishes *The Professor's House.*

1926

The Oriental Theater opens in the Randolph Street theater district, presenting motion pictures and live stage performances, May 8.

The Palace Theatre, also in the Randolph Street district, opens as part of the Orpheum vaudeville circuit, October 4.

Eugene V. Debs dies in Elmhurst, Illinois, October 20.

Benny Goodman records his first solo in Chicago with the Ben Pollack Band, December 17.

Maurine Watkins's play *Chicago* opens on Broadway, December 30.

Carl Sandburg *Abraham Lincoln: The Prairie Years.*

Sherwood Anderson publishes *Tar: A Midwest Childhood; Sherwood Anderson's Notebook.*

Ernest Hemingway publishes *The Torrents of Spring.*

Ring Lardner publishes *The Love Nest and Other Stories.*

Edna Ferber publishes *Show Boat.*

1927

Municipal Airport, later named Midway Airport, opens on the Southwest Side, soon becoming the nation's busiest airfield.

Heavyweight boxer Jack Dempsey loses to Gene Tunney at Soldier Field in the controversial "long count" decision, September 22.

Singer Joe E. Lewis, entertaining at a mobster-run Prohibition-era nightclub on the North Side, is assaulted and severely injured in a contract dispute, November 10.

Richard Wright arrives in Chicago from Memphis, November.

The stage musical version of Edna Ferber's novel *Show Boat* opens in New York, December 27.

Carl Sandburg publishes *The American Songbag.*

Glenway Wescott publishes *The Grandmothers.*

1928

Oscar DePriest is elected the first African American from a northern state to serve in Congress, November 6.

Chicagoan Johnny Weissmuller wins swimming championships for the second time at the Olympic Games, leading to his movie role of Tarzan, created by Chicagoan Edgar Rice Burroughs.

Ben Hecht and Charles MacArthur's play *The Front Page,* set within the milieu of Chicago journalism, opens in New York, August 14.

MacKinlay Kantor publishes *Diversey.*

Vachel Lindsay publishes *Johnny Appleseed and Other Poems.*

1929

St. Valentine's Day Massacre takes place in a warehouse on North Clark Street, leaving seven dead, February 14.

Thorstein Veblen dies in Menlo Park, California, August 3.

The stock market collapses on Black Tuesday, October 29, plunging the nation and the world into the Great Depression.

The Civic Opera House, built by the soon-to-be-ruined mogul Samuel Insull, opens shortly after stock market crash, November 4.

Robert M. Hutchins is inaugurated president of the University of Chicago, November 12.

Tennessee Mitchell dies in Chicago, an apparent suicide, December 20.

The last issue of *Little Review* is published, May.

Henry Blake Fuller dies in Chicago, July 28.

W. R. Burnett publishes *Little Caesar.*

1930

Adler Planetarium opens on May 11, the first planetarium in America.

Sinclair Lewis, exponent of the "revolt from the village," becomes the first American to win the Nobel Prize in literature.

Mary Harris "Mother" Jones dies, November 30; she is buried at the Union Miners Cemetery in Mount Olive, Illinois.

The new Chicago Board of Trade building is completed, its Art Deco style replacing the demolished 1885 building on the same site.

Langston Hughes publishes *Not Without Laughter.*

Jane Addams publishes *The Second Twenty Years at Hull-House.*

BIBLIOGRAPHY

Andrews, Clarence A. *Chicago in Story: A Literary History*. Iowa City, Iowa: Midwest Heritage Publishing Company, 1982.

Asbury, Herbert. *Gem of the Prairie: An Informal History of the Chicago Underworld*. Introduction by Perry Davis. DeKalb: Northern Illinois University Press, 1986.

Bernstein, Arnie. *Hollywood on Lake Michigan: 100 Years of Chicago and the Movies*. Chicago: Lake Claremont Press, 1998.

———. *"The Movies Are": Carl Sandburg's Film Review and Essays, 1920–1928*. Chicago: Lake Claremont Press, 2000.

Bray, Robert C. *Rediscoveries: Literature and Place in Illinois*. Urbana: University of Illinois Press, 1982.

Cronon, William. *Nature's Metropolis: Chicago and the Great West*. New York: W. W. Norton and Company, 1991.

Davis, Allen F. *Spearheads for Reform: The Social Settlements and the Progressive Movement*. New York: Oxford University Press, 1967.

———. *American Heroine: The Life and Legend of Jane Addams*. New York: Oxford University Press, 1973.

Deegan, Mary Jo. *Jane Addams and the Men of the Chicago School, 1892–1918*. New Brunswick, N.J.: Transaction Books, 1988.

Duffy, Bernard. *The Chicago Renaissance in American Letters: A Critical History*. East Lansing: Michigan State College Press, 1954.

Duncan, Hugh Dalziel. *The Rise of Chicago as a Literary Center from 1885 to 1920: A Sociological Essay in American Culture*. Totowa, N.J.: Bedminster Press, 1964.

Foner, Philip S. *Women and the American Labor Movement: From Colonial Times to the Eve of World War I*. New York: Free Press, 1979.

Graf, John, and Steve Skorpad. *Chicago's Monuments, Markers, and Memorials*. Chicago: Acadia Publishing, 2002.

Grube, Oswald W., Peter C. Pran, and Franz Schulze. *100 Years of Architecture in Chicago: Continuity of Structure and Form*. Chicago: Follett Publishing Company, 1977.

Hallwas, John E., ed. *Studies in Illinois Poetry*. Urbana, Ill.: Stormline Press, 1989.

———. *Illinois Literature: The Nineteenth Century*. Macomb: Illinois Heritage Press, 1986.

Hanson, Harry. *Midwest Portraits: A Book of Memories and Friendships*. New York: Harcourt, Brace and Company, 1923.

Hardwick, Elizabeth. *American Fictions*. New York: The Modern Library, 1999.

Hart, James D. *The Popular Book: A History of America's Literary Taste*. Berkeley: University of California Press, 1961.

Hines, Thomas S. *Burnham of Chicago: Architect and Planner*. Chicago: University of Chicago Press, 1979.

Historic City: The Settlement of Chicago. Chicago: City of Chicago, Department of Development and Planning, 1976.

Holman, David Marion. *A Certain Slant of Light: Regionalism and the Form of Southern and Midwestern Fiction*. With an Introduction by Louis D. Rubin Jr. Baton Rouge: Louisiana State University Press, 1995.

Hurt, James. *Writing Illinois: The Prairie, Lincoln, and Chicago*. Urbana: University of Illinois Press, 1992.

Korda, Michael. *Making the List: A Cultural History of the American Bestseller 1900–1999.* New York: Barnes and Noble Books, 2001.

Kramer, Dale. *Chicago Renaissance: The Literary Life in the Midwest, 1900–1930.* New York: Appleton-Century, 1966.

Larson, George A. and Jay Pridmore. *Chicago Architecture and Design.* New York: Harry N. Abrams, Inc., 1993.

Lowe, David Garrard. *Lost Chicago.* New York: Watson-Guptill Publications, 2000.

Miller, Donald L. *City of the Century: The Epic of Chicago and the Making of America.* New York: Simon & Schuster, 1996.

Regnery, Henry. *Creative Chicago: From* The Chapbook *to the University.* Evanston, Ill.: Chicago Historical Bookworks, 1993.

Schultz, Rima Lunin, and Adele Hast, ed. *Women Building Chicago 1790–1990.* Bloomington, Ind.: Indiana University Press, 2001.

Schulze, Franz, and Kevin Harrington, ed. *Chicago's Famous Buildings.* 4th ed., revised and enlarged. Chicago: University of Chicago Press, 1993.

Smith, Carl S. *Chicago and the American Literary Imagination, 1880–1920.* Chicago: University of Chicago Press, 1984.

Stansell, Christine. *American Moderns: Bohemian New York and the Creation of a New Century.* New York: Henry Holt and Company, 2000.

Watson, Steven. *Strange Bedfellows: The First American Avant-Garde.* New York: Abbeville Press, 1991.

Wilson, Edmund. *Patriotic Gore: Studies in the Literature of the American Civil War.* Boston: Northeastern University Press, 1984.

Woolley, Lisa. *American Voices of the Chicago Renaissance.* DeKalb: Northern Illinois University Press, 2000.

INDEX

Page numbers in **boldface** indicate main entry; those followed by *f* indicate a photograph or illustration.

Palmer, Potter 117, 217–218, 251, **252–253**, 252f, 258
Palmer raids **253**
Panama Canal 227, **253**, 284
Panic of 1873 **253**
    and Cooke, Jay 76
    and Coxey's Army 84
    depiction of in *The Financier* (Dreiser) 121
    and the Great Strike of 1877 144
    and Mother Jones 182
    representation of in *The Web of Life* (Herrick) 357
Panic of 1893 **253**, 384
"Paper Pills" (Anderson, S.) 369. *See also Winesburg, Ohio* (Anderson, S.)
Paramount Pictures v–vi, 27, 243, 391
Parsons, Albert 5, 14, 154, 175, **254**, 254
Parsons, Louella 107, **254**
Parsons, Lucy **254–255**, 254f
    on the Chicago Board of Trade 57
    on dynamite 103
    and the Haymarket Affair 154
    and the Industrial Workers of the World 174
    and the International Working People's Association 175
    relationship with Parsons, Albert 254
    "To Tramps" 339
    work with *Alarm* publication 5
Patterson, Joseph Medill 222, 226, **255**
Patti, Adelina 24, **255**, 255f
A Peculiar Treasure (Ferber) 116, 194
Peggy from Paris (Ade and Lorraine) 4, **256**
Pekin Theater 94, **256**
People's Party. *See* Populist Party
Peterson, Julia (character) 209–210, **256**, 284
"Petit, the Poet" (Masters) 316–317. *See also Spoon River Anthology* (Masters)
Phillips, Medora (character) 30–36, 124, 197, **256**
"The Philosopher" (Anderson, S.) 369. *See also Winesburg, Ohio* (Anderson, S.)
Pinkerton, Allan 127, 160, **257**
Pink Marsh: A Story of the Streets and the Town (Ade) 4, **257**
The Pit (Norris) v, 244–245, **257–261**
    characters in 81–82, 84, 88, 151, 177, 218
    compared to *The Cliff-Dwellers* (Fuller) 72
    use of naturalism in 242
Platow, Stephanie (character) 172, **261**
    relationships with other characters 83, 93, 205
    synopsis of *The Titan* (Dreiser) 332–338
Poetry: A Magazine of Verse iv, v, 174, **261–262**
    The Chinese Nightingale and Other Poems (Lindsay) in 67
    "The Code" (Frost) in 128
    "Eros Turannos" (Robinson) in 283
    "The Four Brothers" (Sandburg) in 81
    "I Am the Woman" (Moody) in 237
    "Sanger" (Reed) in 281
    "Sunday Morning" (Stevens) in 322
    "Trees" (Kilmer) in 191

Poor White (Anderson, S.) 17, 20, 160, 178, 238, **262–267**
    characters in 49, 50, 55, 170, 225, 355
    representation of socialism in 305
populist causes 20, 126
Populist Party 69, 132, 142, 191, **267**
Porter, William Sydney 18, **267**
"Portrait of a Motorcar" (Sandburg) 79. *See also Cornhuskers* (Sandburg)
Potowatami (Native American tribe) 191, **267**, 356
Pound, Ezra 6, 138, **268**
    relationships maintained by 16, 97, 106, 128, 207
    style of 127, 149, 173–174, 221, 233
    works in literary journals 94, 127, 203, 234, 249, 262
prairie 92, **268**
"The Prairie" (Sandburg) 77–78, 81, 268, 292. *See also Cornhuskers* (Sandburg)
"The Prairies" (Bryant) 45, 81
Prairie School of Architecture 166, 246, **268–269**, 385
"Prayers of Steel" (Sandburg) 65, 79–80. *See also Cornhuskers* (Sandburg)
primitivism 60, 75, 86, **269**, 309
The Professor's House (Cather) 54, 107, **269–272**
    characters in 216, 249–250, 290–291
    representations in 245, 273
progressive movement 3, 239, **272**
Progressive Party 3, 125, **272**, 285, 305
Prohibition vi, **272–273**
    Anti-Saloon League 19
    and Capone, Al 52
    and the Green Mill Gardens 146
    and jazz 178
    and muckraking 272
    opinions of 76, 87, 326–327, 380
    rental cars during 158
    and Wilson, Pres. Woodrow 362
Prohibition Party 19, 272, **273**
Prokofiev, Sergei 59, 131, 206–207, **273–274**
Provident Hospital 274, 360–361
Provincetown Players 76, 140, **274**
    individuals involved with 92–93, 150–151, 172, 238, 247
    influence of on the Little Theatre 204
    production of "The Eldest" (Ferber) 56
Pullman (town) 44, **274–275**, 275–276
Pullman, George M. 123, 274, **275**
Pullman Palace Car Company **275**
    and the Brotherhood of Sleeping Car Porters 43–44, 279
    Lincoln, Robert Todd, involvement with 201
    membership in the American Railway Union and 7
    opinions of 19, 250
    and the Pullman strike 275–276
Pullman strike 274, **275–276**
    American Railway Union on 7
    Cleveland, Pres. Grover, response to 69, 145
    and Debs, Eugene V. 19, 91–92
    Lincoln, Robert Todd, involvement with 201

    opinions of 117, 281–282
    and the Panic of 1893 253
    as represented in literary works 60, 158, 330

Q

"Queer" (Anderson, S.) 373–374. *See also Winesburg, Ohio* (Anderson, S.)
Quinn Chapel A.M.E. Church **277**

R

race riots of 1919 3, **278**
    and Bronzeville 43
    The Chicago Race Riots, July 1919 (Sandburg) 64
    Farrell, James T., depiction of 114
    and Hull-House 169
    and Packington 251
Radical Republicans 52, 142, 153, 181, **278**, 280
Rainey, Gertrude "Ma" 97, **278–279**
Rainey, Sue (character) 225, **279**, 362–368
Raisa, Rosa (opera singer) 59, 68, **279**
Rand McNally and Company 47, 93, **279**, 303
Randolph, A. Philip **279**
    on the AFL 7
    and the Brotherhood of Sleeping Car Porters 44
    relationships maintained by 250, 256
    Wells, Ida B., support of 358
    work with the *Chicago Bee* 57
    on World War I 385
Randolph, Basil (character) 30–36, 124, **280**
"Ready to Kill" (Sandburg) 62. *See also Chicago Poems* (Sandburg)
realism **280**
    authors who use 105, 130, 133, 167, 231, 286
    examples of 144, 158, 166, 237, 338, 391
    naturalism as the next step 241
    omission of in the *Little Review* 204
    opinions of 76, 117, 132, 295, 322, 354
    and veritism 354
Reconstruction 143, 153, 181, 278, **280–281**
Reed, John 281, 321
Reedy, William Marion 219, **281**, 302, 320
Reefy, Doctor. *See* "Death" (Anderson, S.); "Paper Pills" (Anderson, S.)
regionalism 281
religion 51, 243, 297, 311. *See also* Christian socialism
Remington, Frederic 132, 160, **281–282**
Replenishing Jessica (Bodenheim) 38, 243
"Respectability" (Anderson, S.) 371. *See also Winesburg, Ohio* (Anderson, S.)
"The Return" (Anderson, S.) 89–90, 91, 159, 273. *See also* "Death in the Woods" (Anderson, S.)
"The Return of a Private" (Garland) 208, 210, 304, 309. *See also Main-Travelled Roads* (Garland)
"Reuben Pantier" (Masters) 313–314. *See also Spoon River Anthology* (Masters)
"Rev. Abner Peet" (Masters) 317. *See also Spoon River Anthology* (Masters)